Washington, DC

"All you've got to do is decide to go and the hardest part is over.

So go!"

TONY WHEELER, COFOUNDER – LONELY PLANET

THIS EDITION WRITTEN AND RESEARCHED BY

Karla Zimmerman

Regis St Louis

Contents

Plan Your Trip 4

Explore Washington, DC 76

Understand Washington, DC 255

Survival Guide 287

Washington, DC, Maps 316

(left) **Tidal Basin (p93)** with views of Thomas Jefferson Memorial

(above) **National Air and Space Museum (p86)**

(right) **Kennedy Center (p113)**

Welcome to Washington, DC

The USA's capital teems with iconic monuments, vast museums and the corridors of power where visionaries and demagogues roam.

Museums & Monuments

Thanks, James Smithson, you eccentric antimonarchist Englishman. That $508,318 gift you willed to the USA back in 1826 to create a 'diffusion of knowledge' paid off big time. There's nothing quite like the Smithsonian Institution, a collection of 19 behemoth, artifact-stuffed museums, many lined up in a row along the Mall. The National Air and Space Museum, Museum of Natural History, Museum of American History, Museums of Asian Art – all here, all free, always.

Alongside the museums, Washington's monuments bear tribute to both the beauty and the horror of years past. They're potent symbols of the American narrative, from the awe-inspiring Lincoln Memorial to the powerful Vietnam Veterans Memorial to the controversial Martin Luther King Jr Memorial.

Arts & Culture

Washington is the showcase of American arts, home to such prestigious venues as the National Theatre, the Kennedy Center and the Folger Shakespeare Theatre. Jazz music has a storied history here. In the early 20th century, locals such as Duke Ellington climbed on stages along U St NW, where atmospheric clubs still operate.

Political Life

The president, Congress and the Supreme Court are here, the three pillars of US government. In their orbit float the Pentagon, State Department, World Bank and embassies from most corners of the globe. If you hadn't got the idea, *power* is why Washington exerts such a palpable buzz.

As a visitor, there's a thrill in seeing the action up close – to walk inside the White House, to sit in the Capitol chamber while senators argue about Arctic drilling, and to drink in a bar alongside congresspeople likely determining your newest tax hike over their single-malt Scotch.

History

A lot of history is concentrated within DC's relatively small confines. In a single day, you could gawp at the Declaration of Independence, the real, live parchment with John Hancock's, er, John Hancock scrawled across it at the National Archives; stand where Martin Luther King Jr gave his 'I Have a Dream' speech on the Lincoln Memorial's steps; prowl around the Watergate building that got Nixon into trouble; see the flag that inspired the 'Star Spangled Banner' at the National Museum of American History; and be an arm's length from where Lincoln was assassinated in Ford's Theatre.

RICHARD CUMMINS / LONELY PLANET IMAGES ©

Why I Love Washington, DC

By Karla Zimmerman, Author

It begins with the Mall. How cool is it to have a walkable strip of museums where you can see nuclear missiles, cursed diamonds and exquisite Asian ceramics in a peacock-themed room – for *free*? Further down the path the notes and photos people leave at the Vietnam Veterans Memorial will break your heart, and the Lincoln Memorial just kills with its grandness and sweeping view. H St wins my affection for its pie-and-beer mix. Most of all, I love how Ben's Chili Bowl makes you feel like a local even if you're not.

For more about our authors, see p344.

Capitol (p131)

Washington, DC's Top 10

STEPHEN J BOITANO / LONELY PLANET IMAGES ©

Lincoln Memorial *(p82)*

1 There's something extraordinary about climbing the steps of Abe Lincoln's Doric-columned temple, staring into his dignified eyes, and reading about the 'new birth of freedom' in the Gettysburg Address chiseled beside him. Then to stand where Martin Luther King Jr gave his 'Dream' speech and take in the sweeping view – it's a defining DC moment. At dawn, nowhere in the city is as serene and lovely, which is why the Lincoln Memorial is a popular place for proposals.

National Mall

Washington Monument *(p83)*

2 Tall, phallic and imbued with shadowy Masonic lore, the 555ft obelisk is DC's tallest structure. Workers set the pyramid on top in 1884 after stacking up some 36,000 blocks of granite and marble over the preceding 36 years. A 70-second elevator ride whisks you to the observation deck at the top for what are usually the city's best views. The monument closed for repairs in 2011 after an earthquake, but it's scheduled to reopen (hopefully) in 2013.

National Mall

1

2

STEPHEN J BOITANO / LONELY PLANET IMAGES ©

LEE FOSTER / LONELY PLANET IMAGES ©

5

IMAGEBROKER / LONELY PLANET IMAGES ©

JASON COLSTON / LONELY PLANET IMAGES ©

Vietnam Veterans Memorial *(p84)*

3 The opposite of DC's white, gleaming marble, the black, low-lying Vietnam memorial cuts into the earth, just as the Vietnam War cut into the national psyche. The monument shows the names of the war's 58,267 casualties – listed in the order they died – along a dark, reflective wall. It's a subtle but remarkably profound monument, where visitors leave poignant mementos, such as photos of babies and notes ('I wish you could have met him, Dad').

National Mall

National Gallery of Art *(p85)*

4 It takes two massive buildings to hold the National Gallery's free-to-see trove of paintings, sculptures and decorative arts from the Middle Ages to the present. The East Building gets the modern stuff – Calder mobiles, Matisse collages. The West Building hangs works from earlier eras – El Greco, Monet and the hemisphere's only Leonardo da Vinci. Free films and concerts, a sweet cafe with 20 gelato flavors and an adjoining garden studded with whimsical sculptures add to the awesomeness.

National Mall

White House *(p100)*

5 Thomas Jefferson groused it was 'big enough for two emperors, one Pope and the grand Lama,' but when you tour the White House you get the feeling – despite all the spectacle – that it really is just a *house*, where a family lives. Admittedly, that family gets to hang out in Jefferson's green dining room and Lincoln's old office where his ghost supposedly roams. If you don't get in (tours require serious pre-planning), the visitors center provides the scoop on presidential pets and Oval Office rug design.

White House Area & Foggy Bottom

Capitol Hill *(p131)*

6 City planner Pierre L'Enfant called it 'a pedestal waiting for a monument.' So that's how the Capitol came to sit atop the hill that rises above the city. You're welcome to go inside the mighty, white-domed edifice and count the statues, ogle the frescoes and visit the chambers of the folks who run the country. Afterward, call on the neighbors. The Supreme Court and Library of Congress also reside up here, across the street from the Capitol.

Capitol Hill & Southeast DC

Smithsonian Institution *(p80)*

7 If America was a quirky grandfather, the Smithsonian Institution would be his attic. Rockets, dinosaurs, Rodin sculptures, Tibetan *thangkas* (silk paintings) – even the 45-carat Hope Diamond lights up a room here. The Smithsonian is actually a collection of 19 museums and they're all free, baby. The Air and Space, Natural History and American History museums are the group's rock stars, while the American Indian and Asian Art museums and National Portrait Gallery provide quieter spaces for contemplation.

AMERICAN ART MUSEUM (P154)

National Mall

6

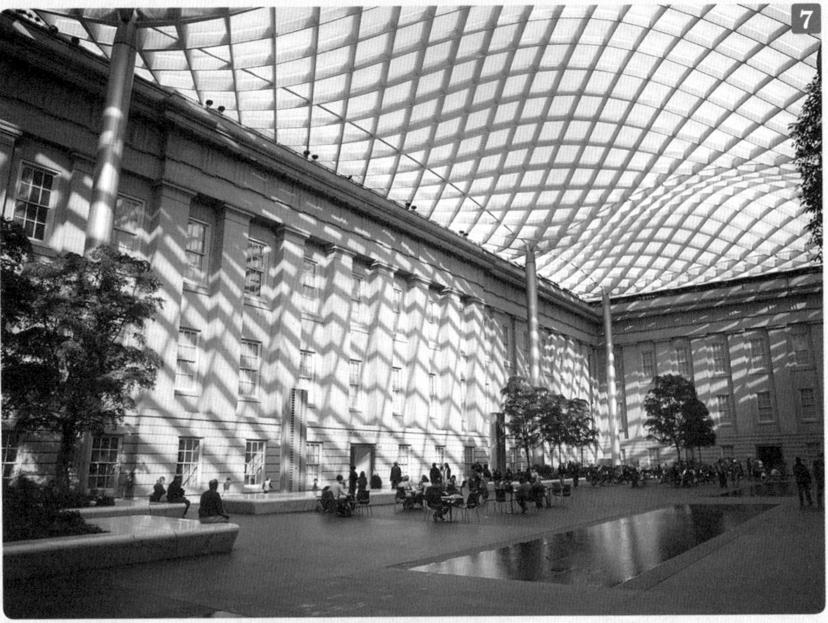

7

DESIGNED BY FOSTER AND PARTNERS / JUSTIN MATHEWS / LONELY PLANET IMAGES ©

8

RICHARD I'ANSON / LONELY PLANET IMAGES ©

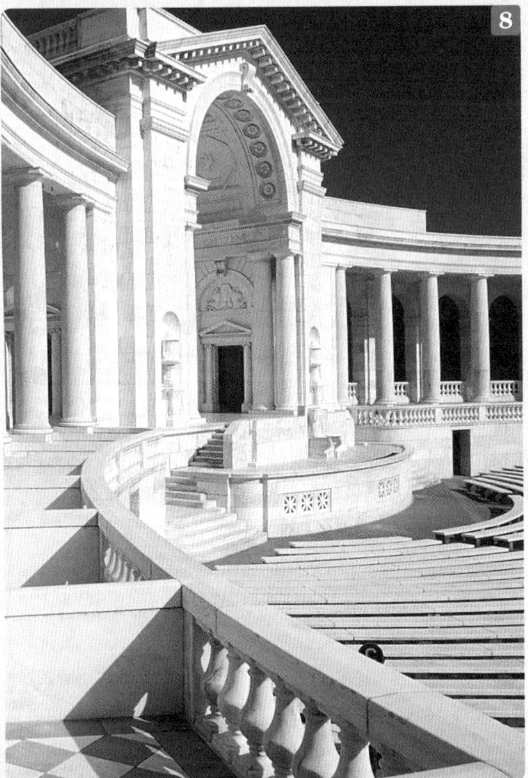

Arlington National Cemetery *(p217)*

8 Soldiers from every war since the Revolution are buried in the 624-acre grounds. Simple white headstones cover the green hills in a seemingly endless procession. Many US leaders and notable civilians are also buried here. An eternal flame flickers over the grave of John F Kennedy. Flowers pile at the marker for the space shuttle *Challenger* crew. Rifle-toting military guards maintain a 24-hour vigil at the Tomb of the Unknowns, affecting in its solemnity.

TOMB OF THE UNKNOWNS

Northern Virginia

Ben's Chili Bowl & U Street Corridor *(p195)*

9 The U St Corridor has had quite a life. It was the 'Black Broadway' where Duke Ellington got his jazz on in the early 1900s. It was the smoldering epicenter of the 1968 race riots. There was a troubled descent, then a vibrant rebirth as an entertainment district. And Ben's Chili Bowl has stood there through most of it. Despite visits by presidents and movie stars, Ben's remains a real neighborhood spot, with locals downing half-smokes and gossiping over sweet iced tea. It's quintessential DC.

U Street, Columbia Heights & Northeast

9

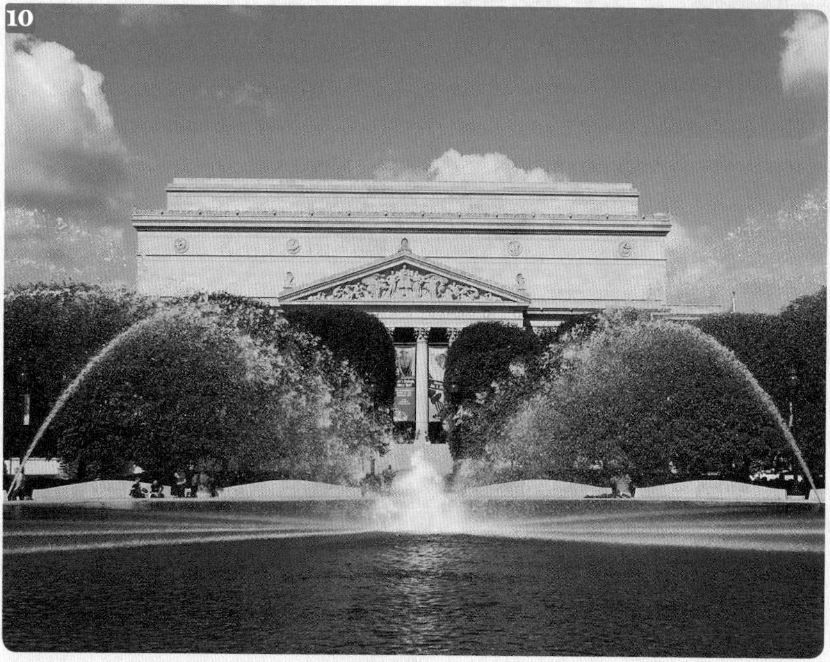

10

National Archives *(p153)*

10 You're in line with all of the school groups, annoyed, thinking maybe your time would be better spent at a local watering hole. Then you enter the dim rotunda and see them – the Declaration of Independence, the Constitution and the Bill of Rights – the USA's founding documents. The National Archives has the real, yellowing, spidery-handwriting-scrawled parchments. And your jaw drops. There's John Hancock's signature, and Ben Franklin's, and Thomas Jefferson's! The archives also display the Magna Carta, George Washington's old letters and Charles 'Pa' Ingalls' homesteading paperwork.

Downtown & Penn Quarter

What's New

Martin Luther King Jr Memorial
A striking, 30ft-tall likeness of Dr King emerges from a mountain of granite in DC's newest monument, which has quickly become a Mall must-see. (p87)

Howard Theatre
Duke Ellington's old jazz joint has reopened after a resplendent, $29-million renovation. Blues and jazz acts have returned to fill the house, along with the Sunday gospel brunch. (p201)

Ford's Theatre Center
A giant visage of Abe Lincoln marks this educational center that examines how and why Lincoln became a national icon; it's across the street from his assassination site. (p156)

Reflecting Pool & Mall
The duck-filled stretch of water in front of the Lincoln Memorial is getting all gussied up, along with the Mall's paths and gardens. (p94)

Georgetown Waterfront Park
The riverfront park now sprawls all the way from Washington Harbour to the Key Bridge, offering plenty of places to sip an alfresco drink and watch the rowing teams. (p118)

Hamilton
Part power-player restaurant, part sushi cafe, part craft-spirit-pouring bar, part live-music club, part late-night milkshake diner: the Hamilton has a *lot* going on. (p112)

H St Corridor/Atlas District
Pie cafes, noodle shops and burlesque palaces are funking up the edgy H St Corridor (aka Atlas District), and a fleet of streetcars is forthcoming. (p145)

DC Brau
The first brewery to launch in the District in more than 50 years pours audacious suds such as the seasonal Fermentation Without Representation. (p201)

American River Taxi
A new fleet of water taxis glides along the Potomac, from Georgetown's Washington Harbour to the Wharf in southwest DC to the Yards by Nationals Park. (p290)

Artisphere
Arlington's fresh, sleek arts center offers world music, film, experimental theater and other performances and exhibits – many for free – along with a cool cafe and bar. (p218)

MyTix
Patrons aged 18 to 30 can get deep discounts – even free tickets – to all opera, ballet, symphony and other Kennedy Center performances via this social media–oriented program. (p113)

For more recommendations and reviews, see **lonelyplanet.com/usa/washington-dc**

Need to Know

Currency
US dollar ($)

Language
English

Visas
Visitors from Canada, the UK, Australia, New Zealand, Japan and many EU countries do not need a visa for stays under 90 days. Other visitors might (see http://travel.state.gov).

Money
ATMs widely available. Credit cards accepted at most hotels, restaurants and shops.

Cell Phones
Europe and Asia's GSM 900/1800 standard does not work in the USA. Consider buying a cheap local phone with a pay-as-you-go plan.

Time
Eastern Standard Time (GMT/UTC minus five hours)

Tourist Information
See www.washington.org or visit the DC Chamber of Commerce Visitor Information Center (☎202-347-7201; 506 9th St NW; ⏲8am-5:30pm Mon-Fri; Ⓜ Gallery Pl-Chinatown).

Your Daily Budget

Budget under $100
- Dorm bed $25-45
- Lunchtime specials for food and happy-hour drinks $15-25
- Metro day pass $9

Midrange $100-350
- Hotel or B&B double room $120-275
- Dinner in a casual restaurant $20-40
- Capitol Steps theater ticket $40

Top end over $350
- Luxury hotel double room $400
- Dinner at Minibar $150
- Washington National Opera ticket $100-150

Advance Planning

Six months Book your hotel, request a White House tour.

Two months Request Pentagon tour and House and Senate visits; sign up for discount tickets from Gold Star and MyTix (ages 18 to 30 only).

Two weeks Reserve tickets online for the National Archives, Holocaust Memorial Museum, Washington Monument and Ford's Theatre.

A few days Check www.washingtoncitypaper.com to see what's on for entertainment and make bookings.

Useful Websites

- **Lonely Planet** (www.lonelyplanet.com/usa/washington-dc) Destination information, hotel bookings, travel forum and photos.
- **Destination DC** (www.washington.org) Official tourism site packed with sightseeing and event info.
- **Cultural Tourism DC** (www.culturaltourismdc.org) Neighborhood-oriented events and tours.
- **DCist** (www.dcist.com) Hip blog about all things DC.
- **Washingtonian** (www.washingtonian.com) Features on dining, entertainment and local luminaries.

WHEN TO GO

Peak season is late March through April. Crowds also throng in May. From late June through August it's crowded and hot. September and October is the shoulder season. December is festive.

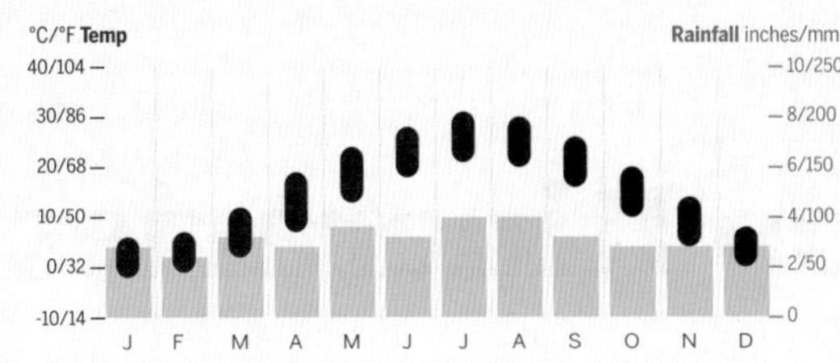

Arriving in Washington, DC

Ronald Reagan National Airport Metro trains ($2) depart every 10 minutes or so; they reach the city center in 20 minutes. A taxi is $12 to $20.

Dulles International Airport The Washington Flyer bus links Dulles to West Falls Church Metro; total time to center is 60 to 90 minutes, total cost $12.50. A taxi is $56 to $64.

Union Station All trains and many buses arrive at this huge station near the Capitol. There's a Metro stop inside for easy onward transport.

For much more on **arrival,** see p288.

Getting Around

The Metro is the main way to move around the city. Buy a day-pass ticket for $9, and remember to use it to enter *and* exit station turnstiles.

- **Metro** Fast, frequent, ubiquitous; operating between 5am and midnight (3am on weekends).
- **DC Circulator bus** Useful for Georgetown, Adams-Morgan and other areas with limited Metro service.
- **Bicycle** The Capital Bikeshare program makes biking a doable option.
- **Taxi** Relatively easy to find (less so at night), but costly.

For much more on **getting around,** see p289.

Sleeping

Accommodations will likely be your biggest expense in DC. The best digs are monuments of Victorian and jazz-era opulence. Chain hotels, B&Bs and apartments blanket the cityscape, too.

Several hostels are sprinkled around, typically in locations that are a bit far-flung. Groovy boutique hotels abound in the core neighborhoods, as do uber-luxury hotels catering to presidents, prime ministers and other heads of state. DC's atmospheric B&Bs (also called guesthouses) are often cheaper than hotels.

Useful Websites

- **Bed & Breakfast DC** (www.bedandbreakfastdc.com) One-stop shop to book B&Bs and apartments.
- **Destination DC** (www.washington.org) Options from the tourism office's jam-packed website.
- **WDCA Hotels** (www.wdcahotels.com) Discounter that sorts by neighborhood, price or eco-friendliness.

For much more on **accommodations,** see p241.

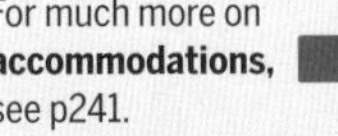

PRE-BOOKING REQUIRED

Many of Washington's top sights require that you plan ahead – way ahead, in some cases. Foremost among these is the White House, for which you should make your tour request three to six months in advance. Sights that need two to three months' leeway include the Pentagon, the Marine Corp parade, the US Naval Observatory, the State Department, the Federal Reserve and the House and Senate chambers at the Capitol.

Top Itineraries

Day One

National Mall (p80)

You might as well dive right into the good stuff, and the **Lincoln Memorial** is about as iconically DC as it gets. It's also a convenient starting point, since Abe sits at the far end of the Mall. Next up as you walk east is the powerful **Vietnam Veterans Memorial**. Then comes the **Washington Monument**, which is pretty hard to miss, being DC's tallest structure and all.

Lunch Munch sandwiches by an artsy waterfall at Cascade Cafe (p96).

National Mall (p80)

After lunch, it's time to explore the **National Gallery of Art**. Pick a side: East, for modern; or West, for Leonardo da Vinci, impressionists and other classics. Afterward, mosey across the lawn to the **National Air and Space Museum** and gape at the stuff hanging from the ceiling. The missiles and Wright Brothers' original plane are incomparably cool.

Dinner Hop the Metro to Afterwords Cafe (p171) in Dupont Circle.

Dupont (p165)

Dupont parties in the evening. Lounge-lovin' types can swill vodka at **Russia House**. Casual types can hoist brews at **Bier Baron**.

Day Two

Capitol Hill (p129)

Do the government thing today. Start in the **Capitol** and tour the statue-cluttered halls. Then walk across the street and up the grand steps to the **Supreme Court**; hopefully you'll get to hear a case argument. The **Library of Congress** and its 500 miles of books blow minds next door.

Lunch Have soup with Congress in the Capitol restaurant (p132).

White House Area (p98)

Hopefully you planned ahead and booked a **White House** tour. If not, make do at the **White House Visitor Center**. Pop into the **Round Robin** to see if any big wigs and lobbyists are clinking glasses. Zip over to the **Kennedy Center** to watch the free 6pm show.

Dinner Speaking of JFK: he proposed to Jackie at Martin's Tavern (p121).

Georgetown (p115)

After dinner, sink a pint in a friendly pub like **J Paul's**. On warm nights the outdoor cafes and boating action make **Georgetown Waterfront Park** a hot spot. And check if anyone groovy is playing at **Blues Alley**.

Day Three

Arlington (p214)

Walking around **Arlington National Cemetery** you can't help but be moved, from the Tomb of the Unknowns' dignified guards to John F Kennedy's eternal flame. One Metro stop south, the **Pentagon** offers another affecting memorial to those who died in the September 11, 2001, attacks.

Lunch Follow the warm-baked-bread smell to Matchbox Pizza (p158).

Downtown (p151)

It's an abundance of riches downtown. See the Declaration of Independence at the **National Archives**, and the seat where Lincoln was shot at **Ford's Theatre**. The **Reynolds Center for American Art** hangs sublime portraits. The **Newseum** has the Unabomber's cabin. The **International Spy Museum** has wiretaps and hidden cameras. You'll have to make some hard choices about which sights to visit.

Dinner It's an absolute must: a half-smoke at Ben's Chili Bowl (p195).

U Street (p189)

Soak up the neighborhood's jazzy vibe at **Bohemian Caverns** or the **Howard Theatre**. Or grab a drink on the outdoor porch at flirty **Marvin**.

Day Four

Upper Northwest DC (p205)

If you have kids, get to the **National Zoo** now. Even without kids, the zoo entertains thanks to its giant pandas and brainy orangutans. Earmark some quality time for **Washington National Cathedral** and its Darth Vader gargoyle, moon rock and Helen Keller's ashes, among other esoteric offerings.

Lunch The thin-crust pizza at 2 Amys (p210) is a religious experience.

Adams-Morgan (p178)

Adams-Morgan is Washington's party zone, but during the day **Meeps Vintage Fashionette**, **Idle Time Books** and **Crooked Beat Records** provide plenty to do. Plus you're well situated for happy hour at **Stetson's Famous Bar & Grill**.

Dinner Stroll into the Diner (p180) any time: it's open round the clock.

National Mall (p80)

End in the 'hood where you began your Washington trip, but experience it from a different perspective this time. Walk along Constitution Ave from east to west. The dramatically lit monuments glow ethereally at night. Climb the **Lincoln Memorial's** steps and turn around for one last, long fantastic view. That'll do it, until you and DC meet again.

If You Like...

Famous Monuments

Lincoln Memorial Abraham Lincoln gazes peacefully across the Mall from his hallowed Doric-columned temple. (p82)

Vietnam Veterans Memorial Simple and moving, the black wall shows the names of the Vietnam War's 58,267 casualties, listed in the order they died. (p84)

Tomb of the Unknowns Military guards maintain a somber, round-the-clock vigil at this crypt in Arlington National Cemetery. (p217)

Martin Luther King Jr Memorial Dr King's 30ft-tall likeness emerges from a mountain of granite at the Mall's newest must-see. (p87)

National WWII Memorial Soaring columns and stirring quotes mark this memorial smack in the Mall's midst. (p94)

Franklin Delano Roosevelt Memorial FDR's monument sprawls across 7.5 acres, an oasis of alcoves, fountains and contemplative inscriptions. (p94)

Thomas Jefferson Memorial TJ's round shrine, set amid a grove of gorgeous cherry trees, represents his famously shaped library. (p94)

Not-So-Famous Monuments

Korean War Veterans Memorial The haunting tribute depicts ghostly steel soldiers marching by a wall of etched faces. (p95)

George Mason Memorial The statesman who wrote the Bill

SCULPTOR: LEI YIXIN / LEE FOSTER / LONELY PLANET IMAGES ©

Martin Luther King Jr Memorial (p87)

of Rights' prototype gets his due via an oasis of flowers and fountains. (p94)

Titanic Memorial The waterside figure honors the men who sacrificed their lives for the women and children aboard the sinking ship. (p140)

National Japanese American Memorial Two cranes bound with barbed wire represent Japanese American citizens held in internment camps during WWII. (p137)

Navy Memorial A large plaza of flags and masts surrounds the lone sailor with his duffel bag. (p156)

National Law Enforcement Officers Memorial Its walls show the names of all US police officers killed in the line of duty since 1794. (p157)

African American Civil War Memorial Rifle-bearing troops who fought in the Union Army are immortalized in bronze. (p191)

Green Spaces

National Arboretum Learn your state tree amid 450 acres of meadowlands and wooded groves. (p192)

Rock Creek Park It's twice the size of New York's Central Park and wild enough to house coyotes. (p208)

Dumbarton Oaks The Georgetown mansion features sprawling, fountain-dotted gardens; big bonus if you visit during spring. (p118)

Botanic Garden Exotic flowers bloom in a glassy Mall greenhouse that looks like London's Crystal Palace. (p92)

Theodore Roosevelt Island Car and bike free, this Potomac River isle floats woodlands, trails and tranquility. (p218)

Georgetown Waterfront Park Sip an alfresco drink, ogle the yachts and watch rowing teams ply the Potomac. (p118)

East Potomac Park Walk, fish and smell the cherry blossoms in this lovely spot a hop and skip from the Mall. (p138)

Black History

Frederick Douglass National Historic Site The hilltop home of the escaped slave and statesman impresses almost as much as the man himself. (p137)

Anacostia Museum This Smithsonian museum rotates exhibits on African American history and culture. (p138)

African American Civil War Museum It goes beyond the war, following black history through the Civil Rights movement. (p191)

Howard Theatre It was the first major theater built to feature black entertainers performing for a predominantly black clientele. (p201)

Mt Zion Cemetery The crumbling headstones belong to free black residents who lived here in the 19th century. (p120)

Alexandria Black History Museum Alexandria was a major slave port, and the museum's small collection documents that experience. (p220)

Metropolitan AME Church Former slaves funded and built the mighty structure where Frederick Douglass used to preach. (p169)

Off-the-Beaten-Path Museums

National Postal Museum A whopping stamp collection and poignant old letters lift this museum beyond its humdrum name. (p136)

Textile Museum The nation's only textile museum unfurls exquisite fabrics and carpets from 3000 BC to the present. (p168)

National Museum of Health and Medicine Home to a giant hairball, Lincoln's assassination bullet and more macabre exhibits. (p194)

Hillwood Museum & Gardens The Russian art–filled manor of cereal heiress Marjorie Post also serves borscht and sparkling wine. (p209)

DEA Museum The war-on-drugs propaganda gives way to a sweet bong collection. (p219)

Stabler-Leadbeater Apothecary Museum Antique glass medicine bottles and Martha Washington's Scouring Compound line the shelves of the 1792 shop. (p219)

Woodrow Wilson House See how genteel Washingtonians lived and socialized in this 1920s-preserved home on Embassy Row. (p168)

Art

Reynolds Center for American Art Portraits on one side, O'Keeffe, Hopper and more of America's best on the other. (p154)

For more top Washington, DC, spots, see

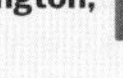

- Eating (p30)
- Drinking & Nightlife (p33)
- Entertainment (p35)
- Shopping (p37)
- Sports & Activities (p39)

National Gallery of Art It takes two massive buildings to hold the trove of paintings, sculptures and decorative arts from the Middle Ages to the present. (p85)

Phillips Collection The country's oldest modern-art museum is a cozy house that puts you face-to-face with Renoirs and Rothkos. (p177)

National Museums of Asian Art An incredible ensemble of ancient ceramics and temple sculptures spreads across two tunnel-connected galleries. (p90)

Hirshhorn Museum Rodin and Brancusi sculptures mingle with Miró and Warhol canvases in the Mall's cylindrical modern-art house. (p91)

Corcoran Gallery of Art Bronze sculptures, provocative special exhibitions and a French princess' salon fill its gilded halls. (p101)

Torpedo Factory Art Center The former arms factory has morphed into three floors of artists' studios offering ceramics, glassworks and jewelry. (p224)

Kid-Friendly Activities

National Zoo Bamboo-nibbling pandas, roaring lions, swinging orangutans, frolicking otters and many more critters roam the 163 acres. (p208)

National Museum of Natural History Dinosaurs! Henry the giant elephant! Insect zoo to watch tarantulas get fed! (p93)

Discovery Theater Cultural plays, puppet shows and storytelling are all part of the repertoire at the Smithsonian children's theater. (p97)

National Air and Space Museum It's a blast, with moon rocks, spaceships, starry films and a wild simulator ride. (p86)

Albert Einstein Statue Einstein's bemused, chubby bronze likeness is a magnet for climbing kids. (p107)

Newseum Junior journalists report 'live from the White House' via the TV studio (and get the take-home video to prove it). (p155)

International Spy Museum Budding James Bonds get to crawl through ductwork, peek through vents and find hidden recording devices. (p163)

Seeing Politics in Action

Capitol Sit in on committee hearings to see how bills start winding their way toward laws. (p131)

White House The protester-fueled political theater outside the building is where to observe democracy at its finest. (p100)

Round Robin The word 'lobbyist' was coined here, and bigwigs still swirl Scotch and cut deals in the gilded bar. (p112)

Cafe Milano Georgetown's premier Italian restaurant has long been the place to twirl spaghetti and spot political big shots. (p124)

Pop-Culture Icons

Watergate Complex The chi-chi apartment-hotel complex is synonymous with political scandal, thanks to Richard Nixon and his wiretaps. (p107)

Lincoln Memorial Steps Where MLK gave his 'dream' speech, and Owen Wilson and Vince Vaughn discussed girls in *Wedding Crashers*. (p82)

Washington Monument Tall, phallic and imbued with shadowy lore, it's also a frequent target of Hollywood destruction (think *2012* and *Mars Attacks*). (p83)

Exorcist Stairs Demonically possessed, head-spinning Reagan from *The Exorcist* sent victims to their screaming deaths in Georgetown. (p118)

Ben's Chili Bowl Everyone who's anyone – rock stars, actors, presidents – takes a counter seat at Ben's for the obligatory photo op. (p195)

Renaissance Mayflower Hotel J Edgar Hoover famously dined here; New York governor Eliot Spitzer infamously trysted with a call girl here. (p246)

Romantic Spots

Lincoln Memorial At dawn, nowhere in DC is as serene and lovely, which is why it's a popular place for proposals. (p82)

Constitution Gardens The shady grove, small pool and old stone cottage form a hidden oasis on the Mall. (p96)

National Sculpture Garden In summer jazz concerts set the mood; in winter the ice rink gets hearts racing. (p92)

Kennedy Center Terrace Grab a glass of wine and watch the city sparkling in every direction. (p113)

National Arboretum Take your sweetie to the Capital Columns Garden, and it's like you're walking amid Greek ruins. (p192)

Bishop's Garden Stroll hand-in-hand along the winding, rosebush-strewn paths in the National Cathedral's Gothic shadow. (p207)

Month by Month

TOP EVENTS

National Cherry Blossom Festival, March

White House Easter Egg Roll, April

Passport DC, May

Smithsonian Folklife Festival, June

Marine Corp Marathon, October

January

January is quiet – unless it's an inauguration year. Then it's madness. Crisp, clear days alternate with gray, frigid days. Every once in a while it will snow, shutting the city down.

Martin Luther King Jr's Birthday

On the third Monday in January and the weekend just prior, the city celebrates MLK's legacy with concerts, films and the recitation of his famous 'I Have a Dream' speech on the Lincoln Memorial steps.

Inauguration Day

Every four years, on January 20, DC is *the* place to be as the new president is sworn in. Dance cards' worth of inaugural balls accompany the peaceful power transition (held in 2013, 2017 etc).

February

The weekend around President's Day (the third Monday) brings crowds, but otherwise it's time for low-season bargains. Several events brighten up the gloomy days.

Chinese New Year

Bringing fire to the cold winter, the Chinatown parade lights up with dancing dragons and firecrackers. It's scheduled around the lunar calendar, meaning it sometimes falls in late January. Festivities occur along H and I Sts between 6th and 8th Sts. (www.chinatownchamber.us)

Washington DC International Wine & Food Festival

Local and celebrity chefs gather to stir up pots and pans. Expect a range of global fare, mouthwatering wines from all corners of the world and demonstrations by celebrated cooks. (www.wineandfooddc.com)

DC Fashion Week

The week-long event brings out an array of emerging talent and lesser-known international designers for runway shows and networking parties. Most events are open to the public, though some require tickets. It's also held in September. (www.dcfashionweek.org)

March

Cherry-blossom season – DC's tourism apex – ramps up mid-month, culminating in the famed festival. The trees are gorgeous, but boy, are you gonna pay for it.

St Patrick's Day

Dancers, bagpipers, marching bands and assorted merrymakers share the Irish love along Constitution Ave NW (from 7th to 17th Sts) at this big annual event. The parade is held on a Sunday, either on or preceding March 17. (www.dcstpatsparade.com)

Blossom Kite Festival

On the last Saturday of March, the skies near the Washington Monument come alive with color as kite lovers swoop on the Mall. This usually kicks off the Cherry Blossom Festival.

National Cherry Blossom Festival

The star of DC's annual calendar celebrates spring's arrival with boat rides in the Tidal Basin, evening walks by lantern light, cultural fairs and a parade. The two-week event, from late March to early April, also commemorates Japan's gift of 3000 cherry trees in 1912. (www.nationalcherryblossomfestival.org)

April

Cherry-blossom season continues to bring mega-crowds (and prices). The park service determines April 4 is the average 'peak bloom,' so if you want to see the trees at their shimmery pink best, this is it.

White House Easter Egg Roll

A tradition since 1878, some 30,000 families from around the US descend on the South Lawn on Easter Monday for storytelling, games, music and dance. The big event is the massive egg hunt, featuring 13,000 wooden eggs. (www.whitehouse.gov/eastereggroll)

FilmFest DC

Featuring over 70 films from across the globe, this 10-day, mid-month fest showcases new and avant-garde cinema at venues around the city. In addition to film screenings, there are guest appearances by directors and other special events. (www.filmfestdc.org)

May

It rains more in May than other months, but the temperature is comfy. It's a busy time for conventions and university graduations, so prices bump up and hotels are often full.

Passport DC

Passport DC offers the chance to peer inside some of the city's grandest embassies when they throw open their doors to the public throughout the month. Expect music, crafts, dancing and cuisine from each country hosting. (www.passportdc.org)

Rolling Thunder Ride for Freedom

Motorcycle-riding Vietnam vets commemorate Memorial Day (last Monday of May) with a ride along the National Mall to draw attention to the POWs and MIAs who were left behind. The route goes from the Pentagon to the Vietnam Veterans Memorial. (www.rollingthunder1.com)

June

Early June is a good time to visit, sort of post-school-group crowds and pre-summer-holiday crowds. The temperature steams up as the weeks go on.

Capital Pride

Some 250,000 people attend the gay pride party held in early to mid-June. The parade along Pennsylvania Ave to the Mall is the focal point, although there are also film screenings as well as performances. Many bars and clubs host special events. (www.capitalpride.org)

Barbecue Battle

Who makes the best barbecue? Teams compete in late June for $40,000 in prizes. In addition to tender ribs, chicken and sausage, you'll find live bands, cooking demonstrations, celebrity chefs and kiddie toys. (www.bbqdc.com)

DC Caribbean Carnival

On the last weekend in June, 300,000 people show up for island revelry on Georgia Ave. The highlights are live bands, food vendors, craft stalls and a brilliantly colorful parade (between Missouri Ave and Barry Pl). (www.dccaribbeancarnival.org)

Smithsonian Folklife Festival

For 10 days around Independence Day, this extravaganza celebrates international and US cultures on the Mall by the Smithsonian Castle. The fest features folk music, dance, crafts, storytelling and ethnic fare, and it highlights a diverse mix of countries. (www.festival.si.edu)

July

The days are exceptionally hot and humid, but that doesn't stop droves of vacationers from touring the sights. Temperatures regularly crack 90°F.

(Top) Fireworks over the National Mall and Washington Monument
(Bottom) Bhutanese monks making a mandala at the Smithsonian Folklife Festival

DENNIS JOHNSON / LONELY PLANET IMAGES ©

LEE FOSTER / LONELY PLANET IMAGES ©

Independence Day

On July 4, huge crowds gather on the Mall to watch marching bands parade and hear the Declaration of Independence read from the National Archives steps. Later, the National Symphony Orchestra plays a concert on the Capitol's steps, followed by mega-fireworks.

Capital Fringe Festival

The mid-month, two-and-a-half-week festival offers 500 wild and wacky performances of theater, dance, music, poetry and puppetry, performed by local and international artists at 30 venues around town. (www.capfringe.org)

September

September gets a gold star for awesomeness. The heat breaks. Kids go back to school. And Congress is not yet in session, so fewer people are in town jacking up rates.

Virgin Mobile FreeFest

Big-name acts plug in at the biggest rock concert around, held every September at Merriweather Post Pavilion in Columbia, MD, 30 miles northeast of the city. The fest runs shuttle buses to the scene. (www.virginmobilefreefest.com)

October

October is another banner month when lovely weather, reduced crowds and lower prices harmoniously converge.

Marine Corps Marathon

This popular road race routes through iconic DC scenery on the last Sunday in October. The course winds along the Potomac and takes in Georgetown, the entire length of the Mall, the Tidal Basin and Arlington Cemetery. (www.marinemarathon.com)

High Heel Drag Race

Outrageously dressed divas strut their stuff before large crowds, then line up for a no-holds-barred sprint down 17th St. An informal block party, with more colorful mayhem, ensues. Traditionally held on the Tuesday before Halloween (October 31) in Dupont.

December

'Tis the holiday season, and the city twinkles with good cheer from Zoo Lights to candlelight tours of historic homes to free holiday concerts. As your holiday gift, rates remain reasonable.

National Christmas Tree & Menorah Lighting

In early December, the president switches on the lights to the national Christmas Tree. Then he does the honors for the National Menorah. Live bands and choral groups play holiday music, which adds to the all-round good cheer. (www.thenationaltree.org)

Like a Local

When in Washington, do as the Washingtonians do. Seek out beer gardens and bountiful happy hours. Make brunch plans and chase down epicurean food trucks. Cheer on the Redskins and Nationals. Get on your bike. Get in line for late-night chow. Romantic strolls are always a fine option, too.

JUSTIN MATHEWS / LONELY PLANET IMAGES ©

Joggers in Constitution Gardens (p96)

Drinking

Hangouts

Neighborhood bars are all around the city, but the best batch for the local vibe are in Capitol Hill (particularly along H St NE and 8th St SE, aka Barracks Row) and Columbia Heights. The hangouts come in many guises: some are watering holes for an older crowd, some are frat-boy-style keg-o-ramas, and some are mod gastro-pubs with sophisticated drink and comfort-food menus.

Alfresco

Rooftop terraces, backyard beer gardens, sidewalk patios – alfresco drinking by any name makes local tipplers happy. The relatively temperate climate means Washingtonians have much of the year to head outdoors and hoist their craft libations. Columbia Heights' nighthawk joints, U St's trendy bars, Georgetown's waterfront and the White House Area's hotel bars are all good spots to get out with a glass in hand.

Happy Hour

Work hard, play hard – and that means hitting the bar right after the office. Washington is a big happy-hour town. Practically all bars (and restaurants that double as bars) have some sort of drink and/or food special for a few hours between 4pm and 7pm. Interns and staffers on a budget pile in to take advantage of half-price burgers and two-for-one mojitos and to decompress over the senator's latest appropriations bill. Downtown, Capitol Hill and Dupont Circle see lots of happy-hour action. Check www.dchappyhours.com.

Post-Bar Bites

While DC isn't known as a late-night town, it must be admitted that sometimes citizens do stay out carousing until 2am or so, and then they need something to soak up the booze. Mini-chain Julia's Empanadas (www.juliasempanadas.com) is often there to meet the need. Post-partiers also make their way to Adams-Morgan or Dupont Circle, where 24-hour establishments like the Diner and Afterwords Cafe sling awesome hash in the wee hours.

Eating

Brunch

This meal is taken seriously on weekends, especially Sunday. Meeting up with friends at midday and lingering over bottomless Bloody Marys and a hulking pile of eggs and potatoes is de rigueur. Many restaurants offer boozy specials around Adams-Morgan, Dupont Circle and Eastern Market. There are even blogs devoted to the subject. Check out the Bitches who Brunch (www.bitcheswhobrunch.com).

Food Trucks

It's official: locals are obsessed with food trucks. They stalk them via Food Truck Fiesta (www.foodtruckfiesta.com) and chase them around Farragut Sq, Foggy Bottom and L'Enfant Plaza at lunchtime, then Dupont Circle, Georgetown and Adams-Morgan toward evening. New vehicles seem to roll out every week, including trucks by big-name chefs selling everything from Iberico pork sandwiches to gourmet mac-and-cheese.

Not a truck per se, Crunk Cakes (www.districtofcrunk.com) is a roving vendor who inspires deep allegiance from DC barflies. The alcohol-infused cupcakes – such as the chocolate-Guinness-whiskey Irish Car Bomb – show up in various bars, frequently around Capitol Hill.

Markets

Eastern Market, near Capitol Hill, is the city's main bazaar and a great place to soak up local flavor. Families shop, browsers browse, friends laugh – oh, and there are good eats (mmm, fried oyster sandwiches), too. The time to go is on the weekends, when a lively craft market and adjoining flea market surround the area.

Most neighborhoods also have their own farmers market one day per week from May through October. Residents flock to these to buy produce, eggs, cheese, honey and cider from nearby small farms.

Pastimes

Spectator Sports

Washingtonians support a full slate of pro sports teams – the Redskins (football), Nationals (baseball), Wizards (basketball), Capitals (hockey) and DC United (soccer) – and all have rabid fans. The surest way to feel like a local is to catch a 'Skins game at a city pub. If they're playing the hated Dallas Cowboys, all the better. DC's transients and natives bond over the Nationals, too; games are good fun and can be cheap if you score $5 grandstand tickets. Imbibing in the park's outdoor beer garden is a pre-game ritual.

Biking

The Capital Bikeshare program prompts many citizens to make short-haul trips on two wheels, and the District's terrific array of long-haul trails brings out droves of weekend cyclists. The 18.5-mile, river-clasping Mount Vernon Trail is a particular favorite with locals, along with the Capital Crescent Trail and C&O Canal & Towpath. Bike-rental companies make it easy to join the action.

Mall Activities

Yes, tourists throng the Mall, but so do locals. Joggers, Ultimate teams and volleyball players are among those hanging out on the scrubby green grass.

Odds & Ends

Romantic Places

If you're looking for places that bestow a 'kiss me' vibe, follow locals to their favorites. Constitution Gardens, the Lincoln Memorial and the National Sculpture Garden win smooching points on the Mall; being there at sunrise or sunset ups the ante. A Mall stroll at night past the dramatically lit monuments is another sure thing. And what lips can resist their beloved's in the Capital Columns Garden at the National Arboretum or the Bishop's Garden at Washington National Cathedral?

Airplane Spotting

There are a couple of well-known sites where residents go for fun views of planes taking off and landing. Hains Point, at the southern tip of East Potomac Park in southwest DC, is one with picnicking opportunities. Gravelly Point in Arlington, VA, is another.

For Free

We're just going to say it: Washington, DC, has the best freebies on the planet. From the Smithsonian Institution's 19 museums, to gratis theater and concerts, to jaunts through the White House and National Archives, you can be entertained for weeks without spending a dime.

SCULPTOR: ED HAMILTON / RICK GERHARTER / LONELY PLANET IMAGES ©

African American Civil War Memorial (p191)

Museum Mania

Smithsonian

Oh, sweet Smithsonian – was ever an eccentric antimonarchist Englishman's endowment better spent (see the box, p91)? The top draws of the institution's 19 museums are the rocket-fueled National Air and Space Museum; the dinosaur- and diamond-stuffed National Museum of Natural History; the pop culture–rich National Museum of American History; and the National Zoo, home to bamboo-lovin' giant pandas.

The Reynolds Center for American Art (part portrait gallery, part who's who of big-name US artists) and the National Museums of Asian Art (incredible temple sculptures, ancient ceramics) are among those that are less packed but equally sublime.

Other Free Museums

There's more beyond the Smithsonian. The National Gallery of Art splits into two massive buildings to show its trove of paintings, sculptures and decorative arts. The US Holocaust Memorial Museum haunts long after your visit ends. The hidden Art Museum of the Americas features a fantastic 20th-century collection. It's a bit farther-flung than the others, but the African American Civil War Museum goes beyond the war between the states and follows black history through the Civil Rights movement.

Free Days at Paid Museums

The intimate, Renoir-filled Phillips Collection is free every Tuesday through Friday. The Corcoran Gallery of Art's gilded halls are free on Saturdays during summer. The regal National Museum of Women in the Arts is free the first Sunday of every month. The Natural History Museum's separate, next-door Butterfly Pavilion is free on Tuesday.

Monument Madness

Monuments pack the Mall and spill off into the surrounding neighborhoods. There are too many for us to list here, but rest assured: they're all free.

JUSTIN MATHEWS / LONELY PLANET IMAGES ©

National Public Radio headquarters (p157)

Lincoln Memorial
Abraham Lincoln's neoclassical temple awes in its own right. Factor in that you can stand where Martin Luther King Jr gave his 'I Have a Dream' speech and have killer views out over the Mall, and it's hard to believe the priceless experience costs nada.

Washington Monument
The iconic obelisk – the District's tallest structure – took a beating in the 2011 earthquake, but once it's back in business, the view from the top is unparalleled.

Tomb of the Unknowns
Military personnel maintain a round-the-clock vigil at this crypt located in Arlington National Cemetery, and the changing of the guard is one of DC's most moving sights.

Government in Action

White House
Unlike many palaces around the globe, the US Presidential Palace (as it was once known) is free to tour. Heck, you might even run into the First Lady or First Dog.

National Archives
Really – we'd pay to see the Declaration of Independence with John Hancock's, er, John Hancock scrawled across the bottom.

Capitol
Guided excursions through the mighty, white-domed sanctum of Congress, cluttered with busts, statues, frescoes and gardens, cost zilch.

Bureau of Engraving & Printing
Though the Treasury tour is about money, it won't be taking any of yours. Watch millions of dollars as they're printed, cut and inspected.

Library of Congress
The world's largest library is more than a stack of books. It's a museum with 500-year-old world maps, historic photographs, concerts and film screenings – all free.

Show Time

Kennedy Center
The show could star the National Symphony, a gospel group or an Indian dance troupe, but whatever it is, count on it happening at 6pm for free at the Kennedy's Millennium Stage.

Busboys & Poets
OK, the Tuesday-night open mic costs $5. But that's nothing for the rollicking, two-hour show of seasoned performers, spoken-word rookies and jammin' musicians.

Politics & Prose
Rock stars, past presidents, Pulitzer winners – if they've written a book, they'll do a free reading at Politics & Prose. Events take place almost daily.

National Theatre
Puppets, magic, ballet and music are all on tap for the free, family-oriented Saturday shows at 9:30am and 11am.

Shakespeare Theatre Company
'Free for All' is an annual end-of-summer tradition: the company picks a Bard classic

and performs it gratis for two and a half weeks.

Museum Concerts

The National Gallery of Art offers free choral and classical concerts at 6:30pm Sunday, which take place in the West Building. It also sponsors Jazz in the Garden outdoors amid the sculptures from 5:30pm to 8:30pm on summer Fridays. The Reynolds Center for American Art hosts free jazz concerts the third Thursday of each month.

History Highlights

Ford's Theatre

The theater where John Wilkes Booth shot Abraham Lincoln provides free tours exploring what happened that fateful night in April 1865. The basement museum shows artifacts such as the murder weapon. Petersen House, where Lincoln died, sits across the street and is included as part of the ticket.

Frederick Douglass National Historic Site

The hilltop home of revered abolitionist Frederick Douglass provides a compelling look into his life via original furnishings, books and personal belongings.

Tours

DC by Foot

Knowledgeable guides working on a tip-only basis share history and lore along routes covering the Mall, Arlington Cemetery and Lincoln's assassination.

Cultural Tourism DC

The tours are DIY using free maps, apps and audio provided by Cultural Tourism DC (www.culturaltourismdc.org). More than 10 neighborhoods have in-depth heritage trails; the tours reveal civil-rights sites, espionage hot spots and more.

National Public Radio

Wave to your favorite correspondents as you walk past the foreign and national desks of the venerable news organization.

Eating

A homegrown foodie revolution has transformed the once buttoned-up DC dining scene. Driving it is the bounty of the mid-Atlantic and Southern farms at the city's doorstep. The number of ethnic eateries has also grown in leaps and bounds, with DC ranking only behind New York and LA in terms of sheer variety.

Global Influence

Washington, DC, is one of the most diverse, international cities of its size in America, heavily populated by immigrants, expats and diplomats from every inhabited continent in the world. People from far away crave the food of home, and so there's a glut of good ethnic eating and international influences around here. Salvadoran, Ethiopian, Vietnamese, French, Spanish, West African – they've all become Washingtonian.

Local Movement

The locally sourced food movement has been a huge boon to the Washington eating scene. Many visitors to the District don't have an understanding of its unique geography, the way it's situated between two of the best food-production areas in America: Chesapeake Bay and the Virginia Piedmont. From the former come crabs, oysters and rockfish; the latter provides game, pork, wine and peanuts.

Southern Influence

Keep in mind that DC also occupies the fault line between two of America's greatest culinary regions: the northeast and the South. The South, in particular, exerts a tremendous pull. The city offers heaps of soul food and its high-class incarnations, so get ready to loosen the belt for plates of fried chicken, catfish, collard greens, sweet-potato hash and butter-smothered grits – all washed down with sweet iced tea, of course.

Half-Smokes

DC's claim to native culinary fame is the half-smoke, a bigger, coarser, spicier and better version of the hot dog. There's little agreement on where the name comes from. But there is general consensus as to what goes on a half-smoke: chili and chopped onions, every time.

Food Trucks

As in most other US cities, the food-truck frenzy has hit Washington. Empanadas, chocolate pie, crab cakes, cupcakes – you name it and there's a truck driving around selling it out the window. Trucks generally prowl office worker–rich hot spots like Farragut Sq, Foggy Bottom and L'Enfant Plaza around lunchtime, and then Dupont Circle, Georgetown and Adams-Morgan toward evening. Food Truck Fiesta (www.foodtruckfiesta.com) tracks their real-time locations.

Eating by Neighborhood

➡ **National Mall** (p96) It's a food desert beyond the museum cafes and food carts.

➡ **White House Area & Foggy Bottom** (p107) Pinnacle of the power lunch and pricy, show-off dinner scene.

➡ **Georgetown** (p120) Elegant old-guard restaurants mix with quick-bite student eateries.

➡ **Capitol Hill & Southeast DC** (p140) Casual burger or pizza joints; burgeoning hipster spots on H St NE and Barracks Row.

➡ **Downtown & Penn Quarter** (p158) Chinatown, chic bistros and small-plates wine bars share the sidewalks.

➡ **Dupont Circle & Kalorama** (p171) Delicious fusion of classy nouveau cuisine, upscale ethnic spots and bohemian cafes.

➡ **Adams-Morgan** (p180) Global smorgasbord of Ethiopian, Latin, Italian, Cajun and late-night booze absorbers.

➡ **U Street, Columbia Heights & Northeast** (p195) Soul food on U Street, Latin and other ethnic chow in Columbia Heights.

➡ **Upper Northwest DC** (p210) Hip, family-friendly pizza and comfort-food places pepper the residential 'hood.

➡ **Northern Virginia** (p221) Cheap Vietnamese and Korean cooks beyond Arlington; upscale and pub-grub spots fill Alexandria.

NEED TO KNOW

Price Ranges

In our listings we've used the following price codes to represent the cost of a main dish at dinner:

$	under $12
$$	$12 to $30
$$$	more than $30

Opening Hours

➡ Most restaurants: breakfast 7am or 8am to 11am, lunch 11am or 11:30am to 2:30pm or 3pm, dinner 5pm or 6pm to 10pm Sunday to Thursday, to 11pm or midnight Friday and Saturday.

Reservations

➡ It's a good idea to make a reservation for eateries in the midrange and upper price bracket, especially on weekends. A phone call that afternoon or the day before is usually sufficient.

➡ Many restaurants let you book online through OpenTable (www.opentable.com).

Tipping

➡ Tipping 15% of the total bill is the accepted minimum. If service is good, 20% is a decent average tip; tip more if service is exceptional.

Credit Cards Versus Cash

➡ Almost all restaurants accept credit cards, aside from a smattering of budget places.

Saving Money

➡ Restaurants around Downtown and the Kennedy Center often have pre- or post-theater menus. This generally means a three-course meal for $30 or so, offered before 7pm or after 9:30pm.

Websites

➡ Yelp (www.yelp.com/dc) Everyday eaters give their restaurant opinions.

➡ Metrocurean (www.metrocurean.com) Covers the local dining scene.

➡ DC Food Finder (www.dcfoodfinder.org) Finds farmers markets.

Lonely Planet's Top Choices

Dangerously Delicious Pies (p140) Sweet and savory slices of flaky goodness.

Ben's Chili Bowl (p195) Gossip with locals while downing a half-smoke.

Birch & Barley (p158) Indulge in toffee-bacon donuts, home-made pastas and other nouveau comfort foods.

Afterwords Cafe (p171) Browse the stacks and feed your face at this bookstore-bistro combo.

Diner (p180) Stuffed pancakes at 4am never tasted so good.

Old Ebbitt Grill (p109) Play spot the politico while carving into a steak.

Best by Budget

$

Toki Underground (p140)

Good Stuff Eatery (p140)

Jimmy T's (p141)

Vace Deli (p211)

Teaism (p159)

$$

Westend Bistro (p173)

Blue Duck Tavern (p172)

Eatonville (p197)

Comet Ping Pong (p210)

$$$

Equinox (p110)

Kinkead's (p110)

Citronelle (p121)

City Zen (p145)

Best by Cuisine

American

Blue Duck Tavern (p172)

Nora (p173)

Palena (p210)

Equinox (p110)

Southern

Eatonville (p197)

Florida Avenue Grill (p197)

Vidalia (p173)

Bayou (p110)

Latin American

Dos Gringos (p198)

Mixtec (p181)

Restaurant Judy (p197)

Chix (p196)

Asian

Kotobuki (p124)

Toki Underground (p140)

Malaysia Kopitiam (p172)

Eden Center (p221)

French

Cafe du Parc (p109)

Montmartre (p141)

Bistrot du Coin (p171)

Bistro D'Oc (p160)

Italian

Obelisk (p172)

Coppi's Organic (p196)

2 Amys (p210)

Matchbox Pizza (p158)

Best Bakeries & Sweets

Dolcezza (p124)

Baked & Wired (p120)

Sticky Fingers (p198)

Pitango Gelato (p144)

BreadLine (p109)

Best Late Night

Afterwards Cafe (p171)

Yechon (p222)

Quick Pita (p124)

Amsterdam Falafelshop (p181)

Julia's Empanadas (p182)

Best Brunch

Tabard Inn (p172)

Perrys (p182)

Crème (p197)

Afterwards Cafe (p171)

Best Seafood

Kinkead's (p110)

BlackSalt (p121)

Market Lunch (p144)

Maine Avenue Fish Market (p144)

Pearl Dive Oyster Palace (p197)

Best Vegetarian

Sticky Fingers (p198)

Rasika (p159)

Amsterdam Falafelshop (p181)

Restaurant Eve (p222)

Etete (p197)

Best for Kids

Good Stuff Eatery (p140)

Jimmy T's (p141)

Ted's Bulletin (p141)

Lebanese Taverna (p211)

Best Burgers

Martin's Tavern (p121)

Good Stuff Eatery (p140)

Granville Moore's (p141)

Desperados (p197)

Ray's Hell Burger (p221)

Drinking & Nightlife

When Andrew Jackson swore the oath of office in 1800, the self-proclaimed populist dispensed with pomp and circumstance and, quite literally, threw a raging kegger. Folks got so gone they started looting art from the White House. The historical lesson: DC loves a drink, and these days it enjoys said tipples in many incarnations besides executive-mansion-trashing throwdowns.

Beer

Beer is the drink on everyone's lips at present. Newish establishments such as Birch & Barley pour it seriously: out of special copper pipes that transport 50 craft brews and cask-aged ales to the taps. In 2011, DC Brau became the District's first brewery to launch in more than 50 years. It has met with great success, distributing zesty suds such as Thyme After Thyme, a herb-spiced Belgian-style ale.

Cocktails

The craft-cocktail craze is in full swing. Mixologists do their thing using small-batch liqueurs, fresh-squeezed juices, hand-chipped ice – and maybe some bacon or charcuterie thrown in for good measure. It may sound pretentious, but most of the bars are actually pretty cool.

Boozy Cupcakes

Here's a trend you don't see often: crunk cakes, as in alcohol-infused cupcakes. They're sold by roving vendors in bars around the city. Have a few Irish Car Bombs (Guinness, Jameson, Baileys and chocolate cake) and let us know how you feel the next morning.

Happy Hour

Washington is a big happy-hour town. Practically all bars have some sort of drink and/or food special for a few hours between 4pm and 7pm. This is particularly welcome at restaurants that double as bars – which many do – because often they'll sell affordable, small-plate versions of menu items during happy hour.

Drinking & Nightlife by Neighborhood

➡ **White House Area & Foggy Bottom** (p112) Wheeler-dealer hotel bars by the White House, scruffy college bars in Foggy Bottom.

➡ **Georgetown** (p125) British-style pubs, sports bars and slick martini lounges compete on M St.

➡ **Capitol Hill & Southeast DC** (p145) Friendly taverns orbit Cap Hill; awesomely offbeat bars line up on H St NE.

➡ **Downtown & Penn Quarter** (p161) Beer lovers' bars lie beyond the VIP clubs and Verizon Center sports bars.

➡ **Dupont Circle & Kalorama** (p174) The gay-nightlife mecca also offers fun dance clubs and sleek lounges.

➡ **Adams-Morgan** (p182) 18th St gets wild on weekend nights, thanks to raucous dives and youthful clubs.

➡ **U Street, Columbia Heights & Northeast** (p199) U St has the flirty 'it' places; trendy nighthawks stake out Columbia Heights' bars.

➡ **Upper Northwest DC** (p211) Drinking spots are quiet and spread out.

➡ **Northern Virginia** (p223) Arlington rocks along Wilson and Clarendon Blvds; Alexandria gets pubby on King St.

NEED TO KNOW

Opening Hours

- Bars: 5pm to 1am or 2am weekdays, 3am on weekends.
- Nightclubs: 9pm to 1am or 2am weekdays, 3am on weekends.
- Places that double as restaurants open around 11:30am.

Taxes

- Sales tax is 6%.

Tipping

- 10-15% per round, minimum per drink $1.

Door Policies

- Some clubs have a dress code that requires closed-toe shoes and long pants, and occasionally no jeans or hats. In most of the places we've reviewed you can come as you are.
- The drinking age is 21. Take your driver's license or passport out at night: you will be asked for ID.

Resources & Websites

The following publications are available online or as free hard-copy newspapers you'll find around town.

- On Tap (www.ontaponline.com) Nightlife and entertainment listings.
- Washington Blade (www.washingtonblade.com) Gay and lesbian happenings.
- Washington City Paper (www.washingtoncitypaper.com) Alternative publication with entertainment coverage.

Lonely Planet's Top Choices

Wonderland (p200) Edgy, eccentric, with oddball folk art and a sweet patio.

H Street Country Club (p146) Booze while playing shuffleboard and DC-themed minigolf.

Little Miss Whiskey's Golden Dollar (p145) Sip killer beer and whiskey amid hallucinogenic decor.

Round Robin (p112) Knock back a Scotch at the place that birthed the lobbyist.

Dan's Cafe (p182) One of DC's great dives, like an evil Elks Club.

Best Cocktails

Fruit Bat (p146)

Firefly (p174)

POV (p112)

Poste (p161)

Black Jack (p200)

Best Lounges

Russia House (p174)

18th Street Lounge (p174)

Science Club (p175)

Tryst (p183)

Continental (p223)

Best Beer

Meridian Pint (p201)

Churchkey (p161)

Birreria Paradiso (p125)

RFD Washington (p161)

Bier Baron (p174)

Best Wine Bars

Cork Wine Bar (p200)

Dickson Wine Bar (p200)

Room 11 (p201)

Bardeo (p211)

Best Outdoor Terraces

Le Bar (p112)

POV (p112)

Sequoia (p125)

Argonaut (p146)

Marvin (p199)

Best Local Scene

Red Derby (p201)

Marvin (p199)

Stetson's Famous Bar & Grill (p183)

Whitlow's on Wilson (p223)

Best Gay & Lesbian

JR's (p175)

Phase One (p146)

Cobalt (p174)

Number Nine (p175)

Nellie's (p200)

Best Clubs

Cobalt (p174)

Cafe Citron (p175)

Bukom (p182)

Chief Ike's Mambo Room (p183)

Habana Village (p183)

Best Pubs

J Paul's (p125)

Star & Shamrock (p146)

Kelly's Irish Times (p146)

Blaguard (p183)

Ireland's Four Courts (p223)

Entertainment

From the evening-wear elegance of the Kennedy Center to punk stripping the paint at an H St club, the nation's capital has an envious slate of performances. It caters to Shakespeare, jazz, classical-music and poetry-slam fans particularly well. Best of all, many shows are free.

Music

JAZZ

Washington's jazz affair started in the early 20th century, when U St NW was known as Black Broadway for its many music theaters. Relics from that era, such as Bohemian Caverns, still host sweet notes.

ROCK

DC's rock scene thrives, and the city is a great place to catch a show. Clubs like the Black Cat are typical: intimate, something indie-cool always going on, and nights of DJ music in the mix.

CLASSICAL

The Kennedy Center is ground zero for symphony, opera and other classical fare. But for all its high-falutin' ways, it's also surprisingly accessible to the masses, with free performances nightly at 6pm.

MILITARY

Military music is big here. The Marine Corps, Air Force, Army and Navy bands alternate performing at 8pm most weeknights on the Capitol's steps in summer.

Theater

Washington has many adventurous small stages and multi-faceted arts centers that do intriguing work. Keep an eye out for Atlas, Studio and Source theaters.

Spoken Word

DC has hundreds of author readings, poetry slams, story slams and open-mic nights. Busboys & Poets (p202) anchors the scene.

Entertainment by Neighborhood

- **National Mall** (p97) Free jazz in the sculpture garden, free films on the lawn.
- **White House Area & Foggy Bottom** (p113) The Kennedy Center runs the show, with performances nightly.
- **Georgetown** (p126) Dizzy Gillespie's old stomping grounds are the main draw.
- **Capitol Hill & Southeast DC** (p147) Vintage jazz, burlesque and Shakespeare make this 'hood top of the heap.
- **Downtown & Penn Quarter** (p162) The majority of theaters, from opulent to comic to experimental, concentrate here.
- **Dupont Circle & Kalorama** (p176) Art galleries cluster in Dupont.
- **Adams-Morgan** (p186) Rowdy live music, cozy jazz and avant-garde theater fill the nights.
- **U Street, Columbia Heights & Northeast** (p201) Splendid mix of historic jazz venues, thrashing rock clubs and poetry slams.
- **Upper Northwest DC** (p212) Cutting-edge dance, a starry outdoor amphitheater and literary events are on tap.
- **Northern Virginia** (p224) Fiddlin' pubs and a sleek, worldly art space make it worth the trip.

NEED TO KNOW

Ticket Shops

➡ **Ticketplace** (www.ticketplace.org; 407 7th St NW; ⏲11am-6pm Wed-Fri, 10am-5pm Fri) sells half-price day-of-show tickets to theater, dance, symphony and opera performances. Some tickets are also available for the weeks ahead. Search by date or by venue. Buy online or in person at the Downtown booth.

Saving Money

➡ Patrons aged 18 to 30 can get deep discounts – even free tickets – to all opera, ballet, symphony and other Kennedy Center performances via **MyTix** (www.kennedy-center.org/offers/mytix).

➡ Arena Stage puts half-price tickets on sale at the box office 30 minutes before show time.

➡ Many theaters, such as Source and Woolly Mammoth, offer 'pay what you can' admission during preview shows.

Websites

➡ **Ticketplace** (www.ticketplace.org) Half-price offers.

➡ **Gold Star** (www.goldstar.com) More half-price offers from national ticket broker.

➡ **Destination DC** (www.washington.org/calendar) Full events listings.

➡ **Culture Capital** (www.culturecapital.com) Arts-specific listings.

➡ **Pink Line Project** (www.pinklineproject.com) Holds salons for artsy mingling; offers discount tickets.

Lonely Planet's Top Choices

Red Palace (p147) Sexy, bizarre, punk-rock-burlesque venue.

HR-57 (p147) A BYO jazz preservation hall with open jam sessions.

Capitol Steps (p162) Theater troupe that takes corny, bipartisan jabs at Congress.

Busboys & Poets (p202) Ground zero for open-mic poetry readings and story slams.

Kennedy Center (p113) DC's performing-arts king of the hill.

Best Jazz & Blues

Madam's Organ (p186)

Bohemian Caverns (p202)

Blues Alley (p126)

Columbia Station (p186)

Basin Street Lounge (p224)

Best Rock & Funk

Rock & Roll Hotel (p147)

9:30 Club (p202)

U Street Music Hall (p202)

DC9 (p202)

Black Cat (p202)

Best Classical & Opera

National Symphony Orchestra (p113)

Washington National Opera (p113)

Phillips Collection Concerts (p176)

Best Theater Shows

Arena Stage (p147)

Folger Shakespeare Theatre (p148)

Atlas Performing Arts Center (p148)

Studio Theatre (p162)

Source Theatre Company (p202)

Best Theater Venues

Howard Theatre (p201)

Carter Barron Amphitheater (p212)

National Theatre (p162)

Warner Theatre (p162)

Best Free & Low Cost

Jazz in the Garden (p97)

Screen on the Green (p97)

Politics & Prose (p212)

Shakespeare Theatre 'Free for All' (p162)

Library of Congress (p148)

Best Art Galleries

Studio Gallery (p171)

District of Columbia Arts Center (p180)

Foundry Gallery (p171)

Touchstone Gallery (p162)

Civilian Art Projects (p163)

Best Cinema

Screen on the Green (p97)

Arlington Cinema & Drafthouse (p224)

Mary Pickford Theater (p148)

AMC Loews Uptown 1 (p212)

Best World & Folk Music

Birchmere (p224)

Tiffany Tavern (p224)

Rock & Roll Hotel (p147)

Shopping

Shopping in DC means many things, from browsing atmospheric antique shops to perusing rare titles at secondhand booksellers. Temptations abound for lovers of vinyl, kitschy home furnishings, one-of-a-kind jewelry and art, and handicrafts imported from all corners of the globe. And, of course, that Abe Lincoln pencil sharpener and rhinestone Obama hat you've been wanting await...

Specialties

No surprise: politically oriented souvenirs are Washington's specialty, from stars-and-stripes boxer shorts to rubber Nixon masks to White House snow globes. Museum shops contain iconic gifts like stuffed pandas from the National Zoo and balsa-wood airplanes from the National Air and Space Museum, as well as more unusual items like weavings from indigenous tribes at the National Museum of the American Indian and Kenyan handicrafts from the National Museum of African Art.

Fashion

Don't be fooled by all the blue suits and khakis you see those government people wearing. This is a city where you'll find an assortment of funky vintage shops, fashion-forward boutiques, couture-loving consignment stores and specialty shops dealing in African robes, hats, lingerie, urban gear and stylish footwear.

Markets

Eastern Market, near Capitol Hill, is the city's main bazaar. It's a splendid place to pick up fresh fruits, vegetables and other edible items. The time to go is on the weekends, when a lively craft market and adjoining flea market surround the area. The U Street Flea Market is another place to soak up local culture on weekends. From May through October most neighborhoods have a farmers market one day a week, where vendors sell a smattering of crafts, soaps and herbal products in addition to produce.

Shopping by Neighborhood

➡ **National Mall** (p95) It's all about museum shops.

➡ **White House Area & Foggy Bottom** (p113) Gems hide in office buildings, but mostly souvenir shops dot the streets.

➡ **Georgetown** (p126) DC's top corridor for upscale brand-name stores, peppered with vintage shops.

➡ **Capitol Hill & Southeast DC** (p148) Eastern Market is the core, along with the Hill's souvenir and campy shops.

➡ **Downtown & Penn Quarter** (p163) It's mostly generic chains, though galleries and museum shops add character.

➡ **Dupont Circle & Kalorama** (p176) A big, quirky variety of bookstores, vintage shops, homewares and artsy stuff.

➡ **Adams-Morgan** (p186) Indie record shops, doorknob shops, bong shops and ethnic handicrafts scatter along 18th St.

➡ **U Street, Columbia Heights & Northeast** (p203) Distinctive antiques and homewares line 14th and U Sts; big-box retailers throng Columbian Heights Metro.

➡ **Upper Northwest DC** (p212) Lots of family-friendly shops, plus a famed bookstore; malls toward Friendship Heights.

➡ **Northern Virginia** (p224) Galleries in Alexandria; malls in Arlington and beyond.

NEED TO KNOW

Opening Hours

➡ Malls: 10am to 8pm or 9pm Monday to Saturday, 11am to 6pm Sunday.

➡ Shops: 10am to 7pm Monday to Saturday, noon to 6pm Sunday.

Taxes

➡ Sales tax is 6% in DC and 5% in Virginia.

Websites

➡ **Refinery 29** (www.refinery29.com/washington-dc) Fashion news, events and sales.

➡ **Daily Candy** (www.dailycandy.com/washington-dc) Local style and trends.

➡ **Washingtonian** (www.washingtonian.com)

Lonely Planet's Top Choices

Miss Pixie's (p203) A trove of timeworn curiosities to sort through.

Meeps Vintage Fashionette (p187) Cowboy shirts, Jackie O sunglasses and magnificent duds from past eras.

Torpedo Factory Art Center (p224) Three floors of artists' studios fill an old munitions factory.

Politics & Prose (p212) Independent, brain-food bookstore that hosts perpetual author events.

International Spy Museum Shop (p163) The place to get that mustache disguise or hidden recording device.

Best Books

Kramerbooks (p176)

Idle Time Books (p187)

Second Story Books (p176)

Big Planet Comics (p203)

American Institute of Architects Bookstore (p114)

Best for Kids

Tugooh Toys (p126)

National Zoo Store (p212)

National Building Museum Shop (p163)

Sullivan's Toy Store (p212)

Best Museum Shops

National Gallery of Art (p95)

National Museum of the American Indian (p95)

National Museum of African Art (p95)

National Air and Space Museum (p95)

National Museum of Natural History (p95)

Best Souvenirs

White House Historical Association Gift Shop (p113)

Archives Shop (p163)

Political Americana (p163)

Indian Craft Shop (p113)

Skynear Designs Gallery (p187)

Best Fashion

Caramel (p187)

Nana (p204)

Coup de Foudre (p163)

Relish (p127)

Redeem (p203)

Best Antiques & Vintage

Hunted House (p148)

Brass Knob (p187)

Annie Cream Cheese (p126)

Old Print Gallery (p126)

Kulturas (p176)

Best Music

Crooked Beat Records (p187)

Second Story Books (p176)

Smash! (p187)

Best Food & Drink

Cowgirl Creamery (p163)

Smucker Farms (p203)

Teaism (p163)

Dean & DeLuca (p126)

Best Homewares

Hunted House (p148)

Home Rule (p203)

Skynear Designs Gallery (p187)

Tabletop (p177)

Good Wood (p204)

Best Arts & Crafts

Renwick Gallery (p114)

Appalachian Spring (p126)

Beadazzled (p176)

Woven History (p149)

Sports & Activities

The nation's capital comes together in ways unexpected and touching when sports are at stake. It's about the only thing that gets citizens as pumped as politics, and it's more accessible, if not quite as cutthroat. But the city doesn't just watch sports, it plays them too, from Ultimate games on the Mall to bocce ball in Capitol Hill.

Spectator Sports

The football-playing Redskins are the most popular team of the lot. The other ties that bind are the Capitals on ice; the failure-prone Wizards pro basketball team; DC United, one of Major League Soccer's most popular and successful clubs; the Howard Bisons, Georgetown Hoyas and other university teams, along with their rabid student-body fans; and the Nationals, with their shiny baseball stadium and 'Racing Presidents' tradition.

Cycling

Acres of parkland along the Potomac River and around the National Mall, plus a relatively flat landscape, make for great bike touring around DC. The miles and miles of off-road bike paths up the ante. Areas with sweet trails include Georgetown, Upper Northwest DC and Northern Virginia.

Hiking & Running

Everyone jogs on the Mall. Rock Creek Park has 15 miles of unpaved trails. A good map is *Trails in the Rock Creek Park Area,* published by the Potomac Appalachian Trail Club.

Paddling

Kayaks and canoes cruise the waters of both the Potomac River and the C&O Canal. The canal is ideal for canoeing between Georgetown and Violettes Lock (mile 22). The Potomac has a great vantage point from which to admire the city skyline, but it also has some dangerous currents.

Sports & Activities by Neighborhood

- **National Mall** Join the locals tossing Frisbees, jogging and otherwise recreating.
- **Georgetown** (p127) Top 'hood for cycling trails and paddling options.
- **Capitol Hill & Southeast DC** (p149) Pro baseball, soccer and football, plus golf.
- **Downtown & Penn Quarter** (p164) Pro basketball and hockey, plus cycle rentals.
- **U Street, Columbia Heights & Northeast** (p204) Golf and far-flung natural areas for hikes.
- **Upper Northwest DC** (p213) Horseback riding and sweet trails in Rock Creek Park.
- **Northern Virginia** (p225) Laced with hiking and biking paths like the Mount Vernon Trail.

NEED TO KNOW

Pro Teams

➡ **DC United** (MLS; www.dcunited.com)

➡ **Washington Capitals** (NHL; capitals.nhl.com)

➡ **Washington Nationals** (MLB; www.nationals.com)

➡ **Washington Redskins** (NFL; www.redskins.com)

➡ **Washington Wizards** (NBA; www.nba.com/wizards)

Tickets

➡ You can try to buy tickets to games direct from teams' websites or stadiums, or from scalpers outside the venues. Or you can try online providers. Most charge an inconvenient 'convenience' fee.

➡ **Dream Tix** (www.dreamtix.com)

➡ **StubHub!** (www.stubhub.com)

➡ **TicketExchange by Ticketmaster** (www.ticketexchangebyticketmaster.com)

➡ **Tickets-Redskins** (www.tickets-redskins.com)

➡ **Craigslist** (washingtondc.craigslist.org) No fee; the site serves as an online scalping service.

Recreational Leagues

➡ **DC Bocce League** (www.dcbocce.com) Lawn bowling league with the motto 'Our balls are harder.'

➡ **DC Kickball** (http://dckickball.org) League for the soccer-meets-baseball activity.

Lonely Planet's Top Choices

Rock Creek Park Trails (p208) Amazingly wild paths for cycling and hiking crisscross a stone's throw from civilization.

Washington Nationals Game (p149) Ya gotta love the cheap tickets and incomparable Racing Presidents.

Mount Vernon Trail (p225) Ride to George's Washington's estate past Arlington Cemetery, airplanes, marshes and birds.

Theodore Roosevelt Park Trails (p218) The Potomac River isle floats boardwalks and trails through tranquil woodlands.

Mall (p81) Nothing inspires a jog like this big green lawn studded with monuments.

Best Websites

Bike Washington (www.bikewashington.org) Trail information.

Running Report (www.runwashington.com) Information on races and training.

DC Front Runners (www.dcfrontrunners.org) Club for GLBT runners and walkers.

Best Trails

C&O Canal & Towpath (p117)

Capital Crescent Trail (p127)

East Potomac Park (p149)

Washington & Old Dominion Trail (p225)

Best Bicycles

Big Wheel Bikes (p128)

Bike & Roll (p164)

Capital Bikeshare (p290)

Thompson Boat Center (p128)

Fletcher's Boathouse (p213)

Best Spectator Sports

Washington Redskins (p149)

DC United (p150)

Washington Wizards (p164)

Washington Capitals (p164)

Best Paddling

Jack's Boathouse (p128)

Thompson Boat Center (p128)

Fletcher's Boathouse (p213)

Best Golf

East Potomac Park Golf Course (p150)

Langston Golf Course (p150)

Rock Creek Park Golf Course (p204)

Best Places for a Walk

Georgetown Waterfront Park (p118)

East Potomac Park (p138)

National Arboretum (p192)

Malcolm X Park (p180)

Best Guided Jaunts

Jack's Boathouse 'Twilight Tours' (p128)

Bike & Roll's 'Monuments @ Night' (p164)

Bike & Roll's Mount Vernon Picnic (p225)

DC by Foot (p291)

ROBERT GINN / GETTY IMAGES ©

The museums of the Smithsonian Institute offer many captivating exhibits for kids

Kids

Oh, have you come to the right town. Washington bursts with kid-friendly attractions. Not only do they hold the nation's best collection of dinosaur bones, rockets and one-of-a-kind historical artifacts, but just about everything is free. Another bonus: green space surrounds all the sights, so young ones can burn off energy to their hearts' content.

Best Sights

The top destination is undoubtedly the National Zoo. For details on it, as well as the best museums, theaters and other attractions for kids overall, see p47. For the best sights by age group, see the lists beginning on p45.

Several popular kids' attractions lie beyond the city limits:

Glen Echo Park (☎301-634-2222; www.glenechopark.org; admission free; 7300 MacArthur Blvd, Glen Echo, MD) This beautiful park 9 miles northwest of downtown has a huge **carousel** (per ride $1.25; ⌚May-Sep) and children's shows by the **Puppet Company** (www.thepuppetco.org; tickets $10; ⌚Wed-Sun) and **Adventure Theatre MTC** (www.adventuretheatre-mtc.org).

National Children's Museum (☎301-686-0225; www.ncm.museum; 112 Waterfront St, National Harbor, MD) Will reopen its expanded doors in 2013 in the National Harbor Complex, 10 miles south of the Mall.

NEED TO KNOW

Advance Reservations

You'll need to make reservations several weeks in advance for the White House, the Marine Barracks drill parade and for House and Senate chamber visits. For the following places, it pays to go online and reserve tickets at least a few days in advance:

- Capitol tours
- Ford's Theatre
- International Spy Museum
- National Archives
- Washington Cathedral tours
- Washington Monument
- Bureau of Engraving and Printing – You cannot reserve in advance, but do remember to show up early. The ticket office opens at 8am.

Saving Money

The Newseum offers a family discount rate of $50 for two adults and two youths, which saves about $20 off regular admission. Tickets must be purchased on site.

Films

- *Night at the Museum 2: Battle of the Smithsonian* (2009) – Museum exhibits come to life for Ben Stiller in the National Air and Space Museum and National Gallery of Art. FYI, the first film was set in the Smithsonian's New York City history museum.
- *National Treasure* (2004) – Nicolas Cage finds a coded map on the back of the Declaration of Independence that leads to – that's right – national treasure! The sequel came out in 2007, and supposedly a third installment is in the works.

Top Tip

- Most museums provide family guide booklets with activities kids can do on site; ask at the information desk, as the guides can enhance visits greatly.

Six Flags America (☎301-249-1500; www.sixflags.com/america; adult/child $57/37; ⊙May-Oct) Amusement park located about 15 miles east of downtown in Largo, MD; offers a full array of roller coasters and tamer kiddie rides.

Tours

Bike & Roll (www.bikethesites.com; adult/child $40/30) Has all-ages, 4-mile cycling tours that zip around the Mall and Tidal Basin. Tours run in the daytime and at night. Children's bikes are provided.

DC by Foot (www.dcbyfoot.com) Offers free, tip-based walking tours. While they're not specifically geared to kids, they are popular with families. The Mall tour takes about two hours and covers a mile; the route is stroller-friendly.

American River Taxi (p290) DIY option that'll take you on the Potomac River from Georgetown to Nationals Park.

Rainy-Day Options

CATCH AN IMAX

The Smithsonian has two IMAX theaters on the Mall: one in the National Museum of Natural History, and the other in the Air and Space Museum. The latter also holds the Einstein Planetarium. Schedules are amalgamated at www.si.edu/imax.

NATIONAL BUILDING MUSEUM

The museum's Building Zone lets kids aged two to six drive bulldozers and other construction play trucks, use giant Lego to build towers, and don gear such as hard hats and tool belts. It's timed entry every hour on the hour; tickets cost $3 and are valid for 45 minutes.

PLAYSEUM

The **Playseum** (☎888-575-2973; www.playseum.com; 545 8th St SE; admission $6; ⊙9am-5:30pm Mon-Sat) is a terrific hands-on play facility by Eastern Market. The main level has a market room, with pretend produce kids collect in baskets and 'buy' at the cash register. A beauty salon provides fingernail painting. Pirate's Cove offers sand, shells and a ship to climb. The lower level has a Chinatown room with woks to stir, kimonos to try on and Asian instruments to play. There are also rooms where kids can bake cupcakes or make a smoothie. The facilitated activities cost an extra $3 each.

FAMILY ROOM

The **Family Room** (☎202-640-1865; www.thefamilyroomdc.com; 411 8th St SE, 2nd fl; admission 1st child $10, per sibling $5; ⊙9am-5pm Mon-Thu, to 8pm Fri, 10am-8pm Sat, noon-6pm Sun) is another indoor playground near

Eastern Market. It's filled with things to climb plus a variety of toys, art supplies and children's books. Scheduled activities (included in the admission fee) include crafts, music and story times.

BOOGIE BABES

See where the **Boogie Babes** (www.boogiebabes.com; per child $5) are jamming. They get the preschool-age crowd rockin' at Eastern Market every Thursday and at Atlas Performing Arts Center on Friday, both at 10:30am.

Eat Streets for Kids

7th Street NW Located by the Spy Museum and National Archives, this street and its environs have quite a few kid-friendly burger and pizza places, such as Matchbox Pizza (p158).

Eastern Market Pick up sandwiches and picnic supplies at the market itself, or head into any of the area's abundant kid-friendly restaurants, such as Ted's Bulletin (p141).

Mall Lunch here is going to be from a vendor cart or a museum cafe. Mitsitam cafe (p96) in the American Indian Museum provides unique options. Or there's old standby McDonald's in the Air and Space Museum.

Zoo area The areas north and south of the Connecticut Ave entrance have heaps of restaurants, such as Lebanese Taverna (p211).

Resources & Games for Kids

Many sights and museums have a section on their website with interactive computer games for children. Favorites include:

International Spy Museum (www.spymuseum.org/kidspy) Loud, booming games to create disguises and to 'diffuse robotic covert pigeons with explosive birdseed.'

Library of Congress (www.americaslibrary.gov) Kids can animate a cartoon, listen to a jukebox of historic recordings and see old videos of buildings being blown up with dynamite. The latter – the Disasters, Devastation & Destruction section – is particularly impressive.

National Gallery of Art (www.nga.gov/kids) Young artists can create portraits and landscapes using interactive tools.

Smithsonian (www.smithsonianeducation.org/students) Lets kids peruse the institution's 142 million objects, from rocks to rockets, baseball cards to brontosaurus bones.

Kennedy Center (artsedge.kennedy-center.org) The ArtsEdge portal has interactive games such as Perfect Pitch (artsedge.kennedy-center.org/interactives/perfectpitch), where kids choose an era (Baroque, Modern etc) and then a 'team' of instruments strolls onto the baseball field. Click on an instrument to see it and hear it. ArtsEdge also has parents' resources, such as 'Five Arty Activities for the Car and Grocery.'

Mount Vernon (www.washingtonsworld.org) Offers video games like Bombarding Yorktown and an interactive jigsaw puzzle.

House of Representatives (kids.clerk.house.gov) Not particularly interactive, but it is educational. The website is broken down by age. Older kids get links to the Clerk of the House YouTube Channel (the thrills!).

Other Fun Projects

WRITE A LETTER TO THE PRESIDENT

There's something pretty cool about writing to the prez while you're in the neighborhood. White House staff respond to every letter, so make sure your child includes a return address both on the letter and on the envelope. Here are some writing tips:

Introduce yourself to the president in one sentence (how old you are, where you live etc).

Explain why you're writing. To ask for help with a certain issue? To approve or disapprove of a decision he made? To ask the president a personal question?

Explain the action you'd like him to take, ie propose legislation, visit your town, send you a photo.

Address it to: President, The White House, 1600 Pennsylvania Ave NW, Washington, DC 20500.

Wait for his response!

CREATE A BLOG

This is a great way for older kids to share their experiences with friends. Check out **Kids Learn to Blog** (www.kidslearntoblog.com), which walks parents through the process of setting up a blog for youngsters, including information on safety and monitoring the blog. Kids also can sign up for blogs on monitored sites like **Kidzworld** (www.kidzworld.com).

Resources for Parents

DC Urban Mom (www.dcurbanmom.com) Has an active forum to post your pressing DC questions; look for the Travel Discussion thread.

Kids by Neighborhood

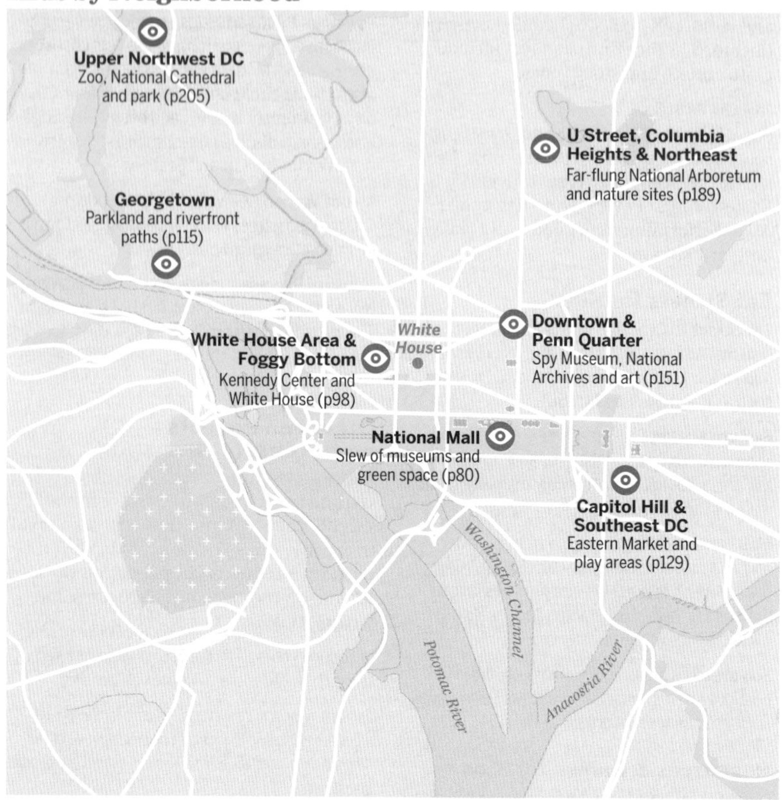

Kid Friendly DC (www.kidfriendlydc.com) A local mom's blog with particularly good events listings.

Our Kids (www.our-kids.com) Local website that has loads of listings for kid-centric shows and events, family-friendly restaurants and activity ideas.

Washington Post (www.washingtonpost.com) Check the 'Saturday's Child' page in the Weekend section of Friday's newspaper.

Washington Parent (www.washingtonparent.com) Free monthly paper available around town at libraries and bookstores.

Destination DC (www.washington.org) Has lots of family-friendly info under the Experience heading.

Apps Several apps on DC travel with children are available. These change frequently, but at press time popular ones included **DC with Kids** (www.FamilyiTrips.com) and **DC Essential Family Guide** (www.sutromedia.com/apps/DC_Essential_Family_Guide).

Lonely Planet's Top Choices

National Zoo (p208) Giant pandas, orangutans and lions roam against a lovely backdrop.

National Museum of Natural History (p93) Dinosaurs, a giant squid and an insect zoo fill the cavernous hall.

National Air and Space Museum (p86) Touch moon rocks and walk through space capsules.

Bureau of Engraving & Printing (p138) Watch money roll off the press.

Washington Nationals (p149) Cheer on the Racing Presidents during a baseball game.

Best Sights For Preschoolers

Carousel on the Mall (p90)

National Building Museum Building Zone (p157)

Georgetown Waterfront Park (p118)

National Sculpture Garden (p92)

Best Sights For Grade-Schoolers

National Museum of American History (p93)

National Gallery of Art (p85)

National Archives (p153)

Washington National Cathedral (p207)

Mount Vernon (p227)

Best Sights For Teens

International Spy Museum (p155)

Newseum (p155)

Capitol (p131)

Frederick Douglass National Historic Site (p137)

United States Holocaust Memorial Museum (p134)

Best Festivals & Events

Blossom Kite Festival (p21)

White House Easter Egg Roll (p22)

DC Caribbean Carnival (p22)

Independence Day (p23)

National Christmas Tree & Menorah Lighting (p24)

Zoo Lights (p206)

Best Restaurants

Good Stuff Eatery (p140)

Jimmy T's (p141)

Ted's Bulletin (p141)

Lebanese Taverna (p211)

Argonaut (p146)

Best Bakeries & Sweets

Baked & Wired (p120)

Dolcezza (p124)

Red Velvet Cupcakery (p161)

Georgetown Cupcake (p125)

Pitango Gelato (p144)

Best Parks & Gardens

East Potomac Park (p138)

Georgetown Waterfront Park (p118)

Rock Creek Park (p208)

Constitution Gardens (p96)

United States National Arboretum (p192)

Best Monuments

Lincoln Memorial (p82)

Thomas Jefferson Memorial (p94)

Washington Monument (p83)

Albert Einstein statue (p107)

Best Government Sites

National Archives (p153)

Library of Congress (p133)

White House (p100)

Capitol (p131)

Best Theaters

National Theatre (p162)

Discovery Theater (p97)

Kennedy Center (p113)

Puppet Theater (p41)

Best Cultural

National Museum of African Art (p90)

National Museum of the American Indian (p92)

Reynolds Center for American Art (p154)

Hirshhorn Museum & Sculpture Garden (p91)

Corcoran Gallery (p101)

Best Lodging

Omni Shoreham Hotel (p254)

Hotel Monaco (p248)

Embassy Suites Washington DC (p250)

Eldon Suites (p249)

Hotel Harrington (p249)

AA WORLD TRAVEL LIBRARY / ALAMY ©

DC for Families

National Zoo

The free National Zoo is the top banana among family sights in DC. Little folks get amped up the moment they enter the gate: elephants! zebras! tigers! Giant pandas Mei Xiang and Tian Tian are the resident rock stars. Follow the Asia Trail to reach their abode and watch for sloth bears, red pandas, clouded leopards and clawed otters en route.

The great apes are another crowd-pleaser. As you near the ape house, look up to see orangutans swinging overhead on the 'O Line,' a series of steel cables and towers that lead to the Think Tank, a building with interactive games on animal intelligence. The Kids' Farm gets youngsters up close to cows, goats and donkeys. There's also a giant pizza to climb on (odd, but cool).

Animal feedings and trainings take place throughout the day. The 11:30am Meet the Ape Keeper and 2pm spider feedings are big hits. Check the schedule at the entrance for others.

When you enter, ask at the visitor center for the free Zoo Crew Training Manual, filled with puzzles, bingo games and educational blurbs on the animals. Stroller rentals are available for $3/4 per single/double.

The zoo grounds sprawl, so don't expect to get to everything in one visit. The park is on a hill – nothing major, but the gradual incline can be tiring to little legs.

For more information, see p208.

TIPS

- ➡ Best Age Group: Preschool, grade school
- ➡ Don't Miss: Giant pandas Mei Xiang and Tian Tian
- ➡ Fun Fact: Adult giant pandas eat 60lb of bamboo per day, along with carrots, apples and sweet potatoes. They're vegetarians and never eat meat.
- ➡ Nearby Restaurant: Panda Place Grill inside the zoo; Lebanese Taverna (p211) outside near the Woodley Park-Zoo/Adams Morgan Metro station

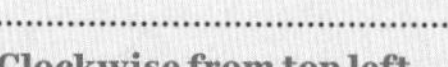

Clockwise from top left

1. Kids enjoying the elephant enclosure **2.** Lion sculpture **3.** Giant panda

DAVID R. FRAZIER PHOTOLIBRARY, INC. / ALAMY ©

2

SCULPTOR: ROLAND PERRY / JASON COLSTON / LONELY PLANET IMAGES ©

1

3

JEAN-PIERRE LESCOURRET / LONELY PLANET IMAGES ©

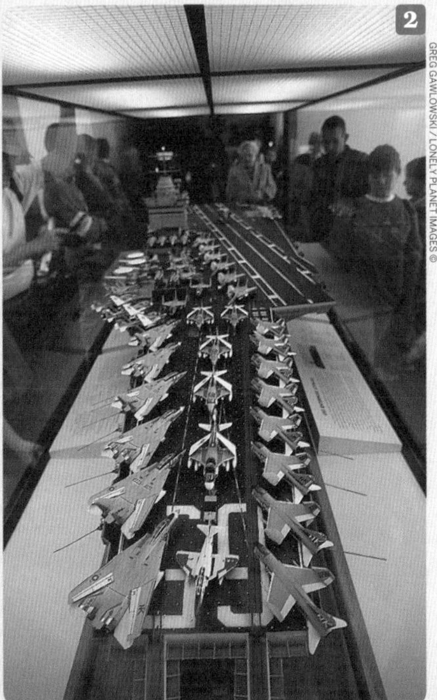

GREG GAWLOWSKI / LONELY PLANET IMAGES ©

National Air & Space Museum

The Air and Space Museum is the Smithsonian's biggest crowd-puller. Families flock in for the mind-blowing array of rockets, airplanes and other contraptions – and all of it is as rousing for adults as kids.

As soon as you walk in the Mall-side entrance, go touch the moon. The lunar rock is one of the few in the world that kids can put their fingers on. Next, stop by the information desk and pick up children's activity guides. Then head next door to the How Things Fly gallery, whooshing with interactive gadgets. Kids can find out their weight on the moon, see a wind tunnel in action and make high-flying paper airplanes.

Other young crowd-pleasers, all on the 1st floor, include the hulking DC-7 airplane to climb aboard in the America by Air gallery; the Skylab orbital workshop, to walk through and see what cramped astronaut life is like, in the Space Race gallery; and the Flight Simulator Zone, which offers two experiences. One is a badass aerial-combat trip, where participants control the action. The other is a more passive 'ride' aboard an F-18 or cosmic coaster. Though the museum is free, the simulators cost $7 to $8 per person.

For more details, including info on tours, the IMAX, the planetarium and the Virginia annex, see p86.

TIPS

- Best Age Group: Grade school
- Don't Miss: How Things Fly gallery, moon rock, DC-7 airplane
- Fun Fact: If you wanted to gift-wrap the moon, you'd need a piece of wrapping paper as large as Africa
- Nearby Restaurant: McDonald's, Donato's Pizza and Boston Market are inside. For something more offbeat, try the Mitsitam Native Foods Cafe (p96) in the American Indian Museum next door.

Clockwise from top left

1. Airplane display **2.** Aircraft carrier exhibit **3.** *Apollo* re-creation in Skylab

National Museum of Natural History

The second-most-popular museum in the Smithsonian will likely be jam-packed. But crowd jostling is a small price to pay for the mummies, meteorites, mammoths and other thrills that stuff 18 giant exhibition halls.

Most families beeline to the Dinosaur Hall (1st floor) and gape at *Tyrannosaurus rex,* still terrifying at 65 million years of age, and *Diplodocus longus,* his 90ft-long hall mate. Nearby, you can peek in at scientists examining their finds in the FossiLab.

The Ocean Hall (1st floor) straps up a North Atlantic right whale to the ceiling. On the 2nd floor, the cursed (so the story goes), blue-tinted Hope Diamond sparkles in the Gem Hall. Mummies, tombs and coffins crowd the spooky Egyptian Hall. Next door live centipedes, roaches, ants and other creepers parade around the Insect Zoo. Big excitement ensues here during the daily tarantula feedings (usually 10:30am, 11:30am and 1:30pm Tuesday through Friday, 11:30am, 12:30pm and 1:30pm on weekends).

There's a Butterfly Pavilion on the 9th St side of the building, where kids can walk among the fluttering denizens. The pavilion costs $6 for adults and $5 for children. Tuesdays are free; stop by the pavilion box office to pick up timed-entry tickets.

For more info on the museum, see p93.

TIPS

- Best Age Group: Preschool, grade school
- Don't Miss: T-rex, Hope Diamond, mummies, tarantula feedings
- Fun Fact: Those tarantulas are picky eaters – they'll only chow on crickets
- Nearby Restaurant: Fossil Cafe on the 1st floor; the tables have fossils under the glass

Clockwise from top left

1. Fish-skeleton exhibit **2.** Rotunda, with African bull-elephant display **3.** *Tyrannosaurus rex* skeleton

KUMAR SRISKANDAN / ALAMY ©

EDDIE BRADY / LONELY PLANET IMAGES ©

Capitol

The Capitol is more low-key than Washington's museums, but families will still find much to grab their attention. Sign up in advance for a tour.

The sky-high rotunda impresses. Look up to see a painting of George Washington surrounded by symbols of American democracy and innovation. The Hall of Statues holds two famous residents per state – some well known, some less so. The statue of Helen Keller at age seven is the youngest person represented (state of Alabama). Other eye-catchers include spear-toting King Kamehameha I of Hawaii; Sakakawea (aka Sacagawea), the woman who helped explorers Lewis and Clark, from North Dakota; and spacesuit-clad astronaut Jack Sigert Jr, from Colorado. Guides also demonstrate the hall's amazing acoustics, and how a whisper on one side of the room can be heard loud and clear on the other, thanks to the ceiling's perfectly smooth, curved surface.

After the tour, head over to the Exhibition Hall (by the information desk on the lower level). The mighty Statue of Freedom standing in front was the plaster cast used for the bronze sculpture that now crowns the Capitol.

To visit the House or Senate chambers you must make separate arrangements via a Member of Congress. To be honest, it's not particularly exciting for kids, plus there's a lot of waiting and security to go through.

For more info on the Capitol, see p131.

TIPS

- Best Age Group: Grade school, teens
- Don't Miss: Hall of Statues, George Washington rotunda painting, Statue of Freedom
- Fun Fact: The Capitol has its own subway. It carries politicians from House and Senate office buildings to the Capitol.
- Nearby Restaurant: Capitol restaurant on the lower level

Clockwise from top left
1. Dome in the rotunda **2.** Guided tour in the National Statuary Hall **3.** Exterior of the Capitol

2

KUMAR SRISKANDAN / ALAMY ©

GREG GAWLOWSKI / LONELY PLANET IMAGES ©

1

KENNETH E. BEHRING CENTER

3

Siege Warfare

Field Artillery

DAVID COLEMAN / ALAMY ©

RICHARD GREEN / ALAMY ©

National Museum of American History

Children get their history lesson hidden in a dose of pop culture at the three-floor, interactive American History Museum.

Train fanatics go gaga over the steam locomotive in the Transportation and Technology hall. Up a level is the tattered flag that inspired Francis Scott Key to write the 'Star-Spangled Banner.' The fragile cloth is now kept in a dark, temperature-controlled chamber. Also on the second level (east side) is the Greensboro, NC, lunch counter where four African American students made history by sitting in the 'whites only' section.

The 1776 gunboat *Philadelphia* drifts on the 3rd floor of the museum's east side, along with a slew of presidential artifacts such as Abraham Lincoln's top hat and George Washington's sword. The west side displays a gallery of pop-culture items, including Dorothy's ruby slippers from *The Wizard of Oz,* Babe Ruth's baseball bat and the original Kermit the Frog puppet.

The museum has been undergoing renovation, so displays tend to move around. Pick up a map at the entrance. For more information on the museum, see p93.

TIPS

- Best Age Group: Preschool, grade school
- Don't Miss: 'Star-Spangled Banner' flag, Kermit, ruby slippers, Lincoln's top hat
- Fun Fact: Dorothy's shoes were silver in L Frank Baum's original novel about Oz. The moviemakers changed them to red so they'd stand out better against the yellow brick road.
- Nearby Restaurant: The Stars & Stripes Cafe inside serves all-American fare.

Clockwise from top left

1. Main foyer of the museum **2.** Abraham Lincoln's death mask **3.** Exhibit on historic military campaigns

1

3

VISIONSOFAMERICA / JOE SOHM / GETTY IMAGES ©

MICHAEL VENTURA / ALAMY ©

National Archives

The National Archives doesn't do the whiz-bang exhibit thing. Its premier display – the Declaration of Independence, Constitution and Bill of Rights – stands on its own.

Prepare to queue to get in during the spring and summer. Then you enter the dim rotunda and see them: America's founding documents, the real deal. The Declaration, penned in 1776, announces the 13 colonies' separation from Great Britain and their right to 'life, liberty and the pursuit of happiness.' Look at the bottom for John Hancock's bold signature, as well as those of Ben Franklin and Thomas Jefferson. The Constitution, from 1787, sets out the system of governance. The Bill of Rights, from 1789, adds the first 10 amendments protecting freedom of speech, press, religion and more. The room beside the rotunda displays the 1297 Magna Carta that states no man – even a king – is above the law. It influenced the Bill of Rights.

Head over to the Public Vaults afterward to see George Washington's old letters.

The film *National Treasure* can stoke families for their visit beforehand. In classic Hollywood fashion, Nicolas Cage busts into the Archives, steals the Declaration and uses the map on the back to find buried treasure.

For more information on the National Archives, see p153.

TIPS

- Best Age Group: Grade school, teens
- Don't Miss: The Big Three in the rotunda, Public Vaults
- Fun Fact: The special case that houses the Declaration of Independence contains the inert gas argon and a controlled amount of humidity to keep the parchment flexible. Light fades the ink, too, which is why the room is so dim.
- Nearby Restaurant: Teaism (p159)

Clockwise from top left
1. A family views the Constitution **2.** Exterior of the National Archives **3.** Rotunda

International Spy Museum

Budding James Bonds will dig the Spy Museum, where they're invited to crack codes, identify disguises and go on secret missions. The slick design brings on booming, screaming-siren sound effects, much like a video game, and lots of interactive spy gadgets. From the get-go you're invited to adopt a 'cover' ID to set the mood.

The exhibits are pretty hard-core. Families will see the Bulgarian assassination umbrella and the 'Kiss of Death' lipstick pistol used by the KGB during the 1960s. One exhibit re-creates a communist interrogator's office; there's a secret entrance to a secret prison that people walked into, never to return. It's seriously cool to see Bond's 1964 tricked-out Aston Martin complete with rotating license plates and hidden machine guns (from *Goldfinger*). Ditto the display of hidden cameras and how they're concealed in clothing and pigeons. A masked ninja shows how to be invisible. The most modern exhibit examines electronic security and the chaos a computer-related threat could cause.

Kids aged 12 and over can take part in Operation Spy, an hour-long interactive game in which they decode messages, crack safes and interrogate a suspected double agent. It's a separate ticket ($15), and does not require museum admission (yes, the Spy Museum is one of the few in Washington you have to pay to visit).

For more information, see p163.

TIPS

- Best Age Group: Teens
- Don't Miss: James Bond's 1964 Aston Martin loaded with machine guns, tire slashers, ejector seat et al
- Fun Fact: Washington, DC, has more spies than any other city on earth
- Nearby Restaurant: Spy City Cafe inside; Matchbox Pizza (p158)

1

3

Clockwise from top left
1. Exterior of the museum **2.** James Bond's Aston Martin **3.** Berlin Tunnel re-creation

PAUL J. RICHARDS / AFP / GETTY IMAGES ©

PAUL J. RICHARDS / AFP / GETTY IMAGES ©

National Gallery of Art

The National Gallery is not only a trove of art but also a treasure trove for families. Programs and resources available for school-age children go way beyond the usual.

First, decide which wing to start in. The West Building displays Renaissance, Dutch Golden Age, Impressionist and other works before the early 20th century. The East Building hangs contemporary art. Each wing has an information desk where you can pick up 'Family Guide' activity booklets that cover different genres (Italian art, American art etc). The West Building also offers a free children's audio tour.

The biggest thrill for younger kids is not in either wing, but between them: the moving sidewalk that connects the two wings underground is sheathed in a sparkly light installation.

The Children's Film Program (☎202-789-3030; www.nga.gov/programs/flmchild) usually screens on Saturday in the East Building auditorium. Family concerts take place once a month in the same space. Artists conduct hands-on family workshops for younger kids, and five-hour painting and drawing classes for teens in the gallery's studios. All programs are free, but some workshops require preregistration. See www.nga.gov/programs/family for details.

Stop by the gallery's next-door sculpture garden. Kids can run around, while grown-ups can get a glass of wine from the cafe.

For more information, see p85.

TIPS

- Best Age Group: Grade school, teens
- Don't Miss: Underground walkway, sculpture garden, free films and concerts
- Fun Fact: Though the Alexander Calder mobile in the East Building looks light and airy, it weighs 1000lb
- Nearby Restaurant: Cascade Cafe (p96) inside

Clockwise from top left

1. Moving walkway connecting the East and West Buildings **2.** Exterior of the East Building **3.** Gallery interior

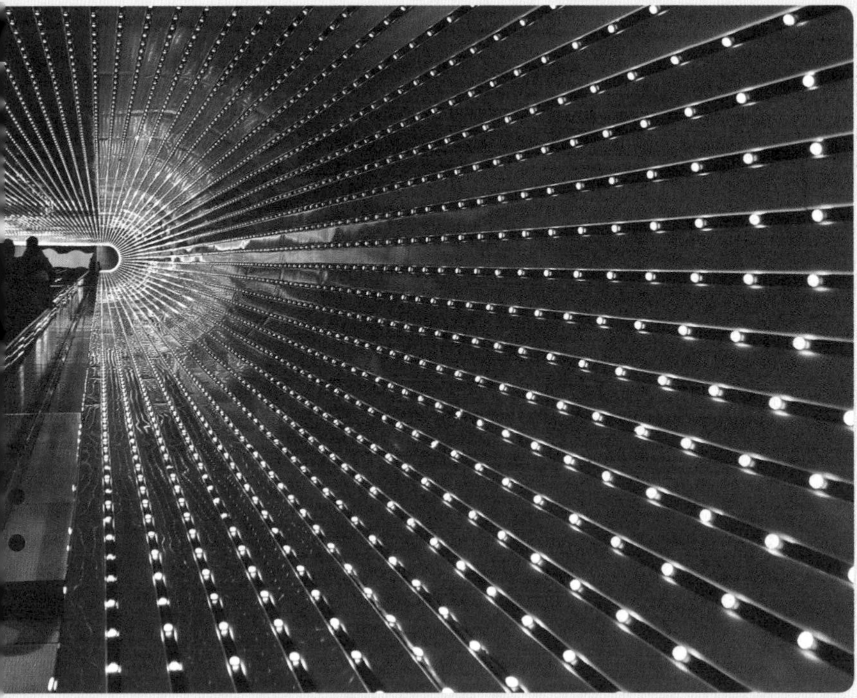

DAVID COLEMAN / ALAMY ©

2

ARCHITECT: I. M. PEI / DENNIS JOHNSON/ LONELY PLANET IMAGES ©

1

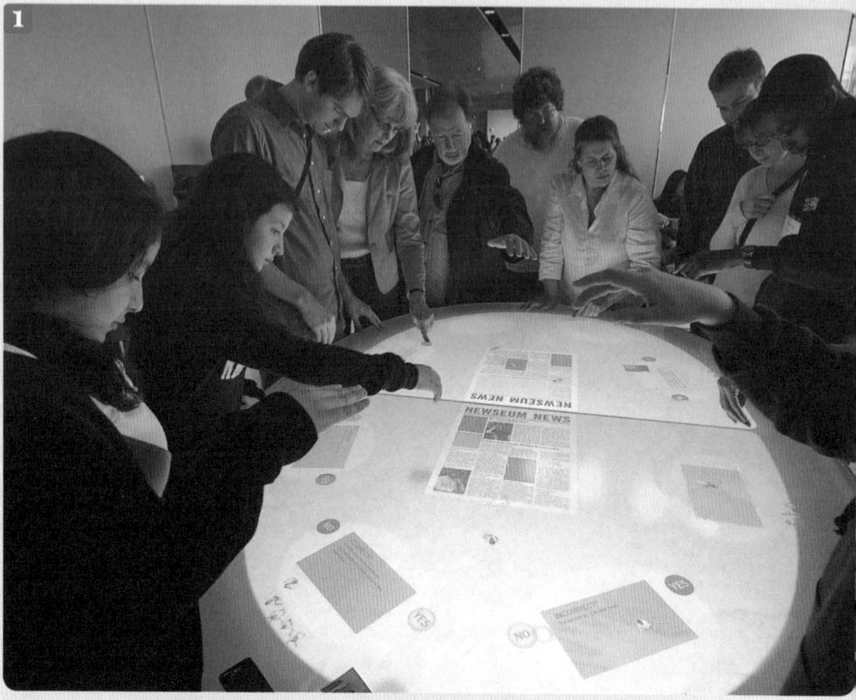

NEWSEUM NEWS

3

VANCES

TED STATES

First Dogs

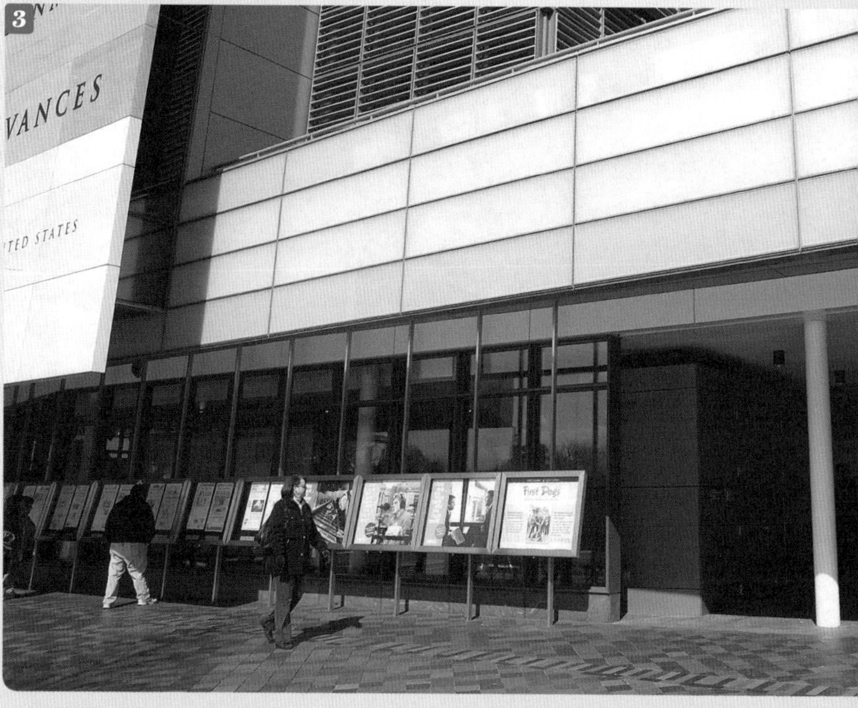

MICHAEL VENTURA / ALAMY ©

ARCHITECT: JAMES POLSHEK / JUSTIN MATHEWS / LONELY PLANET IMAGES ©

Newseum

The Newseum boasts it's 'the most interactive museum' around, and it may well be. There is a *lot* to see in its 15 theaters and 15 galleries spread over six floors. Be aware that some exhibits deal with violence and death – they're hard news, after all – and can be a bit much for younger children.

Probably the coolest thing is the TV studio on Level 2. Here, junior journalists choose a story and a background (the White House, the National Zoo etc), then pick up a microphone, step in front of the TV camera and report 'live' from the site by reading the teleprompter. The experience costs $5, including a take-home DVD. They look really professional!

Nearby on the same level, kids can be in the hot seat of a newsroom. Touch screens let them prepare a news report on deadline, and show what's needed to be complete, timely and accurate under pressure. The Ethics Center's kiosks allow them to deal with real-life reporting dilemmas (is it OK to use an anonymous source? to alter a photo to make it more dramatic?) and see how their responses stack up against journalists' actions.

Level 6 displays the day's front page from newspapers across all 50 states, as well as international newspapers. Step out onto the terrace on this level for a terrific view up Pennsylvania Ave to the Capitol.

For more information, see p155.

TIPS

- Best Age Group: Grade school, teens
- Don't Miss: TV studio to be an on-camera reporter
- Fun Fact: The marble tablet affixed to the museum's front weighs 50 tons and displays the 45 words of the First Amendment (protecting freedom of the press)
- Nearby Restaurant: Wolfgang Puck's stylish Source restaurant is inside; Red Velvet Cupcakery (p161) is four blocks away

Clockwise from top left

1. News display **2.** Kids' interactive game **3.** Exterior of Newseum

Theater

Washington hosts an incredible amount of family-friendly theater. The Smithsonian's Discovery Theater (p97) devotes its entire repertoire to kids. Global music and dance groups take the stage, along with puppet shows and 'tot rock' concerts. Tickets cost around $6.

The Kennedy Center (p113) puts on a series of big, bright musicals for young audiences. The National Symphony Orchestra plays several kids' concerts at the Kennedy, including the popular 'Teddy Bear' shows for wee ones aged three to five. It's not the full orchestra, but smaller groups meant to introduce kids to certain instruments. Ticket prices hover near $18.

The National Theatre (p162) downtown offers free shows for families every Saturday morning at 9:30am and 11am. Puppets, magicians, jugglers, ballet and opera are all possibilities. Get in line 30 minutes before show time to get a seat.

Another popular performing-arts site is Glen Echo Park (p41), 9 miles northwest of downtown. Based here, the Puppet Company specializes in puppet shows, putting on classics such as *Pinocchio* every Wednesday through Sunday for $10 per ticket. Also here is Adventure Theatre MTC, which has been around for more than 60 years and stages musicals based on children's books. Tickets cost around $18.

TIPS

- Best Age Group: Preschool, grade school
- Don't Miss: National Theatre's free Saturday-morning shows
- Nearby Restaurants: Discovery Theater – walk across the Mall to the Fossil Cafe in the National Museum of Natural History (p93). Kennedy Center – hit KC Cafe on the roof terrace. National Theatre – try the food court at the Old Post Office Pavilion (see the box, p158). Glen Echo Park – snack at the ballroom cafe on site, or bring a picnic.

Clockwise from top left

1. Foyer of the Kennedy Center (p113) **2.** Performance on the Millennium Stage, Kennedy Center (p113) **3.** Theater production by the Puppet Company (p41)

1

3

2

DAN HERRICK / LONELY PLANET IMAGES ©

THE WASHINGTON POST / GETTY IMAGES ©

East Potomac Park

East Potomac Park spreads its green goodness across 328 acres directly southeast of the Tidal Basin. It's an enticing place for families, with a playground, an outdoor pool and a mini-golf course. An 18-hole public golf course covers much of the park, along with a 24-court public tennis center.

The playground has a springy, rubberized 'ground' and apparatuses for climbing and sliding. Parents can sit at the surrounding picnic tables. The mini-golf course (adult/child $6.50/5) is in the vicinity. It's an old one, so no bells and whistles at the holes, just nice, shaded, straight-ahead greens. The Olympic-size pool (adult/child $7/4) is near the golf facilities. Open swim is from 4:30pm to 8pm weekdays (except Wednesday, when the pool is closed), and noon to 6pm on weekends. Go to www.dpr.dc.gov to buy a pool pass.

A 5-mile paved trail, great for biking or walking, runs around the park's circumference, paralleling Ohio Dr. Benches along the way provide rest stops and boat watching at the water's edge (which is fenced off, so no worries about falling).

Hains Point lies at the park's southern tip. Lots of families bring picnics and hang out here, since the spot provides great views of the planes taking off from nearby Reagan National Airport.

For more information, see p138.

TIPS

- Best Age Group: Preschool, grade school
- Don't Miss: Playground, mini-golf course, pool, Hains Point planes
- Fun Fact: The park's mini-golf course opened in 1931, making it one of the oldest operating courses in the country
- Nearby Restaurant: The Potomac Grill (972 Ohio Dr SW), by the mini-golf course, serves burgers, salads and snacks

Clockwise from top left

1. Fishing in the Potomac River at Hains Point (p138)
2. Cherry-blossom trees in bloom **3.** Path alongside the Potomac River

CHUCK PEFLEY / ALAMY ©

2

IRINA SILAYEVA / DREAMSTIME ©

1

3

PETER PTSCHELINZEW / LONELY PLANET IMAGES ©

JOHN NEUBAUER / LONELY PLANET IMAGES ©

Library of Congress

For young book lovers, visiting the world's largest library is pretty awesome. John Adams, the USA's second president, established the library in 1800 to prove to Europeans that America was cultured. It all went up in smoke – literally – when British troops burned the area during the war in 1814. The next year Congress decided to rebuild the library, and bought Thomas Jefferson's personal stash of 6487 books to use as the base.

Today the library is made up of three buildings, but the Jefferson Building is where the action is. Volunteers provide family tours aimed at kids aged six to 14 that take in the building's history, art and architecture. Tours run according to demand; ask at the ground-floor information desk about the schedule.

Also on the ground floor is the Young Readers Center (Room LJ-G29), which is set up for all ages. Older children and teens can choose among shelves of current and classic books to read on site. Younger children can participate in facilitated story-time activities. Parents can also pick books to read aloud to their children on their own.

Free concerts, films and other events – some geared toward children – take place daily throughout the complex; check www.loc.gov/loc/events.

For more information, see p133.

TIPS

- Best Age Group: Grade school, teens
- Don't Miss: Young Readers Center, family tours
- Fun Fact: The library holds more than 150 million items, but they're not all books. It also contains photographs, recordings, maps and sheet music.
- Nearby Restaurant: Ted's Bulletin (p141), one stop east on Blue/Orange Line Metro.

Clockwise from top left

1. Library exterior **2.** Main Reading Room **3.** Great Hall

Biking, Paddling & Other Activities

Washington provides great spots for families to get out and get active. The area around Georgetown is rich with opportunities. Georgetown Waterfront Park curves along the Potomac River and has fountains to splash in (at the foot of Wisconsin Ave NW) and a labyrinth to curlicue around (at the foot of 33rd St NW). Fletcher's Boathouse, a few miles upriver, rents canoes, rowboats, fishing gear and bicycles. Back in Georgetown proper, several outfitters rent bikes so you can hop on the C&O path or the Capital Crescent Trail.

In the river across from Georgetown, Theodore Roosevelt Island floats a nature sanctuary. Boardwalk trails slice through car-free, bike-free woodlands and make for fun, adventurous-feeling explorations. Access it via the footbridge from Arlington, VA. Nearby in Alexandria, outfitters can set up biking trips along the popular Mount Vernon Trail to George Washington's estate.

For gentler jaunts, many families rent paddleboats and glide out into Tidal Basin.

For more on outfitters and activities in Georgetown, see p127; for Fletcher's Boathouse, see p213; for Alexandria, see p225; and for the Tidal Basin, see p93

TIPS

- Best Age Group: Preschool, grade school, teens
- Don't Miss: Theodore Roosevelt Island, Tidal Basin paddleboats
- Fun Fact: Union troops were stationed at Roosevelt Island during the Civil War, but other than that, it has been uninhabited since 1831
- Nearby Restaurant: Baked & Wired (p120) in Georgetown

Clockwise from top left

1. Biker passes the Lincoln Memorial (p82) **2.** Ice skaters in the National Sculpture Garden (p92) **3.** Kayaker on the Potomac River

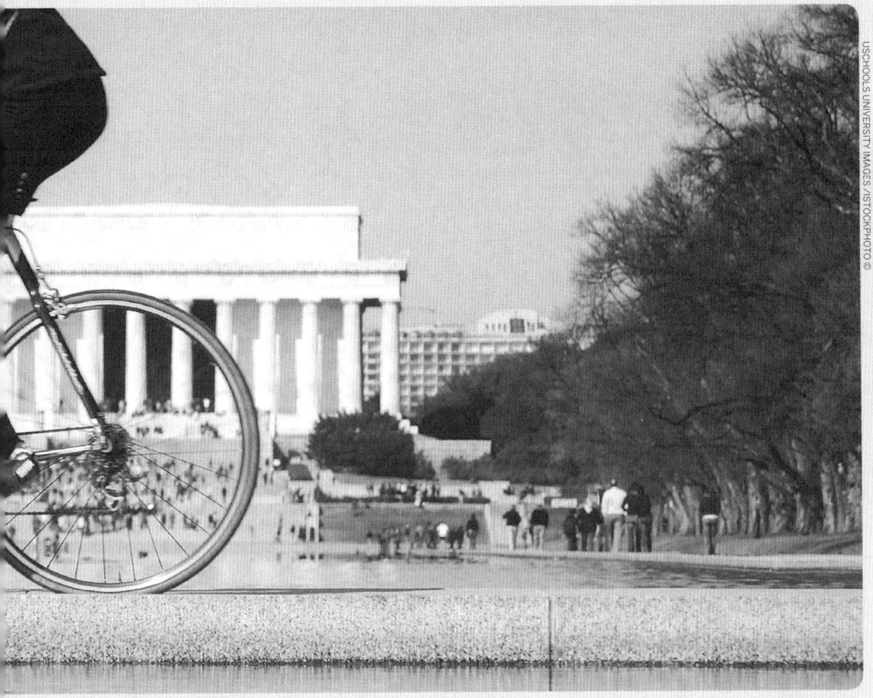

USCHOOLS UNIVERSITY IMAGES /ISTOCKPHOTO ©

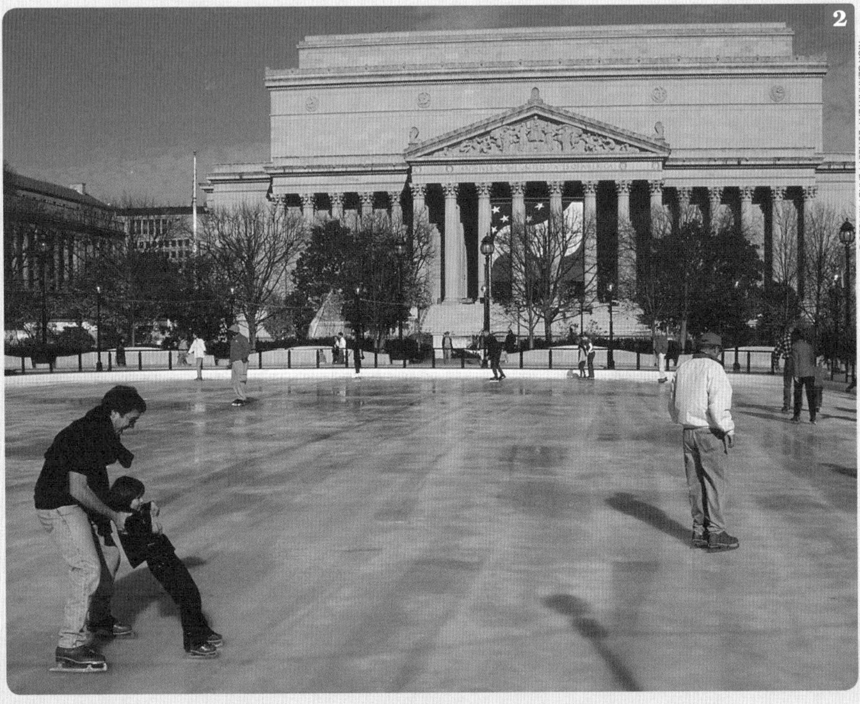

2

RICK GERHARTER / LONELY PLANET IMAGES ©

1

3

BLAINE HARRINGTON III / ALAMY ©

RICK GERHARTER / LONELY PLANET IMAGES ©

RICK GERHARTER / LONELY PLANET IMAGES ©

Washington National Cathedral

A church might seem like a boring attraction for a family, but the Washington National Cathedral is different than most houses of worship. Inside, kids will find beyond-the-norm decor hidden amid the stained glass and chapels. Not far from the entrance, in the Folger Bay, the vivid Lewis and Clark windows depict what the explorers saw on their westward journey; look for teepees. The Space Window nearby has a small moon rock embedded in it that the *Apollo 11* crew brought back. Further on, animal-headed wrought-iron gates lead into the Children's Chapel, with a pint-sized organ and chairs. Back by the entrance, the Lincoln Bay sports a floor of pennies that intrigues kids.

The gargoyles reign supreme as the most popular feature. All manner of odd ones dot the exterior – a cat, frog, alligator and dragon can be seen from the south lawn. The pièce de résistance is the Darth Vader gargoyle, which sits high up on the northwest tower. The best way to explore the bizarre stonework is on a gargoyle tour (adult/child $10/5), usually held on Thursday and Sunday from April through October.

Afterward wander through the enchanted Bishop's Garden, abloom with medieval flowers and herbs, fountains and a koi pond.

Pick up (or download) the *Cathedral for Families* brochure for additional activities.

For more information, see p207.

TIPS

- Best Age Group: Grade school
- Don't Miss: Darth Vader gargoyle; bring binoculars
- Fun Fact: The National Cathedral is the sixth-largest cathedral in the world.
- Nearby Restaurant: 2 Amys (p210)

Clockwise from top left
1. Reflections from the stained-glass windows **2.** Prom tower **3.** Interior of the cathedral

DENNIS JOHNSON / LONELY PLANET IMAGES ©

Explore Washington, DC

WASHINGTON, DC'S
TOP SIGHTS

Neighborhoods at a Glance

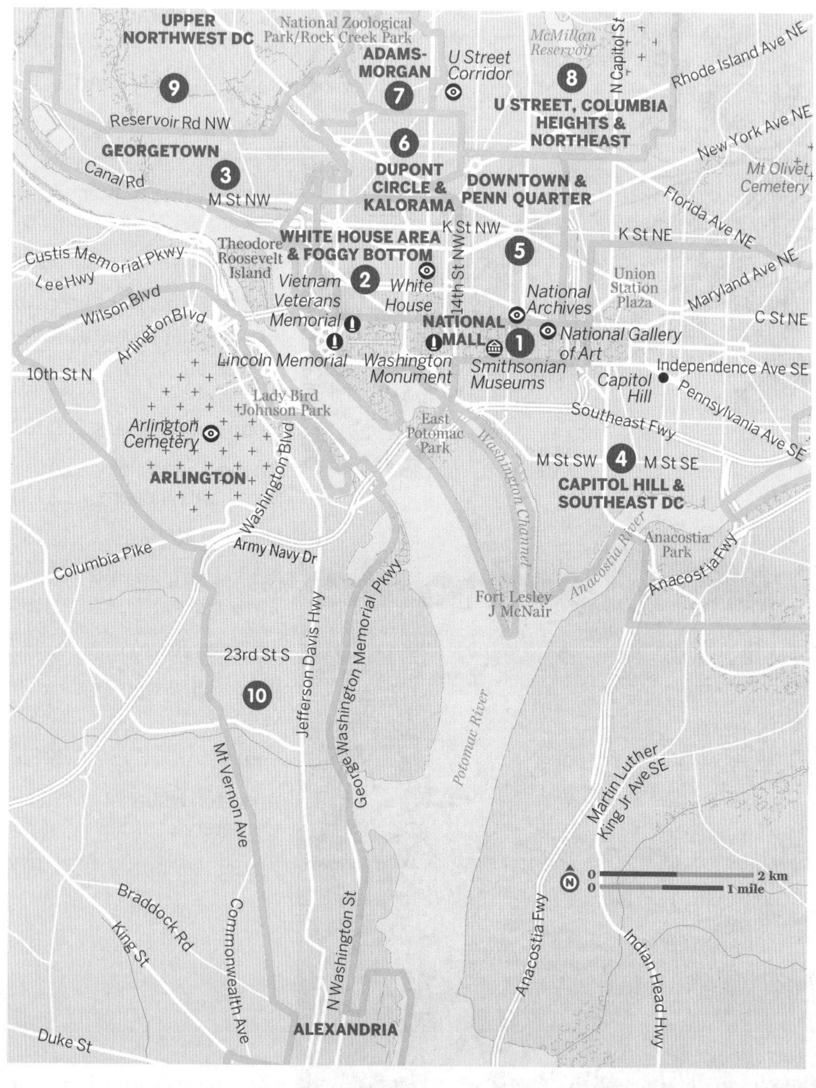

❶ National Mall p80

The Mall – aka 'America's front yard' – holds most of the Smithsonian museums and major monuments. The Lincoln Memorial, Washington Monument, Air and Space Museum, National Gallery of Art and much more crowd around a 2-mile-long strip of scrubby grass.

❷ White House Area & Foggy Bottom p98

The President lives at the center of the 'hood. The State Department, World Bank and other institutions hover nearby in Foggy Bottom. It's mostly a business district by day, and not terribly active by night, with the exception of the Kennedy Center for performing arts.

❸ Georgetown p115

Georgetown is DC's most aristocratic neighborhood, home to elite university students, ivory-tower academics and diplomats. Chi-chi brand-name shops, dark-wood pubs and upscale restaurants line the streets. Lovely parks and gardens color the edges.

❹ Capitol Hill & Southeast DC p129

The city's geographic and legislative heart surprises by being mostly a traditional residential neighborhood. The vast area holds top sights such as the Capitol, Library of Congress and Holocaust Memorial Museum. The areas around Eastern Market and H Street NE are locals' hubs, with good-time restaurants and nightlife.

❺ Downtown & Penn Quarter p151

Penn Quarter forms around Pennsylvania Ave as it runs between the White House and the Capitol. Downtown extends west beyond it. Major sights include the National Archives, International Spy Museum and Ford's Theatre. It's also DC's theater district and home to the basketball/hockey sports arena.

❻ Dupont Circle & Kalorama p165

Dupont offers flash new restaurants, hip bars, cafe society and cool bookshops. It's also the heart of the city's GLBT community. It used to be where turn-of-the-century millionaires lived. Today those mansions hold DC's greatest concentration of embassies. Kalorama sits in the northwest corner and ups the regal reserve.

❼ Adams-Morgan p178

Adams-Morgan has long been Washington's fun, nightlife-driven neighborhood. It's also a global village of sorts. The result today is a raucous mash-up centered on 18th St NW. Vintage boutiques, record shops and ethnic eats poke up between thumping bars and clubs.

❽ U Street, Columbia Heights & Northeast p189

This neighborhood covers a lot of ground. Historic U Street has been reborn as a jazzy arts and entertainment district. Columbia Heights booms with Latino immigrants and hipsters. Northeast DC is a stretch of prosperous residential blocks holding some great far-flung sights.

❾ Upper Northwest DC p205

The leafy lanes of Upper Northwest have long been the place for upper-income Washingtonians to settle their families. Sights scatter across the extensive area. The National Zoo and National Cathedral are foremost. Rock Creek Park and Russian art-filled Hillwood Museum are less well known but equally worthwhile.

❿ Northern Virginia p214

Arlington has the solemn National Cemetery, the imposing Pentagon and ethnic enclaves for good eats. Colonial Alexandria is a posh collection of red-bricked homes, cobblestoned streets, outdoor cafes and a waterfront promenade. Nature areas and trails fringe both towns.

National Mall

Neighborhood Top Five

❶ Climb the steps of the **Lincoln Memorial** (p82), stare into Abe's stony eyes and read his Gettysburg Address chiseled in the wall. Then go stand where Martin Luther King Jr gave his 'I Have a Dream' speech and feel the sweep of history.

❷ Touch the moon and gawp at nuclear missiles at the **National Air and Space Museum** (p90).

❸ Reflect on the sea of names sprawled across the **Vietnam Veterans Memorial** (p84).

❹ Smell the roses, er, cherry blossoms around the **Tidal Basin** (p93) come springtime.

❺ Poke around the monumental trove of paintings and sculpture at the **National Gallery of Art** (p85).

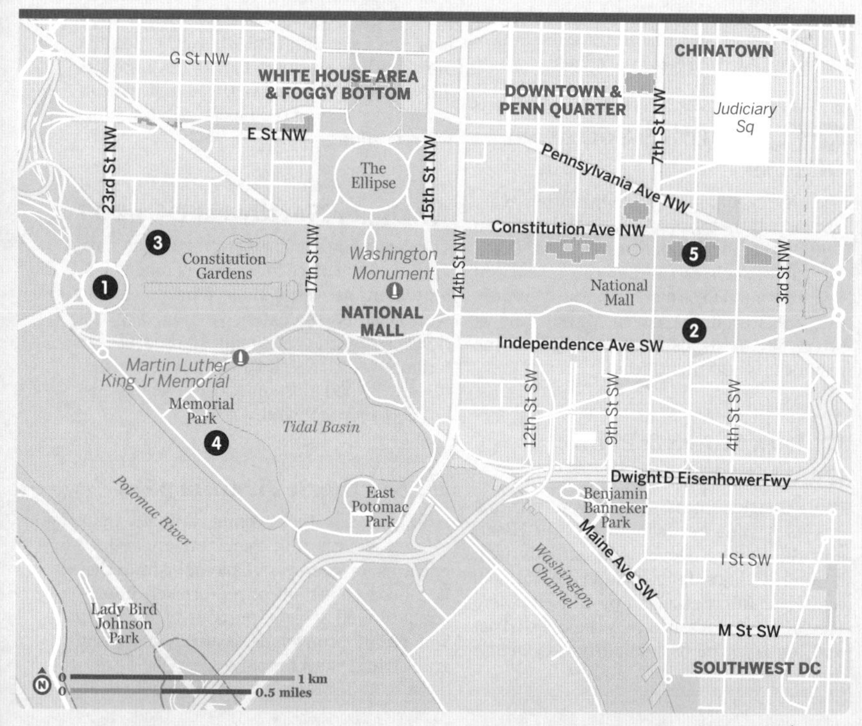

For more detail of this area, see Map p318

Explore the National Mall

A nation is many things: her people, her history, her politics and her amassed knowledge. Somehow, every item listed above is given architectural life on the National Mall, the center of iconography of the most iconic city in America. This is where the nation's ideals are expressed in stone, landscaping, educational institutions, monuments and memorials.

It's also, for you first-timers, a big old lawn. Really, that's the gist of it – about 3 miles of scrubby grass sandwiched between the Capitol and Lincoln Memorial, pinned down by the Washington Monument, flanked by hot-dog vendors and T-shirt stands, and containing therein the American experience. This communal space is where Americans come to protest, to rally, to watch presidents get inaugurated. It's also where locals come to jog, dog-walk and toss a Frisbee.

With all the monuments and museums to see (for free!), you could spend your entire trip here. It's easy to get lost in the National Gallery of Art or the Air and Space Museum for half a day. Whatever places you decide to explore, be prepared to walk. The main row of sights, from the Smithsonian museums west to the Lincoln Memorial, is about 2 miles tip to tip, and there's no public transport that covers the route. Eating and drinking options are thin on the ground beyond the museum cafes. And while the monuments are beautiful at night, there's not much going on after hours.

Local Life

- **Early to Rise** Many locals say the best cherry blossom viewing is from the FDR Memorial (p94) at sunrise.
- **Sunset Kiss** Looking for a romantic place to smooch your sweetie? Constitution Gardens (p96) at sunset is a well-known hot spot.
- **Nighttime Stroll** Don't overlook visiting the Mall at night. A walk along Constitution Ave past the dramatically lit monuments is incredibly atmospheric (and safe).

Getting There & Away

- **Metro** Smithsonian (Blue and Orange Lines) and L'Enfant Plaza (Blue, Orange, Green and Yellow Lines) for the majority of sights; Foggy Bottom-GWU for the Lincoln and Vietnam Memorials – though note they're about a mile walk from the station.

Lonely Planet's Top Tip

Download free apps: www.nps.gov/nama/photosmultimedia/app-page.htm, with maps and background info; and www.si.edu/apps/smithsonianmobile, for browsing the Smithsonian collection.

Best Gardens

- National Sculpture Garden (p92)
- United States Botanic Garden (p92)
- Hirshhorn Sculpture Garden (p91)
- Enid A Haupt Memorial Garden (p90)
- Constitution Gardens (p96)

For reviews, see p90

Best Museums

- National Air and Space Museum (p86)
- National Gallery of Art (p85)
- National Museums of Asian Art (p90)
- National Museum of Natural History (p93)
- Hirshhorn Museum (p91)

For reviews, see p90

Best Monuments

- Vietnam Veterans Memorial (p84)
- Lincoln Memorial (p82)
- Martin Luther King Jr Memorial (p87)
- Franklin Delano Roosevelt Memorial (p94)
- Washington Monument (p83)

For reviews, see p90 

LEE FOSTER / LONELY PLANET IMAGES ©

TOP SIGHTS
LINCOLN MEMORIAL

In a city of icons, the inspiration for the back of the penny stands out in the crowd. Maybe it's the classicism evoked by the Greek temple design, or the stony dignity of Lincoln's gaze. Whatever; a visit here while looking out over the Reflecting Pool is a defining DC moment.

The Design

Plans for a monument to Abraham Lincoln, the 16th president, began in 1867 – two years after his assassination – but construction didn't begin until 1914. Henry Bacon designed the memorial to resemble a Doric temple, with 36 columns to represent the 36 states in Lincoln's union. Carvers used 28 blocks of marble to fashion the seated figure. Lincoln's face and hands are particularly realistic, since they are based on castings done when he was president. The words of his Gettysburg Address and Second Inaugural speech flank the statue on the north and south walls, along with murals depicting his principles. Look for symbolic images of freedom, liberty and unity, among others. More info is available via a **DIY cell phone tour** (☎202-747-3420).

Civil Rights Rallying Point

From the get-go, the Lincoln Memorial became a symbol of the Civil Rights movement. Most famously, Martin Luther King Jr gave his 'I Have a Dream' speech here in 1963. An engraving of King's words marks the spot where he stood. It's on the 18th step and is usually where everyone is gathered, snapping photos of the awesome view out over the **Reflecting Pool** and Washington Monument. Visiting the memorial at nighttime is particularly atmospheric (and there's less crowd jostling).

DON'T MISS...

- Martin Luther King's 'Dream' speech marker
- Lincoln's expressive face and hands
- Gettysburg Address text
- Murals
- Visiting at nighttime

PRACTICALITIES

- Map p318
- ☎202-426-6841
- www.nps.gov/linc
- west end of Mall, at 23rd St
- admission free
- 24hr
- Ⓜ Foggy Bottom-GWU

TOP SIGHTS
WASHINGTON MONUMENT

Oldest joke in DC: 'So, what part of Washington is his monument modeled on?' Yeah, that's right, America has a bigger...obelisk than you. At 555ft the monument is not only the tallest building in DC (by federal law no structure can reach above it), it is also the tallest masonry structure in the world.

DON'T MISS...

- Change in color a third of the way up
- Inscribed stones inside
- Views from the top

PRACTICALITIES

- Map p318
- 202-233-3520
- www.nps.gov/wamo
- admission free
- 9am-5pm, to 10pm Jun-Aug
- M Smithsonian

Exterior

Of course George Washington gets DC's most impressive monument. He was the nation's first president and played a helluva role in its history (revolutionary war hero, statesman, whiskey maker). Construction began in 1848, but a lack of funds during the Civil War grounded the monument at 152ft. President Ulysses S Grant got the ball rolling again in 1876.

There was a problem though. The original marble was drawn from a quarry in Maryland, but the source dried up during the construction delay. Contractors had to turn to Massachusetts for the rest of the rock. If you look closely there is a visible delineation in color where the old and new marble meet about a third of the way up (the bottom is a bit lighter).

In December 1884 workers heaved a 3300lb marble capstone on the monument and topped it off with a 9in pyramid of cast aluminum. It was the culmination of some 36,000 stacked blocks of granite and marble, weighing 81,000 tons. The 'Father of his Country' had his due.

Interior

Inside the monument, a 70-second elevator ride whisks you to the observation deck at the top. In the days before September 11, 2001, it was possible to descend the 897 steps rather than take the elevator – the shaft's interior is decorated with inscribed stones from states, cities and patriotic societies. You can still see some of them from the elevator. Speaking of which: when the monument first opened, the elevator was not considered safe for women. Men got to ride in style to the top, while women had to hoof it.

Queues & Tickets

Same-day tickets for a timed entrance are available at the **kiosk** (15th St, btwn Madison Dr NW & Jefferson Dr SW; 8:30am-4:30pm) by the monument. Make sure you arrive early as tickets are limited. During spring cherry-blossom season, people start queuing at 6:30am. The rest of the year, if you turn up by 9am you should be fine. Alternatively, you can **reserve tickets in advance** (877-444-6777; www.recreation.gov; fee per ticket $1.50) by phone or online, and pick them up at the kiosk's will-call window.

On August 23, 2011, a rare earthquake rattled DC. While there was no catastrophic damage, the quake did cause internal structural harm to the Washington Monument. Repairs are in progress, with the sight expected to reopen in summer 2013.

TOP SIGHTS
VIETNAM VETERANS MEMORIAL

This simple memorial is the most powerful in the city, if not the nation. A black granite 'V' cuts into the Mall, just as the war it memorializes cut into the national psyche. The memorial eschews mixing conflict with glory. Instead, it quietly records the names of service personnel killed in action (KIA) and missing in action (MIA) in Vietnam, honoring those who gave their lives and explaining, in stark architectural language, the true price paid in war.

The Design

Originally planned to reconcile a divided nation, the memorial was conceived by Maya Lin, a 21-year-old Yale architecture student, following a nationwide call for proposed designs in 1982. The two walls of Indian granite meet in a 10ft apex; their polished, mirror surface invites visitors into the roll call of the dead. There are over 58,200 soldiers named on the wall; the number sporadically increases as names are added due to clerical errors in record keeping. Rank is not provided on the wall, and privates share space with majors. Unlike the soaring white Washington Monument and similar structures, the Vietnam Memorial is black, and burrows into the ground.

The Reaction

Paper indices at both ends help you locate individual names. Left mementos such as photos of babies and hand-scrawled notes bring tears to the most hardened hearts; these are collected by rangers and brought to the National Museum of American History (p93).

In 1984 opponents of Maya Lin's design insisted that a more traditional sculpture of soldiers be added to the monument. The **Three Soldiers** depicts a white, African American and Latino soldier who seem to be gazing upon the nearby sea of names. Also nearby is the tree-ringed **Women in Vietnam Memorial** depicting female soldiers aiding a fallen combatant.

Names & Symbols

Soldiers' names are listed on the wall in chronological order according to the date they died (and alphabetically within each day). The list starts at the wall's apex on panel 1E on July 8, 1959 (though later it was discovered there had been earlier casualties). It moves day by day to the end of the eastern wall at panel 70E, then starts again at panel 70W at the western wall's end, before returning to the apex on May 15, 1975. So the war's beginning and end meet in symbolic closure.

What do the symbols beside each name mean? A diamond indicates 'killed, body recovered.' A plus sign indicates 'missing and unaccounted for.' There are approximately 1200 of the latter. If a soldier returns alive, a circle is inscribed around the plus sign. To date, no circles appear on the wall.

DON'T MISS...

- Mementos left at the wall
- Your reflection in the wall
- Three Soldiers monument
- Women in Vietnam Memorial
- Symbols beside the names

PRACTICALITIES

- Map p318
- ☎202-426-6841
- www.nps.gov/vive
- west end of Mall, at 22nd St
- admission free
- 24hr
- M Foggy Bottom-GWU

TOP SIGHTS
NATIONAL GALLERY OF ART

Affiliated with but not a part of the Smithsonian, the National Gallery needs two buildings to house its massive collection of more than 110,000 paintings, sculptures and decorative arts from the Middle Ages to the present. The gallery, being a generalist sort of spot, doesn't quite excel in any one area (the Hirshhorn has better modern art, and the American Art Museum keeps a better national retrospective), but it's still mighty impressive.

The original neoclassical building, known as the West Building, exhibits primarily European works from the Middle Ages to the early 20th century, including pieces by El Greco, Monet and Cézanne. The National Gallery is also the only art museum in the western hemisphere displaying a Leonardo da Vinci (*Ginevra di' Benci,* in Gallery 6). Impressionist fans should head to galleries 72 to 93, where all the big-name brushmen hang. Free audio tours are available inside the main entrance near the coat check.

Across 4th St NW, the angular East Building, designed by IM Pei, holds an incredible atrium mobile designed by Alexander Calder, along with other abstract and modern works by Matisse, Mondrian et al. You know the place is impressive when a five-year-old comes bouncing out squealing 'Jackson Pollock!'

To get between the two buildings, jump on the trippy, twinkling moving sidewalk that connects them underground. The Cascade Cafe buzzes with patrons at the walkway's east end.

The gallery overall is huge and could easily fill a day. If you're short on time, ask for the see-it-in-an-hour highlights brochure; each building has its own, available at the main entrances. For in-depth explorations of French paintings, African American art etc, check out the free podcasts (www.nga.gov/podcasts).

DON'T MISS...

- Leonardo da Vinci's *Ginevra di' Benci*
- Alexander Calder mobile
- Impressionist galleries
- Twinkling-light walkway
- Free films and concerts

PRACTICALITIES

- Map p318
- 202-737-4215
- www.nga.gov
- Constitution Ave NW, btwn 3rd & 7th Sts
- admission free
- 10am-5pm Mon-Sat, 11am-6pm Sun
- M Archives-Navy Memorial

TOP SIGHTS
NATIONAL AIR AND SPACE MUSEUM

The most popular Smithsonian museum is one of the best for kids and kids at heart, full of interactivity and things that go fast/boom/swoosh/etc. When you visit, don't forget to touch the moon. No, really, there's an actual chunk of lunar love here. Other must-sees include Chuck Yeager's sound-barrier-breaking Bell X-1, Lindbergh's *Spirit of St Louis,* the Lunar Lander and the Wright Brothers' original airplane. They all hang from wires off the enormous ceiling, directing your gaze ever upward.

The Air and Space Museum draws seven million visitors a year, and it's typically jam-packed in here. But you gotta come anyway. C'mon – they've got real nuclear missiles! Plus astronaut ice cream (the stuff they actually eat in space; it tastes awful) in the gift shop and the **Lockheed Martin IMAX Theater**, which offers a rotating list of films shown throughout the day. Alternative shows at the **Albert Einstein Planetarium** send viewers hurtling through space on tours of the universe. Buy your tickets as soon as you arrive, or on the museum website before you visit.

To get your bearings in the vast hall remember this: rockets and space flight exhibits fill the museum's east side. Airplanes and aviation are on the west side. Free 90-minute tours depart from the information desk daily at 10:30am and 1pm.

The museum has so much cool stuff they had to build extra hangars for it at the Steven F Udvar-Hazy Center (p218) near Dulles Airport. Together the two sites comprise the world's largest collection of aviation and space artifacts, and folks, that's pretty damn cool.

DON'T MISS...

- Chuck Yeager's Bell X-1
- Lindbergh's *Spirit of St Louis*
- Lunar Lander
- Wright Brothers' original airplane
- Astronaut ice cream

PRACTICALITIES

- Map p318
- ☎202-633-1000
- www.airandspace.si.edu
- cnr 6th St & Independence Ave SW
- admission free
- ⏲10am-5:30pm, to 7:30pm mid-Mar–early Sep
- Ⓜ L'Enfant Plaza

TOP SIGHTS

MARTIN LUTHER KING JR MEMORIAL

The newest memorial on the Mall, and the first one to honor an African American, occupies a lovely space along the Tidal Basin, near the Jefferson and FDR Memorials. The monument conveys themes of democracy, justice and hope, given form in the striking centerpiece: a 30ft-tall likeness of Dr King emerging from a mountain of granite. But like the man who inspired it, the monument has faced a heap of controversy.

Sculptor Lei Yixin carved the piece. Besides Dr King's image, known as the Stone of Hope, there are two blocks behind him that represent the Mountain of Despair. A wall inscribed with King's quotes flanks the statues. King's statue, incidentally, is 11ft taller than those of Lincoln and Jefferson in their memorials.

The MLK monument broke ground in 2006, then got mired in funding difficulties. It finally opened in late 2011. But there was a problem. Chiseled on the Stone of Hope's side is the quote, 'I was a drum major for justice, peace and righteousness.' It's paraphrased from a sermon King gave in Atlanta in 1968, where he said, 'Yes, if you want to say that I was a drum major, say that I was a drum major for justice. Say that I was a drum major for peace. I was a drum major for righteousness. And all of the other shallow things will not matter.' Many have pointed out the 'if' and the 'you' change the quote's meaning from the paraphrased version. Poet Maya Angelou said the way the monument reads now makes King sound like 'an arrogant twit.'

After much debate, the park service has promised to fix the quote. Details on how and when were still being decided at press time.

DON'T MISS...

- Stone of Hope
- Mountain of Despair
- View of Washington and Jefferson monuments
- Wall of quotes
- Paraphrased 'drum major' quote

PRACTICALITIES

- Map p318
- 202-233-3520
- www.nps.gov/mlkm
- Tidal Basin, near Independence Ave & W Basin Dr SW
- admission free
- 24hr
- Smithsonian

Folks often call the Mall 'America's Front Yard,' and that's a pretty good analogy. It is indeed a lawn, unfurling scrubby green grass from the Capitol west to the Lincoln Memorial. It's also America's great public space, where citizens come to protest their government, go for scenic runs and connect with the nation's most cherished ideals writ large in stone, landscaping, monuments and memorials.

You can sample quite a bit in a day, though it'll be a full one that requires roughly 4 miles of walking. Start at the **Vietnam Veterans Memorial** **1**, then head counterclockwise around the Mall, swooping in on the **Lincoln Memorial** **2**, **Martin Luther King Jr Memorial** **3** and **Washington Monument** **4**. You can also pause for the cause of the Korean War and WWII, among other monuments that dot the Mall's western portion.

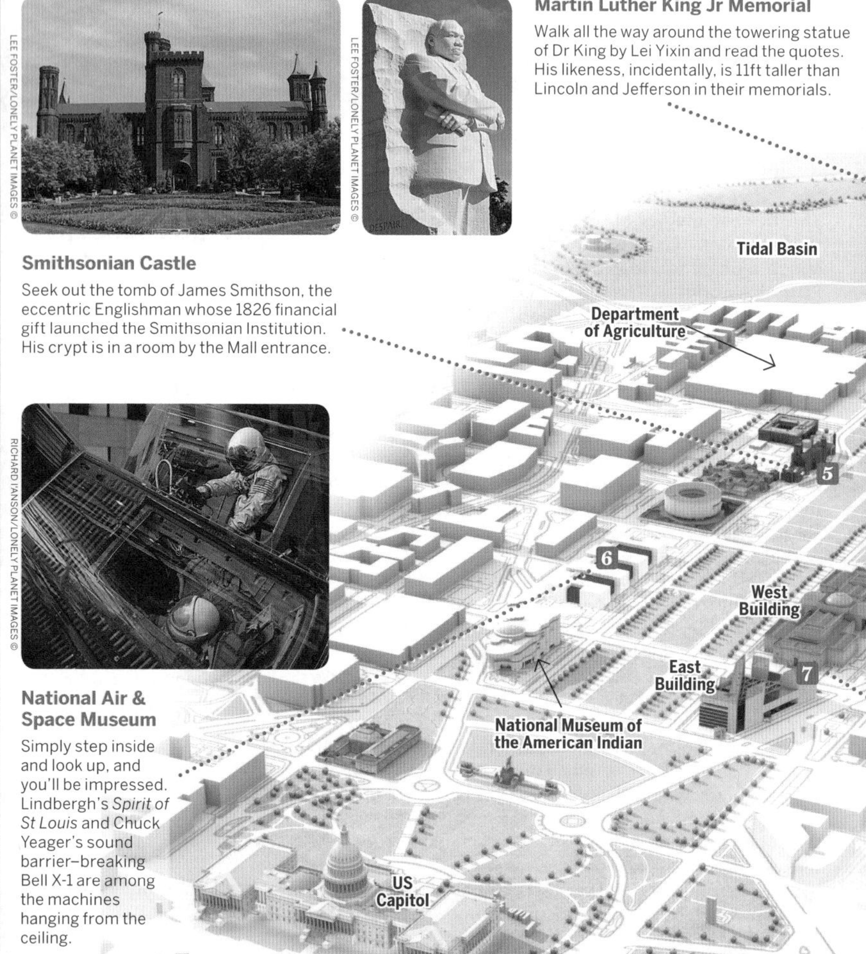

LEE FOSTER/LONELY PLANET IMAGES ©

LEE FOSTER/LONELY PLANET IMAGES ©

RICHARD I'ANSON/LONELY PLANET IMAGES ©

Martin Luther King Jr Memorial

Walk all the way around the towering statue of Dr King by Lei Yixin and read the quotes. His likeness, incidentally, is 11ft taller than Lincoln and Jefferson in their memorials.

Smithsonian Castle

Seek out the tomb of James Smithson, the eccentric Englishman whose 1826 financial gift launched the Smithsonian Institution. His crypt is in a room by the Mall entrance.

National Air & Space Museum

Simply step inside and look up, and you'll be impressed. Lindbergh's *Spirit of St Louis* and Chuck Yeager's sound barrier–breaking Bell X-1 are among the machines hanging from the ceiling.

Then it's onward to the museums, all fabulous and all free. Begin at the **Smithsonian Castle** 5 to get your bearings – and to say thanks to the guy making all this awesomeness possible – and commence browsing through the **National Air & Space Museum** 6, **National Gallery of Art & National Sculpture Garden** 7 and **National Museum of Natural History** 8.

TOP TIPS

Start early, especially in summer. You'll avoid the crowds, but more importantly you'll avoid the blazing heat. Try to finish with the monuments and be in the air-conditioned museums by 10:30am. Also, consider bringing snacks, since the only food available is from scattered cart vendors and museum cafes.

Lincoln Memorial

Commune with Abe in his chair, then head down the steps to the marker where Martin Luther King Jr gave his 'Dream' speech. The view of the Reflecting Pool and Washington Monument is one of DC's best.

Vietnam Veterans Memorial

Check the symbol that's beside each name. A diamond indicates 'killed, body recovered.' A plus sign indicates 'missing and unaccounted for.' There are approximately 1200 of the latter.

STEVEN GREAVES/LONELY PLANET IMAGES ©

1 2 3 4 8

Korean War Veterans Memorial

National WWII Memorial

National Museum of American History

National Sculpture Garden

Washington Monument

As you approach the obelisk, look a third of the way up. See how it's slightly lighter in color at the bottom? Builders had to use different marble after the first source dried up.

National Museum of Natural History

Wave to Henry, the elephant who guards the rotunda, then zip to the 2nd floor's Hope Diamond. The 45.52-carat bauble has cursed its owners, including Marie Antoinette, or so the story goes.

National Gallery of Art & National Sculpture Garden

Beeline to Gallery 6 (West Building) and ogle the Western Hemisphere's only Leonardo da Vinci painting. Outdoors, amble amid whimsical sculptures by Miró, Calder and Lichtenstein. Also check out IM Pei's design of the East Building.

RICHARD CUMMINS/LONELY PLANET IMAGES ©

RICHARD CUMMINS/LONELY PLANET IMAGES ©

SIGHTS

LINCOLN MEMORIAL — MONUMENT
See p82.

WASHINGTON MONUMENT — MONUMENT
See p83.

VIETNAM VETERANS MEMORIAL — MONUMENT
See p84.

NATIONAL GALLERY OF ART — MUSEUM
See p85.

NATIONAL AIR AND SPACE MUSEUM — MUSEUM
See p86.

MARTIN LUTHER KING JR MEMORIAL — MONUMENT
See p87.

SMITHSONIAN CASTLE — VISITOR CENTER, NOTABLE BUILDING
(Map p318; 202-633-1000; www.si.edu; 1000 Jefferson Dr SW; 8:30am-5:30pm; Smithsonian; wi-fi) James Renwick designed this turreted, red-sandstone fairy tale in 1855. Today the castle houses the Smithsonian Visitors Center, which makes a good first stop on the Mall. Inside you'll find an orientation film, multilingual touch-screen displays, a staffed information desk, free maps, a cafe – and the tomb of James Smithson, the institution's founder. His crypt lies inside a little room by the main entrance off the Mall. The castle also sells a useful visitor guide booklet ($2).

In front of the castle, a musical **carousel** (per ride $3.50) pleases the kiddies.

ENID A HAUPT MEMORIAL GARDEN — GARDENS
(Map p318; www.gardens.si.edu; Smithsonian) The pretty green space behind the Smithsonian Castle is actually a rooftop garden, with Asian moon gates and Moorish-style geometric flower beds that reflect the personalities of the Sackler Gallery and Museum of African Art below. It's usually a peaceful retreat from the Mall madness. Shaded benches and tables dot the grounds.

FREE WI-FI FOR FREE APPS

If you didn't already download the handy-dandy **National Mall app** (www.nps.gov/nama/photosmultimedia/app-page.htm) and the **Smithsonian app** (www.si.edu/apps/smithsonianmobile), and you want to save on data costs, swing into the Smithsonian Castle and use the free wi-fi to get them on your mobile device.

FREE NATIONAL MUSEUMS OF ASIAN ART — MUSEUM
(Map p318; www.asia.si.edu; 10am-5:30pm; Smithsonian) The dangling sculpture *Monkeys Grasping for the Moon,* an image of a dozen stylized primates fashioned into the word 'monkey' in a like number of languages (including Japanese, Hebrew, Braille and Urdu) is perhaps the most impressive piece of introductory art to welcome you to a Smithsonian institution – and a reminder that you have just entered a very special museum. Well, two museums actually: the **Arthur M Sackler Gallery** (1050 Independence Ave SW) and **Freer Gallery of Art** (cnr 12 St & Jefferson Dr SW) combine to form the National Museums of Asian Art. Make sure to visit them in tandem for the best effect.

This is simply a lovely spot in which to while away a Washington afternoon. Japanese silk scrolls, Buddha's flashing *Mona Lisa* smiles, rare Islamic manuscripts and a treasure of Silk Road artifacts – many the gift of Dr Arthur M Sackler – are all housed in appealingly spare and well-executed galleries. When you finish in the Sackler, jaunt over to the Freer via the underground tunnel. It offers its own incredible ensemble of ancient ceramics, Southeast Asian temple sculpture and centuries-old Chinese scrolls, a gift from Detroit industrialist Charles Lang Freer. The self-taught connoisseur was also a fan of James McNeill Whistler, whose works, somewhat incongruously, also appear here. Don't miss the blue-and-gold, ceramics-crammed Peacock Room.

Like all Smithsonian institutions, free lectures, film screenings etc are hosted here; check the website for details.

FREE NATIONAL MUSEUM OF AFRICAN ART — MUSEUM
(Map p318; www.nmafa.si.edu; 950 Independence Ave SW; 10am-5:30pm; Smithsonian; family-friendly) Enter the museum's ground-level pavilion through the Enid A Haupt Memorial Garden, then descend into the dim underground exhibit space. Devoted to ancient and modern sub-Saharan African art, the

THANK YOU, JAMES SMITHSON

Englishman James Smithson never set foot in the USA, let alone Washington (or not while he was alive, anyway). Yet he was an inestimable boon to the District and the nation she governs thanks to the $508,318 he willed to America in 1826. The money was to be used to create an 'establishment for the increase and diffusion of knowledge,' and said gift horse was promptly looked in the mouth by the government.

'Every whippersnapper vagabond...might think it proper to have his name distinguished in the same way,' grumbled Senator William Preston, while Senator John C Calhoun argued it was 'beneath American dignity to accept presents from anyone.' Anti-British sentiment informed some of this debate: the 1814 British torching of Washington (see the box, p260) remained fresh in many American minds. Finally, in 1846, Congress deigned to accept the gift and turned a cool half million into the final destination of countless elementary school field trips by constructing the Smithsonian.

So who was Smithson? A mineralogist by trade and shrewd investor by evidence (his gift was a fortune for its time), he was well-educated and wealthy by any measure. But his motivations for bequeathing so much money to the USA, as opposed to his native Britain (or anywhere else, for that matter), remain a mystery. Some say he was an antimonarchist who took a particular shine to the American Republic. He may have just loved learning; to quote Smithson, 'Every man is a valuable member of society who by his observations, researches, and experiments procures knowledge for men.' Today Smithson is entombed in the Smithsonian Castle. His coffin incorrectly states he died at 75; he was 64.

He left behind quite a baby: the collected attic of the American psyche, as it were. Only 1% of the Smithsonian's approximately 140 million artworks, scientific specimens, artifacts and other objects is on display at any given point. Ten of its 18 DC museums are scattered across the National Mall, with the rest found around the city; the organization also operates the National Zoological Park and throws the annual Smithsonian Folklife Festival (www.festival.si.edu) on the Mall every summer. The best part about the Smithsonian museums is that there's no entry fee, so you needn't feel guilty about not staying all day. Plus, if you're traveling with the tykes, free admission means you can come and go in accordance with your little ones' attention spans.

The Smithsonian needs (and is receiving) some expensive upkeep. It has been suggested the museums start charging for admission, but the powers that be won't hear of it, arguing fees would fly in the face of the Smithsonian's mission. The museums will stay free if it kills them, which is a sad possibility. The Arts & Industries Museum (900 Jefferson Dr SW) is closed indefinitely.

quiet galleries display masks, textiles, ceramics, ritual objects and other examples of the visual traditions of a continent of over 900 distinct cultures. Intentionally or not, there's a definite West African focus here – this is the traditional art many people associate with Africa, including wooden masks, statues and fetish dolls, largely from Nigeria, Benin and Cameroon. That said, the museum is making admirable strides in showcasing more contemporary work from the continent. African dance troupes, theater companies and multimedia artists frequently stage shows here. An underground tunnel connects to the Sackler Gallery.

FREE HIRSHHORN MUSEUM & SCULPTURE GARDEN — MUSEUM

(Map p318; www.hirshhorn.si.edu; cnr 7th St & Independence Ave SW; 10am-5:30pm, sculpture garden 7:30am-dusk; M L'Enfant Plaza;) The Smithsonian's cylindrical modern art museum is the best of its kind in Washington. Sculptures and canvases are presented in chronological fashion, from modernism's early days to pop art to contemporary. Rotating exhibits ring the 2nd floor; the permanent collection circles the 3rd floor, where there's also a balcony that offers Mall views. Gallery spaces are usually airy and bright, infused with the right edge of cold showroom chic you expect in modern art

LOCAL KNOWLEDGE

KILROY IS THERE

During WWII, a popular bit of serviceman graffiti was of a bulbous-nosed man peeking over a wall under the words 'Kilroy Was Here.' Old Kilroy graced walls from London to Okinawa by war's end (rumor has it Hitler thought Kilroy was some kind of super spy), and he's snuck onto the WWII Memorial as well – but he's not easy to find.

From the Pacific Tower, walk out of the memorial (ie away from the main plaza). There's a path here; follow it past the wreath-bedecked state and territory columns. After the columns end, you'll see an alcove/niche with metal grating for flooring. Engraved into the surrounding walls is Kilroy, peeping away, safe in the knowledge that he may be the only official graffiti allowed on any monument in the District.

museums. Highlights include sculptures by Rodin, Brancusi, Calder and Moore, along with canvases by Bacon, Miró, O'Keeffe, Warhol, Stella and Kiefer. On Fridays and Saturdays, the Improv Art Room invites children to create their own works of art.

Outside and across Jefferson Dr, the sunken **Sculpture Garden** feels, on the right day, like a bouncy jaunt through a Lewis Carroll Wonderland all prettified up. Young lovers, lost tourists and serene locals wander by sculptures such as Rodin's *The Burghers of Calais*.

FREE NATIONAL MUSEUM OF THE AMERICAN INDIAN

MUSEUM

(Map p318; www.americanindian.si.edu; cnr 4th St & Independence Ave SW; ⏲10am-5:30pm; Ⓜ L'Enfant Plaza; 👪) The award for most impressive external architecture of any museum on the Mall (and perhaps in the city) goes to the Museum of the American Indian. The curving exterior blobs like an art-house amoeba on the eastern edge of the Mall; fashioned from rough Kasota limestone that blushes honey in the sunset, it manages to look rustic and strong, yet liquid and organic all at once. In fact, there are no sharp edges to be found anywhere – the impression is one of nature flowing into the learning space, accentuated by an outside green area of wetlands and microbiomes meant to simulate the ecosystem of the North American continent.

Inside, you'll find the story of Native Americans told in a format not often employed by mainstream museums, with mixed results. The idea, to use native communities' voices and their own interpretations, is imaginative. Unfortunately, by allowing each tribe to promote their own version of their culture, the exhibits can come off as marketing rather than learning material.

That said, the collection, which consists of nearly a million objects (sourced from Canada and Mexico as well as the United States) is impressive, and this museum is certainly worth a few hours of your time. Free tours take place at 1:30pm daily, as well as 11am on weekends. The ground-floor Mitsitam Native Foods Cafe (see p96) is the best dining option on the Mall.

FREE UNITED STATES BOTANIC GARDEN

GARDENS

(Map p318; www.usbg.gov; 100 Maryland Ave SW; ⏲10am-5pm; Ⓜ Federal Center SW; 👪) Resembling London's Crystal Palace, this iron-and-glass greenhouse provides a beautiful setting for displays of exotic and local plants. Make sure to check out the Titan Arum, also known as *Amorphophallus titanum* ('giant misshapen penis'). If you're lucky, the plant's 'corpse flower' will be on display. This Sumatran native only blooms every three to five years, but when it does, it smells like rotten meat. Mmm! Behind the conservatory, across Independence Ave, you'll find the grand **Bartholdi Fountain**.

FREE NATIONAL SCULPTURE GARDEN

GARDENS

(Map p318; www.nga.gov/feature/sculpturegarden/general/index.shtm; cnr 7th St & Constitution Ave NW; ⏲10am-5pm Mon-Sat, 11am-6pm Sun; Ⓜ Archives-Navy Memorial) The National Gallery of Art's 6-acre garden is studded with whimsical sculptures such as Roy Lichtenstein's *House*, a giant Claes Oldenburg typewriter eraser and Louise Bourgeois' leggy *Spider*. They are scattered around a fountain – a great place to dip your feet in summer. From November to March the garden's central fountain becomes an **Ice Rink** (adult/child \$8/7; ⏲10am-9pm Mon-Thu, to 11pm Fri & Sat, 11am-9pm Sun). Skate rental (\$3) is available. During summer the garden is open an hour later than the rest of the year, and evening jazz concerts are held on Fridays from 5:30pm to 8:30pm.

FREE NATIONAL MUSEUM OF NATURAL HISTORY — MUSEUM

(Map p318; www.mnh.si.edu; cnr 10th St & Constitution Ave NW; 10am-5:30pm, to 7:30 Jun-Aug; M Smithsonian, Federal Triangle;) The Smithsonian's second-most popular museum clogs with kids, but adults will find lots to love here too. Say hello to the famous African-elephant statue dominating the entrance rotunda and the nearby carcass of a giant squid (in the Ocean Hall) and get ready to explore one of the most eclectic collections of, well, stuff, anywhere. The exhibits are a bit oddly mashed up – what exactly do Javanese shadow puppets have to do with birds of northern Europe?

Traipse past the Hall of Dinosaurs (1st floor) to the supposedly cursed Hope Diamond (2nd floor, Hall of Gems and Minerals) and Easter Island heads (lobby at the Constitution Ave entrance). Watch tarantula feedings at the insect zoo (2nd floor); ask at the front desk for the schedule. The museum adds new displays constantly, yet it manages to maintain the old-school charm that caused many a metro-area school kid to fall in love with it back in the day.

Almost 200 scientists work here, which the museum claims is the largest concentration of experts in natural history and cultures in the world. In a somewhat political statement, which is uncommon for the Smithsonian, the museum has heavily promoted its Darwin and evolution exhibits as a counter to creationism proponents.

The Johnson IMAX Theater (per ticket $9) shows nature extravaganzas like *Bugs! in 3D* daily. Movies sell out so buy tickets as soon as you arrive, or online in advance.

FREE NATIONAL MUSEUM OF AMERICAN HISTORY — MUSEUM

(Map p318; www.americanhistory.si.edu; cnr 14th St & Constitution Ave NW; 10am-5:30pm, to 7:30pm Jun-Aug; M Smithsonian, Federal Triangle;) This institution has accented itself with the daily bric-a-brac of the American experience – synagogue shawls, protest signs and cotton gins – along with icons such as Dorothy's ruby slippers and Kermit the Frog (yes, he is the cutest thing you'll find in DC. Even the pandas in the zoo can't compete). The centerpiece is a viewing space of the flag that flew over Fort McHenry in Baltimore during the War of 1812 – the same flag that inspired Francis Scott Key to pen *The Star-Spangled Banner*. In general, this is a better museum for children than adults; displays tend to be bright and interactive, perhaps a little too much so for those seeking a more serious engagement with the nation's history. The African American History and Culture Gallery (2nd floor) is a notable exception. It will spin off into the **National Museum of African American History and Culture** (www.nmaahc.si.edu; cnr Constitution Ave & 14th St NW) in 2015.

The building continues to undergo significant renovations, so prime exhibits often disappear. Check the website for updates. Film buffs should scan the schedule for the museum's new film theater (www.americanhistory.si.edu/filmseries), which screens classics for free throughout the year

TIDAL BASIN — WATERFRONT

(Map p318; M Smithsonian) Beloved for the magnificent Yoshino cherry trees that ring it, the Tidal Basin is an elegant aquatic interruption to the stone and grass of the Mall and its surrounding web of roads. The orchard was a gift from Japan in 1912; since then, every year in late March or early April the banks shimmer with pale pink blossoms. When said blossoms start to shed, the effect of soft pink snow against warm spring weather is intoxicating. The National Cherry Blossom Festival celebrates this event – late March and early April draw 750,000 visitors to DC for the festivities, which culminate in a big parade.

The Tidal Basin serves a practical purpose: flushing the adjacent Washington

WHERE THE CROWDS ARE

Expect lots of company at the Smithsonian's most-visited sights. Here are the big boys' visitor numbers for 2011:

- **National Air and Space Museum** 7 million
- **National Museum of Natural History** 6.6 million
- **National Museum of American History** 4.6 million
- **National Zoo** 1.9 million
- **Smithsonian Castle** 1.5 million
- **National Museum of the American Indian** 1.4 million

Channel. At high tide, river waters fill the basin through gates under the Inlet Bridge; at low tide, gates under the Outlet Bridge open and water streams into the channel.

Visit the **Tidal Basin Boathouse** (www.tidalbasinpaddleboats.com; 1501 Maine Ave SW; 2-/4-person boat rental $12/19; ⏲10am-6pm mid-Mar–Aug, Wed-Sun only Sep–mid-Oct, closed mid-Oct–mid-Mar) and rent out a paddleboat. Make sure you bring the camera; there are great views, of the Jefferson Memorial in particular, from the water.

FREE THOMAS JEFFERSON MEMORIAL
MONUMENT

(Map p318; www.nps.gov/thje; ⏲24hr; Ⓜ Smithsonian) Set on the south bank of the Tidal Basin amid the cherry trees (check it out in late March or early April when the blossoms are blazing pink), this memorial honors the third US president, political philosopher, drafter of the Declaration of Independence and founder of the University of Virginia. Designed by John Russell Pope to resemble Jefferson's library at the university, the rounded monument was initially derided by critics as 'the Jefferson Muffin.' We think the circular shape is a nice contrast to the angles jutting out from so many other monuments. Inside is a 19ft bronze likeness, and excerpts from Jefferson's writings are etched into the walls.

FREE GEORGE MASON MEMORIAL
MONUMENT

(Map p318; www.nps.gov/gemm; cnr Ohio Dr & E Basin Dr SW; ⏲24hr; Ⓜ Smithsonian) This little oasis of flowers and fountains honors the famed statesman and author of the Commonwealth of Virginia Declaration of Rights (a forerunner to the US Bill of Rights). A bronze sculpture of Mason sits (literally; his legs are crossed and the man looks eminently relaxed) under a pretty covered arcade, amid wise words against slavery and in support of human rights.

FREE FRANKLIN DELANO ROOSEVELT MEMORIAL
MONUMENT

(Map p318; www.nps.gov/fdrm; W Basin Dr SW; ⏲24hr; Ⓜ Smithsonian) Only good memorials manage to capture the essence of their subject, but the FDR Memorial takes it a step forward, encapsulating the longest-serving president in US history and the era he governed.

On the Tidal Basin's west bank, this landscaped 7.5-acre space is composed of four red-granite 'rooms' that narrate FDR's presidency, from the Depression to the New Deal to WWII. The story of both the man and the 1930s and '40s is told through statuary and inscriptions, punctuated with cascades and peaceful alcoves.

The irony is, FDR didn't want a grand memorial. In fact, when asked about a more traditional memorial, he reportedly responded, 'If any memorial is erected to me, I should like it to consist of a block about the size of this desk and placed in front of the Archives Building. I want it plain, without any ornamentation, with the simple carving "In Memory Of".' This request was honored in 1965, with a small **stone slab** (Map p326; cnr 9th St & Pennsylvania Ave NW).

Come at night. There are few better evening views of the Mall than the sight of reflected marble shimmering in the glossy stillness of the Tidal Basin.

FREE NATIONAL WWII MEMORIAL
MONUMENT

(Map p318; www.wwiimemorial.com; 17th St; ⏲24hr; Ⓜ Smithsonian) Dedicated on Memorial Day (May 29) 2004, the WWII memorial honors the unity that swept the nation during that conflict, plus the 16 million Americans who served in the armed forces during the war, 400,000 who died in it and millions more who helped the effort at home.

The memorial anchors the eastern end of the Reflecting Pool, serving as a balancing axis between the Washington Monument and Lincoln Memorial. The centerpiece is a plaza dominated by dual arches symbolizing victory in the Atlantic and Pacific theaters, surrounded by 56 granite pillars, one for each state and territory plus the District

CLEANING THE POOL

The Reflecting Pool should have a new filtration system by the time you're reading this, so it no longer will be the vat of duck crap from years past. Whereas the old pool allowed water to stagnate, the new one will flush water in from the Tidal Basin. The park service is also upgrading the walking paths around the pool. Ideas are even being floated that the pool could become an ice rink in winter. Stay tuned...

SHOPPING THE NATIONAL MALL

The Mall's museums all have shops where you'll unearth rare finds. Amazonian artwork, West African handicrafts and surreal space food are just a few things on offer.

➡ **National Gallery of Art** (p85) The museum boasts several shops, including a huge one lining the underground corridor linking the East and West Buildings. You'll find framed and unframed reproductions of the museum's best-known works, greeting cards, jewelry, creative games and activities for kids and loads of books.

➡ **National Museum of the American Indian** (p92) The smaller first-floor shop sells pottery, artwork and jewelry made by tribes from across the Americas. The busier store upstairs has books, crafts and native-themed souvenirs (dream catchers, Mola purses, replica arrowheads).

➡ **National Museum of African Art** (p90) This is a great gift-buying spot with African textiles, baskets, musical instruments and dolls. Don't overlook the exquisite Tuareg jewelry.

➡ **National Air and Space Museum** (p86) The three-floor emporium offers books, toys, kites, posters, model aircraft and such iconic DC souvenirs as freeze-dried astronaut ice cream.

➡ **National Museum of Natural History** (p93) It has four different specialty shops, including a bottom-floor store devoted to toys, stuffed dinosaurs and East Asian–themed items (origami sets, silk purses, kimonos). Outside the Geology Hall, the gem store sells fine and costume jewelry, vases, bowls, candleholders and a variety of unpolished stones.

➡ **Freer Gallery of Art** (p90) Browse the antique ceramics from Asia, plus unique prints, scarves, bags and Eastern music. The knowledgeable staff can help with any questions.

➡ **Arthur M Sackler Gallery** (p90) It features Asian art posters and limited-edition prints, exotic jewelry and world crafts.

➡ **National Museum of American History** (p93) Replica souvenirs (brass binoculars, lanterns, wooden model ships) plus books and DVDs on all aspects of American culture and history fill the shelves.

of Columbia. The Freedom Wall is studded with 4048 hand-sculpted gold stars, one for every 100 Americans who lost their lives between 1941 and 1945 (the stars are replicas of those worn by mothers who lost their sons in the war). Today, you'll often see widows and families placing flowers or fading black-and-white photos of handsome young men at the foot of the wall. Bas-relief panels depict both combat and the mobilization of the home front, and quotes – some truly stirring – speckle the entire affair.

Beside the memorial to the south there is an information kiosk where you can look through the registry of war veterans.

FREE DISTRICT OF COLUMBIA WAR MEMORIAL — MONUMENT

(Map p318; West Potomac Park off Independence Ave; ⏲24hr; Ⓜ Foggy Bottom-GWU) This small Greek-style temple commemorates local soldiers killed in WWI, making it the only local District memorial on the Mall. Twelve Doric 22ft-high marble columns support the circular structure; inside are the names of the 26,000 Washingtonians who served in the war and the 499 DC soldiers killed in action. In 2008, Representative Ted Poe of Texas put forward the Frank Buckles WWI Memorial Act (named for the last living US veteran of WWI). If passed, the law would expand the site into a national WWI memorial. He reintroduced it as HR938 in 2011. As of writing the bill – HR938 – was mired in a subcommittee. To follow its progress, check out www.govtrack.us/congress/bills/112/hr938.

FREE KOREAN WAR VETERANS MEMORIAL — MONUMENT

(Map p318; www.nps.gov/kwvm; ⏲24hr; Ⓜ Foggy Bottom-GWU) Nineteen steel soldiers wander through clumps of juniper past a wall bearing images of the 'Forgotten War' that assemble, in the distance, into a panorama of the Korean mountains. Best visited at night, when the sculpted patrol – representing all races and combat branches that served in the war – takes on a phantom cast. In winter, when snow folds over the infantry's field coats, the impact is especially powerful.

FREE CONSTITUTION GARDENS — GARDENS

(Map p318; ⏱24hr; Ⓜ Foggy Bottom-GWU) Constitution Gardens is a bit of a locals' secret. Quiet, shady and serene, it's a reminder of the size of the Mall – how can such isolation exist amid so many tourists? Here's the simple layout: a copse of trees set off by a small kidney-shaped pool, punctuated by a tiny island holding the **Signers' Memorial**, a plaza honoring those who signed the Declaration of Independence. At the northeast corner is an elegantly aged stone cottage, a remnant of the days when the Washington City Canal flowed through this area. The 1835 **C&O Canal Gatehouse** (near cnr Constitution Ave NW & 17th St NW) was the lock-keepers' house for the lock that transferred boats from the City Canal onto the C&O Canal, which begins in Georgetown. If you're in need of a romantic getaway, the 'kiss me' vibes don't get much better than this spot at sunset.

EATING

The Mall has always been a bit of a food desert. There are hot-dog and half-smoke vendors stationed around, while most museums have overpriced restaurants with unremarkable menus. We've listed a few of the exceptions here. Don't forget to get astronaut ice cream from the Air and Space Museum – it's nasty, but novel.

PAVILION CAFE — CAFE $

(Map p318; www.pavilioncafe.com; cnr Constitution Ave & 7th St NW; mains $9-11; ⏱lunch & dinner; Ⓜ Archives-Navy Memorial) Set amid the rambling sylvan serenity of the Sculpture Garden of the National Gallery of Art, this pizza and panini place makes for a green dream on spring days; free jazz concerts enrich Friday evenings in summer (see p97).

CASCADE CAFE — CAFE $

(Map p318; www.nga.gov/dining; East Bldg, National Gallery of Art, cnr 4th St & Constitution Ave NW; mains $7-14; ⏱11am-3pm Mon-Sat, to 4pm Sun; Ⓜ Archives-Navy Memorial; 👪) Oh what a lovely place for a bowl of tortellini or a croissant sandwich. Located at the juncture of the wings of the National Gallery of Art, the Cascade offers views of just that: a shimmering, IM Pei-designed artificial waterfall. It's one of the best coffee stops in any Washington museum. Food is of the soup and sandwich sort, and is available for picnic wrap if you'd like to eat outdoors. The adjoining espresso bar scoops 19 flavors of gelato.

MITSITAM NATIVE FOODS CAFE — NATIVE AMERICAN $$

(Map p318; www.mitsitamcafe.com; National Museum of the American Indian, cnr 4th St & Independence Ave SW; mains $8-18; ⏱11am-5pm; Ⓜ L'Enfant Plaza) Without a doubt the most intriguing museum food on the Mall, the Mitsitam introduces visitors to the palette of five regional Native American cuisines, from the blue corn tortillas and slow-smoked barbecue of the southwest, to wild rice and cranberry-stuffed turkey in the eastern woodlands. Menus rotate daily, and mixed among the tourists are a fair few regular local office workers seeking an indulgent lunch.

LOCAL KNOWLEDGE

CHOW BEYOND THE MALL

Granted, it's not particularly convenient, but for better food choices than the museums and Mall carts offer, hop on the Metro at the Smithsonian or Archives-Navy Memorial stations and make the quick trip to **Eastern Market** (p137).

Another option, especially from the Mall's north-side institutions, is to walk a quarter-mile or so along 12th St NW to the food court in the **Old Post Office Pavilion** (cnr 12th St NW & Pennsylvania Ave NW).

And it's possible, just possible, that DC's food trucks will be allowed on the Mall by the time you're reading this. City officials were pushing for it as this book went to press, though many issues still had to be worked out. Check **Food Truck Fiesta** (www.foodtruckfiesta.com) for locations.

LOCAL KNOWLEDGE

FARMERS MARKET

The US Department of Agriculture hosts a smallish **farmers market** (Map p318; cnr 12th St & Independence Ave SW; ⏲10am-2pm Fri Jun-mid-Nov; Ⓜ Smithsonian) on Fridays in its parking lot, featuring produce from the surrounding states of Maryland, Virginia, Delaware and Pennsylvania. Cooking demonstrations with well-known DC chefs add to the scene the first Friday of each month.

ENTERTAINMENT

FREE JAZZ IN THE GARDEN — LIVE MUSIC

(Map p318; www.pavilioncafe.com/jazz.html; cnr Constitution Ave & 7th St NW; ⏲5:30-8:30pm Fri late May–early Sep; Ⓜ Archives-Navy Memorial) Lots of locals show up for these outdoor jazz concerts at the National Gallery of Art's Sculpture Garden. Pack a picnic, and supplement with wine and beer from the Pavilion Cafe.

FREE SCREEN ON THE GREEN — CINEMA

(Map p318; www.hbo.com/screenonthegreen; Mall btwn 8th & 14th Sts NW; ⏲8pm Mon late Jul-late Aug; Ⓜ Smithsonian) Classic movies such as *One Flew Over the Cuckoo's Nest* and *Gentlemen Prefer Blondes* flicker on a large outdoor screen set up on the Mall. Bring a blanket, picnic fixin's and plenty of bug spray. Films start at sunset, usually around 8pm. Check the location before heading out, as it can vary due to construction on the Mall.

DISCOVERY THEATER — THEATER

(Map p318; www.discoverytheater.org; tickets adult/child $8/6; 1100 Jefferson Dr SW; Ⓜ Smithsonian; 👪) In the basement of the Ripley Center, it stages delightful productions for kids, such as puppet shows.

White House Area & Foggy Bottom

WHITE HOUSE AREA | FOGGY BOTTOM

Neighborhood Top Five

❶ It doesn't matter how many times you've seen it on TV: strolling through the **White House** (p100) thrills. From the ceremonial East Room, to Thomas Jefferson's green dining room to Lincoln's ghost roaming the halls.

❷ Knock back a Scotch at the **Round Robin** (p112), birthplace of the lobbyist.

❸ Watch a free performance any night of the week at the **Kennedy Center** (p113).

❹ Browse exquisite rooms of Hopper, Picasso and Warhol at the **Corcoran Gallery of Art** (p101).

❺ Play spot-the-politician while carving into a steak at the **Old Ebbitt Grill** (p109).

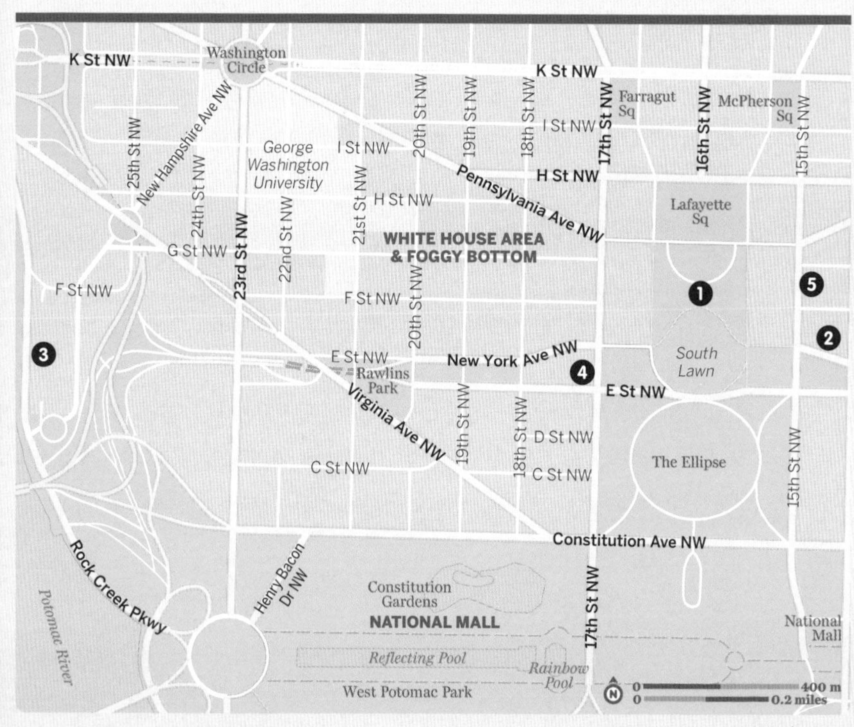

For more detail of this area, see Map p320

Explore White House Area & Foggy Bottom

When you play image association with the words 'Washington, DC,' the mental snapshot most people have of the city is the White House, a pale flame slipped into a grid of dark, manicured grounds. The president's pad does take your breath away the first time you see it, if only because you're standing in front of the *real thing,* the building you've seen a thousand times before in photos and on TV.

All in all, there's a sense of regal importance on these streets, blended with the bustle of a very alive nerve cluster of federal power. By day the area hums with the comings and goings of office workers, diplomats, lobbyists, tourists and bureaucrats. At night it dies a sudden death, like most urban business districts, aside from scattered fine dining restaurants and hotel bars mixing Manhattans.

West of the White House Area is Foggy Bottom, deriving its name from its low-lying geography, which serves as a catchment for Potomac mists. Foggy Bottom is synonymous with the State Department, World Bank, IMF and other hefty institutions. George Washington University infuses it with a bit of youthful energy.

With worthy art museums such as the Corcoran Gallery and Renwick Gallery, a slew of terrific architecture to browse – including that big white house – and the Kennedy Center for evening performances, plan on a full day here.

Local Life

➡ **Cheap Eats** Follow local office workers to the food trucks (p109) and lunch spots like BreadLine (p109) for economical fare in this neighborhood of power-player dining.

➡ **Romantic Drink** The terraces at the Kennedy Center (p113) and POV (p112) unfurl fantastic views and are perfect for a romantic cocktail.

➡ **Smell the Roses** Students and workers looking for a green respite grab a bench in rosebush-strewn University Yard (p107).

Getting There & Away

➡ **Metro** The Orange and Blue Lines run in tandem here. Get off at Federal Triangle or McPherson Sq for the White House; Farragut West for the Corcoran, Renwick and other museums; and Foggy Bottom-GWU for the university and Kennedy Center.

➡ **Bus** A free shuttle runs every 15 minutes between the Foggy Bottom-GWU Metro station and the Kennedy Center.

Lonely Planet's Top Tip

Plan ahead! To visit the White House you need to make a tour request 21 days to six months in advance. For the best chance of success, do it at least three months beforehand. You also need to make advance arrangements to tour the Federal Reserve and the Department of the Interior – at least two weeks notice for both. Visits to the Octagon are enhanced if you download the audio tours first.

Best Places to Eat

- Old Ebbitt Grill (p109)
- Cafe du Parc (p109)
- BreadLine (p109)
- Founding Farmers (p109)
- Georgia Brown's (p110)

For reviews, see p107

Best Places to Drink

- Round Robin (p112)
- Off the Record (p112)
- Le Bar (p112)
- Hamilton (p112)
- POV (p112)

For reviews, see p112

Best Art Museums

- Corcoran Gallery of Art (p101)
- Renwick Gallery (p104)
- Art Museum of the Americas (p106)
- Octagon Museum (p106)
- Daughters of the American Revolution (p106)

For reviews, see p104

TOP SIGHTS
WHITE HOUSE

LEE FOSTER / LONELY PLANET IMAGES ©

The White House is a home as well as a symbol. It stuns visitors with its sense of pomp and circumstance, yet it also charms with little left traces of those who have lived here before, which includes every US president since John Adams. Icon of the American presidency? Yeah. But it's also someone's front yard.

The Presidential Palace, as it was once known, has changed a great deal over history. It was not originally white, for example. After the British burned the building in the War of 1812, it was restored and painted. Presidents have customized the property over time: Grant put in a personal zoo; Franklin Roosevelt, a pool; Bush Sr, a horseshoe-throwing lane; and Clinton, a jogging track. Some residents never leave: it's said that Eleanor Roosevelt and Harry Truman both sighted Lincoln's ghost in Abe's old study.

Tours

It ain't easy to get into the White House. Tours are free, but you need to plan ahead. Americans must make a request through their Member of Congress. You can submit up to six months in advance, but no less than 21 days in advance (three months is advisable). Foreigners should contact their embassy in Washington, which can submit a tour request on your behalf. You choose the dates; White House staff then contact you to confirm, usually a month beforehand.

The self-guided half-hour tour covers the ground and 1st floors of the main residence (sorry, no east wing or west wing traipsing). See p102 for an armchair walk-through.

DON'T MISS...

- View from E St NW across South Lawn
- East Room
- Blue Room
- State Dining Room
- Rose Garden (on west side)

PRACTICALITIES

- Map p320
- ☎202-456-7041
- www.whitehouse.gov
- 1600 Pennsylvania Ave NW
- admission free (prebooking required)
- 7:30am-11am Tue-Thu, to noon Fri, to 1pm Sat
- Ⓜ Federal Triangle, McPherson Sq

TOP SIGHTS
CORCORAN GALLERY OF ART

You'd think the largest private museum in the city couldn't compare to the Smithsonian – and you'd think wrong. The Corcoran's permanent gallery of American, European and contemporary art is grand enough, but special exhibitions, which span themes such as Roy Lichtenstein's work, the art of the Harlem Renaissance and the theses projects culled from the Corcoran's own school of design, are the real standout. It's all located in a beautiful 1897 beaux-arts building overlooking the Ellipse.

Permanent Collection

The 1st floor houses most of the permanent collection. Here you'll find Edward Hopper's *Ground Swell* (room 5) and works by Pablo Picasso (room 6) and Thomas Gainsborough (Large Mantle Room). Bronze sculptures by American artists including Augustus Saint-Gaudens and Frederic Remington stud rooms 10 and 11.

The pièce de résistance is the 18th-century Salon Doré, or gilded room, originally part of the Parisian mansion of the Count d'Orsay. He built the room to be fit for a princess – aka his new bride Marie-Louise-Albertine-Amélie – and bedazzled it with the floor-to-ceiling Corinthian pilasters, carved panels, gilded garlands and huge framed mirrors. The salon became famous throughout Paris for its splendor. This didn't bode well during the French Revolution, and the government seized it, dispersing the furnishings. Pieces such as the bronze and alabaster corner tables disappeared for more than 200 years before landing at the Corcoran. The alabaster, incidentally, is antique and believed to be from the palace of Caligula.

Special Exhibitions

The crowds amass at the 2nd floor's special exhibitions. There are usually three simultaneous shows, each bringing together big-name artists around an edgy and thought provoking theme. For example, the recent '30 Americans' focused on racial and historical identity through works by Jean-Michel Basquiat, David Hammons and other African American artists. Photojournalist Tim Hetherington's war pictures and videos comprised another popular exhibition.

The Corcoran is also an art school, and a rotating display of students' work fills Gallery 31 (room 31), behind the 1st-floor museum shop. Peek in to see the next potential art world star.

The museum offers free half-hour gallery tours at noon daily, plus 3pm on weekends and 7pm on Thursdays. Lectures, concerts, films and family workshops also pack the schedule. The Corcoran is not overwhelmingly large like some of the other art museums in town. You can swing through in an hour if need be. Admission is free on Saturdays in summer.

Behind the Corcoran, on E St NW between 18th and 20th Sts NW, pretty **Rawlins Park** is named for President US Grant's Secretary of War. With goldfish in its little pond and blooming magnolias in spring and summer, it's among downtown DC's more charming oases.

DON'T MISS...

- The gilded Salon Doré
- Students' art in Gallery 31
- The bronze sculpture rooms
- Noontime tours
- Rawlins Park

PRACTICALITIES

- Map p320
- 202-639-1700
- www.corcoran.org
- 500 17th St NW
- adult/child $10/free
- 10am-5pm Wed & Fri-Sun, to 9pm Thu
- Farragut West

TOP SIGHTS
WHITE HOUSE

The most striking thing about the White House is how much it feels like a house. A 55,000-sq-ft house, but still a real one where a family lives. If you're lucky enough to get inside on a public tour, you'll see several rooms in the main residence, each rich in presidential lore: this is where Thomas Jefferson ate; Abe Lincoln's coffin stood over there...

The walk-through is self-guided and starts at the visitor entrance by the White House's southeast gate. From there you pass by the **Library** 1, Vermeil Room and China Room, all on the ground floor (they're roped off, so you don't actually go in). Next you go up a flight of stairs to the State Floor and continue on through the **East Room** 2, Green Room, **Blue Room** 3, Red Room and **State Dining Room** 4. Unlike the floor below, you can enter these rooms. The Secret Service guys standing guard everywhere are ace at answering questions – really.

The White House's 2nd and 3rd floors, as well as the east and west wings, are off-limits. So you won't get to see two of the most famous rooms – the **Lincoln Bedroom** 5 and the **Oval Office** 6 – but you'll feel their aura.

You depart from the building's front (north) side. Before leaving the neighborhood, swing over to 15th St NW and stroll south to E St NW. Turn right and walk along the South Lawn, and you'll have a picture-perfect **view** 7 of the house you just visited.

WALLY MCNAMEE / CORBIS ©

Oval Office
West Wing, Ground Floor
Suppose you were allowed into the west wing. You'd see the Oval Office, the president's official workspace. Each president has changed it to suit his taste, even designing his own carpet.

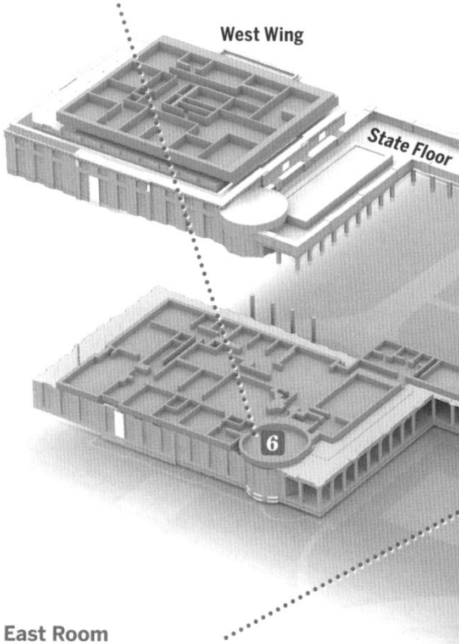

East Room
Residence, State Floor
Admire the White House's largest room, used for ceremonies and press conferences. Lincoln, Kennedy and five other presidents have lain in state here. Note how gilded eagles hold up the piano.

CHRISTOPHER MORRIS / VII / CORBIS ©

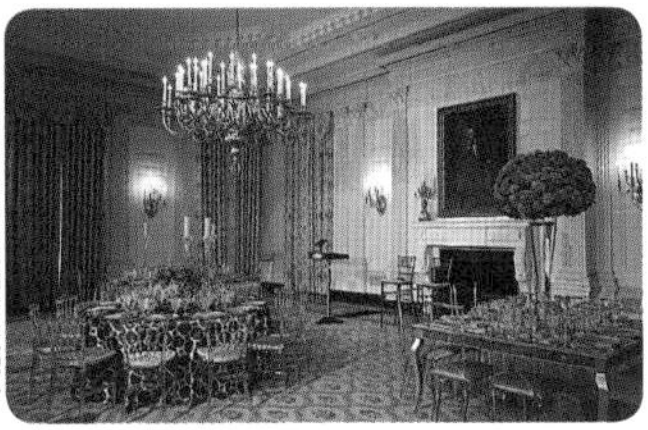

ALEX WONG / GETTY IMAGES ©

State Dining Room

Residence, State Floor

Imagine inviting over 130 of your closest kings, prime ministers and movie stars for a little poached lobster. The fireplace mantel's quote is from a letter John Adams wrote in 1800.

Lincoln Bedroom

Residence, 2nd Floor

Keep watch for Lincoln's ghost, said to roam the White House from here. The room was formerly Abe's office, where he signed the Emancipation Proclamation. His Gettysburg Address draft sits on the desk.

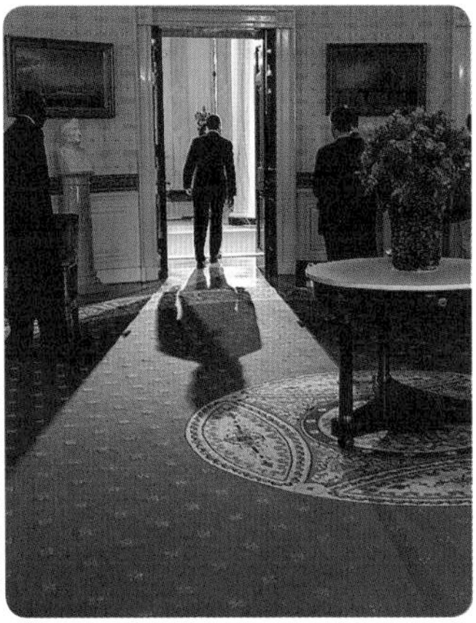

WHITE HOUSE PHOTO / ALAMY ©

Blue Room

Residence, State Floor

Pretend the president is receiving you here, as he does other guests. Fifth prez James Monroe bought the gilded French Empire decor. Eighth prez Martin Van Buren painted the room blue.

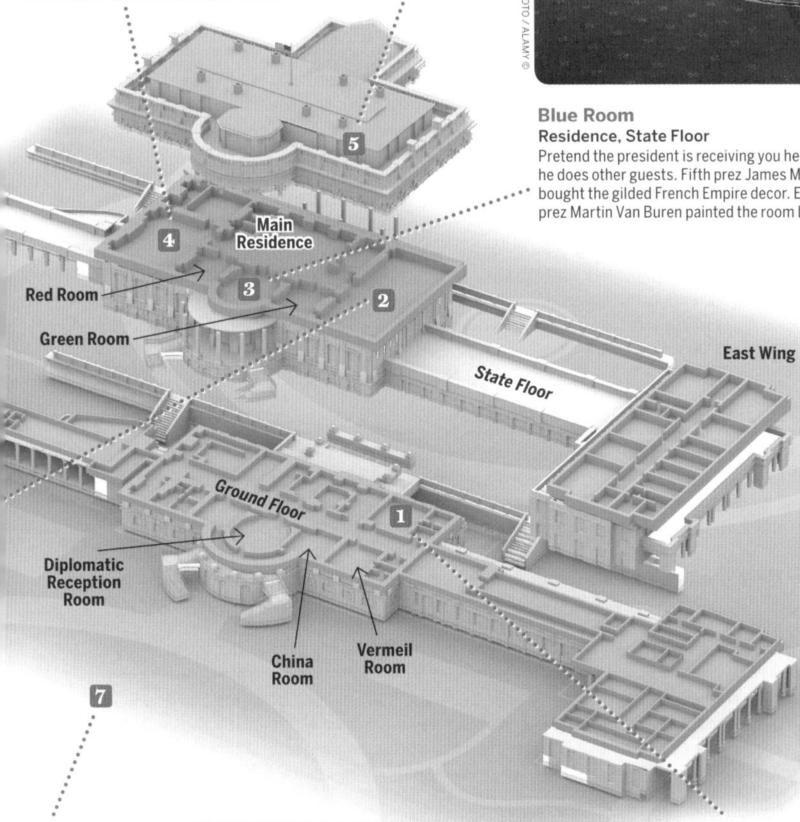

5
Main Residence
4
3
2
Red Room
Green Room
East Wing
State Floor
Ground Floor
1
Diplomatic Reception Room
China Room
Vermeil Room
7

View from E St NW

Snap your keepsake pictures across the South Lawn (taking photographs inside the White House is forbidden). Recognize the view? It's commonly used as the backdrop to TV news reports.

STEPHEN BOITANO / LONELY PLANET IMAGES ©

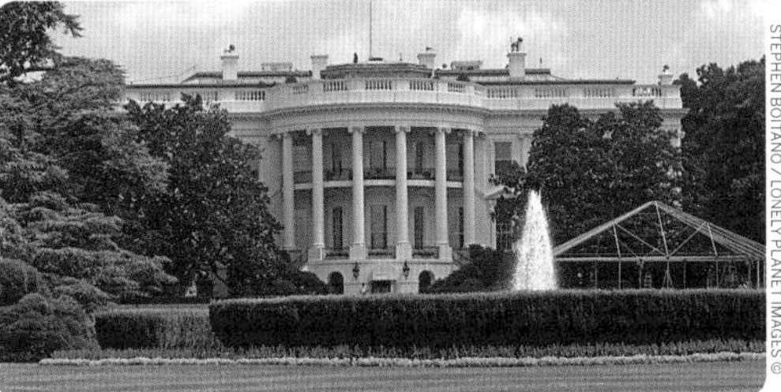

Library

Residence, Ground Floor

Scan the shelves of history, fiction and biography, and check out that chandelier. It belonged to the family of James Fenimore Cooper (author of *Last of the Mohicans*, 1826).

SIGHTS

White House Area

WHITE HOUSE LANDMARK

See p100.

CORCORAN GALLERY OF ART MUSEUM

See p100.

FREE WHITE VISITOR CENTER VISITOR CENTER

(Map p320; www.nps.gov/whho; 1450 Pennsylvania Ave NW; 7:30am-4pm; M Federal Triangle, McPherson Sq) Getting inside the White House can be tough (see White House, p100), so here is your backup plan. Browse exhibits, watch historic reenactments and take a video tour of the White House in the Malcolm Baldrige Hall in the Department of Commerce building. It's obviously not the same as seeing the real deal first-hand, but the center does do its job very well, giving good history sprinkled with great anecdotes on presidential spouses, kids and pets. Betcha didn't know each president designs their own Oval Office rug?

ELLIPSE PARK

(Map p320; Constitution Ave btwn 15th & 17th Sts NW) That elliptical road that circles the expansive park on the south side of the White House? It's imaginatively known as the Ellipse. The park is studded with a random collection of monuments, such as the **Zero Milestone** (the marker for highway distances all across the country) and the **Second Division Memorial**. But the more important function of the Ellipse is hosting sporting events, parades and festivals – from lighting the national Christmas tree, to military drill performances to Lance Armstrong's final ride.

FREE RENWICK GALLERY MUSEUM

(Map p320; www.americanart.si.edu; 1661 Pennsylvania Ave NW; 10am-5:30pm; M Farragut West;) Part of the Smithsonian American Art Museum, the Renwick highlights the American tradition of decorative arts and crafts. Housed in a regal 1859 mansion, there's a sense of eccentricity and loving whimsy; the 'crafts' here straddle a line between utilitarian and artistic expression. The many playful pieces make this a wonderful place to introduce kids to art.

PECULIAR PRESIDENTIAL PETS

Most of you have probably heard of Bo Obama (or as everyone calls him, 'Bobama'), the Portuguese water dog that is America's current first pet. Before Bo was Barney the terrier, preceded by Socks the cat, Buddy the Labrador and then...well, here are some suitably awesome pets you may never have known graced the presidential digs.

➡ **Billy the pygmy hippo** Rubber-maker Harvey Firestone brought Billy all the way from Liberia for Calvin Coolidge in 1927, who, for the record, already owned a wallaby, a duiker (a kind of African antelope) and a raccoon. Billy ended up in the National Zoo when (contrary to his species name) he got too big for the White House.

➡ **The Adams alligators** Let's say you're the Marquis de Lafayette and you want to get a present for John Quincy Adams, the kind of guy who likes to go swimming, naked, in the Potomac every morning. How about: two alligators! In the 1820s, Adams, skinny-dipping badass that he was, happily housed the two reptiles in the White House bathtub.

➡ **Pauline Wayne the cow** William Taft let Pauline, a Holstein gift from a Wisconsin Senator, graze the front lawn of the White House from 1909 to 1913, during his term. The trade-off? Pauline provided milk for the first family during Taft's last three years in office.

➡ **Josiah the badger** All of the above animals were thoughtful presents to sitting presidents. Josiah, on the other hand, was apparently a furry assassination attempt. In 1903, a girl in Kansas threw ornery Josiah directly at Theodore Roosevelt. Roosevelt, the kind of guy who hunted lions and charged fortified positions like San Juan hill on foot, ended up taking the little guy back to Washington.

We love Kim Schmahmann's *Bureau of Bureaucracy,* a hilariously accurate expression of the futility of dealing with official ineptitude realized in a cabinet plucked from MC Escher's nightmares. Head upstairs for it and several other terrific art-stuffed rooms; special exhibits fill the downstairs galleries.

LAFAYETTE SQUARE SQUARE

(Map p320; Pennsylvania Ave btwn 15th & 17th Sts NW) The land north of 1600 Pennsylvania was originally deeded as part of the White House grounds. However, in 1804 President Thomas Jefferson decided to divide the plot and give half back to the public in the form of a park, now known as Lafayette Sq. A statue of Andrew Jackson astride a horse holds court in the center, while the statues anchoring the four corners are all of foreign-born revolutionary leaders, a nice reminder that non-American freedom fighters helped ensure American independence.

In the southeast corner check out the likeness of the Marquis de Lafayette, a revolutionary war general by the age of 19. Although Lafayette was branded a traitor in his native France following the war, he was consistently lauded in the young America. In the northeast corner is a memorial to Tadeusz Kościusko, a Polish soldier and prominent engineer in Washington's army. The sculpture is one of the more in-your-face ones in town: Kosciusko towers over an angry imperial eagle killing a snake atop a globe, and an inscription at the base, taken from Scottish poet Thomas Campbell, reads: 'And Freedom shrieked as Kosciusko fell!'

ST JOHN'S CHURCH CHURCH

(Map p320; www.stjohns-dc.org; 1525 H St NW; ⌚9am-3pm, services 12:10pm Mon-Sat, 7:45am, 9am & 11am Sun; Ⓜ McPherson Sq) A small building, St John's isn't DC's most imposing church, but it is arguably its most important. That's because it's the 'Church of the Presidents' – every president since Madison has attended services here at least once, and pew 54 is reserved for the Big Guy (er, the president; not God).

DECATUR HOUSE MUSEUM

(Map p320; www.decaturhouse.org; 748 Jackson Pl NW, visitor entrance 1610 H St NW; Ⓜ Farragut West) Designed in 1818 by Benjamin Latrobe for the War of 1812 naval hero Stephen Decatur, Decatur House sits at Lafayette Sq's northwest corner. It holds the honor of being the first and last house on the square to be occupied as a private residence and, architecturally, it's an interesting mash-up of austere Federal and wedding cake Victorian influences. Famous tenants include Martin Van Buren and Henry Clay. The White House Historical Association bought the building in 2010. It has been closed for renovations, but plans are to reopen it to visitors. Check the website for updates.

K STREET STREET

(Map p320; K St; Ⓜ Farragut North, McPherson Sq) K St is the center of the Washington lobbying industry. This is where high-powered lawyers, consultants and, of course, lobbyists ('K St' and 'lobbyist' have practically become synonymous since the 1990s) bark into their smartphones and enjoy expensive lunches. Come nightfall, the same power set comes back with hair considerably slicked and/or flattened to drink expensive cocktails while surrounded by the sort of people who swoon over everything we've just described.

In total contrast are some lovely nearby green spaces. **Franklin Square** (between 13th and 14th Sts NW) is a large stretch of green open space thick with trees, paths and benches. Check out the Victorian-era redbrick Franklin School keeping watch over the patch. The architecture around **McPherson Square**, named for Civil War general James B McPherson who once commanded the Army of Tennessee, is fabulous. Keep an eye out for the 1924 neoclassical, limestone **Investment Building** (cnr 15th & K Sts).

BLAIR & LEE HOUSES NOTABLE BUILDING

(Map p320; 1653 Pennsylvania Ave NW; ⌚closed to public; Ⓜ Farragut West) The 1824 **Blair House** has been the official presidential guesthouse since 1942, when Eleanor Roosevelt got sick of tripping over dignitaries in the White House. A plaque on the front fence commemorates the bodyguard killed here while protecting president Truman from a 1950 assassination attempt by pro-independence militants from Puerto Rico (Truman was living here while the White House was undergoing renovations).

The neighboring 1858 **Lee House** was built by Robert E Lee's family. This is where Lee declined command of the Union Army when the Civil War erupted.

FREE **OCTAGON MUSEUM** MUSEUM

(Map p320; ☎202-638-3221; www.theoctagon.org; 1799 New York Ave NW; ⏲1-4pm Thu & Fri; MFarragut West) The apex of the Federal style of architecture pioneered in the USA also happens to be the oldest museum in America dedicated to architecture and design. Designed by William Thornton (the Capitol's first architect) in 1800, the building is a symmetrically winged structure designed to fit an odd triangular lot. Behind it, the American Institute of Architects' (AIA) large modern offices wrap around like a protective older brother. AIA operates Octagon House. It's open Thursday and Friday afternoons for self-guided audio tours; download the four different routes from the website. Inside you'll get a feel for the stunning design, as well as see some original furnishings.

FREE **ORGANIZATION OF AMERICAN STATES** MUSEUM, GARDENS

(Map p320; OAS; www.oas.org; 201 18th St NW; ⏲10am-5pm Tue-Sun; MFarragut West) A forerunner to the UN, the OAS was founded in 1890 to promote cooperation among North and South American nations. Its main building at 17th St and Constitution Ave NW is a marble palazzo surrounded by the sculpture-studded **Aztec Gardens**. In the small building behind it, the OAS operates the **Art Museum of the Americas** (www.museum.oas.org), featuring a fine collection of art that spans the 20th century and the western hemisphere.

FREE **DAUGHTERS OF THE AMERICAN REVOLUTION** MUSEUM

(Map p320; DAR; www.dar.org/museum; 1776 D St NW; ⏲8:30am-4pm Mon-Fri, 9am-5pm Sat; MFarragut West) The DAR's neoclassical behemoth, also known as Constitution Hall, is supposedly the largest complex of buildings in the world owned exclusively by women. They own the entire city block! Enter from D St to reach the museum, where'll you find a sweet spread of silver teapots, quilts, portrait paintings, crystal decanters and folk art.

If the group's name sounds familiar, it's because in 1939 the DAR barred African American contralto Marian Anderson from singing at its hall. Anderson then performed her famous civil rights concert on the Lincoln Memorial's steps. The DAR eventually changed its policies and mended fences with Anderson.

FREE **FEDERAL RESERVE** BUILDING

(Map p320; ☎202-452-3324; www.federalreserve.gov; 20th St NW btwn C St & Constitution Ave; ⏲tours by reservation; MFarragut West) 'The Fed,' which resembles a cross between a Greek temple and a Soviet-era bunker, is the Olympus of the Gods of the American Economy. Unfortunately, you won't see too much fiscal action on tours; these focus on the architecture of the Eccles Building, which houses the reserve. You do get to visit the board room, which looks like the place where the world's economy is batted about like a big ball of yarn between some very powerful cats. That said, the tour – which must be pre-arranged by calling at least two weeks in advance – is recommended for adults only (kids will get bored).

Another option, which requires only five days' advance notice, is to view the **Fed's art collection** (reserve by calling ☎202-452-3778), part of which is displayed in the atrium of the Eccles Building. The permanent collection is a survey of American art from the 1830s to the present. The board also presents rotating exhibitions of borrowed art on varied themes like currency design.

FREE **DEPARTMENT OF THE INTERIOR MUSEUM** MUSEUM

(Map p320; ☎202-208-4743; www.doi.gov/interiormuseum; 1849 C St NW; ⏲tours 2pm Tue & Thu, reservations required; MFarragut West) Responsible for managing the nation's natural resources, the Department of the Interior operates this small, but excellent, museum to educate the public about its current goals and programs. It includes landscape art, Native American artifacts and some great historical photos of Native American life, as well as exhibits on wildlife and resource management. The museum was closed for renovation at press time, but staff was offering tours of the building's tremendous New Deal murals from the 1930s and 1940s. The collection includes 26 photographic murals by Ansel Adams, plus panels by Maynard Dixon and Allan Houser. The hour-long jaunts are at 2pm Tuesday and Thursday, but you must call to make a reservation two weeks in advance. Adults need photo identification to enter.

to reserve a tour spot, and bring photo ID; no kids under 12 are admitted.

Foggy Bottom

GEORGE WASHINGTON UNIVERSITY — UNIVERSITY

(Map p320; www.gwu.edu; 801 22nd St NW; Ⓜ Foggy Bottom-GWU) The university that shares the District's namesake spreads throughout the streets of Foggy Bottom. Known as 'G-dub' or 'GW', this school has been a bedrock of Washington identity since its founding in 1821. Besides shaping much of the American political landscape, GW has shaped the capital itself, buying up townhouses on such a scale that it is now the city's second-biggest landowner after the federal government. Plenty of famous alumni have studied here: Edgar Hoover, Jacqueline Kennedy Onassis, Colin Powell, Brian Williams and Haddaway (you know, the guy who sang 'What Is Love?').

The school is spread over several blocks between F, 20th and 24th Sts and Pennsylvania Ave in Foggy Bottom. The best bit of the campus is **University Yard**, between G, H, 20th and 21st Sts, where Colonial-revival buildings flank a green park bedecked with roses and a statue of – who else? – Washington.

ST MARY'S EPISCOPAL CHURCH — CHURCH

(Map p320; www.stmarysfoggybottom.org/smc; 730 23rd St NW; 9:30am-3pm Mon-Thu; Ⓜ Foggy Bottom-GWU) Built in 1887, St Mary's was home to the first black Episcopal congregation in DC. James Renwick, designer of the Smithsonian Castle, created the beautiful redbrick building especially for the congregation. Above the altar are French-made painted-glass windows that depict, among others, the African bishop and martyr St Cyprian.

FREE STATE DEPARTMENT — BUILDING

(Map p320; US Department of State; 202-647-3241; www.state.gov, https://receptiontours.state.gov; cnr 22nd & C Sts NW; tours by reservation 9:30am, 10:30am & 2:45pm Mon-Fri; Ⓜ Foggy Bottom-GWU) The headquarters of the American diplomatic corps is a forbidding, well-guarded edifice, all modernist, blocky and unfriendly. In stark contrast are the elegant grand diplomatic reception rooms, where Cabinet members and the Secretary of State entertain visiting potentates amid ornate 18th-century American antiques. Call at least 90 days beforehand to reserve a tour spot, and bring photo ID; no kids under 12 are admitted.

NATIONAL ACADEMY OF SCIENCES — BUILDING

(Map p320; NAS; 202-334-2000; www.nasonline.org; 2101 Constitution Ave NW; 9am-5pm Mon-Fri; Ⓜ Foggy Bottom-GWU) Made up of approximately 2100 members, including almost 200 Nobel Prize winners, these are the guys the government hits up for scientific advice (whether the government listens to them or not is, as you may have guessed, entirely up to the government). The NAS hosts scientific and art exhibitions and symposiums, and concerts are often held on Sunday afternoons. The building was slated to reopen in late 2012 after a renovation.

The nicely landscaped grounds along Constitution Ave feature DC's most huggable monument (well, besides the Kitten and Puppy Memorial – kidding): the **Albert Einstein statue**. The larger-than-life, sandal-shod, chubby bronze reclines on a bench, while little kids crawl all over him and frolic on a 'star map,' which depicts the heavens that his theories reshaped for humanity.

WATERGATE COMPLEX — BUILDING

(Map p320; www.watergatehotel.com; 2650 Virginia Ave NW; Ⓜ Foggy Bottom-GWU) The Watergate is an iconic bit of Washingtonia. The riverfront complex of private apartments, designer boutiques and deluxe hotel is an integral feature of the city's facade. And then there's that little break-in that occurred here in 1972, when the Democratic National Committee headquarters was raided by Nixon's Committee to Re-elect the President – aka CREEP. Monica Lewinsky, Ruth Bader Ginsburg and Condoleezza Rice have all lived here. As of writing, the interior of the complex was still closed to the public for renovations.

EATING

As you might guess, this is high-end eating territory, the pinnacle of the power lunch and show-off dinner school of sartorial activity. With all that said, you usually get what you pay for – there's too much competition around for local chefs to rest lazily on their laurels.

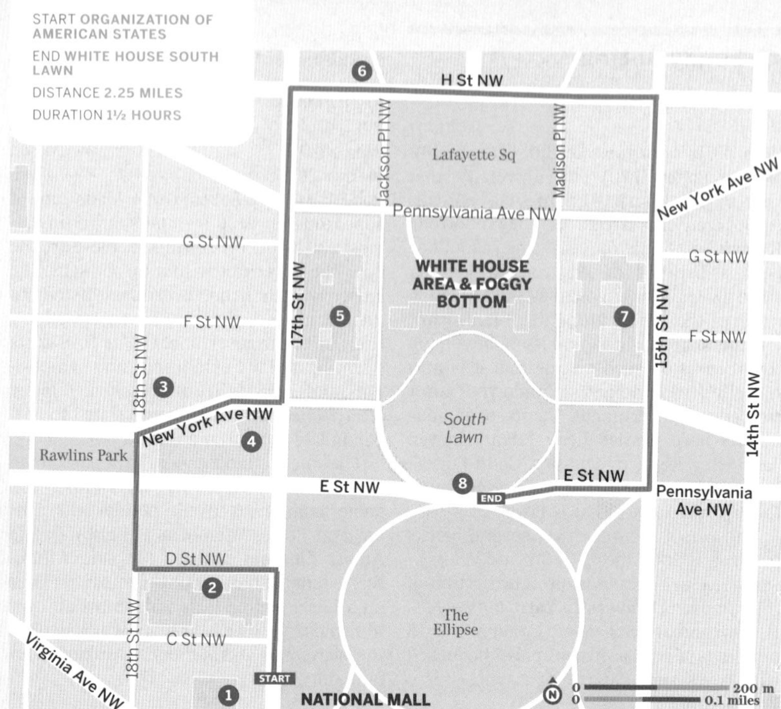

Neighborhood Walk

Architectural Accents

Powerful architecture rises throughout the neighborhood that is USA's seat of, well, power. Start at the **1 Organization of American States**, a marble palazzo offering pretty gardens and an impressive art museum. Stroll up to D St NW and check out the headquarters of the **2 Daughters of the American Revolution**. Also known as Constitution Hall, it's a great example of neoclassical architecture; go inside for a peek.

Onward to the **3 Octagon Museum**. The American Institute of Architects owns the 1801 Federal-style beauty, where President James Madison lived after the British burned Washington. The beaux-arts **4 Corcoran Gallery of Art** stands across the street, fresh from a facade renovation.

At the corner of 17th St & Pennsylvania Ave, the **5 Eisenhower Building** is done up with all the baroque flair of the late 19th-century, also known as the Gilded Age. The sloped mansard roof is European in origin, while its 900 columns are wonderfully ostentatious. Currently the building is used as an office wing of the executive branch.

Walk north on 17th to H St and turn right. An office building by any other name, the designers of **6 800 Connecticut Ave** knew lobbyists and politicos would be using it. As a result it prickles with terraces and corner offices that provide excellent lines of sight to the White House.

Head past Lafayette Sq to 15th St NW and turn south toward the **7 Treasury Building**. It took a while to find a place to plop the building, and legend has it President Andrew Jackson, ticked off by foot-dragging, stood on the current spot and yelled, 'Build it here!' As a result, Pierre L'Enfant's planned clear line of sight between the White House and the Capitol was ruined.

Last stop: E St NW, for the quintessential view of the city's most famous building, the **8 White House**, strutting its stuff across the South Lawn.

LOCAL KNOWLEDGE

FOOD TRUCKIN'

A heapin' fleet of food trucks rolls in DC. They generally prowl Farragut Square and Foggy Bottom around lunchtime, as well as other office-worker-rich hotspots like L'Enfant Plaza, Metro Center, Chinatown and Union Station. **Food Truck Fiesta** (www.foodtruckfiesta.com) tracks them down via Twitter. Some of our favorites:

➡ **Fojol Brothers** (twitter.com/fojolbros) Clad in turbans and framed by their droopy mustaches, the brothers Fojol – Ababa-Du, Gewpee, Kipoto and Dingo – patrol city streets in their colorful van, blaring circus music, screaming 'It's a traveling culinary carnival,' and attracting all kinds of hungry followers. They were one of the first trucks on the scene, and they now have three vehicles: Merlindia (serving Indian fare), Benethiopia (Ethiopian) and Volathai (Thai). They're all delicious, less than $10 for a full meal, plus they use biodegradable packaging.

➡ **Sweetflow Mobile** (twitter.com/Sweetflowmobile) It is the on-the-go version of local mini-chain Sweetgreen, purveyor of macrobiotic salads and frozen yogurt. It's basically a healthy ice-cream truck.

➡ **DC Pie Truck** (twitter.com/ThePieTruckDC) The folks from Dangerously Delicious Pies (see p140) swing out in big red truck. Sweet and savory slices emerge from the window. Pies range from spinach with goat cheese to chocolate cream to coconut chess.

➡ **Red Hook Lobster Truck** (twitter.com/LobsterTruckDC) Take your pick: mayo-based, Maine-style lobster rolls or butter-slathered Connecticut-style rolls. Prepare to shell out (pun!) $15 per sandwich.

TOP CHOICE **OLD EBBITT GRILL** AMERICAN $$
(Map p320; ☎202-347-4800; www.ebbitt.com; 675 15th St NW; mains $12-22; ⏰7:30am-1am, from 8:30am Sat & Sun; Ⓜ Metro Center) The Grill is something of an institution, having occupied its prime, adjacent-to-just-about-everything (the White House, the Mall, Penn Quarter) real estate since 1846. This is as down to earth as fine DC dining gets. Political players (and lots of tourists) pack into the brass and wood interior, the sound of their conversation rumbling across a dining room where good burgers, oysters and fish-and-chip type fare are rotated out almost as quickly as the clientele. It's a fine place to pop in for a drink, too.

CAFE DU PARC FRENCH $$
(Map p320; ☎202-942-7000; www.cafeduparc.com; 1401 Pennsylvania Ave NW; mains $23-29; ⏰breakfast, lunch & dinner; Ⓜ Metro Center, Federal Triangle) Du Parc is one of the best bistros in town, a place for French fare devoid of embellishment but ripping in honest, strong flavors and deceptively simple preparation. The mussels and beef tartar may be the best in the city, which would be reason enough to visit. However, the calf liver, kissed perfectly by the pan and a drizzle of shallots, olive-crusted local rockfish and crisp shavings of pork belly make us want to pitch a tent on the terrace. Which is a good spot for outdoor dining, by the way. Breakfast here is lovely – a nice blend of American and Continental dishes – and presents a good opportunity for politico spotting.

BREADLINE BAKERY $
(Map p320; ☎202-822-8900; www.breadline.com; 1751 Pennsylvania Ave NW; sandwiches $8-11; ⏰7:30am-3:30pm Mon-Fri; Ⓜ Farragut West) 'Food is ammunition – don't waste it!' commands a WWII-era poster on the wall of this polished bakery and sandwich shop. Come here for a good, cheap lunch, but don't be surprised if you end up waiting in lines stretching out the door; office workers love it here, and with reason. The fresh and filling sandwiches are gorgeous, as are the to-die-for sweet treats.

FOUNDING FARMERS AMERICAN $$
(Map p320; ☎202-822-8783; www.wearefoundingfarmers.com; 1924 Pennsylvania Ave NW; mains $14-26; ⏰breakfast, lunch & dinner Mon-Fri, brunch, lunch & dinner Sat & Sun; Ⓜ Foggy Bottom-GWU, Farragut West) They serve bacon cocktails here. No, really. And they're awesome, as is the frosty decor of pickled

goods in jars overlooking an art gallery of a dining space. It's a combination of made-from-scratch and modern art that reflects the nature of the food: locally sourced, New American – figs, prosciutto, fried chicken and ricotta ravioli with creamed corn. Our one complaint is the location – the rustic Americana thing isn't well served by essentially occupying the ground floor of an office building.

GEORGIA BROWN'S SOUTHERN **$$**

(Map p320; 202-393-4499; www.gbrowns.com; 950 15th St NW; mains $16-32; lunch & dinner Mon-Sat, brunch & dinner Sun; M McPherson Sq) Georgia Brown's treats the humble ingredients of the American South (shrimp, okra, red rice, grits and sausage) with the respect great French chefs give their provincial dishes. The result is consistently excellent regional American cuisine: high-class Southern food from the Carolina Lowcountry served in a warm, autumnal interior. This was a favorite spot for the Clintons during Bill's presidency (we're not sure if it still is during Hillary's Secretary of Stateship).

KINKEAD'S SEAFOOD **$$$**

(Map p320; 202-296-7700; www.kinkead.com; 2000 Pennsylvania Ave NW; mains $26-34; lunch Mon-Fri, dinner daily; M Foggy Bottom-GWU) Robert Kinkead's restaurant is one of the most revered of DC's old-line establishments. Where others have let quality slip and slide as their name has grown, or vanished altogether, this place endures and improves. Long before being a foodie or locavore was popular – in fact, back when a sign of status was having your Japanese tuna flown in from across the ocean – this seafood powerhouse was concentrating on artfully teasing the best flavors it could find from nearby fisheries and farms. For this commitment to the region and good food in general, we give our enthusiastic endorsement. Try the brioche-crusted flounder and thank us later.

BAYOU CAJUN **$$**

(Map p320; 202-223-6941; www.bayouonpenn.com; 2519 Pennsylvania Ave NW; mains $17-22; lunch & dinner Tue-Fri; M Foggy Bottom-GWU) Here's your slice of New Orleans in DC. Is it the most phenomenal Cajun/Creole you'll ever have? No, but it's mighty fine. All the classics arrive at the jazzy red booths with heat and spice. Bite into oyster po' boy sandwiches, crawfish cheesecake (not a dessert!), seafood gumbo and sides of jalapeno grits. There's even a fried green tomato po' boy for vegetarians. Wash it down with a mason jar of Hurricane. Then get your dance on at the live blues, jazz and R&B shows weekend nights at 10pm.

BOMBAY CLUB INDIAN **$$**

(Map p320; 202-659-3727; www.bombayclubdc.com; 815 Connecticut Ave NW; mains $20-32; lunch Mon-Fri, dinner daily, brunch Sun; M Farragut West) No bad sitar music and clunky curry here; this is Indian food moved up several notches. The seafood curries like the Goan fish or lobster cooked in fenugreek and garam masala are solidly wonderful, and plates like wild boar vindaloo are as tasty as they are novel. Action stars agree – Bombay Club is popular with the likes of Harrison Ford and Bruce Willis.

EQUINOX AMERICAN **$$$**

(Map p320; 202-331-8118; www.equinoxrestaurant.com; 818 Connecticut Ave NW; mains $31-34; lunch Mon-Fri, dinner daily; M Farragut West) Equinox is as mom-and-pop as high-end White House-adjacent dining gets – Todd Gray and wife Ellen Kassoff are the respective chef and manager. The intimacy of the restaurant's executive staff extends into the menu, which has long eschewed pricey export ingredients in favor of meat, fish, fowl and fruit sourced from the Shenandoah and Chesapeake Bay. That said, while Gray's ingredients are rooted in the mid-Atlantic, he can cross the pond for cooking inspiration; the duck breast served over black Indian rice is juicy and comforting, the rice pillow soft, and the accompaniment of roasted cherries plucked from the best rural French traditions.

MARCEL'S FRENCH **$$$**

(Map p320; 202-296-1166; www.marcelsdc.com; 2401 Pennsylvania Ave NW; 3-/5-/7-course menus $65/105/145; dinner; M Foggy Bottom-GWU) The trick with French cuisine is keeping true to the classics while adding the right edge of modern embellishment. Marcel's has this tricky formula down. Old school, fill-you-up-by-a-fire fare like pork belly and turbot with peas is hearty and thick, inducing pleasant drowsiness and a satisfied sense of stuffed. But the sprucing on the side – quail egg and cornichons, or the miso that accompanies the Alaskan cod – is just understated enough to ratchet the dining experience into a level approaching, and even dipping into, greatness. A classy touch: Marcel's offers a complimentary limousine service to the Kennedy Center, so this is an ideal spot for pre-theater dining.

OVAL ROOM AMERICAN **$$**

(Map p320; ☎202-463-8700; www.ovalroom.com; 800 Connecticut Ave NW; mains $25-36; ⏲lunch & dinner Mon-Fri, dinner Sat; Ⓜ Farragut West) The Oval Room occupies some pretty prime real estate, sitting in the equidistant center of a Polygon of Power formed by the Hay-Adams Hotel, Army & Navy Club, Eisenhower Building and Decatur House. (We can imagine a Dan Brown character drawing marker lines between all of the above to the Oval, whispering, 'It all *fits*!' But we digress.) You could plop the Oval anywhere and it'd still serve standout food, generally of the American-hint-of-Mediterranean genre. The Oval eschews heavy sauces in favor of allowing ingredients to hold their own intensity, such as foie gras with lemon and lavender, or bass laced with a delicate mix of anise and toasted almonds, works wonders. Condoleezza Rice agrees – this is her favorite restaurant in town.

CIRCLE BISTRO FRENCH **$$**

(Map p320; ☎202-293-5390; www.circlebistro.com; 1 Washington Circle NW; mains $23-28; ⏲breakfast, lunch & dinner, closed lunch Sat; Ⓜ Foggy Bottom-GWU) When it comes to intimate French dining, the Circle ups the romance level, brings the price point down a notch and presents a menu that's solid if not particularly inspiring. This is fine dining with American ingredients, and while you may not be surprised by dishes such as trout with artichoke hearts or a squid-ink pasta (such things seem *de rigueur* of late), that doesn't mean you won't be delighted by them – the food is, simply, quite good. The service is generally even better, which adds to the appeal of using this spot for a date night.

SICHUAN PAVILION CHINESE **$$**

(Map p320; ☎202-466-7790; sichuanpavilion.googlepages.com; 1814 K St NW; mains $11-18; ⏲noon-9pm; Ⓜ Farragut North) Why do we think this unassuming spot may be the best Chinese in the city? Because so many Chinese come here, far from any ethnic enclaves out in the 'burbs, to dine on fiery, oily classics of the old school. Piquant Sichuan (or Szechuan) cuisine is often blanded-up for Western customers around the world, but these guys keep it real for all their clientele, Asian or otherwise. The *ma-po tofu* (includes pork, fermented black beans and fiery peppercorns) is particularly stinky and sublime.

KAZ SUSHI BISTRO JAPANESE **$$**

(Map p320; ☎202-530-5500; www.kazsushibistro.com; 1915 I St NW; lunch specials $10, mains $20-30; ⏲lunch & dinner Mon-Fri, dinner Sat; Ⓜ Farragut West) Fusing East and West, chef Kaz Okochi presents his own invention, 'free-style Japanese cuisine.' The sushi on its own is fresh and flavorful and good enough. Many clever combinations, however, add a certain *je ne sais quoi* to the traditional tastes.

DC COAST SEAFOOD **$$**

(Map p320; ☎202-216-5988; www.dccoast.com; 1401 K St NW; mains $26-30; ⏲lunch & dinner Mon-Fri, dinner Sat; Ⓜ McPherson Sq) If Poseidon hired an art deco revivalist to redo his temple, the final result would probably end up looking something like DC Coast's interior. It's a beautiful space, more chaotic for the constant hum of lobbyist lunchers. Join the crowd indulging in pan-roasted trout and smoked lobster.

PRIME RIB STEAKHOUSE **$$$**

(Map p320; ☎202-466-8811; www.theprimerib.com; 2020 K St NW; mains $26-48; ⏲lunch Mon-Fri, dinner Mon-Sat; Ⓜ Farragut North) There are lots of K St restaurants that serve up fusiony, modernist, wasabi-crusted-panko-seaweed-octopus-brioche kinda fare. Not

LOCAL KNOWLEDGE

FARMERS MARKETS

The neighborhood has two bountiful spreads that are part of the Fresh Farm Market (www.freshfarmmarket.org) program, one of the leaders of the Chesapeake Bay region local food movement:

- **Foggy Bottom Market** (Map p320; cnr I St & New Hampshire Ave NW; ⏲3-7pm Wed Apr-Nov; Ⓜ Foggy Bottom-GWU)
- **By the White House Market** (Map p320; 810 Vermont Ave NW; ⏲3-7pm Thu May-Oct; Ⓜ McPherson Sq)

the Prime Rib. Excuse a bit of stereotyping, but power, friends, is still best exemplified by sitting in a dark-wood dining room cutting deals over huge hunks of seared cow, then stepping outside for a cigar (damned smoking ban) and coming back in for a cognac. With a side of testosterone. The wait staff, clad in tuxedos, dress the part, and you'd better too – that means ties and jackets, men. Actually, you don't need the jacket at lunch, at which time the Rib delivers a $25 set menu that is quite a good deal. The food lives up to the atmosphere; while this place may not be cutting edge, that doesn't mean it isn't good at what it does.

OCCIDENTAL GRILL STEAKHOUSE **$$$**

(Map p320; ☎202-783-1475; www.occidentaldc.com; 1475 Pennsylvania Ave NW; mains $28-37; ⊗lunch & dinner; MMetro Center) This DC institution is practically wallpapered with mug shots of congressmen and other political celebs who have dined here throughout the years. Although the Occidental isn't the nerve center it once was, plenty of bigwigs still roll up their pinstripes to dive into hamburgers, chops, steaks and seafood.

DRINKING & NIGHTLIFE

College kids, doctors and journalists coexist in this neighborhood. For the most part the vibe is sort of white-yuppie-meets-college-scruffy at the local pub, although there are some genuine wheeler-dealer bars in the bigger hotels.

TOP CHOICE **ROUND ROBIN** BAR

(Map p320; Willard InterContinental Hotel; 1401 Pennsylvania Ave NW; ⊗4:30pm-1am Sun-Thu, from 3pm Fri, from noon Sat; MFederal Triangle) The bar at the Willard InterContinental Hotel is likely the most famous drinking institution in the city. The word 'lobbyist' was invented here during the Grant administration, and too many politicians, heads of state, journalists and other bigwigs have passed through for this book to list. The small, circular drinking space is done up in Gilded Age accents, all dark wood and 19th-century flourishes, and while it's a bit touristy, you'll still see folks here likely determining your latest tax hike over a single-malt Scotch.

OFF THE RECORD BAR

(Map p320; Hay-Adams Hotel, 800 16th St NW; ⊗11:30am-midnight Sun-Thu, to 12:30am Fri & Sat; MMcPherson Sq) Chintzy chairs, brass fixtures, Manhattan cocktails, location in the basement of one of the city's most prestigious hotels, and right across from the White House. If you came to DC to see important people get drunk, saunter on down to Off the Record (there's a reason it has the name – the politicos who imbibe here don't need the nearby reporters capturing their quotes). The on-site Steinway piano was a gift from the Kennedy family.

LE BAR BAR

(Map p320; Sofitel Lafayette Square, 806 15th St NW; ⊗10am-midnight; MMcPherson Sq) Ah, Le Bar, *elle est si belle*. This is the kind of spot you should rightly enter in a trench coat in the midst of occupied Paris whilst delivering secret documents to a very attractive member of the Resistance…er, we're getting carried away again, aren't we? But seriously, that's kind of the vibe: all chandelier-like European glitz mixed with a bit of Washington power-player muscle, a heady combination that's as strong as the bourbon. The outdoor patio is wonderful on spring and humid summer nights.

HAMILTON BAR

(Map p320; www.thehamiltondc.com; 600 14th St NW; MMetro Center) The Hamilton is a newcomer to the scene and it's working hard to be all things to all people. Upstairs it's a power-player restaurant, all dark wood and pork chops and silver pots of coffee. The space is so vast you almost don't see the mahogany-paneled bar tapping 20 craft beers. Downstairs it's a 500-person live music club that genre-jumps from Ramblin' Jack Elliott to Roy Hargrove to Shemekia Copeland. Then there's the sushi bar, the breakfast burritos, the toasted marshmallow milkshakes…

POV LOUNGE

(Map p320; W Hotel Washington, 515 15th St NW; MMetro Center) The sky terrace of POV, which sits atop the W Hotel Washington, is one of the best spots to watch the sunset on a hot summer night. From the rooftop the entire city stretches out in front of you, and the panoramic view is nothing short of spectacular. The actual drinks are great too (although do you ever pay for them) – there's a healthy respect for mixology here, and you won't find the sort of watered-down pre-mixes that occasionally rear their ugly heads in other bars around town.

FROGGY BOTTOM PUB BAR

(Map p320; www.froggybottompub.com; 2142 Pennsylvania Ave NW; MFoggy Bottom-GWU) This popular GWU hangout attracts students with grub-and-pub deals, a frat-boy-esque atmosphere and the sort of shot specials that make you want to down a lot of hard alcohol very quickly. As you might have guessed, things can get messy in here, but in a good, all-American college kinda way.

ENTERTAINMENT

KENNEDY CENTER PERFORMING ARTS

(Map p320; 202-467-4600; www.kennedy-center.org; 2700 F St NW; MFoggy Bottom-GWU) Sprawled across 17 riverside acres, the Kennedy Center is Washington's main cultural jewel. It hosts a staggering array of performances – more than 2000 each year – among its multiple venues. These include the Concert Hall, Opera House, Eisenhower Theater and Film Theater. In addition, the National Symphony Orchestra, Suzanne Farrell Ballet and Washington National Opera are all based here.

Reduced-rate tickets are available for people age 18 to 30 via the MyTix program; details are on the Kennedy website. Students can sometimes get half-price tickets for certain performances. Call or visit the box office.

It's about a half-mile walk from the Metro to the Kennedy Center. Alternatively, a free shuttle bus runs between the two points every 15 minutes from 9:45am to midnight Monday to Saturday, and noon to midnight on Sunday. Follow the signs toward the left as you exit the escalator. There's also paid parking underneath the Kennedy Center.

KENNEDY CENTER FREEBIES

Don't have the dough for a big-ticket show? No worries. Each evening the Kennedy Center hosts the **Millennium Stage** (www.kennedy-center.org/millennium), a series of first-rate music and dance performances at 6pm in the Grand Foyer. The cost is absolutely nada. Check the website to see who's playing.

The Kennedy also offers **free tours** (10am-5pm Mon-Fri, to 1pm Sat & Sun). They depart every 10 minutes from the tour desk on Level A, and include a stop on the viewtastic rooftop terrace.

NATIONAL SYMPHONY ORCHESTRA PERFORMING ARTS

(www.kennedy-center.org/nso) Directed by Christoph Eschenbach, this is the affiliate orchestra of the Kennedy Center and one of the best chamber symphonies in the nation.

WASHINGTON NATIONAL OPERA PERFORMING ARTS

(www.dc-opera.org) Another Kennedy Center affiliate, the Washington Opera puts on a varied showcase throughout the year. Placido Domingo helmed the company until 2011, when he stepped down after 15 years for Francesca Zambello.

WASHINGTON BALLET PERFORMING ARTS

(www.washingtonballet.org) The Washington Ballet hasn't been known for many groundbreaking productions, although its reputation is beginning to change as it explores the work of younger choreographers. The troupe leaps at the Kennedy Center and THEARC in Southeast DC.

SHOPPING

WHITE HOUSE HISTORICAL ASSOCIATION GIFT SHOP SOUVENIRS

(Map p320; www.whitehousehistory.org/shop; 740 Jackson Pl NW, Lafayette Sq; 9am-4pm Mon-Fri; MFarragut West) Peruse a wide selection of books, videos, gifts, posters, Christmas ornaments, jewelry, postcards and educational materials, all on the theme of the big house across the square. This is the place to buy your dad a White House necktie. There is a similarly stocked store in the White House Visitors Center.

INDIAN CRAFT SHOP ARTS & CRAFTS

(Map p320; www.indiancraftshop.com; 1849 C St NW, No 1023 Dept of Interior; 8:30am-4:30pm Mon-Fri; MFarragut West) Representing over 45 tribal groups in the US, this crowded one-room shop sells gorgeous but costly basketry, weavings, pottery, beadwork and carvings made by Native Americans. It's hidden inside the Department of the Interior; show photo ID to enter the building.

AMERICAN INSTITUTE OF ARCHITECTS BOOKSTORE BOOKS

(Map p320; 1735 New York Ave NW; 9am-5pm Mon-Fri; M Farragut West) Architecture buffs are in good company in this small specialty shop, which stocks the latest architecture and design titles and periodicals. For the classic overview on the city's iconic buildings, pick up the AIA *Guide to the Architecture of Washington, DC.*

RENWICK GALLERY ARTS & CRAFTS

(Map p320; www.americanart.si.edu; 1661 Pennsylvania Ave NW; 10am-5:30pm; M Farragut West) In one of DC's best museum shops, handmade textiles and hand-dyed silks are available, as is glasswork, woodwork and unique jewelry, much of it rather affordable. Its excellent choice of books includes how-to manuals on jewelry- and fabric-making, ceramics, glassblowing and cabinetry, many appropriate for kids.

CHOCOLATE MOOSE HOUSEWARES, TOYS

(Map p320; www.chocolatemoosedc.com; 1743 L St NW; 10am-6pm Mon-Sat; M Farragut North) In an otherwise staid stretch of L Street, Chocolate Moose lures in shoppers with its campy window displays and smiling brown moose. Among the array of temptations are leopard-printed wine glasses, candy-colored jewelry and wallets, dog-faced cake servers, wind-up toys and the famous punching nun puppet.

Georgetown

Neighborhood Top Five

❶ Escape the concrete jungle by hiking or biking the waterside **C&O Canal & Towpath** (p117) past waterwheels, stone bridges and historic homes speckling the bucolic green trail.

❷ Swirl a cocktail in the same room where JFK proposed to Jackie at **Martin's Tavern** (p121).

❸ Meander the ponds, pools and terraced formal gardens of **Dumbarton Oaks** (p118).

❹ Paddle past DC's stony monuments on a sunset tour with **Jack's Boathouse** (p128).

❺ Sip an alfresco drink, ogle the yachts and watch rowing teams at **Georgetown Waterfront Park** (p118).

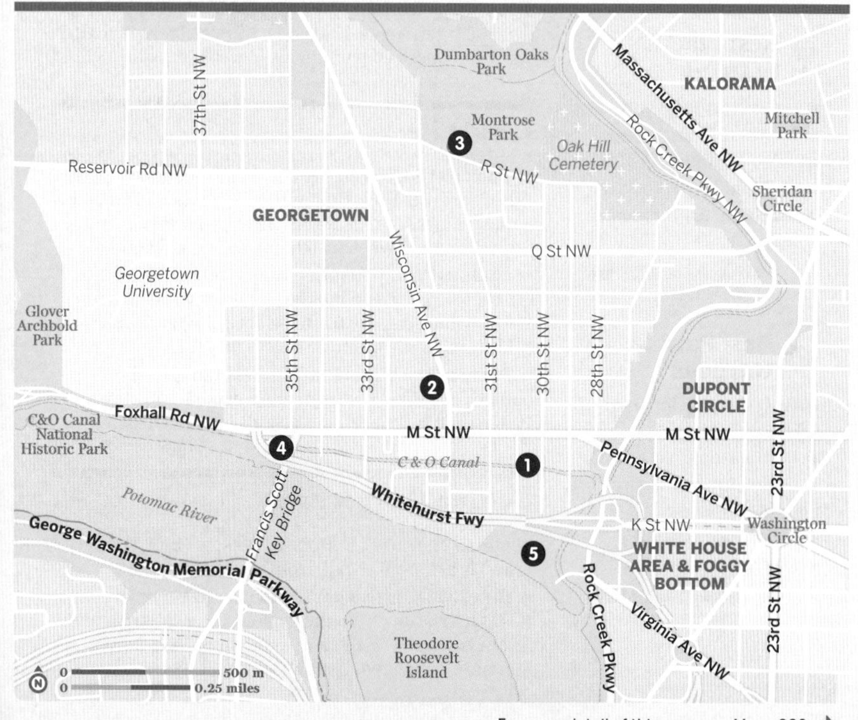

For more detail of this area, see Map p332 ➡

Lonely Planet's Top Tip

Georgetown is a terrific biking spot. Two top trails are the C&O Canal towpath, which is flat, wide, forested and scenic; and the Capital Crescent Trail, a paved path built on an old railroad bed that provides beautiful lookouts over the Potomac River. The neighborhood has several bike rental shops that make it easy to get rolling.

Best Places to Eat

- Baked & Wired (p120)
- Martin's Tavern (p121)
- Sweetgreen (p121)
- 1789 (p121)
- Ching Ching Cha (p121)

For reviews, see p120 ➡

Best Places to Drink

- Birreria Paradiso (p125)
- Tombs (p125)
- J Paul's (p125)
- Mr Smith's (p125)
- Rhino Bar & Pumphouse (p125)

For reviews, see p125 ➡

Best Parks & Gardens

- C&O Canal & Towpath (p117)
- Dumbarton Oaks (p118)
- Georgetown Waterfront Park (p118)
- Tudor Place (p120)
- Oak Hill Cemetery (p120)

For reviews, see p118 ➡

Explore Georgetown

Thousands of the bright and beautiful, from students to academics and diplomats, call this leafy, aristocratic neighborhood home. Georgetown is Washington's house on the hill. To be more accurate, it's a series of beautiful houses, reflecting the best of American Federal and Victorian architecture, interspersed with velvet green gardens, high-end shopping arcades, hushed restaurants and a nightlife scene seemingly inhabited by J Crew catalogues given preppie life. Then there's the collegiate name behind the game: Georgetown University, the city's most prestigious school (sorry, GWU, but it's true).

This is an evocative place. In spring and summer, it's green and gorgeous, the trees waving over filigreed brick romance, laughing co-eds and well-off families. In fall and winter, Georgetown becomes dignified and reserved, her old-school atmosphere enhanced by the change of leaves or the flicker of gas lamps on snowy nights.

There's a subtle but palpable sense of exclusivity in many haunts, and to keep the commoners out, Georgetown residents killed any Metrorail extensions into their neighborhood in 1980. The other hitch: Georgetown is expensive.

Still, it's hard not to fall for the allure of the capital's equivalent of the prettiest, most popular girl in school. Shopaholics have their chic boutiques lined up in a row along M St, hikers and cyclists have idyllic trails, and garden lovers have genteel landscapes to stroll through. Afterward, the cafes and pubs invite lingering into the night.

Local Life

➡ **Book Hill** Wisconsin Ave between P St and Reservoir Rd is known as Book Hill for its art galleries, cafes and antique shops. The area holds the popular French Market festival in April, when merchants set up outdoors.

➡ **La Dolce Vita** When DC sweet tooths need a fix, Georgetown delivers: hulking pastries at Baked & Wired (p120), creamy frosted Georgetown Cupcakes (p125) and exotic gelato at Dolcezza (p124).

➡ **Party at the Waterfront** On warm nights the outdoor cafes and boating action make Georgetown Waterfront Park (p118) the neighborhood hot spot.

Getting There & Away

➡ **Metro** The Foggy Bottom-GWU stop (Blue/Orange Lines) is a 0.75-mile walk from the M St action.

➡ **Bus** The DC Circulator's Dupont-Georgetown-Rosslyn line runs from the Dupont Circle Metro station (south entrance), with stops along M St. The Union Station-Georgetown line runs via K St.

TOP SIGHTS
C&O CANAL & TOWPATH

There are all kinds of green escapes from Washington's urban jungle, but the C&O is one of the best. With wooden waterwheels, a green canal and a cobbled path running alongside, it's so bucolic you expect hobbits to emerge from the bushes with fiddles and ale.

Past Life

The C&O Canal runs 185 miles from Georgetown to Cumberland, MD. It was built starting in 1828 to connect the Chesapeake Bay and Ohio River (hence the initials). Its mission: transport goods and passengers from the capital westward. It became a national park in 1971.

On Your Bike

Today the canal's towpath (so-called because boats were once hauled by mule) marks the start of a fabulous hiking-biking trail. If you follow it out of the city and into Maryland (heads up: this isn't a casual undertaking as you'll be heading several miles upstream before you cross the District line), there are many places to get off the path and venture down to the river – some spots are all rocks and rapids, others calm and sandy holes. The 14-mile ride to Great Falls is sublime. The park's website and **Bike Washington** (www.bikewashington.org/canal) have trail maps. Or stop in the **visitor center** (1057 Thomas Jefferson St NW; ⏲10am-4pm Wed-Sun mid-Apr–mid-Sep) for information. You can also enquire about barge trips farther along the waterway.

DON'T MISS...

- Biking to Great Falls
- Old stone bridges
- Rangers dressed as 19th-century boatmen

PRACTICALITIES

- Map p332
- ☎202-653-5190
- www.nps.gov/choh
- 1057 Thomas Jefferson St NW
- admission free
- ⏲24hr

SIGHTS

C&O CANAL & TOWPATH — PARK, BIKING

See p117.

GEORGETOWN WATERFRONT PARK — PARK

(Map p332; www.georgetownwaterfrontpark.org; K St NW & Potomac River) The Waterfront is a favorite with couples on first dates, singles hoping to hook up, families on an evening stroll and yuppies showing off their big yachts. The park begins at **Washington Harbour** (look for it east of 31st St NW), a modern complex of towers set around a circular terraced plaza filled with fountains (they light up like rainbows at night). Here you'll find loads of restaurants and alfresco bars, as well as the docks for sightseeing boats that ply the Potomac to Alexandria, VA. The park then curves along 10 riverside acres east to the Key Bridge. Trees shade the clot of pedestrian-friendly lanes, and benches dot the way where you can sit and watch the rowing teams out on the water. Kids splash in the fountains at Wisconsin Ave's foot. At 33rd St there's a labyrinth in the grass; walk the circles and see if you feel more connected to the universe.

GEORGETOWN UNIVERSITY — UNIVERSITY

(Map p332; www.georgetown.edu; cnr 37th & O Sts NW) The namesake of the neighborhood is the cornerstone of its identity, infusing the surrounding streets with its mixed patrician/party atmosphere. Founded in 1789, Georgetown was America's first Roman Catholic university. Notable Hoya (derived from the Latin *hoya saxa,* 'what rocks') alumni include Bill Clinton; notable lecturers include Madeleine Albright. The campus is handsome, if not overwhelmingly so. Near the east gate, the imposing, Flemish-style 1879 **Healy Building** is impressive with its tall clock tower. Lovely **Dahlgren Chapel** and its quiet courtyard are hidden behind.

EXORCIST STAIRS — FILM LOCATION

(Map p332; 3600 Prospect St NW) Across from the Key Bridge is a steep set of stairs that happens to be 1) a popular track for joggers and 2) the spot where demonically possessed Reagan of *The Exorcist* sent victims to their screaming deaths. Come on foggy nights, when the steps really are creepy as hell, and don't try and walk them drunk (trust us).

DUMBARTON OAKS — MUSEUM, GARDENS

(Map p332; www.doaks.org; 1703 32nd St NW; museum admission free, gardens adult/child $8/5; ⌚museum 2-5pm Tue-Sun, gardens 2-6pm Tue-Sun) One of the finest mansions in DC is set in some of its finest gardens, a multi-terraced study in pruned elegance. Nineteen ponds and pools are dolloped over 16 acres of landscaped goodness. In springtime, the blooms are stunning. In the mansion itself is a collection of fine Byzantine and pre-Columbian art, an intricately painted beamed ceiling and El Greco's *The Visitation*. As a bonus, diplomatic meetings took place here that laid the groundwork for the UN. The trustees of Harvard University operate the house, so Harvard students, faculty and staff get in for free. The garden entrance is at R and 31st Sts NW.

FUELED BY MULE

When work began on the C&O in 1828, the canal was considered an engineering marvel. Unfortunately, by the time it was completed in 1850, the waterway was already obsolete, rendered out of date by the railroad. Nonetheless, the C&O remained in operation for 74 years until a series of floods closed it in 1924.

Mules typically were the 'engines' of the canal boats, pulling them along the water from the roadside. The 1000lb creatures were sturdier and cheaper than horses. Some mules worked on the C&O for more than 20 years.

After the canal closed, it almost became a highway but for the efforts of Supreme Court Justice William Douglas. Douglas was one of the most committed civil libertarians and environmentalists to sit the court. He felt the towpath should be set aside for future generations, and to prove his point he organized a creative publicity stunt. In March 1954, the judge led an eight-day hike from Cumberland to DC; of the 58 people who set out, only nine (including Douglas) made it to Georgetown. The ploy worked: press coverage of the hike was positive, as was the public reaction, and the towpath became a national park.

START **MT ZION CEMETERY**
END **GEORGETOWN WATERFRONT PARK**
DISTANCE **3 MILES**
DURATION **3 HOURS**

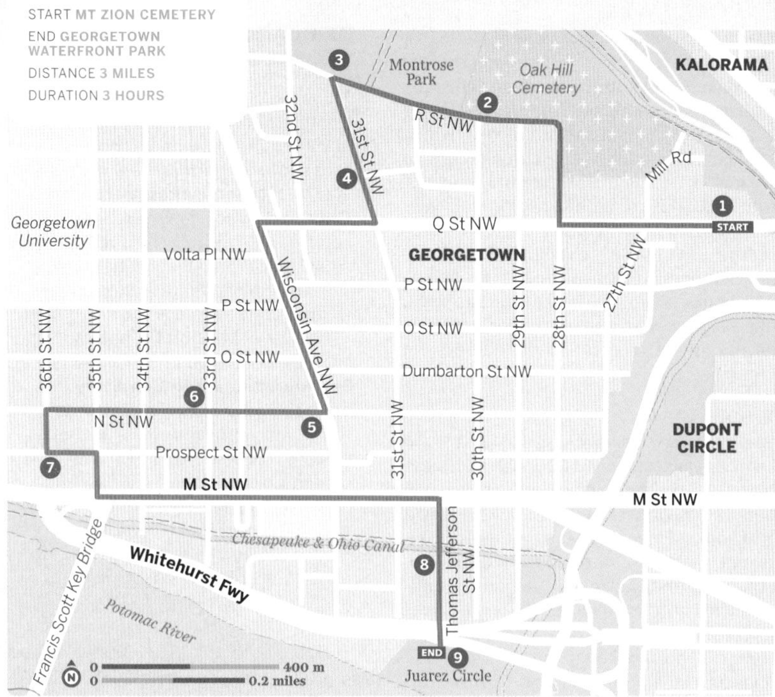

Neighborhood Walk

Genteel Georgetown

If ever a neighborhood was prime for ambling, it's Georgetown, in all its leafy, filigreed-manor glory.

African American **1 Mt Zion Cemetery**, near the intersection of 27th and Q Sts, dates from the early 1800s. The nearby church was a stop on the Underground Railroad; escaping slaves hid in a vault in the cemetery.

2 Oak Hill Cemetery's entrance is a few blocks away at 30th and R Sts NW. Stroll the obelisk-studded grounds and look for gravesites of prominent Washingtonians such as Edwin Stanton (Lincoln's war secretary). Up the road **3 Dumbarton Oaks** offers exquisite Byzantine art inside and sprawling, fountain-dotted gardens outside. The blooms in springtime are stunning.

George Washington's step-granddaughter Martha Custis Peter owned **4 Tudor Place**, the neoclassical mansion at 1644 31st St NW. It has some of George's furnishings from Mount Vernon on show and pretty landscaped grounds.

Head over to Wisconsin Ave NW, and stop in **5 Martin's Tavern**, where John F Kennedy proposed to Jackie. Walk onward on N St and you'll pass several Federal-style townhouses in the 3300 block. JFK and Jackie lived at **6 3307 N St** between 1958 and 1961, when they left for the White House.

At the corner of 36th St and Prospect Ave, stare down the **7 Exorcist Stairs**. This is the spot where possessed Reagan of *The Exorcist* sent victims to their screaming deaths. Joggers use the stairs by day; at night they are legitimately creepy as hell.

Go down to M St NW, popping in to whatever tony boutiques and high-end chain stores your wallet permits. At Jefferson St turn right and sniff your way to **8 Baked & Wired** to replenish with a monster cupcake and cappuccino. From there you can stroll down to **9 Georgetown Waterfront Park** to watch the boats and other action along the Potomac River.

DUMBARTON HOUSE MUSEUM

(Map p332; www.dumbartonhouse.org; 2715 Q St NW; adult/child $5/free; ⏲11am-3pm Tue-Sun) Often confused with Dumbarton Oaks (the mansion and gardens), Dumbarton House is a modest Federal historic house, which was constructed by a wealthy family in 1798. Now it's run by the Colonial Dames of America, who are on hand to provide genteel but gently witty commentary. The focus isn't just the house – chockablock with antique china, silver, furnishings, rugs, gowns and books – but quaint Federal customs, like passing round the chamber pot after formal dinners so gentlemen could have a group pee.

TUDOR PLACE MUSEUM

(Map p332; www.tudorplace.org; 1644 31st St NW; 1-hr house tour adult/child $8/3, self-guided garden tour $3; ⏲10am-3pm Tue-Sat, from noon Sun) This 1816 neoclassical mansion was owned by Thomas Peter and Martha Custis Peter, granddaughter of Martha Washington. The urban estate stayed in the Peter family until it opened to the public in 1984, so it preserves pieces of the family's, as well as the country's, history. Today the mansion functions as a small museum, and features furnishings and artwork from Mount Vernon, which give a nice insight into American decorative arts. The 5 acres of grounds are beautifully landscaped.

OAK HILL CEMETERY CEMETERY

(Map p332; www.oakhillcemeterydc.org; cnr 30th & R Sts NW; ⏲9am-4:30pm Mon-Fri, 1-4pm Sun) This 24-acre, obelisk-studded cemetery contains winding walks and 19th-century gravestones set into the hillsides of Rock Creek. It's a fantastic spot for a quiet walk, especially in spring, when it seems like every wildflower in existence blooms on the grounds. James Renwick designed the lovely gatehouse and charming gneiss chapel.

LOCAL KNOWLEDGE

HIDDEN DIARY

At the labyrinth in Georgetown Waterfront Park, look for the semi-circular teak bench. Underneath you should find a diary, where passers-by stop to write their thoughts, poems and messages. Feel free to browse and/or add to the book.

AFRICAN AMERICAN GEORGETOWN

Three sites recall the history of Georgetown's 19th-century free black community, who lived in an area known as Herring Hill. Founded in 1816, **Mt Zion United Methodist Church** (Map p332; www.mtzionumcdc.org; 1334 29th St NW) is DC's oldest black congregation. Its original site, on 27th St NW, was a stop on the Underground Railroad.

Nearby, at **Mt Zion Cemetery** (Map p332; 2700 Q St NW) and the adjacent **Female Union Band Cemetery** (Map p332; behind 2515-2531 Q St NW) are the crumbling, overgrown headstones of many free black residents. The church hid escaping slaves in a vault here. You can reach the cemeteries from Wisconsin Ave by heading east on Q St NW and turning left at the path just before 2531 Q St NW.

FREE **OLD STONE HOUSE** MUSEUM, GARDENS

(Map p332; www.nps.gov/olst; 3051 M St NW; ⏲11am-6pm) Built in 1765, the capital's oldest surviving building has been a tavern, brothel and boardinghouse (sometimes all at once) and today, despite sitting in the middle of M St, serves as a gardens and small museum on 18th-century American life. It was almost demolished in the 1950s, but a persistent (albeit false) rumor that L'Enfant used it as a workshop while designing DC saved it for posterity.

EATING

TOP CHOICE **BAKED & WIRED** BAKERY $

(Map p332; www.bakedandwired.com; 1052 Thomas Jefferson St NW; snacks $3-6; ⏲7am-8pm Mon-Thu, to 9pm Fri, 8am-9pm Sat, 9am-8pm Sun) With one of the nation's great universities a spilled cappuccino away, you'd think Georgetown would have more hip coffee shops, but alas, there's a lack. B&W makes up for this lost ground with a studio-chic interior and, more importantly, great coffee and freaking huge cupcakes that are also DC's best. It's a supremely cheerful, smile-at-the-world sort of place, just the right kind of sunny disposition this occasionally stuffy neighborhood needs.

MARTIN'S TAVERN AMERICAN **$$**

(Map p332; ☎202-333-7370; www.martins-tavern.com; 1264 Wisconsin Ave NW; mains $12-25; ⏲lunch Mon-Fri, breakfast Sat & Sun, dinner daily) John F Kennedy proposed to Jackie in booth three at Georgetown's oldest saloon, and if you're thinking of popping the question there today, the attentive waitstaff keep the champagne chilled for that very reason. With an old-English country scene, including the requisite fox-and-hound hunting prints on the wall, this DC institution serves a mean cheeseburger and icy-cold pints of beer to college students and senators alike.

SWEETGREEN HEALTH FOOD **$**

(Map p332; ☎202-337-9338; www.sweetgreen.com; 3333 M St NW; mains $8-11; ⏲11am-10pm; ✎) One day, we'll catch the guys at Sweetgreen selling polar-bear-cub tacos to lumberjacks in the back room. We're sure that's the dark secret to this place – no business can be so cutely macrobiotic! Until then, we admit these are some of the freshest, most gigantic salads in the city. Just leave room for the nonfat Sweetflow frozen yogurt – every time you buy one, an acre of the Amazon Rainforest grows back. No, not really, but you get the sense it could happen – everyone here is such a damn do-gooder. Sweetgreen has four other locations in DC, plus its food truck, Sweetflow Mobile (twitter.com/sweetflowmobile), which trundles around town.

PIZZERIA PARADISO ITALIAN **$$**

(Map p332; ☎202-337-1245; www.eatyourpizza.com; 3282 M St NW; mains from $11; ⏲11:30am-11pm Mon-Thu, to midnight Fri & Sat, noon-10pm Sun) This casual restaurant serves wood-oven Neapolitan-style pizzas with scrumptious toppings to crowds of starving patrons with rave results. The pizza crust is perfect – light, crisp and a little flaky. Great people-watching from the big plate-glass windows, popular happy hours, and a hand-picked beer and ale selection heighten the appeal. There's a second location in Dupont Circle and a third in Alexandria's Old Town.

CHING CHING CHA ASIAN **$$**

(Map p332; www.chingchingcha.com; 1063 Wisconsin Ave NW; snacks $2-5, 3-course lunch $14; ⏲11am-9pm) This atmospheric wood-paneled teahouse feels a world away from the shopping mayhem of M St. Stop in for a pot of rare tea (they brew more than 70 varieties) and steamed dumplings, coconut tarts, or a three-course lunch along the lines of green squash and miso salmon. CCC also stocks books, ceramic tea sets and teapots.

1789 AMERICAN **$$$**

(Map p332; ☎202-965-1789; www.1789restaurant.com; 1226 36th St NW; mains $34-45; ⏲dinner) If one restaurant were to exemplify not only Georgetown, but all that Georgetown represents – the brownstone political aristocracy of Washington, DC – it would be 1789. Located in a smart Federal row house, the setting is colonial, cozy and distinguished all at once. As a bonus, the food is excellent. This kitchen was one of the first high-end geniuses of the 'rustic New American' genre, so if you're going to try local ingredients sexed up with provincial flare, such as roasted Virginia rabbit with country ham and English peas, this is the spot to indulge your taste buds. Formal wear (jacket) is not only expected, but required for dinner.

BLACKSALT SEAFOOD **$$$**

(off Map p332; ☎202-342-9101; www.blacksaltrestaurant.com; 4883 MacArthur Blvd NW; mains $29-35; ⏲lunch Mon-Sat, dinner daily, brunch Sun) There are many who claim BlackSalt serves both the best seafood and operates the best fish market in the city. We won't lay those laurels down yet, but we're also acknowledging that we hate having to drive or bus out here. As fish markets go, this one is very Georgetown-oriented, which is to say fresh, artesian, organic – and expensive. As restaurants go...well, we give it to the chef. The man loves cooking fish, finding new flavors, delving into whatever culinary pleasure one can ratchet out of a sole, skate or soft-shell crab. The shifting, innovative menu is spot-on about 80% of the time, which is a fine ratio by our math. Five- and seven-course tasting menus ($78/94) are also available.

CITRONELLE FRENCH **$$$**

(Map p332; ☎202-625-2150; www.citronelledc.com; Latham Hotel, 3000 M St NW; 4-course menu $110; ⏲dinner Tue-Sat) Citronelle regularly lurks near the very top of every Washington best restaurant list ever compiled. Big name Michel Richard started this show, a split-level study in the most creative twists tweakable on the American palate, yet

1

RICK GEHARTER / LONELY PLANET IMAGES ©

2

4

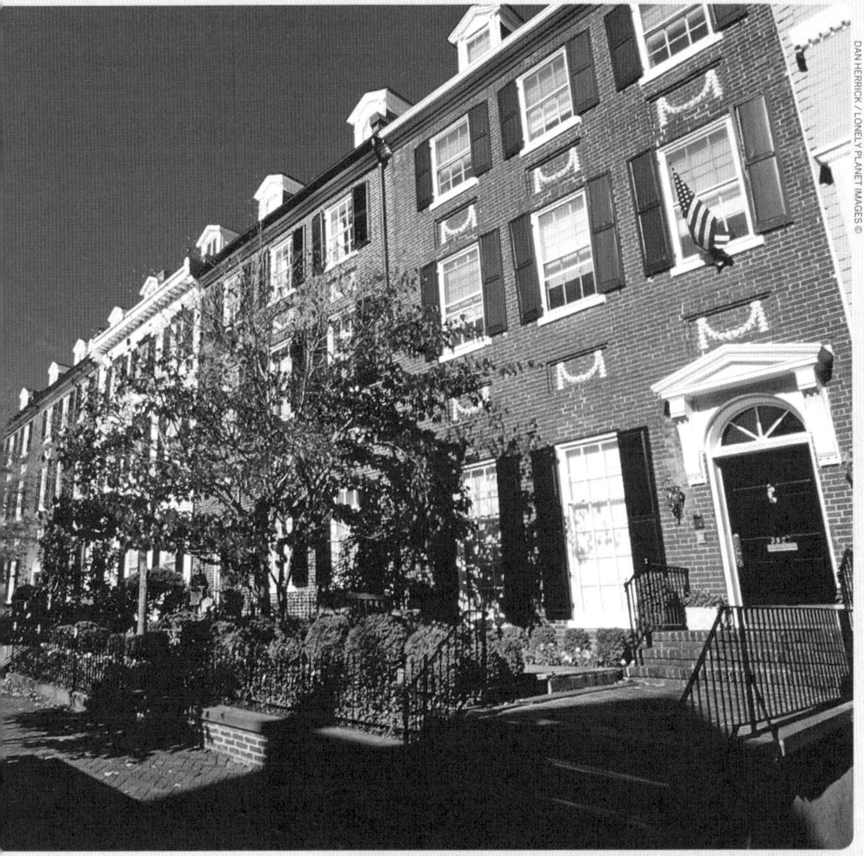

DAN HERRICK / LONELY PLANET IMAGES ©

1. Georgetown University (p118)
Founded in 1789, Georgetown was the USA's first Roman Catholic university.

2. Neighborhood streets
Georgetown's leafy streets, filled with handsome row houses, are evocative places to stroll.

3. Dumbarton Oaks (p118)
One of DC's finest mansions is set amid elegant gardens and formal courtyards.

4. Blues Alley (p126)
A former haunt of Dizzy Gillespie, this is still one of the city's best jazz and blues bars.

3

RICHARD CUMMINS / LONELY PLANET IMAGES ©

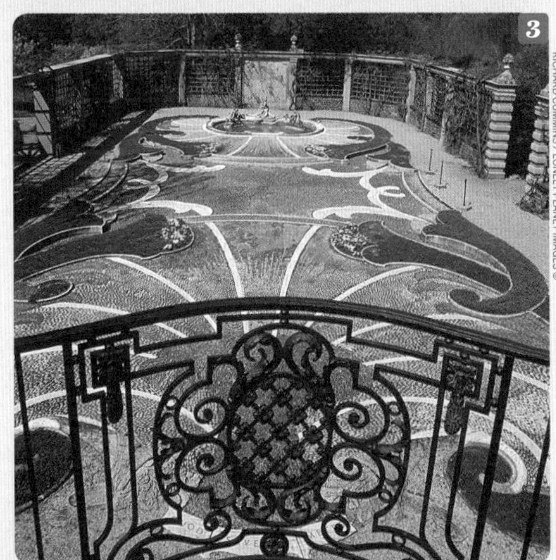

grounded in French classicism. Part of what makes dining here so special is the emphasis on fun over formality. The cooks seem to laugh through their creations, such as salmon in a chicken (?!) *jus*, or the famous short ribs, braised for three days, then pan-seared (?!?) into something...well, medium-rare and amazing. This is the silly envelope's edge of what can be done in DC cuisine; if you're a visiting foodie, this should go on your 'can't miss' list. Jackets preferred; ties optional. The attached lounge serves a pared-down menu of Richard's fare on Mondays.

KOTOBUKI — JAPANESE $$

(off Map p332; ☎202-281-6679; www.kotobukiusa.com; 4822 MacArthur Blvd NW; sushi $7-15; ⏲lunch from noon Mon-Sat, dinner daily) Kotobuki is one of the better spots for sushi in the city, both by dint of its excellent sushi and sashimi platters (at around $12 for a lunch and $18 for a dinner platter, a good deal), its tucked-away location, which adds a feeling of random discovery, and its oh-so-Japanese interior, all stripped-down aesthetic overlaid by running cursive kanji script on the walls. It's upstairs above a more expensive sushi joint. Take Reservoir Rd NW west a few miles to MacArthur Blvd NW.

QUICK PITA — MIDDLE EASTERN $

(Map p332; ☎202-338-7482; 1210 Potomac St NW; sandwiches $5-6; ⏲11:30am-3am Sun-Thu, to 4:30am Fri & Sat) There's a million late-night joints in Georgetown selling falafel to drunk kids. This is the one we go to. Why? The yogurt is a little saltier, the stools a little more stable so we don't fall on our faces, the shawarma (a meat-in-pita sandwich) a little greasier and the guys behind the counter curse at each other in Arabic with just a little more vehemence. It's cozy like that.

MAKOTO — JAPANESE $$$

(off Map p332; ☎202-298-6866; 4844 MacArthur Blvd NW; mains from $30; ⏲lunch Tue-Sat, dinner Tue-Sun) When we want sushi in the city we often opt for Makoto, simply because it's so classically...*Japanese*. We probably need to clarify that comment. See, we don't just mean the staff are Japanese or there's flute and funny one-string-guitar music playing in the back (although they are, and there is). It's that special Japanese attention to detail. The napkins look like origami. The wasabi is fresh grated. You leave your shoes at the door. The waitresses are so attentive they might as well wipe your mouth and hold your hand in the toilet. And the food, needless to say, is excellent. There's no mucking about; this is old-school stuff prepared with the height of focus and technique. For a splurge (around $60), try the *kaiseki*, a 10-course seasonal tasting menu. Reservations are a good idea, since the place is tiny. Take Reservoir Rd NW west a few miles to MacArthur Blvd NW.

LA CHAUMIERE — FRENCH $$

(Map p332; ☎202-338-1784; www.lachaumieredc.com; 2813 M St NW; mains $19-33; ⏲lunch Mon-Fri, dinner Mon-Sat) There's artists and there's craftsmen, and La Chaumiere's kitchen seems to fall into the second category. This isn't a bad thing; there's no fooling around with funny envelope pushing here, just very good classical French food prepared in an intimate dining room that screams 'expensive date.' This is hearty, stick-to-your-bones stuff straight from the *terroir* – duck breast, saddle of rabbit, calf brains – things that are long- and slow-braised with love. Screw art. We'll take the loving work of these craftsmen any day.

CAFE MILANO — ITALIAN $$$

(Map p332; ☎202-333-6183; www.cafemilano.net; 3251 Prospect St NW; mains $25-45; ⏲lunch from 11:30am, dinner from 4pm) Widely regarded as one of the best bring-your-date-out-for-some-upscale-Italian eateries in the city, Milano has been racking up political bigwigs and besotted Georgetown couples for years with its executions of northern Italian favorites. It is ridiculously pricey, though; while we accept you're paying for atmosphere along with food, self-importance and the (admittedly good) chance of some DC celebrity-spotting don't warrant some of the price tags on this menu. For a good deal that still translates into some pretty good eating, order one of the pastas.

DOLCEZZA — ICE CREAM $

(Map p332; www.dolcezzagelato.com; 1560 Wisconsin Ave NW; ice cream $4-7; ⏲noon-9pm Sun-Fri, to 10pm Fri & Sat;) Dolcezza serves amazingly good gelato from a menu that changes weekly. Recent hits include lime cilantro, Mexican coffee and lemon ricotta cardamom. A second outpost scoops in Dupont Circle.

GEORGETOWN CUPCAKE BAKERY $

(Map p332; www.georgetowncupcake.com; 3301 M St NW; cupcakes $2.75; ⏲10am-9pm Mon-Sat, to 7pm Sun) We're really not into the whole cupcake craze, and we don't think these are the best in town (though they are pretty damn good). We bring Georgetown Cupcake to your attention because here's what's going to happen: you'll be walking down M St and see a gigantic line spill out of a small shop. Mommies with kids, preppy students and ladies-who-lunch types will be in it. Shouts of 'They have salted caramel! I'm getting the lava fudge!' will fill the air. And you won't be able to resist and will fall in behind them. For the record, we give the cupcake prize to Baked & Wired (p120).

SNAP CAFE CREPERIE $

(Map p332; www.snap-restaurant.com; 1062 Thomas Jefferson St NW; mains $5-8; ⏲11am-11pm; 📶) Sweet and savory crepes are the specialty in this cute little pea-green spot. The execution can be inconsistent, but it's one of the cheapest fill-ups you'll find in Georgetown.

DRINKING & NIGHTLIFE

Several British-style pubs with heavy wood and dark nooks line up on M St. Drinks can be amazingly expensive in this cashed-up 'hood.

BIRRERIA PARADISO BAR

(Map p332; www.eatyourpizza.com; 3282 M St NW) The basement of Pizzeria Paradiso (see p121) is Birreria Paradiso, Italian for 'paradise of beer' (more or less). Despite the low-level environs, the place gets lots of sunlight and has a warm Mediterranean vibe, but look, you're here for some hops, and you won't be disappointed: the menu feels something like an atlas for beer lovers who want to engage in some sudsy globetrotting.

TOMBS BAR

(Map p332; www.tombs.com; 1226 36th St NW; ⏲from 11:30am Mon-Sat, from 9:30am Sun) Every school of a certain pedigree has 'that' bar – the one where faculty and students alike sip pints and play darts under athletic regalia of the old school. The Tombs is Georgetown's contribution to the genre, and also happened to be a shooting set for *St Elmo's Fire*. The house is usually filled with students, professors and the occasional Jesuit priest; walls are decked with rowing accoutrement and, oddly, WWI-era posters.

NEIGHBORHOOD RESOURCE

The **Georgetown Business Improvement District** (www.georgetowndc.com) has maps, transport and parking info, and a directory of bars, restaurants and shops on its website.

J PAUL'S PUB

(Map p332; www.j-pauls.com; 3218 M St NW; from 11:30am Mon-Fri, from 10:30am Sat & Sun) Politicians, lobbyists, students and other locals belly up at J Paul's to knock one back. Join them at the long mahogany shotgun bar, especially during happy hour when deals on oysters and other items off the restaurant menu prevail. This is one of the old-fashioned saloon-type places that are common along M St, but we think it's the most inviting of the bunch.

MR SMITH'S BAR

(Map p332; www.mrsmiths.com; 3104 M St NW) This is as divey as they come in Georgetown – sawdust and dusky interior concealing patrons that only get more rowdy and roaring with the night. That said, Mr Smith's is as popular with Georgetown Jonathan as Average Joe, which makes for an intriguing and generally affable atmosphere. Most nights a sing-a-long piano player gets the crowd crooning; you can escape by heading to the patio.

RHINO BAR & PUMP HOUSE SPORTS BAR

(Map p332; www.rhinobardc.com; 3295 M St NW) This is a good spot to see Hoyas behaving badly – a college-age crowd checks its inhibitions at the door here most weekends. DJs play dance music on weekends, and the scene gets crazy in an undergrad kinda way, but for the rest of the week this is pretty much the bar for watching sports and downing wings in the Georgetown area.

SEQUOIA BAR

(Map p332; www.sequoiadc.com; Waterfront Harbour, 3000 K St NW) On a steamy summer night, Sequoia's patio is the spot to be. Plop down on a plastic chair on its cascading terrace overlooking the Potomac and check out the rich people messing around in boats. Or fight your way through the throng at the bar, grab an overpriced Corona, then start flirting and talking politics with the hottie of your choice. This bar attracts all types – from pretty gays to trustafarian college kids to 30-something lawyers – and has a reputation as a pick-up spot.

MIE N YU LOUNGE

(Map p332; www.mienyu.com; 3282 M St NW) Georgetown's most popular lounge-bar is also an Asian-Mediterranean-Middle-Eastern-kitchen-sink fusion restaurant, but we come to see really, really good-looking people sip really, really expensive drinks. It can be a bit pretentious at times, but if you're into the slick lounge-itini scene, this will be right up your alley.

ENTERTAINMENT

BLUES ALLEY JAZZ BAR

(Map p332; www.bluesalley.com; 1073 Rear Wisconsin Ave; admission from $20; ⏲shows 8pm & 10pm) Calling the Alley an establishment is like calling the Lincoln Memorial a landmark. If you grew up around the way, your parents likely went on dates here to watch greats like Dizzy Gillespie back in the day. The talent today is just as sterling for the most part, and the setting just as sophisticated. If big names are playing, you'll want to reserve a ticket in advance. Enter through the alley just off M, south of Wisconsin.

SHOPPING

M St and Wisconsin Ave are the main thoroughfares packed with Urban Outfitters, Juicy Couture, Apple and a slew of other tony brand stores. Stroll down the side streets to find the more imaginative stores.

OLD PRINT GALLERY MAPS, PRINTS

(Map p332; www.oldprintgallery.com; 1220 31st St NW; ⏲10am-5:30pm Tue-Sat) This small store sells a fine array of vintage maps and prints, from the botanical to the architectural, with American portraits, gardens, locomotives, birds and New England scenes all on view. Prints are arranged by category and you can pay extra to have them framed. It's a great place to browse and hold a bit of history in your hands.

ANNIE CREAM CHEESE VINTAGE

(Map p332; www.anniecreamcheese.com; 3279 M St NW) One of several vintage shops in Georgetown, Annie's has some of the best selections, at least for women. You'll find tennis skirts, oversized sunglasses, sexy skirts and tops, glammy high heels – with a bevy of top designers represented. The men's selection is poor, unless monochrome polyester shirts and pleather jackets strike your fancy.

APPALACHIAN SPRING ARTS & CRAFTS

(Map p332; www.appalachianspring.com; 1415 Wisconsin Ave NW; ⏲10am-6pm Mon-Sat, from noon Sun) Touting its motto, 'fine American craft,' this local chain features handmade pottery, woodcarvings, quilts and jewelry. The carved wooden boxes and hand-blown glass bowls make nice gifts.

AS SEEN ON TV GIFTS

(Map p332; bottom level, Shops at Georgetown Park, 3222 M St NW) The objects for sale here don't exactly represent the zenith of American culture, but they make for a good laugh nonetheless; and it's true, many items are sold on TV (or at least they were before the 1980s came screeching to a halt). You'll find Tae-Bo videos (not DVDs), supercharged potato peelers, abdominal rockers, battery-operated scissors, snuggies (that most beloved of wearable blankets), electric hair clipper-brush combos and all manner of products endorsed by George Foreman. ASOT also sells poorly dubbed kung-fu movies to complete the walk down memory lane.

TUGOOH TOYS CHILDREN

(Map p332; www.yirostores.com; 1319 Wisconsin Ave NW; ⏲10am-6pm Mon-Sat, 11am-5pm Sun) This splendid store is a great place to browse, even if you're not packing a rug rat on your hip. You'll find eco-friendly toys and games, including racecars made of bamboo and lots of cuddly animals made with high-quality organic cotton. Lots of items made of wood and other natural substances give an old-fashioned charm to the place.

DEAN & DELUCA FOOD & DRINK

(Map p332; www.deananddeluca.com; 3276 M St NW; ⏲8am-9pm Mon-Sat, to 8pm Sun) The New York gourmet chain has an overwhelming and mouthwatering selection of produce, meat and baked goods in this revamped brick warehouse. Outside is a lovely canopied dining area for noshing on ready-made sandwiches, soups and pastries.

SECONDHAND ROSE — WOMEN'S CLOTHING

(Map p332; www.secondhandrosedc.com; 1516 Wisconsin Ave NW; ⏲11:30am-6pm) This small, cramped secondhand shop sells consignment clothing, usually well-known labels and nothing more than two years old. It isn't a place for bargain hunters – no $10 dresses here – but Secondhand Rose has a speedy turnover and all items are in good condition.

RELISH — WOMEN'S CLOTHING

(Map p332; www.relishdc.com; 3312 Cady's Alley NW; ⏲10am-6pm Mon-Sat) Set on peaceful Cady's Alley, Relish sells high-end fashion for the girls. The two-level store boasts top-name labels and indie designers alike, including pieces by Marni, Jil Sander and Nicole Farhi. Shoes, bags and accessories all make nice eye candy.

LOST BOYS — MEN'S CLOTHING

(Map p332; www.lostboysdc.com; 1033 31st St NW; ⏲closed Mon) Lost Boys sells stylish but staid men's clothing for that well-tailored, slightly preppy Georgetown look. Super soft James Perse polos, Earnest Sewn jeans, candy-striped Steven Alan button-downs and skinny ties by Band of Outsiders are a few recent hits.

SHOPS AT GEORGETOWN PARK — MALL

(Map p332; www.shopsatgeorgetownpark.com; 3222 M St NW) Set in a 19th-century cast-iron building that once sheltered horse-drawn omnibuses, this elegant mall (with skylights and hanging plants) contains more than 100 shops. On the bottom level, you'll find a meager food court, trickling fountains and a few shops, while the other levels contain well-known stores like H&M, Anthropologie, Intermix and Victoria's Secret.

CADY'S ALLEY — HOMEWARES

(Map p332; www.cadysalley.com) Not a store per se, Cady's Alley is exactly that, a small street lined with ubercool (and often expensive) interior-design boutiques selling everything from concept furniture to faucets of the future. It runs parallel to M St NW, between 33rd and 34th Sts NW; you can enter off M St NW.

APPLE STORE — ELECTRONICS

(Map p332; www.apple.com; 1229 Wisconsin Ave NW) iPads, iPhones and 'i' everything else for Mac enthusiasts are splayed across this bright, airy store. Plenty of clued-up staff are on hand to answer product questions, and there's free internet access on machines throughout the store.

ZARA — CLOTHING

(Map p332; www.zara.com; 1238 Wisconsin Ave NW) New products arrive weekly and inventory changes biweekly at Spanish fashion house Zara. It's sort of Gap meets H&M, with youthful, off-the-runway styles at low prices in women's, men's and kids' clothing.

LUSH — BEAUTY

(Map p332; www.twitter.com/lushgeorgetown; 3066 M St NW) A cleaner world awaits inside sweet-smelling Lush. A purveyor of handmade, all-natural soaps, Lush brings high art to the common bath experience. Top selections include honey- and toffee-scented lump soap, rosebud-filled bath bombs (which fizz in the tub) and bergamot-and-lemon bubble bars (for the bubble-bath experience).

PATAGONIA — OUTDOOR EQUIPMENT

(Map p332; www.patagonia.com; 1048 Wisconsin Ave NW) Staffed with knowledgeable sales clerks and stocked with everything you need for a trip to the great outdoors, this tri-level shop has a giant collection of Patagonia's trusted gear, including trendy garb for women and men along with camping supplies, down jackets and hiking shoes and shorts.

SPORTS & ACTIVITIES

CAPITAL CRESCENT TRAIL — BIKING

(Map p332; www.cctrail.org; Water St) Stretching between Georgetown and Bethesda, MD, the constantly evolving Capital Crescent Trail is a fabulous (and very popular) jogging and biking route. Built on an abandoned railroad bed, the 11-mile trail is paved and is a great leisurely day trip. It has beautiful lookouts over the Potomac River, and winds through woodsy areas and upscale neighborhoods. It also links up with the C&O Canal & Towpath and trails through Rock Creek Park.

In Georgetown, the trail begins under the Key Bridge on Water St (which is what K St becomes as it moves west along the waterfront); the trailhead is clearly marked. In Bethesda, it starts at the Wisconsin Ave Tunnel, on Wisconsin Ave just south of Old Georgetown Rd (it's clearly marked here, too, and accessible from Bethesda Metro station).

JACK'S BOATHOUSE — WATER SPORTS

(Map p332; www.jacksboathouse.com; 3500 K St NW; watercraft/paddleboards per hr $14/25; ⏲hr vary Mar-Oct) Located beneath the Key Bridge, Jack's rents canoes, kayaks and stand-up paddleboards. It also offers guided, 90-minute kayak trips (per person $50) in summer at 7pm that glide past the Lincoln Memorial as the sun sets. If you have a bike, Jack's is a mere few steps from the Capital Crescent Trail.

THOMPSON BOAT CENTER — KAYAKING, BIKING

(Map p332; www.thompsonboatcenter.com; 2900 Virginia Ave NW; watercraft per hr/day from $10/24, bikes per hr/day from $7/28; ⏲8am-5pm Mar-Oct) Just across the street from the Kennedy Center, Thompson Boat Center rents canoes and kayaks and offers rowing classes. This is also a convenient place to rent bicycles.

BIG WHEEL BIKES — BIKING

(Map p332; www.bigwheelbikes.com; 1034 33rd St NW; per 3hr/day $21/35; ⏲11am-7pm Tue-Fri, 10am-6pm Sat & Sun) Big Wheel is a short way up the hill from the Capital Crescent Trail. Look for the bright yellow building with a huge bicycle on it. There's a three-hour minimum with rentals.

Capitol Hill & Southeast DC

CAPITOL HILL | SOUTHEAST DC | SOUTHWEST DC

Neighborhood Top Five

❶ Count the statues, ogle the frescoes, eat the bean soup and visit the chambers of the guys and gals who run the country under the big white dome of the **Capitol** (p131).

❷ Be wowed by the sheer volume of, well, volumes at the **Library of Congress** (p133).

❸ Immerse in the good and bad sides of human nature at the haunting **United States Holocaust Memorial Museum** (p134).

❹ Listen in on case arguments at the **Supreme Court** (p135).

❺ Catch a baseball game and see the famous racing presidents at **Nationals Park** (p149).

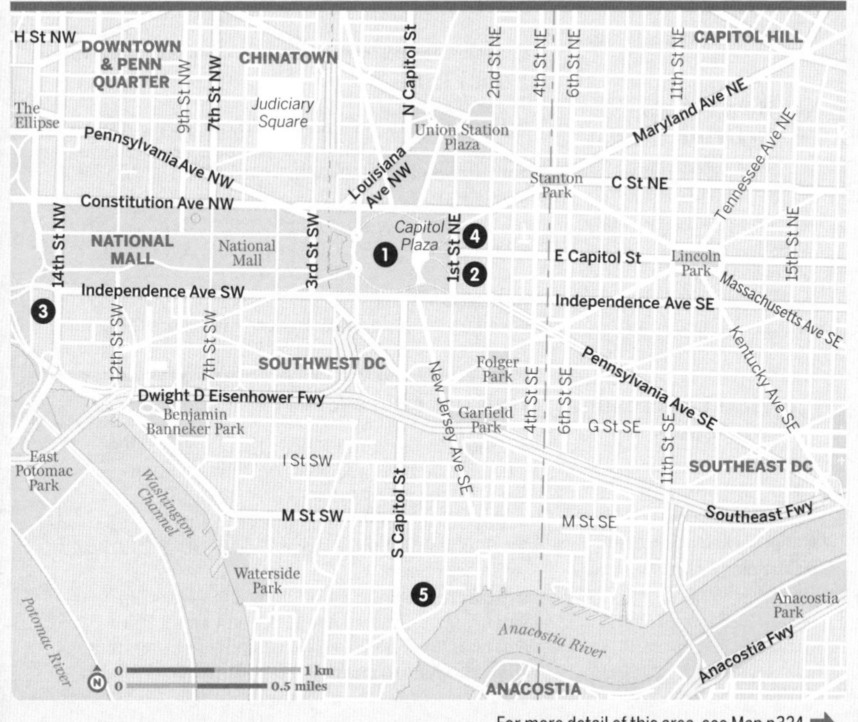

For more detail of this area, see Map p324

Lonely Planet's Top Tip

During the March to April peak season, it pays to plan ahead for certain sights, given the crowds and potential sell-out of tickets. The Capitol lets you reserve tours online for free. The United States Holocaust Memorial Museum lets you reserve tickets for a $1 fee. The Bureau of Engraving and Printing does not take advance bookings, so show up around 8am to get a ticket. For the Marines' drill parade, book online weeks in advance.

Best Places to Eat

- Dangerously Delicious Pies (p140)
- Toki Underground (p140)
- Maine Avenue Fish Market (p144)
- Good Stuff Eatery (p140)

For reviews, see p140

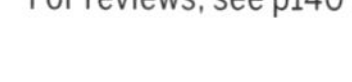

Best Places to Drink

- Little Miss Whiskey's Golden Dollar (p145)
- H Street Country Club (p146)
- Argonaut (p146)
- Red Palace (p147)

For reviews, see p145

Best Underrated Museums

- Folger Shakespeare Library & Theatre (p135)
- Frederick Douglass National Historic Site (p137)
- National Postal Museum (p136)
- Sewell-Belmont House (p139)

For reviews, see p135

Explore Capitol Hill & Southeast DC

First-time visitors will be forgiven for assuming Capitol Hill, the city's geographic and legislative heart, is all about power-broking, wheeling-dealing and backroom bargains. Truth is, it's pretty much a traditional neighborhood, where people live in brownstone row houses clumped into a community that revolves around Eastern Market. The feel of the area is more cozy borough than clandestine backroom.

But there's no denying that the big domed building grabs all the attention. The Capitol, appropriately, sits atop Capitol Hill (what Pierre L'Enfant called 'a pedestal waiting for a monument') across a plaza from the almost-as-regal Supreme Court and Library of Congress. They're all DC highlights, and touring them requires the better part of a day. The Holocaust Memorial Museum and money-churning Bureau of Engraving and Printing are other must-sees. They're in Southwest DC, a little sliver of spillover from the Mall. Beyond, in far-flung Southeast, are the Nationals' stadium and Frederick Douglass's historic home, but not much else for tourists among the hardscrabble communities out this way.

The neighborhood is quite large, so plan on some serious Metro-ing to get between sights. And count on lingering into the night. The eating and entertainment options rock, especially along H St NE and around Eastern Market.

Local Life

- **Hangout** Eastern Market (p137) is the true heart of Capitol Hill: a neighborhood hangout, covered bazaar and all-round great place to soak up local flavor.
- **Bard's B-day** On April 23 – Shakespeare's birthday – the Folger Shakespeare Library (p135) throws a party with jugglers, jesters, cake and sonnet contests. It's a big DC to-do for families.
- **Jazz Jam** Local musicians gather at HR-57 (p147) for open jam sessions on Wednesday and Thursday nights.

Getting There & Away

- **Metro** Union Station (Red Line), Capitol South (Orange and Blue) and Eastern Market (Orange and Blue) are the main stations.
- **Bus** To reach H St's nightlife from Union Station, bus X8 runs along Maryland Ave. Exit at 13th St and walk two blocks north.
- **Streetcar** The city is building a streetcar line that will bring easier access to H St and Capitol Hill's northern area. It's slated for completion in summer 2013; check progress at www.dcstreetcar.com.

TOP SIGHTS
CAPITOL

The political center of the US government and geographic heart of the District, the Capitol sits atop a high hill overlooking the National Mall and the wide avenues flaring out to the city beyond. The towering 285ft cast-iron dome topped by the bronze *Statue of Freedom*, the ornate fountains and marble Roman pillars set on sweeping lawns and the flowering gardens scream: 'This is DC.'

Background & History

Since 1800, the Capitol is where the legislative branch of American government – ie Congress – has met. The lower House of Representatives (435 members) and upper Senate (100 members) meet respectively in the south and north wings of the building.

Pierre L'Enfant chose the site for the Capitol in his original 1791 city plans; construction began in 1793. George Washington laid the cornerstone, anointing it with wine and oil in Masonic style. In 1814, midway through construction, the British marched into DC and burnt the Capitol (and much of the city) to the ground. The destruction tempted people to abandon Washington altogether, but the government finally rebuilt both city and structure. In 1855 the iron dome (weighing nine million pounds) was designed, replacing a smaller one; the House and Senate wings were added in 1857. The final touch, the 19ft *Freedom* sculpture, was placed atop the dome in 1863.

DON'T MISS...

- Constantino Brumidi frieze around rotunda
- *Freedom* sculpture atop dome
- Hall of Statues
- Grotto
- Senate bean soup

PRACTICALITIES

- Map p324
- 202-225-6827
- www.visitthe capitol.gov
- 1st St NE & E Capitol St
- admission free
- 8:30am-4:30pm Mon-Sat
- Capitol South

VISITING THE HOUSE & SENATE FLOORS

To watch Congress in action, you need a separate pass. US citizens must get one from their representative or senator; foreign visitors should take their passports to the House and Senate Appointment Desks on the upper level. Congressional committee hearings are actually more interesting (and substantive) if you care about what's being debated; check for a schedule, locations and to see if they're open to the public (they often are) at www.house.gov and www.senate.gov. Prepare to go through rigid security; you'll have to store most of your belongings before entering the chambers.

The Capitol's restaurant (8:30am-4pm Monday through Saturday) on the lower level has the same numbers of seats as there are Congressional members. Order the famous Senate bean soup – it's on the menu daily. Who knows who you'll be slurping it next to (which is why it's best to hold the jokes about politicians, beans and flatulence).

Visiting the Building

The **Capitol Visitor Center** (www.visitthecapitol.gov; 1st St NE & E Capitol St; 8:30am-4:30pm Mon-Sat) sits below the East Plaza and is where all visits begin. Tours are free, but you need a ticket. Get one at the information desk, or reserve online in advance (there's no fee). It's a good idea to make reservations between March and August.

The hour-long jaunt starts with a cheesy film where you'll hear a lot about 'E Pluribus Unum' (Out of Many, One) and how the US government works. Then staff lead you to the good stuff.

Inside the halls and ornate chambers you really get a feel for the power-playing side of DC. The centerpiece of the Capitol is the magnificent Rotunda (the area under the dome). Guides explain the height this way: if you took the Statue of Liberty off its base and put it in here, there would be room to spare above it. A Constantino Brumidi frieze around the rim replays more than 400 years of American history. Look up into the eye of the dome for the *Apotheosis of Washington,* an allegorical fresco by the same artist. Other eye-catching creations include enormous oil paintings by John Trumbull depicting scenes from the American Revolution. And be on the lookout for sculptures of two famous residents per state in the Hall of Statues.

After the tour, swing by the Exhibition Hall (on the lower level near the information desk). It has an 11ft scale model of the Capitol dome, as well as historic Congressional documents from the National Archives and Library of Congress.

Capitol Grounds

The Capitol's sweeping lawns owe their charm to famed landscape architect Frederick Law Olmsted, who also designed New York City's Central Park. During the Civil War, soldiers camped in Capitol halls and stomped around its lawns. In 1874, spring cleaning was in order: Olmsted added lush greenery and majestic terraces, creating an elegant landscape that gave rise to over 4000 trees from all 50 states and many countries. Northwest of the Capitol is the charming 1879 **grotto**, a redbrick hexagon with black-iron gates and an interior well. Its official name is the Summer House, so-called because this is where women back in the day came to stay cool in their big hoop dresses during the warmer months.

At the base of Capitol Hill, the **Capitol Reflecting Pool** echoes the larger, rectangular Reflecting Pool at the other end of the Mall. This pool actually caps the I-39 freeway, which dips under the Mall here. The ornate **Ulysses S Grant Memorial** dominates its eastern side, showing the general in horseback action.

TOP SIGHTS
LIBRARY OF CONGRESS

The White House and the Capitol may be more iconic, but for our money (well, none, seeing as admission is free), the Library of Congress (LOC) – the world's largest library – is the most impressive structure in DC. It's just the sheer scope of the thing: approximately 120 million items, including 22 million books, plus manuscripts, maps, photographs, films and prints shelved along 500 miles of library stacks in the three main buildings.

The centerpiece of the LOC tourist experience is the historic 1897 Jefferson Building, where you can wander around the spectacular Great Hall, with stained glass, marble, cherubs and goddesses representing different fields of knowledge. The LOC's purpose is simple: to collect all the knowledge in the world. Multimedia kiosks provide the minutest details of the art, architecture and book collection.

Pick up a map at the entrance, which will take you to other sweet spots such as the Gutenberg Bible (c 1455) on the 1st floor. The 2nd floor holds Thomas Jefferson's round library, the Waldseemuller World Map from 1507 (the first to show America) and the overlook into the Main Reading Room. Guides lead free 45-minute tours from the ground floor at 10:30am, 11:30am, 1:30pm, 2:30pm and 3:30pm that take you through the building.

The **Madison Building** (1st St SE btwn Independence Ave & C St SE) and **Adams Building** (cnr 2nd St & Independence Ave SE) are the LOC's other structures, but they don't have as much eye candy for visitors. Free concerts, lectures, films and other events take place throughout the complex daily; check www.loc.gov/loc/events.

DON'T MISS...

- Great Hall
- 1507 Waldseemuller World Map
- Main Reading Room overlook
- Thomas Jefferson's library
- Gutenberg Bible

PRACTICALITIES

- Map p324
- ☎202-707-8000
- www.loc.gov
- 10 1st St SE
- admission free
- 8:30am-4:30pm Mon-Sat
- Ⓜ Capitol South

TOP SIGHTS
UNITED STATES HOLOCAUST MEMORIAL MUSEUM

Both grim summation of human nature and fierce confirmation of basic goodness, the Holocaust Museum is unlike any other museum in Washington, DC. In remembering the millions murdered by the Nazis, it is brutal, direct and impassioned. Visitors are given the identity card of a single Holocaust victim, narrowing the scope of suffering to the individual level while paying thorough, overarching tribute to its powerful subject. Many visitors leave in tears, and few are unmoved.

Design

James Ingo Freed designed the extraordinary building in 1993, and its stark facade and steel-and-glass interior echo the death camps themselves. Look up at the skylight in the Hall of Witness when you enter the building. Many survivors say this reminds them of the sky above the camps. For them it was symbolic, the only thing the Nazis couldn't control.

Permanent Exhibit

The permanent exhibit presents the Holocaust's history chronologically from 1933 to 1945. Galleries span three floors and use more than 900 artifacts, 70 video monitors, historic film footage and eyewitness testimonies.

Start on the 4th floor, which is titled 'Nazi Assault' and covers the period between 1933 and 1939. You can watch propaganda videos of Hitler, Goebbels and others, and learn how the Nazis used modern techniques such as video to craft their message to sway citizens.

The 3rd floor is 'The Final Solution,' covering the period between 1940 and 1945. Here you'll see a railcar used to transport people to the camps, a wooden bunk bed from Auschwitz and a harrowing scale model of Crematorium II at Auschwitz. There's also a listening room where you can hear recordings of people speaking about their experiences in the camps.

The 2nd floor is the 'Last Chapter,' where old film footage shows the camps' liberation, and videos flicker across screens illuminating individual survivors telling their stories. From here you come out into the candlelit Hall of Remembrance, a sanctuary for quiet reflection. The Wexner Center is likewise on this floor, featuring exhibits on other genocides around the world. The museum is a major advocate against, and information clearing house on, ongoing genocides such as in Darfur. Here's something you'll learn: the word genocide didn't exist until 1944. That's when Raphael Lemkin, a Jewish refugee from Poland, coined it to describe what was happening in German-occupied Europe.

If you have young children, a gentler kids' installation – 'Remember the Children: Daniel's Story' – is on the 1st floor.

Entry Tickets

Same-day passes to view the permanent exhibit are required March through August, available at the pass desk on the 1st floor. The passes allow entrance at a designated time; arrive early because they do run out. Alternatively, for a $1 surcharge, tickets are available in advance at the museum's website.

DON'T MISS...

- Hall of Remembrance
- Skylight in the Hall of Witness
- Propaganda videos
- Survivor testimonies
- Wexner Center

PRACTICALITIES

- Map p324
- ☎202-488-0400
- www.ushmm.org
- 100 Raoul Wallenberg Pl SW
- admission free
- ⏲10am-5:20pm, to 6:20pm Mon-Fri Apr & May
- Ⓜ Smithsonian

SIGHTS

Capitol Hill

CAPITOL LANDMARK

See p131.

LIBRARY OF CONGRESS LANDMARK

See p133.

FREE **SUPREME COURT** LANDMARK

(Map p129; ☎202-479-3030; www.supremecourt.gov; 1 1st St NE; ⌚9am-4:30pm Mon-Fri; MCapitol South) The highest court in the land is also the head of the least prominent branch of government: the United States judiciary. As such, the actual Supreme Court building, one of the last Greek classical structures built in DC, isn't as iconic as the Capitol or the White House (the respective centers of the legislative and executive branches). This suited a few folks just fine in the past: when the building came up in 1935, some justices felt it was too large, and didn't properly reflect the subdued influence of the nine justices within.

The design scheme was to create, in typical federal-government style, a Greek Temple of Justice. The seated figures in front of the building represent the female Contemplation of Justice and the male Guardian of Law; panels on the 13,000lb bronze front doors depict the history of jurisprudence. The interior grand corridor and Great Hall are no less impressive. Downstairs is an exhibit on the history of the court. Friezes within the courtroom also depict legal history and heroes, which has caused no little debate among Americans.

On days when court's not in session you can hear lectures (every hour on the half-hour) about the Supreme Court in the courtroom. When court is in session, try to hear the oral arguments (10am Monday to Wednesday, for two weeks every month from October to April). Lines form out front starting at 8am: choose the appropriate one depending on whether you wish to sit through the entire argument or observe the court in session for a few minutes. The release of orders and opinions, open to the public, takes place in May and June. Check the court's website for case details.

FREE **FOLGER SHAKESPEARE LIBRARY & THEATRE** LIBRARY

(Map p324; www.folger.edu; 201 E Capitol St SE; ⌚10am-5pm Mon-Sat, noon-5pm Sun; MCapitol South) The world's largest collection of the bard's works, including seven First Folios, is housed at the Folger Library: its Great Hall exhibits Shakespearean artifacts and other

ONE THOUSAND ARGUMENTS OVER THE 10 COMMANDMENTS

The issue of separating church and state is one of the main battlefronts in US culture wars, and Supreme Court architecture has often been in the middle of the cross fire.

The sculpture *Justice the Guardian of Liberty,* on the east (ie back) pediment of the court's exterior, displays Moses bearing two tablets. In addition, an interior frieze in the main courtroom also depicts Moses, again with tablets in hand. This is proof, according to some, that the Ten Commandments should be displayed in American courthouses and schools, a traditional aim of the antiseparation of church and state movement.

The problem is, these claims take Moses out of artistic context. In the exterior sculpture he is presented with Solon of Athens and Confucius; the figures are meant to represent great lawgivers of 'the East' and Moses' tablets are deliberately left blank. In the interior frieze, Moses' tablets are numbered, Roman-style, I to X, but Adolph Weinman, who designed the frieze, told the court (his letter is kept in court archives) the numbers represent the Bill of Rights, not the Ten Commandments.

Moses is also represented with 17 other lawgivers in a frieze that runs along the north and south walls of the main courtroom. Included among these lawgivers are Hammurabi, Napoleon and the Islamic Prophet Muhammad. The Council on American Islamic Relations has asked for the Muhammad depiction to be removed as Islamic law forbids depictions of the prophet, but that request was turned down by Justice William Rehnquist, who argued the depiction is a respectful one meant to honor Muhammad's jurisprudence.

rare Renaissance manuscripts. Most of the rarities are housed in the library's reading rooms, closed to all but scholars, except on Shakespeare's birthday (April 23), but you can peek electronically via the multimedia computers in the Shakespeare Gallery.

The **Folger Theatre** replicates a theater of Shakespeare's time. With its woodcarvings and sky canopy, it's an intimate setting for plays, readings and performances, including the stellar annual PEN/Faulkner readings. East of the building is the **Elizabethan Garden**, full of flowers and herbs that were cultivated during Shakespeare's time, as well as statues of the bard's characters. Staff give daily tours (11am and 3pm Monday through Friday, 11am and 1pm Saturday, 1pm Sunday) of the building and exhibitions.

The Folger building itself is notable for being the most prominent example of the modernist-classical hybrid movement that swept Washington, DC, during the Great Depression. Jokingly referred to as 'Stark Deco,' it tends to inspire strong feelings; lovers say it elegantly pays homage to Greek classicism and 20th-century modernism, while haters say it ruins both styles.

SEWALL-BELMONT HOUSE — MUSEUM

(Map p324; www.sewallbelmont.org; 144 Constitution Ave NE; admission $5; noon-5pm Wed-Sun; Union Station, Capitol South) The District, sadly, lacks a specific monument and museum to the women's rights movement, but it does have this historic house – home base of the National Woman's Party since 1929, and 43-year residence of the party's legendary founder, suffragette Alice Paul. Paul spearheaded efforts to gain the vote for women (enshrined in the 19th Amendment) and wrote the Equal Rights Amendment. Docents show off historical exhibits, portraits, sculpture and a library that celebrates feminist heroes. The entrance is on 2nd St, next to the Hart Senate Office Building.

STREET ADDRESSES

In Capitol Hill, different streets in close proximity can have the same letter, depending on whether they are north or south of E Capitol St (ie A St NE is just two blocks north of A St SE). Pay attention to the directional (NE or SE) to avoid confusion.

UNION STATION — LANDMARK

(Map p324; www.unionstationdc.com; 50 Massachusetts Ave NE; Union Station) How beautiful is Union Station? Well, even commuters who use it to get to work – people who should loathe the sight of it – say the grand entrance hall, meant to resemble a Roman triumphal arch, never fails to impress. This was the first structure built in accordance with the McMillan plan, the 1901 campaign to revitalize DC's then dead urban core. Union is one of the pinnacles of the beaux-arts and city-beautiful movements that transformed the American urban landscape in the 20th century. Besides being an architectural gem, Union also has a small arcade of shops and fast-food restaurants and serves as Washington's main rail hub.

The main hall, known as the Grand Concourse, is patterned after the Roman Baths of Diocletian (although shields are strategically placed across the waists of the legionnaire statues – for the record, they're supposed to be anatomically correct, but rumor holds only one was built that way). In the station's east wing is the old Presidential Waiting Room (now B Smith's restaurant), where dignitaries and celebrities once alighted when they traveled to DC.

The station's exterior offers vistas of the Capitol and avenues radiating south toward the Mall. Just south along Louisiana Ave NW you'll find **Union Station Plaza**, a grassy park with a large fountain cascade, and the **Taft Memorial Carillon**, whose bells ring every quarter-hour.

FREE NATIONAL POSTAL MUSEUM — MUSEUM

(Map p324; www.postalmuseum.si.edu; 2 Massachusetts Ave NE; 10am-5:30pm; Union Station;) Philatelists, rejoice. In the National Capitol Post Office Building, just west of Union Station, the kid-friendly Postal Museum has exhibits on postal history from the Pony Express to modern times. Gawk at the world's largest stamp collection, antique mail planes and touching exhibits of old letters (from soldiers, pioneers and others). Some of the stamp galleries are undergoing renovation until late 2013. Make due by going into the museum's stamp shop, browsing the catalog and having the 'philatelic clerk' (excellent job title!) fetch your selection from the zillions available. A lot of hard-core stamp collectors hang out in here, since many of the stamps are hot-off-the-press and aren't available elsewhere.

NATIONAL JAPANESE AMERICAN MEMORIAL MONUMENT

(Map p324; www.njamf.com; Louisiana Ave btwn New Jersey Ave & D St; 24hr; Union Station) During WWII, thousands of West Coast Japanese American citizens were held in internment camps as suspected 'enemy aliens.' Even as this discrimination occurred under government mandate, hundreds of their relatives enrolled in the all Japanese American 442nd Infantry Regiment, which would go on to become the most decorated American combat unit of the war. Both soldiers and interred civilians are honored in this plaza, centered on a statue depicting two cranes bound with barbed wire.

LINCOLN PARK PARK

(Map p324; E Capitol St btwn 11th & 13th Sts SE) Lincoln Park is the lively center of Capitol Hill's east end. Freed black slaves raised the funds to erect the 1876 **Emancipation Memorial**, which portrays the snapping of slavery's chains as Abraham Lincoln proffers the Emancipation Proclamation. The **Mary McLeod Bethune Memorial**, DC's first statue of a black woman, honors the educator and founder of the National Council of Negro Women. Near the park, the **Car Barn** (cnr 14th & E Capitol Sts), now private housing, was DC's 19th-century trolley turnaround. South of here on 11th St SE, an 1860s builder constructed the lovely **Philadelphia Row** (124-54 11th St SE) for his homesick Philly-born wife.

EASTERN MARKET MARKET

(Map p324; www.easternmarket-dc.org; 225 7th St SE; 7am-7pm Tue-Fri, to 6pm Sat, 9am-5pm Sun; Eastern Market) The Capitol dome might win the word-image association game with visitors, but 'the' Market probably sweeps the title among locals when it comes to Capitol Hill. That's because Eastern Market makes the Hill a neighborhood as opposed to...well, a hill. Packed with good food, crafts and every ethnicity in the area, this roofed bazaar is a must-visit on weekends. Built in 1873, it is the last of the 19th-century covered markets that once supplied most of DC's food. South Hall has food stands, bakeries, flower stands and delis. North Hall is an arts center where craftspeople sell handmade wares. Come Christmas, this is the best place in town to buy a tree.

Southeast DC

FREE MARINE BARRACKS BUILDING, PARADE

(Map p324; http://www.marines.mil/unit/barracks/pages/welcome.aspx; cnr 8th & I Sts SE; parade 8:45pm Fri May-Aug; Eastern Market) The 'Eighth and Eye Marines' are on largely ceremonial duty at the nation's oldest Marine Corps post. Most famously, this is the home barracks of the Marine Corps Band, once headed by John Philip Sousa, king of the military march, who was born nearby at 636 G St SE. On Friday evenings in summer the two-hour ceremonial drill parade featuring the band, drum and bugle corps and silent drill team is a must-see. Make reservations online weeks in advance, or show up for general admission at 8pm when they distribute any unclaimed tickets.

NATIONALS PARK STADIUM

(Map p324; www.nationals.com; 1500 S Capitol St SE; Navy Yard) When it opened in 2008, everyone held their breath hoping that the new home of the Washington Nationals (DC's Major League Baseball team) could serve as a cornerstone for regeneration in tough Southeast. While some corners have spruced up, development hasn't been as pervasive as hoped for. But it may happen yet: at the time of writing, a brewery, park and other projects were in the works. In the meantime, catch a game if you can. The Nats act as a strong social glue among DC's transients and natives.

FREE FREDERICK DOUGLASS NATIONAL HISTORIC SITE HISTORIC SITE

(877-444-6777; www.nps.gov/frdo; 1411 W St SE; 9am-5pm Apr-Oct, to 4:30pm Nov-Mar; B2, B4 from Anacostia Metro) The hilltop home – Cedar Hill – of the escaped slave, abolitionist, man of letters and icon of the American Civil Rights movement is maintained as a nice museum that overlooks, in a figurative and literal way, the city and neighborhood that represents his nation's highest hopes and harshest realities. Douglass lived here from 1878 until his death in 1895. The house still contains most of his original furnishings, down to his wire-rim eyeglasses on his roll-top desk. Visits into the home are by organized tour only, of which there are five or six daily. Call for times and to reserve a space ($1.50 reservation fee per ticket). The site is about 2 miles southeast of Nationals Park.

FREE **ANACOSTIA MUSEUM** MUSEUM

(☎202-633-4820; www.anacostia.si.edu; 1901 Fort Pl SE; ⏰10am-5pm; 🚌W2, W3 from Anacostia Metro) This Smithsonian museum wears several hats: as community hall and museum for the surrounding black neighborhood of Anacostia, and as a place for rotating exhibits from the nomadic Museum of African American culture (to have its own home on the Mall in 2015). Call ahead, as the museum often closes between installations. Be aware that you can't really walk here; you'll either need a taxi, your own wheels or the bus. From the Metro station, take the 'Local' exit to Howard Rd and transfer to the W2 or W3 bus. The W2 runs during rush hours, the W3 every 30 minutes.

THEARC ARTS CENTER

(www.thearcdc.org; 1901 Mississippi Ave SE; Ⓜ Southern Ave) The Town Hall Education, Arts and Recreation Campus (THEARC) has been a cornerstone for community redevelopment in River East/Far Southeast. A multipurpose community center, arts education campus and performance space, the building was the first one of its kind in what was then a neglected area of town, and its impact has really brought some of the surrounding blocks back to life. If you want a sense of the pulse of contemporary African American DC, catch a show or see one of the center's frequent special exhibitions. THEARC is about 3.5 miles southeast of Nationals Park, and three-quarters of a mile from the closest Metro; it's best to drive here.

Southwest DC

Washington's smallest quadrant consists of Smithsonian spillover from the Mall, the federal center (which includes several executive branch department buildings) and the two residential neighborhoods of Southwest Waterfront and Bellevue.

LOCAL KNOWLEDGE

HAINS POINT

The southern tip of East Potomac Park that juts out into the river is called Hains Point. Lots of folks come here to picnic, and the spot provides great views of the planes taking off from nearby Reagan National Airport.

UNITED STATES HOLOCAUST MEMORIAL MUSEUM MUSEUM

See p134.

FREE **BUREAU OF ENGRAVING AND PRINTING** LANDMARK

(Map p324; www.moneyfactory.gov; cnr 14th & C Sts SW; ⏰8:30am-3pm Mon-Fri, to 7:30pm summer; Ⓜ Smithsonian; 👪) Cha-ching! The Bureau of Engraving and Printing, aka the most glorified print shop in the world, is where all the US paper currency is designed. Some $450 million of it rolls off the presses daily. Forty-minute guided tours demonstrate how money is designed, printed and cut, from wads of green ink to the stuff that ends up in your wallet.

During peak season (March through August), line up at the **NBEP ticket kiosk** (Raoul Wallenberg Pl, aka 15th St) for tickets. Arrive early (it opens at 8am), as only a limited number are distributed. For the rest of the year you can come in through the main entrance at 14th & C Sts; note there are no tours between 10:45am and 12:30pm during low season.

EAST POTOMAC PARK PARK

(Map p324; Ohio Dr SW; Ⓜ Smithsonian) Although only a stone's throw from the National Mall, as far as tourists go, East Potomac Park may as well be in Siberia. A very pleasant, green, cherry-blossom-lined Siberia that is a lovely spot for walking, fishing and general gamboling (not that you can't do any of that stuff in the real Siberia). A 5-mile paved trail, great for biking or in-line skating, runs around the park's circumference, paralleling Ohio Dr. The center of the park is the East Potomac Park golf course; see p150 for details.

The park sits on a finger of land that extends southward from the Tidal Basin into the Potomac River. On foot, you can access it by following trails that lead from the Thomas Jefferson Memorial (p94) under the bridges. If you drive out this way, you can park on the shoulder of Ohio Dr.

WATERSIDE PARK PARK

(Map p324; Ⓜ Waterfront-SEU) A few historic homes – curiosities in this neighborhood – survived the 1950s urban clearance. The **Law House** (1252 6th St SW) is a Federal-style row house that was built by one of

START EASTERN MARKET METRO
END UNION STATION
DISTANCE 2 MILES
DURATION 3 TO 4 HOURS

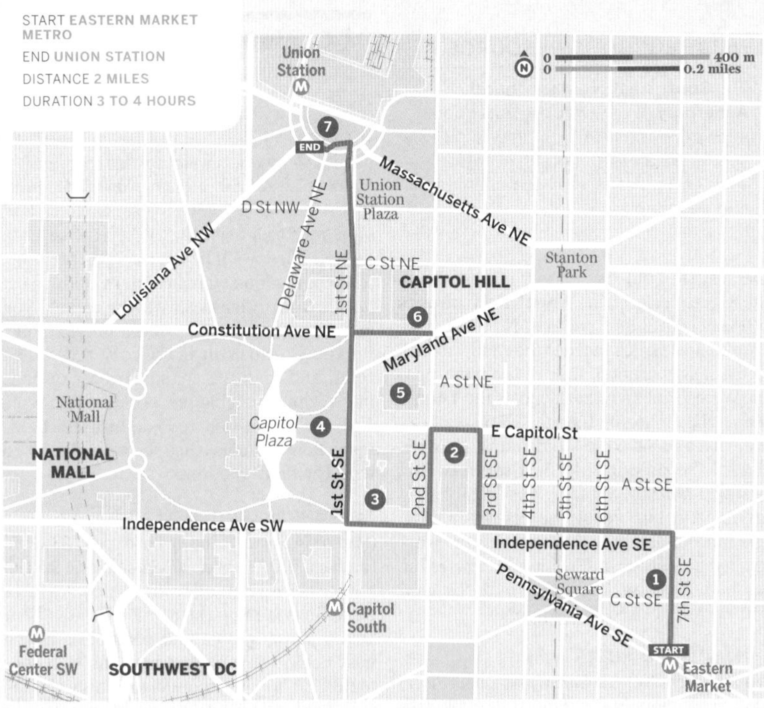

Neighborhood Walk

Cap Hill Crawl

If it's a big impressive building and it sits on Capitol Hill, we'll check it out on this jaunt.

Start by fueling up at 1 **Eastern Market** (get out of Eastern Market Metro and walk about 20m north). This is the true heart of Capitol Hill: a neighborhood hangout, covered bazaar and just generally great place to soak up local flavor.

Walk west on Independence Ave SE toward the Capitol Dome, which is pretty hard to miss. At 3rd St SE, detour a couple of blocks north to the 2 **Folger Shakespeare Library**. The building, jokingly referred to as 'Stark Deco,' holds the world's largest collection of Shakespeare's works, along with cool exhibits. Get ready for a literary comparison, because our next stop is the 3 **Library of Congress**. Pop in for an excellent guided tour of a building that's almost as impressive as its mission: to gather all of the knowledge in the world under one roof.

Now go underground into the 4 **Capitol Visitor Center**. You can easily spend two or more hours here learning about the seat of the legislative branch of government (ie Congress). Across the street the government's judiciary branch – the 5 **Supreme Court** – rises up in Greek temple-esque splendor. If you happen to stumble upon the day of an interesting case, you may find that your tour has come to an abrupt, albeit serendipitous end – watching oral arguments conducted in front of the nine justices is an opportunity that shouldn't be passed up.

Make another little detour to the 6 **Sewell-Belmont House**, home base of the National Woman's Party since 1929, and 43-year residence of the party's legendary founder, suffragette Alice Paul. Ladies: she's why you can vote.

Return to 1st St NE and head north until you get to 7 **Union Station**. This is one of the masterpieces of the early 20th-century beaux-arts movement, patterned after the Roman Baths of Diocletian. We like to think even an emperor would be awed by the sights just traversed.

NEIGHBORHOOD RESOURCE

The **Southwest Neighborhood Assembly** (www.swdc.org) has good information on the community's museums, theaters, parks and events such as jazz concerts in local churches and trapeze classes.

the first DC land speculators in 1796. From the same period, the **Wheat Row houses** (1313-1321 4th St SW), south of N St SW, have human-scale brick facades that add warmth to the neighborhood. Also in the park, near the Waterfront's southern end, is the **Titanic Memorial**, honoring the men who sacrificed their lives to save the women and children aboard the sinking ship. Just south is **Fort Lesley J McNair**, an army post established in 1791 and burned by the British in 1814. The Lincoln-assassination conspirators were hanged at McNair in 1865; it now houses the National Defense University and National War College (closed to the public).

BENJAMIN BANNEKER PARK PARK
(Map p324; cnr 10th & G Sts SW; ML'Enfant Plaza) This park honors Benjamin Banneker, a free black, self-taught astronomer, mathematician and one of the original surveyors of the 10-sq-mile plot that would define the District. It's a grassy little circle near the Waterfront, swiped by a tangle of highways, about a half-mile from the Metro.

EATING

Capitol Hill has long been an outpost for the DC burger bar, the sort of unpretentious spot where you roll up your sleeves and slather on some ketchup and – 'Sorry, yes Senator? I'll be back on the Hill right away! Damn, there goes my lunch.' Hipper upscale spots are popping up, especially along Pennsylvania Ave and around Barracks Row (ie 8th St SE, near the Marine Barracks). H St NE, near Union Station, has seen the most action. The formerly beat-up section of town is being transformed by a glut of fun, offbeat restaurants and bars, most clustered between 12th and 14th Sts NE.

Capitol Hill

TOP CHOICE **DANGEROUSLY DELICIOUS PIES** AMERICAN $
(Map p324; www.dangerouspiesdc.com; 1339 H St NE; slices $6.50; 11am-midnight Mon-Thu, to 3:30am Fri, 9am-3:30am Sat, 9am-10pm Sun; X8 from Union Station;) When the gates of heaven open, we'll be led into this pie shop. The eponymous wares come in both sweet and savory varieties, which means you can – without shame – make a meal of pie. Pull up a retro chair in the cozy, red-walled room and scan the chalkboard for options like vegan vegetable pie, pork barbecue pie and the mega-rich, cookie-infused Baltimore Bomb. Bonus: they serve alcohol to go with the flaky goodness.

TOKI UNDERGROUND ASIAN $
(Map p324; www.tokiunderground.com; 1234 H St NE; mains $10; dinner; X8 from Union Station) Spicy, belly-warming ramen noodles and dumplings sum up the menu in wee, 15-seat Toki. Steaming pots and pans obscure the busy chefs, while diners slurp and sigh contentedly. The eatery doesn't take reservations and there's typically a long wait. Use it as an opportunity to explore the surrounding bars; Toki will text you when your table is ready. Despite the name, Toki Underground is on the second floor. It's not marked; look for the Pug bar sign, and the restaurant is above it.

GOOD STUFF EATERY AMERICAN $
(Map p324; www.goodstuffeatery.com; 303 Pennsylvania Ave SE; burgers $6-8; 11:30am-11pm Mon-Sat; MEastern Market, Capitol South;) Good Stuff chef Spike Mendelsohn is one of the most buzzed-about young chefs in the District. He brings good food at a good price to the masses: he does reality shows like *Top Chef*, and he works his kitchen – a celebrity chef who actually cooks your meal. The burgers, salads, shakes and fries – that's the sum of the menu – are done with nice attention to detail and fresh ingredients. Random things we like: you can top off fries at the 'dipping bar' of various sauces; the toasted marshmallow milkshake comes with an honest-to-god toasted marshmallow; and salads come with cornbread. The ambience is that of a fast-food joint, and seats are at premium weekend nights when Cap Hill youth descend on the place.

MONTMARTRE FRENCH $$$

(Map p324; ☎202-544-1244; www.montmartredc.com; 327 7th St SE; mains $25-40; ⏰lunch & dinner Tue-Fri, brunch & dinner Sat & Sun; Ⓜ Eastern Market) One of the better pure French spots in town, Montmartre is ensconced in a warm, neighborly location, cluttered in a *maman's* dining room kinda way, and complimented by great wines and some very fine steak, served bloody and yummy. This is more of a neighborhood spot than a political dinner date, which adds to the feeling of cozy authenticity. The homemade pâté is silky and rich, desserts are delightful, and all in all this is a place French expats take their friends to give them a taste of home. The praise doesn't come much higher than that.

GRANVILLE MOORE'S BELGIAN $$

(Map p324; www.granvillemoores.com; 1238 H St NE; mains $12-16; ⏰5pm-midnight Sun-Thu, to 3am Fri & Sat; 🚌X8 from Union Station) Walking into Granville's is like walking into a medieval pub where the hobbits have tattoos and a bit of attitude. It's sweetly dark, redolent with the pure smells of beer and slow-cooking meat (oh yeah). The whole place screams cozy, and the food is fantastic: big meaty burgers, sandwiches, smoky bacon, runny cheese and bowls of shellfish, all accompanied by mountains of perfectly prepared frites. The fireside setting is ideal on a winter's eve, and locals have been known to fall on their faces over the bison cheese steak.

SIDAMO COFFEE & TEA CAFE $

(Map p324; www.sidamocoffeeandtea.com; 417 H St NE; sandwiches $3-6; ⏰7am-7pm Mon-Fri, 8am-6pm Sat, 8am-5pm Sun; Ⓜ Union Station; wi-fi) DC is lacking in the cafe department. Yeah, we've got Starbucks and some other chains out the wazoo, but indies where you can use the wi-fi and smell the beans roasting and write books while blustery days go by? Not so much. Sidamo, thankfully, makes up for us in this regard. Owned by an Ethiopian family, Sidamo offers excellent, organic African coffee, tasty and strong as hell. There's friendly staff and that right bohemian atmosphere, which, while overplayed in other parts of the world, doesn't get enough play in the capital. On Sundays at 2pm, the family puts on a free Ethiopian coffee ceremony; all customers are invited to participate.

B SMITH'S SOUTHERN $$

(Map p324; ☎202-289-6188; www.bsmith.com; Union Station, 50 Massachusetts Ave NE; mains $19-31; ⏰lunch & dinner; Ⓜ Union Station) With its spectacular vaulted ceilings, marble floors and Ionic columns, you can't beat this place's location in the former Presidential Waiting Hall at Union Station. It is a remarkable contrast to the down-home Southern fare served here by former model Barbara Smith (whose unclouded complexion once graced Oil of Olay ads). Which is not to say the food is not delicious: it is. She upgrades Southern classics to sophisticated oeuvres in fun and unexpected ways, eg vegetarian ribs and the 'Swamp Thang,' a mess of crawfish, scallops and shrimp on collard greens swimming in Dijon cream. The restaurant attracts an affluent crowd and is as popular for après-work drinks as it is for dinner. The ambience is soul soothing, with mellow lights and music, muted colors and mod art on the walls.

JIMMY T'S DINER $

(Map p324; 501 E Capitol St SE; mains $6-10; ⏰7am-3pm Tue-Sun; Ⓜ Eastern Market; family-friendly) Jimmy's is a neighborhood joint of the old school, where folks come in with their dogs, cram in to read the *Post,* have a burger or a coffee, or an omelet (breakfast all day, by the way), and basically be themselves. If you're hungover on Sunday and in Cap Hill, come here for a greasy cure. Cash only.

TED'S BULLETIN AMERICAN $$

(Map p324; ☎202-544-8337; www.tedsbulletin.com; 505 8th St SE; mains $10-18; ⏰breakfast, lunch & dinner; Ⓜ Eastern Market; family-friendly) Plop into a booth in the art-deco-meets-diner ambience, and loosen the belt. Ted's doles out a rich plateful. Beer biscuits and sausage gravy for breakfast, meatloaf with ketchup glaze for dinner and other hipster spins on comfort foods hit the tables throughout the day. You've got to admire a place that lets you substitute pop tarts for toast (breakfast is available all day).

LOCAL KNOWLEDGE

FARMERS MARKET

In addition to Eastern Market, locals buy their fruit and veg from the **H St Market** (Map p324; www.freshfarmmarket.org; 625 H St NE; ⏰9am-noon Sat mid-Apr–mid-Nov). It's part of the Fresh Farm program, a leader in the Chesapeake Bay local food movement.

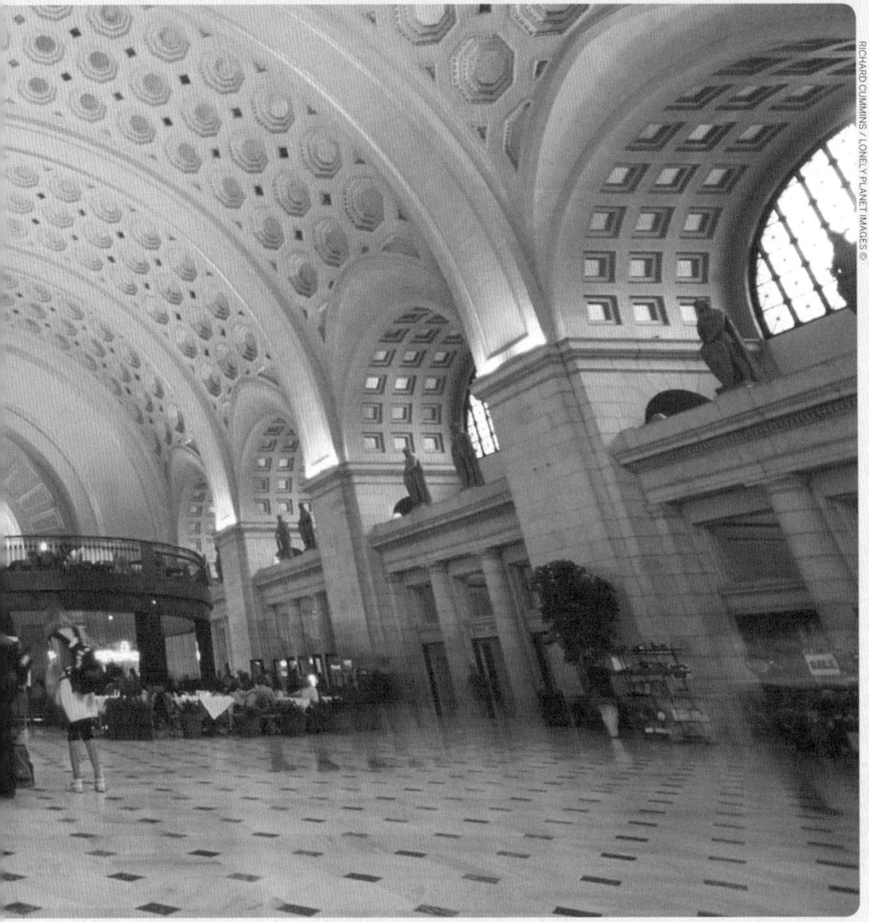

RICHARD CUMMINS / LONELY PLANET IMAGES ©

1. Union Station (p136)
Union Station is one of the best examples of the US beaux-arts movement.

2. Frederick Douglass National Historic Site (p137)
The hilltop home of the escaped slave, abolitionist, man of letters and icon of the US Civil Rights movement.

3. Eastern Market (p137)
Going strong since 1873, the market is a local favorite for food and crafts.

2

LEE FOSTER / LONELY PLANET IMAGES ©

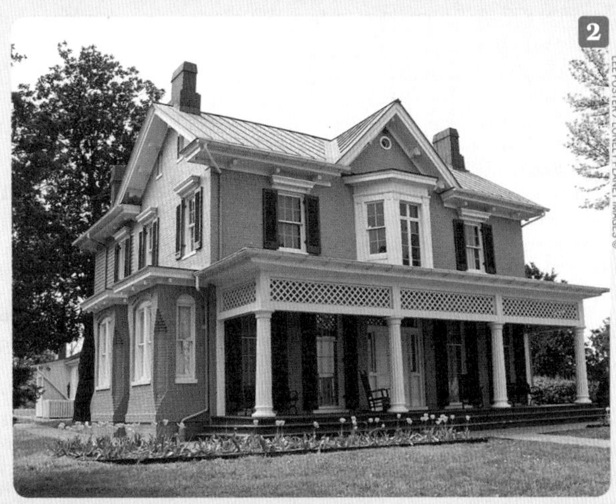

POUND CAFE $

(Map p324; www.poundcoffee.com; 621 Pennsylvania Ave SE; mains $5-8; 7am-9:30pm Mon-Sat, 8am-8pm Sun; Eastern Market;) In Capitol Hill, Pound serves high-quality coffees amid an elegant rustic interior (exposed brick and timber, original plaster ceilings, wood floors and nicely lit artwork). Breakfast quesadillas, panini and daily lunch specials are tops – as is the Nutella latte.

PITANGO GELATO ICE CREAM $

(Map p324; www.pitangogelato.com; 660 Pennsylvania Ave SE; ice cream $3-6; from noon; Eastern Market) Pitango scoops terrific all-natural gelato, but the sorbet is the standout. Fruity flavors made from Haitian mangoes, white grapefruits and Bosc pears from a nearby farm explode on the tongue. Staff are very sweet (pun!) about letting you try lots of samples.

MARKET LUNCH SEAFOOD $

(Map p324; www.easternmarket-dc.org; 225 7th St SE; mains $9-12; breakfast & lunch Tue-Sun; Eastern Market) Smack in the middle of Eastern Market, this food stall is our favorite. The ingredients are obviously local and fresh, plucked from surrounding vendors. The fried oyster sandwich and lemonade lead the pack of our favorite DC weekend lunches. Eat at the long communal table, or outside at the picnic tables. Cash only. The stall also serves burgers and breakfast dishes like blueberry buckwheat pancakes.

TAYLOR GOURMET DELI $

(Map p324; www.taylorgourmet.com; 1116 H St NE; sandwiches $7-11; 11am-9pm Sun-Thu, to 3am Fri & Sat; X8 from Union Station) When you just need a good sandwich, Taylor has got you covered. For about $10 you can walk out of here with a foot of excellent anything between two pieces of bread, dressed with nicely shredded lettuce and brilliant oil and vinegar. We race here for the Race Street – turkey, prosciutto, pesto and mozzarella. There's a good Italian deli in the back.

LA PLAZA LATIN AMERICAN $

(Map p324; 202-546-9512; 629 Pennsylvania Ave SE; mains from $8; lunch & dinner; Eastern Market) There are two prime times to go to La Plaza: for lunch, when it's occupied by Hill types seeking some cheap, filling (and very tasty) Tex-Mex and Salvadorian fare, and at night, when they serve margaritas that will *kick your ass*. The staff are crazy friendly; if you shoot the breeze with them enough, the tequila starts pouring so quick you don't even know when you shtart shlurrin' yer speesh…uh oh.

ARMAND'S PIZZERIA PIZZERIA $$

(Map p324; www.armandspizza.com; 226 Massachusetts Ave NE; pizzas $11-17; 11:30am-9:30pm Mon-Thu, to 10pm Fri & Sat, 4-9:30pm Sun; Union Station) The best pizza on the hill is served Chicago-style (deep crust) and pleasantly greasy. It's almost next door to the right-wing Heritage Foundation, so depending on your politics, you can share some pie with Newt Gingrich or throw it at him.

SONOMA RESTAURANT & WINE BAR AMERICAN $$

(Map p324; 202-544-8088; www.sonomadc.com; 223 Pennsylvania Ave SE; mains $12-28; lunch Mon-Fri, dinner daily; Capitol South) Wine bars became all the buzz in DC for a few years in the mid-noughties, and Sonoma has long stood out from the pack. The decor is sleek-chic but warm, like a fireplace den decorated by a Scandinavian couture designer's grandmother. The food is fantastic, a nice sampling of Mid-Atlantic delicacies like blue bay mussels with chorizo and rainbow trout laid out with summer pumpkins. You can rely on the staff to pick good wine pairings, but if you're an oenophile the extensive grape menu shouldn't disappoint.

MONOCLE AMERICAN $$$

(Map p324; 202-546-4488; www.themonocle.com; 107 D St NE; mains $18-36; lunch & dinner Mon-Fri; Union Station) The Monocle's food – very American surf-and-turf type stuff – is 3.5 stars out of 5. Generally good, occasionally great, sometimes disappointing. But people don't come here to eat so much as to celebrity spot, and seeing as this good ol' boys' club is just behind the Capitol, your chances of seeing Senator Smith aren't bad. The dark bar and the walls help hit home the fact that this is a politicians' place first and foremost; note the quotes ('If you want a friend in Washington, get a dog').

Southwest DC

MAINE AVENUE FISH MARKET SEAFOOD $

(Map p324; 1100 Maine Ave SW; meals from $7; 8am-9pm; L'Enfant Plaza) In case you didn't know, Washington, DC, is basically

ATLAS DISTRICT ASCENDANT

H St NE between 12th and 14th Sts was once one of Washington's major shopping strips. That was before the race riots of 1968, which sadly gutted the area. No more – this is one of DC's most interesting areas once again thanks to a rapid profusion of bars, restaurants and entertainment venues over the past few years. The quick rise is all the more amazing given that this was once, if not the ghetto, a poorer part of town that was rarely visited by outsiders. The whole thing is flanked by two Chinese takeout places – Danny's and Good Danny's (we can't tell you which one is better) – and anchored by the Atlas Performing Arts Center (see p148). This beautiful deco structure has lent its name to what is now known as the Atlas District, or more commonly the H St Corridor (or just H St). The neighborhood – though still a bit edgy – is one of the best places for dinner and drinks in the city, a place where new and old DC seem to not so much collide as mesh.

The only barrier to perfection is easy access by public transportation. The Atlas District is about a 25-minute, desolate walk from Union Station. You can always catch a cab (about $8) from there, or take the bus (X8 runs along Maryland Ave; exit at 13th St and walk two blocks north). Then again, the issue may be solved by the time you're reading this: plans are underway to put Czech streetcars into service in the neighborhood. Check progress at www.dcstreetcar.com.

in Maryland, and Maryland does the best seafood in America. You get it fresh as hell – still flopping – here, where locals will kill, strip, shell, gut, fry, broil or whatever your fish, crabs, oysters etc in front of your eyes. Have a seat and a beer on the nearby benches and bliss out. If you haven't had steamed hard crabs with Old Bay seasoning, or a fried soft-shell crab sandwich, have some, now, *now* for God's sake. Over a dozen vendors line the wharf selling the smelly goods.

CITY ZEN AMERICAN **$$$**

(Map p324; 202-787-6148; www.mandarinoriental.com/washington/dining/cityzen; Mandarin Oriental Hotel, 1330 Maryland Ave SW; set menus $90-120; dinner Tue-Sat; Smithsonian) James Beard–award-winning chef Eric Zeibold heads the kitchen at one of DC's most acclaimed restaurants. Zeibold is something of a legend in US culinary circles; he came up in California's French Laundry (arguably the best restaurant in America, some say the world) and approaches food with what we'd call *fierce* innovation. This is the kind of guy who mixes red snapper skin with lentils and can make you think a monkfish liver was a slice of perfect foie gras. The tasting menu of most foodies' fantasies is served in a dining room that's almost blinding in its ritzy opulence. To cut a very fine deal, treat yourself to the $50 bar tasting menu.

DRINKING & NIGHTLIFE

The boozing atmosphere on Capitol Hill, still very much a residential neighborhood, is one of cozy pubs where policy talk gives way to Redskins predictions in the NFL. H St NE, otherwise known as the Atlas District, is a lovingly funky contrast to the Hill's red-brick conviviality.

LITTLE MISS WHISKEY'S GOLDEN DOLLAR BAR

(Map p324; www.littlemisswhiskeys.com; 1104 H St NE; from 5pm; X8 from Union Station) If Alice got back from Wonderland so traumatized by a near-beheading that she needed to start engaging in heavy drinking, we'd imagine she'd often pop down to Little Miss Whiskey's. She'd love the decor: somewhere between Wonderland's most whimsical moments of surrealism and the dark nightmares of a lost drug addict, all mixed with a heavy dose of Cure video *Goth-Glam*. And she'd probably go ape-poo for the excellent beer and whiskey menu, served by savvy bartenders who are hand-picked veterans of the DC nightlife scene. These guys have specifically been selected to run this spot, and as such Little Miss Whiskey's feels like a bartender's bar. Although, to be fair, it also gets pretty fun for run-of-the-mill folk who enjoy a weirdly fantastic back patio and the thumping bass of an upstairs dance floor on weekends.

H STREET COUNTRY CLUB — BAR

(Map p324; www.thehstreetcountryclub.com; 1335 H St NE; ⏲from 5pm Mon-Thu, from 4pm Fri-Sun; 🚌X8 from Union Station) The Country Club is two levels of fantastic-ness. The bottom floor is packed with pool tables, skeeball and shuffleboard, while the top contains (seriously) its own minigolf course ($7 to play) done up to resemble a tour of the city on a small scale. You putt-putt past a trio of Lego lobbyists, through Beltway traffic snarls and past a King Kong–clad Washington monument. The whole vibe of the place just facilitates a relaxed atmosphere where it's very easy to strike up conversations with strangers – if you're shy and new to town, we'd highly recommend joining the Country Club, as it's hard to leave here without hitting up some random in conversation ('Nice chip, dude').

ARGONAUT — BAR

(Map p324; www.argonautdc.com; 1433 H St NE; ⏲from 5pm Mon & Tue, from 11:30am Wed & Thu, from 4pm Fri, from 10am Sat & Sun; 🚌X8 from Union Station; 👪) The 'Naut looks and feels like a corner spot where folks repair for a beer after work, and in truth, people still do so here. The lengthy suds list flows with craft brews. Many draughts are half-price during happy hour (from 5pm to 7pm), and you can order a four-beer sampler to get acquainted with the options. Take your drinks out to the dog-friendly patio, play a little cornhole (beanbag toss), and if hunger strikes, try the fish tacos or sweet potato fries. Children are welcome and get their own menu. Hipster enough to be different, but not so much that locals have fled the premises, the Argonaut is a great date spot for someone who's a little off-kilter.

GRANVILLE MOORE'S — PUB

(Map p324; www.granvillemoores.com; 1238 H St NE; ⏲from 5pm Mon-Fri, from 11am Sat & Sun; 🚌X8 from Union Station) Besides being one of the best places to grab a steak sandwich in the District, Granville Moore's has an extensive Belgian beer menu that should satisfy any fan of low-country boozing. With its raw, wooden fixtures and walls that look as if they were made from daub and mud, the interior resembles nothing so much as a medieval barracks. When they get the fire going in here, this is one of our favorite bars to repair into on a cold winter night.

STAR & SHAMROCK — PUB

(Map p324; www.starandshamrock.com; 1341 H St NE; ⏲from 11am; 🚌X8 from Union Station) It's not every day you come across an Irish pub–Jewish deli fusion. So fork right in to fried matzo balls with 'au Jew' dipping sauce, chopped chicken livers and latkes (though the latter will not be as good as your bubbe's) while sipping Guinness or Harp. Of course, Manischewitz sangria and Hebrew Genesis ale are also part of the shtick.

PHASE ONE — LESBIAN

(Map p324; www.phase1dc.com; 525 8th St SE; ⏲from 7pm Thu-Sun; Ⓜ Eastern Market) 'The Phase' claims to be the oldest lesbian bar in the country; it's certainly the best lesbian dive in DC, not that there's much competition for the crown. It's great, friendly fun by any measure, chockablock with jelly wrestling, free pizza nights and an unpretentious but raucous enough atmosphere for ladies on the prowl. Come early to mingle in peace and quiet, or late to shake your booty on the packed dance floor.

KELLY'S IRISH TIMES — IRISH PUB

(Map p324; www.kellysirishtimesdc.com; 14 F St NW; ⏲from 11am; Ⓜ Union Station) Kelly's implores: 'Give me your tired, your hungry, your befuddled masses,' and the masses respond. Fans of the on-tap Guinness and the Wednesday to Saturday live music tend to be younger than the patrons next door at the Dubliner – students and staffers and other suds-drinkers. The layout is like every Irish pub you've ever been in, but it's an exemplar of the genre.

18TH AMENDMENT — BAR

(Map p324; www.18thdc.com; 613 Pennsylvania Ave SE; Ⓜ Eastern Market, Capitol South) The Amendment embraces a speakeasy theme – hence the name. Gangsters and bootleggers should head directly to the basement, where the furniture is made from beer barrels and whiskey crates, and there are pool tables on which to fight your duel. Upstairs there's a late-1920s art-deco air, reminiscent of prohibition-era Chicago. It has ample seating and eight beers on tap.

FRUIT BAT — BAR

(Map p324; www.dcfruitbat.com; 1236 H St NE; ⏲from 5:30pm Tue-Sat; 🚌X8 from Union Station) The low-hanging fruit is literal at Fruit Bat, in the baskets that dangle over the bar. It's also what goes into the eclectic, fruit-filled cocktails. Barkeeps squeeze a wild array of juices – persimmon, papaya and ginger-apple cider, to name a few. After your drink has been boozeified, take it to the condiment station to sweeten or spice some more. A vegetarian-friendly, South American street-food menu (yuca fries etc) soaks it up so you don't get too fruit-loopy.

UGLY MUG SPORTS BAR

(Map p324; www.uglymugdc.com; 723 8th St SE; ⏲from 11am; Ⓜ Eastern Market) The Mug is typical of the dives in this part of town: kinda grotty, but self-consciously so, attracting an interesting mix of preppie Hill-rats, Marines from the nearby barracks and Capitol Hill locals. The predominating crowd is usually pretty loud and raucous, making this the 8th St SE option for those wanting a bit more of a frattish ambience.

LOLA'S BARRACKS BAR & GRILL BAR

(Map p324; www.lolasbarracksbarandgrill.com; 711 8th St SE; ⏲from 11am; Ⓜ Eastern Market) If the Ugly Mug is the 20-something's bar of choice around this stretch of Capitol Hill, Lola's is geared more toward 30-somethings and older. The mood is darker, a little more sophisticated; a spot to watch Cap Hill professionals drink wine instead of shots. Although Lola's isn't sedate by any stretch: it's just that the buzz here is low and constant, compared with the roar at the spots next door.

LOCAL KNOWLEDGE

CRUNK CAKES

A couple of enterprising vendors sell **Crunk Cakes** (www.districtofcrunk.com; per cake $3.50), aka alcohol-infused cupcakes, at many DC dive bars, especially around H St and the Rock & Roll Hotel. Each confection supposedly contains an ounce of liquor, meaning that consuming one is roughly equivalent to knocking back a shot. The Fat Elvis is a rum-soaked banana cake topped with Frangelico-peanut-butter icing. The chocolaty Irish Car Bomb stirs in Guinness, Jameson whiskey and Bailey's. It will knock you out – literally, if you demolish too many. Find the vendors' location via Twitter (@crunkcakesdc).

ENTERTAINMENT

RED PALACE LIVE MUSIC, BURLESQUE

(Map p324; www.redpalacedc.com; 1212 H St NE; ⏲from 5pm; 🚌X8 from Union Station) When the Red and Black (a down-and-dirty rock club) married its next-door neighbor, the Palace of Wonders (a freak-show venue), in 2011, the two became one: the Red Palace. A pillar of the frenzied H St scene, the sexy, bizarre space draws a punkish crowd for its mix of burlesque shows and live bands, with an abundance of indie rock and experimental sounds. Three bars pouring a decent craft-beer selection ensure no one suffers from thirst.

ROCK & ROLL HOTEL LIVE MUSIC

(Map p324; www.rockandrollhoteldc.com; 1353 H St NE; 🚌X8 from Union Station) The Hilton this hotel ain't, unless the Hilton went to hell and came back on a screaming motorcycle while wailing on guitars made of fire. Right; that's a tad hyperbolic, but this is a great, grotty spot to catch rockin' live sets from the likes of Thurston Moore, Mudhoney and the Vivian Girls. Don't let the name fool you; this hotel hosts all kinds of music genres from Afrofunk to the city's freshest hip-hop acts, with rock 'n' roll, indie, punk and metal, too.

HR-57 JAZZ

(Map p324; www.hr57.org; 816 H St NE; ⏲from 8pm Wed & Thu, from 9pm Fri & Sat; tickets $8-15; Ⓜ Union Station) Named after the Congressional bill that designated jazz 'a rare and valuable national treasure,' HR-57 is a preservation hall for the genre. The atmospheric little club hosts open jam sessions on Wednesday and Thursday nights, and snappy bands Friday and Saturday. There's a bar, but you're welcome to bring your own wine for a $3 corkage fee. The club also fries up chicken, greens and a smattering of other soul-food dishes.

ARENA STAGE THEATER

(Map p324; www.arenastage.org; 1101 6th St SW; tickets from $35; Ⓜ Waterfront-SEU) Fresh from a mod, glassy revamp in 2010, the striking Arena Stage is now the second-largest performing arts complex in Washington after the Kennedy Center. The three theaters inside (including a theater-in-the-round) are top venues for traditional and experimental theatrical works, especially American classics, premieres of new plays and contemporary stories. Arena Stage was the city's first racially integrated theater and has continued its progressive tradition through performances addressing African American history.

FOLGER SHAKESPEARE LIBRARY & THEATRE THEATER

(Map p324; www.folger.edu; 210 E Capitol St SE; tickets from $30; Ⓜ Capitol South) The magnificent Globe-style theater attached to the Folger Shakespeare Library stages classic and modern interpretations of Shakespeare plays. Exhibitions, poetry readings and great programs for children are all part of the repertoire at this venue, in addition to world-class Shakespearean theater.

ROSE'S DREAM BAR & LOUNGE CLUB

(Map p324; ☎202-398-5700; 1370 H St NE; 🚌X8 from Union Station) Go-go, the DC style of local music that's a cross between funk and an improvised drum line, occasionally dusted with a bit of hip-hop, has been a fading genre in the District. But Rose's keeps the beat alive. It's one of the few go-go clubs left where an out-of-towner won't feel like they're interloping in someone else's territory. Coming here is a DC cultural experience – go-go really is the city's own brand of music – but beyond that, Rose's is plenty fun, with good bartenders working the line, and karaoke, dance nights and live shows blowing up the house for the better part of the week.

ATLAS PERFORMING ARTS CENTER THEATER

(Map p324; www.atlasarts.org; 1333 H St NE; tickets $5-25; 🚌X8 from Union Station) The art-deco Atlas theater is the backbone of the H St NE revival. All kinds of indie goodness gets performed here, from operettas to contemporary classics and innovative new works to chamber music.

FREE **MARY PICKFORD THEATER** CINEMA

(Map p324; ☎202-707-5677; 101 Independence Ave SE, 3rd fl, Madison Bldg; ⊙call for schedule; Ⓜ Capitol South) This theater at the Library of Congress screens films on historical or cultural themes, relevant to current events. Seating is limited to only 64 people, but reservations can be made by telephone up to one week in advance. Call for the schedule.

LOCAL KNOWLEDGE

LIBRARY OF CONGRESS FREEBIES

In addition to the Mary Pickford Theater's films, the Library of Congress (p133) offers free lectures, concerts and other events throughout its multi-building complex each day. Famous actors, Nobel laureates and world musicians pepper the schedule. Check www.loc.gov/loc/events.

SHOPPING

HUNTED HOUSE HOMEWARES

(Map p324; ☎202-549-7493; www.huntedhousedc.com; 510 H St NE; ⊙1-7pm Thu, 11am-6pm Fri-Sun; Ⓜ Union Station) Every piece of vintage furniture stuffing this walk-up, laid out to resemble a functioning (quite attractive) apartment, is a gem of the deco or modernism design movement. We could spend hours staring at the Jetsonsesque TV in the sitting room, which is sadly never for sale. Open Tuesday by appointment.

EASTERN MARKET MARKET

(Map p324; www.easternmarket-dc.org; 225 7th St SE; ⊙7am-7pm Tue-Fri, to 6pm Sat, 9am-5pm Sun; Ⓜ Eastern Market) Eastern Market's South Hall is the closest DC gets to foodie heaven. In its friendly confines are a bakery, dairy, fish counter, poultry counter, butcher, flower stalls, and a beautiful selection of fruits and vegetables (including organic items). You can put together a real Southern feast here – the Southern Maryland Seafood Company serves up the blue crabs and shrimp, and there's also a stand selling cooked food.

On weekends, both the artists and the farmers markets spill out onto the sidewalks. Besides fresh produce, you can pick up scarves, prints, handmade soaps and candles, colorful pottery, painted ceramics, art prints and unusual jewelry. Across the street at the weekend **flea market** (www.easternmarket.net; 7th & C Sts SE; ⊙9am-5pm Sun), you'll find yet more crafty items, plus a handful of antique vendors.

BACKSTAGE CLOTHING

(Map p324; www.backstagecostumes.com; 545 8th St SE; ⊙closed Sun; Ⓜ Eastern Market) This

PRESIDENTIAL PHOTO OP

There's no better keepsake photo than one where you're surrounded by the Washington Nationals' Racing Presidents while at the ballpark. After George, Abe, Tom and Teddy race in the middle of the fourth inning, they hang out in the CF Picnic area until the end of the fifth inning to take pictures with fans. Just do it.

costume store caters to both the drag crowd and government types in search of unusual attire for masquerade parties. It rents outfits, and you can buy funky face paints, wigs and masks – including those creepy rubber presidential masks (covering every president from Nixon to Obama).

WOVEN HISTORY ARTS & CRAFTS
(Map p324; www.wovenhistory.com; 315 7th St SE; 10am-6pm Tue-Sun; Eastern Market) It's like a Silk Road caravan got lost and pitched up near the Eastern Market. This lovely emporium is stuffed with crafts, carpets and tapestries from across Central Asia, Tibet and Mongolia. Unlike a lot of stores of this genre, this feels more like an authentic tented bazaar than a hippie hangout.

HOMEBODY HOMEWARES
(Map p324; www.homebodydc.com; 715 8th St SE; closed Mon; Eastern Market) A good stop on your way to or from Eastern Market is the fun and colorful Homebody. Here you'll encounter a range of eye-catching gift ideas, including painted candelabras, decorative wall clocks, painted drinking glasses, graphic dinner plates and windup robot insects.

UNION STATION MALL
(Map p324; www.unionstationdc.com; 50 Massachusetts Ave NE; Union Station) Not only an architectural landmark and a train depot, Union Station is also a good-sized mall, complete with food court, restaurants and dozens of shops. The options are fairly run of the mill, though the East Hall has unique vendors, including **Appalachian Spring** (www.appalachianspring.com), with its arts and crafts. For more on Union Station, see p136.

SPORTS & ACTIVITIES

BIKE & ROLL BIKING
(Map p324; 202-962-0206; www.bikethesites.com; Union Station, 50 Massachusetts Ave NE; bikes per hr/day from $6/30; year-round; Union Station) Rent a bike to explore the city; the rental price includes safety equipment. The company has branches downtown at the Old Post Office Pavilion and in Alexandria, VA; you can drop off your bike at these other locations for a $5 surcharge if you don't want to pedal back here.

WASHINGTON NATIONALS BASEBALL
(Map p324; www.nationals.com; 1500 S Capitol St SE; Navy Yard) DC's Major League Baseball team (the Washington Nationals) bats at Nationals Park. Games include the 'running of the president' – an odd, middle-of-the-fourth-inning race between caricatures of George Washington, Abraham Lincoln, Thomas Jefferson and Teddy Roosevelt. It's good fun, more so in the rare event the Nationals win. Grandstand seats start at $5; infield boxes go for around $70.

WASHINGTON REDSKINS FOOTBALL
(301-276-6800; www.redskins.com; 1600 Fedex Way, Landover, MD; tickets from $60) Washington's NFL team, the Redskins, play September through January at FedEx Field, but rare is the opportunity to actually see them play here. There is a miles-long waiting list to buy season tickets, so there are never tickets left for individual games. The only exception is when some are returned to the box office by the opposing team, which you can find out about by calling the stadium two or

BIKING EAST POTOMAC PARK

East Potomac Park (p138) makes a fine biking destination. Ohio Dr starts at the Tidal Basin and circumnavigates the peninsula that contains the park. A wide, paved sidewalk runs parallel for cyclists who are not at ease sharing the road with cars. The 5-mile loop runs along the Washington Channel on one side and the Potomac River on the other. It's easy, breezy and pleasing.

three days before the game. If you have your heart set on seeing the 'Skins in person, online agents such as **Tickets-Redskins** (www.tickets-redskins.com) will be pleased to sell you tickets with a hefty markup.

Drive to FedEx Field by taking the Central Ave exit from I-495, or walk to the field from Morgan Blvd Metro station (1 mile). Or just watch the game in a local bar – everyone else in the city will be doing it.

DC UNITED SOCCER

(off Map p324; www.dcunited.com; 2400 East Capitol St; Ⓜ Stadium-Armory) Multiple-time Major League Soccer champions DC United play March through October at RFK Stadium. Tickets start at around $20.

EAST POTOMAC PARK GOLF COURSE GOLF

(Map p324; www.golfdc.com; Ohio Dr SW; 18 holes weekday/weekend $27/31, 9 holes from $10/13; dawn-dusk; Ⓜ Smithsonian) It's a bit scrubby, with three courses.

LANGSTON GOLF COURSE GOLF

(off Map p324; www.golfdc.com; 26th St NE & Benning Rd NE; 18 holes weekday/weekend $24/30, 9 holes $17/22; dawn-dusk; X1, X2 or X3 from Union Station) The fairways are flat, with lots of trees on the back nine.

Downtown & Penn Quarter

PENN QUARTER | JUDICIARY SQUARE | CHINATOWN & THE CONVENTION CENTER

Neighborhood Top Five

❶ Gawp at the Declaration of Independence, Constitution and Bill of Rights – the real, live, yellowing, spidery-handwriting-scrawled documents themselves – at the **National Archives** (p153).

❷ Browse the world's largest collection of US art at the **Reynolds Center for American Art** (p154).

❸ See the very seat where Abraham Lincoln was assassinated at **Ford's Theatre** (p155).

❹ Read the day's newspapers from around the globe and learn the journalist lifestyle at the **Newseum** (p155).

❺ Identify disguises, listen to bugs and spot hidden cameras at the **International Spy Museum** (p155).

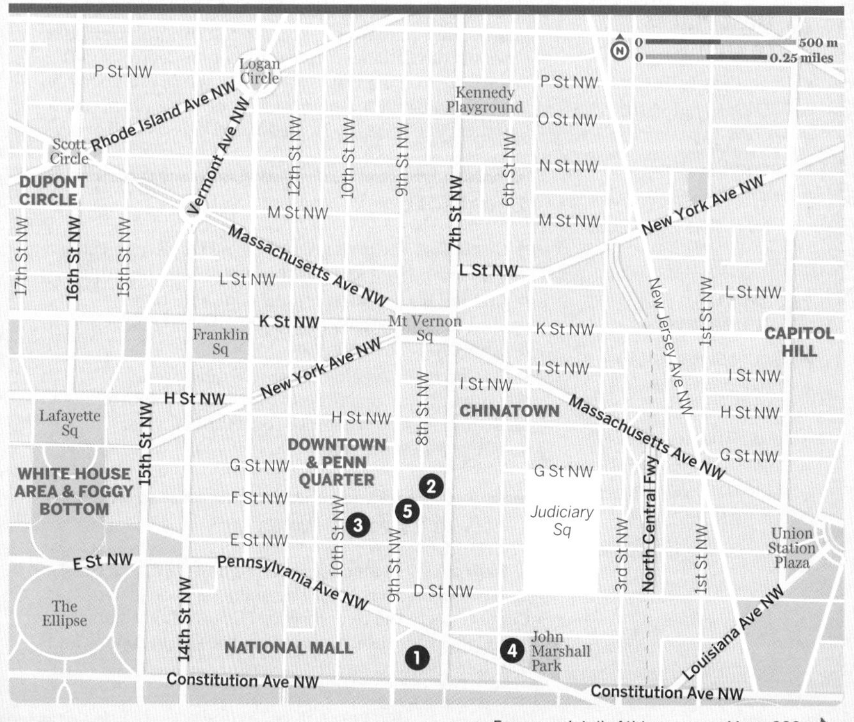

For more detail of this area, see Map p326 ➡

Lonely Planet's Top Tip

Many restaurants in the neighborhood offer pre- and post-theater menus. This generally means a three-course meal for around $30, offered before 7pm or after 9:30pm. Our favorite is Bistro D'Oc ($25, including a glass of wine). Jaleo, Rasika, Zola and Poste are among the others that offer theater menus.

Best Places to Eat

- Birch & Barley (p158)
- Matchbox Pizza (p158)
- Minibar (p159)
- Rasika (p159)
- Teaism (p159)

For reviews, see p158

Best Places to Drink

- Churchkey (p161)
- RFD Washington (p161)
- Poste (p161)
- Rocket Bar (p161)
- Green Lantern (p162)

For reviews, see p161

Best Theaters

- Capitol Steps (p162)
- Shakespeare Theatre (p162)
- Ford's Theatre (p162)
- Studio Theatre (p162)
- Woolly Mammoth Theatre Company (p162)

For reviews, see p162

Explore Downtown & Penn Quarter

Washington's downtown is less conventional city center and more of a gussied-up transition space between the National Mall and Washington's residential communities. The neighborhood both emerges from and is attached to Penn Quarter, a corridor formed by the line Pennsylvania Ave creates between the White House and the Capitol. There are the usual chain stores and bright lights, but the area revolves around the enormous, gaudy Verizon Center, home of DC's professional basketball and hockey teams, and some of the city's best museums.

We're talking about the National Archives, where the Declaration of Independence lies enshrined for viewing; the Reynolds Center for American Art, filled with famed portraits and a who's who of big-name artists' works; Ford's Theatre, where John Wilkes Booth shot Abraham Lincoln; the International Spy Museum, revealing sneaky tricks of the trade; and the Newseum, a whiz-bang, multistory collection of artifacts and current-events exhibits. You'll need a few days to do them all justice.

Downtown is also the theater district. The Capitol Steps do their political shtick. Shakespeare Theatre puts on well-regarded productions of the bard's plays (including a free summer series). Studio Theatre and Woolly Mammoth Theatre Company stage contemporary and experimental works.

In case you hadn't figured it out, the neighborhood bustles day and night. Trendy restaurants and bars cater to conventioneers (the Convention Center is in the 'hood), theatergoers and sports fans. While this good life tends to come with a not-so-lovely price tag, there are a few cheap surprises to be discovered here as well.

Local Life

- **Circle & P** The area around Logan Circle, especially along P St, is a hot spot for restaurants and nightlife.
- **Cheesy** It's crowded at lunchtime with office workers, because Cowgirl Creamery (p163) makes a helluva good sandwich.
- **Oasis** Locals seeking peace and quiet from downtown's hullabaloo head to the American Art Museum's first floor interior courtyard of trees, gurgling water and free wi-fi.

Getting There & Away

- **Metro** All five Metro lines cross downtown, so there are several stations here. The main ones are Metro Center (where the Red, Blue and Orange Lines hub), and Gallery Pl-Chinatown (where the Green, Yellow and Red Lines merge).

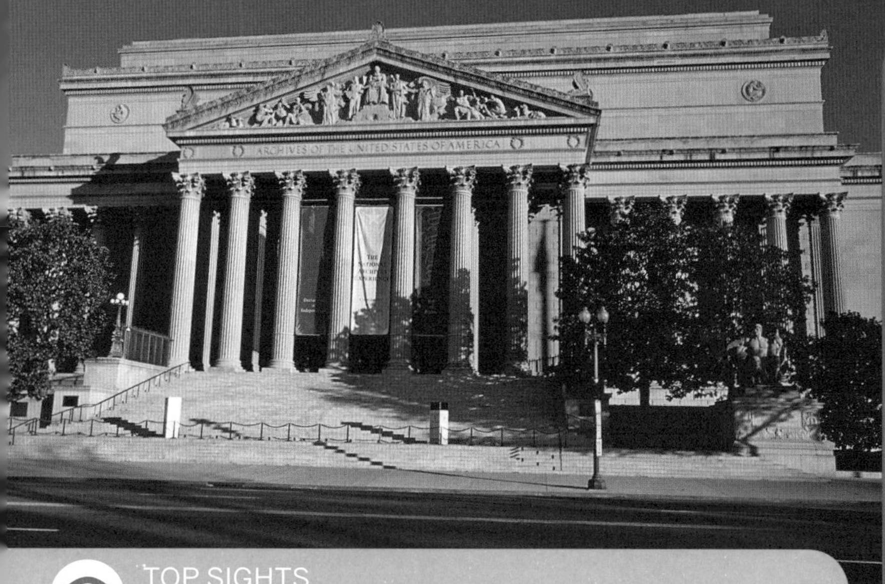

TOP SIGHTS
NATIONAL ARCHIVES

DAN HERRICK / LONELY PLANET IMAGES ©

The importance of the archives, or more specifically what is contained within them, cannot be overstated. Herein lies the Constitution, the Declaration of Independence and the Bill of Rights. If the USA has a mission statement, it's here. Seeing these documents in person is one of those DC experiences that gets even hard-bitten locals to whisper 'Wow.'

The documents are contained in a dimly lit rotunda within the grand neoclassical building. Just before you reach the Big Three, you'll see a 1297 version of the Magna Carta. Don't expect to linger over any of the documents – guards make you keep moving. Editors in the group can try to spot the error in the Constitution (hint: look at the list of signatories, at the word that starts with 'p' and ends with 'sylvania').

After the rotunda, head over to the Public Vaults on the same floor. Here you can browse a 1792 letter from George Washington in which he declines an artist's request to paint him because he's 'heartily tired of irksome sitting.' View hand-scrawled Congressional acts from 1790 about taxation and debt reduction. There's a nifty piece of paperwork from Charles 'Pa' Ingalls (of *Little House on the Prairie* fame) showing his grant application for 154 acres in the Dakota Territory under the 1862 Homestead Act. You can also watch vintage D-Day reels.

In spring and summer, it's best to reserve tickets in advance at the website for $1.50 each. This lets you go through the fast-track entrance on Constitution Dr (to the right of the steps) versus the general entrance (to the left of the steps).

DON'T MISS...

- Declaration of Independence
- Constitution
- Bill of Rights
- Magna Carta
- Pa Ingalls' land grant

PRACTICALITIES

- Map p326
- ☎866-272-6272
- www.archives.gov
- 700 Pennsylvania Ave NW
- admission free
- 🕒10am-5:30pm Sep–mid-Mar, to 7pm mid-Mar–Aug
- Ⓜ Archives-Navy Memorial

TOP SIGHTS

REYNOLDS CENTER FOR AMERICAN ART

If you only visit one art museum in Washington, DC, make it the Reynolds Center for American Art, which combines the National Portrait Gallery with the American Art Museum.

There is, simply put, no better collection of American art in the world than at these two Smithsonian museums. Both occupy three floors in the 19th-century US Patent Office building, a neoclassical quadrangle that hosted Lincoln's second inaugural ball and a Civil War hospital. Walt Whitman based *The Wound-Dresser* upon his experiences as a volunteer nurse here ('The hurt and wounded I pacify with soothing hand/I sit by the restless all the dark night…').

Winslow Homer, John Singer Sargent, Andy Warhol, Roy Lichtenstein and loads more celebrated artists fill the galleries. Highlights on the 1st floor include Georgia O'Keeffe's flowery pink *Manhattan* and Edward Hopper's trapped woman in *Cape Cod Morning* on the American Art side, and *Benjamin Franklin* (the same image that graces the $100 bill) on the Portrait side. Gilbert Stuart's *George Washington* is a must on the 2nd Floor Portrait side. The top floor is one of the most impressive spaces in the city. Be sure to hit the Luce Center up here – an open storage area stuffed with 3500 paintings, sculptures, miniatures and folk art pieces. The Luce information kiosk provides free audio tours.

The museum's other bit of awesomeness is the 1st-floor interior courtyard with trees and peaceful fountains, a cafe and wi-fi. Free jazz concerts fill the space the third Thursday of each month.

DON'T MISS...

- Luce Center
- Gilbert Stuart's *George Washington*
- Joseph Siffred Duplessis' *Benjamin Franklin*
- Edward Hopper's *Cape Cod Morning*
- Georgia O'Keeffe's *Manhattan*

PRACTICALITIES

- Map p326
- ☎202-275-1500
- www.americanart.si.edu, www.npg.si.edu
- cnr 8th & F Sts NW
- admission free
- ⌚11:30am-7pm
- Ⓜ Gallery Pl-Chinatown

SIGHTS

Penn Quarter

NATIONAL ARCHIVES LANDMARK

See p153.

REYNOLDS CENTER FOR AMERICAN ART MUSEUM

See p154.

INTERNATIONAL SPY MUSEUM MUSEUM

(Map p326; ☎202-393-7798; www.spymuseum.org; 800 F St NW; adult/child $20/14; ⏱10am-8pm Apr-Oct, to 6pm Nov-Mar; Ⓜ Gallery Pl-Chinatown; 👪) One of DC's most popular museums is flashy, over the top, and probably guilty of overtly glamming up a life of intelligence gathering. But who cares? You basically want to see Q's lab, and that's what a trip to the International Spy Museum feels like. Kids go crazy for this spot, but be warned: lines form long and early. You can ease the wait somewhat by reserving tickets online (per ticket surcharge of $2).

There are all kinds of artifacts, anecdotes and interactive displays on the inside, and guests are invited to play the role of a secret agent by adopting a cover at the start of their visit. Throughout the museum, you can try to identify disguises, listen to bugs and spot hidden cameras. A lot of the exhibit is historical in nature, focusing on the Cold War in particular (a re-creation of the tunnel under the Berlin Wall is an eerie winner).

The museum also offers several tours. 'Spy in the City' ($15) is a sort of GPS-driven scavenger hunt across DC with an attached plotline that Jack Bauer from *24* would appreciate. 'Spy at Night' ($20) takes place the second Friday of each month, when the museum stays open late and serves alcohol. The two-hour 'Spy City Tour' ($59) takes in 25 skullduggery-associated sites across the city via bus; there's an interactive mission component to this tour as well. All of the above are great fun, and can be booked through the museum's website.

NEWSEUM MUSEUM

(Map p326; www.newseum.org; 555 Pennsylvania Ave NW; adult/child $22/13; ⏱9am-5pm; Ⓜ Archives-Navy Memorial, Judiciary Sq; 👪) Unaffiliated with the Smithsonian (ergo the cost of admission), the 'most interactive museum in the world' is dedicated to the craft of news gathering and dissemination. There's a ton to see here, and it's spread out over six levels.

The concourse level displays FBI artifacts from prominent news stories, such as the Unabomber's cabin and John Dillinger's death mask. Level 3 holds a memorial to journalists killed in pursuit of the truth. If you're visiting on Sunday morning, keep an eye out for George Stephanopoulos, who tapes *This Week* in TV Studio A on Level 3. Level 4 has twisted wreckage from the September 11, 2001, attacks and haunting final images from Bill Biggart's camera (Biggart was the only journalist to be killed that day). Level 6 offers a terrace with awesome views of Pennsylvania Ave up to the Capitol. It's also worth your time to wander in front of the Newseum, where the front pages of newspapers from around the world are displayed every day.

Tickets are usable for two consecutive days, so you don't have to view everything at once. Ask for the '2-Hour Highlights Tour' brochure at the front desk. Buying tickets online nets a 10% discount.

FREE **FORD'S THEATRE** HISTORIC SITE

(Map p326; ☎202-426-6924; www.nps.gov/foth, www.fords.org; 511 10th St NW; ⏱9am-4:30pm; Ⓜ Metro Center, Gallery Pl-Chinatown) On April 14, 1865, John Wilkes Booth, actor and Confederate sympathizer, assassinated Abraham Lincoln, as the president and Mrs Lincoln watched *Our American Cousin* in the Presidential Box of Ford's Theatre. The box remains draped with a period flag to this day.

The theater is open during the day to visitors (except during rehearsals or matinee performances), but you'll need to get a (free) ticket with timed entry from the theater box office (open from 8:30am). It's a good idea to reserve tickets in advance in spring and summer; there's a $2.50 per ticket surcharge to do it in person, and a few dollars more to reserve via **Ticketmaster** (☎202-397-7328; www.ticketmaster.com). It's *always* smart to check the theater's closure schedule before heading out; Ford's posts it online, or you can call the box office.

The ticket also provides entry to the **Lincoln Museum** in the basement, which maps out the assassination's details and displays related artifacts. You'll see the .44 caliber pistol Booth used to kill Lincoln, the muddy boot Dr Mudd had to cut through to treat

Booth's leg, Mrs Lincoln's opera glasses and much more.

FREE PETERSEN HOUSE HISTORIC SITE

(Map p326; www.nps.gov/foth, www.fords.org; 516 10th St NW; 9:30am-5:30pm; Metro Center, Gallery Pl-Chinatown) After being shot at Ford's Theatre, the unconscious president was carried across the street to die at Petersen House. Its tiny, unassuming rooms create a moving personal portrait of the president's slow and tragic death. You'll need a ticket to enter; these are given in conjunction with the Ford's Theatre tickets at the box office there. Another assassination-related site is nearby: Surratt House, now the restaurant **Wok & Roll** (604 H St NW), is where the Lincoln-assassination conspirators met in 1865. Its owner, Confederate spy Mary Surratt, was eventually hanged at Fort McNair.

FREE FORD'S THEATRE CENTER EDUCATIONAL CENTER

(Map p326; www.fords.org; 514 10th St NW; 9am-5pm; Metro Center, Gallery Pl-Chinatown) It's hard to miss this new addition to the Ford's complex: a giant Abe peers out from a glass window, and a 34ft stack of Lincoln books (they're actually an aluminum sculpture) rises in the window. The focus here is not on Lincoln's death – as at the theater itself and at next-door Petersen House – but on Lincoln's legacy: how and why he became an icon. Exhibits on the 3rd and 4th floors show the assassination's aftermath and how presidents across the spectrum have sought to evoke Abe's spirit. The 2nd floor has classrooms and lecture halls. The 1st floor holds the Lincoln-stuffed gift shop.

LOCAL KNOWLEDGE

THE FBI

If you're just dying to make your eyes bleed, why not take a gander at the headquarters of the **Federal Bureau of Investigation** (10th St & Pennsylvania Ave). This concrete, brutalist affront to all that is good and holy should be seen, if only to say you have laid eyes on – and we're not kidding – the single ugliest building in the entire District.

NATIONAL MUSEUM OF WOMEN IN THE ARTS MUSEUM

(Map p326; www.nmwa.org; 1250 New York Ave NW; adult/child $10/free; 10am-5pm Mon-Sat, from noon Sun; Metro Center) The only US museum exclusively devoted to women's artwork resides in this Renaissance-Revival mansion. Its collection – 2600 works by almost 700 female artists from 28 countries – moves from Renaissance artists such as Lavinia Fontana to 20th-century works by Kahlo, O'Keeffe and Frankenthaler. The bulk of the permanent collection, from the 19th and 20th centuries, hangs on the 3rd floor. Special exhibits take up the 2nd floor; these are incredibly varied, ranging from Maria Sibylla Merian's natural history engravings to Native American pottery. Placards giving feminist interpretations of various art movements accompany the works. The museum is free the first Sunday of each month.

FREE NAVY MEMORIAL & NAVAL HERITAGE CENTER MONUMENT

(Map p326; www.navymemorial.org; 701 Pennsylvania Ave NW; memorial 24hr, center 9:30am-5pm; Archives-Navy Memorial) The hunched figure of the *Lone Sailor,* warding off the wind with his flipped-up pea coat, waiting quietly by his duffel, is our favorite service (rather than war) memorial in the city. No other work of art quite captures the quiet strength that drives enlisted personnel on and brings them home after years away. The sailor waits in a circular plaza bordered by masts sporting semaphore flags; the space is meant to evoke both the vastness and ubiquity of the sea. The Naval Heritage Center, on the same grounds, displays artifacts and a couple of ship models.

FREE MARTIN LUTHER KING JR MEMORIAL LIBRARY LIBRARY

(Map p326; www.dclibrary.org; 901 G St NW; 9:30am-9pm Mon & Tue, to 5:30pm Wed-Sat; Metro Center; @) Designed by Mies van der Rohe, this low-slung, sleek central branch of the DC public library system is as warm and fuzzy as a goodnight story on the inside, especially the colorful mural portraying the Civil Rights movement. This is an important community and cultural center, sponsoring readings, concerts, films and children's activities. You can also access the internet here.

FREE **OLD POST OFFICE PAVILION** LOOKOUT

(Map p326; www.oldpostofficedc.com; 1100 Pennsylvania Ave NW; ⊙10am-8pm Mon-Sat, to 7pm Sun; Ⓜ Federal Triangle) The landmark 1899 Old Post Office Pavilion – nicknamed 'Old Tooth' for its spiky clock tower – is a downtown success story. Threatened with demolition during much of the 20th century, the Romanesque building was restored in 1978 and became a key Penn Quarter attraction. Its beautiful, bunting-draped, 10-story central atrium holds shops, a large (and pretty good, as these things go) food court and government agencies. The Park Service operates a glass elevator that takes visitors to the 270ft-high **observation deck** for a broad view of downtown and close-up look at the carillon bells. If the Washington Monument is still closed when you visit, the Old Post Office provides the next best panorama. Everything closes a few hours earlier from September through May.

Judiciary Square

NATIONAL BUILDING MUSEUM MUSEUM

(Map p326; www.nbm.org; 401 F St NW; adult/child $8/5; ⊙10am-5pm Mon-Sat, from 11am Sun; Ⓜ Judiciary Sq; 👪) Devoted to the architectural arts, this museum is appropriately housed in an architectural jewel: the 1887 Old Pension Building. Four stories of ornamented balconies flank the dramatic 316ft-wide atrium, and the Corinthian columns are among the largest in the world, rising 75ft high. An inventive system of windows and archways keeps the so-called Great Hall constantly glimmering in natural light, and this space has hosted 17 inaugural balls – from Grover Cleveland's in 1885 to Barack Obama's in 2009.

It is free to enter the building and look around. Pick up a self-guided tour brochure at the information desk, or join a free 45-minute docent-led **tour** (⊙11:30am, 12:30pm and 1:30pm daily). There's also a nice cafe and nifty bookstore inside.

The admission fee is only for the exhibits, which are great if you're an architecture buff. 'Washington: City and Symbol' examines the deeper symbolism of DC architecture; other exhibits rotate. Kids get their own hands-on displays, such as the past 'LEGO Architecture.' Check the website for a schedule of concerts and family programs.

NATIONAL LAW ENFORCEMENT OFFICERS MEMORIAL MONUMENT

(Map p326; www.nleomf.com; E St btwn 4th & 5th Sts NW; ⊙24hr; Ⓜ Judiciary Sq) The memorial on Judiciary Sq commemorates US police officers killed on duty since 1794. In the style of the Vietnam Veterans Memorial, names of the dead are carved on two marble walls curving around a plaza; new names are added during a moving candlelight vigil each year in May. Peeking over the walls, bronze lion statues protect their sleeping cubs (presumably as law enforcement officers protect us).

The nearby **visitor center** (400 7th St NW; ☎9am-5pm Mon-Fri, from 10am Sat, from noon Sun) houses a small shop and a couple of exhibits about the memorial's history and the law enforcement officers it honors. The group has broken ground on the National Law Enforcement Museum, which will open across from the memorial in 2013 or 2014.

HISTORICAL SOCIETY OF WASHINGTON, DC MUSEUM

(Map p326; www.historydc.org; 800 Mount Vernon Sq; Ⓜ Mt Vernon Sq/7th St-Convention Center, Gallery Pl-Chinatown) As of mid-2012, the Historical Society was closed until further notice. Keep an eye on it though. Plans are to re-open, and if it does, it's a great place to learn about DC as a living, breathing city of neighborhoods, immigrants and working lives outside of the Federal scene. The extensive library of books, photographs, maps and other archives is a treasure. Staff are a trove of knowledge and opinions on the current state of DC. It's located in the Carnegie Library building at Mount Vernon Sq.

Chinatown & the Convention Center

FREE **NATIONAL PUBLIC RADIO** BUILDING

(Map p326; www.npr.org; 635 Massachusetts Ave NW; ⊙tours 11am Tue & Thu; Ⓜ Mt Vernon Sq/7th St-Convention Center) If, like us, you cannot complete the day without *Morning Edition, All Things Considered* and *This American Life,* may we direct you to the wedge-like headquarters of NPR, the best thing to happen to radio since...nah, pretty much ever. Tours include strolls past the foreign and national desks and a peek into the organization's satellite control room. Just show up; no reservations required. If you can't make the tour, you can still pop in during business hours and pick up free postcards, buttons, stickers and other marketing swag by the front desk.

CHINATOWN NEIGHBORHOOD

(Map p326; 7th & H Sts NW; MGallery Pl-Chinatown) Most visitors to DC's dinky Chinatown are surprised they didn't trip over it. Anchored on H and 7th Sts NW, this was once a major Asian entrepôt, but today most Asians in the Washington area live in the Maryland/Virginia 'burbs. However small she may be, Chinatown is still entered through **Friendship Arch**, the largest single-span arch in the world – local wags say the structure should be renamed the 'Starbucks-Fuddruckers Gateway' seeing as both chains now flank Chinatown's entrance. This used to be an infamous boozer strip, now scrubbed and shiny thanks to the nearby Verizon Center, but if you miss the old 'hood you can still buy a bottle of Mad Dog for under $3 at **Chinatown Market** (cnr H St & 6th St NW).

VERIZON CENTER STADIUM

(Map p326; www.verizoncenter.com; 601 F St NW; MGallery Pl-Chinatown) When the $200 million, 20,000ft-high stadium opened in 1997, the streets surrounding it were, to put it lightly, a bit gritty. Families definitely didn't wander out this way. All that changed within a few months of the stadium opening – sports bars, shops and restaurants bloomed like neon flowers, luxury condominiums replaced old tenements and all of a sudden the most dangerous thing on the block was bad traffic and rude teenagers. The NBA's Washington Wizards and NHL's Capitals both call the center their home turf (see p164). The spot also hosts major concerts, and even when there are no events, it functions as a ghastly shopping mall.

FREE **BETHUNE COUNCIL HOUSE** HISTORIC SITE

(Map p326; www.nps.gov/mamc; 1318 Vermont Ave NW; 9am-4pm; MMcPherson Sq) Mary McLeod Bethune, founder of the Daytona Educational and Industrial School for Negro Girls, served as President Franklin Roosevelt's special advisor on minority affairs. In Washington, DC, she rose through the political ranks to become the first African American woman to head a federal office. Her Vermont Ave home, where she lived for seven years, has been transformed into an archive, research center and small museum administered by the National Park Service. Rangers lead tours and show videotapes about Bethune's life, and exhibits, lectures and workshops on black history are held here as well.

EATING

Restaurants are thick on the ground along 7th and 8th Sts NW as well as H St NW in Chinatown.

TOP CHOICE **BIRCH & BARLEY** AMERICAN $$

(Map p326; 202-567-2576; www.birchandbarley.com; 1337 14th St NW; mains $16-27; dinner Tue-Sun, brunch Sun; MDupont Circle) Birch & Barley shimmers a coppery glow in Logan Circle. It's partially from candlelight, but also from the wall of organesque pipes in the back that transport 50 draught beers to the taps. The menu of nouveau comfort foods pleases the belly with housemade pastas and the crowd-favorite brat burger. Sunday's 'boozy brunch' (prix fixe $30) pulls crowds for the donut appetizer (toffee-bacon and lemon-poppy-glazed), entree, bottomless cups of coffee and two mind-altering cocktails. The upstairs bar is Churchkey (see p161).

MATCHBOX PIZZA PIZZA $$

(Map p326; 202-289-4441; www.matchboxdc.com; 713 H St NW; pizzas $12-14, mains $14-28; lunch & dinner; MGallery Pl-Chinatown) Lines stretch round the block, the buzz is deafening and happy, the smells lead you in like a lost, cheesy lover: welcome to one of the

LOCAL KNOWLEDGE

CHEAP EATS

For a quick bite, Downtown offers a couple of food courts popular with office workers. One is inside the **Old Post Office Pavilion** (www.oldpostofficedc.com; 1100 Pennsylvania Ave NW), which has Greek, Indian and Chinese fare among its stash. The other is the **Shops at National Place** (529 W 14th St NW), inside the National Press Club Building, where Five Guys wafts its burgery goodness.

most popular pizzerias in town. The pie here has rocketed into the DC gastronomic universe, and you can't come here now without finding Matchbox packed with the curious and the satisfied. What's so good about it? Fresh ingredients, a thin, blistered crust baked by angels and more fresh ingredients.

MINIBAR AMERICAN **$$$**

(Map p326; ☎202-393-0812; www.minibarbyjoseandres.com; 405 8th St NW; tasting menu $150; ⏲6pm & 8:30pm Tue-Sat; Ⓜ Archives-Navy Memorial) A wee restaurant within a restaurant, Minibar is foodie nirvana, where the lucky six (just six seats, folks) get wowed by animal bits spun into cotton candy and cocktails frothed into clouds. The tasting menu, entirely determined by chef Jose Andres, is often delicious and never dull. There's a sense of madcap experimentation among the 25 to 30 courses, as you'd expect from a molecular gastronomist like Andres. Reserve exactly one month in advance. Minibar is on the second floor of America Eats Tavern.

RASIKA INDIAN **$$**

(Map p326; ☎202-637-1222; www.rasikarestaurant.com; 633 D St NW; mains $17-26; ⏲lunch Mon-Fri, dinner daily; Ⓜ Archives-Navy Memorial; ✎) Rasika ('flavors,' in Sanskrit) is incredible, and likely the best Indian food in town. This ain't your average McMasala's. Rather, it's as cutting edge as Indian food gets, both in terms of menu and presentation. The latter resembles a Jaipur palace decorated by a flock of modernist art gallery curators; the former...well, it's *good*. Narangi duck is juicy, almost softly unctuous, but pleasantly nutty thanks to the addition of cashews; the deceptively simple dal (lentils) have the right kiss of sharp fenugreek. Vegans and vegetarians will feel a lot of love here.

TEAISM ASIAN **$**

(Map p326; www.teaism.com; 400 8th St NW; mains $6-11; ⏲breakfast, lunch & dinner; Ⓜ Archives-Navy Memorial) This teahouse is unique in the area for its very affordable lunch options – hot noodle dishes and fresh bento boxes – and its pleasantly relaxing atmosphere. It's a grand spot for a bite after a day of Mall sightseeing. The salty oat cookies are gorgeous. It has locations in Dupont Circle and Foggy Bottom as well.

PING PONG ASIAN **$$**

(Map p326; ☎202-506-3740; 900 7th St NW; pingpongdimsum.us; dim sum $5-7; ⏲11:30am-11pm Mon-Sat, 11am-10pm Sun; Ⓜ Gallery Pl-Chinatown) At Ping Pong, you can enjoy delectable dim sum any time. In fact, the stylish and open dining room gathers the liveliest crowds at night. The pan-Asian menu features delicate steamed dumplings, honey-roasted pork buns, seafood clay pots and other hits, plus tasty libations like plum wine and elderflower *saketini* (sake-based cocktail).

JALEO SPANISH **$$**

(Map p326; ☎202-628-7949; www.jaleo.com; 480 7th St NW; tapas $7-15; Ⓜ Archives-Navy Memorial) The whole tapas thing has been done to death, but Jaleo helped start the trend in DC and it still serves some of the best Spanish cuisine in town. The interior is an Iberian pastiche of explosive color and vintage mural-dom, which all underlines, rather than overpowers, the quality of the excellent food. Opt for the tapas over the main dishes, which are a bit overpriced. Garlicky shrimps, beet salad with pistachios and housemade pork sausage with white beans are favorites.

CAFE MOZART GERMAN **$$**

(Map p326; ☎202-347-5732; www.cafemozartonline.com; 1331 H St NW; mains $16-27; ⏲breakfast, lunch & dinner; Ⓜ Metro Center) Germans don't get enough credit for their food. Sure, a lot of it is meat and potatoes, but let's not forget it's often very good meat and potatoes. This rather excellent German grocery store has a nice restaurant in the back that serves great sauerkraut, spaetzle and schnitzel; hell, they'll probably do you up a *currywurst* (pork sausage with curry ketchup) if you ask nice. Best of all, they host (wait for it) accordion concerts on Tuesdays, Wednesdays and Sundays, and classical piano concerts on Sundays; they all start at 6pm. *Das ist* awesome!

ACADIANA SOUTHERN **$$**

(Map p326; ☎202-408-8848; www.acadianarestaurant.com; 901 New York Ave NW; mains $24-29; ⏲lunch Mon-Fri, dinner daily, brunch Sun; Ⓜ Gallery Pl-Chinatown, Metro Center) Louisiana probably has the best homegrown culinary tradition in the USA, and all over the country different chefs try to capture the richness of our greatest gift to regional cooking. Acadiana is the DC effort, and it's a good one. This is rich, heart-attack stuff, so come prepared for duck glazed in pepper jelly, sweet watermelon salad set off by spicy pecans, and veal dunked in mushroom gravy set atop a hot bed of jalapeno grits. The interior is a bit sterile – not nearly colorful enough for a Louisiana restaurant – but the food makes up for this decor deficit.

VERANDA MEDITERRANEAN **$$**

(Map p326; ☎202-234-6870; www.verandaonp.com; 1100 P St NW; mains $16-21; ⏰dinner daily, brunch Sat & Sun; Ⓜ Mt Vernon Sq/7th St-Convention Center) This convivial little spot cooks up lamb shanks, butternut squash risotto, moussaka and other hearty Greek and Italian dishes for neighborhood folks who appreciate the good value. Tuesdays bring crowds for half-price bottles of wine. Dog owners can bring Fido to dinner on the outdoor patio.

POSTE FRENCH **$$$**

(Map p326; ☎202-783-6060; www.postebrasserie.com; Hotel Monaco, 555 8th St NW; mains $25-32; ⏰breakfast, lunch & dinner; Ⓜ Gallery Pl-Chinatown) Named for its previous incarnation as the mail sorting room for the city post office, Poste does the nouveau brasserie thing with style. Fork into top-notch beef Bourguignon, smoked trout rillettes, and roasted beet and goat cheese crepes, among other dishes, each with a subtle Southern spin. The outdoor courtyard is one of the best alfresco dining spaces in the city. Come evenings, the bar slings impressive cocktails. Poste gets green points by using vegetables and herbs from its organic garden, composting its food waste and offering a list of organic and local Virginia wines.

NANDO'S PERI-PERI FAST FOOD **$$**

(Map p326; www.nandosperiperi.com; 819 7th St NW; mains $9-14; ⏰lunch & dinner; Ⓜ Gallery Pl-Chinatown; 📶) South African chain Nando's is about hot-spiced, flame-grilled chicken. Peri peri, for the uninitiated, is a vinegary, chili-laden sauce in which they marinate the meat. Choose the spice level you want (it ranges from tongue-scorching to plain), order at the counter (including beer and wine), and staff brings the meal to your table. It's akin to fast food, but a winning step up. Check out the walls: they hang original artworks by South African artists.

FULL KEE CHINESE **$$**

(Map p326; www.fullkeedc.com; 509 H St NW; mains $10-20; ⏰11am-2am; Ⓜ Gallery Pl-Chinatown) Although you may find more atmosphere on the moon, you won't find a better Chinese dive in the city limits. Fill yourself for next to nothing with a simple noodle dish or stir-fry, but make sure you leave some room for the duck, which is divine stuff. Try it with some mambo sauce (DC's almost citrusy version of sweet and sour). Cash only.

ZOLA AMERICAN **$$**

(Map p326; ☎202-654-0999; www.zoladc.com; International Spy Museum, 800 F St NW; mains $22-28; ⏰lunch Mon-Fri, dinner daily; Ⓜ Gallery Pl-Chinatown) A subtle but playful theme of espionage runs through this hip restaurant, named for French author Émile Zola, who championed the case of Alfred Dreyfus when he was falsely accused of being a spy. Located inside the International Spy Museum, it's only appropriate that guests should be able to monitor the kitchen through discreet one-way mirrors in the booths, or slip off to the restroom through a hidden door. Black-and-white photographs and projections of coded text further add to the mysterious air in the restaurant. In the midst of this secrecy, Zola's cuisine is pretty straight up. Most dishes take comfort food and kick it up a notch, such as roasted chicken with curry aioli, *chia* seed gnocchi, and lobster mac and cheese.

PROOF AMERICAN **$$**

(Map p326; ☎202-737-7663; www.proofdc.com; 775 G St NW; small plates $9-14, mains $21-29; ⏰lunch Tue-Fri, dinner daily; Ⓜ Gallery Pl-Chinatown) Everything at this wine bar/small plates restaurant is excellent, but if you want to keep costs down and still eat well, opt for the excellent cheese and charcuterie dishes, which are likely the best compliments to the epic wine menu. The four-course $56 tasting menu is also a winner that gives you a good idea of what the kitchen is capable of. If you're in a group, try to mix and match off sexy small plates like cozy flatbread under creamy ricotta.

BISTRO D'OC FRENCH **$$**

(Map p326; ☎202-393-5444; www.bistrodoc.com; 518 10th St NW; mains $19-28; ⏰lunch Mon-Sat, dinner daily; Ⓜ Metro Center) D'Oc is widely acknowledged as Washington's best place to impress with old-school French cuisine.

LOCAL KNOWLEDGE

FARMERS MARKET

Chefs from neighborhood restaurants, such as Poste, shop at the **Penn Quarter Market** (Map p326; www.freshfarmmarket.org; 450 8th St NW; ⏱3-7pm Thu late-Mar–late-Dec; Ⓜ Gallery Pl-Chinatown, Archives-Navy Memorial), part of the Fresh Farm group that sources from the Chesapeake Bay region.

It's supremely cozy, more Languedoc basement than lobbyist banter-bar. Think rich cassoulet and heavenly cheese plates, then stop thinking and order them.

BURMA BURMESE $

(Map p326; ☎202-638-1280; 740 6th St NW; mains $9-11; ⏱11am-3pm & 6-10pm Mon-Fri, 6-10pm Sat & Sun; Ⓜ Gallery Pl-Chinatown) If you haven't had Burmese food (hell, even if you have), get ye to this walkup and order some *ohn no kauk swe,* a coconut milk chicken soup that drives off winter chills with its amassed armies of deliciousness. Dishes are not too spicy, and the setting is serene compared with the usual Chinatown chophouse.

RED VELVET CUPCAKERY BAKERY $

(Map p326; www.redvelvetcupcakery.com; 501 7th St NW; cupcakes from $3; ⏱9am-11pm Mon-Fri, 10am-11pm Sat & Sun; Ⓜ Gallery Pl-Chinatown, Metro Center) A lot of locals go nuts for this place, and we feel the need to say: calm down. It's just a cupcake. Yes, yes, a very good cupcake, but sheesh...anyways, you can't convince the converted. The titular pastry is well described by its name: soft, rich and all around decadent.

BUSBOYS & POETS AMERICAN $$

(Map p326; www.busboysandpoets.com; 1025 5th St NW; mains $8-14; ⏱8am-midnight Mon-Thu, to 1am Fri, 9am-1am Sat, 9am-midnight Sun; Ⓜ Gallery Pl-Chinatown; 📶) The artsy cafe that started life in the U Street Corridor has another outpost downtown. Same intellectual, multiracial, opinionated, creative vibe; same well-priced sandwiches, pizzas, coffee, beer, wine and other cafe fare; same open-mics and literary readings; but a calmer, dialed-down atmosphere and crowd that skews slightly older.

DRINKING & NIGHTLIFE

The areas around Penn Quarter, Chinatown and Logan Circle are good nightlife bets.

CHURCHKEY BAR

(Map p326; www.churchkeydc.com; 1337 14th St NW; ⏱from 4pm Mon-Fri, noon Sat & Sun; Ⓜ Dupont Circle) Churchkey is the upstairs counterpart to restaurant Birch & Barley (see p158) and glows with the same coppery, mod-industrial, loungey ambience. Fifty beers flow from the taps, including five brain-walloping, cask-aged ales. If none of those please you, another 450 types of brew are available by bottle. You can also order much of Birch & Barley's food menu up here.

RFD WASHINGTON BAR

(Map p326; www.lovethebeer.com; 810 7th St NW; ⏱from 11am; Ⓜ Gallery Pl-Chinatown) RFD – the initials stand for 'Real Food and Drink,' although the food is just greasy bar fare – has one of the most extensive beer menus in town. Compared with other bars of the 'hundreds of varieties' of booze genre, RFD has a slick, corporate feel, but the service is fast, it's rarely out of any one brand and the actual drinking space is huge; if you've got a large group, this is a good spot to hit up. If you're looking for a local draught, try DC Brau.

POSTE LOUNGE

(Map p326; www.postebrasserie.com; Hotel Monaco, 555 8th St NW; ⏱to 10pm; Ⓜ Gallery Pl-Chinatown) Located in the back of the Hotel Monaco, Poste is a fantastic spot for a strong cocktail and some eye candy. The bartenders take their trade seriously and they serve genuine absinthe, which is a sure method of getting yourself silly. The outdoor courtyard is an enormous, friendly space that's especially lovely on humid summer nights. In winter, heat lamps warm the area, and you can snuggle under the blankets draped over the couches.

ROCKET BAR BAR

(Map p326; www.rocketbardc.com; 714 7th St NW; ⏱from 4pm; Ⓜ Gallery Pl-Chinatown) Rocket Bar is an almost inexplicably popular pool hall, although there's lots more going on than some stick – shuffle board, Golden Tee, all the oldies and goodies. It's a good spot on the singles' circuit, especially if you're looking for a place to check out members of the opposite sex without all the pomp, circumstance and dressing up that comes with a night of clubbing.

GREEN LANTERN & TOOL SHED GAY

(Map p326; www.greenlanterndc.com; 1335 Green Ct NW; McPherson Sq) The gay Green Lantern is downstairs, with leather-lovers' Tool Shed on the 2nd floor. This place attracts a slightly older crowd, and there are all kinds of daily promotions – free beer for shirtless men Thursday nights (10pm to 11pm), Monday karaoke etc. The Lantern has a nice, long happy hour too – from 4pm till at least 9pm, sometimes till close. All in all there's a hairier, bear-ier crowd here, so if you like 'em young and waxed, stick to Dupont.

ENTERTAINMENT

TOP CHOICE **CAPITOL STEPS** COMEDY

(Map p326; www.capsteps.com; Ronald Reagan Bldg & International Trade Center Amphitheater; tickets $40.25; shows 7:30pm Fri & Sat; Federal Triangle) This troupe claims to be the only group in America that tries to be funnier than Congress. It's actually composed of current and former congressional staffers, so they know their stuff, although sometimes it can be overtly corny. The best of political comedy, this DC tradition pokes satirical bipartisan fun at both sides of the spectrum.

SHAKESPEARE THEATRE THEATER

(Map p326; www.shakespearetheatre.org; 450 7th St NW; tickets from $30; box office 10am-6pm Mon-Sat, noon-6pm Sun; Archives-Navy Memorial) Under artistic director Michael Kahn, this little theater on Gallery Row has been called 'one of the world's three great Shakespearean theaters' by the *Economist*. Its home company stages a half-dozen works annually, plus a free summer Shakespeare series onsite from mid-August to early September.

FORD'S THEATRE THEATER

(Map p326; www.fordstheatre.org; 511 10th St NW; tickets from $25; box office 10am-6pm Mon-Fri; Gallery Pl-Chinatown) The historical theater – where John Wilkes Booth killed Abraham Lincoln – has staged world-premiere musicals, mostly about Lincoln's life and times. For more information about visiting the theater as a historic attraction and museum, see p155.

STUDIO THEATRE THEATER

(Map p326; www.studiotheatre.org; 1501 14th St NW; tickets from $35; Dupont Circle) The contemporary four-theater complex has been staging Pulitzer Prize–winning and premiere plays for more than 25 years. It cultivates a lot of local actors.

NATIONAL THEATRE THEATER

(Map p326; www.nationaltheatre.org; 1321 Pennsylvania Ave NW; box office 10am-9pm Mon-Sat, noon-8pm Sun; Federal Triangle) Established in 1835 and renovated in 1984, the National is Washington's oldest continually operating theater. This is where you would catch *Les Misérables* and *Wicked*. Students and seniors can check at the box office for half-price tickets for Tuesday and Wednesday shows. Saturday mornings feature free performances for children at 9:30am and 11am. Grown-ups get their free show Monday evenings September through May.

WARNER THEATRE THEATER

(Map p326; www.warnertheatredc.com; 513 13th St NW; tickets from $25; box office 11am-3pm Mon-Fri; Federal Triangle) The beautifully restored 1924 art-deco theater was originally built for vaudeville and silent films, but it now stages headliner concerts, comedians and national runs of Broadway musicals.

WOOLLY MAMMOTH THEATRE COMPANY THEATER

(Map p326; www.woollymammoth.net; 641 D St NW; tickets from $35; box office 10am-6pm Mon-Fri; Archives-Navy Memorial) Woolly Mammoth is the edgiest of DC's experimental groups. Fifteen-dollar 'stampede' seats are available at the box office two hours before performances, assuming the show is not a sell-out.

TOUCHSTONE GALLERY ART GALLERY

(Map p326; www.touchstonegallery.com; 901 New York Ave NW; 11am-6pm Wed-Fri, noon-5pm Sat & Sun; Gallery Pl-Chinatown, Metro Center) Artist-owned Touchstone Gallery exhibits contemporary works created by its 30-plus member artists. Works cover multiple media, including sculpture, painting and the occasional esoteric installation.

CIVILIAN ART PROJECTS ART GALLERY

(Map p326; www.civilianartprojects.com; 1019 7th St NW; ⏲1-6pm Wed, Thu & Sat; Ⓜ Mt Vernon Sq/7th St-Convention Center) It's one of the flashier new galleries holding together the downtown gallery scene. Features contemporary work.

SHOPPING

INTERNATIONAL SPY MUSEUM SOUVENIRS

(Map p326; www.spymuseumstore.org; 800 F St NW; ⏲10am-6pm; Ⓜ Gallery Pl-Chinatown) Let's face it, every so often everyone needs a pair of reverse-mirrored sunglasses, whether you are being followed or you just want to check out the hottie behind you in the elevator. Now you know where to get them, and piles of other nifty spy gadgets you may need some day. Other Bond-gear that might come in handy includes concealed video and listening devices, disguise kits, micro cameras and recorder pens.

ARCHIVES SHOP SOUVENIRS

(Map p326; www.archives.gov; 700 Pennsylvania Ave NW; Ⓜ Archives-Navy Memorial). Archives Shop is awesome – whether you're looking for a Thomas Jefferson biography, a Declaration of Independence inscribed ruler, a John Adams stuffed toy or Elvis meets Nixon magnet

COWGIRL CREAMERY FOOD & DRINK

(Map p326; www.cowgirlcreamery.com; 919 F St NW; ⏲7:30am-7pm Mon-Fri, from 11am Sat; Ⓜ Gallery Pl-Chinatown) Don't know your Gouda from your gruyere? Cowgirl Creamery, a California-based artisan cheesemonger, can help. The knowledgeable staff gives lots of samples, so you can try before you buy. They also prepare tasty sandwiches for takeaway. The compact storefront crowds with office workers at lunchtime.

NATIONAL BUILDING MUSEUM ART

(Map p326; www.nbm.org; 401 F St NW; ⏲10am-5pm Mon-Sat, 11am-5pm Sun; Ⓜ Judiciary Sq) This museum shop is an amateur architect's dream, with small pieces of furniture, rich coffee-table books, paper models of famed buildings, and a collection of books on American and international architecture. There's also a big selection of build-it-yourself educational toys for kids.

NATIONAL MUSEUM OF WOMEN IN THE ARTS ART

(Map p326; www.nmwa.org; 1250 New York Ave NW; ⏲10am-5pm Mon-Sat, noon-5pm Sun; Ⓜ Metro Center) This unique institution dedicated to women artists has an equally unique shop. A small room left of the museum entrance, it holds books, prints, posters, jewelry and handicrafts – all created by women.

POLITICAL AMERICANA SOUVENIRS

(Map p326; ☎202-737-7730; 1331 Pennsylvania Ave NW; ⏲9am-8pm Mon-Sat, 10am-6pm Sun; Ⓜ Federal Triangle) Well, you can't leave without one presidential mug, right? Red-white-and-blue tat is ubiquitous in Washington, but this shop's collection of paraphernalia is a standout, from Truman posters to Mondale buttons to Barack Obama everything.

COUP DE FOUDRE WOMEN'S CLOTHING

(Map p326; www.coupdefoudrelingerie.com; 1008 E St NW; ⏲11am-6pm Mon-Sat; Ⓜ Metro Center) Local men dream of the day their girlfriends take them here and say, 'What should I get, honey?' Women also love Coup; the lingerie makes Victoria's Secret look gauche, and the mom-and-daughter owners have a passion for prettying up your bottom drawer.

PUA NATURALLY WOMEN'S CLOTHING

(Map p326; www.puanaturally.com; 701 Pennsylvania Ave NW; ⏲noon-6:30pm Mon-Fri, from 1pm Sat & Sun; Ⓜ Archives-Navy Memorial) Women head here to splurge on high-end ethnic clothing, like long flowing skirts and handwoven jackets from southern Asia.

TEAISM FOOD & DRINK

(Map p326; www.teaism.com; 400 8th St NW; Ⓜ Archives-Navy Memorial) Next to the inviting cafe of the same name, Teaism sells dozens of loose-leaf teas, from smoky Lapsang souchong to organic jasmine and rich green teas – all concealed in artful boxes behind the counter. You can also buy teapots, mugs, strainers and ornate display boxes (covered with handmade paper).

OLD POST OFFICE PAVILION MALL

(Map p326; www.oldpostofficedc.com; 1100 Pennsylvania Ave NW; ⏲10am-8pm Mon-Sat, to 7pm Sun; Ⓜ Federal Triangle) It's not exactly a shopping center, but it does have a tourist-crowded food court, as well as souvenir shops, newsstands and stores. It's worth a visit just for a look around the gorgeous central atrium. For more details, see p157.

SPORTS & ACTIVITIES

BIKE & ROLL — BIKING

(Map p326; ☎202-842-2453; www.bikethesites.com; Old Post Office Pavilion, 1100 Pennsylvania Ave; bikes per hr/day from $6/30; ⊙mid-Mar–early Dec; Ⓜ Federal Triangle) Rent a bike to explore DIY style, or go on a guided tour (from adult/child $40/30). The latter covers the Capital's main sites or the monuments; tours also do the jaunts at night (highly recommended!). The rental price includes safety equipment, while the tour price includes the bike, bottled water and a snack. The company has branches at Union Station and in Alexandria, VA; you can drop off your bike at these other locations for a $5 surcharge if you don't want to pedal back here.

WASHINGTON WIZARDS — BASKETBALL

(Map p326; www.nba.com/wizards; 601 F St NW; ⊙box office 10am-5:30pm Mon-Sat; Ⓜ Gallery Pl-Chinatown) The Wizards are DC's NBA basketball team. The season runs from October through April, with home games played at the Verizon Center. Tickets are as cheap as $15 for the nosebleed section; $60 for decent seats in the upper concourse; $90 or so for the club concourse; and higher and higher.

DC's WNBA team, the **Washington Mystics** (www.wnba.com/mystics) also play here from May to September. The popular **Georgetown Hoyas** (www.guhoyas.com), part of the National College Athletic Association (NCAA), play here during the same timeframe as the NBA.

WASHINGTON CAPITALS — HOCKEY

(Map p326; http://capitals.nhl.com; 601 F St NW; ⊙box office 10am-5:30pm Mon-Sat; Ⓜ Gallery Pl-Chinatown) The Verizon Center turns to ice when DC's rough-and-tumble NHL team, the Capitals, are playing from October through April. Tickets start from around $40.

Dupont Circle & Kalorama

Neighborhood Top Five

❶ Travel to India, Kenya, Laos, Luxembourg, Malawi, Morocco and Zambia during an hour's walk (literally – embassy grounds are technically another nation's territory) along **Embassy Row** (p167).

❷ Stand face-to-face with Renoirs and Rothkos in the intimate setting of the **Phillips Collection** (p168).

❸ Browse the stacks, sip cocktails and stuff your face at **Kramerbooks** (p176).

❹ Shake a tail at clubtastic **Cobalt** (p174).

❺ Experience the genteel Washingtonian lifestyle, both past and present, at **Woodrow Wilson House** (p168).

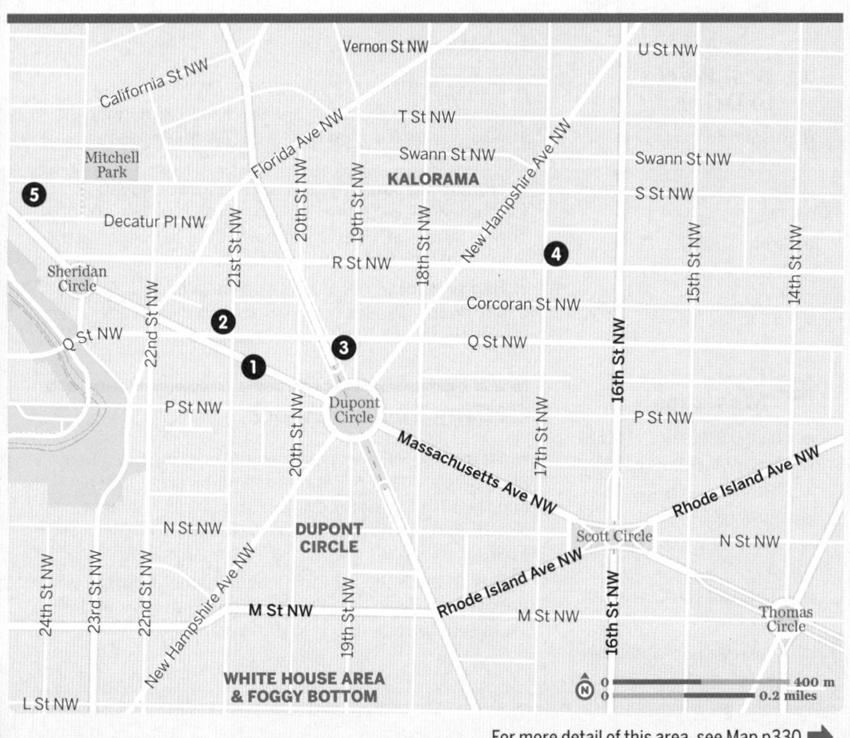

For more detail of this area, see Map p330 ➡

Lonely Planet's Top Tip

If you really want to take advantage of the embassy scene, check out the International Club (www.internationalclubdc.com). It organizes concerts, dinners and cultural events – many held at embassies – for 'internationally minded' locals to socialize. Anyone can join and be off to dinners at the Ukrainian Embassy, concerts at the Austrian Embassy and more.

Best Places to Eat

- Afterwords Cafe (p171)
- Bistrot du Coin (p171)
- Tabard Inn (p172)
- Obelisk (p172)
- Malaysia Kopitiam (p172)

For reviews, see p171

Best Places to Drink

- Russia House (p174)
- Bier Baron (p174)
- Beacon Martini Sky-Bar (p174)
- Firefly (p174)
- Science Club (p175)

For reviews, see p174

Best Museums

- Phillips Collection (p168)
- Textile Museum (p168)
- National Geographic Museum (p169)
- Woodrow Wilson House (p168)
- Society of the Cincinnati (p168)

For reviews, see p168

Explore Dupont Circle & Kalorama

A well-heeled splice of gay community and DC diplomatic scene, Dupont Circle – or much more commonly, Dupont – is city life at its best. Here you'll find flash new restaurants, hip bars, cafe society and folk-singer-esque bookstores. The neighborhood has Washington's highest concentration of embassies, many set in captivating historic mansions along Massachusetts Ave (aka Embassy Row). Dupont is also the out-and-about heart of DC's gay and lesbian community. This combination gay and international pulse tends to beat out the social rhythm for young professionals of all stripes and persuasions.

Kalorama adjoins Dupont to the northwest. Greek for 'beautiful view,' it was named for an estate built by Jefferson confidant Joel Barlow that dominated this hilly area in the 19th century. These days it's a sort of Dupont with an extra helping of regal reserve and mansions.

The neighborhood is easy to explore, since almost everything radiates from the literal Dupont Circle, the traffic rotunda. Spend the morning getting cultured in under-the-radar museums. An embassy stroll coupled with artsy shopping is a fine way to spend the afternoon. Have dinner in one of the sublime international bistros, then take your pick of thumping dance clubs to end the night (or start the morning, as the case may be).

Local Life

- **Midnight Bite** Afterwords Cafe (p171) hops late-night on weekends, when it slings chow – and tomes at attached store Kramerbooks – 24/7. Brunch is equally jam-packed.
- **Lunchtime Journey** During the spring and fall, the National Geographic Museum (p169) shows a free documentary on Tuesdays at noon. Join locals on their lunch break to explore distant lands.
- **Happy Hours** Lots of bars and clubs mean lots of happy hours. Dupont is a great spot for post-work tipples that won't flatten your wallet.

Getting There & Away

- **Metro** Access most points from Dupont Circle (Red Line). Use the Q St exit for destinations north of P St, and the 19th St exit for destinations south. Farragut North (Red Line) is the closer station to points near M St.
- **Bus** To catch the DC Circulator's Dupont-Georgetown-Rosslyn bus, depart the Dupont Metro station from the south exit; the bus stop is at 19th and N Sts.

TOP SIGHTS

EMBASSY ROW

How quickly can you leave the country? It takes about five minutes; just stroll north along Massachusetts Ave from Dupont Circle and you pass roughly 50 embassies housed in mansions ranging from the elegant to the imposing. Technically, they're on foreign soil – embassy grounds are another nation's territory.

Embassies sprinkle the District, but Dupont possesses Washington's highest concentration of them. This was once Millionaire's Row, and the mansions of the old elite are still thick on the ground. Most embassies were once private residences dating from the turn of the century – a time when industrialists and financiers dealt with insecurity complexes by turning their homes into brick wedding cakes. The Great Depression caused many to lose their manors, which then stood gracefully decaying until WWII's aftermath. As nations came to Washington to set up shop, the old homes were uniquely fit to be embassies.

The **Indonesian Embassy** (2020 Massachusetts Ave NW), pictured above, is an impressive example. Gold-mining magnate Thomas Walsh commissioned the home in 1903, when it was said to be the costliest house in the city (not surprising, considering the gold-flecked marble pillars). The **Luxembourg Embassy** (2200 Massachusetts Ave NW) is another show-stopper. Congressman Alexander Stewart built the home in 1909 in the grand court style of Louis XIV. In 1941 the Grand Duchess of Luxembourg bought it and lived here in exile during WWII. Edward Everett, inventor of the grooved bottle cap, built the structure that is now the **Turkish Ambassador's Residence** (cnr Sheridan Circle & 23rd St). George Oakley Totten designed the building, which has some Ottoman influences. Totten was the official architect of the Ottoman Sultan Abdul Hamid II.

DON'T MISS...

- Indonesian Embassy
- Luxembourg Embassy
- Turkish Embassy
- Diplomats' shiny black Mercedes Benzes

PRACTICALITIES

- Map p330
- www.embassy.org
- Massachusetts Ave btwn Observatory & Dupont Circles NW
- M Dupont Circle

SIGHTS

EMBASSY ROW
STREET

See p167.

PHILLIPS COLLECTION
MUSEUM

(Map p330; www.phillipscollection.org; 1600 21st St NW; admission free weekdays, $10 Sat & Sun; ⏲10am-5pm Tue-Sat, to 8:30pm Thu, 11am-6pm Sun; MDupont Circle) Don't think of the oldest modern art museum in the country as a gallery. It's more like a house, immaculately designed and dappled with some of the best creativity you'll ever see for free (Monday through Friday). The intimate rooms put you unusually close to the artworks. Van Gogh, Bonnard and O'Keeffe grace the permanent collection, while special exhibits pull in conceptual talent like Christo. Highlights include Renoir's *Luncheon of the Boating Party* and the Rothko Room, which hangs four of the abstract expressionist's pieces. The free app (www.phillipscollection.org/apple or/android) provides details on it all. Extra admission fees apply to special exhibits. The Sunday **chamber music series** (per ticket $20; ⏲4pm Sun Oct-May) has been playing sweet music since 1941.

FREE SOCIETY OF THE CINCINNATI
MUSEUM

(Map p330; www.societyofthecincinnati.org; 2118 Massachusetts Ave NW; ⏲tours 1:15pm, 2:15pm & 3:15pm Tue-Sat; MDupont Circle) The Society of the Cincinnati is a private patriotic group dedicated to educating the public about the Revolutionary War. Who knew? What's key here is the chance to go inside the Renaissance Revival mansion (aka Anderson House) where it has its headquarters and check out the opulent interior. The gilded ballrooms, chandeliers, tapestries, sweeping staircases and marble pillars drop the jaw.

TEXTILE MUSEUM
MUSEUM

(Map p330; www.textilemuseum.org; 2320 S St NW; suggested donation $8; ⏲10am-5pm Tue-Sat, from 1pm Sun; MDupont Circle) This gem is the country's only textile museum, and is as unappreciated as the art itself. In two historic mansions, cool, dimly lit galleries hold exquisite fabrics and carpets. Exhibits revolve around a theme, say Asian textiles depicting dragons or Kuba cloth from the Democratic Republic of Congo, and rotate a few times a year. Accompanying wall commentary explains how the textiles mirror the social, spiritual, economic and aesthetic values of the societies that made them. Founded in 1925, the collection includes rare kimonos, pre-Columbian weaving, American quilts and Ottoman embroidery. (Find the flaw: traditional textile artists, from Islamic carpet makers to Appalachian quilters, weave intentional flaws into their work to avoid mimicking God's perfection.)

Upstairs, the learning center will keep older kids entertained – and learning – for hours. Hands-on (literally) exhibits demonstrate weaving patterns, dying techniques and lots more.

In 2014 the museum is scheduled to move into a new building on the George Washington University campus.

WOODROW WILSON HOUSE
MUSEUM

(Map p330; www.woodrowwilsonhouse.org; 2340 S St NW; adult/child $10/free; ⏲10am-4pm Tue-Sun; MDupont Circle) This Georgian-revival mansion offers guided hour-long tours focusing on the 28th president's life and legacy. Genteel elderly docents discuss highlights of Wilson's career (WWI, the League of Nations) and home, which has been restored to the period of his residence (1921–24). The tour features a garden, a stairwell conservatory, European bronzes, 1920s-era china and Mrs Wilson's elegant dresses, all of which offer a glamorous portrait of Roaring '20s DC society. The docents' entertaining stories spread beyond the Wilson house: they can point out the rich eccentrics and ambassadors who live nearby and give you directions to the Clinton's Georgian Colonial pad about a mile up the road.

HEURICH HOUSE
MUSEUM

(Map p330; www.heurichhouse.org; 1307 New Hampshire Ave NW; tours $5; ⏲11:30am & 1pm Thu & Fri, 11:30am, 1pm & 2:30pm Sat; MDupont Circle) We like to call this place 'the castle that beer built.' Heurich House is immediately recognizable, a medieval manor in the midst of modern America. While there are a lot of baroque and Renaissance swishes, this was also the first District building to appreciably rely on reinforced concrete. The 31-room mansion was designed by John Granville Myers for German-born brewer Christian Heurich, a man who loved beer with a passion we can appreciate. One quote along the walls states: '*Raum ist in der kleinsten Kammer fur den grossten Katzenjammer*' ('There is room in the smallest chamber for the biggest hangover'), a sentiment you may blearily agree with after a night out in Dupont. Entry is by guided tour only, though DIY explorations of the **gardens** (admission free; ⏰11am-3pm Apr-Oct) are permitted.

MANSION ON O STREET NOTABLE BUILDING

(Map p330; www.omansion.com; 2020 O St NW; tours $5; ⏰10am-4pm Sun & Mon; Ⓜ Dupont Circle) This 100-room 1892 mansion is part inn, part gallery performance space and part private club. In this latter incarnation, it has hosted Hollywood celebrities and Chelsea Clinton's sweet-16 party. Its owner, grande dame HH Leonards, has done the place up like a wedding at Castle Dracula: swags of velvet drapery, ornate chandeliers and lampshades, candelabras and concealed doorways. And it's all for sale! The mansion serves food and drinks, but we recommend sticking to the bizarro self-guided tour. Register online for a time slot at least 24 hours in advance.

NATIONAL GEOGRAPHIC MUSEUM MUSEUM

(Map p330; ☎202-857-7588; events.nationalgeographic.com/events/locations/center/museum; cnr 17th & M Sts NW; adult/child $8/4; ⏰10am-6pm; Ⓜ Farragut North) The museum at National Geographic Society headquarters can't compete with the Smithsonian's more extensive offerings, but it can be worth a stop, depending on what's showing. Exhibits are drawn from the society's well-documented expeditions to the far corners of the Earth (and beyond), and they change every three months or so. Check the schedule before heading out.

The society's year-round series, **National Geographic Live** (www.nglive.org/dc), includes films, concerts and lectures by famed researchers and explorers. It is held at the Grosvenor Auditorium, located across the courtyard from the museum. Most programs have a fee; the **free movie** every Tuesday at noon (spring and fall) is the exception. The **photography exhibit** in the lobby (accessed via the M St entrance) is also free and merits a peek.

FREE **CHARLES SUMNER SCHOOL & ARCHIVES** MUSEUM

(Map p330; www.sumnerschool.tumblr.com; 1201 17th St NW; ⏰10am-5pm Mon-Fri; Ⓜ Dupont Circle) The stately, dignified Sumner building is a great example of solidly beautiful redbrick 19th-century urban design, but it is an even better testament to civil rights and education. Back in 1877, this was where the first high-school class of African Americans was graduated out of the school system. Today you can find the DC Public School archives here, as well as a museum that displays local public school memorabilia along with exhibits on statesman and orator Frederick Douglass.

METROPOLITAN AME CHURCH CHURCH

(Map p330; Metropolitan African Methodist Episcopal Church; www.metropolitanamec.org; 1518 M St NW; ⏰10am-6pm Mon-Sat; Ⓜ McPherson Sq) Built and paid for in 1886 by former slaves (quite a feat considering its impressive size), the Metropolitan AME Church occupies an imposing redbrick Gothic structure and is one of the city's most handsome, yet striking, churches. Frederick Douglass often preached here, and his state funeral was held here in February 1895. On the day of his burial, black schools closed, crowds packed the exterior to pay respect and flags flew at half-mast.

CAPITALLY KOSHER

Two of Washington's most prominent Judaica sights can be found amid the brown-red bricks of Dupont Circle. The **Washington DC Jewish Community Center** (www.washingtondcjcc.org; 1529 16th St NW; Ⓜ Dupont Circle) hosts plenty of arts activities, interfaith dialogues, community action programs and the like. The community center's sleek, boxlike headquarters is a treat in itself, resembling the exterior of a modern art museum.

The **National Museum of American Jewish Military History** (www.nmajmh.org; 1811 R St NW; admission free; ⏰9am-5pm Mon-Fri; Ⓜ Dupont Circle) is a small but fascinating peek into the wartime exploits of American Jews. The permanent exhibition is currently being renovated into a more modern, interactive multimedia experience. In the meantime, displays on Jewish Medal of Honor recipients and the history of death-camp liberation – among others – are a cool enough reason to pop in.

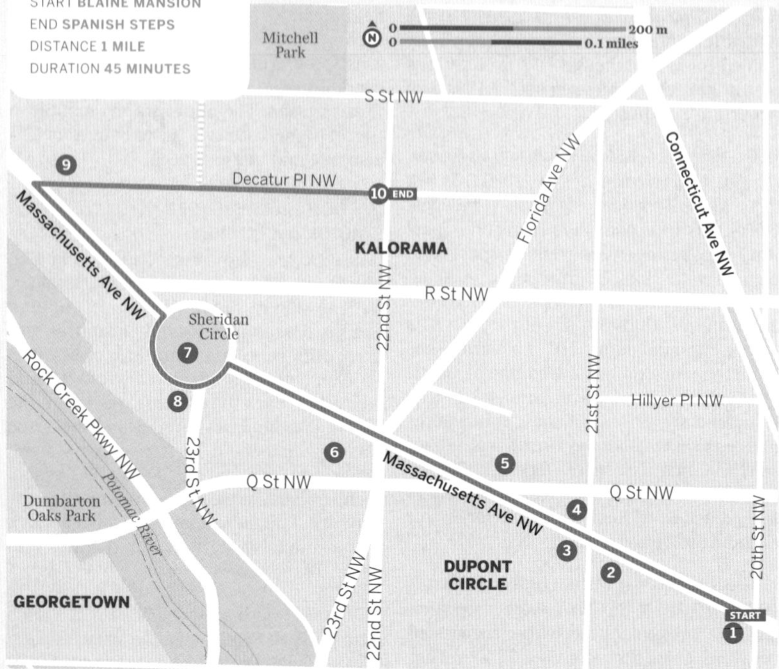

Neighborhood Walk

Embassy Row Ramble

In 1881 Republican party founder 'Slippery Jim' Blaine built the haunted-house-creepy **1 Blaine Mansion** at 2000 Massachusetts Ave, the oldest mansion in Dupont.

The Walsh-McLean House at No 2020 is now the **2 Indonesian Embassy**. Gold-mining magnate Thomas Walsh commissioned the home in 1903. He embedded in the foundation a gold nugget, which has never been found.

Continue up Massachusetts Ave to the grand **3 Anderson House**, base of the Society of the Cincinnati. It's one of the few homes you can go inside. Across the street, a simple statue of **4 Mahatma Gandhi** marks the Indian embassy.

The rich mansion at No 2121, designed to resemble Petit Trianon at Versailles, is the **5 Cosmos Club**, the most prominent social club of DC's intellectual elite: it oozes culture and class. The **6 Luxembourg Embassy** at No 2200 was built in the grand court style of Louis XIV for congressman Alexander Stewart.

Now you are approaching **7 Sheridan Circle**, centered on Gutzon Borglum's equestrian statue of Civil War General Philip Sheridan. Borglum later sculpted Mt Rushmore. The **8 Turkish Ambassador's Residence** is on the corner of Sheridan Circle and 23rd St.

At No 2343 Massachusetts Ave, a cross-legged sculpture of St Jerome dreams over his book. This masterpiece was the work of renowned Croatian sculptor Ivan Meštrović; appropriately, it fronts the **9 Croatian Embassy**.

Detour east on Decatur Pl to 22rd St. The rise up to S St NW was deemed too steep, so city planners constructed a delightful pedestrian staircase, dubbed the **10 Spanish Steps** for its resemblance to Rome's Piazza di Spagna. Climb up and stare across the area you've just traversed.

CATHEDRAL OF ST MATTHEW THE APOSTLE CHURCH

(Map p330; www.stmatthewscathedral.org; 1725 Rhode Island Ave NW; MDupont Circle) The sturdy redbrick exterior doesn't hint at the marvelous mosaics and gilding within this 1889 Catholic cathedral, where JFK was laid in state and his funeral mass was held. Its vast central dome, altars and chapels depict biblical saints and eminent New World personages – from Simón Bolívar to Elizabeth Ann Seton – in stained glass, murals and scintillating Italianate mosaics; almost no surface is left undecorated. Evening is the best time to visit, when flickering candles illuminate the sanctuary, but you can attend mass on Sunday morning or slip in almost any time to look around. Pick up a self-guided tour brochure by the entrance (beneath the guest register).

FOUNDRY GALLERY GALLERY

(Map p330; www.foundrygallery.org; 1314 18th St NW; 1-7pm Wed-Fri, noon-6pm Sat & Sun; MDupont Circle) A nonprofit member-run organization, this gallery features a diverse range of super-contemporary art made in the last decade – mediums include painting, sculpture and drawings – all created by local artists. Openings are held on various Fridays.

STUDIO GALLERY GALLERY

(Map p330; www.studiogallerydc.com; 2108 R St NW; 1-7pm Wed-Fri, 1-6pm Sat; MDupont Circle) A 30-artist cooperative featuring canvases and sculpture, this is the longest-running artist-owned gallery in the area. There are both solo and group exhibits in all mediums. Openings are held on the first Friday of the month.

SCOTTISH RITE TEMPLE NOTABLE BUILDING

(Map p330; www.scottishrite.org; 1733 16th St NW; adult/child $8/free; 9am-4pm Mon-Thu; MDupont Circle) The regional headquarters of the Scottish Rite Freemasons, also known as the House of the Temple, is one of the most eye-catching buildings in the District. That's because it looks like a magic temple lifted out of a comic book, all the more incredible for basically sitting amid a tangle of residential row houses. It's as if someone plopped the Parthenon in the middle of Shady Acres suburbia.

There's a lot of heavy Masonic symbolism and ritual associated with the building. Thirty-three columns surround the building, representing the 33rd Degree, an honorary distinction conferred on outstanding Masons. Two sphinxes, Wisdom and Power, guard the entrance, and past the gates of bronze that front the building (really), the grand atrium looks like a collision zone between the Egyptian and Greek antiquities departments of a major museum. Note the pharaonic statues and chairs modeled to resemble thrones from the Temple of Dionysus. For a secret society, the Masons ain't exactly subtle interior decorators. Guides provide tours of all this fascinating minutiae.

EATING

Classy nouveau cuisine and upscale ethnic eateries cater to the flocks of diplomats and businesspeople, while casual cafes cater to the more bohemian.

TOP CHOICE AFTERWORDS CAFE AMERICAN $$

(Map p330; 202-387-1462; www.kramers.com; 1517 Connecticut Ave; mains $11-19; 7:30am-1:30am Sun-Thu, 24hr Fri & Sat; MDupont Circle) Attached to Kramerbooks, this buzzing spot is not your average bookstore cafe. The packed indoor tables, wee bar and outdoor patio overflow with good cheer. The menu features tasty bistro fare and an ample beer selection, making it a prime spot for happy hour, brunch and at all hours on weekends (open 24 hours, baby!). Browsing the stacks before stuffing our guts is a favorite way to spend Washington weekends.

BISTROT DU COIN FRENCH $$

(Map p330; 202-234-6969; www.bistrotducoin.com; 1738 Connecticut Ave; mains $14-24; lunch & dinner; MDupont Circle) How do you know if a French bistro is the real thing? The decor? Du Coin does up its dining rooms with a lovely tricolor spread come Bastille Day. Resistance to smoking bans? Du Coin held the line longer than any DC restaurant we know of. But really, it's the food, and this is still our favorite spot for roll-up-your-sleeves, working-class French fare: steak *frites, moules, cassoulet* and the like. Not because it's necessarily the best (although it's quite good), but because the atmosphere feels plucked out of Orwell's *Down and Out* descriptions of Paris, the clientele is a fun mix of Dupont yuppies and nostalgic Euros and the prices are very reasonable. *Nous t'aimons,* du Coin.

LOCAL KNOWLEDGE

FARMERS MARKET

The **Dupont Circle Market** (Map p330; www.freshfarmmarket.org; 1560 20th St NW; ⌚8:30am-1pm Sun, from 10am Jan-Mar; Ⓜ Dupont Circle) teems with locals on Sunday mornings. It's part of the Fresh Farm Market program, one of the leaders of the Chesapeake Bay region local food movement.

TABARD INN — AMERICAN $$

(Map p330; ☎202-331-8528; www.tabardinn.com/restaurant; 1739 N St NW; mains $24-32, brunch $12-17; ⌚breakfast, lunch & dinner; Ⓜ Dupont Circle) In a city that loves its brunches, it's unfair Dupont gets two standouts of the genre (the other is Afterwords Cafe), but the gods put the Tabard here and we mortals must contend. Dinners are great, but it's the deceptively normal weekend brunch menu – poached eggs, pecan waffles etc – that stands out. The ingredients (including oysters caught specifically for the inn) are just so good it's like brunch enlightened.

OBELISK — ITALIAN $$$

(Map p330; ☎202-872-1180; 2029 P St NW; prix-fixe from $75; ⌚6-9:30pm Tue-Sat; Ⓜ Dupont Circle) Oh the pleasure of dining at Obelisk. You need only do it once, but you need to do it, especially if you're a fan of pushing the boundaries of what can be done in an Italian *cucina*. The small and narrow dining room feels almost like eating at someone's kitchen table, and the set-course Italian feasts are lovingly prepared with first-rate ingredients; the antipasti in particular is a revelation of just how powerful a start can be. The menu changes daily, but doesn't give you much selection (picky eaters should call ahead). Reservations are a good idea.

KOMI — FUSION $$$

(Map p330; ☎202-332-9200; www.komirestaurant.com; 1509 17th St NW; set menu $135; ⌚dinner Tue-Sat; Ⓜ Dupont Circle) Many critics point to Komi as serving the best food in the capital. There's an admirable simplicity to the changing menu, which is rooted in Greece and influenced by everything, primarily genius. Suckling pig for two; scallops and truffles; a roasted baby goat. It all comes together, because here it's not just the food, but the incredible attention and measured pacing provided by the staff. You pay for Komi, but what you get is one of Washington's most knockout dining experiences. Komi's Venetian fairytale of a dining space doesn't take groups larger than four, and you need to reserve way in advance – like, now.

MALAYSIA KOPITIAM — MALAYSIAN $$

(Map p330; ☎202-833-6232; www.malaysiakopitiam.com; 1827 M St NW; mains $9-15; ⌚lunch & dinner; Ⓜ Dupont Circle) If you are familiar with Malaysian food, this is as close as you get to a Penang street stall in Washington. If you're not, may we introduce you to: *laksa* (bowls of noodle soup cut with coconut milk and pillowy chunks of chicken), spiced dry fish, and anything cooked in a banana leaf. It's all a few steps from Camelot, DC's most (in)famous stripper bar.

HANK'S OYSTER BAR — SEAFOOD $$

(Map p330; ☎202-462 4265; www.hanksdc.com; 1624 Q St NW; mains $15-23; ⌚dinner daily, lunch Fri, brunch Sat & Sun) There are a fair few oyster bars in Washington (slurping raw boys is good for political puffery, apparently) and Hank's is our favorite of the bunch. It's got the right testosterone combination, a bit of power-player muscle mixed with good-old-boy ambience, which isn't to say women won't love it here. Just that guys really do. Needless to say, the oyster menu is extensive and excellent; there are always at least four varieties on hand. Quarters are cramped, and you often have to wait for a table – nothing a saki oyster bomb won't fix.

BLUE DUCK TAVERN — AMERICAN $$

(Map p330; ☎202-419-6755; www.blueducktavern.com; 1201 24th St NW; mains $14-28; ⌚breakfast, lunch & dinner; Ⓜ Dupont Circle) The Blue Duck tries to create a rustic kitchen ambience in the midst of one of M St's uber-urbanized concrete corridors. Design-wise, it doesn't quite work for us; the Amish quilts and hand-crafted wood accents seem to clash with the modernist clean lines and art-gallery interior. Food-wise, the experiment is a smashing success: the menu sources from farms across the country, bringing diners lovely mains like a pork terrine and trotter croquette made from pigs in Virginia, crab cakes sourced from the waters of Louisiana, and sturgeon caviar plucked from the Columbia River in Washington State.

NORA AMERICAN $$$

(Map p330; ☎202-462-5143; www.noras.com; 2132 Florida Ave; mains $29-36; ⊙dinner Mon-Sat; MDupont Circle) Nora Pouillon remains the queen of the Washington food scene. She made her reputation serving food from farmers and ranchers – this was by many accounts the first organic restaurant in the country – and a list of the farms that provided your food is included on the menu. The way these fresh ingredients are combined is in the New American style – Nora was one of the originals and still executes it so well that each bite is like rediscovering what the nation can do with its ingredients: Alaskan halibut arrives on a bed of corn succotash, while Amish chicken livers soak deliciously in their own jus. All this happens in a quaint carriage house on one of Dupont's loveliest corners.

WESTEND BISTRO FRENCH $$

(Map p330; ☎202-974-4900; www.westendbistrodc.com; 1190 22nd St NW; mains $16-35; ⊙lunch Mon-Fri, dinner daily; MDupont Circle) There's some intimidating talent behind Westend's kitchen: the restaurant was founded by Eric Ripert, who has a small constellation of Michelin stars under his belt, and the chef de cuisine is Joe Palma, who has come up through some of the best kitchens in DC and New York, including Citronelle and Le Bernardin. Those sort of names attract some gushing hype, attention which is pretty justified in this gem of wood and warm tones. The French-American menu is a mix of rich haute cuisine and a playful wink; you can snack on truffled popcorn at the bar, then enjoy a fish burger dressed with a delicate saffron aioli that hits like a delicious whisper – and at $16, that burger isn't costing you much more than a night at Red Lobster. Good food, good deals – what's keeping you?

VIDALIA SOUTHERN $$$

(Map p330; ☎202-659-1990; www.vidaliadc.com; 1990 M St NW; mains $30-34; ⊙lunch Mon-Fri, dinner daily; MDupont Circle) Is it fair to call Vidalia 'Southern?' Chef Jeff Buben, who also runs the kitchen in Bistro Bis in the Hotel George, is a man who likes his French influences. But there's clear Southern roots in his focus on mixing the rich with the filling – 'Southern' ain't just grits, after all. Although with that said, the shrimp and grits here are something else, a sort of Platonic ideal of the shrimp and grits concept. The menu changes regularly, but it always revolves around unique, approachable flavors, say sweetbreads and waffles under bacon fondue. The signature side is a slow-cooked version of the titular onion. The subterranean dining room, wallpapered in sultry-sweet magnolia, is exquisitely lovely.

SUSHI TARO JAPANESE $$$

(Map p330; ☎202-462-8999; www.sushitaro.com; 1503 17th St NW; dinner from $50; ⊙lunch & dinner Mon-Fri, dinner Sat; MDupont Circle) The argument over best sushi in town comes down to this place and Makoto in Georgetown. Like Makoto, the kitchen here obsesses over serving the finest, freshest fish possible arranged with beautiful sides and garnishes, presented with that attention to detail where the Japanese exist in a league of their own. A quivering bit of fatty tuna comes with a side of wasabi freshly grated from one long stem of Japanese horseradish into slivers of nose-tingling happiness. The tastes have almost mathematical layers of complexity, yet this intricacy is arrived at from the simple combination of a few fresh ingredients. The look and feel of the place is contemporary Japanese, and the service is Americanized. Loosen the belt and prepare to eat very, very well.

ZORBA'S CAFE GREEK $$

(Map p330; ☎202-387-8555; www.zorbascafe.com; 1612 20th St NW; mains $11-15; ⊙lunch & dinner; MDupont Circle; 👪) Generous portions of moussaka and souvlaki, as well as pitchers of Rolling Rock, make this Greek diner one of DC's best bargain haunts. Contrary to the menu's promise, you will probably not confuse this for being in the Greek Isles (despite the bouzouki music). But the fresh food and quick service make this family-run place a good option.

FILTER CAFE $

(Map p330; www.filtercoffeehouse.com; 1726 20th St NW; ⊙7am-7pm Mon-Fri, 8am-7pm Sat & Sun; MDupont Circle; 📶) On a quiet street in Dupont, Filter is a jewel-box sized cafe with a tiny front patio, a hipsterish laptop-toting crowd and, most importantly, great coffee. Aussies and those who seek caffeinated perfection can get a decent flat white here.

SWEETGREEN HEALTH FOOD $

(Map p330; www.sweetgreen.com; 1512 Connecticut Ave NW; mains $8-11; ⊙11am-10pm; 🖉) Dupont Circle's branch of the uber-healthy salad and frozen yogurt purveyor often has a line out the door. Order your ginormous bowl of curry-yogurt-sauced roasted chicken and greens (or other equally wholesome dish) at the counter, then take it to the communal tables to consume with the rest of the young and fit.

DOLCEZZA ICE CREAM $

(Map p330; www.dolcezzagelato.com; 1704 Connecticut Ave NW; ice cream $4-7; 8am-11pm Mon-Sat, 8am-8pm Sun; M Dupont Circle; wi-fi) DC's best gelateria spreads over a dozen unique, delectable flavors (like Thai coconut milk, wildflower honey and champagne mango). There is good coffee, vintage-chic decor and free wi-fi.

WELL-DRESSED BURRITO TEX-MEX $

(Map p330; www.cffolks.com; 1220 19th St NW; mains $6-9; 11:45am-2:15pm; M Dupont Circle) Brought to you by CF Folks, a local catering firm, Well-Dressed Burrito deals in...well, do we need to spell it out? These burritos are a good antidote to overly hungry stomachs. Enter through the alley between M and N Sts.

DRINKING & NIGHTLIFE

DC's gay and lesbian nightlife mecca, this neighborhood is packed with bars ranging from raunchy to ritzy. Regardless of your sexual orientation, there's something to keep you drinking around the circle. Chill coffeehouses, super-sleek lounges and ramshackle joints known for cheap happy hours abound.

RUSSIA HOUSE LOUNGE

(Map p330; www.russiahouselounge.com; 1800 Connecticut Ave NW; from 5pm Mon-Fri, from 6pm Sat & Sun; M Dupont Circle) Russophiles flock to this faded but elegant Dupont gem, with its brassy chandeliers, candlelit chambers and stupefying vodka selection. It's a great spot for conversation and caviar – or heartier continental classics like *pelmeni* (dumplings), braised stuffed rabbit and *shashlik* (shish kebab).

18TH STREET LOUNGE LOUNGE

(Map p330; www.eighteenthstreetlounge.com; 1212 18th St NW; from 9:30pm Sat & Sun, from 5:30pm Tue-Fri; M Dupont Circle) Chandeliers, velvet sofas, antique wallpaper and a ridiculously good-looking, dance-loving crowd adorn this multi-floored mansion. The DJs here – spinning funk, soul and Brazilian beats – are phenomenal, which is not surprising given Eric Hilton (of Thievery Corporation) is co-owner. The lack of a sign on the door proclaims the club's exclusivity, and bouncers are famed for leaving lesser patrons out in the cold. No denim or sneakers. Cover charges range from $5 to $15.

BIER BARON BAR

(Map p330; www.bierbarondc.com; 1523 22nd St NW; from 5pm Sun-Thu, from 11:30am Fri & Sat; M Dupont Circle) Since changing name and ownership, the former Brickskeller serves better food and has better service, with the same dark, pubby ambience and venerable selection of beer. Fifty types flow from the taps and 500 more are available in the bottle. Aim for a corner seat, order a sampler and settle in for an impressive taste tour of global and local brews.

BEACON MARTINI SKY-BAR LOUNGE

(Map p330; www.bbgwdc.com; Beacon Hotel & Corporate Quarters, 1615 Rhode Island Ave NW; May-Oct; M Dupont Circle) On top of the swank Beacon Hotel, this patio on the roof offers ample sky-high (well, for DC) city views and an opportunity to mingle with new friends over signature martinis. Events are often held here, and while it can get crowded, this is a cool spot to listen to a DJ spin while surveying the greater capital area like the pimp you are.

COBALT GAY CLUB

(Map p330; www.cobaltdc.com; 1639 R St NW; 5pm-2am; M Dupont Circle) Cobalt pretty much rules the roost of the DC club scene. The music is great, the bartenders are ripped and sufficiently shirtless and the scene is equal parts all about the hook-up and getting down to some good (if pounding) dance music. Honestly, this place is such an epitome of a gay club it ought to come with its own five-piece costume ensemble of an Indian, a cop, a motorcycle rider etc. If you're in the mood for that sort of thing, this is pretty much a guaranteed good time. There's no cover charge early in the week; it ranges from $3 to $10 Thursday through Saturday.

FIREFLY BAR

(Map p330; www.firefly-dc.com; 1310 New Hampshire Ave NW; to 10pm Sun-Thu, to 10:30pm

Fri & Sat; Ⓜ Dupont Circle) Firefly is a restaurant first – the Hotel Madera's restaurant, to be precise – but we're not listing it for those merits. We can say it's one of the coolest bars in Dupont, decked out with its surreal, magically happy 'firefly trees,' all candle-lit and reminiscent of childhood summer evenings, and romantic as hell to boot. The cocktail menu is a glorious thing. Knock back a bourbon cream soda and see if the world doesn't just glow a little more... wait, that's the firefly trees. Whatever – still happy!

SCIENCE CLUB — LOUNGE

(Map p330; www.scienceclubdc.com; 1136 19th St NW; ⏲ from 5pm, closed Sun; Ⓜ Dupont Circle) In a warren of rooms scattered about a townhouse, the Science Club attracts a varied crowd of interns, transplants and young geeky types. They bond over wine, vegetarian snacks and nightly DJ music.

LUCKY BAR — BAR

(Map p330; www.luckybardc.com; 1221 Connecticut Ave NW; ⏲ from 3pm Mon-Fri, from noon Sat & Sun; Ⓜ Dupont Circle) Lucky's interior is nothing special – your standard double-decker dark wood and cozy chairs. It's the crowd that sets it apart: an amalgamation of capital subcultures ranging from politicos, Dupont gay couples, club kids needing a break from thumpa-thumpa and the occasional tourist, everyone enjoying each other over a happy booze-fueled drone. Lots of sports, including international soccer, flicker on the 22 TVs and big screens.

CAFE CITRON — CLUB

(Map p330; www.cafecitrondc.com; 1343 Connecticut Ave NW; ⏲ closed Sun & Mon; Ⓜ Dupont Circle) So here's the thing, ladies: when guys want to go out dancing, that's usually because they're trying to pick up girls. So here's the thing guys: when girls go out dancing, they're usually just interested in dancing (or 'letting off steam,' 'chilling with my chicas' etc). Sociology lesson finished, nothing personifies this dichotomy of affairs more than Cafe Citron, one of DC's most popular Latin music bars (in fairness, it plays everything, but the focus is salsa, samba et al). Girls dance; guys watch; the hours tick on. Late night it morphs to an all-dance crowd. Nights out here are really fun, if only to observe the above unfolding epic.

JR'S — GAY BAR

(Map p330; www.jrsbardc.com; 1519 17th St NW; ⏲ from 4pm Mon-Fri, from 1pm Sat & Sun; Ⓜ Dupont Circle) At JR's weekday happy hour you might think you've stepped into a living Banana Republic ad: chinos and button-downs are *de rigueur* at this popular gay hangout frequented by the 20- and 30-something, work-hard and play-hard set. Some DC residents claim that the crowd at JR's epitomizes the conservative nature of the capital's gay scene; but even if you love to hate it, as many do, JR's is the happy-hour spot in town and is packed more often than not.

LAURIOL PLAZA — BAR

(Map p330; www.lauriolplaza.com; 1835 18th St NW; ⏲ 11:30am-11pm Mon-Thu, to midnight Fri & Sat, to 3pm Sun; Ⓜ Dupont Circle) Lauriol doubles as a decent Mexican restaurant by day; by night, she's extremely popular with the young and the restless and the hot. The theme being south of the border, most folks go for multicolored margaritas. Y'know, the ones that don't taste like they've got any booze in them, and you really shouldn't have ordered another three but aw whatever man, there's nothing in these...(30 minutes later)...Wooh! I love you, bro!

BIG HUNT — BAR

(Map p330; www.thebighunt.net; 1345 Connecticut Ave NW; Ⓜ Dupont Circle) If you just said the name of this bar and smiled a little inner smile (or turned red), well, that's kinda the point. The irreverence is carried on inside via two floors of general tomfoolery, including one of the city's better rooftop patios and some pool, should you need to get some stick on.

BUFFALO BILLIARDS — POOL HALL

(Map p330; www.buffalobilliards.com; 1330 19th St; ⏲ from 4pm Mon-Thu, noon Sat & Sun; Ⓜ Dupont Circle) The 30 pool and snooker tables pull college kids and yuppies into this bright, below-street-level cave. There's usually a wait for a table, so trash yourself a bit before taking up some stick.

NUMBER NINE — GAY BAR

(Map p330; www.numberninedc.com; 1435 P St NW; Ⓜ Dupont Circle) Number Nine looks like it should be a total den of obnoxiousness, what with its super-sleek spaceship-style furniture and Euro I'm-too-cool-for-school vibe, but then you go inside and it's a totally friendly, even laid-back gay bar. This is a great bar for gay meet-and-greet early in the evening, although things definitely get a bit more cruise-y as the night wears on.

SIGN OF THE WHALE BAR

(Map p330; www.signofthewhaledc.com; 1825 M St NW; ⌚from 11:30am; Ⓜ Dupont Circle) The Sign (which is next to strip club Camelot) attracts a raucous GWU crowd, plus a fair few lawyers, on weekends. On other days of the week it comes off as a divey pub with low-level buzz.

ENTERTAINMENT

DC IMPROV COMEDY

(Map p330; www.dcimprov.com; 1140 Connecticut Ave NW; tickets from $10; ⌚closed Mon; Ⓜ Farragut North) DC Improv is comedy in the more traditional sense, featuring stand-up by comics from Comedy Central, Mad TV and HBO, among others. It also offers workshops for those of us who think we're pretty funny.

THEATER J THEATER

(Map p330; www.washingtondcjcc.org/center-for-arts/theater-j; 1529 16th St NW; Ⓜ Dupont Circle) Well-respected Theater J addresses the urban American Jewish experience.

SHOPPING

The shopping action in Dupont Circle centers on Connecticut Ave north and south of the roundabout.

KRAMERBOOKS BOOKS

(Map p330; www.kramers.com; 1517 Connecticut Ave NW; ⌚7:30am-1:30am Sun-Thu, 24hr Fri & Sat; Ⓜ Dupont Circle) With the Afterwords Cafe and bar behind the shop, this round-the-clock bookstore is as much a spot for schmoozing as for shopping. You can grab a meal, have a pint and flirt with comely strangers (the store is a fabled pick-up spot for straights and gays). This flagship independent – which leapt into First Amendment history when it firmly refused to release Lewinsky's book-buying list to Starr's snoops – features fine current literature, travel and politics sections.

> **LOCAL KNOWLEDGE**
>
> **PHILLIPS COLLECTION CONCERTS**
>
> If you like chamber music, don't forget about the Sunday concerts at the **Phillips Collection** (www.phillipscollection.org; 1600 21st St NW; per ticket $20; ⌚4pm Sun Oct-May). They have been a local tradition since 1941.

CLAUDE TAYLOR PHOTOGRAPHY ART

(Map p330; www.travelphotography.net; 1627 Connecticut Ave NW; ⌚10am-9pm Mon-Sat, to 8pm Sun; Ⓜ Dupont Circle) Claude Taylor's glossy travel photographs feature people and landscapes from around the world. The photographer has a keen eye for color and composition, and the prints (which come in all shapes and sizes) run from $35 to $100 or so, for small to large format. You can also purchase them framed.

BEADAZZLED JEWELRY

(Map p330; ☎202-265-2323; www.beadazzled.net; 1507 Connecticut Ave NW; Ⓜ Dupont Circle) Crafty types and jewelry lovers should not miss this specialty shop, which carries all things small and stringable. The selection from around the world ranges from 5¢ clay doohickeys to expensive pearls. Helpful staff will tell you how to put them together, and classes are offered on weekends (call to register).

SECOND STORY BOOKS BOOKS & MUSIC

(Map p330; www.secondstorybooks.com; 2000 P St NW; ⌚10am-10pm; Ⓜ Dupont Circle) Packed with dusty secondhand tomes, this atmospheric Dupont Circle bookstore also sells secondhand CDs (mostly jazz and classical). The prices are decent, and the choices are broad (particularly in the realm of history and Americana).

KULTURAS VINTAGE

(Map p330; www.kulturasbooks.vpweb.com; 1728 Connecticut Ave NW; ⌚noon-8pm Mon-Wed, 11am-10pm Thu-Sat, 11am-7pm Sun; Ⓜ Dupont Circle) Kulturas is a jack-of-all-trades bohemian shop selling used art and foreign language books, CDs, vintage clothes and original paintings by area artists. While not extensive, the clothing selection packs a punch, hanging everything from zebra-striped jeans to pearl-button cardigans on the rack. Bring your books to trade (no self help, mysteries or romance).

PROPER TOPPER ACCESSORIES

(Map p330; www.propertopper.com; 1350 Connecticut Ave NW; Ⓜ Dupont Circle) Fedoras, panama hats, short- and wide-brimmed straw hats – they're all for sale at the Proper Topper, along with children's books, wallets, jewelry, scarves and a few snazzy black dresses.

TABLETOP HOMEWARES

(Map p330; www.tabletopdc.com; 1608 20th St NW; ⏲noon-8pm Mon-Sat, to 6pm Sun; Ⓜ Dupont Circle) Also known as the best little design store in Dupont, Tabletop is evidence that DC is a lot more chic than some give it credit for. With the kooky candles, postmodern purses and postindustrial housewares taken together, your living space will be pampered.

PHILLIPS COLLECTION ART

(Map p330; www.phillipscollection.org; 1600 21st St NW; ⏲10am-5pm Tue-Sat, 11am-6pm Sun; Ⓜ Dupont Circle) The museum shop has a good collection of posters, pop and scholarly art books, and knickknacks imprinted with famous paintings, such as umbrellas sporting Renoir's *Luncheon of the Boating Party* and Monet water-lily mugs.

GINZA HOMEWARES

(Map p330; www.ginzaonline.com; 1721 Connecticut Ave NW; ⏲11am-7pm Mon-Sat, noon-6pm Sun; Ⓜ Dupont Circle) Japan is the theme at Ginza. There is a nice selection of beautiful (looking and sounding) indoor fountains, scented candles and other interesting elements of Asian decor.

SECONDI WOMEN'S CLOTHING

(Map p330; www.secondi.com; 1702 Connecticut Ave NW; ⏲11am-6pm Mon & Tue, to 7pm Wed-Fri, to 6pm Sat, 1-5pm Sun; Ⓜ Dupont Circle) Up a narrow row of stairs, Secondi is filled with beautiful top labels like Marc Jacobs jackets and slightly loved Manolo Blahniks. It's not the cheapest shop in the city, but it has a good collection of big-name designers.

BETSY FISHER WOMEN'S CLOTHING

(Map p330; www.betsyfisher.com; 1224 Connecticut Ave NW; Ⓜ Dupont Circle) The sales team at this classy women's boutique makes you feel like a queen while trying on fantastic pieces by designers like Diane von Furstenberg and Nicole Miller. The styles run the gamut from funky and fashion forward to elegant, but a touch on the conservative side.

Adams-Morgan

Neighborhood Top Five

❶ Explore **18th St NW** (p180), where Africans, Latin Americans and hard drinkers collide in a row of restaurants, music clubs, dive bars, vintage boutiques, and indie book and record shops.

❷ Stroll through **Malcolm X Park** (p180), a surprising green space of statuary and hilltop views.

❸ Make a bleary-eyed stumble into the **Diner** (p180) to quell late-night munchies.

❹ Soak up the previous night's debauchery with a drag queen brunch at **Perrys** (p182).

❺ Catch a band at **Madam's Organ** (p186) and snap a photo under the bawdy mural.

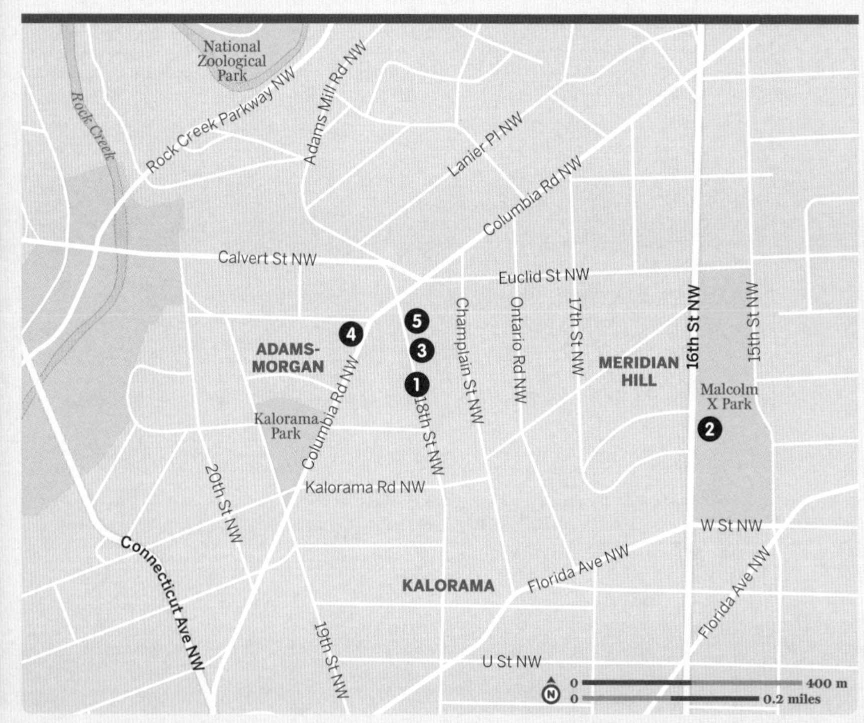

For more detail of this area, see Map p334

Explore Adams-Morgan

Adams-Morgan has long been Washington's fun, nightlife-driven neighborhood. It's also a global village of sorts, from an earlier time when rents were cheap and immigrants set up shop. The result is a raucous mash-up centered on 18th St NW. Walk the half-mile stretch between Columbia Rd and Florida Ave and you'll sniff shish kebabs, Ethiopian lamb stew, jerk chicken and vegetable biryani mingling in the air. Vintage boutiques, arty homewares stores and record shops poke up between the ethnic eats, and make for good browsing by day.

But nighttime is when AdMo (as it's called in local text message-ese) really lets loose. Whether you love it or hate it – and everyone in DC seems to experience both emotions at some point – 18th St becomes one of the great bar crawls in town. Bored kids from the 'burbs, the international crowd, Hill rats, Dupont cats, Georgetown brats, a multiracial crew of young professionals and even a fair amount of party people from the rough side of town all throw aside their differences for a while to shake a tail feather and scream in your face. If you're looking for a quiet night out, this is *not* your place.

The neighborhood's only real sight is Malcolm X Park, off the beaten path to the east and well worth a walkabout.

Local Life

➡ **Long Weekend** It starts on Thursday in Adams-Morgan, when many bars and clubs offer 'college night' promotions that draw crowds.

➡ **Bang on the Drum All Day** When the weather warms, a multicultural group gathers in Malcolm X Park (p180) for a drum circle 3pm to 9pm Sunday.

➡ **Block Party** The Adams Morgan Festival rocks the second Sunday of September. International bands, dance and food vendors take over the streets for DC's biggest neighborhood bash.

Getting There & Away

➡ **Metro** To reach most of 18th St, use the Woodley Park-Zoo/Adams Morgan station (Red Line). For points on 18th St south of Kalorama Rd, the Dupont Circle station (Red Line) is closer. For U St destinations, go to U St-Cardozo (Green Line). Each station is about a 15-minute walk from its hot spots.

➡ **Bus** The DC Circulator runs from the Woodley Park-Zoo/Adams Morgan Metro to the corner of 18th and Calvert Sts (a block north of Columbia Rd), before heading east out of the neighborhood.

Lonely Planet's Top Tip

While 18th St grabs the glory for its wide-ranging bounty of bars and cafes, and Columbia Rd is well known for its Latin clubs and restaurants, don't overlook U St in the neighborhood's Southeast quadrant. It has its share of cool-cat shops and bars, and they extend east into the historic U St Corridor.

Best Places to Eat

➡ Diner (p180)

➡ Bardia's (p180)

➡ Meskerem (p181)

➡ Amsterdam Falafelshop (p181)

➡ Rumba Cafe (p181)

For reviews, see p180

Best Places to Drink

➡ Dan's Cafe (p182)

➡ Tryst (p183)

➡ Black Squirrel (p183)

➡ Stetson's Famous Bar & Grill (p183)

➡ Bukom (p182)

For reviews, see p182 ➡

Best Places to Shop

➡ Crooked Beat Records (p187)

➡ Brass Knob (p187)

➡ Meeps Vintage Fashionette (p187)

➡ Idle Time Books (p187)

➡ Skynear Designs Gallery (p187)

For reviews, see p186

SIGHTS

18TH STREET NW & COLUMBIA ROAD — STREET

(Map p334; Ⓜ Woodley Park-Zoo/Adams Morgan) If you're looking for DC's most easily accessed international side with a fair helping of food and nightlife thrown in, wander up 18th St NW and nearby Columbia Rd. Close to 40 restaurants and nightspots line 18th St between Florida Ave and Columbia Rd, a stretch of blocks that also packs stores selling African, Asian and Latin American bric-a-brac. During the day the area can feel a little listless, but as soon as that sun starts to set the strip comes alive. Nearby Columbia Rd has become one of the main thoroughfares for DC's Latino community, and the spot where these two streets intersect is the launching point of many a capital night out.

DISTRICT OF COLUMBIA ARTS CENTER — ARTS CENTER

(Map p334; www.dcartscenter.org; 2438 18th St NW; ⏲gallery 2-7pm Wed-Sun; Ⓜ Woodley Park-Zoo/Adams Morgan) The grassroots DCAC offers emerging artists a space to showcase their work. The 750-sq-ft gallery features rotating visual arts exhibits, while plays and other theatrical productions take place in the theater (see p186). The gallery is free and worth popping into to see what's showing.

LOCAL KNOWLEDGE

NAME GAME: MALCOLM X OR MERIDIAN HILL?

Officially, the park's name is Meridian Hill, because it's located on the exact longitude of DC's original milestone marker. Locals started calling it Malcolm X Park in 1970, after activist Angela Davis gave a speech there and rechristened it. Leaders then introduced a bill in Congress to change the moniker, but it was shot down because – wait for it – the park contains DC's only memorial to President James Buchanan (the nation's 15th commander in chief). Thus the park's name cannot represent another person, according to the National Park Service. Locals pay the rule no mind, and everyone still calls it Malcolm X. Peculiar statues of Dante and Joan of Arc also dot the grounds.

MALCOLM X PARK — PARK

(Map p334; www.nps.gov/mehi; btwn 15th, 16th, Euclid & W Sts NW; ⏲sunrise-sunset; Ⓜ U St-Cardozo) This is an incredible bit of green space that gets short shrift in the list of America's great urban parks. What makes the park special is the way it emphasizes its distinctive geography. Lying on the fall line between the upland Piedmont Plateau and flat Atlantic Coastal Plain, the grounds are terraced like a hanging garden replete with waterfalls, sandstone terraces and assorted embellishments that feel almost Tuscan. Out-of-towners call it Meridian Hill Park.

MERIDIAN INTERNATIONAL CENTER — CULTURAL BUILDING

(Map p334; www.meridian.org; 1630 Crescent Pl; ⏲2-5pm Wed-Sun; Ⓜ U St-Cardozo) Many people who have lived in Washington for years haven't even heard of Meridian House, which isn't surprising – this impressive mansion does spring out of nowhere, looking like the headquarters for some world-dominating secret society. In fact, it's an education and hospitality center for DC's international community; the interior grounds are as impressive as the exterior facade. John Russell Pope built the structure to resemble a French country chateau, complete with a stately walled entrance, a charming cobblestone courtyard and a decorated limestone facade.

EATING

TOP CHOICE DINER — AMERICAN $$

(Map p334; www.dinerdc.com; 2453 18th St NW; mains $8-16; ⏲24hr; Ⓜ Woodley Park-Zoo/Adams Morgan; 🚸) The Diner serves hearty comfort food, any time of the day or night. It's ideal for wee-hour breakfast scarf-downs, weekend bloody-Mary brunches (if you don't mind crowds) or any time you want unfussy, well-prepared American fare. Omelets, stuffed pancakes, mac & cheese, grilled Portobello sandwiches and burgers hit the tables with aplomb. It's a good spot for kids too; they'll even hang their Diner-made colorings on the wall.

BARDIA'S — CAJUN $$

(Map p334; www.bardiasneworleanscafe.com; 2412 18th St NW; mains $8-16; ⏲11am-10pm Tue-Fri, 10am-10pm Sat & Sun; Ⓜ Woodley Park-Zoo/

Adams Morgan) We have it on good authority (a bunch of stoners stumbling out of B&K Newsstand) that this New Orleans–style cafe is the best cure for munchies in town. But that stereotype is a disservice. Bardia's food – the po' boys, the breakfasts and especially the beignets – is fantastic whatever your mental state. The fare stacks up to what you'd find in the Big Easy: rich, silky luxurious, silly decadent, and while the setting isn't as attractive as Faubourg Marginy, it's pretty damn close.

TRYST CAFE **$**

(Map p334; www.trystdc.com; 2459 18th St NW; breakfast & sandwiches $5-9; ⏲6:30am-midnight Sun-Wed, to 2am Thu, to 3am Fri & Sat; Ⓜ Woodley Park-Zoo/Adams Morgan; wi-fi) 'So-and-so is Trysting' seems to be a perennial Facebook status/Twitter update in DC, which automatically tells you what to expect here: good coffee, good sandwiches and lots of Macs (no wi-fi on weekends, though). Come nightfall, baristas become bartenders, and rather good ones too. Tryst is the sibling eatery of the Diner.

MESKEREM ETHIOPIAN **$**

(Map p334; ☎202-462-4100; www.meskerem ethiopianrestaurantdc.com; 2434 18th St NW; mains $9-12; ⏲lunch & dinner; Ⓜ Woodley Park-Zoo/Adams Morgan; vegetarian) As you make your way across DC, you'll see loads of places offering Ethiopian food, but Meskerem, named for the first month of the Ethiopian calendar, remains near the top of the heap. The spot is a stalwart of quality despite many years on the block. It's the just-seared lamb served in spicy sauce, the *wat* (stew) scooped with spongy *injera* (pancake-like bread) and the vegetables, all deliciously spiced, not hot but rich, complex and savory. This is remarkably easy food for the most conservative palette, best washed down with some imported honey wine.

AMSTERDAM FALAFELSHOP MIDDLE EASTERN **$**

(Map p334; www.falafelshop.com; 2425 18th St NW; items $4-7; ⏲11am-midnight Sun-Mon, to 2:30am Tue-Thu, to 4am Fri & Sat; Ⓜ Woodley Park-Zoo/Adams Morgan; vegetarian) Cheap and cheerful, fast and delicious, the Falafelshop rocks the world of vegetarians and those questing for late-night munchies. Bowl up to the counter, order your falafel sandwich, then take it to the topping bar and pile on pickles, tabbouleh, olives and 20 other items.

LOCAL KNOWLEDGE

MIDNIGHT BITES & BRUNCH

In addition to ethnic fare, Adams-Morgan is famed for its late-night eateries. Lots of people come here post-party on weekend nights to soak up the booze. Huge slices of pizza are a traditional DC post-bar snack; they're sold everywhere around the neighborhood and are uniformly greasy and delicious after several libations. Other places to stuff your face in the wee hours:

- Diner (p180)
- Amsterdam Falafelshop (p181)
- Julia's Empanadas (p182)

Brunch is another favorite meal in the 'hood. It's usually decadent at:

- Perrys (p182)
- Cashion's Eat Place (p182)
- Diner (p180)

French fries are the only other dish on the menu, and they head to the bar too, best slathered with a mayo/peanut sauce combination. Take away, or dribble away at the scattering of stools and tables.

RUMBA CAFE BRAZILIAN **$$**

(Map p334; ☎202-588-5501; www.rumbacafe.com; 2443 18th St NW; tapas $7-13, mains $18-28; ⏲dinner Mon-Fri, brunch Sat & Sun; Ⓜ Woodley Park-Zoo/Adams Morgan) Sit outside on the sidewalk and watch life pass you by while sipping some of the mintiest mojitos in the city and munching on mouthwatering morsels from South America. This tiny, eclectic restaurant's menu is mainly Brazilian, although it pops around the rest of the continent. We love the empanadas and, as is the Brazilian wont, anything steak-based is usually delicious. After dinner Rumba hosts live Latin bands in its shabby-chic, red-and-mirror-clad interior.

MIXTEC MEXICAN **$$**

(Map p334; ☎202-332-1011; 1792 Columbia Rd NW; mains $8-16; ⏲9am-10pm; Ⓜ Woodley Park-Zoo/Adams Morgan) Budget Mexican that eschews the taco/burrito/enchilada drabness of the genre, Mixtec is justifiably popular with Anglos and Latinos. The *moles* are freshly prepared, the meat authentically spiced (rumors say they use more than 200 seasonings) and the huevos rancheros are a great hangover cure. The hot chocolate – bittersweet and pretty much made of silk – is the best in town.

PASTA MIA ITALIAN **$$**
(Map p334; 1790 Columbia Rd NW; mains $10-16; dinner Tue-Sat; Woodley Park-Zoo/Adams Morgan) Long lines, stiff wait staff, crowded conditions, $15 per person minimum. This is the price of good, cheap Italian, friends. But that's OK. Sip your red, twirl one of 20-some types of pasta perfection and try not to break into operatic praise. It gets crowded inside, so this may not be the best place for romantic candlelight and Chianti, although it is grand for big groups and gregariousness. By the way, we mean it when we say 'long lines' – there are no reservations here, and if you're coming for dinner on a weekend night, you'll want to arrive early. They won't seat groups until everyone has arrived. Cash only.

PERRYS ASIAN **$$**
(Map p334; 202-234-6218; www.perrysadamsmorgan.com; 1811 Columbia Rd NW; mains $17-22; dinner Mon-Sun, brunch Sat & Sun; Woodley Park-Zoo/Adams Morgan) Three words: drag queen brunch. What, you need more? *Drag queen brunch,* people! Fine; in addition to the above, you can also munch sushi at Perrys, but the creative fusion fare really deserves your tongue's attention. The only problem is deciding whether to dine in the attractive lounge or under the stars. This place can be hard to spot because there's no real sign – the doorway canopy uses rebus symbols (like a pear) to spell out the name.

CASHION'S EAT PLACE AMERICAN **$$$**
(Map p334; 202-797-1819; www.cashionseatplace.com; 1819 Columbia Rd NW; mains $25-32; dinner Tue-Sun, brunch Sun; Woodley Park-Zoo/Adams Morgan) With an original menu and inviting decor, this little bistro is lauded as one of the city's very best. The mismatched furniture and flower boxes create an unpretentious setting to enjoy rich dishes such as scallion-cream-sauced crab and bison rib-eye with wild mushroom bordelaise. The bar serves fancy late-night fare, like pork cheek and goat cheese quesadillas, till 2am on Friday and Saturday.

LOCAL KNOWLEDGE

FARMERS MARKET

On Saturday mornings the **Adams-Morgan Farmers Market** (Map p334; www.starhollowfarm.com/market; bank plaza, cnr Columbia Rd NW & 18th St NW; 9am-noon Sat May-Nov; Woodley Park-Zoo/Adams Morgan) pops up for a few brief hours. Join locals filling their reusable bags with produce, eggs, cheese, honey and cider from nearby small farms.

JULIA'S EMPANADAS LATIN AMERICAN **$**
(Map p334; www.juliasempanadas.com; 2452 18th St NW; empanadas from $3.50; 11am-2am; Woodley Park-Zoo/Adams Morgan) A frequent winner in DC's 'best late night eats' polls, Julia's stuffs its dough bombs with chorizo, Jamaican beef and curry, spinach and more. Flavors peak if you've been drinking. The little chain has a handful of takeaway shops around town. Cash only.

DRINKING & NIGHTLIFE

TOP CHOICE **DAN'S CAFE** BAR
(Map p334; 2315 18th St NW; from 7pm, closed Sun & Mon; Woodley Park-Zoo/Adams Morgan) Dan's dive is all the more grotty for its location: smack in the middle of the 18th St skimpy-skirt parade. Inside this barely-signed bar is dim lighting, old locals, J Crew-looking types slumming it and DIY flasks of whiskey, coke and a bucket of ice on sale for under $12(!). This is one of DC's great dives; the interior looks like the sort of place an evil Elks Club would have designed, all un-ironically old school 'art,' cheap paneling and dim lights barely illuminating the unapologetic slumminess. Cash only.

BUKOM CAFE
(Map p334; www.bukom.com; 2442 18th St NW; shows 9pm Mon-Thu, 10pm Fri & Sat; Woodley Park-Zoo/Adams Morgan) Come see DC's West African expats get their weekend going, and be prepared for sore but happy hips the next morning, 'cause these cats can move. There's an interesting vibe here when the African clientele gets joined by ex-Peace Corps types who've learned their dancing chops on the continent; this is one of those very DC moments when immigrants plus

an internationally experienced population merge into one happy scene of dancing goodness. The cafe serves chicken yassa, ox-tail stew and other homeland specialties.

TRYST CAFE

(Map p334; www.trystdc.com; 2459 18th St NW; Ⓜ Woodley Park-Zoo/Adams Morgan) This Greenwich Village–style place is a coffeehouse by day, cushy bar bordering on lounge by night. The couches, armchairs and bookshelves, and the light flooding through street-side windows, lure patrons so faithful they probably should pay rent. Sweet alcoholic concoctions flow along with caffeine (sometimes in the same glass), nice complements to the menu of waffles, muffins and cake. It's a swell place to meet up with old friends or make new ones, hence the name.

BLACK SQUIRREL BEER BAR

(Map p334; www.blacksquirreldc.com; 2427 18th St NW; ⏲from 5pm Mon-Fri, from noon Sat & Sun; Ⓜ Woodley Park-Zoo/Adams Morgan) Sometimes in Adams-Morgan all you want is a good friggin' beer – no suds in plastic cups, no Jaeger shots – just a succulent microbrew. The warm, exposed-brick Squirrel stocks more than 100 unusual ales, from Mexican-spiced elixirs to abbey-style triple brews. Hungry? Pair them with the gastropub grub, say mac and locally sourced cheese or Gruyere-smothered, house-ground burgers, per the menu's recommendations. Burgers ring up half price on Thursdays.

STETSON'S FAMOUS BAR & GRILL BAR

(Map p334; www.stetsons-dc.com; 1610 U St NW; Ⓜ U St-Cardozo) Famous? Maybe. But Stetson's is a great bar, period: the floors are scuffed, the outdoor courtyard is packed with smokers, the staff are friendly in that surly friendly way great bar staff can be and the shots come quick. It's popular with congressional Democratic staffers, although it attracts a mixed crowd of anyone you please on weekends.

CHIEF IKE'S MAMBO ROOM BAR

(Map p334; www.chiefikes.com; 1725 Columbia Rd NW; admission free-$8; ⏲9pm-2am; Ⓜ Columbia Heights) What we love about Ike's is how it's a place to get a good Latin groove going…while surrounded by leering *Evil Dead*-esque murals of psychedelic voodoo zombies and assorted other undead. There are punk and hip-hop clubs upstairs if you tire of monster movie mambo, but they don't quite match the awesomeness of the whole Mexican Day of the Dead funfest on the bottom floor.

BOSSA LOUNGE

(Map p334; www.bossaproject.com; 2463 18th St NW; admission from $5; Ⓜ Woodley Park-Zoo/Adams Morgan) Dark, intimate, close and sexy – that's the scene in this Adams-Morgan watering hole. The soundtrack, if you couldn't guess, grooves: jazz, flamenco and bossa nova played in the candlelit lounge. Come drink mojitos and martinis, and taste the delectable tapas during happy hour.

REEF BAR

(Map p334; www.thereefdc.com; 2446 18th St NW; Ⓜ Woodley Park-Zoo/Adams Morgan) We mainly come to Reef for the roof, which is heavenly on hot capital nights, but somehow, everyone always ends up in the aquarium-studded main lounge. That's probably because the roof of the Reef, despite (or because of) it being an amazing space, is often too crowded to really enjoy, at least on weekends. Wherever you end up, every floor is usually packed with the hot and hot-to-trot, so sink a pint and, if you can't make it outside, make a friend next to the fishies.

BLAGUARD IRISH PUB

(Map p334; www.blaguarddc.com; 2003 18th St NW; Ⓜ Dupont Circle) The Blaguard is a great bar in which to finish an Adams-Morgan night. After you've had too much time dancing and screaming into someone's ear, you want a place that'll keep the party going, but is a few notches lower on the crazy scale than a club. This youthful, slightly grungy, neighborhood spot delivers.

HABANA VILLAGE BAR

(Map p334; www.habanavillage.com; 1834 Columbia Rd NW; ⏲from 6:30pm Wed-Sat; Ⓜ Woodley Park-Zoo/Adams Morgan) Squeezed into an old townhouse with a cosmopolitan bar and romantic back room is the Village, which is as close as the capital gets to Cuba. That's not particularly close, but you do get some good, stiff mojitos here, and the music – salsa, meringue, mambo, tango and bossa nova – could make you imagine you were in Miami when the dance floor gets packed, which happens every now and then. Instructors give salsa lessons ($10) each evening at 7:30pm.

1

STEPHEN BOITANO / LONELY PLANET IMAGES ©

2

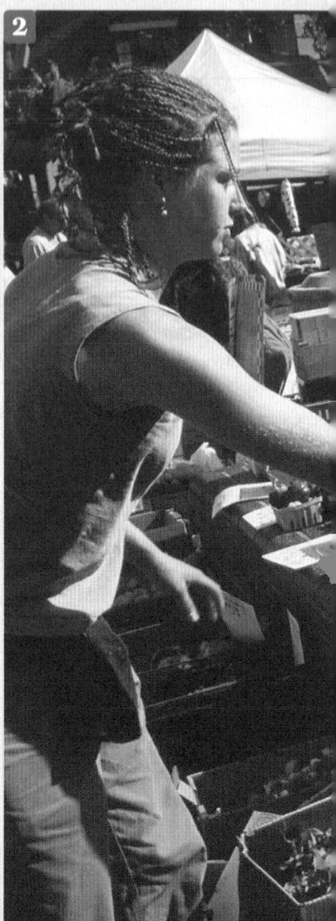

4

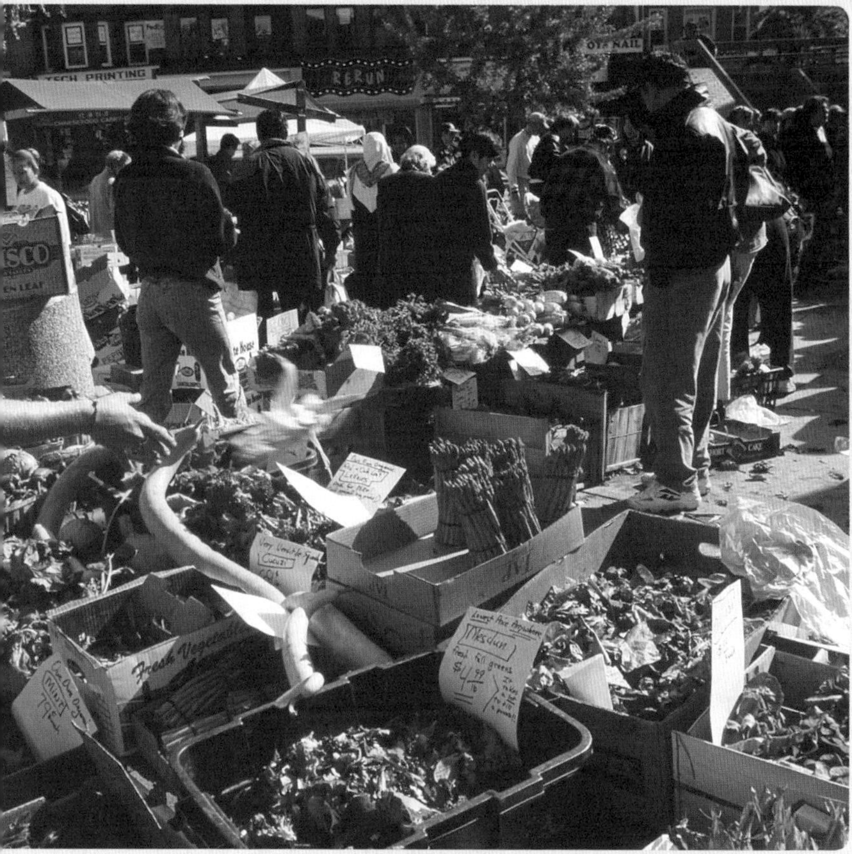

RICK GEHARTER / LONELY PLANET IMAGES ©

1. Madam's Organ (p186)
Patrons gather on the balcony of this famously quirky bar.

2. Adams-Morgan Farmers Market (p182)
Shoppers abound at this Saturday-morning fresh-produce market.

3. Rumba Cafe (p181)
Minty mojitos and mouthwatering South American cuisine are on offer at Rumba.

4. Diner (p180)
The Diner serves hearty, around-the-clock breakfasts and comfort food.

STEPHEN BOITANO / LONELY PLANET IMAGES ©

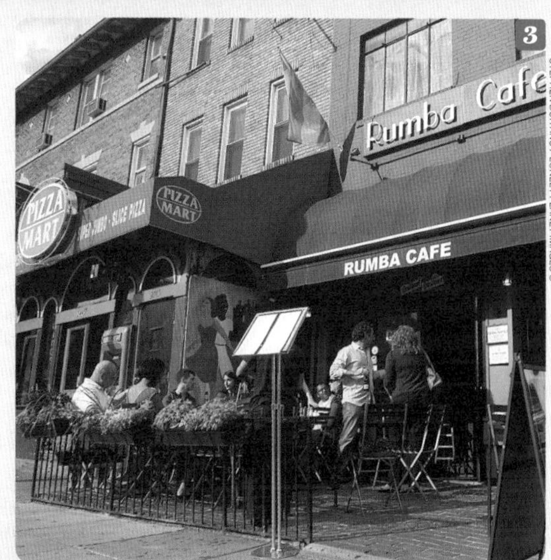

NEIGHBORHOOD RESOURCE

AdMo's businesses work together under the banner **Adams Morgan Main Street** (www.ammainstreet.org). Check the website for neighborhood events and deals at local restaurants, bars and shops.

CHI-CHA LOUNGE LOUNGE

(Map p334; www.latinconcepts.com/chicha.php; 1624 U St NW; MU St-Cardozo) On first thought, Arabic *arguilehs* (hookahs) and Andean food don't seem a felicitous combination, but Chi-Cha makes it work. Curl into velvet settees, nibble Ecuadorian tapas and order a pipe of Bahrainian fruit-and-honey-cured tobacco. A sort of double dose of swarthy clientele pays its respects as a result: Middle Eastern and South American accents are in evidence. Hookahs are available weekdays only.

MILLIE & AL'S BAR

(Map p334; www.millienals.com; 2440 18th St NW; from 4pm; MWoodley Park-Zoo/Adams Morgan) This comfortably worn dive is an Adams-Morgan institution, famous for its $2 drafts, Jell-o shots and hit-the-spot pizza (best consumed in that order). Two TVs show a constant stream of sports. M&A has always been, and probably will always be, a yuppie bar with a frat-house flavor – the kind of place where you can expect to be hit on and have beer spilled on you in the same night.

LOCAL 16 BAR

(Map p334; www.localsixteen.com; 1602 U St NW; MU St-Cardozo) Local 16 has such a great layout – the feel of a hip, semi-Victorian mansion that happens to have been crossed with a slamming bar and sweaty dance club. The problem is it gets too damn sweaty – this is one of those places where you have to elbow someone just to get to the bathroom on weekends, although that said, the person you elbow is probably pretty attractive. The rooftop deck sees plenty of action.

HEAVEN & HELL BAR

(Map p334; www.clubheavenandhelldc.com; 2327 18th St NW; admission from $5; MWoodley Park-Zoo/Adams Morgan) A perennial favorite with the college crowd, this hot spot hosts Heaven (upstairs), with thematic dance parties to flashing disco lights and a cool, airy interior; and Hell (downstairs), grittier, darker, hotter and packed with hard drinkers. The large outdoor patio in Heaven overlooks the 18th St strip and is popular on steamy nights.

ENTERTAINMENT

MADAM'S ORGAN LIVE MUSIC

(Map p334; www.madamsorgan.com; 2461 18th St NW; admission $3-10; MWoodley Park-Zoo/Adams Morgan) 'Where the beautiful people go to get ugly,' according to the T-shirt. It's not far off the mark – this is the kind of perfect dive where you'll see a beautiful girl dancing on the bar one minute and puking in the bathroom the next. A ramshackle place that's been around forever, Madam's Organ was once named one of *Playboy* magazine's favorite bars in America. The live jazz, blues and bluegrass can be downright riot-inducing. There is a roving magician, a raunchy bar-dancing scene, and funky decor with stuffed animals and bizarre paintings on the 1st floor. The big-boobed mural outside is a classic. God bless you, you weird and wonderful Organ – keep DC strange.

COLUMBIA STATION LIVE MUSIC

(Map p334; www.columbiastationdc.com; 2325 18th St NW; admission free; closed Mon; MWoodley Park-Zoo/Adams Morgan) Columbia Station is an intimate spot to listen to nightly jazz and blues, and if you're on a budget it's especially appealing – it doesn't have a cover charge. It's a good date spot (well, assuming your date likes jazz), with lots of low light and, natch, romantic music.

DISTRICT OF COLUMBIA ARTS CENTER THEATER

(Map p334; www.dcartscenter.org; 2438 18th St NW; tickets $10-20; MWoodley Park-Zoo/Adams Morgan) DCAC's theater is a 50-seat black-box venue hosting avant-garde comedy, improv, musicals, dramas and interview shows. Peek in the free art gallery during the day; it's open from 2pm to 7pm Wednesday through Sunday.

SHOPPING

Funky boutiques, antique shops and stores selling ethnic knickknacks are the strong suits here.

CROOKED BEAT RECORDS MUSIC

(Map p334; www.crookedbeat.com; 2116 18th St NW; ⏲1:30-8pm Mon, noon-9pm Tue-Sat, noon-7pm Sun; Ⓜ Woodley Park-Zoo/Adams Morgan) Go underground to enter this excellent record shop, the sort of place that in the '90s could have been its own movie about a bunch of aimless 20-somethings finding love amid stacks of indie, hip-hop and vinyl...you get the idea. Trust us; it's a cool music shop, and to their enormous credit, the folks behind the counter are eminently down to earth.

BRASS KNOB ANTIQUES

(Map p334; www.thebrassknob.com; 2311 18th St NW; ⏲10:30am-6pm Mon-Sat, noon-5pm Sun; Ⓜ Woodley Park-Zoo/Adams Morgan) This unique two-floor shop sells 'rescues' from old buildings: fixtures, lamps, tiles, mantelpieces and mirrors. The store's raison d'être though is the doorknob – brass, wooden, glass, elaborate, polished and antique. If you need to accent your crib like the interior of the best old DC row houses, look no further. Staff can help you find whatever you need, and the classical music overhead adds to the charm.

MEEPS VINTAGE FASHIONETTE VINTAGE

(Map p334; www.meepsdc.com; 2104 18th St NW; ⏲noon-7pm Mon-Sat, to 5pm Sun; Ⓜ Dupont Circle) There's this girl you know: extremely stylish and never seems to have a brand name on her body. Now, picture her wardrobe. Mod dresses, cowboy shirts, suede jackets, beaded purses, leather boots, Jackie O sunglasses and denim jumpsuits: there's Meeps mapped out for you. The store also carries a selection of clever, locally designed T-shirts.

IDLE TIME BOOKS BOOKS

(Map p334; www.idletimebooks.com; 2467 18th St NW; ⏲11am-10pm; Ⓜ Woodley Park-Zoo/Adams Morgan) Three creaky wooden floors are stuffed with secondhand literature and nonfiction, including one of the best secondhand political and history collections in the city. Its sci-fi, sports and humor sections are top-notch, and there's a good newsstand in its front window.

SKYNEAR DESIGNS GALLERY HOMEWARES

(Map p334; www.skyneardesigns.com; 2122 18th Ave NW; Ⓜ Dupont Circle) How much hip can fit over several floors of fab, and what is hip anyway? Barack Obama T-shirts where the president's face is assembled from rhinestones? Bronze candelabras and kitschy coffee tables? How about Japanese-style removable room partitions? It's all for sale in Skynear.

CARAMEL CLOTHING

(Map p334; www.caramelfashion.com; 1603 U St NW; ⏲noon-8pm Thu & Fri, 11am-7pm Sat, noon-6pm Sun; Ⓜ U St-Cardozo) This dapper little boutique on U St sells a well-edited selection of men's and women's clothing and accessories that aim for a stylish effortlessness. Look for comely I-Shandi dresses, eye-catching Leather Island belts and incredibly soft denim apparel. The artwork on the walls is also for sale – all created by local artists.

TORO MATA HANDICRAFTS

(Map p334; www.toromata.com; 2410 18th St NW; ⏲noon-8pm Tue-Fri, 10am-8pm Sat, noon-6pm Sun; Ⓜ Woodley Park-Zoo/Adams Morgan) If your Andean trip fell through this year, Toro Mata provides a good backup plan. Inside the handsomely laid-out store you'll find a well-curated selection of Peruvian objects, including fluffy Alpaca rugs and cuddly stuffed animals, hand-carved chess sets and folk-art tableau, colorful tapestries, furniture and woven hats and sweaters. The friendly owners have a wealth of knowledge on Peru.

SMASH! MUSIC, CLOTHING

(Map p334; www.smashrecords.com; 2314 18th St NW; ⏲noon-9pm Mon-Thu, to 10pm Fri & Sat, to 7pm Sun; Ⓜ Woodley Park-Zoo/Adams Morgan) There's a slightly punk-rock vibe to this small upstairs shop. In addition to a solid selection of vinyl (covering mostly classic and indie rock and soul), Smash! sells used and new CDs, punky T-shirts, Doc Martens and secondhand clothing.

COMMONWEALTH CLOTHING

(Map p334; www.cmonwealth.com; 1781 Florida Ave NW; Ⓜ Dupont Circle) With a purely hip-hop aesthetic, this shop sells one-of-a-kind sneakers and graphic T-shirts. You can add to the wardrobe at a couple of other street-fashion shops in the same building.

FLEET FEET SHOES

(Map p334; www.fleetfeetdc.com; 1841 Columbia Rd NW; Ⓜ Woodley Park-Zoo/Adams Morgan) Shoes for every sporting activity are on sale at this outlet of the national chain, and the personalized service ensures your feet get what they need. The store hosts free runs at 9am Sunday; they're typically 5 miles and often swing through nearby Rock Creek Park. Women-only runs take place Wednesdays at 6pm.

B&K NEWSSTAND PIPE SHOP

(Map p334; 2414 18th St NW; 9am-9pm; M Woodley Park-Zoo/Adams Morgan) No one asks for the *New York Times,* because B&K is really a head (pipe) shop, one of the most famed among the city's stoner set. All of the glassware is, of course, to be used for tobacco smoking. Beyond all of the cigars, pipes and bongs is an almost clichéd array of Bob Marley paraphernalia along with other Amsterdam-esque accoutrements.

U Street, Columbia Heights & Northeast

U ST & SHAW | COLUMBIA HEIGHTS & MT PLEASANT | NORTHEAST DC

Neighborhood Top Five

❶ Wander along U St and take in its jazzy history, troubled descent and vibrant rebirth as an arts and entertainment district, then contemplate it over a meal at **Ben's Chili Bowl** (p195).

❷ Walk through wooded groves at the **National Arboretum** (p192).

❸ Fork into meatloaf and cornbread at soul-food joints like **Florida Avenue Grill** (p197).

❹ Discuss politics, sip free-trade coffee or spout verse at **Busboys & Poets** (p196).

❺ Gawk at Lincoln's assassination bullet and more macabre exhibits at the **National Museum of Health and Medicine** (see the boxed text, p194).

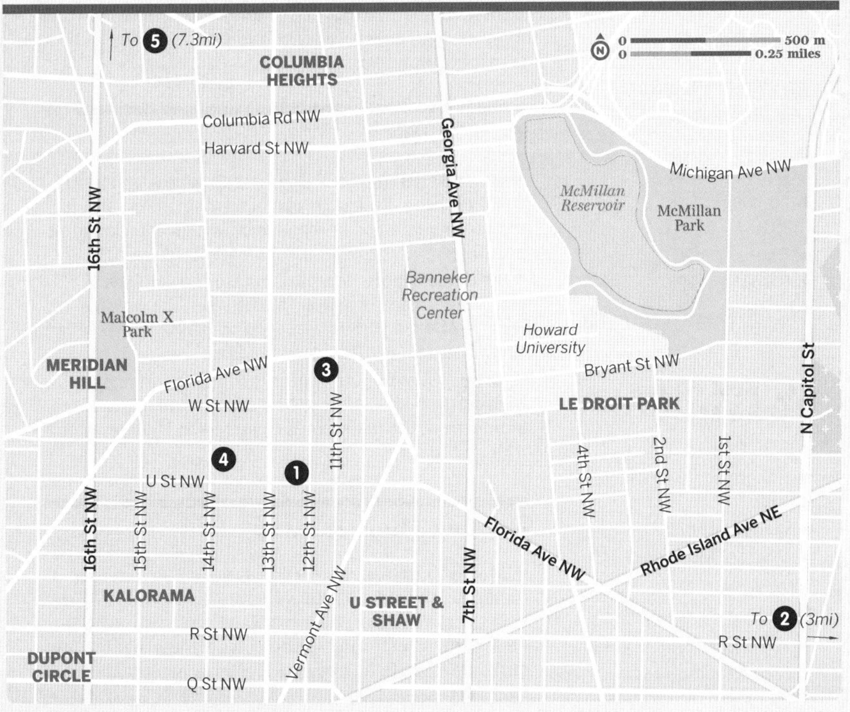

For more detail of this area, see Map p336 ➡

Lonely Planet's Top Tip

Keep an eye out for all the murals splashed across the neighborhood's walls, especially around U St. A painting of local son Duke Ellington, by G Byron Peck, stares out from the True Reformer Building at 1200 U St. Across the way *The Alchemy of Ben Ali*, by Eric B Ricks, pays colorful homage to the founder of Ben's Chili Bowl. *Community Rhythms*, by Alfred J Smith, fills the U Street Metro station tunnel.

Best Places to Eat

- Ben's Chili Bowl (p195)
- Busboys & Poets (p196)
- Sticky Fingers (p198)
- Coppi's Organic (p196)
- Hitching Post (p198)

For reviews, see p195

Best Places to Drink

- Wonderland (p200)
- Marvin (p199)
- Looking Glass Lounge (p201)
- Room 11 (p201)
- Saloon (p199)

For reviews, see p199

Best Places for Music

- 9:30 Club (p202)
- Bohemian Caverns (p202)
- Black Cat (p202)
- U Street Music Hall (p202)
- Velvet Lounge (p202)

For reviews, see p201

Explore U Street, Columbia Heights & Northeast

The U St Corridor and Columbia Heights have changed more in recent years than probably any other neighborhoods. U St's story, in particular, is remarkable. By the early 1900s, it was one of the most vibrant African American neighborhoods in the country, akin to New York's Harlem. Duke Ellington, Ella Fitzgerald and Louis Armstrong all made sweet music in the Great Black Way's clubs. Then came a long period of neglect, punctuated by the 1968 riots. Revitalization started in the 1990s when the city built the U St Metro station. Cheap rents reeled in restaurants, artists, clubs and creative types, until it became what it is today: a multicultural 'hood of good eats, fab music and eccentric indie boutiques. A dose of scholarliness and activism spill over from Howard University, in nearby Shaw. Between U St's heritage sites, diners and slew of jazz and rock venues, plan on a full day here.

To the north, Columbia Heights and neighboring Mt Pleasant have a reputation as an enclave for Latino immigrants and hipsters. There are no real sights here, but the cheap ethnic food and unassuming punk dive bars can occupy many an evening.

Northeast DC is a vast stretch of leafy residential blocks holding several far-flung sights. Nature lovers have a couple of groovy, free landscapes to explore, as long as you have a car or don't mind lengthy public-transportation trips.

Local Life

- **Be at Ben's** The Chili Bowl (p195) is no secret, and you'll probably find a busload of tourists inside. But it remains a real neighborhood spot, with locals downing half-smokes and gossiping over sweet iced tea.
- **Alfresco Tipple** Beer gardens are chockablock in this part of DC, where everyone heads when the weather warms. Marvin (p199), Wonderland (p200) and Looking Glass Lounge (p201) set the standard.
- **Groovy Shops** Join residents filling their bags with comic books, vintage brooches and ties-turned-handbags at the little stores clustered on U St between 15th and 16th Sts.

Getting There & Away

- **Metro** The Green and Yellow Lines run in tandem to most of the sites. Useful stops are U St-Cardozo (for U St Corridor sites), Columbia Heights (for it and Mt Pleasant hot spots) and Georgia Ave-Petworth (for a few outlying bars). Religious sites cluster near Brookland-CUA (Red Line).

SIGHTS

U Street & Shaw

AFRICAN AMERICAN CIVIL WAR MEMORIAL — MONUMENT

(Map p336; www.afroamcivilwar.org; cnr U St & Vermont Ave NW; MU St-Cardozo) Standing at the center of a granite plaza, this bronze statue depicting rifle-bearing troops is DC's first major art piece by black sculptor Ed Hamilton. The sculpture is surrounded on three sides by the Wall of Honor, listing the names of 209,145 black troops who fought in the Union Army, as well as the 7000 white soldiers who served alongside them. You can use the directory to locate individual names within each of the regiments. Exit the Metro station at 10th St (just follow the 'memorial' signs as you leave the train).

FREE AFRICAN AMERICAN CIVIL WAR MUSEUM — MUSEUM

(Map p336; 202-667-2667; www.afroamcivilwar.org; 1925 Vermont Ave NW; 10am-6:30pm Tue-Fri, to 4pm Sat, noon-4pm Sun; MU St-Cardozo) Located behind the memorial, across Vermont Ave, the museum opened in 2011 in a spacious old schoolhouse. It makes the point that for some, the Civil War was about secession versus union, but for others, it was a matter of breaking human bondage. The permanent exhibit includes photographs, documents and audiovisual programs following African American history from the Civil War through the Civil Rights movement. The **Civil War Soldiers and Sailors Project** allows visitors to search for ancestors in databases of black troops, regiments and battles.

HOWARD UNIVERSITY — UNIVERSITY

(Map p336; www.howard.edu; 2400 6th St NW; MShaw-Howard U) The Shaw neighborhood is as defined by Howard University as Georgetown is by her titular school. Founded in 1867, this remains the nation's most prestigious traditionally African American institute of higher education. Distinguished alumni include the late Supreme Court Justice Thurgood Marshall (who enrolled after he was turned away from the University of Maryland's then all-white law school), Ralph Bunche, Nobel laureate Toni Morrison and former New York City mayor David Dinkins. Today Howard enrolls around 12,000 students in 18 schools. There are campus **tours** (www.howard.edu/explore) and a friendly **Welcome Center** (1739 7th St NW). The surrounding streets are largely filled with vegan cafes serving ital (Rastafarian-approved) food, bookstores selling Pan-African and black nationalist lit, and record stores stocked with funk, jazz, blues and hip-hop.

Founders' Library, a handsome Georgian building with a gold spire and giant clock, is the campus' architectural centerpiece. It houses the **Moorland-Spingarn Research Center** (www.howard.edu/msrc; 9am-4:45pm Mon & Wed, to 4:30pm Fri), which boasts the nation's largest collection of African American literature. Nearby the **Howard University Gallery of Art** (Childers Hall; 9:30am-5pm Mon-Fri, noon-4pm Sun) has an impressive collection of work, largely dominated by African and African American artists.

ST AUGUSTINE CATHOLIC CHURCH — CHURCH

(Map p336; www.saintaugustine-dc.org; cnr 15th & V Sts NW; mass 10am & 12:30pm Sun; MU St-Cardozo) Let the spirit move you at DC's oldest black Catholic congregation. Clad in Kente cloth and sporting soloists just waiting to bust their lungs, the 165 members of the St Augustine gospel choir rock the house every Sunday at 12:30pm. The mass is long, but it's a hell of a lot of fun and spiritually nourishing to boot. For calmer

VISITORS CENTER & DIY TOURS

The **Greater U Street Visitors Center** (1211 U St; 10am-6pm) sits on the floor above Ben's Next Door. It's a partnership between the restaurant and **Cultural Tourism DC** (www.culturaltourismdc.org), with photos and simple exhibits on U Street's history, info on local businesses and, of course, Ben's Chili Bowl souvenirs. Pick up the free booklet *City Within a City: Greater U Street Heritage Trail* or download it from the website. It's also available as an excellent **free audio tour** (www.audisseyguides.com/ustreet); to access it via smartphone, go to dc.toursphere.com.

but equally beautiful music, come for 10am mass, when the church chorale sings traditional Catholic hymns.

Founded in 1858, St Augustine's congregation moved to the Gothic-revival building at 15th and V Sts NW in 1961. It was a bold move, and marked a merger with an all-white congregation; the joined churches became known as Sts Paul & Augustine. The name reverted to St Augustine in 1982, but the congregation continues to welcome members of all races and ethnic groups. If you go, wear your Sunday best.

PROJECT 4 GALLERY

(Map p336; www.project4gallery.com; 1353 U St NW; noon-6pm Wed-Sat; U St-Cardozo) Extremely hip Project 4 showcases some of the best of the contemporary and pop-art scene.

Columbia Heights & Mt Pleasant

MT PLEASANT STREET STREET

(Map p336; Columbia Heights) There's no consensus as to why so many immigrants in the Metro area are Central American as opposed to Mexican, but what can be confirmed is Mt Pleasant St is the *corazón* of DC's Latino, largely Salvadoran community. Every few businesses advertise money-transfer services to San Salvador or surrounds, or sell cheap, delicious *pupusas* (Salvadoran baked turnovers stuffed with cheese and pork), or both. Look out for the 7-Eleven, popularly known as **El Seven** (cnr Kenyon St & Mt Pleasant St NW); the storefront is a popular informal hangout (inside, it's just a 7-Eleven).

LOCAL KNOWLEDGE

RESERVOIR BOG

On Michigan Ave and North Capitol St, you'll notice a string of cylindrical concrete structures that look like the entrance to the Kingdom of the Mole People sticking out of a grassy field. This is the **McMillan Reservoir Sand Filtration Plant**; the buildings are ruins of old water reservoirs. It is a huge, open and basically unused area. The District hasn't been able to decide what to do with it since 1987 – suggestions range from a new park to more housing. In the meantime, those old reservoir towers look pretty cool from the road.

Northeast DC

FREE **UNITED STATES NATIONAL ARBORETUM** GARDENS

(202-245-2726; www.usna.usda.gov; 3501 New York Ave NE; tram tours adult/child $4/2; 8am-5pm, tram tours Sat, Sun & holidays mid-Apr–mid-Oct) The best things in life – or this city – require a little effort. In this case, you need wheels to reach the greatest green space in Washington, almost 450 acres of meadowland, sylvan theaters and a pastoral setting that feels somewhere between bucolic Americana countryside and a Romantic artist's conception of classical Greek ruralscapes.

Stop at the **Administration Building** near the R St gate for a map and self-guided walking tour information. Highlights include the **Bonsai & Penjing Museum** (10am-4pm Mar-Oct), east of the Administration Building, and the **Capitol Columns Garden**, south along Ellipse Rd. The latter is studded with Corinthian pillars removed from the Capitol in the 1950s. A short distance further south, the **National Grove of State Trees** rises up. The Admin Building offers the complete list and map, so Ohioans can navigate quickly to the buckeye tree, New Yorkers to the sugar maple, Californians to the giant sequoia etc.

The best times to visit are spring (March to May, when the azaleas bloom) and fall (September to November, for colorful autumn leaves). No direct buses serve the gardens and they're hard to negotiate on foot, so drive or cycle.

FREE **KENILWORTH AQUATIC GARDENS** GARDENS

(202-426-6905; www.nps.gov/keaq; 1550 Anacostia Ave NE; 7am-4:30pm, to 5pm Jun-Aug; Deanwood) DC was built on a marsh, a beautiful, brackish, low-lying ripple of saw grass and steel-blue water, wind-coaxed and tide touched by the inflow of the Potomac from the Chesapeake Bay. You'd never know all that now, of course, unless you come to the only national park in the USA devoted to water plants. The aquatic gardens were begun as the hobby of a Civil War veteran and operated for 56 years as a commercial

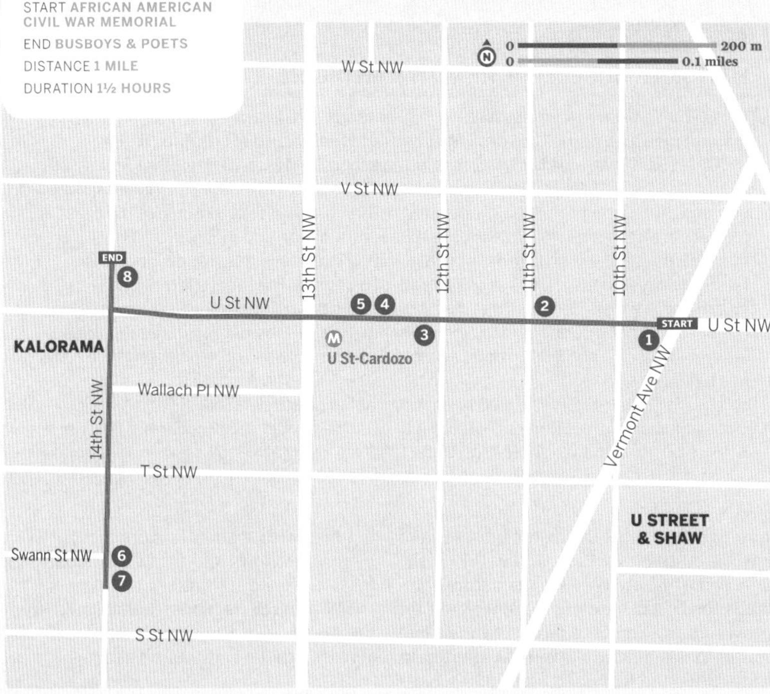

Neighborhood Walk

U Street Stroll

Wander and learn about the U St Corridor's rich African American heritage and renewal.

Exit the U St-Cardozo Metro station at the 10th St exit and wander around the ❶ **African American Civil War Memorial** plaza. Why is this sculpture here? Because the Metro stop, which opened in 1991, was one of the first heralds of new development in the formerly downtrodden area. The memorial reminds black residents that the rebuilding of their community has been accomplished before, by ancestors who fought for their people's freedom.

Now walk west along U St – the numbered cross streets should be going up. At the corner of U and 11th Sts, the legendary jazz club ❷ **Bohemian Caverns** hosted names like Miles, Coltrane and Ellington. Speaking of the latter: at 1200 U St there's a ❸ **Mural of Duke Ellington**, perhaps DC's most renowned musical native son, who grew up just around the way on Bates St.

Cross the street and pop into ❹ **Ben's Chili Bowl**, one of the city's most iconic restaurants and one of the few businesses to survive since the 1950s. Grab a counter stool and chow down a chili half-smoke.

Next door, the ❺ **Lincoln Theatre** is the heart of what was once termed 'Black Broadway' – Billie Holiday, Ella Fitzgerald, Louis Armstrong and Cab Calloway all graced the stage. The '68 riots shut it down. Revitalization projects in the early '90s reopened it.

Spirited shops and clubs dot 14th St. Turn left (south), and after passing T St you'll run into the ❻ **Black Cat**. The Foo Fighters' Dave Grohl started the club, and it hosts ripping rock sets most nights. Nearby ❼ **Home Rule** sells brightly painted homewares. Artists made the counter mosaic with smashed glass from the 1968 riots.

Now head north until you reach ❽ **Busboys & Poets**, a cafe and progressive bookstore that hosts readings and performances. It remains one of the artistic linchpins of the U St revival.

WORTH A DETOUR

NATIONAL MUSEUM OF HEALTH & MEDICINE

Once you've seen a giant hairball, you never forget it. Generations have had that distinct pleasure at the **National Museum of Health and Medicine** (NMHM; ☎301-319-3349; www.nmhm.washingtondc.museum; 2500 Linden Lane, Silver Spring, MD; admission free; ⏰10am-5:30pm). Opened in 1862, it's one of the oldest museums in the city and one of the few partially operated by the military. That's because the focus of the museum's eclectic collection is military medicine – the displays on Civil War combat 'nursing' are gruesome and fascinating in equal measure. It's not for the faint-hearted – visitors will see the effects of diseases, the tools used to battle them and all the messy side and after effects. Probably the most popular exhibit remains the paraphernalia connected to Abraham Lincoln's assassination, including the bullet that killed him and bits of bone and hair from Lincoln's skull. And then there's the hairball...

The museum recently moved to new digs at Fort Detrick's Forest Glen Annex. That's officially out of the District, but just over the border in Silver Spring, MD (about 8 miles north of the White House). Unfortunately, the Metro won't get you very close, so it's easiest to drive out. Parking is free. Bring photo ID.

water garden, until the federal government purchased them in 1938. Today this is the only place in the city to see the natural wetlands the District sprang from; look out for beaver dams, clouds of birds and the more traditional manicured grounds, quilted in water lilies and lotus.

The park is about a mile walk from the Metro. Depart the station from the lower Polk St exit and take the pedestrian overpass across Kenilworth Ave. Go left on Douglas St, then go right on Anacostia Ave and enter any gate on your left.

BASILICA OF THE NATIONAL SHRINE OF THE IMMACULATE CONCEPTION — CHURCH

(www.nationalshrine.com; 400 Michigan Ave NE; ⏰7am-7pm Apr-Oct, to 6pm Nov-Mar; Ⓜ Brookland-CUA) The largest Catholic house of worship in North America can host 6000 worshippers. (Some might say that's when the building is at critical *mass*. Get it?) This is an enormous, impressive, but somehow unimposing edifice, more Byzantine than Vatican in its aesthetic. Outlaid with some 75,000 sq ft of mosaic work and a crypt modeled after early Christian catacombs, the (literal) crowning glory is a dome that could have been lifted off the Hagia Sophia in Istanbul. The Marian shrine sports an eclectic mix of Romanesque and Byzantine motifs, all anchored by a 329ft minaret-shaped campanile. Downstairs, the original Eastern-style crypt church has low, mosaic-covered vaulted ceilings lit by votives and chandeliers. Upstairs, the main sanctuary is lined with elaborate saints' chapels, lit by rose windows and fronted by a dazzling mosaic of a stern Christ.

The church is about a half-mile from the Metro. Exit the station and head west across Catholic University's campus.

POPE JOHN PAUL II SHRINE & CULTURAL CENTER — MUSEUM

(www.jp2cc.org; 3900 Harwood Rd NE; suggested donation adult $5; ⏰10am-5pm Tue-Thu; Ⓜ Brookland-CUA) An adjunct for many devotees who visit the Basilica of the National Shrine of the Immaculate Conception, this modernist-style structure is an unexpected setting for a museum of the Catholic Church. Galleries explore the history of the church, personal faith, and its relation to science, community and social service. At the time of writing, the center was undergoing renovation, with the building open on a limited basis while new exhibits are being developed. The center is about a quarter mile north of the basilica on Harewood Rd.

FRANCISCAN MONASTERY — MONASTERY, GARDENS

(www.myfranciscan.com; 1400 Quincy St NE; admission by donation; ⏰hourly tours 9am-4pm Mon-Sat, 1-4pm Sun; Ⓜ Brookland-CUA) This honey-colored compound leaps out like an unexpected religious slap from the surrounding parkland and residential row houses. Also known as Mt St Sepulchre, the building is pretty but not particularly unique; more interesting are the carefully maintained grounds, threaded with walkways that lead past 44 acres of tulips, dogwoods, cherry trees and roses – and some unintentionally tacky recreations of venerated places. The Order of St Francis is charged with the guardianship of the Holy Land's sacred sites, and it has interpreted that task in a unique – and broad – way here, constructing replicas for the faithful on its grounds. There are life-size fake-granite reproductions of the Tomb of Mary and the Grotto at Lourdes, and within Mt St Sepulchre itself are reproductions of the Roman Catacombs under the sanctuary floor. These dark, narrow passages wind past some fake tombs and the very real remains of Sts Innocent and Benignus; claustrophobes need not apply. It's all creepy and fascinating, like a holy Disneyland. Reach it from the Metro station by walking north on Michigan Ave NE to Quincy St; it's about three-quarters of a mile.

GALLAUDET UNIVERSITY UNIVERSITY

(off Map p336; www.gallaudet.edu; 800 Florida Ave NE; MUnion Station) The first university for deaf and hard-of-hearing students in the world occupies a lovely manicured campus of bucolic green and Gothic accents north of Capitol Hill. Notable buildings include **College Hall**, an antique vision in brownstone, and **Chapel Hall**, a gorgeous Gothic structure that screams academia. The American football huddle was invented here when the Bisons (the school team) noticed other teams were trying to interpret their sign language while they plotted their plays. If you speak sign language, note that Gallaudet is a bilingual institution where English sign language and ASL are both practiced. Union Station is the closest Metro stop, but it's a little over a mile walk (25 minutes); you may want to take a cab or drive out here.

FREE FORT STEVENS PARK HISTORIC SITE

(www.nps.gov/cwdw; cnr 13th & Quackenbos Sts NW; 70, 79 from Gallery Pl-Chinatown) In a raid on July 11, 1864, Confederate General Jubal Early attacked Fort Stevens, the northernmost of the defensive ramparts ringing the city. A small but fierce battle raged – the only time the Civil War touched District soil – until Early's men withdrew across the Potomac. Abraham Lincoln himself was drawn into the shooting: the president, observing the battle from Fort Stevens' parapet, popped his head up so many times that Oliver Wendell Holmes, Jr, then a Union captain, yelled 'Get down, you damn fool, before you get shot!' The fort has been partially restored, and 41 Union men who died in its defense are buried at tiny **Battleground National Cemetery** (6625 Georgia Ave NW), a half-mile north.

EATING

U Street & Shaw

TOP CHOICE BEN'S CHILI BOWL AMERICAN $

(Map p336; www.benschilibowl.com; 1213 U St; mains $5-9; breakfast, lunch & dinner daily, to 4am Fri & Sat; MU St-Cardozo) Ben's is to DC dining what the White House and Capitol are to sightseeing: a must-visit. To take that analogy a little further, while the White House and Capitol are the most recognizably important symbols of DC as capital, Ben's holds the same status as regards DC, the place where people live. Opened and operated by Ben and Virginia Ali and family (Ben died in 2009; the alley adjacent is named in his honor), the diner-style Bowl has been around since 1958. It's one of the only businesses on U St to have survived the 1968 riots and the disruption that accompanied construction of the U Street

LOCAL KNOWLEDGE

FARMERS MARKETS

If you miss the following weekend markets, swing by Smucker Farms (p203), a brick-and-mortar shop stocked with from-the-countryside wares.

14th & U Farmers' Market (Map p336; www.marketsandmore.net; 14th & U Sts NW; 9am-1pm Sat May–mid-Nov; MU St-Cardozo)

Bloomingdale Farmers' Market (Map p336; www.marketsandmore.net; 102 R St NW; 10am-2pm Sun mid-May–mid-Nov; MShaw-Howard U)

Mt Pleasant Farmers' Market (Map p336; www.mtpfm.org; Lamont Park, 3200 Mt Pleasant St NW; 9am-1pm Sat year-round; MColumbia Heights)

Metro stop. The main stock in trade are half-smokes, DC's meatier, smokier version of the hot dog, usually slathered in mustard and the namesake chili. Until recently, Bill Cosby was the only person who ate here for free, but Michelle Obama and daughters Sasha and Malia get the nod too – though apparently, not their presidential dad. That's a short list, as a *lot* of famous faces have passed through these doors, from Bono to both Bushes. Cash only.

BEN'S NEXT DOOR AMERICAN **$$**

(Map p336; ☎202-667-0909; www.bensnextdoor.com; 1211 U St; mains $17-28; ⏰lunch & dinner daily; Ⓜ U St-Cardozo) Ben's Next Door is, yes, next door to Ben's Chili Bowl. It offers more upscale Southern fare (steak, trout etc), along with beer and cocktails, in a warm, wood-floored room. That said, you can also get half-smokes and the rest of the Chili Bowl items over here (though we prefer to scarf them while sitting at the counter in their original environment).

BUSBOYS & POETS AMERICAN **$$**

(Map p336; ☎202-387-7638; www.busboysandpoets.com; 2021 14th St NW; mains $8-14; ⏰8am-midnight Mon-Thu, to 2am Fri, 9am-2am Sat, 9am-midnight Sun; Ⓜ U St-Cardozo; 📶) Busboys (named for a Langston Hughes poem) has become as much a keystone of the U St scene as Ben's Chili Bowl. It seems to capture that sense of what DC really *is*. So what is DC? Intellectual, multiracial, opinionated, creative, takes itself a little too seriously (just perhaps), supportive of its local community, but sometimes a bit too obsessed by its own laptop. Everything we've just described is pretty much the daily scene inside B&P, the sort of place where everyone gathers for coffee, wi-fi and a progressive vibe (and attached bookstore) that makes San Francisco feel conservative. The food is upscale diner: sandwiches, burgers, pizzas and the like, all quite tasty and reasonably priced. There are a couple of other B&P locations, but this one is the flagship.

WHAT'S A HALF-SMOKE?

DC's claim to native culinary fame is the half-smoke, a bigger, coarser, spicier and better version of the hot dog. There's little agreement on where the name comes from – half beef/half pork? (But some are all beef!) Because the sausage is usually split down the middle? Because they can be grilled or steamed? Who knows? But there is general consensus as to what goes on a half-smoke. New Yorkers like their mustard and relish, Chicagoans dress their dogs with a freakin' garden, and in DC? Chili and chopped onions, baby.

COPPI'S ORGANIC ITALIAN **$$**

(Map p336; ☎202-319-7773; www.coppisorganic.com; 1414 U St NW; pizza from $16, mains $19-27; ⏰dinner daily, brunch Sat & Sun; Ⓜ U St-Cardozo) Coppi's is an old-school U St restaurant that fires up the wood-burning oven nightly to serve perfectly crusted, crispy pizzas along with other seasonal and traditional Italian delicacies. The owner is crazy about bicycles and the cozy restaurant is jammed with biking memorabilia. More importantly, the owner obsesses over fresh, high-quality ingredients, a consuming passion that shines through in the Italian fare. Coppi's gets packed on weekends, when locals flock in to partake of all of the above, plus some good cheap wine.

CHIX LATIN AMERICAN **$**

(Map p336; ☎202-234-2449; www.chixdc.com; 2019 11th St NW; mains $9-13; ⏰11:30am-10pm Mon-Fri, from noon Sat & Sun; Ⓜ U St-Cardozo; 📶) The DC area takes its Peruvian chicken seriously. If you haven't had the stuff, it's slow-roasted, rotisserie style, and is it good: succulent, juicy, the savory skin complementing the comforting pillows of meat. Most of the best Peruvian chicken *(pollo a la brasa)* in the area is actually outside of the city in the Maryland and Virginia 'burbs, but Chix is about as good as it gets in the District itself. Plus, Chix is green and good: it was built with sustainable materials and the cups are made out of fast-degrading corn. Vegetarian dishes – mostly sides such as black beans and seasonal greens – are available, too.

OOHH'S & AAHH'S SOUTHERN **$$**

(Map p336; ☎202-667-7142; www.oohhsnaahhs.com; 1005 U St NW; mains $14-26; ⏰noon-10pm Mon-Thu, to 4am Fri & Sat, to 7pm Sun; Ⓜ U St-Cardozo) Some of DC's best soul food is on offer at this barebones U St joint popular with everyone from the homeless to sports superstars. The down-home Southern cooking comes in plentiful portions; it's hard to walk away from the fish platter with some mac 'n' cheese and greens without being filled up, unless you're some kind of human trash compacter. The clientele is very much made up of the U St that was before this part of town became gentrified.

EATONVILLE SOUTHERN $$

(Map p336; ☎202-332-9672; www.eatonvillerestaurant.com; 2121 U St NW; mains $16-21; ⏰lunch & dinner Mon-Fri, brunch & dinner Sat & Sun; Ⓜ U St-Cardozo) Novelist Zora Neal Hurston is the unconventional theme at this restaurant. Eatonville was her home town; we're not sure if the easy pun 'Eating-ville' was another source of the name. What do you expect of the guys who opened next-door Busboys & Poets? The atmosphere is superb, a sort of bayou dripped through impressionist-style murals of the South, then resurrected upon a modernist, cavernous dining hall that looks like nothing less than a cathedral to black intelligentsia. And the food? Very fine. Catfish come correct with cheese grits, and the andouille-and-sweet-potato hash…don't get us started. Wash it down with lavender lemonade, which, on hot summer days, is sort of like drinking sex.

FLORIDA AVENUE GRILL SOUTHERN $$

(Map p336; ☎202-265-1586; www.floridaavenuegrill.com; 1100 Florida Ave NW; mains $9-16; ⏰8am-9pm Tue-Sat, to 4:30pm Sun; Ⓜ U St-Cardozo) Besides the Hitching Post, we deem the Grill DC's quintessential diner. Be they president, Harlem globetrotter or college student, they've all come here for almost 70 years to eat turkey legs, catfish and meatloaf served with sides of sweet tea and more character than Shakespeare's collected works.

RESTAURANT JUDY LATIN AMERICAN $$

(Map p336; ☎202-265-2519; 2212 14th St; mains $7-15; ⏰breakfast, lunch & dinner; Ⓜ U St-Cardozo) When we asked a Honduran friend where to get good Central American food, her unhesitating answer was: 'Judy's.' Everything's good, but the breakfasts, consisting of tamales, white cheese and other odds and ends, are tops. Come at night for the best Spanish-language karaoke in town; if you don't speak Spanish, work on your hand gesturing.

SANKOFA CAFE $

(Map p336; ☎202-332-1084; www.sankofa.com; 2714 Georgia Ave NW; mains $7; ⏰9:30am-8pm Mon-Sat, 11am-6pm Sun; Ⓜ Columbia Heights; 📶✍) Good for your soul and your body, Sankofa is basically a black intellectual cafe expounding the old school Pan-African ideal. In the 21st century it still fronts an excellent African/African American-themed bookstore and video place, but don't miss the sandwiches, salads and wraps; the wraps constitute some of the best vegan fare in town. We're all about the Gaston Kaboré garlic hummus, honey Dijon, olives etc served in an excellent tortilla.

CRÈME SOUTHERN $$

(Map p336; ☎202-234-1884; www.cremedc.com; 1322 U St NW; mains $13-24; ⏰dinner Mon-Sat, brunch Sat & Sun; Ⓜ U St-Cardozo) Crème's upscale soul attracts a multiculti crowd and is particularly popular with buppies (black yuppies), who enjoy a stick-to-your-ribs menu served in a slick dining room of soft beiges and buffed metal. Fight for seats at Sunday brunch; the chicken and waffles might be our favorite night-after nosh in DC, and based on the lines out the door, we're not the only folks sharing that opinion.

PEARL DIVE OYSTER PALACE SEAFOOD $$

(Map p336; www.pearldivedc.com; 1612 14th St NW; mains $19-25; ⏰noon-3pm Fri & Sat, 11am-3pm Sun, dinner daily; Ⓜ U St-Cardozo) Flashy Pearl Dive serves exceptional, sustainable oysters from both coasts, along with braised duck and oyster gumbo, crab cakes and insanely rich peanut butter chocolate pie. Fresh air from the big front windows wafts through the open industrial space, done up in a nautical, weathered-wood motif. They don't take reservations. Instead you'll need to pull a number (like at a deli) and watch for it to flash up while hanging at either the oyster bar on the main floor or Black Jack's bar upstairs.

ETETE ETHIOPIAN $$

(Map p336; ☎202-232-7600; www.eteterestaurant.com; 1942 9th St NW; mains $10-20; ⏰11:30am-11pm; Ⓜ U St-Cardozo; ✍) In the small ethnic enclave on 9th St sometimes called 'Little Ethiopia', Etete serves authentic and high-quality food – fiery *yebeg wat* (spicy lamb stew), tender *goden tibs* (marinated short beef ribs), bountiful vegetarian platters and tangy *injera* (spongy flatbread) for soaking it all up.

DESPERADOS BURGERS $

(Map p336; www.desperadosburgers.com; 1342 U St NW; burgers & sandwiches $9-11; ⏰11am-1am;

Ⓜ U St-Cardozo) Subterranean Desperados is a sweet dive in which to grab a burger and beer with friends. The eponymous patty comes topped with roasted pork, Swiss cheese and rémoulade sauce. Shrimp po' boys and frickles (fried pickles) add joy to your brewski, too.

Columbia Heights & Mt Pleasant

STICKY FINGERS VEGAN **$**

(Map p336; ☎202-299-9700; www.stickyfingersbakery.com; 1370 Park Rd NW; mains $5-10; ⏰breakfast, lunch & dinner; Ⓜ Columbia Heights; 📶🖉) The sesame udon, soy barbecue nuggets, gluten-free pancakes and tofu scramble are but foreplay to the screamingly yum peanut butter fudge and raspberry cream cupcakes. Sticky Fingers is primarily a bakery, with a wee dining area attached. Order at the counter, then salivate over your purchases at the close-quartered retro tables where fellow vegans tap away on their Macbooks.

HEIGHTS AMERICAN **$$**

(Map p336; ☎202-797-7227; www.theheightsdc.com; 3115 14th St NW; mains $10-19; ⏰lunch & dinner; Ⓜ Columbia Heights) Heights' food is excellent Americana stuff – the fried chicken and mashed potatoes is wonderful, and wasabi-crusted fish is gorgeous, but whatever you do, come on a weekend and order off the greatest Bloody Mary menu on Earth. Select from 10 different types of vodka, or tequila, or gin, then add from a glut of options, including beef broth, clam juice, Old Bay seasoning, lump crabmeat, bacon – well, we could go on. By the way, you can order all of the above *together*. Of course, then time would stop and the universe would implode upon itself, so you probably shouldn't.

RED ROCKS PIZZERIA PIZZA **$$**

(Map p336; ☎202-506-1402; www.redrocksdc.com; 1063 Park Rd NW; pizza from $12; ⏰lunch Tue-Sun, dinner daily; Ⓜ Columbia Heights) Red Rocks has been voted best pizza in the city in a glut of DC publications since its opening. That's testament to the unswerving excellence of their irregularly shaped, brick-fired pies, all of which feel like they were individually crafted – because they have been. You're not gonna be shocked by any of the ingredients, except when it comes to their quality, which is impeccable: fresh basil, and flour, tomatoes and cheese all imported from Italy.

HITCHING POST SOUTHERN **$$**

(☎202-726-1511; 200 Upshur St NW; mains $11-18; ⏰11am-10pm Tue-Sat; Ⓜ Georgia Avenue-Petworth) 'This is East Coast jazz,' says the owner behind the counter. 'No one listens to this anymore.' Another song comes up; The Drifters. Really? The Drifters and jazz in a diner so neighborly it should put on a cardigan and loafers when it comes inside? Let's try the fried chicken…which is seriously like a whole, fried chicken. Served with two sides. And another man comes in and the owner calls him by name and the customer asks, 'This the Chi-lites?' and we know we're in love. It's about a mile northeast of the Metro station, off the beaten path enough that you'll want a car to get here.

W DOMKU INTERNATIONAL **$$**

(☎202-722-7475; www.domkucafe.com; 821 Upshur St NW; mains $12-18; ⏰6-11pm Tue-Thu, noon-midnight Fri, 10am-midnight Sat, 10am-10:30pm Sun; Ⓜ Georgia Avenue-Petworth) A gem in the midst of an uninspiring stretch of Petworth, W Domku spreads a broad mix of Polish, Russian and Scandinavian fare – from goulash, fish stew and gravlax to house-infused aquavit. Retro furnishings (one fan referred to it as 'Ikea on good drugs') and an easy-going vibe add to the appeal. You'll get here easiest if you have wheels; otherwise it's about a half-mile northeast of the Metro stop (take Georgia Ave north to 9th St, go right and continue to Upshur).

DOS GRINGOS LATIN AMERICAN **$**

(Map p336; ☎202-462-1159; www.dosgringoscafe.com; 3116 Mt Pleasant St NW; mains $5-8; ⏰7:30am-8pm Tue-Thu, to 9pm Fri, 9am-9pm Sat, 9am-4pm Sun; Ⓜ Columbia Heights; 🖉) You gotta chuckle at both the nerve and the self-deprecation of putting this, well, gringo (white) owned cafe in the middle of Mt Pleasant and naming it as such. Not that anyone resents Dos Gringos' presence; Latinos and Anglos alike line up to order off a bilingual menu that includes fresh veg burritos, cheap cups of coffee, curry chicken salads and portobello sandwiches served in an Ikea-chic interior.

PETE'S APIZZA PIZZA $$

(Map p336; 202-332-7383; www.petesapizza.com; 1400 Irving St NW; per slice average $3, pizzas $19-26; lunch & dinner; M Columbia Heights) The specialty pizza at Pete's is New Haven–style. No, that doesn't mean it comes dressed with Yale flair, that's a white pizza (ie no tomato sauce) with olive oil and clams, with a NYC-style thin crust. Take our word on this: it's really good. There's dozens of other combinations on the menu, but we'll opt for the white pizza with clams most days. It can all be cushioned by gluten-free crust, too.

DON JUAN RESTAURANT LATIN AMERICAN $

(Map p336; 1600 Lamont St NW; mains $6-9; 9am-2am; M Columbia Heights) Don Juan's is the keystone of the Mt Pleasant St arch (along with nearby Best Way Groceries, one of DC's biggest Latino supermarkets). While it may not serve the best Latin American food in the city, the chow is still good. Try the black bean soup for a pleasant, easy-on-a-conservative-stomach breakfast. More importantly, Don Juan's is a bedrock for local Central Americans, where they meet, greet, eat and gossip.

ADAM EXPRESS KOREAN $

(Map p336; 202-328-0010; 3211 Mt Pleasant St NW; mains $7-13; lunch & dinner Tue-Sat; M Columbia Heights) An older Korean couple cooks up *bi bim bap* (mixed beef, veggies, egg and rice), *bulgogi* (marinated barbecued beef) and other fare from their homeland in this postage-stamp-sized eatery. Service can be slow, but it's worth it for the home-cooked flavors and kindly attention you receive.

PHO 14 VIETNAMESE $

(Map p336; 202-986-2326; www.dcpho14.com; 1436 Park Rd NW; mains $8-13; lunch & dinner; M Columbia Heights) Smart, solid Pho 14 ladles out steaming bowls of the namesake noodle soup, as well as stir-fry dishes and *banh mi* sandwiches (baguettes filled with meat and/or spicy vegies) to brisk lunchtime and dinner crowds.

PUPUSERIA SAN MIGUEL LATIN AMERICAN $

(Map p336; 202-387-5140; 3110 Mt Pleasant Ave NW; mains $4-8; M Columbia Heights) For quick eats, Pupuseria San Miguel fries up great, very cheap *pupusas*.

DRINKING & NIGHTLIFE

The U St Corridor has evolved into one long strip of bars, plus a fair few jazz spots and concert halls. Further north, Columbia Heights and beyond – the periphery of DC development – has already become trendy among nighthawks. That makes sense, as the first people to settle gentrification lines are the daring: the drinkers and dancers and DJs.

U Street & Shaw

MARVIN BAR

(Map p336; www.marvindc.com; 2007 14th St NW; M U St-Cardozo) Named for native son Marvin Gaye, this bar-lounge has a great setting (in this case a clubby little back room and expansive porch that's one of the best alfresco drinking spaces in the city), an excellent Belgian beer menu, Southern-French bistro fare and good DJs on weekends. But it gets *packed* some nights, with lines stretching around the block. Also, guys: no shorts or sandals on weekend nights.

SALOON BAR

(Map p336; 1207 U St NW; closed Sun & Mon; M U St-Cardozo) The Saloon takes a firm stand against packing patrons in like sardines, with posted rules against standing between tables. That's great, because the added elbow room better allows you to enjoy a brew ordered off one of the most extensive beer menus in town (Belgian ales are the tour de force). For a casual drink or place to start the night in the U St area, it's arguably your best bet. Keep in mind the Saloon is usually closed for the month of August, when the owners build schools in developing countries around the world.

BAR PILAR BAR

(Map p336; www.barpilar.com; 1833 14th St NW; M U St-Cardozo) Bar Pilar is a laid-back option for those prowling the U St Corridor, although 'laid-back' is a relative term in these parts. The narrow drinking area doesn't accommodate too many guests, but those who can squeeze in are treated to a dark, intimate drinking space that is simultaneously buzzy come busy weekend nights. A good spot for those who want to have fun on U St minus the meat-market atmosphere you get in some spots.

CORK WINE BAR WINE BAR

(Map p336; www.corkdc.com; 1720 14th St NW; ⏲closed Mon; Ⓜ U St-Cardozo) This dark 'n' cozy wine bar manages to come off as foodie magnet and friendly neighborhood hangout all at once, which is a feat. Smart wine choices plus small plates equals culinary bliss – a brioche of prosciutto is graced by fontina cheese and a smiling, sunny-side-up egg, while chicken livers arrive on a rosemary bruschetta accompanied by a dollop of intriguing shallot marmalade. With this innovative menu (and excellent cheese selection) you generally can't go wrong, although those little dishes do add up on the wallet.

CAFE SAINT-EX BAR

(Map p336; www.saint-ex.com; 1847 14th St NW; Ⓜ U St-Cardozo) Reminiscent of the Parisian Latin Quarter crossed with a U St lounge, Saint-Ex is always good for a night of sweaty flirting and heavy imbibing. Different DJs spin tunes every night and there's never a cover charge, although there's often a crowd. A bar salvaged from a 1930s Philadelphia pub, seats from an old movie theater and classic movies running on the TVs all lend a nostalgic air, but the folks inside are anything but: this is young, hip, popped-collar country. The downstairs lounge plays up the aeronautic theme with a wooden propeller from the owner's grandfather's WWI fighter plane.

BLACK JACK LOUNGE

(Map p336; www.blackjackdc.com; 1612 14th St NW; ⏲from 6pm Tue-Fri, from 3pm Sat & Sun; Ⓜ U St-Cardozo) The bar above Pearl Dive Oyster Palace is very much the 'it' place right now, all velvet curtains and exposed brick and beam. Tattooed, fedora-wearing bartenders mix quality cocktails along the lines of the Cigar (mezcal, smoked peach ice and a toothpick-twirled slice of charcuterie); the young and glamorous suck it down. Then they go play boccie (Italian lawn bowling) in the attached room.

DICKSON WINE BAR WINE BAR

(Map p336; www.dicksonwinebar.com; 903 U St NW; ⏲from 6pm Mon-Sat; Ⓜ U St-Cardozo) Cozy and candlelit, with walls covered in wine bottles, Dickson pours romantic, first-date ambience throughout a three-story row house. The entrance is not marked by name; look for 'Dickson Building 903' above the door. It's a cool spot to swing into before a show at the 9:30 Club.

SOLLY'S BAR

(Map p336; www.sollystavern.com; 1942 11th St NW; Ⓜ U St-Cardozo) Solly's is always a good kick-off to the U St stumble: a neighborhood corner tavern on one floor and a meat market/hormone perfumery on the second. It's a beer and shot kinda place, but on weekends the clientele is as young and beautiful as anywhere else in the city (although all ages are well represented). This is a big rugby bar, so if you like to scrum, here's your spot.

TABAQ BISTRO LOUNGE

(Map p336; www.tabaqdc.com; 1336 U St NW; Ⓜ U St-Cardozo) Ignore the restaurant downstairs and head for the top floors, all frosted glass, good views and a Middle Eastern/Asian/buppie crowd getting down to R&B and stiff drinks. We admit we've never been to a super-posh sky club in Beirut, but we imagine that it'd have the look and feel of this sexily swish spot.

NELLIE'S GAY BAR

(Map p336; www.nelliessportsbar.com; 900 U St NW; Ⓜ U St-Cardozo) The vibe here is low-key, and Nellie's is a good place to hunker down among a friendly crowd for tasty bar bites (including Venezuelan corn muffins), event nights (including drag Bingo Tuesdays) or early drink specials. Twelve plasma screens show sporting events; there's also a roof deck and board games on hand.

Columbia Heights & Mt Pleasant

TOP CHOICE **WONDERLAND** BAR

(Map p336; www.thewonderlandballroom.com; 1101 Kenyon St NW; Ⓜ Columbia Heights) She's gotten almost too popular over the years, but Wonderland is still one of our favorite bars in DC. A sawdust-and-sweat mix of punk and hip-hop, this bar embodies the Columbia Heights vibe – kinda edgy, always eccentric and up for a good time. The interior is clapped out in vintage signs and found objects to the point it could be a folk-art museum, the outdoor patio is a good spot for meeting strangers, and the upstairs dance floor is a good place to take said strangers for a bit of bump and grind. This used to be Nob Hill, which was the longest-operating gay bar in the country (from 1953 to 2004), a major stop on the African American drag-queen circuit, and (of course) famous for its Sunday evening gospel concerts.

LOOKING GLASS LOUNGE BAR

(off Map p336; www.thelookingglasslounge.com; 3634 Georgia Ave NW; MGeorgia Avenue-Petworth) Here's who you expect to find when you look through the Looking Glass: an old guy, one who's owned his chair at the bar for decades, in a broad-brimmed cap and clutching a highball of Jameson as if to prove it. And that guy is here. But drinking next to him is a crowd of 20- and 30-somethings who respect his presence, even as they crank the music under dark chandelier-ish lighting and commiserate in the beer garden out back. If the scene in CoHi (Columbia Heights) is getting too raucous, this is a good alternative for a quiet tipple. It's a stone's throw south of the Metro station.

ROOM 11 WINE BAR

(Map p336; www.room11dc.com; 3234 11th St NW; MColumbia Heights) Room 11 is a little too accurately named: this place really isn't much bigger than an ambitious living room, and as such it can get pretty crowded. On the plus side, everyone here is friendly, the intimacy is warmly inviting on chilly winter nights and there's a nice, spacious outdoor area for when it gets too hot inside. The crowd is hip sans pretension, munching tapas off an evolving menu, sipping excellent wines hand-selected by the management and enjoying some frankly kick-ass cocktails. There's beer, too, of course, but we really recommend you order something that was once a grape, or order off the mixed-drink menu – that's where these cats excel.

MERIDIAN PINT BEER BAR

(Map p336; www.meridianpint.com; 3400 11th St NW; MColumbia Heights) Staffed by locals from the neighborhood, Meridian Pint is the quintessential corner tavern for hipster Columbia Heights. Sports flicker on TV, folks play pool and shuffleboard, and impressive American craft beers flow from the taps. Try a pop by DC Brau. Meridian Pint poured the local brewery's first glassful in 2011, and it continues to stock the newest recipes.

RED DERBY BAR

(off Map p336; www.redderby.com; 3718 14th St NW; MColumbia Heights) There's no sign – always a good sign – just the symbol of a red hat. Underneath that cap is a hipster-punk lounge where the 'tenders know the names, the sweet-potato fries soak up the beer ordered off an impressively long menu and – why yes, that is *The Princess Bride* – cult movies play on a projector screen. The lighting is blood red and sexy, natch; you can't help but look good under it. It's about a 10-minute walk from the Metro north on 14th St.

LOCAL KNOWLEDGE

LOCAL BREW

Northeast DC has its own brewery: **DC Brau** (www.dcbrau.com; 3178B Bladensburg Rd). It launched in 2011 with bodacious beers like Thyme After Thyme and seasonal specialties like the pumpkin porter Fermentation Without Representation. Keep an eye on the taps around the District for their slurpable suds. You can also visit the brewery, which offers free tours on most Saturdays at 1:30pm, 2:30pm and 3:30pm. It's north of the National Arboretum near the Maryland border.

RAVEN BAR

(Map p336; 3125 Mt Pleasant St NW; from noon; MColumbia Heights) The best jukebox in Washington, a dark interior crammed with locals and lovers, that neon lighting that casts you under a glow Edward Hopper should paint and a tough but friendly bar staff are the ingredients in this shot, which, when slammed, hits you as DC's best dive by a mile. A $20 bill gets you roughly a case of Schlitz or other cheap beer from the bar.

☆ ENTERTAINMENT

☆ U Street & Shaw

HOWARD THEATRE THEATER

(Map p336; www.thehowardtheatre.com; 620 T St NW; MShaw-Howard U) This historic jazz venue reopened in 2012 after a $29 million renovation. Hoo-wee, does it sparkle, from the black walnut paneling to the oak floors and huge portraits of Duke Ellington, Ella Fitzgerald, Billie Holiday and other famed names who once performed here. Built in 1910, the Howard was the first major theater built to feature black entertainers performing for a predominantly black clientele. It shuttered in 1980 when the neighborhood declined. Now big-name comedians, blues and jazz acts have returned to fill the house, as does the Sunday gospel brunch. Don't forget to check out the steel-and-granite statue out front of Ellington pounding the keys of a swirling treble clef.

BUSBOYS & POETS — LITERARY

(Map p336; www.busboysandpoets.com; 2021 14th St; M U St-Cardozo; wi-fi) This cafe holds a full slate of open-mic poetry readings (Tuesday nights are the big event), story slams, film screenings and discussion series about race, labor and religion. Most events are free; Tuesday poetry costs $5.

9:30 CLUB — LIVE MUSIC

(Map p336; www.930.com; 815 V St NW; admission from $10; M U St-Cardozo) The 9:30, which can pack 1200 people into a surprisingly intimate venue, is the granddaddy of the live-music scene in DC. Pretty much every big name that comes through town ends up on this stage, and a concert here is the first-gig memory of many a DC-area teenager. The calendar is packed with a random assortment of big names – Justin Timberlake, The Violent Femmes, George Clinton, Wolfmother and the Yeah Yeah Yeahs, to name a few. Concerts usually include around three acts, with the headlining band taking the stage between 10:30pm and 11:30pm.

BOHEMIAN CAVERNS — JAZZ CLUB

(Map p336; www.bohemiancaverns.com; 2001 11th St NW; admission $7-22; M U St-Cardozo) One of Washington's most pedigreed grand dames reopened in 2000; before, it hosted the likes of Miles, Coltrane, Ellington and Ella. There are frequent open-mic nights and an increasing crop of names headlining to reestablish the title of this icon of American jazz.

BLACK CAT — LIVE MUSIC

(Map p336; www.blackcatdc.com; 1811 14th St NW; admission $5-15; M U St-Cardozo) Still one of the best places in town for rock or indie, the Cat always keeps something good going on the back stage, from soul-funk nights to heavy-metal dance-offs to big-band-era bashes. For DC, this is an iconic spot, the love child of Foo Fighter Dave Grohl, who cut his chops drumming in DC-area bands while still a Northern Virginia teenager.

U STREET MUSIC HALL — LIVE MUSIC

(Map p336; www.ustreetmusichall.com; 1115 U St NW; admission $10-20; closed Sun; M U St-Cardozo) Two local DJs own and operate this basement club, a relative newcomer on the scene. It looks like a no-frills rock bar, but it has a pro sound system, cork-cushioned dance floor and other accoutrements of a serious dance club. Alternative bands also thrash a couple of nights per week to keep it fresh.

VELVET LOUNGE — LIVE MUSIC

(Map p336; www.velvetloungedc.com; 915 U St NW; admission from $5; M U St-Cardozo) Velvet is tiny, red and awesome. It's a hole in the wall, almost literally given its diminutive size, but that doesn't stop a steady stream of great rock and hip-hop artists taking the stage, or top DJs spinning house, funk and R&B on weekends.

DC9 — LIVE MUSIC

(Map p336; www.dcnine.com; 1940 9th St NW; admission $8-15; M U St-Cardozo) DC9 is as intimate as DC's big-name venues get, and about as divey as well. Not that we're complaining; there's always a good edge on in this spot. Up-and-coming local bands, with an emphasis on indie rockers, play most nights of the week; when the live music finishes (often around 11pm) DJs keep the place spinning until about 3am. On the 2nd floor, zodiac murals and diner booths set the mellow vibe; downstairs you'll find a narrow shotgun bar that's often packed wall to wall.

SOURCE THEATRE COMPANY — THEATER

(Map p336; www.sourcedc.org; 1835 14th St NW; M U St-Cardozo) In the heart of the U district, Source stages mostly new works across an array of disciplines. You might see improv, Spanish-language opera or a dreamy interpretation of Strindberg in the 150-seat theater. The popular Source Festival in June puts on a slew of 10-minute plays.

TOWN DANCEBOUTIQUE — GAY CLUB

(Map p336; www.towndc.com; 2009 8th St NW; admission $5-12; Fri & Sat; M U St-Cardozo) With a great sound system and fine DJs, Town is the go-to spot for dancing, with two floors, various rooms (including an outdoor smoking area) and hilarious drag shows on weekends.

LINCOLN THEATRE — THEATER

(Map p336; www.thelincolntheatre.org; 1215 U St NW; M U St-Cardozo) The District renovated this historic cinema in the 1990s to host music and theater. It's classy, but it kind of limps along with sporadic performances.

☆ Columbia Heights & Mt Pleasant

DANCE PLACE DANCE

(www.danceplace.org; 3225 8th St NE; Ⓜ Brookland-CUA) The only truly cutting-edge dance space in the capital is tucked away up in Northeast DC. It's run by five resident modern-dance companies offering a year-round calendar of new work, which includes festivals featuring African dance, tap dancing, step dancing and other genres. It also hosts the work of top-notch national companies. The theater is a few blocks south of the Metro station.

GALA HISPANIC THEATRE THEATER

(Map p336; www.galatheatre.org; 3333 14th St NW; Ⓜ Columbia Heights) The Gala maintains a 30-year tradition of annual Spanish-language productions.

SHOPPING

The still-edgy U St area unfurls upscale boutiques, quirky design and furniture shops, galleries and vintage stores along both 14th and U Sts. In Columbia Heights, Target, Staples, Giant Foods and other big-box retailers throng the area around the Metro station.

TOP CHOICE **MISS PIXIE'S** ANTIQUES

(Map p336; www.misspixies.com; 1626 14th St NW; ⏲11am-7pm; Ⓜ U St-Cardozo) One of the best places to browse in the neighborhood, Miss Pixie's is piled high with relics from the past, from stuffed leather armchairs to 1960s lawn ornaments. You'll find dishes, ashtrays, rocking chairs, black-and-white photos and plenty of other curiosities. There's a cafe upstairs.

HOME RULE HOMEWARES

(Map p336; www.homerule.com; 1807 14th St NW; Ⓜ U St-Cardozo) Tired of Pottery Barn homogeneity around your house? Check out Home Rule's amusingly original stock: frog-shaped toothbrush holders, brightly colored martini glasses, animal-shaped salt-and-pepper sets, and rugs and linens, too. The mosaic decorating the front counter symbolizes the U St district's revitalization – it's made with smashed glass from the 1968 riots.

LOCAL KNOWLEDGE

NEIGHBORHOOD NEWS

Several bloggers in the neighborhood post information on restaurants, bars and shops that are opening, as well as political goings-on. They're a great source for the local lowdown. For instance, we just learned that Ben's Chili Bowl is opening a second outlet at 10th and H Sts NE. Read more at:

- ➡ **Prince of Petworth** (www.princeofpetworth.com)
- ➡ **U Street Beat** (www.ustreetbeat.wordpress.com)
- ➡ **Borderstan** (www.borderstan.com)

SMUCKER FARMS FOOD & DRINK

(Map p336; www.smuckerfarmsdc.com; 2118 14th St NW; ⏲9am-9pm; Ⓜ U St-Cardozo) Do you ever get that urge for shoofly pie or fresh-churned butter, but find you're nowhere near an Amish community to satisfy the craving? Smucker to the rescue. The small grocery store brings in meat, produce and other farm-fresh goods straight from Lancaster County, PA, one of the nation's largest Amish communities. Dairy products and baked items are the strong suits; handicrafts such as carved wooden toys and beeswax candles fill the shelves, too.

REDEEM CLOTHING

(Map p336; www.redeemus.com; 1734 14th St NW; ⏲closed Tue; Ⓜ U St-Cardozo) 'It's never too late to change,' is the motto of this enticing little clothier on 14th St. Redeem carries indie labels and a small selection of local designers, and targets urban and hip but cashed-up customers. Look for Earnest Sewn denim, Colcci ankle boots, Corpus sweaters and other unique labels.

BIG PLANET COMICS BOOKS

(Map p336; www.bigplanetcomics.com; 1520 U St NW; ⏲11am-7pm Mon, Tue, Thu & Fri, to 8pm Wed, to 6pm Sat, noon-5pm Sun; Ⓜ U St-Cardozo) Not just for comic-book-loving geeks, Big Planet appeals to a surprisingly diverse audience, with an excellent collection of limited editions and graphic novels, plus posters, T-shirts, manga material and collectible stuff.

GOOD WOOD ANTIQUES

(Map p336; www.goodwooddc.com; 1428 U St NW; noon-7pm Mon-Sat, to 5pm Sun; U St-Cardozo) Even if you're not in the market for a mid-century armoire, Good Wood is well worth a visit. This warm, atmospheric store has a fine selection of antiques, including handcrafted chairs and tables, elegant lamps and wall hangings, plus other decorative items.

PULP GIFTS

(Map p336; www.pulpdc.com; 1803 14th St NW; U St-Cardozo) Quirky, kitschy Pulp has all kinds of things you weren't looking for – funky frames, funny cards, silly toys, smelly candles, retro art and tons of political gag gifts. It's a good place to come looking for a gift (as long as you don't know what you are looking for).

NANA WOMEN'S CLOTHING

(Map p336; www.nanadc.com; 3068 Mt Pleasant St NW; closed Mon; Columbia Heights) Nana is a sweet little boutique selling a mix of funky and classic fashions. Look for Holly Aiken bags, Dagg & Stacey coats and blouses, dresses and skirts by Classic Girl, Uppsee Daisies and Elaine Perlov. Nana throws in a few well-placed vintage pieces to complete the look.

U STREET FLEA MARKET MARKET

(Map p336; cnr U & 9th St NW; 9am-5pm Sat & Sun; U St-Cardozo) You won't (likely) find a cute vintage frock here – this is a real flea market, patronized by folks who consider secondhand shopping a necessity rather than just a diversion. That said, there are usually awesome albums for sale, a few local crafts and a sense of U St's vibe c 1980s BG (Before Gentrification).

SPORTS & ACTIVITIES

ROCK CREEK PARK GOLF COURSE GOLF

(202-723-8499; www.golfdc.com; 1600 Rittenhouse St NW; 18 holes weekday/weekend $20/25; 6am-7pm Apr-Oct, 7am-6pm Nov-Mar; S1, S2, S4) The hilly and narrow fairways have large elevation changes. Dense woods on either side replace water hazards.

Upper Northwest DC

Neighborhood Top Five

❶ Seek out the sacred and profane in the architectural treasures of **Washington National Cathedral** (p207). A Darth Vader gargoyle, floor of pennies, moon rock, Helen Keller's ashes and a secret garden are but a fraction of the esoteric offerings.

❷ Wave to the giant pandas and swinging orangutans at the **National Zoo** (p208).

❸ Hike, bike or saddle up a horse in **Rock Creek Park** (p208).

❹ Inspect the Fabergé egg collection and slurp borscht at **Hillwood Museum & Gardens** (p209).

❺ Browse books by big-name authors, then meet them in person at **Politics & Prose Bookstore** (p212).

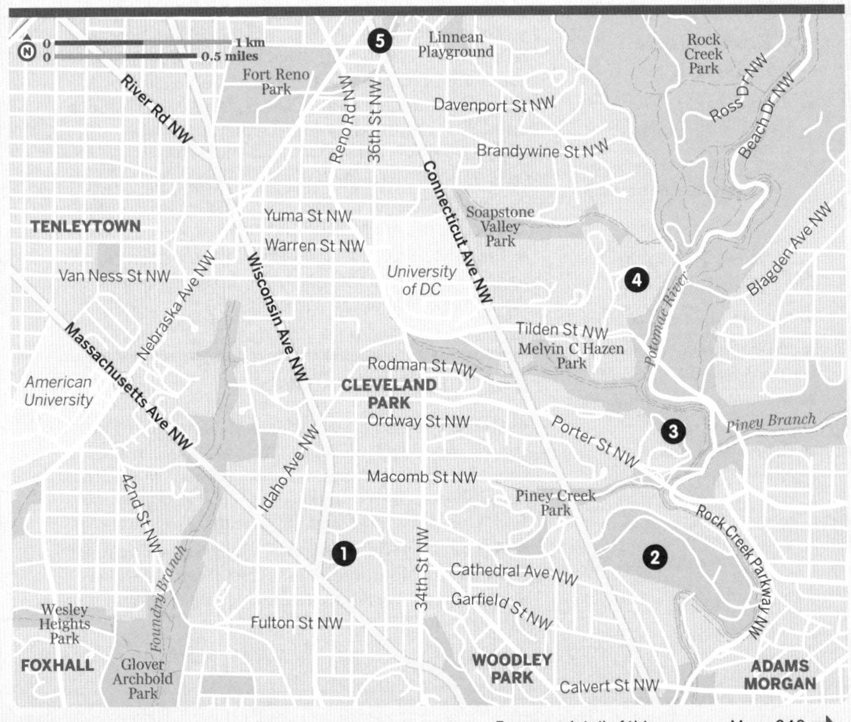

For more detail of this area, see Map p340

Lonely Planet's Top Tip

Remember your geography. The Upper Northwest may seem far from the action, but it's right next door to Georgetown (to the southwest), Dupont (to the southeast) and Adams-Morgan (to the west). You can easily walk to any of these neighborhoods and their rich stock of restaurants and nightlife.

Best Places to Eat

- Comet Ping Pong (p210)
- Palena (p210)
- 2 Amys (p210)
- Buck's Fishing & Camping (p210)
- Nam Viet (p211)

For reviews, see p210

Best Places to Drink

- Bardeo (p211)
- Nanny O'Brien's Irish Pub (p211)

For reviews, see p211

Best Parks & Gardens

- Rock Creek Park (p208)
- Hillwood Museum & Gardens (p209)
- Kahlil Gibran Memorial Garden (p209)
- Glover Archbold Park (p210)
- Battery Kemble Park (p210)

For reviews, see p208

Explore Upper Northwest DC

The long, leafy lanes of Upper Northwest have long been the place for upper-income Washingtonians to settle their families. While Georgetown houses more of the city's elite, the presence of its university and the traffic snarls have made it less appealing to folks seeking a quiet place to raise their children. The Upper Northwest's stretching serenity and supremely pleasant clumps of residential bliss do the job. It's no surprise Sidwell Friends School is here, where presidents Clinton and Obama sent their daughters.

Upper Northwest's sights could fill a day. The National Cathedral and National Zoo are foremost. Rock Creek Park and Hillwood Museum (the amazing Russian art-filled manor of cereal heiress Marjorie Post) are less well known but equally worthwhile.

Some of the city's most exciting restaurants have posted up this way, attracted by a population that has disposable income to spend and an increasingly savvy attitude toward food. The nightlife scene hasn't quite caught up, but it's hardly boring either. Lots of sights and eateries cluster around Metro stops, but be prepared to bus or walk a fair distance to others.

Local Life

- **Zoo Lights** At the National Zoo in December, local businesses compete with each other to showcase elaborate Christmas-light displays fashioned to resemble animals. It's a great holiday treat to wander amid the brightness on sharp winter evenings.
- **Poetry Stars** On summer evenings, local poets read under the stars in Rock Creek Park's planetarium (p208). The Joaquin Miller Poetry Series takes place Thursdays at 7pm in June and July.
- **Picnic Basket** Vace Deli (p211) is the perfect place to grab cheeses, sandwiches and drinks for picnics in Rock Creek Park or the National Zoo.

Getting There & Away

- **Metro** The Red Line is your main-vein train. Stations include Woodley Park-Zoo/Adams Morgan (for the zoo), Cleveland Park (for restaurants), Van Ness-UDC (for Hillwood Museum, bookstore, restaurants) and Tenleytown-AU (National Cathedral).
- **Bus** L1, L2 and L4 buses roll along Connecticut Ave NW and pick up from the first three Metro stations mentioned above; 30-series buses run along Wisconsin Ave NW and pick up from Tenleytown-AU.

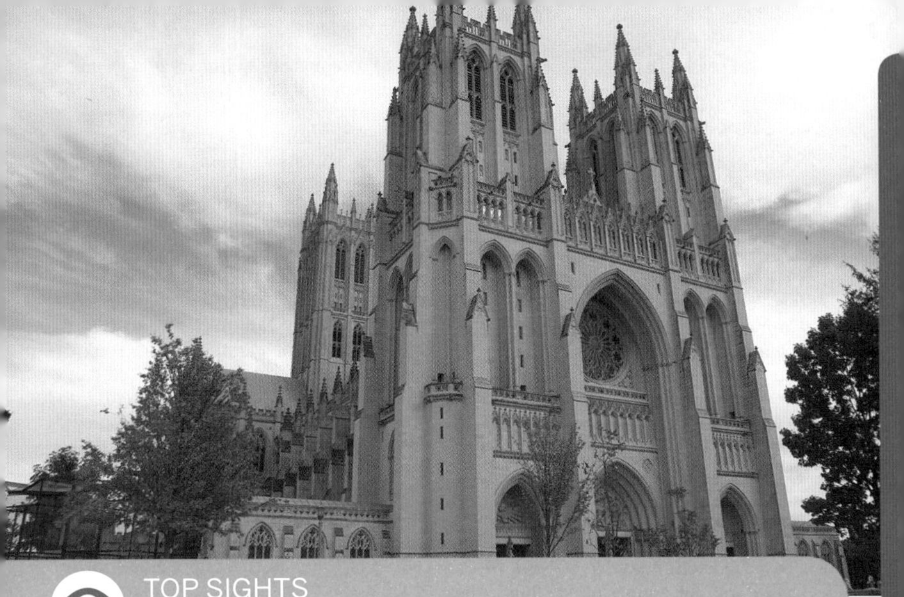

TOP SIGHTS
WASHINGTON NATIONAL CATHEDRAL

The Episcopal diocese runs this house of worship, but it's open to all faiths and creeds. Presidents attend multi-faith services following their inauguration, state funerals are hosted inside and this was where Martin Luther King Jr gave his last Sunday sermon. It took 82 years to build the edifice – Teddy Roosevelt laid the cornerstone in 1908, and construction didn't technically stop until 1990. The cathedral provoked strong opposition early on, but the multi-faith character of worship helped mollify the arguments.

The building is neo-Gothic, but it's embellished by distinctive American accents. A moon rock studs one of the interior stained-glass windows, and Darth Vader's head shares space with the exterior gargoyles (bring binoculars). In the main sanctuary, chapels honor Martin Luther King Jr (in the Kellogg Bay) and Abe Lincoln. Helen Keller and Woodrow Wilson, among others, are buried in the crypt. Themed tours ($5 to $10) take in all of the above; it's a good idea to make advance bookings online in spring and summer.

Other highlights... Take the elevator to the tower overlook for expansive city views. Meander outside through the peaceful winding paths in the Bishop's Garden. The 11am Sunday service features lovely choral music and a 10-bell peal of the carillon afterwards. Choristers sing Evensong at 5:30pm Monday to Thursday during the school year.

The 2011 earthquake damaged some of the cathedral's pinnacles and buttresses. Repairs are underway, but they don't affect most interior sights.

DON'T MISS...

- Darth Vader gargoyle
- Lincoln Bay floor of pennies
- Helen Keller tomb
- Evensong
- Bishop's Garden

PRACTICALITIES

- Map p340
- ☎202-537-6200
- www.nationalcathedral.org
- 3101 Wisconsin Ave NW
- suggested donation adult/child $10/5
- ⌚10am-5:30pm Mon-Fri, to 8pm some days May-Sep, 10am-4pm Sat, 8am-4pm Sun
- M Tenleytown-AU to southbound bus 31, 32, 36, 37

SIGHTS

WASHINGTON NATIONAL CATHEDRAL CHURCH

See p207.

FREE **NATIONAL ZOO** ZOO

(Map p205 ; www.nationalzoo.si.edu; 3001 Connecticut Ave NW; 10am-6pm Apr-Oct, to 4:30pm Nov-Mar; M Cleveland Park, Woodley Park-Zoo/Adams Morgan) Home to over 2000 individual animals (400 different species) in natural habitats, the National Zoo is famed for its giant pandas Mei Xiang and Tian Tian. Other highlights include the African lion pride, Asian elephants and dangling orangutans swinging 50ft overhead from steel cables and interconnected towers (aka the 'O Line').

This Smithsonian Institution zoo was founded in 1889 and planned by Frederick Law Olmsted, designer of New York's Central Park. The zoo's grounds follow the natural contours of a woodland-canyon, and the exhibits are noted for their natural-habitat settings. The zoo is intensively involved in worldwide ecological study and species-preservation work. High points in the past decade include giant panda and lowland gorilla births – a happy change from the early 2000s, when the zoo faced controversy over mismanagement and the deaths of several animals.

Even non-zoo fans will find the National entertaining. The panda house offers fun facts on the creatures' sex lives (they only go at it three days per year) and bowel production (behold the hefty replica poo). Big-cat fans will love the cheetahs' display, while the 'What's for Dinner?' feature has overly honest scales that inform you who would like to feast on you ('100lb to 150lb – you're a female warthog. A pack of lions could finish you off in an hour.') The interactive 'Think Tank' examines animal intelligence (including yours) and displays a cabinet of brains. The zoo's snack stands even sell decent beer.

EASIEST WAY TO THE ZOO

The National Zoo is pretty much equidistant between the Cleveland Park and Woodley Park-Zoo/Adams Morgan Metro stops, but the walk is downhill if you get off at Cleveland Park.

The grounds are well-marked, but maps are available for $2 at the main entrance for easier navigation. Check the sign there for the day's schedule of animal feedings. The elephant exhibits are being renovated and expanded through 2013.

ROCK CREEK PARK PARK

(Map p340; www.nps.gov/rocr; sunrise-sunset; M Cleveland Park, Woodley Park-Zoo/Adams Morgan) At 1700 acres, Rock Creek is twice the size of New York's Central Park and feels a hell of a lot more wild. You can be out here and feel utterly removed from the city. Even coyotes have settled into the wilderness (they're not dangerous, by the way). Rock Creek Park begins at the Potomac's east bank near Georgetown and extends to and beyond the northern city boundaries. Narrow in its southern stretches, where it hews to the winding course of the waterway it's named for, it broadens into wide, peaceful parklands in Upper Northwest DC. Terrific trails for hiking, biking and horseback riding extend the entire length, and the boundaries enclose Civil War forts, dense forest and wildflower-strewn fields.

There are visitor centers at the Nature Center & Planetarium and Peirce Mill where you can pick up maps and sign up for ranger-led programs. Cell phone 'tours' are stationed around the park; when you see a dial-and-discover sign, just enter the listed number. Southwest of the Nature Center, the **Soapstone Valley Park** extension, off Connecticut Ave at Albemarle St NW, preserves quarries where the area's original Algonquin residents dug soapstone for shaping their cookware.

In summer, check what's on at the Carter Barron Amphitheater (p212).

FREE **NATURE CENTER & PLANETARIUM** NATURE CENTER

(off Map p340; www.nps.gov/rocr; 5200 Glover Rd NW, off Military Rd; 9am-5pm Wed-Sun; M Friendship Heights for bus E2, E3) The Nature Center & Planetarium is the main visitor center for Rock Creek Park. Besides exhibits on park flora, fauna and history, it has two small nature trails, tons of information, and maps and field guides to the city. A 'touch table' is set up for kids, and rangers lead child-oriented nature walks. If you're coming via public transportation, take the E2 or E3 bus to the intersection of Military

CIVIL WAR FORTS

The remains of Civil War forts that dot Rock Creek Park are among its most fascinating sites. During the war, Washington was, essentially, a massive urban armory and supply house for the Union Army. Its position near the Confederate lines made it vulnerable to attack, so forts were hastily erected on the city's high points. By spring 1865, 68 forts and 93 batteries bristled on hilltops around DC. See **Civil War Defenses of Washington** (www.nps.gov/cwdw) for more on the subject.

and Glover Rds; look to your left and follow the trail up to the Nature Center.

A bit further north of here, on the west side of Beach Dr, is the **Joaquin Miller Cabin**, a log house that once sheltered the famed nature poet.

PEIRCE MILL — HISTORIC BUILDING

(Map p340; www.nps.gov/pimi; Tilden St; ⏲10am-4pm Sat & Sun; Ⓜ Van Ness-UDC) Alongside the creek, the 1820 Peirce Mill is a beautiful fieldstone building that was once a water-driven gristmill. It is slowly being restored, and you can see it churning on various weekends.

HILLWOOD MUSEUM & GARDENS — MUSEUM, GARDENS

(Map p340; www.hillwoodmuseum.org; 4155 Linnean Ave NW; suggested donation adult/child $15/5; ⏲10am-5pm Tue-Sat; Ⓜ Van Ness-UDC) Hillwood, the former estate of Marjorie Merriweather Post (of Post cereal fame) and her third husband, the ambassador to the USSR, contains the biggest collection of Russian imperial art to be found outside of Russia. Post convinced Stalin and the Soviets to sell her loads of Czarist swag, and her impressive collection includes furniture, paintings and a shockingly gorgeous collection of Fabergé eggs and jewelry. As a bonus, the 25-acre estate incorporates some lovely gardens (which include Post's dog cemetery), a greenhouse and a museum shop. The on-site caf serves up Russian treats (borscht, blintzes and the like) and afternoon tea. It's a mile walk from the Metro to Hillwood.

FREE US NAVAL OBSERVATORY — OBSERVATORY

(Map p340; ☎202-762-1438; www.usno.navy.mil/USNO; 3450 Massachusetts Ave NW; ⏲tours by reservation 8:30pm Mon) If you're ever late to an appointment after visiting this place, you've got no excuse, buddy: the Naval Observatory is the official source of time for the US military and by extension, the country, so you know the clocks are set right here. Framed by a pair of stately white ship's anchors, the observatory, created in the 1800s, is here 'to determine the positions and motions of celestial objects, provide astronomical data, measure the Earth's rotation, and maintain the Master Clock for the US.' Modern DC's light pollution prevents important observational work these days, but that cesium-beam atomic clock is still tickin'. Tours let you peek through telescopes and yak with astronomers, but they fill up weeks in advance, may be cancelled at any time and are only offered on select Mondays at 8:30pm, so reserve early – check the website or phone. On observatory grounds above Massachusetts Ave NW is the official **Vice President's Residence (Admiral's House)**, which is closed to the public. Driving is the best way to reach the observatory.

KAHLIL GIBRAN MEMORIAL GARDEN — GARDEN

(Map p340; 3100 Massachusetts Ave NW; Ⓜ Dupont Circle) In the midst of the wooded ravine known as Normanstone Park, the Kahlil Gibran garden memorializes the arch-deity of soupy spiritual poetry. Its centerpieces are a moody bust of the Lebanese mystic and a star-shaped fountain surrounded by flowers, hedges and limestone benches engraved with various Gibranisms: 'We live only to discover beauty. All else is a form of waiting.' From a trailhead just north of the garden, you can hop onto trails that link to Rock Creek and Glover Archbold Parks.

ISLAMIC CENTER — MOSQUE

(Map p340; www.theislamiccenter.com; 2551 Massachusetts Ave NW; ⏲10am-5pm; Ⓜ Dupont Circle) Topped with a 160ft minaret, this pale limestone structure is the national mosque for American Muslims. Inside, the mosque glows with bright floral tiling, thick Persian rugs and gilt-trimmed ceilings detailed with more Quranic verse. You can enter to look around; remove your shoes, and women must bring scarves to cover their hair.

KREEGER MUSEUM MUSEUM

(off Map p340; 202-338-3552; www.kreegermuseum.org; 2401 Foxhall Rd NW; adult/child $10/free; tours by reservation 10:30am & 1:30pm Tue-Thu, without reservation 10am-4pm Fri & Sat, closed Aug) One of DC's more obscure attractions, this little-known museum is tucked away in the hills northwest of Georgetown and houses a fantastic collection of 20th-century modernist art. The art – by Renoir, Picasso and Mark Rothko, among many others – represents the amassed collection of David and Carem Kreeger. Their individual taste adds a charming degree of intimacy to the experience; you feel more like you're popping into a home than visiting a museum. Speaking of visiting, you must do so on 90-minute, reservation-only tours unless you come for the Friday and Saturday open houses. Exhibits are constantly rotated, so you're just as likely to see Monet's dappled impressionism as Edvard Munch's dark expressionism. Head west on Reservoir Rd NW about a half-mile to Foxhall Rd; turn right and the museum is about a mile onward.

GLOVER ARCHBOLD PARK PARK

(Map p340; M Dupont Circle for bus D1) Glover is a sinuous, winding park, extending from Van Ness St NW in Tenleytown down to the western border of Georgetown University. Its 180 tree-covered acres follow the course of little Foundry Branch Creek, along which runs a pretty nature trail. It's a good birdwatching destination.

BATTERY KEMBLE PARK PARK

(off Map p340; cnr Garfield St NW & 49th St NW; M Dupont Circle for bus D3, D6) Skinny Battery Kemble Park, about a mile long but less than a quarter-mile wide, separates the wealthy Foxhall and Palisades neighborhoods of far northwestern DC. Managed by the National Park Service, the park preserves the site of a little two-gun battery that helped defend western DC against Confederate troops during the Civil War.

EATING

Restaurants cluster around the Metro stops in Cleveland Park, Tenleytown and Woodley Park-Zoo/Adams Morgan.

COMET PING PONG PIZZA $$

(off Map p340; www.cometpingpong.com; 5037 Connecticut Ave NW; mains $13-17; brunch Sat & Sun, dinner daily; M Van Ness-UDC;) Dinner time and the kids are as restless as your spirit, which longs to sit on a stool that's too high for you. To satisfy all nostalgic parties involved, may we suggest: Comet. A round of ping pong on the tables in the back is perfectly complemented by the Smoky – smoked bacon, Gouda, mushrooms and…oh yeah (drool). A nice brewski selection helps wash it all down. It's possibly the most fun restaurant in the city, a sort of Chuck E. Cheese's that's been beat over the head with an awesome stick several times.

PALENA AMERICAN $$$

(Map p340; 202-537-9250; www.palenarestaurant.com; 3529 Connecticut Ave NW; 3-/5-course menu $75/100; dinner Tue-Sat; M Cleveland Park) Set a night aside with a loved one or a good friend and get ready for a culinary ride past the limits of taste into innovative gastro-orgasm land. Palena's menu defies conventions, deliciously. Red snapper with ramps and oyster mushrooms, artichoke risotto and celery root soup with shrimp and almonds are recent favorites. The approach is often unexpected; the rewards are uniformly mouthwatering. The interior is warm but oddly modern in its crafted rusticity. Reserve ahead or eat in the more casual cafe (mains $14 to $27), which serves dinner daily and brunch on weekends.

2 AMYS PIZZA $$

(Map p340; www.2amyspizza.com; 3715 Macomb St NW; mains $9-13; lunch Tue-Sun, dinner daily; M Tenleytown-AU to southbound bus 31, 32, 36, 37;) A stone's throw from Washington National Cathedral, 2 Amys serves some of DC's best thin-crust pizzas. Pies are sprinkled with market-fresh ingredients and baked to perfection in a wood-burning oven. Avoid the weekend crowds.

BUCK'S FISHING & CAMPING AMERICAN $$

(off Map p340; 202-364-0777; www.bucksfishingandcamping.com; 5031 Connecticut Ave NW; mains $14-26; dinner Tue-Sun; M Van Ness-UDC) We love Buck's for its vibe: haute lakeside fishing camp. Really? Yep – modern banquettes, canoes on the walls. The food is American comfort cooking at its best, with the kitchen cranking out rabbit pot pie and wood-grilled burgers. Make reservations on weekend evenings or you'll be waiting ages for a seat. When you do score one of the chairs at the communal tables you could be sharing it with your state's senator and the guy selling books at the coffee shop across the street. The same folks who own Buck's also own Comet Ping Pong.

NAM VIET VIETNAMESE **$$**

(Map p340; ☎202-237-1015; www.namviet1.com; 3419 Connecticut Ave NW; mains $10-17; ⊙lunch & dinner; MCleveland Park) Probably the best Vietnamese within the city lines is served here. The cooking is uncomplicated, but that doesn't mean it isn't excellent, especially the rich *pho*. The layout is from the 'every-Vietnamese-restaurant-you've-ever-been-in' cookie cutter, but the quality of the food elevates Nam Viet several notches above the pack.

VACE DELI ITALIAN **$**

(Map p340; ☎202-363-1999; 3315 Connecticut Ave NW; whole pizza $9; ⊙9am-9pm Mon-Fri, to 8pm Sat, 10am-5pm Sun; MCleveland Park) If you're going on a picnic in Rock Creek Park, may we suggest getting a bit of meat, a parcel of cheese, and some bread, olives, wine and general happiness from Vace, perhaps the best deli in DC? Treat yourself to some of their pizza, too; it's divine.

ROCKLANDS BARBECUE SOUTHERN **$$**

(Map p340; ☎202-333-2558; www.rocklands.com; 2418 Wisconsin Ave NW; mains $7-16; ⊙lunch & dinner; MTenleytown-AU for bus 30, 32, 34, 36) We say Southern, but really, it's just about the barbeque here: slow smoked, red oak and hickory, no electricity, no gas, Texas-style and pretty good for the East Coast. The ribs, as you might guess, are the way to go. While you wait for your order, check out the huge selection of hot sauces ('From the Depths of Hell'), then take a seat at the wooden counter in the window and watch the passers-by drool.

ARDEO INTERNATIONAL **$$**

(Map p340; ☎202-244-6750; www.ardeobardeo.com; 3311 Connecticut Ave NW; small plates $9-10, mains $14-24; ⊙brunch Sat & Sun, dinner daily; MCleveland Park) Ardeo's is one of the original small plates/wine bars in the city, and still one of the best. There are a lot of rich pastas, fresh fish and juicy meat selections, plus a few salads and sandwiches. Try a local specialty like succulent, pan-roasted rockfish served with a ragout of prosciutto, sweet corn and plantains. The well-curated wine list hits the right note alongside the dishes.

LEBANESE TAVERNA MIDDLE EASTERN **$$**

(Map p340; ☎202-265-8681; www.lebanesetaverna.com; 2641 Connecticut Ave NW; mains $17-26; ⊙lunch & dinner; MWoodley Park-Zoo/Adams Morgan;) Lebanese Taverna has been cooking kibbe, shawarma, eggplant, lamb and other traditional dishes for more than three decades. It's pretty routine fare, but everyone we know with kids loves it for the 'little ones' menu and the staff's genuine friendliness toward the younger set. Eat in the high-ceiling, gold-hued room or outside under the shade umbrellas.

DRINKING & NIGHTLIFE

Most places tend to be of the quiet neighborhood pub variety where upper-middle-class couples linger over bottles of vintage Chardonnay. The exception is a cluster of rowdy Irish bars around Connecticut Ave in Cleveland Park, near the Uptown movie theater. This is probably Upper Northwest's most concentrated nightlife strip, and the crowd here is young, international and determined to party.

BARDEO WINE BAR

(Map p340; www.ardeobardeo.com; 3311 Connecticut Ave NW; MCleveland Park) Next door and attached to Ardeo, Bardeo is a favorite spot for starting a night out on the town thanks to its excellent vino. Sip among the menu's wine flights (three 3oz glasses) or go rogue and make your own flight.

NANNY O'BRIEN'S IRISH PUB IRISH PUB

(Map p340; www.nannyobriens.com; 3319 Connecticut Ave NW; ⊙from noon; MCleveland Park) Washington's most authentic Irish pub, Nanny O'Brien's has been a favorite with real and wannabe Irish people for decades. You won't find any cheesy shamrock schlock or shameless promotions here; no, this bar would rather concentrate on serving stiff drinks along with fantastic music. The place is packed and gets pretty rowdy most nights.

ENTERTAINMENT

CARTER BARRON AMPHITHEATER THEATER

(www.nps.gov/rocr; 4850 Colorado Ave NW, near 16th St NW, Rock Creek Park; box office noon-8pm show days; McPherson Sq for bus S2, S4) In a lovely wooded setting inside Rock Creek Park, the 4000-seat outdoor amphitheater stages a mix of theater, dance and music (jazz, salsa, classical, reggae) on summer evenings. Some events are free; ticketed shows cost $25.

FREE **POLITICS & PROSE BOOKSTORE** LITERARY

(off Map p340; www.politics-prose.com; 5015 Connecticut Ave NW; Van Ness-UDC for bus L1, L2 or L4) This independent bookstore is known for hosting brain-food readings and discussions on a regular basis. If you miss your favorite author, go to the website and download an MP3 of the reading for free. From the Metro, it's a one-mile walk north on Connecticut Ave, or you can take the bus from the station.

LA MAISON FRANÇAISE MUSIC, THEATER

(Map p340; www.la-maison-francaise.org; 4101 Reservoir Rd NW; 10am-4pm Mon-Fri) La Maison is otherwise known as the French Embassy. The beating heart of Gallic DC occupies eight elegantly landscaped acres, anchored by the marble, modernesque embassy itself. Countless cultural activities pop off here every week; check the website for listings. Not to stereotype, but if you'd like to sip good wine (via tasting classes) and gaze at interesting art, theater, dance and the like, this is the place to visit. Reservations are required for all events.

AMC LOEWS UPTOWN 1 CINEMA

(Map p340; www.amctheatres.com; 3426 Connecticut Ave NW; Cleveland Park) First-run movie theater near the Cleveland Park Metro.

SHOPPING

POLITICS & PROSE BOOKSTORE BOOKS

(off Map p340; www.politics-prose.com; 5015 Connecticut Ave NW; 9am-10pm Mon-Sat, 10am-8pm Sun; Van Ness-UDC for bus L1, L2 or L4) Way up in Northwest DC is a key literary nexus and coffeehouse. The active independent has an excellent selection of literary fiction and nonfiction – it's fiercely supportive of local authors – plus it has dedicated staff, high-profile readings, steaming mugs of chai and 15 active book clubs. It's a one-mile walk north on Connecticut Ave from the Metro, or you can take the bus from the station.

NATIONAL ZOO SOUVENIRS

(Map p340; 3001 Connecticut Ave NW; Woodley Park-Zoo/Adams Morgan) The National Zoo has several shops on its grounds that sell toys and products featuring all manner of charismatic fauna: ostriches, seals, tigers, wolves, elephants and the inevitable pandas. (Bring home a plastic hyena for less-beloved relatives.) It also has the Zoo Bookstore, in the Education Building on the Connecticut Ave NW side, which has a decent natural-history and field-guide section.

WAKE UP LITTLE SUZIE GIFTS

(Map p340; www.wakeuplittlesuzie.com; 3409 Connecticut Ave NW; Cleveland Park) This funny and original gift shop sells stuff like neon clocks, bright metal-and-ceramic jewelry, polka-dotted pottery, cards and T-shirts. If you have a need for an *Invasion of the Monster Women* lunch box or boxing-rabbi windup doll, Suzie's your woman.

SULLIVAN'S TOY STORE TOYS

(Map p340; www.facebook.com/sullivanstoys; 4200 Wisconsin Ave NW; Tenleytown-AU) This independent toy store specializes in European and educational toys that are a nice antidote to the video-game fare of many children's toy stores.

MAZZA GALLERIE MALL

(off Map p340; www.mazzagallerie.com; 5300 Wisconsin Ave NW; Friendship Heights) If you need an upscale mall, this one has the requisite Neiman-Marcus, Williams-Sonoma, Sak's etc. Downstairs is a seven-screen movie theater. It's right beside the Metro, a stone's throw from the Maryland border.

KRÖN CHOCOLATIER FOOD & DRINK

(off Map p340; www.krondc.com; Mazza Gallerie, 5300 Wisconsin Ave NW; Friendship Heights) This shop is known for hand-dipped truffles and amusing novelties, like edible chocolate baskets, milk-chocolate telephones and cars.

SPORTS & ACTIVITIES

ROCK CREEK HORSE CENTER HORSE RIDING
(off Map p340; www.rockcreekhorsecenter.com; 5100 Glover Rd NW; guided rides $40) Thirteen miles of wide dirt trails crisscross the northern part of Rock Creek Park, with an Equitation Field nearby. The Rock Creek Horse Center offers guided trail rides, lessons and pony rides. Reservations required. Weekday rides are only available during summer; weekend rides run from April to October. There are one to three rides per day; check the website for times.

FLETCHER'S BOATHOUSE WATER SPORTS, BIKING
(off Map p340; www.fletcherscove.com; 4940 Canal Rd NW; watercraft per hr/day from $10/24; 7am-5pm Mar-Nov) This boathouse is a few miles upriver from Georgetown (accessible by bike from the C&O Canal & Towpath or by car from Canal Rd). Canoes, rowboats, bicycles and fishing licenses are available. Take Reservoir Rd west, which merges with Canal Rd.

Northern Virginia

ARLINGTON | ALEXANDRIA

Neighborhood Top Five

❶ Walk around **Arlington National Cemetery** (p217) and you can't help but be moved: from the Tomb of the Unknowns' dignified guards; to John F Kennedy's eternal flame; to the simple white headstones sparkling out in every direction.

❷ Get lost amid space shuttles and jets in the mammoth hangars of the **Steven F Udvar-Hazy Center** (p218).

❸ Cycle the **Mount Vernon Trail** (p225) to Roosevelt Island, Old Town Alexandria or beyond to George Washington's estate.

❹ Admire ingenious homemade bongs at the **DEA Museum** (p219).

❺ Browse ceramics, glassworks and the artists who make them at the **Torpedo Factory Art Center** (p219).

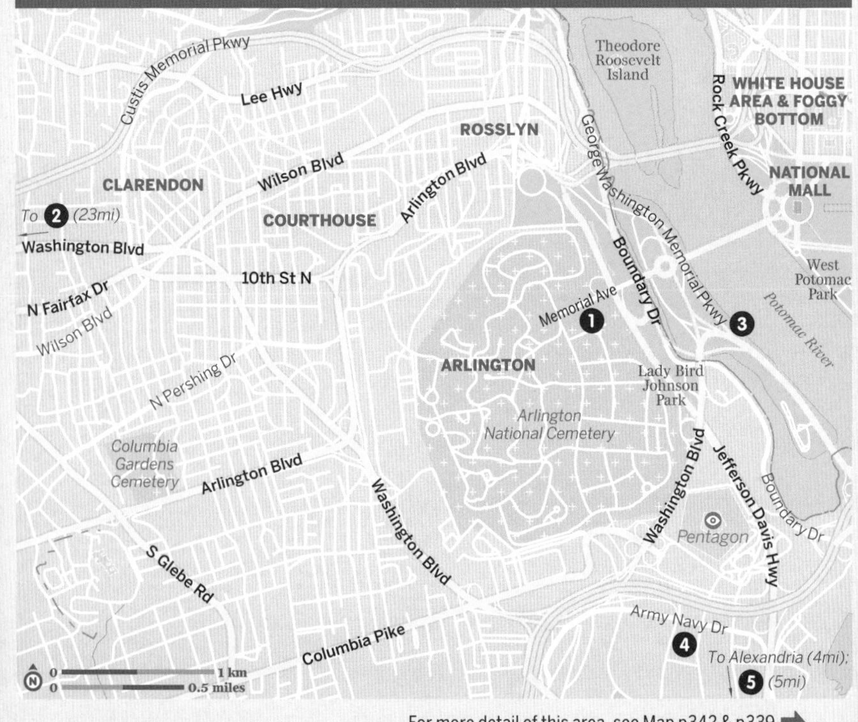

For more detail of this area, see Map p342 & p339

Explore Northern Virginia

Safe, green-conscious, well-trimmed, smells nice. Northern Virginia (NoVa) is DC's perfect neighbor, just across from the picket fence of the Potomac River. NoVa communities are basically suburbs of Washington, attached via the Metro. For the purposes of this book, we concentrate on the towns of Arlington and Alexandria, which combine crucial capital sites with cozy pubs, kickin' pool halls and most of the trappings of suburban bliss.

Start with Arlington. It's quite close, just a Metro stop from DC, and it holds the two main reasons to cross the border: Arlington National Cemetery and the Pentagon. Plan on a half-day for these two sights alone. Beyond Arlington you'll find the un-freaking-believable Udvar-Hazy Center, aka the annex of the National Air and Space Museum, which holds three times as many jets and rockets as the Mall building. Also out this way are the Eden Center, a Saigon-style market and mall where the Vietnamese community clusters, and Annandale, the Korean community's hub. Unfortunately, you'll be hard-pressed to reach these places without a car.

The charming village of Alexandria is 5 miles and 250 years away from Washington. Once a salty port, Alexandria – known as 'Old Town' to locals – is today a posh collection of red-brick homes, cobblestone streets, gas lamps and a waterfront promenade. Boutiques, outdoor cafes and bars pack the main thoroughfare, making the town a fine afternoon or evening jaunt. It's also a jumping-off spot for excursions to Mount Vernon (see p227).

Local Life

➡ **Stay Cool** When temperatures rise, those in the know head to Theodore Roosevelt Island (p218). It's quiet too, since no bikes or cars are permitted.

➡ **Hangout** Whitlow's (p223) is everything a neighborhood hangout should be: boisterous, brunch-awesome, beer-rich and band savvy on weekends.

➡ **Art Attack** Artisphere (p218 and p224) is a secret even to locals. The arts center hosts (often free) exhibitions, performances and films.

Getting There & Away

➡ **Metro** Guess what Arlington Cemetery (Blue Line) and Pentagon (Blue and Yellow Lines) stations are near? Use King St (Blue and Yellow Lines) station for most of Alexandria's sights.

➡ **Trolley** In Alexandria, a free trolley runs along King St between the Metro station and waterfront every 15 minutes from 11:30am to 10:15pm.

➡ **Boat** Tour boats float from Alexandria to Georgetown.

Lonely Planet's Top Tip

Take a day and cycle to Mount Vernon along the eponymous trail. If you start in Alexandria, it's about 12 miles onward. The path clasps the river much of the way and you'll pedal past a lighthouse, bird-filled marsh and 19th-century fort before heading uphill to George Washington's manor. Outfitters have packages where you cycle one way and return via boat.

Best Places to Eat

For reviews, see p221 ➡

Best Places to Drink

For reviews, see p223 ➡

Best Museums

For reviews, see p218 

TOP SIGHTS
PENTAGON

More than 23,000 people work in the massive polygon, the largest office building in the world. As the headquarters of the US Department of Defense, the Army, Navy and Air Force top brass are all here, as are the Joint Chiefs of Staff. With serious pre-planning, you can tour inside. The outdoor Pentagon Memorial is open to anyone, any time.

Just how big is the Pentagon? The entire Capitol could fit into any one of the its five wedge-shaped sections. It has three times the floor space of New York's Empire State Building. The parking lots hold 8770 cars. The building's 17.5 miles of corridors hold 284 bathrooms (side note here: architects designed the building with twice the number of bathrooms needed per number of employees, because segregated Virginia required separate facilities for 'white' and 'colored' persons). The Pentagon's post office handles 1.2 million pieces of mail monthly.

Unlike other monumental federal buildings around DC, the Pentagon was built without using marble. That's because, when construction was going on during WWII, Italy – the source of marble – was an enemy country.

DON'T MISS...

- Memorial audio tour
- Flight 77 point of impact
- Memorial age lines
- Building tours (via pre-registration)
- Medal of Honor

PRACTICALITIES

- Map p342
- 703-697-1776
- pentagon.osd.mil
- Arlington, VA
- admission free
- memorial 24hr, tours by appointment
- Pentagon

Pentagon Memorial

While the formidable edifice appears impenetrable, 184 people were killed here on September 11, 2001, when American Airlines Flight 77 crashed into the side of the building. Just outside of the Pentagon is a tranquil memorial to these victims, including passengers of flight 77. The grounds consist of 184 benches, each engraved with a victim's name, reaching over a small pool of water. The benches are arranged according to the victims' ages and where they were during the crash (Pentagon versus the airplane). The youngest victim was three-year-old Dana Falkenberg (who was on board flight 77); the oldest was John Yamnicky, 71, a Navy veteran also on the flight.

Download the audio tour (www.pentagonmemorial.org) before visiting, or access it on-site by calling 202-741-1004, and it will lead you through the site's features.

To reach the memorial, follow the signs from the Pentagon Metro station and go all the way through the parking lot to the end; it's about a 10-minute walk. It is OK to take photos at the memorial, but nowhere else on Pentagon grounds.

Building Tours

The Pentagon offers free, hour-long **tours** (9am-3pm Mon-Fri). During the 1.5-mile jaunt, guides discuss the military divisions (Army, Air Force, Navy, Marine Corps) housed here; show you the Hall of Heroes and a Medal of Honor; and take you through the Pentagon Memorial. Tours depart from the Metro station. No electronics allowed inside.

To get in, you need to make a reservation eight to 90 days in advance. US citizens can book online (pentagon.osd.mil/tour-selection.html) or through their Member of Congress. Visitors from other countries must contact their embassy for reservations.

TOP SIGHTS

ARLINGTON NATIONAL CEMETERY

Washington's marble often celebrates America's victories and achievements, but this place makes an elegiac counterpoint: commemorating her losses. Simple white headstones mark the sacrifice of over 300,000 service members and their dependents. The 624-acre grounds contain the dead of every war the US has fought since the Revolution.

At the end of Memorial Dr, the first site you'll see is the **Women in Military Service for America Memorial** (www.womensmemorial.org). On the slopes above are the **Kennedy gravesites**. An eternal flame marks the grave of John F Kennedy, next to those of Jacqueline Kennedy Onassis and their two children who died in infancy. Don't forget to visit Arlington House (p218) while you're in the area.

The **Tomb of the Unknowns** contains the remains of unidentified US servicemen from both World Wars and the Korean War. Military guards maintain a round-the-clock vigil and the changing of the guard (every half-hour April through September, every hour October through March) is one of Arlington's most moving sights.

Other points of interest include the **Challenger memorial**, the **Confederate Monument**, the **tomb of Pierre L'Enfant** and the **mast of the battleship USS Maine**. The **Iwo Jima Memorial**, displaying the famous raising of the flag over Mt Suribachi, is on the cemetery's northern fringes.

Pick up a cemetery map at the **visitors center**; the gift shop inside rents audio tours ($6.30). **Bus tours** (☎202-488-1012, ext 200; www.tourmobile.com; adult/child $8.75/4.50) depart out front and are an easy way to hit all the highlights.

DON'T MISS...

- Kennedy graves and eternal flame
- Tomb of the Unknowns
- Iwo Jima Memorial
- Challenger Memorial
- Women in Military Memorial

PRACTICALITIES

- Map p342
- ☎877-907-8585
- www.arlingtoncemetery.mil
- admission free
- 8am-5pm Oct-Mar, to 7pm Apr-Sep
- Ⓜ Arlington Cemetery

SIGHTS

Arlington

ARLINGTON NATIONAL CEMETERY — CEMETERY

See p217.

PENTAGON — BUILDING

See p216.

FREE ARLINGTON HOUSE — HISTORIC SITE

(Map p342; www.nps.gov/arho; 9:30am-4:30pm, to 5:30pm Jun-Aug; M Arlington Cemetery) In one of the great spite moves of American history, thousands of Union war dead were buried in the 1100-acre grounds of Confederate General Robert E Lee's home. After the war, the Lee family sued the federal government for reimbursement: the government paid them off, and Arlington Cemetery was born. The historic house is open for public tours, and is a lovely example of Virginia grand manor architecture.

ARTISPHERE — ARTS CENTER

(Map p342; www.artisphere.com; 1101 Wilson Blvd; M Rosslyn;) For something completely different than memorials and museums, check out the excellent exhibits at this sleek, modern, multistory arts complex, which opened in 2011. Its several theaters host live performances (many free), including world music, film and experimental theater. There's also a cafe, restaurant and bar. While you're here, head up to **Freedom Park**, an elevated greenway that rests in an old road overpass running by Artisphere. It's a nice spot to sit for a while and contemplate.

GEORGE WASHINGTON MEMORIAL PARKWAY — DRIVING TOUR

(Map p342; www.nps.gov/gwmp) The 25-mile Virginia portion of the highway honors its namesake with recreation areas and memorials all the way south to his old estate at Mount Vernon. It's lined with remnants of George Washington's life and works, such as his old Patowmack Company canal (in Great Falls National Park) and parks that were once part of his farmlands (Riverside Park, Fort Hunt Park). The road is a pleasant alternative to the traffic-choked highway arteries further away from the river, but you need to pull off to really appreciate the sites. The 18.5-mile-long Mount Vernon Trail parallels the parkway; see p225 for details.

THEODORE ROOSEVELT ISLAND — PARK

(Map p342; www.nps.gov/this; dawn-dusk; M Rosslyn) This 91-acre wooded island, in the Potomac off Rosslyn, is a wilderness preserve honoring the conservation-minded 26th US president. A large memorial plaza and statue of Teddy dominate the island's center, and trails and boardwalks snake around the shorelines. The island's swampy fringes shelter birds, raccoons and other small animals. There are great views of the Kennedy Center and Georgetown University across the river. The island is accessible from the Mount Vernon Trail and is a convenient stop on a long bike ride or jog –

WORTH A DETOUR

AIR & SPACE MUSEUM ANNEX

The National Air and Space Museum on the Mall is so awesome they made an attic for it: the **Steven F Udvar-Hazy Center** (www.nasm.si.edu/udvarhazy; 14390 Air and Space Museum Parkway; admission free; 10am-5:30pm, to 6:30pm late May-early Sep;), in Chantilly, VA. It's three times the size of the DC museum and sprawls through massive hangars near Dulles Airport. Highlights include the SR-71 Blackbird (the fastest jet in the world), space shuttle *Discovery* (fresh from the clouds after its 2011 retirement) and the Enola Gay (the B-29 that dropped the atomic bomb on Hiroshima). Visitors can hang out in the observation tower and watch the planes take off and land at Dulles, or catch shows at the on-site **Airbus IMAX Theater**. Free tours through the collection are offered at 10:30am and 1pm daily.

To get out here, you'll need to either drive (take I-66 West to VA 267 West, then VA 28 South, then follow the signs; parking costs $15) or take Metrobus 5A to Dulles (see p288 for details). From there, it's an $8 to $12 taxi ride, or you can take the Virginia Regional Transit Association shuttle bus (50¢), which departs from the same stop at the airport as Metrobus and goes direct to the museum every 45 minutes.

but note bikes aren't permitted on the island itself; lock them up in the parking lot.

NATIONAL AIR FORCE MEMORIAL MONUMENT
(Map p342; www.airforcememorial.org; 1300 block of Columbia Pike; 24hr; M Pentagon) Overlooking the Pentagon and adjacent to Arlington National Cemetery, this memorial is (somewhat oddly) especially attractive from the highway. It pays tribute to the millions of men and women who served in the air force and its predecessor organizations via a series of twisting metal arcs, meant to evoke the contrails of jets.

FREE **DEA MUSEUM** MUSEUM
(Map p342; United States Drug Enforcement Agency Museum; www.deamuseum.org; 7200 Army Navy Dr; 10am-4pm Tue-Fri; M Pentagon City) If you've got issues with the US War on Drugs, you may want to give the Drug Enforcement Agency (DEA) Museum a pass. If, on the other hand, you think all drug users and pushers should go to jail for a very long time and drugs and terrorism go hand in hand – or if you just have a thing for heavy-handed propaganda – well, stop on by. We're not trying to be flip, by the way – most Washington museums do a good job of presenting all sides of controversial issues such as the Vietnam War versus the antiwar movement, but there's no such nuance here. Then again, this is the only place in official Washington that displays bongs.

Alexandria

GEORGE WASHINGTON MASONIC NATIONAL MEMORIAL MONUMENT, LOOKOUT
(off Map p339; www.gwmemorial.org; 101 Callahan Dr at King St; adult/child $8/free; 9am-4pm Mon-Sat, noon-4pm Sun; M King St Metro) Alexandria's most prominent landmark features a fine view from its 333ft tower, where you can see the Capitol, Mount Vernon and the Potomac River. It is modeled after Egypt's Lighthouse of Alexandria, and honors the first president (who was initiated into the shadowy Masons in Fredericksburg in 1752 and later became Worshipful Master of Alexandria Lodge No 22). The only way up is via a guided tour; they depart at 10am, 11:30am, 1:30pm and 3pm (on Sunday the first one is at 12:30pm).

ALEXANDRIA VISITOR CENTER

The town's **visitor center** (703-838-5005; www.visitalexandriava.com; 221 King St; 9am-5pm) issues parking permits and discount tickets to historic sights, as well as maps.

FREE **TORPEDO FACTORY ART CENTER** ARTS CENTER
(Map p339; www.torpedofactory.org; 105 N Union St; 10am-6pm, to 7pm Thu; M King St for trolley) What do you do with a former munitions dump and arms factory? How about turn it into one of the best art spaces in the region? Three floors of artist studios and free creativity are on offer in Old Town Alexandria, as well as the opportunity to buy paintings, sculptures, glassworks, textiles and jewelry direct from their creators. The Torpedo Factory anchors Alexandria's revamped waterfront with a marina, parks, walkways, residences and restaurants.

FREE **ALEXANDRIA ARCHAEOLOGY MUSEUM** MUSEUM
(Map p339; alexandriava.gov/archaeology; 105 N Union St; 10am-3pm Tue-Fri, to 5pm Sat, 1-5pm Sun; M King St for trolley) Also housed at the Torpedo Factory is the Alexandria Archaeology Museum, the laboratory where archaeologists clean up and catalog the artifacts they have unearthed at local digs. First-hand observation of the work, excavation exhibits and hands-on discovery kits allow visitors to witness and participate in the reconstruction of Alexandria's history.

STABLER-LEADBEATER APOTHECARY MUSEUM MUSEUM
(Map p339; www.alexandriava.gov/apothecary; 105-107 S Fairfax St; adult/child $4/2; 10am-5pm Mon-Sat, 1-5pm Sun; M King St for trolley) In 1792 Edward Stabler opened up his apothecary (pharmacy) – a family business that would operate for the next 141 years, until the Depression forced the shop to close. Quite a bit of history was shut inside at that time, including over 8000 medical objects. Now the shop is a museum; its shelves are lined with 900 beautiful hand-blown apothecary bottles and strange old items such as Martha Washington's Scouring Compound.

GADSBY'S TAVERN MUSEUM MUSEUM

(Map p339; www.gadsbystavern.org; 134 N Royal St; adult/child $5/2; ⏱10am-5pm Tue-Sat, 1-5pm Sun & Mon; Ⓜ King St for trolley) Once a real tavern (operated by John Gadsby from 1796 to 1808), this building now houses a museum demonstrating the prominent role of the tavern in Alexandria during the 18th century. As the center of local political, business and social life, the tavern was frequented by anybody who was anybody, including George Washington, Thomas Jefferson and the Marquis de Lafayette. The rooms are restored to their 18th-century appearance, and the tavern occasionally still hosts pricey balls. Guided tours take place at quarter to and quarter past the hour.

CHRIST CHURCH CHURCH

(Map p339; www.historicchristchurch.org; 118 N Washington St; admission by donation; ⏱9am-4pm Mon-Sat, 2-4pm Sun; Ⓜ King St for trolley) Since 1773, this redbrick Georgian-style church has welcomed worshipers from George Washington to Robert E Lee. The cemetery contains the mass grave of Confederate soldiers.

FRIENDSHIP FIREHOUSE MUSEUM MUSEUM

(Map p339; www.alexandriava.gov/friendship firehouse; 107 S Alfred St; admission $2; ⏱1-4pm Sat & Sun; Ⓜ King St for trolley; 👪) This 1855 Italianate firehouse displays historic firefighting gear – a great draw for kids. Local legend has it that George Washington helped found this volunteer fire company, served as its captain and even paid for a new fire engine.

> **WORTH A DETOUR**
>
> **FORT WARD MUSEUM & HISTORIC SITE**
>
> Fort Ward is the best-restored of the 162 Civil War forts known as the Defenses of Washington. The Northwest Bastion of the **fort** (www.alexandriava.gov/FortWard; 4301 W Braddock Rd; admission free; ⏱park 9am-dusk, museum 10am-5pm Tue-Sat, noon-5pm Sun) has been completely restored, and the remaining earthwork walls give a good sense of the defenses' original appearance. The on-site museum features exhibits on Civil War topics. The site is about 4 miles northwest of Old Town Alexandria; take King St for 3 miles to Braddock Rd and turn left.

LEE-FENDALL HOUSE HISTORIC BUILDING

(Map p339; ☎703-548-1789; www.leefendall house.org; 614 Oronoco St; adult/child $5/3; ⏱10am-3pm Wed-Sat, 1-3pm Sun, tours on the hr; Ⓜ Braddock Rd) Between 1785 and 1903 generations of the storied Lee family lived in this architecturally impressive house. Guided tours show the restored house as it probably was in the 1850s and 1860s, showcasing Lee family heirlooms and personal effects, and period furniture. The Georgian-style **town house** (607 Oronoco St; ⏱closed to public) across the street was Robert E Lee's childhood home from 1810.

ALEXANDRIA BLACK HISTORY MUSEUM MUSEUM

(Map p339; www.alexblackhistory.org; 901 Wythe St; admission $2; ⏱10am-4pm Tue-Sat; Ⓜ Braddock Rd) Paintings, photographs, books and other memorabilia documenting the African American experience in Alexandria, one of the nation's major slave ports, are on display at this small resource center (enter from Wythe St). Pick up a brochure for self-guided walking tours of important African American–history sites in Alexandria. In the next-door annex, the **Watson Reading Room** has a wealth of books and documents on African American topics.

Operated by the museum, the **African American Heritage Park** (500 Holland Lane) is worth a stop to see headstones from a 19th-century African American cemetery. The park is about a half-mile southeast of the King St Metro. From the station, take Reinekers Lane south, go left on Duke St, then right on Holland Lane.

FREE **NATIONAL INVENTORS HALL OF FAME & MUSEUM** MUSEUM

(☎571-272-0095; www.invent.org; 600 Dulany St, Madison Bldg; ⏱9am-5pm Mon-Fri, noon-5pm Sat; Ⓜ King St) This museum, in the atrium of the US Patent and Trademark Office, tells the history of the United States patent. Step inside to see where the story started in 1917 in Memphis, Tennessee, when a wholesale grocer named Clarence Saunders invented and patented what he called 'self-servicing' stores, now commonly known as supermarkets. Incidentally, he went from rags to riches and almost back to rags again, but you'll have to visit the museum to get the rest of the story, along with displays depicting other famous and influential patents. It is about a third of a mile from the King St Metro station; take Diagonal Rd south to Dulany St.

EATING

Northern Virginia offers two kinds of eating experiences: cheap ethnic eateries, mainly in Arlington, and more upscale, traditional sit-down fare, plus pub-grub type spots, in Alexandria.

LOCAL KNOWLEDGE

FARMERS MARKETS

Virginia's farmland bounty is on display weekend mornings at:

Arlington Farmers' Market (Map p342; www.arlingtonfarmersmarket.com; cnr N Courthouse Rd & N 14th St; ⌚8am-noon Sat Apr-Dec, from 9am Jan-Mar; Ⓜ Courthouse)

Old Town Farmers Market (Map p339; 301 King St, Alexandria; www.alexandriava.gov/farmersmarket; ⌚5:30am-11am Sat; Ⓜ King St Metro)

Arlington

RAY'S HELL BURGER BURGERS $
(Map p342; www.rayshellburger.com; 1713 Wilson Blvd; burgers from $8; ⌚11:30am-10pm Sun-Thu, to 11pm Fri & Sat; Ⓜ Rosslyn) Do Ray's burgers taste as good as they sound? Hell yes. What makes them hellishly good? The free jalapenos, and the massive amounts of meat, and the way the meat drip kinda melts the bun the way your dad's burgers did, and any of the stupendous cheeses you can melt on that bad boy. Barack Obama and Joe Biden came here for impromptu burgers right after they got into office; needless to say, everyone who was just kinda waiting at the counter sort of had the meal of their lives.

WEENIE BEENIE AMERICAN $
(off Map p342; 2680 S Shirlington Rd; under $10; ⌚6am-6pm) Ah Weenie, thy half-smokes descend upon mine tongue like a benediction of sausagey grace from on high, melting upon the mouth of the hungry with thy spicy chili topping and onions – so sweet! – and mustard and cheese – so greasy! – leaving upon the memory naught but sweet remembrance, until next I hold you, piping fresh buns and all, 'twixt my fingers, which even now long for thy half-smoky goodness. Your barbecue ain't half bad either, come to think of it. It's about 4 miles southwest of Arlington cemetery via Arlington Blvd.

EL POLLO RICO LATIN AMERICAN $
(Map p342; ☎703-522-3220; www.elpollorico restaurant.com; 932 N Kenmore St; chicken with sides $6-12; ⌚11am-10pm; Ⓜ Clarendon, Virginia Sq-GMU) Drooling locals have flocked to this Peruvian chicken joint for decades now in search of tender, juicy, flavor-packed birds served with succulent (highly addictive) dipping sauces, crunchy fries and sloppy 'slaw. Lines form outside the door come dinnertime. EPR is one of the first purveyors of Peruvian chicken in the metro area, and age hasn't hurt quality at one of the original kings of *polla a la brasa* (rotisserie chicken).

EDEN CENTER VIETNAMESE $$
(off Map p342; www.edencenter.com; 6571 Wilson Blvd, Falls Church; mains $9-15; ⌚9am-9pm; ✍) One of Washington's most fascinating ethnic enclaves isn't technically in Washington. Instead, drive west past Arlington to Falls Church, Virginia and the Eden Center, which is, basically, a bit of Saigon that got lost in America. And we mean 'Saigon' – this is a shopping center/strip mall entirely occupied and operated by South Vietnamese refugees and their descendants. You can buy Vietnamese DVDs, shop for odd fruits and unusual medicines and, of course, eat – anywhere. It's all as fresh as a Southeast Asian street stall. There's even a vegan Vietnamese restaurant (Thanh Van) as part of the mix.

ABAY MARKET ETHIOPIAN $$
(off Map p342; ☎703-998-5322; 3811 S George Mason Dr, Falls Church; mains from $13; ⌚lunch & dinner) Tucked into a strip mall between a bunch of hideous apartment blocks and corporate towers is the best Ethiopian food we've had in the metro area. Abay is the real deal, run by an Ethiopian former air-force officer, with clientele straight out of Addis and food that will no doubt blow your mind – if you're adventurous. Because this ain't for the faint of heart. Abay specializes in raw or barely cooked meat, either ground up and cooked with spices (and, according to the owner, a bit of Coca-Cola), *kifto* style,

or served in intimidating, chewy, and for our money, delicious slabs, yellow fat still definitely attached. The above comes with a very soft cheese that adds a nice, creamy complement, and should be sopped up with spongy *injera* bread. You'll need to drive to get out here, but it's cheaper than flying to the Horn of Africa, which is about the only way to beat Abay for authenticity.

MYANMAR BURMESE **$**

(off Map p342; ☎703-289-0013; 7810 Lee Hwy, Falls Church; mains under $10; ⏰11am-10pm) Myanmar's decor is barebones; the service is slow; the portions are small; and the food is delicious. This is home-cooked Burmese: curries cooked with lots of garlic, turmeric and oil, chili fish, mango salads and chicken swimming in rich gravies. Try the *mohingar,* the Burmese take on Southeast Asian noodle soup: thin noodles, plump bits of fish and a garlicky, in-depth complexity that will have you smiling into the bottom of your soon-to-be-empty bowl. For an ethnic eating experience, it doesn't get much more authentic. It's located a bit west of Falls Church on Lee Hwy.

YECHON KOREAN **$$**

(off Map p342; ☎703-914-4646; www.yechon.com; 4121 Hummer Rd, Annandale; mains $10-15; ⏰24hr; Ⓜ Rosslyn) Annandale, a suburb on the edge of the beltway west of Arlington and Alexandria, is the center of the Washington, DC, Korean community – and as you'd guess, the Korean culinary scene. Debates over who does the best Korean in the DC area have been the source of much gastronomic bickering; we like Yechon. It's an oldie but a goodie, always packed with Koreans (good sign) and curious Westerners. The *kalbi* (barbecue ribs) is rich, smoky and, well, *meaty* – it's fantastic stuff, true stick-to-your-ribs Seoul food. Contrast it with the complex seaweed and searing kimchi and this is a Korean feast that is affordable, delicious and (important point coming) *open 24/7.* Nothing works off the *soju* (Korean alcoholic drink) like 3am tofu and chili, after all...

Alexandria

Unless stated otherwise, the free trolley from the King St Metro station will get you to Alexandria's eateries.

RESTAURANT EVE AMERICAN **$$$**

(Map p339; ☎703-706-0450; www.restauranteve.com; 110 S Pitt St; 5-/7-course tasting menus $120/135; ⏰lunch Mon-Fri, dinner Mon-Sat; 🖉) While 'fusion' may be an overused adjective when it comes to describing restaurants, the best kitchens always fuse. Innovation and tradition, regional and international influences, comfort and class. Eve contains everything we have described, a combination of great American ingredients, precise French technique and some of the highest levels of service we've encountered in the area. Splurge here on the tasting menus, which are simply on another level of gastronomic experience. This is one of the few vegan-friendly high-end restaurants in the DC metro area; just make sure to call a day ahead and chef-owner Cathal Armstrong's team will be happy to accommodate you.

BRABO TASTING ROOM BELGIAN **$$**

(off Map p339; www.braborestaurant.com; 1600 King St; mains $14-17; ⏰11:30am-11pm Mon-Sat, to 10pm Sun) The inviting and sunlit Brabo Tasting Room serves its signature mussels, tasty wood-fired tarts and gourmet sandwiches (like slow-roasted Angus beef with caramelized mushrooms) with a good beer and wine selection. Brabo restaurant, next door, is the high-end counterpart serving seasonal fare.

EAMONN'S DUBLIN CHIPPER FISH & CHIPS **$**

(Map p339; www.eamonnsdublinchipper.com; 728 King St; mains $7-10; ⏰11:30am-11pm, to 1am Fri & Sat) You'll find no better execution of the fish and chips genre than at this upscale temple to battered and fried potato. How authentic is it? Folks: they import the mushy peas from Ireland, and also serve deep-fried Mars Bars, Milky Way and Snickers. Like many resto-pubs in this part of Old Town, Eamonn's is a good place for a drink on weekend nights.

KING STREET BLUES SOUTHERN **$$**

(Map p339; ☎703-836-8800; www.kingstreetblues.com; 112 N St Asaph St; mains $10-15; ⏰lunch & dinner) King Street Blues is a crazy Southern 'roadhouse' diner that serves really good baked meatloaf, country-fried steak, Southern fried catfish and other diner favorites. The interior is strewn with colorful papier-mâché figures floating across its three levels, while shiny chrome furniture and multicolored tablecloths lend a retro air. Is there blues music, you ask? Very sporadically.

GADSBY'S TAVERN RESTAURANT AMERICAN **$$**

(Map p339; ☎703-548-1288; www.gadsbystavernrestaurant.com; 138 N Royal St; mains $22-30; ⏰lunch & dinner) Set in the building of an 18th-century tavern, Gadsby's is named after the Englishman who operated the tavern from 1796 to 1808 (when it was the center of Alexandria's social life). This place tries to emulate an 18th-century hostelry; the overall effect is rather kitsch, but it's good, clean, historical fun. Besides, who wouldn't want to try 'George Washington's Favorite' (duck stuffed with tart fruit and topped with Madeira gravy)?

MOMO SUSHI & CAFE JAPANESE **$$**

(Map p339; www.mymomosushi.com; 212 Queen St; sushi combos $10-23; ⏰lunch & dinner Mon-Sat, dinner Sun) Momo is tiny and has just 13 seats, but it serves excellent sushi.

DRINKING & NIGHTLIFE

Head to Wilson and Clarendon Blvds in Arlington or King St in Alexandria for good bar-hopping with a crowd of folks who seem to be perpetually enrolled in the University of Virginia, Virginia Tech or George Mason University.

Arlington

CONTINENTAL LOUNGE

(Map p342; www.continentalpoollounge.com; 1911 N Fort Myer Dr; ⏰11:30am-2am Mon-Fri, 6pm-2am Sat & Sun; Ⓜ Rosslyn) A stone's throw from many Rosslyn hotels, this posh pool hall isn't your average billiards club. There's no stale-beer-and-cigarette stink here, where spaghetti lights form constellations on the ceiling and columns are painted like palm trees. Tiki heads and bars painted with silver glitter complete the picture. The owner says Disneyland was the inspiration for his style faux pas that somehow manages to epitomize cool.

WHITLOW'S ON WILSON BAR

(Map p342; www.whitlows.com; 2854 Wilson Blvd; ⏰11am-2am Mon-Fri, 9am-2am Sat & Sun; Ⓜ Clarendon) Occupying almost an entire block just east of Clarendon Metro, Whitlow's on Wilson has something for everyone: burgers, brunch and comfort food on the menu; happening happy hours and positive pick-up potential; plus 12 brews on tap, a pool table, jukebox, live music and an easygoing atmosphere. It's a favorite with singles.

IRELAND'S FOUR COURTS IRISH PUB

(Map p342; www.irelandsfourcourts.com; 2051 Wilson Blvd; ⏰11am-2am Mon-Sat, 10am-2am Sun; Ⓜ Courthouse) Buckets of Guinness lubricate the O'Connors and McDonoughs at Arlington's favorite Irish pub. The sidewalk seating draws a lunchtime crowd for shepherd's pie and fish and chips, while the verdant Irish grass-green interior attracts an evening crowd for cold drafts and live tunes.

Alexandria

UNION STREET PUBLIC HOUSE PUB

(Map p339; www.unionstreetpublichouse.com; 121 S Union St; ⏰from 11:30am; Ⓜ King St for trolley) Gas lamps out front welcome tourists and locals into this spacious taproom for frosty brews, raw-bar delights and nightly dinner specials. Inside, the vibe is equally inviting: a wide bar, heavy wooden furniture and exposed brick provide equal parts retro-and-warm atmosphere.

MISHA'S COFFEE ROASTER CAFE

(Map p339; www.mishascoffee.com; 102 S Patrick St; pastries $3-4; ⏰6am-8pm, from 6:30am Sun; 📶) Sip a lovely latte next to jars of strong-smelling beans imported from Indonesia and Ethiopia, bang out your play on your laptop (or procrastinate with the free wi-fi), check out the cute nerds at the other tables and reach caffeinated nirvana at this very hip indie cafe. Croissants and cookies add to the buzz.

BIRRERIA PARADISO BAR

(Map p339; www.eatyourpizza.com; 124 King St; ⏰from 11:30am Mon-Sat, noon Sun; Ⓜ King St for trolley) Yeah, OK: this is a pizza restaurant (the same Pizza Paradiso chain as in Georgetown), but the bar's beer list kicks ass. It's a comfy spot for hopheads to sit back and indulge in cask ales and gallons of global and small batch suds.

ENTERTAINMENT

Arlington

TOP CHOICE IOTA LIVE MUSIC

(Map p342; www.iotaclubandcafe.com; 2832 Wilson Blvd; most tickets from $10; from 8am; M Clarendon;) With shows almost every night of the week, Iota is the best venue for live music in Clarendon's music strip. Bands span genres; folk, reggae, traditional Irish and Southern rock are all distinct possibilities. Tickets are available at the door only (no advance sales) and this place packs 'em in (the seating is first come, first served). The free open-mic Wednesdays can be lots of fun or painfully self-important, as these things are wont to be. The venue is a panini-serving cafe by day.

TOP CHOICE ARTISPHERE LIVE MUSIC, THEATER

(Map p342; www.artisphere.com; 1101 Wilson Blvd; M Rosslyn;) The multistory arts complex hosts world music, film and experimental theater. Many performances are free; for those that have an admission price, it's generally between $8 and $18.

ARLINGTON CINEMA & DRAFTHOUSE CINEMA

(off Map p342; www.arlingtondrafthouse.com; 2903 Columbia Pike; M Pentagon City) Ice-cold beers and second-run films at bargain-basement prices? Who could resist that? Not many people. You need to be 21 to enter (or with a parent), but once inside you will find comfy chairs for flick-viewing, a menu of sandwiches, pizzas and, of course, popcorn, as well as a selection of alcoholic drinks (this is one of the few places in DC where you can drink and catch a movie at the same time). Some nights the theater skips the movies and hosts stand-up comedy instead. Check the website. There are also family-oriented programs some weekends. It's about a mile from the Metro; grab a cab or the route 16 bus from the station.

CLARENDON BALLROOM LIVE MUSIC

(Map p342; www.clarendonballroom.com; 3185 Wilson Blvd; cover charge varies; M Clarendon) A gorgeous ballroom done up to look like a big band–era dance hall, the Ballroom is a NoVa cornerstone that attracts throngs of young professionals coming to hear emerging local artists, DJs and big names on national tours. The upstairs deck is perfect for lingering over a sunset Cosmopolitan.

Alexandria

FREE TIFFANY TAVERN LIVE MUSIC

(Map p339; www.tiffanytavern.com; 1116 King St; M King St) The food is kind of lame and the beer selection weak, but the live bluegrass (from 8:30pm Friday and Saturday) hits the spot at the well-worn Tiffany Tavern. It gets a little rough and a lot raucous on the best nights, when Yuengling on tap, mandolin and fiddle equal hours of roots-music magic.

BASIN STREET LOUNGE JAZZ BAR

(Map p339; www.219restaurant.com; 219 King St; admission Fri & Sat $5; shows 8pm Tue-Thu, 9pm Fri & Sat; M King St for trolley) Wire-rimmed glasses and black turtlenecks may be the uniform at this sophisticated jazz venue, located in the back of the 219 restaurant. The downstairs lounge boasts quaint French Quarter Victorian decor, which is appropriate for the swinging piano, saxophone and bluesy jazz performances. The crowd is a bit older and if the music is good, the scene is pleasantly sedate.

BIRCHMERE LIVE MUSIC

(off Map p339; www.birchmere.com; 3701 Mount Vernon Ave; tickets $15-35; box office 5-9pm, shows 7:30pm; M Pentagon City for bus 10A) Known as 'America's Legendary Music Hall,' this is the DC area's premier venue for folk, country, Celtic and bluegrass music. The talent that graces the stage is reason enough to come, but the venue is pretty great too: it sort of looks like a warehouse that collided with an army of LSD-savvy muralists. Located north of Old Town Alexandria off Glebe Rd.

SHOPPING

The most charming shopping here is in Alexandria, along cobbled King St in Old Town. Here you'll find craft stores and antique shops, art galleries, used booksellers and more.

TORPEDO FACTORY ART CENTER ARTS & CRAFTS

(Map p339; www.torpedofactory.org; 105 N Union St; M King St for trolley) Built during WWI to manufacture torpedoes, the complex today manufactures art. It houses more than 160 artists and craftspeople who sell their creations directly from their studios. It is a very cool, distinctive set up, and there's a good chance you'll head home with a reasonably priced, one-of-a-kind painting, textile or piece of jewelry.

PRINCIPLE GALLERY — ART

(Map p339; www.principlegallery.com; 208 King St; Ⓜ King St for trolley) One of a growing number of galleries along King St, this approachable place often assembles some of the best collections. Principle represents artists from across the globe, and even if you're not in the art market, it's worth a peek inside.

FASHION CENTRE AT PENTAGON CITY — MALL

(Map p342; 1100 S Hayes St, Arlington; 10am-9:30pm Mon-Sat, 11am-6pm Sun; Ⓜ Pentagon City) It houses 170 shops, including Macy's, Nordstrom, a cinema and a food court beneath skylights. It's your average, convenient mall – with the fun bonus of being where Monica Lewinsky got busted by Ken Starr's troopers back in '98.

POTOMAC MILLS — MALL

(off Map p342; 2700 Potomac Mills Circle, Woodbridge, VA; 10am-9pm Mon-Sat, 11am-6pm Sun) A fire-breathing monster of mid-Atlantic outlet malls, just a half-hour drive south of DC, Potomac Mills features about 250 discount shops, including Ikea, Saks and Spiegel. The place now draws more tourists (about 24 million per year) and tour buses than Williamsburg or Virginia's other historic sites, which might say something about Americans' priorities. Take Exit 158-B off I-95.

SPORTS & ACTIVITIES

Despite its dense suburbs, northern Virginia is laced with hiking and biking trails.

TOP CHOICE MOUNT VERNON TRAIL — BIKING

(Map p342; www.nps.gov/gwmp/mtvernontrail.htm; Ⓜ Rosslyn) The 18.5-mile-long Mount Vernon Trail is a paved riverside path that is a favorite with local cyclists. From the Francis Scott Key Bridge, it follows the Potomac River south past Roosevelt Island, Arlington Cemetery and Reagan National Airport, through Old Town Alexandria, all the way to Mount Vernon (p227). Groovy sights along the way include **Lady Bird Johnson Park**, which commemorates the First Lady who tried to beautify the capital via greenery-planting campaigns; tulips and daffodils go wild here in spring. **Gravelly Point**, just north of the airport, provides a vantage point for watching the planes take off and land. **Roaches Run Waterfowl Sanctuary** lets you check out naturally airborne creatures including ospreys and green herons.

The course is mostly flat, except the long climb up the hill to George Washington's house at the end. The scenery is magnificent – DC skylines and all – and the historical component is certainly unique.

WASHINGTON & OLD DOMINION TRAIL — BIKING

(off Map p342; W&OD; www.nvrpa.org/park/w_od_railroad; Ⓜ East Falls Church) The Washington & Old Dominion Trail starts in southern Arlington and follows the old railway bed through historic Leesburg and on to Purcellville, in the Allegheny foothills. Its 45 miles are paved and spacious, winding their way through the Virginia suburbs. The path allows horseback riding between Vienna and Purcellville. The easiest place to pick up the trail is outside the East Falls Church Metro station: exit right and turn right again onto Tuckahoe St, then follow the signs.

For the truly ambitious, it's a short jump from here to the 2000 miles of Appalachian Trail going south to Georgia and north to Maine.

BIKE & ROLL — BIKING

(Map p339; 703-548-7655; www.bikethesites.com; One Wales Alley; hire per 2hr $12; mid-Mar–Nov; Ⓜ King St for trolley) Rent a bike and hop on the Mount Vernon Trail one block south. Ask about package deals (including picnic provisions, admission fees and one-way boat trips), to George Washington's estate. The shop is located off Strand St.

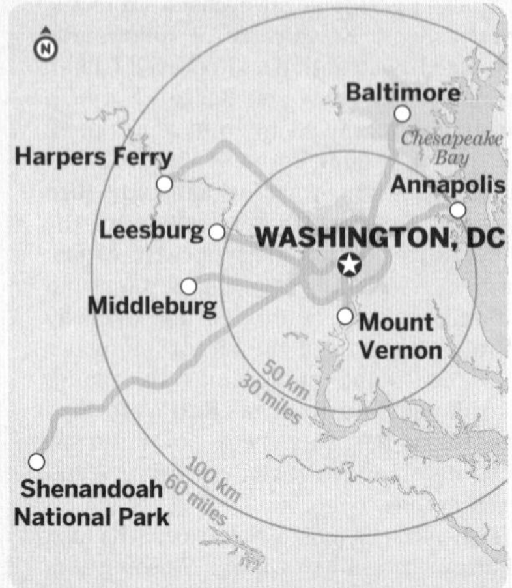

Day Trips from Washington, DC

Mount Vernon p227

The beautifully preserved estate of George Washington is a great place to explore the legacy of one of America's great visionaries.

Baltimore p228

The city has a vibrant waterfront, with a fantastic maritime museum, a sprawling aquarium and top-notch art and history museums.

Annapolis p231

Maryland's small, historic capital has 18th-century architecture, great seafood restaurants and a scenic harbor. Sleepy waterfront towns and islands dotting the Chesapeake Bay are a slice of maritime life.

Harpers Ferry p234

Set on the Potomac and Shenandoah Rivers, peaceful Harpers Ferry is packed with heritage museums and charming B&Bs. There are also great outdoor activities.

Leesburg & Middleburg p236

Two of Virginia's many small-town gems, Leesburg and nearby Middleburg have historic homes and estates and delightful restaurants and B&Bs. Virginia's up-and-coming wine region is nearby.

Shenandoah National Park p238

This vast wilderness has hundreds of miles of hiking trails, plus plenty of scenic overlooks to take in the rolling verdure of the Blue Ridge Mountains.

TOP SIGHTS

MOUNT VERNON

A visit to George Washington's Virginia home, Mount Vernon, is an easy escape from the city – one that the president himself enjoyed. It's also a journey through history: the country estate of this quintessential gentleman has been meticulously restored and affords a glimpse of rural gentility from a time long gone. On the Potomac banks, the 19-room mansion displays George and Martha's colonial tastes, while the outbuildings and slave quarters show what was needed for the functioning of the estate. George and Martha are both buried here, as requested by the first president in his will.

Ford Orientation Center

This modern center is a must-see on the grounds. It features a 20-minute film that shows Washington's courage under fire, including his pivotal crossing of the Delaware River (the do-or-die moment of the Revolutionary War).

Reynolds Museum & Education Center

These galleries and theaters gives more insight into Washington's life through interactive displays, short films and life-size models of Washington himself. The museum also features period furnishings, clothing and jewelry (Martha was quite taken with finery) and George's unusual dentures.

George Washington's Distillery & Gristmill

Three miles south of Mount Vernon, you can learn about Washington's prowess at farming and making whiskey, with actors in period costume demonstrating how it all worked.

DON'T MISS...

- Mount Vernon in Miniature
- The Greenhouse
- Real, live Martha Washington (aka Mary Wiseman)
- Pioneer Farm Site

PRACTICALITIES

- ☎703-780-2000
- www.mountvernon.org
- 3200 George Washington Memorial Parkway
- adult/child $15/7
- 8am-5pm Apr-Aug, shorter hours off season
- M Huntington, then Fairfax Connector bus 101 to Mount Vernon
- The *Spirit of Mount Vernon* departs from Pier 4, at 6th & Water Sts SW

Baltimore

Explore

Baltimore's dramatic and continuing redevelopment has transformed the gritty city into an exciting historical and modern destination. There's much to see here, and you could easily spend four or five days exploring without running out of things to do. If time is short, focus on the Inner Harbor, with its waterfront promenade, superb National Aquarium and sprawling Maritime Museum. It's the most touristic part of the city, but worth seeing. The upscale neighborhood of Mount Vernon lies to the north and has notable art museums (including the celebrated Walters Art Gallery), and a good selection of locally owned restaurants and bars. For nightlife, head east of the Inner Harbor to the bar-lined brick streets of Fell's Point or to Federal Hill, just south of Inner Harbor.

The Best

- **Sight** National Aquarium (p228)
- **Place to Eat** Blue Hill Tavern (p230)
- **Place to Drink** Brewer's Art (p231)

Top Tip

A 10-minute drive north of downtown, **Hampden** is a self-consciously hip urban neighborhood that's packed with bohemian-style restaurants and kitsch-filled shops. Start exploring on the **Avenue** (also known as W 36th St).

Getting There & Away

Car Take I-95 or I-295 (Baltimore-Washington Parkway) north to Russell St, which terminates west of the Inner Harbor. Or take I-95 north to I-395, which spills out downtown as Howard St. Beware of this drive during rush hour; outside of peak times it should take 45 to 60 minutes.

Train Both **Amtrak** (800-872-7245; www.amtrak.com) and the **Maryland Rail Commuter** (MARC; 866-743-3682; www.mtamaryland.com; 6:30am-10:30pm Mon-Fri) travel between Washington, DC's Union Station and Baltimore's Penn Station. MARC is cheaper but runs only on weekdays. Buses 3 and 11 travel up Charles St past Penn Station at 1515 N Charles St.

Need to Know

- **Area Code** 410
- **Location** 45 miles northeast of Washington, DC
- **Tourist Office** (800-282-6632; www.baltimore.org; 100 Light St; 9am-6pm)

SIGHTS

NATIONAL AQUARIUM AQUARIUM

(410-576-3800; www.aqua.org; Piers 3-4, 501 E Pratt St; adult/child $25/15; 9am-5pm Sat-Thu, to 8pm Fri) The National Aquarium in Baltimore put the city on the map as a tourist destination when it opened in 1981. Stretching seven stories high over two piers, its tanks house more than 10,000 marine animals, including sharks, rays and porpoises, plus dolphins in the Marine Mammal Pavilion.

BALTIMORE MARITIME MUSEUM SHIPS

(410-396-3453; www.baltomaritimemuseum.org; Piers 3 & 5, 301 E Pratt St; admission 1/2/4 ships $10/13/16; 10am-5:30pm) For manufactured aquatic wonders, visit the Baltimore Maritime Museum, which consists of a lighthouse (admission free) and four US Navy vessels that visitors can tour. These include a 1930s double-masted lightship, a submarine, a warship that saw action in Pearl Harbor and, most impressive of all, the three-masted 1854 USS *Constellation*.

AMERICAN VISIONARY ART MUSEUM MUSEUM

(410-244-1900; www.avam.org; 800 Key Hwy; adult/child $14/8; 10am-6pm Tue-Sun) One of the most distinctive museums around here is the American Visionary Art Museum, on the south side of the harbor. This avant-garde gallery showcases the raw genius of 'outsider' artists: broken mirror collages, a maniacally embroidered last will, a giant model ship constructed from toothpicks, and other oddities.

MARYLAND SCIENCE CENTER MUSEUM

(410-685-5225; www.mdsci.org; 601 Light St; adult/child $15/11, IMAX film $12; 10am-5pm Wed-Fri, 10am-6pm Sat, 11am-5pm Sun) Baltimore boasts two top stops for kids, both within a few blocks of the Inner Harbor.

The Maryland Science Center sits at the harbor's southeast corner. The excellent rotating exhibits and IMAX films are the highlight.

PORT DISCOVERY MUSEUM

(☎410-727-8120; www.portdiscovery.org; 35 Market Pl; admission $13; ⊙10am-4:30pm Tue-Sat, noon-5pm Sun) Two blocks north, Port Discovery is a converted fish market, which has a playhouse, a laboratory, a TV studio and even Pharaoh's tomb. Wear your kids out here.

CAMDEN YARDS BASEBALL FIELD

(☎888-848-2473; www.theorioles.com; 333 W Camden St; tickets $15-80; ⊙box office 10am-5pm Mon-Sat, noon-5pm Sun) The Orioles' baseball park, Camden Yards, occupies an entire city block west of the Inner Harbor. It was the first 'retro' ball park, which reconciled Major League Baseball's need for more space with fans' nostalgia.

BABE RUTH MUSEUM MUSEUM

(☎410-727-1539; www.baberuthmuseum.com; 216 Emory St; adult/child $6/3; ⊙10am-5pm) Painted baseballs on the sidewalk lead two blocks northwest to the birthplace of a baseball legend; it's now the Babe Ruth Museum, which pays homage to one of the sport's all-time greats. It's open to 7pm on Orioles game days.

B&O RAILROAD MUSEUM MUSEUM

(☎410-752-2490; www.borail.org; 901 W Pratt St; adult/child $14/8; ⊙10am-4pm Mon-Sat, 11am-4pm Sun; 👪) The Baltimore & Ohio railway was (arguably) the first passenger train in America, and the museum is a loving testament to both that line and American railroading in general. Train spotters will be in heaven among more than 150 different. Train rides cost an extra $3; call for the schedule.

LEXINGTON MARKET MARKET

Four blocks north of Camden Yards is Lexington Market. A city market has thrived on this site since 1782. More than 140 merchants hawk everything from homemade kielbasa (Polish sausage) to Korean barbecue.

WESTMINSTER CEMETERY CEMETERY

Around the corner, Edgar Allan Poe is buried in Westminster Cemetery. If you are here around his birthday, January 19, you may see roses and cognac decorating the gravesite.

LITTLE ITALY NEIGHBORHOOD

Behind the power plant is the delightful Little Italy neighborhood, packed with exquisite restaurants, a bocce ball court and a giant brick wall that doubles as an outdoor movie screen in summer.

STAR-SPANGLED BANNER FLAG HOUSE & 1812 MUSEUM MUSEUM

(☎410-837-1793; www.flaghouse.org; 844 E Pratt St; adult/child $7/5; ⊙10am-4pm Tue-Sat) For a dose of American nostalgia head to the Star-Spangled Banner Flag House & 1812 Museum. It opens the home where Mary Pickersgill sewed the flag that inspired Francis Scott Key's 'Star-Spangled Banner' poem.

FREE WALTERS ART MUSEUM MUSEUM

(☎410-547-9000; www.thewalters.org; 600 N Charles St; ⊙10am-5pm Wed-Sun) On Mount Vernon Sq you'll find Walters Art Museum, the city's finest museum. Its art collection spans 55 centuries, from ancient to contemporary, with excellent displays of Asian treasures, rare and ornate manuscripts and books, and a comprehensive collection of French paintings; there's also a great atrium cafe.

FREE CONTEMPORARY MUSEUM MUSEUM

(www.contemporary.org; 100 W Centre St; ⊙noon-5pm Wed-Sun) So modern it's probably 'post,' this museum loves to ride the cutting edge of art. Auxiliary to the on-site exhibits is the museum's mission of bringing art to unexpected spots around the city.

MARYLAND HISTORICAL SOCIETY MUSEUM

(www.mdhs.org; 201 W Monument St; adult/child $6/4; ⊙10am-5pm Wed-Sat, noon-5pm Sun) With more than 5.4 million artifacts, this is one of the largest collections of Americana in the world, including Francis Scott Key's original manuscript of the 'Star-Spangled Banner'. There are often excellent temporary exhibits, as well as a fascinating permanent exhibition tracing Maryland's maritime history.

FORT MCHENRY NATIONAL MONUMENT & HISTORIC SHRINE HISTORIC SITE

(☎410-962-4290; 2400 E Fort Ave; adult/child $7/free; ⊙8am-5pm) The Fort McHenry National Monument & Historic Shrine is one of the most-visited sites in Baltimore, and was instrumental in saving the city from the British attack during the War of 1812.

FELLS POINT NEIGHBORHOOD

Cobblestones fill Market Sq between the Broadway Market and the harbor in the historic maritime neighborhood of Fells Point. Here, you'll find the city's liveliest restaurants and nightlife.

CANTON NEIGHBORHOOD

Further east, the slightly more sophisticated streets of Canton fan out around a grassy square surrounded by more great restaurants and bars.

TOP OF THE WORLD OBSERVATION DECK LOOKOUT

(www.viewbaltimore.org; 401 E Pratt St; adult/child $5/4; ⏲10am-6pm Wed-Thu, 10am-7pm Fri & Sat, 11am-6pm Sun) For a bird's-eye view of Baltimore, head to the observation deck at the World Trade Center.

NATIONAL GREAT BLACKS IN WAX MUSEUM MUSEUM

(www.greatblacksinwax.org; 1601 E North Ave; adult/child $12/10; ⏲9am-5pm Tue-Sat, noon-5pm Sun) In East Baltimore stands one of the country's best African American history museums, with exhibits on Frederick Douglass, Jackie Robinson, Martin Luther King Jr and even Barack Obama, as well as lesser-known figures like explorer Matthew Henson. The museum also covers slavery, the sickening Jim Crow era and African leaders – all told in surreal fashion through Madame Tussaud–style figures.

FEDERAL HILL NEIGHBORHOOD

On a bluff overlooking the harbor, **Federal Hill Park** lends its name to the comfortable neighborhood that's set around Cross Street Market and comes alive after sundown.

CROSS STREET MARKET MARKET

(1065 Cross St, btwn Light & Charles Sts; ⏲7am-7pm Mon-Sat) This well-located food emporium has tempting stalls hawking oysters, crab cakes, sushi, fresh-baked goodies, rotisserie chicken, and plenty of fruit, veg and picnic fare – plus beer (big ones) near the Charles St entrance.

SLEEPING IN BALTIMORE

Inn at Henderson's Wharf (☎410-522-7777, 800-522-2088; www.hendersonswharf.com; 1000 Fell St; r from $209; P ❄ 📶) A complimentary bottle of wine upon arrival sets the tone at this marvelously situated Fell's Point hotel, which began life as an 18th-century tobacco warehouse. Consistently rated one of the city's best lodges.

Inn at 2920 (☎410-342-4450, 877-774-2920; www.theinnat2920.com; 2920 Elliott St; r incl breakfast $175-235; ❄ @ 📶) Housed in a former bordello, this boutique B&B has five individual rooms, high-thread-count sheets, sleek, avant-garde decor and the nightlife-charged neighborhood of Canton right outside your door.

Mount Vernon Hotel (☎410-727-2000; www.mountvernonbaltimore.com; 24 W Franklin St; d $150; P ❄ 📶) The historic 1907 Mount Vernon Hotel has comfortable, heritage-style rooms in a good location near the restaurant scene along Charles St.

TOURS

BALTIMORE GHOST TOURS WALKING

(☎410-357-1186; www.baltimoreghosttours.com; adult/child $15/10; ⏲7pm Fri & Sat Mar-Nov) Offers several walking tours exploring the spooky and bizarre side of Baltimore. The popular Fells Point ghost walk departs from Max's on Broadway, 731 S Broadway. There's also a Fell's Point haunted pub crawl ($20, must be over 21) and a walk around the city's Mount Vernon neighborhood.

EATING & DRINKING

BLUE HILL TAVERN MODERN AMERICAN **$$**

(☎443-388-9363; 938 S Conkling St; mains $25-31; ⏲5-10pm Mon-Thu, to 11pm Fri & Sat, 4-9pm Sun) The dining room has blue shimmery fabrics and dark wood furnishings, a subtle backdrop to the bold and flavorful dishes at this award-winning spot. Recent hits include grilled octopus on endive with cloves and a sous vide (tender slow-cooked) lamb loin. Good service (and wine recommendations), and an outdoor rooftop bar in summer.

OBRYCKI'S SEAFOOD **$$**

(☎410-732-6399; 1727 E Pratt St; mains $19-30; ⏲11:30am-10pm Mon-Thu, to 11pm Fri & Sat, to 9:30pm Sun Mar-Nov) Despite its somewhat touristy reputation, Obrycki's is the go-to spot for crab lovers, with crab soup, crab balls, crab cakes, steamed crabs and soft-shelled crabs. It's only open during crab season, ie March to November.

BLUEGRASS TAVERN MODERN AMERICAN **$$**
(☎410-244-5101; 1500 S Hanover St; mains $12-28; ⊙5-10pm Tue & Wed, to 11pm Thu-Sat, 10am-10pm Sun) Warm woods and boutique bourbons set the scene at this welcoming bar and upscale eatery. You'll find house-made charcuterie, unique beers and cocktails and market-fresh fare with Southern accents. Superb Sunday brunches (fresh donuts).

BREWER'S ART MODERN AMERICAN **$$**
(☎410-547-6925; 1106 N Charles St; sandwiches $9-12, mains $19-26; ⊙4pm-2am Mon-Sat, 5pm-2am Sun) In a lovely early-20th-century townhouse, Brewer's Art serves delicious Belgian-style microbrews to a laid-back Mount Vernon crowd. You can enjoy tasty pub fare in the bar or enter the heritage dining room in back for innovative grilled-meat and seafood dishes. Head downstairs for a more raucous atmosphere.

CITY CAFE CAFE **$$**
(1001 Cathedral St; mains lunch $10-14, dinner $15-29; ⊙7:30am-10pm Mon-Fri, 10am-10pm Sat, 10am-8pm Sun; 📶) Bright, inviting cafe with floor-to-ceiling windows; on offer are desserts and gourmet sandwiches. The dining room in back serves high-end bistro fare.

Annapolis

Explore

Sailors and seafood-lovers will relish exploring the coves and waterways of the Chesapeake Bay. A day trip to endearing Annapolis is the easiest way to get a dose of both treats.

Boasting some of the tastiest seafood in the region, Maryland's capital city, Annapolis is a tribute to the Colonial era. The historic landmark is a perfectly preserved tableau of narrow lanes, brick houses and original 18th-century architecture (one of the largest concentrations of such buildings in the country).

Home of the US Naval Academy since 1845, Annapolis Harbor and its connecting tidal creeks shelter dozens of marinas where thousands of cruising and racing sailboats tie up, earning the city the title of Sailing Capital. If you have time to spare, check out the charming villages and waterfront allure of the Eastern Shore (p232).

The Best

- **Sight** Robert Morris Inn (see the box, p232)
- **Outdoor Activity** Going for a sail around the Chesapeake Bay (p231)
- **Place to Eat** Robert Morris Inn (see the box, p232)

Top Tip

Eating at a crab shack, where the dress code stops at shorts and flip-flops, is the quintessential Chesapeake Bay experience. To beat the crowds, avoid going on summer weekends.

Getting There & Away

Bus Greyhound runs buses to Washington, DC (once daily, $16). **Dillon's Bus** (www.dillonbus.com; tickets $5) has 26 weekday-only commuter buses between Annapolis and Washington, connecting with various DC metro lines.

Car Rte 50 east goes straight into downtown Annapolis. To Eastern Shore destinations, continue east over the Chesapeake Bay Bridge and head south on Rte 50.

Need to Know

- **Area Code** ☎410
- **Location** 35 miles east of Washington, DC
- **Tourist Office** (☎410-263-9591; 26 West St; ⊙9am-5pm)

SIGHTS

HISTORIC HOMES & BUILDINGS HISTORIC SITES
The collection of historic homes and buildings clustered on Cornhill and Fleet Sts between the State House and the harbor is extraordinary. Guided walking and bus tours

WORTH A DETOUR

EASTERN SHORE

Just across the Chesapeake Bay Bridge, nondescript suburbs and jammed highways give way to unbroken miles of bird-dotted wetlands, serene waterscapes, endless cornfields, sandy beaches and friendly little villages. For the most part, the Eastern Shore retains its charm despite the growing influx of former city-dwellers and day-trippers. This area revolves around the water. Working waterfront communities still survive off Chesapeake Bay and its tributaries. Boating, fishing, crabbing and kayaking are a part of local life.

St Michaels, one of the prettiest villages on the Eastern Shore, lives up to its motto as 'The Heart & Soul of Chesapeake Bay.' It's a mix of old Victorian homes, quaint B&Bs, boutique shops and working docks, where escape artists from Washington mix with salty-dog crabbers. On weekends, the village can get crowded with out-of-town boaters. During the War of 1812, inhabitants rigged up lanterns in a nearby forest and blacked out the town. British naval gunners shelled the trees, allowing St Michaels to escape destruction. The building now known as the **Cannonball House** (Mulberry St) was the only structure to have been hit.

At the lighthouse, the **Chesapeake Bay Maritime Museum** (www.cbmm.org; 213 N Talbot St; adult/child $13/6; ⌚9am-6pm summer) delves into the deep ties between Shore folk and America's largest estuary. Narrated 60-minute cruises aboard the **Patriot** (☎410-745-3100; www.patriotcruises.com; Navy Point; adult/child $25/13) leave from the dock near the Crab Claw several times a day.

The Victorian red-brick **Parsonage Inn** (☎410-745-8383; www.parsonage-inn.com; 210 N Talbot St; r incl breakfast $150-210; P ❄) offers floral decadence (curtains, duvets) and brass beds, plus a friendly welcome by its hospitable innkeepers.

Next door to the Maritime Museum the **Crab Claw** (☎410-745-2900; 304 Burns St; mains $15-30; ⌚11am-10pm) has a splendid open-air setting at the water's edge. Get messy eating delicious steamed crabs ($36 to $60 per dozen) at picnic tables, or head upstairs for more refined seafood feasting.

At the end of the road over the Hwy 33 drawbridge, tiny **Tilghman Island** still runs a working waterfront where local captains take visitors out on graceful oyster skipjacks; the historic **Rebecca T Ruark** (☎410-829-3976; www.skipjack.org; 2hr cruises adult/child $30/15), built in 1886, is the oldest certified vessel of its kind.

Oxford is a small village with a history dating back to the 1600s and a fine spread of leafy streets and waterfront homes. Although you can drive there via US-333, it's well worth taking the old-fashioned **ferry** (☎410-745-9023; www.oxfordbellevueferry.com; 1 way car/additional passenger/pedestrian $11/1/3; ⌚9am-sunset Apr-Nov) from Bellevue. Try to go around sunset for memorable views.

Once in Oxford, don't miss the chance to dine at the celebrated **Robert Morris Inn** (☎410-226-5111; www.robertmorrisinn.com; 314 N Morris St; mains $17-29; ⌚7:30-10am, noon-2:30pm & 5:30-9:30pm) near the ferry dock. Award-winning crab cakes, grilled local rockfish and medallions of spring lamb are nicely matched by wines and best followed by pavlova with berries and other desserts. You can also overnight in one of the inn's heritage-style rooms (from $200).

abound, or you can pick up a free brochure at the Annapolis & Anne Arundel County Conference & Visitors Bureau. Some of the highlights that are open to the public include the jewel **Hammond Harwood House** (☎410-263-4683; www.hammondharwoodhouse.org; 19 Maryland Ave; adult/child $6/3; ⌚noon-5pm Tue-Sun Apr-Oct) and the **William Paca House & Garden** (☎410-990-4543; www.annapolis.org; 186 Prince George St; adult/child $8/5; ⌚10am-5pm Mon-Sat, noon-5pm Sun Apr-Dec, 10am-4pm Sat, noon-4pm Sun Jan-Mar).

US NAVAL ACADEMY ARMEL LEFTWICH VISITORS CENTER
COLLEGE CAMPUS

(☎410-293-8687; www.navyonline.com; 52 King George St; tours adult/child $9/7; ⌚9am-3pm Mar-Dec, 9am-4pm Jan & Feb, tours 10am-3pm Mon-Sat, 12:30-3pm Sun) The lovely Navy Campus is northwest of the Annapolis historic district; enter via Gate 1 (at the intersection of King George, East and Randall Sts) and head to the US Naval Academy Armel Leftwich Visitors Center, which features a film, some exhibits and guided tours.

FREE **US NAVAL ACADEMY MUSEUM** MUSEUM

(☎410-293-2108; www.usna.edu/museum; 118 Maryland Ave; ⊙9am-5pm Mon-Sat, 11am-5pm Sun) Preble Hall contains the US Naval Academy Museum with lots of artifacts, including remnants of the famed battleship USS *Maine*.

FREE **MARYLAND STATE HOUSE** HISTORIC BUILDING

(☎410-974-3400; 91 State Circle; ⊙9am-5pm Mon-Fri, 10am-4pm Sat & Sun, tours 11am & 3pm) The heart of Annapolis is the Maryland State House. A dignified domed building built in 1792, it served as the first capitol of the fledgling United States and as a meeting place for the Continental Congress from 1783 to 1784. The period artwork and furnishings are worth a peek; guided tours are also available.

ACTIVITIES

WOODWIND CRUISE

(☎410-263-7837; www.schoonerwoodwind.com; 80 Compromise St; sunset cruise adult/child $39/25; ⊙May-Oct) This beautiful 74ft schooner offers two-hour day and sunset cruises. Or splurge for the Woodwind 'boat and breakfast' package (rooms $295, including breakfast), one of the more unique lodging options in town.

WATERMARK CRUISES CRUISE

(www.watermarkcruises.com; City Dock; 40-min cruise adult/child $13/5) The best way to explore the city's maritime heritage is on the water. Watermark, which operates the Four Centuries Walking Tour, offers a variety of cruise options, with frequent departures.

FOUR CENTURIES WALKING TOUR WALKING TOUR

(www.watermarkcruises.com; adult/child $16/10) A costumed docent will lead you on this great introduction to all things Annapolis. The 10:30am tour leaves from the visitor center and the 1:30pm tour leaves from the information booth at the City Dock; there's a slight variation in sights visited by each, but both cover the country's largest concentration of 18th-century buildings, influential African Americans and colonial spirits who don't want to leave. The associated one-hour **Pirates of the Chesapeake Cruise** (adult/child $16/13; ⊙late May-early Sep) is good 'yar'-worthy fun, especially for the kids.

EATING & DRINKING

MIDDLETON TAVERN SEAFOOD $$

(2 Market Space; mains $10-33; ⊙11:30am-1:30am Mon-Sat, from 10am Sun) This is one of the oldest continuously operating pubs in the country. As you'd expect from a waterside pub, the menu features some of the freshest seafood around. Live music most nights.

SLEEPING IN ANNAPOLIS

Historic Inns of Annapolis (☎410-263-2641; www.historicinnsofannapolis.com; 58 State Circle; r $100-170; ❄📶) The Historic Inns comprise three boutique guesthouses, each set in a heritage building in the heart of old Annapolis: the Maryland Inn, the Governor Calvert House and the Robert Johnson House. Common areas are packed with period details, and the best rooms boast antiques, a fireplace and attractive views (the cheapest are small and could use an update).

1908 William Page Inn (☎410-263-1506; www.1908-williampageinn.com; 8 Martin St; r incl breakfast $175-235; P❄📶) For a romantic getaway, nothing beats this Victorian B&B. Beautifully decorated, comfortable rooms are capped with wonderful hospitality and delicious breakfast.

ScotLaur Inn (☎410-268-5665; www.scotlaurinn.com; 165 Main St; r $95-140; P❄📶) The folks from Chick & Ruth's Delly offer 10 simple pink-and-blue rooms with private bath at their B&B (bed and bagel) above the deli.

49 WEST CAFE **$$**

(☎410-626-9796; 49 West St; mains lunch $8-10, dinner $15-23; ⏱8am-11pm) This art-filled hideaway serves eclectic cuisine – breakfast standards, gourmet sandwiches and salads for lunch, seafood and bistro fare (seared tuna with pesto, mojito-glazed chicken) by night, and good wines and cocktails. Live music most nights.

GALWAY BAY PUB **$$**

(☎410-263-8333; 63 Maryland Ave; mains $8-15; ⏱11am-midnight Mon-Sat, from 10:30am Sun) The epitome of a power-broker bar, this Irish-owned and -operated restaurant-pub is the dark sort of hideaway where political deals go down over Jameson, stouts and mouth-watering seafood specials.

CHICK & RUTH'S DELLY DINER **$**

(165 Main St; mains $6-10; ⏱6:30am-10pm Sun-Thu, to 11:30pm Fri & Sat) This cornerstone of Annapolis bursts with affable quirkiness and a big menu, heavy on sandwiches and breakfasts. Patriots can relive grade-school days reciting the Pledge of Allegiance, weekdays at 8:30am (9:30am on weekends).

ANNAPOLIS ICE CREAM COMPANY ICE CREAM **$**

(196 Main St; ice creams $4-5; ⏱11am-10pm; 👪) Creamy ice cream made in-house from organic ingredients – good variety including seasonal flavors. Huge servings.

Harpers Ferry

Explore

History lives on in this attractive town, set with steep cobblestone streets framed by the Shenandoah Mountains and the confluence of the rushing Potomac and Shenandoah Rivers. The lower town functions as an open-air museum, with over a dozen buildings that you can wander through and thereby get a taste of 19th-century life here. Exhibits narrate the town's role at the forefront of westward expansion, American industry and, most famously, the slavery debate. In 1859 old John Brown tried to spark a slave uprising here and was hanged for his efforts; the incident rubbed friction between North and South into the fires of Civil War.

In addition to the historic sites, there's great outdoor adventure to be had, with excellent hiking trails just steps from Harpers Ferry. Nearby are scenic spots for biking, kayaking and rafting.

HIKING IN HARPERS FERRY

There are great hikes in the area, from three-hour (round-trip) scrambles to the scenic overlook from the Maryland Heights Trail, past Civil War fortifications on the Loudoun Heights Trail or along the Appalachian Trail – all are easily accessible from the historic district. You can also bike or walk along the **C&O Canal towpath**. The Harpers Ferry National Historic Park Visitor Center has maps and details on outfitters.

The Best

➡ **Sight** Master Armorer's House (p235)

➡ **Outdoor Activity** Hiking up to the top of the Maryland Heights Trail (see the box, p234)

➡ **Place to Eat** Canal House (p235)

Top Tip

Parking is extremely limited in Harpers Ferry. Instead head to the **Harpers Ferry National Historic Park Visitor Center** (171 Shoreline Dr) off Hwy 340, where you can park and take a free shuttle.

Getting There & Away

Train Trains to Washington's Union Station are operated by **Amtrak** (www.amtrak.com; 1 daily; 71min; fare $14) and **MARC** (mta.maryland.gov; 3 daily Monday to Friday; fare $11).

Car From Washington take I-495 north to the I-270, which turns into I-70. Merge onto US-340 west and follow the signs for downtown Harpers Ferry. Travel time is 90 minutes.

Need to Know

➡ **Area Code** ☎540

➡ **Location** 66 miles northwest of Washington, DC

➡ **Tourist Office** (☎304-535-6029; www.nps.gov/hafe; 171 Shoreline Dr, off Hwy 340)

SIGHTS

MASTER ARMORER'S HOUSE HISTORIC SITE
Among the many sites you can freely wander through in the historic district, this 1858 house explains how rifle technology developed here revolutionized the firearms industry.

APPALACHIAN TRAIL CONSERVANCY HIKING
(☎304-535-6331; www.appalachiantrail.org; cnr Washington & Jackson Sts; ⊙9am-5pm Mon-Fri Apr-Oct) The 2160-mile Appalachian Trail is headquartered at this tremendous resource for hikers.

STORER COLLEGE BUILDING MUSEUM
Long ago a teachers' college for freed slaves, this museum now traces the town's African American history.

JOHN BROWN MUSEUM MUSEUM
(http://johnbrownwaxmuseum.com; 168 High St; adult/child $7/5; ⊙9am-4:30pm) This laughably tacky museum tells the story of Brown's life and raid through music, voice recordings and life-size wax figures.

ACTIVITIES

RIVER RIDERS ADVENTURE SPORTS
(☎800-326-7238; www.riverriders.com; 408 Alstadts Hill Rd) The go-to place for rafting, canoeing, tubing, kayaking and multi-day biking trips, plus bike hire ($20 for four hours).

O BE JOYFULL WALKING TOURS
(☎732-801-0381; www.obejoyfull.com; 175 High St; adult/child from $8/5) Offers a variety of historical walking tours around Harpers Ferry, including a spooky 90-minute evening tour.

EATING

CANAL HOUSE AMERICAN $$
(1226 Washington St; mains $7-14; ⊙11am-3pm Wed-Sat, 5:30-8:30pm Thu-Sat, noon-6pm Sun; 👪) Roughly 1 mile west (and uphill) from the historic district, Canal House is a perennial favorite for delicious sandwiches and friendly service in a flower-trimmed stone house. Outdoor seating.

ANVIL AMERICAN $$
(☎304-535-2582; 1270 Washington St; lunch mains $8-12, dinner mains $15-24; ⊙11am-9pm Wed-Sun) Local trout melting in honey-pecan butter and an elegant Federal dining room equals excellence at Anvil, in Bolivar, a neighborhood just uphill from the historic district.

BEANS IN THE BELFRY AMERICAN $$
(☎301-834-7178; 122 W Potomac St, Brunswick, MD; ⊙9am-9pm Mon-Sat, to 7pm Sun; @📶👪) Across the river in Brunswick (roughly 10 miles east), you'll find this converted church, sheltering mismatched couches and kitsch-laden walls, light fare (chili,

SLEEPING IN HARPERS FERRY

Jackson Rose (☎304-535-1528; www.thejacksonrose.com; 1167 W Washington St; r weekday/weekend $135/150; ❄📶) This marvelous brick 18th-century residence with stately gardens has three attractive guestrooms, including one where Stonewall Jackson briefly lodged during the Civil War. It's a 600m walk downhill to the historic district. No children under 12.

Town Inn (☎304-702-1872, 877-489-2447; www.thetownsinn.com; 175 & 179 High St; r $70-140; ❄) Spread between two neighboring pre–Civil War residences, the Town Inn has rooms ranging from small and minimalist to charming heritage-style quarters. It's set in the middle of the historic district with an indoor-outdoor restaurant as well.

HI-Harpers Ferry Hostel (☎301-834-7652; www.hiusa.org; 19123 Sandy Hook Rd, Knoxville, MD; dm $20; ⊙mid-Apr–mid-Oct; P❄@📶) Located 2 miles from downtown on the Maryland side of the Potomac River, this friendly hostel has plenty of amenities including a kitchen, a laundry and a lounge area with games and books.

sandwiches) and a tiny stage where live folk, blues and bluegrass bands strike up most nights. Sunday jazz brunch ($16) is a hit.

Leesburg & Middleburg

Explore

Leesburg is one of northern Virginia's oldest towns and its colonial-era center is lined with historic sites, plus antique shops, galleries and restaurants. Leesburg sits along the Washington & Old Dominion Trail, and makes an excellent destination for cyclists.

Lying 19 miles southwest of Leesburg, smaller Middleburg is another quaint northern Virginia town, with colonial buildings that hide some enticing restaurants and shops. Either town makes a fine base for visiting the wineries in the area.

The Best

- **Sight** Loudoun Museum (p236)
- **Place to Eat** Lightfoot (p238)
- **Place to Drink** Bluemont Vineyard (see the box, p237)

Top Tip

On the first Friday of every month, you can join in **Leesburg's First Friday** (www.leesburgfirstfriday.com; ⌚6-9pm), when shops and galleries stay open till 9pm and offer drinks and special sales.

Getting There & Away

Bicycle Pick up the Washington & Old Dominion Trail just outside the East Falls Church Metro in Arlington and head west.

Car Take I-495 or Rte 66 to the Dulles Toll Rd exit (Rte 267) – look for signs to Dulles International Airport. When it turns into the Dulles Greenway, continue 13 miles to the end. Exit left and take the first right exit to Leesburg Business. Follow King St to Loudoun St, the center of historic Leesburg. Middleburg is 19 miles southwest of Leesburg. Take US-15 south and turn right on US-50. Travel time is 40 minutes by car.

Need to Know

- **Area Code** ☎703
- **Location** Leesburg: 40 miles northwest of DC, Middleburg: 42 miles west of DC
- **Tourist Office** (☎703-669-2002; www.visitloudoun.org; 112G South St, Market Station, Leesburg; ⌚9am-5pm)

SIGHTS

FREE **LOUDOUN MUSEUM** MUSEUM

(☎703-777-7427; www.loudounmuseum.org; 16 Loudoun St, Leesburg; guided city tours adult/child $10/3; ⌚10am-5pm Mon & Wed-Sat, 1-5pm Sun) For historical sights, start at the Loudoun Museum, which narrates the history of northern Virginia from the first Native American settlements to the present day. You can also arrange walking tours of historic Leesburg here.

SLEEPING IN LEESBURG & MIDDLEBURG

Norris House Inn (☎703-777-1806; www.norrishouse.com; 108 Loudoun St SW, Leesburg; d $115-150) A renovated 1760 redbrick colonial; tea is served in the lovely Stone House Tearoom. The rate here is for weekends; weekday rates are cheaper.

Best Western Leesburg Dulles (☎703-777-9400; www.bestwestern.com; 726 E Market St, Leesburg; r $100; ❄📶🏊) The rooms boast green carpeting and orange bedspreads, but friendly service and all the extras (pool, free hot breakfast and wi-fi, in-room fridge and microwave) make up for aesthetic shortcomings.

Welbourne B&B (☎540-687-3201; www.welbourneinn.com; 22314 Welbourne Farm Lane, Middleburg; r $143; ❄📶🏊) Located 6 miles west of Middleburg, the Welbourne is set in a historic landmark house (c 1770), surrounded by 520 acres. Guests stay in one of five heritage rooms with fireplaces. Hearty Southern-style breakfast included.

VINEYARDS OF VIRGINIA

Back in the 1980s, when a single vineyard operated in Loudoun County, a Virginian bottle of wine was likely to earn about as much respect as a convicted felon running for office. Much has changed in the last generation, and today this rich farming area has become one of the country's fastest-growing wine regions – with more than 20 vineyards at last count. While largely unknown outside Virginia, Loudoun County wines are garnering critical attention after winning awards at international competitions.

For the traveler, going wine tasting makes a fine day's outing from DC. You can explore the rolling hills and leafy lanes of this pretty countryside, stopping at excellent restaurants and local farmers' markets en route. Both Leesburg and Middleburg are fine bases to begin the viticultural journey.

A useful guide to the vineyards, with detailed information on the wineries, is the *Touring Guide to DC's Wine Country,* available free at the Leesburg tourist office.

Here are a few favorites from the wine country:

Bluemont Vineyard (☎540-554-8439; www.bluemontvineyard.com; 18755 Foggy Bottom Rd, Bluemont; tasting $5; ⏲noon-6pm Fri-Sun) Bluemont produces ruby red Nortons and crisp Viogniers, though it's equally famous for its spectacular location – at a 950ft elevation with sweeping views over the countryside. It's open outside hours by appointment.

Breaux Vineyards (☎540-668-6299; www.breauxvineyards.com; 36888 Breaux Vineyards Lane, Hillsborough; tasting $10; ⏲11am-6pm) One of Virginia's largest vineyards, with over 17 varietals, Breaux produces award-winning reds including an exceptional Merlot Reserve. Breaux hosts three culinary festivals throughout the summer.

Chrysalis Vineyards (☎540-687-8222; www.chrysaliswine.com; 23876 Champe Ford Rd, Middleburg; tasting $5-10; ⏲10am-5pm) Proudly using the native Norton grape (which dates back to 1820), Chrysalis produces highly drinkable reds and whites – including a refreshing Viognier. The pretty estate hosts a bluegrass fest in October.

Fabbioli Cellars (☎703-771-1197; www.fabbioliwines.com; 15669 Limestone School Rd, Leesburg; tasting $5; ⏲11am-5pm Fri-Sun) This eco-friendly winery provides an intimate but informal tasting experience, where you can learn about the wines from innovative winemaker Doug Fabbioli himself. It's open outside hours by appointment.

Tarara Vineyard (☎703-771-7100; www.tarara.com; 13648 Tarara Lane, Leesburg; tasting $5-10; ⏲11am-5pm) On a bluff overlooking the Potomac, this 475-acre estate provides guided tours showing the grape's journey from vine to glass. The winery is located in a 6000-sq-ft cave, and visitors can pick fruit in the orchard or hike the 6 miles of trails through rolling countryside. Tarara also hosts summertime Saturday-evening concerts and three major wine festivals.

MORVEN PARK — HISTORIC SITE

(☎703-777-2414; www.morvenpark.org; 17263 Southern Planter Lane, Leesburg; admission to grounds free, mansion tours adult/child $7/1; ⏲grounds 7am-6pm daily, tours 11am-4pm Mon, Fri & Sat, 1-4pm Sun) Morven Park is a 1000-acre property that was once the home of Virginia governor Westmoreland Davis. The Greek Revival mansion, with its manicured boxwood gardens, resembles a transplanted White House, and its antique carriage museum includes more than 100 horse-drawn vehicles. Morven Park is 1 mile west of Leesburg off Rte 7 (Market St). Heading west, turn right onto Morven Park Rd and follow it to the property.

OATLANDS PLANTATION — HISTORIC SITE

(☎703-777-3174; 20850 Oatlands Plantation Lane, Leesburg; adult/child $10/7, grounds only $7; ⏲10am-5pm Mon-Sat, 1-5pm Sun Apr-Dec) Six miles south of Leesburg, Oatlands Plantation was established in 1803 by a great-grandson of Robert 'King' Carter, a wealthy pre-Revolutionary planter. The carefully restored Greek Revival mansion is surrounded by 4 acres of formal gardens and connecting terraces. It's located on US-15, about 5 miles south of Leesburg.

EATING

LIGHTFOOT MODERN AMERICAN $$

(☎703-771-2233; 11 N King St, Leesburg; mains lunch $9-18, dinner $22-30; ⌚11:30am-2:30pm & 5:30-10pm Sun, to 11pm Mon-Thu, to midnight Fri & Sat) Lightfoot is an award-winning restaurant featuring delicious, progressive American fare such as slow-braised pork shank, swordfish *au poivre* and artichoke gratin-crusted salmon.

TUSCARORA MILL MODERN AMERICAN $$

(☎703-771-9300; 203 Harrison St, Leesburg; mains $19-28; ⌚11am-11pm Mon-Sat, to 9pm Sun) In the Market Station complex (where the tourist office is), Tuscarora Mill serves market-fresh fare, including rack of lamb, ahi tuna steak with roasted portobello mushrooms and a delectable seafood stew.

LA CHOCITA LATIN AMERICAN $

(☎703-443-2319; 210 Loudoun St SE, Leesburg; mains $5-12; ⌚11am-10pm) This casual, welcoming spot serves Latin American food, including satisfying enchiladas, tacos and *pupusas* (maize flatbreads), although its rotisserie chicken is famous. Outside seating in back.

MARKET SALAMANDER MODERN AMERICAN $

(☎540-687-8011; 200 W Washington St, Middleburg; mains $7-13; ⌚11am-5pm Sun, to 6pm Mon-Thu, to 7pm Fri & Sat) Well worth the trip to Middleburg, Market Salamander is a small gourmet food shop with a low-key restaurant serving delicious market fare such as roasted chicken, crab cakes, mac 'n' cheese and bourbon pecan chicken salad. Save room for dessert.

Shenandoah National Park

Explore

Shenandoah National Park is easy on the eyes, set against a backdrop of the dreamy Blue Ridge Mountains, granite and metamorphic formations that are more than one billion years old. The park itself is almost 70 years old, founded in 1935 as a retreat for East Coast urban populations. It is an accessible day-trip destination from DC, but stay longer if you can. The 500 miles of hiking trails, 75 scenic overlooks, 30 fishing streams, seven picnic areas and four campgrounds are sure to keep you entertained.

The Best

- **Sight** Old Rag Mountain (p240)
- **Scenic Drive** Skyline Dr (p239)
- **Place to Stay** Big Meadows Lodge (see the box, p239)

Top Tip

To beat the crowds, avoid going on weekends – especially in the summer – when there's a lot of traffic in the park.

Getting There & Away

Car From Washington, DC, take I-66 west to Rte 340. Front Royal is 3 miles south; Luray is 27 miles south. The drive to the northern entrance at Front Royal is 90 minutes.

Need to Know

- **Area Code** ☎540
- **Location** 75 miles west of Washington, DC
- **Tourist Office** Dickey Ridge Visitors Center (☎540-635-3566; Skyline Dr, mile 4.6; ⌚9am-5pm Apr-Nov)

SIGHTS

SHENANDOAH NATIONAL PARK

(☎540-999-3500; www.nps.gov/shen; week passes per car Mar-Nov $15) One of the most spectacular national parks in the country, Shenandoah is like a smile from nature: in spring and summer the wildflowers explode, in fall the leaves burn bright red and orange, and in winter a cold, starkly beautiful hibernation period sets in. White-tailed deer are a common sight and, if you're lucky, you might spot a black bear, a bobcat or a wild turkey. Whatever your agenda, don't miss a visit to this amazing wonderland.

Your first stop should be the **Dickey Ridge Visitors Center** (☎540-635-3566; Skyline Dr, mile 4.6; ⌚9am-5pm Apr-Nov), close to the northern end of Skyline Dr, or **Byrd Visitors Center** (☎540-999-3283; Skyline Dr, Mile 50; ⊙9am-5pm Apr-Nov). Both places have exhibits on flora and fauna, as well as maps and information about hiking trails and activities.

SKYLINE DRIVE SCENIC DRIVE

Skyline Dr is the breathtaking road that follows the main ridge of the Blue Ridge Mountains and winds 105 miles through the center of the park. You're constantly treated to an impressive view, but keep in mind the road is bendy, slow going (the limit is 35mph) and (in peak season) congested. There are two visitor centers in the park; they have maps, backcountry permits and information on horseback riding, hang gliding, bicycling (only on public roads) and other wholesome goodness.

The drive begins in Front Royal near the western end of I-66 and ends in the southern part of the range close to Rockfish Gap near I-64. Mile markers at the side of the road provide a reference.

FRONT ROYAL TOWN

The town of Front Royal, at the northern end of Skyline Dr, is a convenient jumping-off point for the park. It's a good place to pack your picnic before heading into the wilderness.

OASIS WINERY WINERY

(☎540-635-9933; www.oasiswine.com; 14141 Hume Rd; tasting $5-10; ⊙10am-5pm) If you have some free time, visit the Oasis Winery, off Rte 635 near Front Royal. The sparkling wines produced here have a solid reputation.

SKYLINE CAVERNS CAVES

(☎800-296-4545; www.skylinecaverns.com; entrance to Skyline Dr; adult/child $16/8; ⊙9am-5pm) Front Royal is also home to the Skyline Caverns, whose interiors are decked with unusual anthodites ('cave flowers'). Unlike stalactites and stalagmites, these spiky nodes defy gravity and grow in all directions, one inch every 7000 years.

LURAY CAVERNS CAVES

(☎540-743-6551; www.luraycaverns.com; Rte 211; adult/child $21/10; ⊙9am-7pm Jun-Aug, 9am-6pm Sep-Nov, Apr & May, 9am-4pm Mon-Fri Dec-Mar) The small town of Luray sits snug between Massanutten Mountain, in George Washington National Forest, and Shenandoah National Park. The eastern US's largest and most popular caves, Luray Caverns, are 9 miles west of here on Rte 211.

EATING

BIG MEADOWS MODERN AMERICAN $$

(☎800-999-4714; www.visitshenandoah.com; Skyline Dr, mile 51.2; ⊙late May-Oct) One of several resorts in the park, Big Meadows has a restaurant and tavern with nightly live music. Highlights from the wide-ranging menu include rainbow trout, oven-roasted turkey, and spicy red lentil cakes, with many locally sourced ingredients – all of which go nicely with Virginia wines and local microbrews. It also offers the most services, including gas, laundry and camp store. It's best to bring your own food into the park if you're going camping or on extended hikes.

SLEEPING IN SHENANDOAH NATIONAL PARK

Big Meadows Lodge (☎540-999-2255; www.nps.gov/shen; Skyline Dr, Mile 51.2; r $85-150, cabins $100-110; ⊙late May-Oct) The historic Big Meadows Lodge has 29 cozy wood-paneled rooms and several rustic cabins. The on-site Spotswood Dining Room serves three hearty meals a day; reserve well in advance.

Skyland Resort (☎540-743-5108, 800-999-4714; Skyline Dr, mile 41.7; r $90-152, cabins $75-140; ⊙Apr-Oct) Founded in 1888, this beautifully set resort has fantastic views over the countryside. You'll find simple, wood-finished rooms and a full-service dining room, and you can arrange horseback rides from here.

Lewis Mountain Cabins (☎540-999-2255; www.nps.gov/shen; Skyline Dr, mile 57.6; cabins $90-100, campsites $16; ⊙Apr-Oct) Lewis Mountain has several suitably rustic but pleasantly furnished cabins complete with private bathrooms for a hot shower after a day's hiking. The complex also has a campground with a store, a laundry and showers.

SPORTS & ACTIVITIES

SKYLAND STABLES HORSE RIDING

(540-999-2210; guided group rides 1/2½hr $30/50; 9am-5pm May-Oct) Horseback riding is allowed on designated trails. Pick up your pony at Skyland Stables, near mile 41.7.

HIKING TRAILS HIKING

Shenandoah has more than 500 miles of hiking trails, including 101 miles of the famous Appalachian Trail. Access the trail from Skyline Dr, which roughly parallels the trail. Following are just a few of the great hikes that await, listed from north to south:

Old Rag Mountain This is a tough 8-mile circuit trail that culminates in a rocky scramble only suitable for the physically fit. Your reward is the summit of Old Rag Mountain and, along the way, some of the best views in Virginia.

Skyland Four easy trails here, none exceeding 1.6 miles, with a few steep sections throughout. Stony Man Trail gives great views for not-too-strenuous trekking.

Big Meadows Very popular area, with four easy-to-mid-level-difficulty hikes. The Lewis Falls and Rose River Trails run by the park's most spectacular waterfalls, and the former accesses the Appalachian Trail.

Bearfence Mountain A short trail leads to a spectacular 360-degree viewpoint. The circuit hike is only 1.2 miles, but it involves a strenuous scramble over rocks.

Riprap Three trails of varying difficulty. Blackrock Trail is an easy 1-mile loop that yields fantastic views. You can either hike the moderate 3.4-mile Riprap Trail to Chimney Rock, or detour and make a fairly strenuous 9.8-mile circuit that connects with the Appalachian Trail.

Sleeping

DC's lodgings enjoy a scope of history other American cities have a hard time matching: when rooms here are called the 'Roosevelt suite,' it's because Teddy actually slept in them. The best digs are monuments of Victorian and jazz-era opulence. Chain hotels, B&Bs and apartments blanket the cityscape, too. But nothing comes cheap...

Seasons & Prices

The high-season apex is late March through April (cherry-blossom season). Crowds and rates also peak in May, June, September and October. Book well in advance if you're traveling then. Prices are lowest in January (assuming it's not an inauguration year) and February. Rates on weekends (Friday and Saturday) are typically less than on weekdays.

Hotels

There are roughly 30,000 hotel rooms in DC, seemingly rising up on every corner around downtown, the Capitol and the White House Area. All big-box chains have outposts (usually several) here. Groovy boutique hotels abound, as do uber-luxury hotels catering to presidents, prime ministers and other heads of state.

B&Bs

DC has loads of B&Bs (often called 'guesthouses'). Set in elegant old row houses and Victorian mansions, they cluster around Dupont Circle and Adams-Morgan. Many are redolent of Old Washington (in a sip-sherry-at-noon way) and are atmospheric as hell. They're generally cheaper than big hotels.

Hostels

The District has one **Hostelling International** (www.hiusa.org) property and several independent hostels that do not require membership. Browse listings at **Hostels.com** (www.hostels.com) and **Hostelworld.com** (www.hostelworld.com).

Apartments

Apartments and suites are common, given all the interns, politicos and business folk who come to town for extended stays. The properties may be vanilla, but they're often good value, providing more space than hotel and B&B rooms, plus fully equipped kitchens for self-catering.

Amenities

In-room wi-fi, air-conditioning and a private bathroom are standard, unless noted otherwise. Here are some other general guidelines:

TOP END

Onsite concierge services, fitness and business centers, spas, restaurants, bars and white-glove room service are all par for the course. There's often a fee for wi-fi ($10 to $15). Breakfast is rarely included.

MIDRANGE

Rooms have a phone, cable TV and free wi-fi; many also have a mini-refrigerator, microwave and hairdryer. Often a small fitness center is on site. Rates often include a continental breakfast.

BUDGET

Besides hostels – which provide no-frills, bunk-bed dorms – budget options are thin on the ground. Expect shared bathrooms and wi-fi that is free but may be available in common areas only.

NEED TO KNOW

Price Ranges
In our listings we've used the following price codes to represent the cost of an en suite double room in high season (excluding tax and breakfast, unless stated otherwise).

$	less than $150
$$	$150 to $350
$$$	more than $350

Tax
Washington, DC's room tax is 14.5%. Northern Virginia's tax is around 10% (exact amount varies by county).

Parking Costs
Figure on $20 to $40 per day for in-and-out privileges.

Tipping
- **Hotel bellhops** $2 per bag
- **Housekeeping staff** $2 to $5 daily (higher end of range for suites or particularly messy rooms)
- **Parking valets** At least $2 when handed back your car keys
- **Room service** 15% to 20%
- **Concierges** Nothing for simple information, up to $20 for securing last-minute restaurant reservations, sold-out show tickets, etc

Check-In/Check-Out Times
Normally 3pm/noon. Many places will allow early check-in if the room is available (or will store your luggage if not).

Lonely Planet's Top Choices

Tabard Inn (p249) Quirky, vintage inn with a literary bent.

Chester Arthur House (p247) B&B for those who want to explore DC beyond the norm.

Embassy Circle Guest House (p250) French country–style home that'll feed you silly near Embassy Row.

Jefferson Hotel (p251) Luxurious, romantic, Parisian and often considered DC's top address.

Hotel Lombardy (p244) European-style, Venetian-furnished boutique catering to worldly guests.

Morrison-Clark Inn (p248) A historic 1864 mansion that channels the antebellum South.

Best by Budget

$
William Penn House (p246)

Hostelling International – Washington DC (p248)

DC Lofty (p249)

Windsor Inn (p253)

$$
Adam's Inn (p252)

Hotel Helix (p248)

Carlyle Suites (p250)

Intown Uptown Inn (p253)

Hotel Monticello (p246)

George Washington University Inn (p244)

$$$
Hay-Adams Hotel (p245)

W Hotel Washington (p245)

St Regis Washington (p245)

Willard InterContinental Hotel (p245)

Madison (p252)

Best Contemporary Cool

Hotel George (p247)

Hotel Palomar (p250)

Hotel Helix (p248)

Sofitel Lafayette Square (p244)

Hotel Rouge (p251)

Latham Hotel (p246)

Best for Political Intrigue

Hay-Adams Hotel (p245)

Willard InterContinental Hotel (p245)

St Regis Washington (p245)

Renaissance Mayflower Hotel (p246)

Washington Hilton (p252)

Best Small Gems

Inn at Dupont North (p250)

American Guest House (p252)

Woodley Park Guest House (p253)

Taft Bridge Inn (p252)

Akwaaba (p250)

Best for Families

Omni Shoreham Hotel (p254)

Hotel Monaco (p248)

Embassy Suites Washington DC (p250)

Eldon Suites (p249)

Hotel Harrington (p249)

Best Apartments & Suites

Carlyle Suites (p250)

One Washington Circle (p244)

Capitol Hill Suites (p247)

Georgetown Suites (p246)

Eldon Suites (p249)

Where to Stay

Neighborhood	For	Against
White House Area & Foggy Bottom	Central location dripping with monumental buildings and luxury lodgings where DC's powerbrokers concentrate	Expensive, not much of a neighborhood feeling
Georgetown	Lovely, leafy, moneyed neighborhood with accommodations to match	There's no Metro service, so it's not as convenient as other areas for getting around
Capitol Hill & Southeast DC	Still amid the political intrigue, but more laid-back than the White House Area; wide range of hotels, suites and guesthouses	The area gets pretty quiet come nighttime
Downtown & Penn Quarter	Bustles with trendy bars, restaurants and theaters; near the Mall for tourists and convention center for business travelers	Pricey, and the scene can be a bit raucous
Dupont Circle & Kalorama	Great B&Bs and boutique hotels mix among town homes and embassies; cool shops, bistros, bars and sights at your doorstep	It is DC's most lodging-laden 'hood; main areas can be congested and rowdy at night
Adams-Morgan	Young, quirky, B&B-filled area with a cache of ethnic eateries and musical nightlife	Isolated from the Metro; most properties are a 15-minute walk to the nearest station
Columbia Heights & Northeast	Gentrifying region with small, far-flung lodgings, good for urban explorer types	The neighborhood has groovy dining/nightlife pockets, but you'll have to travel to reach them
Upper Northwest DC	Quiet, family-oriented residential enclave; accommodations cluster around Woodley Park, convenient to the Metro and restaurants	Far from the top-draw sights
Northern Virginia	Cheaper than the District, especially if you have a car (many places offer free parking)	Lodgings tend to be big-box chains without much character

White House Area & Foggy Bottom

Foggy Bottom tends to be cheaper than the White House Area, and has more fun boutique options.

TOP CHOICE **HOTEL LOMBARDY** BOUTIQUE HOTEL **$$**

(Map p320; 202-828-2600, 800-424-5486; www.hotellombardy.com; 2019 Pennsylvania Ave NW; r $180-340; M Foggy Bottom-GWU; P) Done up in Venetian decor (shuttered doors, warm gold walls), and beloved by World Bank and State Department types, this European boutique hotel has multilingual staff and an international vibe – you hear French and Spanish as often as English in its halls. The attitude carries into rooms decorated with original artwork, and Chinese and European antiques. While there is no pool on site, guests receive passes to use the outdoor pool at a nearby property.

SOFITEL LAFAYETTE SQUARE HOTEL **$$**

(Map p320; 202-730-8800; www.sofitel.com; 806 15th St NW; r from $220; M McPherson Sq; P @) In a fabulous corner location with lots of windows, the Sofitel's airy rooms let in loads of natural sunlight (try to reserve one of the 2nd- or 3rd-floor rooms facing 15th or H Sts; they are the brightest). Rooms in the historic building, erected in 1880, have a whiff of Parisian art deco about them; embroidered armchairs and marble fireplaces are fanciful embellishments in otherwise modern rooms done up in geometric design schemes that impart a pleasing feng shui. Wi-fi costs $10 per day.

GEORGE WASHINGTON UNIVERSITY INN HOTEL **$$**

(Map p320; 202-337-6620, 800-426-4455; www.gwuinn.com; 824 New Hampshire Ave NW; r $180-310; M Foggy Bottom-GWU; P @) As you might guess, a lot of parents (of GWU students) find themselves staying in this pleasant hotel, situated on a quiet tree-lined street in the midst of tweedy academics and the occasional drunken undergrad. A little bit of colonial furnishing brightens up rooms that are fine if not particularly memorable; ask the staff to show you a few, as some have good views out onto the Potomac.

PETS

A fair number of DC hotels allow pets, but they charge a $25 to $100 non-refundable cleaning fee. In this book, we have used the icon to denote places that not only permit pets but also waive fees and/or provide special programs for our four-legged friends.

RIVER INN BOUTIQUE HOTEL **$$**

(Map p320; 202-337-7600, 888-874-0100; www.theriverinn.com; 924 25th St NW; r $160-300; M Foggy Bottom-GWU; P) On a quiet residential street (despite the name, it's not actually on the river) a block away from the Kennedy Center, this building looks like a generic bit o' brick. No worries: the real reason to stay here is easy access to Georgetown on one end, and the White House on the other. Rooms have mod, neutral-toned decor, snug pillowtop mattresses and flat-screen TVs. Guests have use of free bikes for two-hour increments (if available: they're first come, first served).

ONE WASHINGTON CIRCLE APARTMENT **$$**

(Map p320; 202-872-1680; www.thecirclehotel.com; 1 Washington Circle; apt from $280; M Foggy Bottom-GWU; P) At its eponymous address, this sleek, modern all-suite hotel has always attracted high-profile guests; for example, Nixon maintained offices here after the Watergate scandal totaled his presidency. On-site kitchens make for easy self-catering, and the rooms themselves are actually a good deal, all shimmering sheets and spaces that look like a swinging (but tasteful) '60s bachelor pad. Bonus: each suite has a balcony. The outdoor pool opens in summer.

DOUBLETREE GUEST SUITES WASHINGTON DC APARTMENT **$$**

(Map p320; 202-785-2000; www.doubletree.com; 801 New Hampshire Ave NW; apt $170-310; M Foggy Bottom-GWU; P) Doubletree may mean bland corporatism to some, but in this case all that money has translated into an all-suites extravaganza. This is a good choice for families or small groups – the one- and two-bedroom digs are large enough to accommodate both, especially if you're self-catering via the fully equipped kitchen. That said, you are trading style for size; there's not much to distinguish these rooms from a Holiday Inn but the extra space. Wi-fi costs $10 per day. The outdoor pool opens in late May.

HAY-ADAMS HOTEL LUXURY HOTEL $$$

(Map p320; ☎202-638-6600; www.hayadams.com; 800 16th St NW; r from $450; Ⓜ McPherson Sq; P ❄ @ ☜) One of the city's great heritage hotels, the Hay is a beautiful old building where 'nothing is overlooked but the White House.' It's named for two mansions that once stood on the site (owned by secretary of state John Hay and historian Henry Adams) that were the nexus of Washington's political and intellectual elite. Today the hotel has a palazzo-style lobby and probably the best rooms of the old-school luxury genre in the city, all puffy mattresses like clouds shaded by four-poster canopies and gold-braid tassels, the sort of chamber you call a *chambre,* where you drink champagne from a crystal shoe and light cigars with $100 bills. There's a tasteful soupçon of Washington scandal on top of all this: back in the 1980s, this hotel was a site where Oliver North wooed contributors to his illegal contra-funding scheme.

W HOTEL WASHINGTON HOTEL $$$

(Map p320; ☎202-661-2400; www.wwashingtondc.com; 515 15th St NW; r from $370; Ⓜ Metro Center; P ⊖ ❄ @ ☜ 🐾) When the oldest continuously operating hotel in Washington, DC, was bought out by the W Hotel chain, everyone connected to the DC accommodations scene had a small heart attack. Would the famously hip W brand do away with the class, tradition and storied sense of history that has sat around the corner from the White House since 1918? It kinda did. Now rooms and suites are decked out in a sort of *Mad Men* meets *Wallpaper* magazine blend of retro-futuristic, all smooth lines and pared-down furnishings, polished and occasionally playful. The rooftop bar has killer views of the city. In-room internet access costs $15 per day; wi-fi is free in the lobby.

MELROSE HOTEL BOUTIQUE HOTEL $$

(Map p320; ☎202-955-6400; www.melrosehoteldc.com; 2430 Pennsylvania Ave NW; r $220-340; Ⓜ Foggy Bottom-GWU; P ⊖ ❄ ☜) For that chintzy, European luxury boudoir feel, you can't go wrong with the Melrose, which also boasts a fine, fine location: a few blocks from the Metro, steps from Rock Creek Park, just over the bridge from Georgetown and a plush spot overlooking a happening span of Pennsylvania Ave. Rooms are all terry-cloth soft and dark-wood style, though they're a bit faded in elegance. The Library Bar adds a classy touch. Wi-fi costs $10 per day.

ACCOMMODATIONS WEBSITES

Lonely Planet (hotels.lonelyplanet.com) Find reviews and make bookings.

Bed & Breakfast DC (www.bedandbreakfastdc.com) One-stop shop to book B&Bs and apartments.

WDCA Hotels (www.wdcahotels.com) Discounter that sorts by neighborhood, price or eco-friendliness.

Destination DC (www.washington.org) Options from DC's official website.

ST REGIS WASHINGTON LUXURY HOTEL $$$

(Map p320; ☎202-638-2626; www.stregis.com/washington; 923 16th St NW; r from $665; Ⓜ McPherson Sq; P ❄ @ ☜ 🐾) The American Institute of Architects describes the St Regis as 'indisputably one of the grandest hotels in the city' – and those guys don't throw such praise about lightly. What else can you say about a freestanding building designed to resemble nothing less than an Italian grand palace? Rooms are as gilded as you'd expect, with hand-carved armoires, double-basin marble sinks and TVs embedded in the bathroom mirrors. Room 1012 is famed for being the place where Monica Lewinsky spilled details of her now infamous shenanigans with President Clinton to Ken Starr's investigators. Wi-fi costs $15 per day.

WILLARD INTERCONTINENTAL HOTEL LUXURY HOTEL $$$

(Map p320; ☎202-628-9100; www.washington.intercontinental.com; 1401 Pennsylvania Ave NW; r $300-1600; Ⓜ Federal Triangle; P ⊖ ❄ @ ☜) You can't sleep much closer to DC history than here. This is where MLK wrote his 'I Have a Dream' speech; where the term 'lobbyist' was coined (by President Grant to describe political wranglers trolling the lobby); and where Lincoln, Coolidge and Harding have all lain their heads. Nathaniel Hawthorne observed that it could 'much more justly [be] called the center of Washington...than either the Capitol, the White House, or the State Department.' The building is a masterpiece of the beaux arts movement, all fancy crenellations and soaring, dignity-laden elegance – upon entering the marble lobby, you'd be forgiven for expecting Jay Gatsby to stumble down the stairs clutching a bourbon. The chandelier-hung hallways are still thick with lobbyists and corporate aristocrats buffing their loafers on the dense carpets. The rooms are just as opulent: flowy curtains framed by potted palms, power-player views over the city and scandalously comfy beds. The stunning presidential suites are often utilized by visiting heads of state. Don't miss the Round Robin bar, which claims to be the mint julep's birthplace. Wi-fi costs $25 per day.

RENAISSANCE MAYFLOWER HOTEL HOTEL $$$

(Map p320; ☎202-347-3000; www.renaissancehotels.com; 1127 Connecticut Ave NW; r from $350; M Farragut North; P ⊖ ❄ @ ☎) J Edgar Hoover dined here; John F Kennedy reportedly sampled the charms of the fairer sex here; and NY Governor Eliot Spitzer infamously rendezvoused with a call girl here (in room 871). Although not the exclusive enclave it once was, this hotel remains regal in its public spaces, with lots of frills and marble, and a beautiful grand ballroom. The contemporary guest rooms are businesslike and not particularly spacious, though they do sport marble bathrooms and posh bedding. Wi-fi costs $17 per day.

Georgetown

HOTEL MONTICELLO HOTEL $$

(Map p332; ☎202-337-0900, 800-388-2410; www.monticellohotel.com; 1075 Thomas Jefferson St NW; r incl breakfast $160-260; M Foggy Bottom-GWU to DC Circulator; P ⊖ ❄ @ ☎) Set smack in the heart of Georgetown, Hotel Monticello is one of the better deals in Washington. The rooms, with brass-and-crystal chandeliers, colonial-reproduction furniture, high-end mattresses and tasteful flower arrangements, have a Euro-townhouse feel, like those cramped but cozy hotels you get in central London. Staff says the look (and prices) will remain the same, even after the property's renovation in late 2012.

LATHAM HOTEL BOUTIQUE HOTEL $$

(Map p332; ☎202-726-5000; www.thelatham.com; 3000 M St NW; r $170-330; M Foggy Bottom-GWU to DC Circulator; P ❄ @ ☎ ≋) Hot with visiting celebrities and European jet-setters, this chic redbrick boutique hotel in the midst of the M St scene exudes European charm. The two-story Carriage House suites are luxe in a 19th-century kind of way; standard rooms possess a mannerly, off-white monochrome scheme overlaid by antique charm. One of DC's finest restaurants, Citronelle (p121), is on site. The rooftop sundeck by the pool is a fine place to relax.

GEORGETOWN SUITES APARTMENT $$

(Map p332; ☎202-298-7800; www.georgetownsuites.com; 1111 30th St NW; apt incl breakfast $165-265; M Foggy Bottom-GWU to DC Circulator; P ⊖ ❄ @ ☎ 👪) If you don't mind trading style for ho-hum practicality (and 1980s decor), the Georgetown Suites provide good value for the neighborhood. The most common units are 500-sq-ft studios and 800-sq-ft one-bedroom suites; larger options are also available. It's more space than you'll get in a hotel room, plus all units have kitchens for self-catering. M St's shopping and dining bonanza, the waterfront and C&O Canal are within spitting distance. Note the property has a second building at 1000 29th St (a block away), which tends to be noisier.

GEORGETOWN INN HOTEL $$

(Map p332; ☎202-333-8900, 888-587-2388; www.georgetowninn.com; 1310 Wisconsin Ave NW; r $200-380; M Foggy Bottom-GWU to DC Circulator; P ⊖ ❄ ☎) The blue-blooded Georgetown Inn with a Revolutionary War–period look (think old Europe meets American colonial) is a gorgeous property favored by Georgetown University alumni and parents on college weekends. The inn spreads rooms through a collection of restored 18th-century townhouses and its stately decor (four-poster beds, furniture with feet) is matched by stately service. Wi-fi costs $11 per day.

Capitol Hill & Southeast DC

WILLIAM PENN HOUSE HOSTEL $

(Map p324; ☎202-543-5560; www.williampennhouse.org; 515 E Capitol St SE; dm incl breakfast $40-50; M Capitol South, Eastern Market; ⊖ ❄ @ 👪) On a peaceful street five blocks east of the Capitol, this friendly Quaker-run guesthouse with garden offers clean, well-maintained dorms, though it could use more bathrooms. There are 30 beds total, including a four-bed room for families ($135 per night). The facility doesn't require religious observance, but there is a religious theme throughout, and it prefers guests be active in progressive causes. The curious and spiritually minded can rise for the 7:30am worship service.

HOTEL GEORGE BOUTIQUE HOTEL **$$**
(Map p324; ☎202-347-4200; www.hotelgeorge.com; 15 E St NW; r from $290-370; Ⓜ Union Station;) George was the first DC hotel to take the term 'boutique' to a daring, ultramodern level. The stylish interior is framed by clean lines, chrome-and-glass furniture and modern art, with rooms that exude a cool, creamy-white Zen. The pop-art presidential accents (paintings of American currency, artfully rearranged and diced up) are a little overdone, but that's a minor complaint about what is otherwise the hippest lodging on the Hill. The free-vino happy hour each evening and free in-room yoga gear ice the cake (thanks, Kimpton hotel family).

CAPITOL HILL SUITES APARTMENT **$$**
(Map p324; ☎202-543-6000; www.capitolhillsuites.com; 200 C St SE; ste incl breakfast $220-420; Ⓜ Capitol South;) This all-suite property is ideally located in the heart of Hill legislative action. It's the only hotel that is actually *on* the Hill, and it's heavily favored by congressional interns (even a few congresspeople and senators rent suites). And no wonder: the place is good value, especially since weekly and monthly rates are available. Thanks to expansive renovation work, rooms are a fair deal larger than the shoeboxes you often find in smaller DC properties, and they're attractive too, all clean lines, soft blue walls and subtle chocolate embellishments that add a bit of warmth to otherwise contemporary chambers. Smaller rooms have kitchenettes, while larger rooms have a full kitchen.

PHOENIX PARK HOTEL HOTEL **$$**
(Map p324; ☎202-638-6900, 800-824-5419; www.phoenixparkhotel.com; 520 N Capitol St NW; r $160-390; Ⓜ Union Station;) It may look like a corporate-bland block from the outside, but you could host a wake, or a meeting of the Dail (Irish parliament), or at least a rowdy Guinness-downing session here. Right, enough Irish stereotyping, but really, the rooms – upstairs from the Dubliner pub – do have the feel of a Trinity College reading chamber that Joyce could have penned a novel in. Plus, this spot has been home away from home for visiting Irish politicians like Gerry Adams, so when they lay on the Emerald Isle kitsch, it's genuine.

THOMPSON-MARKWARD HALL APARTMENT **$**
(Map p324; ☎202-546-3255; www.tmhdc.org; 235 2nd St NE; apt incl breakfast & dinner per month $925; Ⓜ Union Station;) Young women staying at least two weeks might consider this communal option, which is open to women 18 to 34 who are working or studying in Washington. (In summer, 90% of its guests are Hill interns.) The rates include two meals a day plus Sunday brunch, which is good value considering the average price of a sublet apartment in Washington. All rooms are small, furnished singles with phones, computer hookups and shared bathroom. The mood is like that of an upscale dorm, with a spacious courtyard, sundeck, pretty dining room and sitting areas. Drawbacks: you can't drink, smoke or bring male guests above lobby level. (Thompson-Markward's second name is The Young Woman's Christian Home but, apart from these rules, you'd never know it.) If you start missing the Y-chromosome set, the Capitol Hill bar scene is just a couple of blocks away.

CAPITOL CITY HOSTEL HOSTEL **$**
(off Map p324; ☎202-328-3210; 2411 Benning Rd NE; dm $20-28; Ⓜ Union Station for bus X2;) This is a cheap and cheerful hostel with decently clean dorms that tend to have a good communal vibe if there are enough people around. The real pleasure here is the staff and management; we've found them to be unfailingly helpful and considerate, going out of their way to make guests feel at home. The hostel is about 2 miles east of Union Station, in a neighborhood that looks sketchier than it is. You'll have to rely on buses, but they are dependable, and you'll be close to the excellent nightlife on H St NE. From Union Station, take bus X2 going east (it'll say 'Minnesota Ave'); exit at 23rd Pl and Benning Rd.

Downtown & Penn Quarter

TOP CHOICE **CHESTER ARTHUR HOUSE** B&B **$$**
(Map p326; ☎877-893-3233; www.chesterarthurhouse.com; 13th & P Sts NW; r incl breakfast $175-275; Ⓜ U St-Cardozo;) Run by a delightful couple with serious travel experience

under their belts – they both have *National Geographic* credentials – this is a good option for those wanting to explore beneath Washington's surface. Accommodation is in one of three rooms in a beautiful Logan Circle row house that's filled with antiques and collected ephemera from the hosts' global expeditions. The location is an equidistant, 15-minute walk from the U St Corridor's cache of clubs and restaurants (to the north), Dupont Circle's nightlife (to the west) and the convention center (to the southeast).

HOTEL HELIX BOUTIQUE HOTEL **$$**
(Map p326; ☎202-462-9001, 866-508-0658; www.hotelhelix.com; 1430 Rhode Island Ave NW; r $215-350; M Dupont Circle; P ⊖ ❄ @ ☎ ♿ 🐾) Modish and highlighter bright, the Helix is playfully hip – the perfect hotel for the bouncy international set that makes up the surrounding neighborhood. Little touches suggest a youthful energy (Pez dispensers in the minibar) balanced with worldly cool, like the pop-punk decor – just camp enough to be endearing. Specialty rooms include Bunk (that's right, bunk beds) and studios with kitchenettes; all rooms have comfy, crisp-sheet beds and 37in flat-screen TVs. As part of the Kimpton Hotels family, with the requisite free evening wine hour and morning coffee, Helix is the group's eccentric standout. It's an easy walk to the food and drink bounty at either the U St Corridor or Dupont Circle.

MORRISON-CLARK INN HISTORIC HOTEL **$$**
(Map p326; ☎202-898-1200; www.morrisonclark.com; 1015 L St NW; r $200-350; M Mt Vernon Sq/7th St-Convention Center; P ⊖ ❄ @ ☎) The only hotel in DC on the Register of Historic Places, this elegant inn comprises two 1864 Victorian residences filled with fine antiques, chandeliers, richly hued drapes and other features evocative of the pre–Civil War South. Some rooms come with private balconies or decorative marble fireplaces. Be aware that since it is a *historic* home, rooms can be on the small side. A doting staff and super-central location round out the package.

HOSTELLING INTERNATIONAL – WASHINGTON DC HOSTEL **$**
(Map p326; ☎202-737-2333; www.hiwashingtondc.org; 1009 11th St NW; dm incl breakfast $29-45; M Metro Center; ⊖ ❄ @ ☎) Top of the hostel picks, this friendly, 250-bed facility attracts a laid-back international crowd and has loads of amenities – lounge rooms, pool table, movie nights, kitchen and laundry. The dorm rooms are clean and well kept, in configurations ranging from four to 10 beds; there are a few private, en-suite rooms, too. Volunteers organize a variety of free outings: night tours of the monuments, Dupont Circle pub crawls, concerts at the Kennedy Center and the like. Reservations are highly recommended March to October.

HOTEL MONACO BOUTIQUE HOTEL **$$**
(Map p326; ☎202-628-7177; www.monaco-dc.com; 700 F St NW; r from $240-360; M Gallery Pl-Chinatown; P ⊖ ❄ @ ☎ ♿ 🐾) The neoclassical facade has aged with considerable grace at this marble temple to stylish glamour. Free goldfish on request and a geometric, deco-inspired interior help polish the 1930s, cool-daddy-o vibe, all set in the historic, grand, Corinthian-columned, all-marble 1839 Tariff Building. Bold artwork and modern furniture blend masterfully in the wood-paneled lobby; funky prints and jewel tones add new life to the arched ceilings and wood molding in the guestrooms. The location works well for families: it's across the street from the Spy Museum, Smithsonian American Art Museum and Metro; four blocks from the Mall; and attached to the popular Poste restaurant, which has a kids menu. Sip free wine in the evening, as per all Kimpton-brand properties.

HAMPTON INN HOTEL **$$**
(Map p326; ☎202-842-2500; www.washingtondc.hamptoninn.com; 901 6th St NW; r incl breakfast $135-260; M Gallery Pl-Chinatown; P ⊖ ❄ @ ☎ ≋ ♿) Cookie cutter? Yeah, well. You know what you're getting at the Hampton, and it's usually a solid deal here. The 13-story property opened in 2005 and offers the requisite restful bedding, small indoor pool and hot (if spare) breakfast buffet. The location is slightly isolated, meaning you'll have to walk four blocks or so to reach downtown's theaters and nightlife.

HENLEY PARK HOTEL BOUTIQUE HOTEL **$$**
(Map p326; ☎202-638-5200, 800-222-8474; www.henleypark.com; 926 Massachusetts Ave NW; r $200-350; M Mt Vernon Sq/7th St-Convention Center; P ⊖ ❄ ☎) A beautiful Tudor building with gargoyles and stained glass makes a fine setting for this historic hotel. The

rooms – decked in prints and brass furniture – are as elegant as the edifice; some look like a piece of Delft porcelain given bedroom form. Others are slightly more understated, with solid color wallpaper worked over with flowery patterns; they're just as beautiful.

ELDON SUITES APARTMENT $$

(Map p326; ☎202-540-5000, 877-463-5336; www.eldonsuites.com; 933 L St NW; apt $250-380; Ⓜ Mt Vernon Sq/7th St-Convention Center; P ⊖ ❄ ☎ ♿) Given its location right by the Convention Center, Eldon Suites puts up plenty of business folk. Families dig it, too. You get much more space than in hotel rooms in the same price bracket. Even the smallest unit – the Independence – has 600 sq ft and room for four people (if two are willing to crash on a sleeper couch), along with a big, fully equipped kitchen and separate living area. Freedom Suites are slightly larger one-bedroom units, while Liberty Suites have two bedrooms. Decor is pleasant if nondescript, along the lines of your everyday hotel.

HOTEL HARRINGTON HOTEL $$

(Map p326; ☎202-628-8140, 800-424-8532; www.hotel-harrington.com; 436 11th St NW; r $130-200; Ⓜ Federal Triangle; P ❄ ☎ ♿) One of the most affordable options near the Mall, the aging, family-run Harrington has small, basic rooms that are clean but in definite need of an update. Helpful service and a prime location make it a great value for travelers who don't mind roughing it a bit. It's a popular crash pad for school groups, budget-minded families and international guests.

DC LOFTY HOSTEL $

(Map p326; ☎202-506-7106; www.capitalhostels.com; 1333 11th St NW; dm from $33; Ⓜ Mt Vernon Sq/7th St-Convention Center; ⊖ ❄ @ ☎) Located in a crisp row house near the Convention Center, Lofty, with its brick walls and smooth wood floors vaguely delivers on the implied hipness and semiluxury its name suggests. The dorms – some mixed gender, others single sex, each with four to nine beds – are nothing to go wild over, but this is a good central location for backpackers wanting to explore the District on the cheap. A renovation in early 2012 included mattress upgrades, individual reading lights for most beds, and bathroom and kitchen improvements. The hostel has a couple of extra quirks: guests must go shoeless inside, and there's a $20 surcharge for arrivals outside the 10am to 10pm office hours.

HILTON GARDEN INN HOTEL $$

(Map p326; ☎202-783-7800; www.washingtondcdowntown.stayhgi.com; 815 14th St NW; r $135-295; Ⓜ McPherson Sq; P ❄ @ ☎ ≋ ♿) Part of the stalwart chain, this outpost near the White House caters to lots of business travelers. Rooms are decent-sized and good quality, but if the rates skew toward the high end of the range you'll probably find more for your money elsewhere.

DISTRICT HOTEL HOTEL $

(Map p326; ☎202-232-7800; www.thedistricthotel.com; 1440 Rhode Island Ave NW; r incl breakfast $120-150; Ⓜ Dupont Circle; P ⊖ ❄ ☎) Home to some of the smallest rooms in DC, the District Hotel has spartan quarters that are comfy enough if you're low maintenance. It's in a decent location within walking distance to downtown and Dupont Circle. The small parking area is first come, first served.

CAPITAL VIEW HOSTEL HOSTEL $

(Map p326; ☎202-450-3450; www.capitalhostels.com; 301 I St NW; dm from $33; Ⓜ Gallery Pl-Chinatown; ⊖ ❄ @ ☎) Capital View is the sister property of DC Lofty (p249), and it offers a similar vibe and room set-up. But try Lofty first, since it benefits from newer facilities and a better location. The setting at Capital View feels a bit more forlorn (though it is only four blocks from the Metro).

Dupont Circle & Kalorama

TOP CHOICE TABARD INN BOUTIQUE HOTEL $$

(Map p330; ☎202-785-1277; www.tabardinn.com; 1739 N St NW; r incl breakfast $165-250, with shared bathroom $125-145; Ⓜ Dupont Circle; P ⊖ ❄ @ ☎) Named for the inn in *The Canterbury Tales,* this delightful, historic hotel is set in a trio of Victorian-era row houses. The 40 rooms are hard to generalize: all come with vintage quirks like iron bed frames, overstuffed sofas and wing-backed chairs, but little accents distinguish – a Matisse-like painted headboard here, Amish-looking quilts there. Downstairs the parlor, beautiful courtyard restaurant and bar have low ceilings and old furniture, highly conducive to curling up with a vintage port and the *Sunday Post*. It's a good place to catch up on your Chaucer, as most rooms do not have TVs.

TOP CHOICE EMBASSY CIRCLE GUEST HOUSE B&B $$

(Map p330; ☎202-232-7744, 877-232-7744; www.dcinns.com; 2224 R St NW; r incl breakfast $180-240; MDupont Circle;) Embassies surround this 1902 French country-style home, which sits a few blocks from Dupont's nightlife hubbub. The 11 big-windowed rooms are decked out with Persian carpets and original art on the walls; they don't have TVs or radios, though they do each have wi-fi. Staff feeds you well throughout the day, with a hot organic breakfast, afternoon cookies, and an evening wine and beer soiree. Embassy Circle's sister property – the Woodley Park Guest House (p253) – is another hot spot.

INN AT DUPONT NORTH B&B $$

(Map p330; ☎202-467-6777; www.thedupontcollection.com; 1620 T St NW; r incl breakfast $115-270; MDupont Circle;) If you're craving a good range of B&B coziness in the heart of the capital, check out the class-act heritage properties run by the Dupont Collection. Our favorite is the Victorian, eight-room Inn at Dupont North, which feels like the modern home of a wealthy friend. Most of the handsome, dark-wood chambers have a writing desk and fireplace. Lower-price-spectrum rooms share a bathroom; those at the higher end have a Jacuzzi tub. The filling breakfast includes from-the-oven breads.

INN AT DUPONT SOUTH B&B $$

(Map p330; ☎202-467-6777; www.thedupontcollection.com; 1312 19th St NW; r incl breakfast $115-230; MDupont Circle;) This is the Dupont Collection's other neighborhood property, with eight Victorian-inspired rooms that evoke a chintz-and-lacy-linen sensibility. The location is right in the thick of Dupont's action.

CARLYLE SUITES APARTMENT $$

(Map p330; ☎202-234-3200, 800-964-5377; www.carlylesuites.com; 1731 New Hampshire Ave NW; apt $200-320; MDupont Circle;) Inside this all-suites art-deco gem, you'll find sizeable, handsomely furnished rooms with crisp white linens, luxury mattresses, 37in flat-screen TVs and full kitchens. The friendly staff is first rate, and the added extras include free use of laptops and complimentary access to the Washington Sports Club. Plus the onsite bar pours a mean martini. Parking is limited to 20 spaces (out of about 170 rooms), and it's first come, first served.

EMBASSY SUITES WASHINGTON DC HOTEL $$

(Map p330; ☎202-857-3388; www.washingtondc.embassysuites.com; 1250 22nd St NW; r incl breakfast $240-380; MDupont Circle;) You probably know the drill at the Embassy: how all the units are two-room suites (living room with sofa bed in front, bedroom in back), how there's always a cooked-to-order bacon, egg and pancake breakfast each morning, how there's free wine each evening, and how there's an indoor, kiddie-mobbed pool. It may leave little to the imagination, but this outpost of the chain does a fine job with those basics, plus the location between Georgetown and Dupont Circle is handy. Families will appreciate being two blocks from Rock Creek Park, where the little ones can let off steam. Rooms on the 8th and 9th floors have views over Georgetown. Wi-fi costs $12 per day.

HOTEL PALOMAR HOTEL $$

(Map p330; ☎202-448-1800, 877-866-3070; www.hotelpalomar-dc.com; 2121 P St NW; r $260-380; MDupont Circle;) The Palomar brings in a stylish business clientele, plus a whole lot of pooches. Room decor is matter-of-fact compared to its Kimpton-chain brethren, with an emphasis on nicely powered-up work desks. Then there's the pet-friendly vibe, which the hotel does up big time. Not only does your dog get pampered each night with gourmet treats at turndown, he can also get a massage. If he wants to socialize, head to the Bark Bar, a three-tiered water bar for thirsty pets just outside the hotel. Or drop him off at the Dish, the hotel's pet lounging area. Palomar's free evening wine hour is always a jam-packed scene. The outdoor pool and deck go beyond the norm.

AKWAABA B&B $$

(Map p330; ☎866-466-3855; www.akwaaba.com; 1708 16th St NW; r $150-265; MDupont Circle;) Akwaaba is a small chain of B&Bs that puts an emphasis on African American heritage in its properties. Its DC outpost is ensconced in a fine, late-19th-century mansion; rooms are themed from abstractions ('Inspiration,' which has fine, airy ceilings and a slanting skylight) to authors ('Zora,' an all-red room that's romantic as all hell, perfect for a lovey-dovey weekend). The cooking gets rave reviews, and the Dupont vibe is at your doorstep.

EMBASSY INN HOTEL $$

(Map p330; 202-234-7800, 800-423-9111; www.embassy-inn-hotel-dc.com; 1627 16th St NW; r incl breakfast $130-190; MDupont Circle;) Run by the genial folks who also operate the District Hotel (p249) and Windsor Inn (p253), the Embassy is in the same plain-Jane vein, but with the benefit of a more recent rehab. Rooms are smallish with thin walls, but there's a veneer of quaintness here.

SWANN HOUSE B&B $$

(Map p330; 202-265-4414; www.swannhouse.com; 1808 New Hampshire Ave NW; r incl breakfast $200-350; MDupont Circle;) A dozen rooms are peppered around an exquisite 1883 Romanesque mansion, all just set off enough from Dupont to be quiet, but close enough to the action for you to get raucous, if you so choose. The rooms are highly individualized; some are too frilly for our tastes (although if you like doilies and porcelain, check out the Blue Sky suite), but others we just love. The Parisienne suite, with its fireplace and modern paintings, has a feeling of set-off seclusion; the hip Shanghaid'away has rich colors and is overlaid with a well-executed Asian theme.

HOTEL MADERA BOUTIQUE HOTEL $$

(Map p330; 202-296-7600, 800-368-5691; www.hotelmadera.com; 1310 New Hampshire Ave NW; r $290-400; MDupont Circle; P) Cozy yet cosmopolitan, this hotel is another Kimpton property, the focus here being more of an intimate, small boutique than large funk-da-house hipster haunt. It's a little more staid than fellows such as Helix, Rouge and Topaz, but more romantic for that, as well as classier. Here the modern art doesn't feel fun so much as tasteful. Rooms are outfitted in dark earth tones, colors as smooth as the thick, silky sheets.

TOPAZ HOTEL BOUTIQUE HOTEL $$

(Map p330; 202-393-3000, 800-775-1202; www.topazhotel.com; 1733 N St NW; r $250-360; MDupont Circle; P) Abracadabra: the door automatically swings open at the Topaz to reveal an Arabian Nights–type decor. Jewel-tone colors dominate the rooms – purple love seats, sapphire-blue drapes and pale-green lamps, all set off by satiny white beds and pillows. This is a Kimpton hotel all the way, with the hip mod-cons, genial service and free-flowing wine you expect. It also provides passes to the YMCA workout facility on the next block.

HOTEL ROUGE BOUTIQUE HOTEL $$

(Map p330; 202-232-8000, 800-738-1202; www.rougehotel.com; 1315 16th St NW; r $250-360; MDupont Circle; P) Rouge is another playful Kimpton winner. The decor is definitively red, with bold designs, funky furniture and hip posters decorating the rooms. Specialty rooms have bunk beds and Xbox 360 games, while others come with kitchenettes. As funky as the hotel, Bar Rouge attracts a regular stream of locals, especially for its Thursday happy hours. Rates can skew lower here than at sibling properties.

DUPONT AT THE CIRCLE B&B $$

(Map p330; 202-332-5251; www.dupontatthecircle.com; 1604 19th St NW; r incl breakfast $215-275, ste $295-400; MDupont Circle;) This upscale inn is housed in a stately brick Victorian row house, one block north of the circle. Its six guestrooms and three suites are furnished differently with tasteful antiques from varying periods – room three is named after Lincoln, another after Cuba – but all have private bathrooms with claw-foot tubs or Jacuzzis. Breakfasts are modest affairs: muffins, granola and fruit. Check out the Pinnacle for a special romantic evening: the inn's poshest suite boasts 22ft ceilings, a stained-glass window, a giant Jacuzzi for two and flat-screen plasma TV on a private floor perched at the very top of the inn.

JEFFERSON HOTEL LUXURY HOTEL $$$

(Map p330; 866-270-8118; www.jeffersondc.com; 1200 16th St NW; r from $450; MFarragut North; P) This luxury boutique is regularly near the top of Washington's best-hotel lists. The elegant, two-winged 1923 mansion has an ornate porte cochere, beaux-arts architecture and a luxurious interior full of crystal and velvet, all meant to evoke namesake Thomas Jefferson's digs when he lived in Paris. Favored by diplomatic visitors, the hotel's antique-furnished rooms waft silk sheets, four-poster luxury, tobacco and earth tones, and Gilded Age class. The best praise we can give: the suites live up to the name presidential, which *means* something in this town.

MADISON LUXURY HOTEL $$$

(Map p330; ☎202-862-1600; www.madisonhoteldc.com; 1177 15th St NW; r from $340; MFarragut North, McPherson Sq; P) The Madison has hosted every US president since JFK. Rooms are attractive in a Washington-power-player kinda way, all warm chocolates, leather furniture and 300-thread-count sheets that are screaming for you to don a smoking jacket. As a side note, the Madison is supposedly the first hotel in the world to have introduced the minibar – thanks, guys.

Adams-Morgan

ADAM'S INN B&B $$

(Map p334; ☎202-745-3600; www.adamsinn.com; 1746 Lanier Pl NW; r incl breakfast $139-179, with shared bathroom $109-139; MWoodley Park-Zoo/Adams Morgan; P) Tucked on a shady residential street, the 26-room inn is known for its personalized service, fluffy linens and handy location just a few blocks from 18th St's global smorgasbord. Inviting, homey rooms sprawl through two adjacent townhouses and a carriage house. The common areas have a nice garden patio, and there's a general sense of sherry-scented chintz. Breakfast is DIY continental style. It's a good seven blocks from the Metro, which can be problematic with lots of luggage.

TAFT BRIDGE INN B&B $$

(Map p334; ☎202-387-2007; www.taftbridgeinn.com; 2007 Wyoming Ave NW; r incl breakfast $175-200, with shared bathroom $95-140; MDupont Circle; P) Named for the bridge that leaps over Rock Creek Park just to the north, this beautiful 19th-century Georgian mansion is an easy walk to 18th St or Dupont Circle. The inn has a paneled drawing room, classy antiques, six fireplaces and a garden. Some rooms have a colonial Americana theme, accentuated by Amish quilts and the like; others are more tweedy, exuding a Euro-renaissance in their decor.

MERIDIAN MANOR B&B $$

(Map p334; ☎202-328-3510, 877-893-3233; www.meridianmanordc.com; cnr 16th & U Sts NW; r incl breakfast $155-250, with shared bathroom $125-155; MU St-Cardozo; P) Unlike in many similar B&Bs, the six rooms here have a contemporary vibe. They're all decked out with designer furniture and monochrome color schemes, which stands in nice contrast to the 'manor' itself, a lovely old DC residence that blends in easily with nearby embassies. The gracious hosts can direct you to action in the U St Corridor (a few blocks away), 18th St (about a half-mile) and Dupont Circle (about three-quarters of a mile away). Breakfast is continental style.

AMERICAN GUEST HOUSE B&B $$

(Map p334; ☎202-588-1180; www.americanguesthouse.com; 2005 Columbia Rd NW; r $160-220; MDupont Circle; @) The 12-room American Guest House earns high marks for its intimate sense of service, bountiful omelet-y breakfasts and elegant, individualized rooms. Decor runs the gamut from Victorian vibe (Room 203) to New England cottage (Room 304) to colonial love nest (Room 303). Some quarters are rather small.

BED & BREAKFAST ON U STREET B&B $$

(Map p334; ☎202-328-3510, 877-893-3233; www.bedandbreakfastonustreet.com; cnr 17th & U Sts NW; r incl breakfast $165-275, with shared bathroom $125-155; MU St-Cardozo; P) With hardwood floors, carved-wood trim, decorative fireplaces and high ceilings, this five-room, Victorian-era B&B is comfortable, though nothing lavish. The 2nd-floor suite, with a sleeper sofa and sitting room, is a good choice for families – mom and dad even get their own space. The two 3rd-floor rooms share a bathroom. It's near the heart of the U St Corridor, 18th St and Dupont Circle. The B&B is the sister property of Meridian Manor (p252).

WASHINGTON HILTON HOTEL $$

(Map p334; ☎202-483-3000; www.hilton.com; 1919 Connecticut Ave NW; r $175-325; MDupont Circle; P) The 1960s-style semicircular structure has all the amenities you expect from a Hilton. It is famed as the site of John Hinckley's attempt to assassinate President Ronald Reagan, on March 30, 1981. Hoping to impress the actor Jodie Foster, the disturbed young man shot Reagan, his press secretary and an FBI agent near the T St NW entrance. The rooms here are corporate, but considering the service you get and the nifty location near food and drink hot spots, it's not a bad deal. Wi-fi costs $12 per day.

WINDSOR INN HOTEL $

(Map p334; ☎202-667-0300, 800-423-9111; www.windsor-inn-hotel-dc.com; 1842 16th St NW; r incl breakfast $100-150; Ⓜ U St-Cardozo;) The Windsor offers pretty much the same spare, fusty rooms as sibling properties the District Hotel (p249) and Embassy Inn (p251). Non-fussy travelers will be fine, and grateful for the affable service and happenin' Dupont Circle/U St Corridor location.

WASHINGTON INTERNATIONAL STUDENT CENTER HOSTEL $

(Map p334; ☎202-667-7681; www.dchostel.com; 2451 18th St NW; dm incl breakfast $25; Ⓜ Woodley Park-Zoo/Adams Morgan;) This ranks low on the hostel totem pole, but it *is* in a rollicking location in the heart of Adams-Morgan, and it *is* cheap. Backpackers used to spick-and-span facilities and friendly, well-organized service might want to look elsewhere, though…

U Street, Columbia Heights & Northeast

INTOWN UPTOWN INN B&B $$

(off Map p336; ☎202-541-9400; www.iuinn.com; 4907 14th St NW; r incl breakfast $135-205; Ⓜ Columbia Heights to bus 52, 53 or 54;) The 10-room Intown is one of the better urban B&Bs out there. We love it for its ability to combine crucial, sometimes disparate elements of an intimate stay in a city: owners who are knowledgeable about town, a design that fuses traditional style (the main sitting and dining rooms) with a more cutting-edge aesthetic (the guestrooms, especially the red-and-white 'Room With a View' and airy 'Soho' chamber), plus a good host of mod-cons. Two rooms share a bathroom; the rest have private facilities. The only drawback is you're not near much here; talk with the owners about connections to the city center on the 14th St bus.

ASANTE SANA GUEST QUARTERS B&B $

p336; ☎202-570-3440; www.asantesana.us; 1207 Kenyon St NW; r incl breakfast $125-145; Ⓜ Columbia Heights;) There's nothing fancy in the four rooms at Asante Sana, which isn't a traditional B&B. Breakfast is a basket of packaged pastries and fruit delivered to your room, and kitchen facilities enable self-catering for other meals (there's a grocery store nearby). The selling point is it's a cool, offbeat neighborhood to stay in for adventurous types, near ethnic eats, hipster dive bars and the Metro.

HILLTOP HOSTEL HOSTEL $

(☎202-291-9591; www.hosteldc.com; 300 Carroll St; dm $24; Ⓜ Takoma;) The rough-and-ready Hilltop is in the bohemian, politically leftist neighborhood of Takoma Park, in far northeast DC. Set in a century-old Victorian mansion, the spot is frequented by crowds of backpackers from all over the world. The backyard BBQ and hammock inspire frequent impromptu parties. Don't be frightened off by the hostel's distance from downtown: it's across the street from the Metro, which gets you to Capitol Hill in about 15 minutes. Besides, Takoma has its own strip of antique shops and vegetarian restaurants to explore.

Upper Northwest DC

WOODLEY PARK GUEST HOUSE B&B $$

(Map p340; ☎202-667-0218, 866-667-0218; www.dcinns.com; 2647 Woodley Rd NW; r incl breakfast $185-230, with shared bathroom $145-165; Ⓜ Woodley Park-Zoo/Adams Morgan;) This elegant, 1920s-era home is excellent value. Fifteen sunny rooms have antique furniture, hardwood floors and white coverlets. The front porch is a wonderful perch for a summer afternoon. The owners are incredibly friendly, and many guests are faithful regulars. Note rooms that share a bathroom have an occupancy of one person only. Woodley Park's sister property – the Embassy Circle Guest House (p250) near Dupont Circle – is another winner.

KALORAMA GUEST HOUSE B&B $$

(Map p340; ☎202-588-8188; www.kalorama guesthouse.com; 2700 Cathedral Ave NW; r incl breakfast $175-235, with shared bathroom $89-99; Ⓜ Woodley Park-Zoo/Adams Morgan;) Set in a cozy Victorian row house, the Kalorama offers 11 flowery, antique-furnished rooms. Seven of them have private baths; the other four rooms share two baths. Some rooms are in the basement, so let them know when booking if you prefer a brighter upstairs unit. Breakfast is a self-serve affair consumed at a long communal table. In winter staff pours sherry or sangria in the evenings; in summer, it's fresh lemonade throughout the day.

OMNI SHOREHAM HOTEL HOTEL **$$**

(Map p340; 202-234-0700; www.omnishorehamhotel.com; 2500 Calvert St NW; r $250-350; M Woodley Park-Zoo/Adams Morgan; P) The Omni may be an 836-room behemoth swarmed by conventioneers, but we're recommending it for its family friendliness. It is a stroller's roll to the National Zoo and Rock Creek Park, and just a couple blocks to the Metro that can whisk you to DC's main sights in four stops. Out the front door, restaurants line Connecticut Ave, including family favorite Lebanese Taverna (p211). Children receive backpacks with toys and games, as well as a milk-and-cookie service their first night. And you'll have a helluva time extracting them from the lovely heated outdoor pool.

Northern Virginia

Chain hotels pepper Arlington, which offers the cheapest options. Many are near the Metro and almost as convenient as staying in the District. Old Town Alexandria's lodgings are more awkward to reach Metro-wise and prices are higher, but the neighborhood is way more charming.

MORRISON HOUSE BOUTIQUE HOTEL **$$**

(Map p339; 703-838-8000; www.morrisonhouse.com; 116 S Alfred St; r from $180-370; M King St Metro to Old Town Shuttle; P) In the heart of Old Town Alexandria, Morrison House captures the neighborhood's charm with its Georgian-style building and Federal-style reproduction furniture. Rooms are beautifully decorated with two- or four-poster beds and some with decorative fireplaces. The on-site restaurant, including its Saturday high tea service, is well respected. Perks include a free shuttle to Reagan airport, free pool access at a nearby sibling hotel, and a free wine happy hour each evening (a Kimpton hotel brand hallmark).

ALEXANDRIA TRAVEL LODGE MOTEL **$**

(Map p339; 703-836-5100; www.travelodge.com; 700 N Washington St; r incl breakfast $80-160; M King St Metro; P) This motel – on a busy section of Washington St – is about a mile north of Old Town's historic district. It is a good bet for budget travelers who have their own car, as parking is free. Basic rooms have TV and wi-fi. Amenities are otherwise limited.

Understand Washington, DC

Washington, DC, Today

Washington has come a long way in the last 15 years. The not-so-distant days of crime-ridden streets and a dysfunctional local government have receded. Today, the economy is booming, with billions of dollars of investments pouring in. In fact, Washington was one of the few metropolitan areas in the USA to survive the recession relatively unscathed. Economics aside, the District is forging a new identity with a range of cutting-edge sustainable initiatives, a celebrated new restaurant scene and ambitious building projects.

Best on Film

All the President's Men (1976) Dramatic portrayal of two journalists who uncover the USA's biggest political scandal: Watergate.

Mr Smith Goes to Washington (1939) Frank Capra classic of idealist do-gooder (played by Jimmy Stewart) taking on the established power brokers of Washington.

Slam (1998) True-to-life portrait of a young man (and budding poet) growing up in a blight-stricken area of DC.

Best in Print

Katharine Graham's Washington (edited by Katharine Graham; 2002) Illuminating essays about the Washington experience, by presidential insiders, novelists, journalists, socialites and humorists.

Lost in the City (Edward P Jones; 1992) Critically acclaimed collection of short stories set in African American DC during the tumultuous 1960s and '70s.

A Long Distance Life (Marita Golden; 1989) Epic tale of Southern sharecroppers who seek a new life in DC, set against the backdrop of the Civil Rights movement and other historic events.

Boom Days

Between 2007 and 2012, the District's economy grew some 14%, compared with 3% across the rest of the country. Even during the darkest days of the recession, unemployment never surpassed 7%. The growth of the federal workforce (and the size of the government) has played a major role in fueling the local economy. It has also helped shield the District from the downturn experienced in the rest of the country.

It's not just the public sector that's doing well. Washington's tech sector is also growing (faster even than California's), and tourism continues to be a huge draw (contributing some $5 billion to the local economy). In fact, the District dynamo shows no sign of letting up: the Bureau of Labor Statistics ranked DC number one (out of 100 surveyed metro areas) for job growth through to 2020. This helps explain why the Washington area remains the wealthiest and best educated in the country.

New Projects

As the economy expands, Washington has seen a spate of new building projects and dramatic renovations. The Martin Luther King Jr Memorial, more than two decades in the making, finally opened in 2011, paying tribute to one of the world's great peacemaking visionaries. Nearby, the much-heralded National Museum of African American History and Culture held its groundbreaking in 2012 (with President Obama and the First Lady present). This Smithsonian museum, scheduled to open on the Mall in 2015, will showcase the tragedies and triumphs of African Americans in a 20,000-piece collection spanning 400 years of history.

Far from being a figment of the past, African American culture remains stronger than ever in Washington. The reopening of the Howard Theatre – a legendary showcase for jazz greats – following a $29-million renovation, attests to the continued renaissance of one of the USA's most vibrant African American neighborhoods.

Culinary Revolution

It wasn't so long ago that Washingtonians craving a first-class meal had few options aside from heading up to New York for the weekend. Things have taken a dramatic turn since then, with a homegrown foodie revolution transforming the once buttoned-up DC dining scene. The buzzwords of the day are 'local' and 'sustainable', with the bounty of the mid-Atlantic and organic Southern farms at the city's doorstep. Celebrated chefs such as Spaniard José Andrés, who has brought molecular gastronomy to the capital; Frenchman Michel Richard, who fuses French and American cuisines; and Food Network star Teddy Folkman have all left their mark on DC. International luminaries such as Alain Ducasse and Wolfgang Puck have also joined the act, opening award-winning restaurants in the District.

The number of ethnic eateries has also grown in leaps and bounds, with DC ranking only behind New York and LA in terms of sheer variety. Speaking of variety, the food-truck craze has also hit the capital, and Washingtonians can feast on lobster rolls, empanadas, curry chicken, gourmet hot dogs, savory quiches, Korean tacos and dozens of other mouthwatering meals by following the trucks (over 100 strong) on Twitter. Fruit and vegetable markets are also on the rise all across the District.

Greening DC

Washington is looking a lot greener these days. It currently leads the country in the number of eco-friendly buildings per capita, and around 50% of the electric power used in District government facilities comes from renewable sources. A bike-sharing program (the first in North America) has quickly grown to become one of the nation's largest, with over 1200 bicycles at 140 stations. Tens of thousands of commuters – as well as casual users – now use Capital Bikeshare, which has helped to get more and more vehicles off the street.

Building on DC's strong environmental record, Mayor Vincent Gray launched an even more ambitious environmental initiative in 2011 in the hope of making the city a model for clean energy, green spaces, urban farming and car-free transportation options. The scheme will include more solar panels on public buildings, gardens on empty lots, the transforming of waste into fuel and more trails for walkers and bikers.

if Washington, DC, were 100 people

49 would be African American
37 would be White
3 would be Asian
2 would be persons reporting two or more races

birthplace

(% of population)

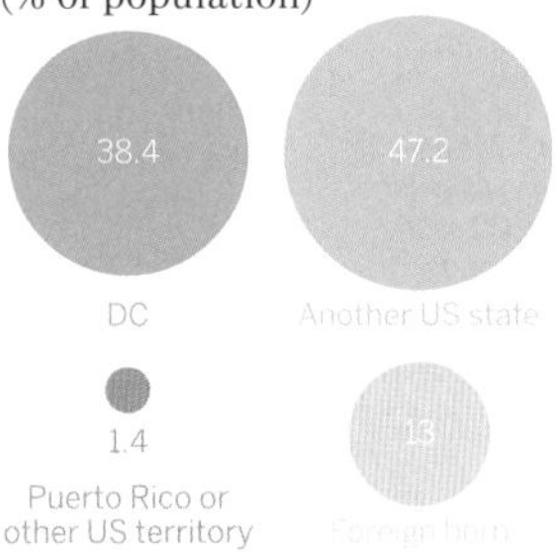

population per sq mile

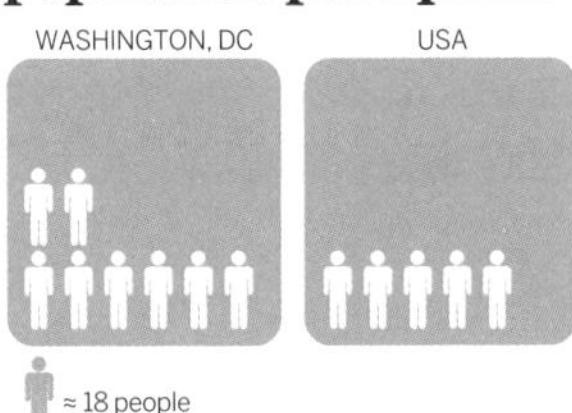

History

A compromise in a fragile new nation, Washington, DC, was built from scratch on a strategically chosen site between north and south. In the aftermath of the devastating Civil War, tiny Washington grew quickly, and became a vital player (and job creator) during the Great Depression and World War II. The 20th century brought turmoil: communist witch hunts, the fight for civil rights, a scandal that brought down the presidency, and urban blight. By the 21st century, however, Washington's stricken neighborhoods were revitalized, and the city continues to be a focal point for America's increasingly divided political views.

EARLY SETTLEMENT

Before the first European colonists sailed up from Chesapeake Bay, Native Americans, primarily the Piscataway tribe of the Algonquin language group, made their home near the confluence of the Potomac and Anacostia Rivers. The first recorded white contact with the Piscataway was in 1608 by the English Captain John Smith, who set out from Jamestown colony to explore the upper Potomac.

Relations with the peaceful Piscataway were amicable at first, but soon turned ruinous for the Native Americans, who suffered from European diseases. By 1700, the few remaining Piscataway migrated out of the region to Iroquois territory in Pennsylvania and New York.

The first European settlers in the region were traders and fur trappers, who plied the woodlands beyond the Allegheny Mountains, often working with local Algonquin communities. English and Scots-Irish settlers followed, turning the forests into farmland.

By the late 1600s, expansive agricultural estates lined both sides of the Potomac. These tidewater planters became a colonial aristocracy, dominating regional affairs. Their most lucrative crop was the precious sotweed – tobacco – which was tended by African indentured servants and slaves. The river ports of Alexandria and Georgetown became famous for their prosperous commercial centers.

Historical Reads

A People's History of the United States (Howard Zinn)

Capital Speculations: Writing and Building Washington, DC (Sarah Luria)

Washington Goes to War (David Brinkley)

TIMELINE

1608

Piscataway people, who live around the Potomac and Anacostia Rivers, encounter Captain John Smith on his journey up the Potomac – a word that may mean 'trading place' in Algonquin.

1791–92

As a compromise to the growing antagonism between north and south, the site for the new federal capital is chosen. Virginia and Maryland both cede land for the 100-sq-mile territory.

1800

Congress convenes in Washington for the first time. Despite the grandeur of L'Enfant's plan, the new capital remains a sparsely populated, muddy frontier town.

FIGHT FOR INDEPENDENCE

In the 1770s, growing hostilities with Britain led the colonies (now calling themselves states) to draft the Declaration of Independence, severing ties with Britain. Perhaps the most empowering section of the declaration stated that Americans were 'resolved to die free men rather than live as slaves.'

At the outset of the war, the colonies faced tremendous obstacles. The colonial leaders' belief in their ultimate success was both visionary and utterly improbable. They had neither a professional army nor navy – only a ragtag group of poorly trained militiamen fighting against the most powerful army and navy on the planet. The king expected a quick suppression of the revolt.

Instead, the British faced off against George Washington, a highly skilled and charismatic military tactician whose courage under fire (in the French and Indian War) was well known. Washington was appointed commander in chief of the 20,000-odd men – a number that would swell to more than 200,000 by the war's end.

Incredibly, the war would rage on for eight years, with more soldiers dying from disease and exposure during the long bitter winters than from battle wounds. The war also brought other European powers into the fray, with France providing arms and munitions, and eventually troops and naval power.

Despite numerous losses, Washington's army prevailed. The British surrendered at Yorktown in 1783 and later ceded all formerly British-held territories to the American colonies.

Presidential Reads

- *Washington (Ron Chernow)*
- *Thomas Jefferson (RB Bernstein)*
- *Lincoln (David Herbert Donald)*
- *Mornings on Horseback (David McCullough)*
- *The Bridge (David Remnick)*

A VISIONARY NEW CITY

Following the Revolutionary War, the fledgling US Congress set up a temporary capital in Philadelphia while searching for a more permanent home. The Constitution, ratified in 1788, specified that a federal territory, no greater than 10 sq miles, should be established for the nation's capital. Northerners and Southerners both wanted the capital in their territory, and archrivals Thomas Jefferson (a Virginian) and Alexander Hamilton (a New Yorker) struck a compromise, agreeing to construct a new city on the border between north and south. The precise location was left up to the newly inaugurated and wildly popular President George Washington.

Washington chose a site some 20 miles from his own Mount Vernon estate – a place he loved and knew well. The site on the Potomac proved a strategic location for commerce and river traffic, and was politically

Want to read the Constitution, Emancipation Proclamation, Federalist Papers and much, much more? Peruse the National Archives at www.archives.gov or '100 Milestone Documents' at www.ourdocuments.gov.

1814

As the War of 1812 rages, British troops attack the fledgling capital, destroying many public buildings (including the White House and the Capitol). President Madison flees to Virginia.

1835

Issue of slavery is dividing the nation. The Snow Riots erupt in Washington, with white mobs attacking blacks. In response, congress passes laws restricting blacks' economic rights.

1846

Allying themselves more with slaveholders and Southern interests, Alexandria County residents successfully petition to return the area to Virginia. It's an indication of the growing north-south divide.

1860

Abraham Lincoln is elected president. The South secedes from the Union and war is declared. Washingtonians live in constant fear of attack from rebels, camped across the river in Virginia.

pleasing to both Northern and Southern concerns. Maryland and Virginia agreed to cede land to the new capital.

Over drinks at Suter's tavern in Georgetown, Washington persuaded local landowners to sell their holdings to the government for $66 an acre. In March 1791 the African American mathematician Benjamin Banneker and surveyor Andrew Ellicott mapped out a diamond-shaped territory that spanned the Potomac and Anacostia Rivers. Its four corners were at the cardinal points of the compass, and it embraced the river ports of Georgetown and Alexandria (the latter eventually returned to Virginia). Pierre Charles L'Enfant, a French officer in the Revolutionary War, sketched plans for a grand European-style capital of monumental buildings and majestic boulevards. It was named the 'Territory of Columbia' (to honor Christopher Columbus), while the federal city within would be called 'the city of Washington.'

L'Enfant, despite his great vision for the city, would be dismissed within a year. He refused to answer to anyone aside from Washington, and when he challenged the commissioning authority above him, he was eventually fired. Nevertheless, his plan for the city would play a major role in its eventual design – and no one, aside from Washington, had a greater influence upon its development. After Washington fired his planner, land speculators grabbed prized properties and buildings sprang up haphazardly along mucky lanes. In 1793, construction began on the President's House and the Capitol, the geographic center points of the city. In 1800, John Adams became the first president to occupy the still uncompleted mansion. His wife Abigail hung the family's laundry in the East Room. The city remained a half-built, sparsely populated work in progress.

City residents for their part still associated themselves with the states from which they'd come. This began to change in 1801 when DC residents lost the right to vote in Virginia and Maryland elections. According to the Constitution, Congress alone would control the federal district, which intentionally or not, disenfranchised District residents. In 1820, DC held its first mayoral and city council elections, which voters took part in – though this would not always be the case.

FOUNDATIONS

Despite popular belief (asserted even by some congressmen), Washington, DC, was not built on a swamp. When surveying the capital, L'Enfant found fields, forests and bluffs. Some marshy areas near the river were prone to tidal fluctuations and periodic floods, but most of the new federal city was not marshy.

WAR OF 1812: WASHINGTON BURNS

In the early 19th century, the young nation had yet to become a formidable force in world affairs. US merchants and seamen were regularly bullied on the high seas by the British Navy. Responding to congressional hawks, President James Madison declared war in 1812. In retaliation for the razing of York (Toronto) by US troops, the British assaulted Washington. Work was barely complete on the Capitol in August 1814

1862

Slavery is abolished throughout DC. Washington becomes an army camp as the Civil War continues. Supply depots, warehouses and factories bring workers into the city.

1863

President Lincoln issues the Emancipation Proclamation, freeing all slaves. By the end of the Civil War, some four million African Americans will be freed.

1864

The war comes to Washington when the Confederate army attacks Fort Stevens – the only battle fought on capital soil. After a two-day skirmish, the Union army prevails.

1865

After Sherman's crippling, scorched-earth drive across the South, Confederate General Robert E Lee surrenders to Ulysses S Grant at Appomattox Court House in Virginia.

when redcoats marched into Washington and sacked and burned the city's most important buildings (but left private houses largely unharmed). President Madison fled to the Virginia suburbs. Upon returning, the president took up temporary residence in the Octagon (now the Octagon Museum), the home of Colonel John Taylor, where he ratified the Treaty of Ghent, which ended the war. He remained there until the refurbishing of the White House was complete.

Although the British were expelled and the city rebuilt, Washington was slow to recover. A congressional initiative to abandon the dispirited capital was lost by just nine votes.

The miniseries *John Adams* (2008) is a riveting story, told from all sides, of the years when the American Revolution hung in the balance and fate could have swung either way.

SLAVERY IN THE FEDERAL CITY

When Congress first convened in Washington in 1800, the city had about 14,000 residents. It was even then a heavily African American populated town: slaves and free blacks composed 29% of the population. Free blacks lived in the port of Georgetown, where a vibrant African American community emerged. They worked alongside and socialized with the city's slaves.

Since its introduction in Jamestown colony in 1619, slave labor had become an essential part of the regional tobacco economy. In 1800, more than half of the nation's 700,000 slaves lived in Maryland and Virginia. The capital of America's slave trade at that time, Washington, DC, contained slave markets and holding pens.

The city's slave population steadily declined throughout the 19th century, while the number of free blacks rose. They migrated to the city, establishing their own churches and schools.

Washington, DC, became a front line in the intensifying conflict between the North and South over slavery. The city was a strategic stop on the clandestine Underground Railroad, shuttling fugitive slaves to freedom in the northern states. The abolitionist movement fueled further racial tensions. In 1835, the Snow Riots erupted as white mobs set loose on black Washingtonians. When the rampage subsided, legislation was passed restricting the economic rights of the city's free blacks. At last, Congress outlawed the slave trade in Washington in 1850; the District Emancipation Act abolished slavery outright in 1862.

THE CIVIL WAR & ITS AFTERMATH

The 1860 election of Abraham Lincoln meant that the office of president would no longer protect Southern interests in the increasingly irreconcilable rift over slavery. Rather than abide by the electoral

1865

Five days after the Confederate surrender, Lincoln is shot in the head by the well-known actor John Wilkes Booth in Washington's Ford's Theatre. He dies hours later.

GREG GAWLOWSKI / LONELY PLANET IMAGES ©

Ford's Theatre (p155)

1865

Andrew Johnson takes office and does little to help newly freed blacks. For violating the Tenure of Office Act, he is impeached and narrowly avoids being removed from office in 1868.

1865–67

After the war, Congress establishes the Freedman's Bureau to help former slaves transition to free society. In 1867, Howard University, the nation's first African American university, is founded.

FROM SLAVE TO STATESMAN: FREDERICK DOUGLASS

Born Frederick Augustus Washington Bailey in 1818 on a slave plantation along Maryland's Eastern Shore, Frederick Douglass is remembered as one of the country's most influential and outstanding black 19th-century leaders.

In 1838, at 20 years old, he escaped wretched treatment at the hands of Maryland planters and established himself as a freeman in New Bedford, Massachusetts, eventually working for abolitionist William Lloyd Garrison's antislavery paper, the *Liberator*. His years as a slave had led Douglass to a profound personal truth: 'Men are whipped oftenist who are whipped easiest.' After his escape, he took his new last name from a character in the Sir Walter Scott book, *The Lady of the Lake*. Largely self-educated, Douglass had a natural gift for eloquence. In 1841, he won the admiration of New England abolitionists with an impromptu speech at an antislavery convention, introducing himself as 'a recent graduate from the institution of slavery,' with his 'diploma' (ie whip marks on his back).

Douglass' effectiveness so angered proslavery forces that his supporters urged him to flee to England to escape seizure and punishment under the Fugitive Slave Law. He followed their advice and kept lecturing in England until admirers contributed enough money ($710.96) to enable him to purchase his freedom and return home in 1847.

Douglass then became the self-proclaimed 'station master and conductor' of the Underground Railroad in Rochester, New York, working with other famed abolitionists like Harriet Tubman and John Brown. In 1860, Douglass campaigned for Abraham Lincoln, and when the Civil War broke out, helped raise two regiments of black soldiers – the Massachusetts 54th and 55th – to fight for the Union.

After the war, Douglass went to Washington to lend his support to the 13th, 14th and 15th Constitutional Amendments, which abolished slavery, granted citizenship to former slaves and guaranteed citizens the right to vote.

In 1895, Douglass died at his Anacostia home, Cedar Hill, now the Frederick Douglass National Historic Site.

outcome, Southern secessionists opted to exit the Union, igniting a horrific four-year war that would leave over half a million dead. Washington was a prized target and the front lines of fighting often came quite near the capital. Indeed when the war began, city residents (including Lincoln) remained fearful of a siege from the Confederates, whose campfires were visible just across the Potomac in Virginia. Had Maryland joined the Confederate side – and it very nearly did – the capital would have been completely isolated from the North, with disastrous results for the city and country. A ring of earthwork forts was hastily erected, but Washington saw only one battle on its soil: Confederate General Jubal Early's unsuccessful attack on Fort Stevens

1870–80

The city doubles in size during the postwar boom. Board of Public Works Alexander 'Boss' Shepherd helps modernize the city with paved streets, sewers, gaslights and parks.

1901

The McMillan Commission revives L'Enfant's original design for the rapidly growing capital, beautifying the Mall and solidifying the grandeur of Washington.

1907

The grand beaux arts–style Union Station opens and serves as a key terminus between north and south (with 200,000 passengers a day). Today it receives over 32 million visitors annually.

1913

President Woodrow Wilson institutes a policy of segregation in federal offices (including lunchrooms and bathrooms) for the first time since 1863. Segregation continues through the 1950s.

in northern DC, in July 1864. Nevertheless, Washingtonians lived in constant anxiety, as bloody battles raged nearby at Antietam, Gettysburg and Manassas.

As the war raged on, soldiers, volunteers, civil servants and ex-slaves flooded into the capital. Within three months of the first shots fired at Fort Sumter, over 50,000 enlistees descended on the capital to join the Union Army. Throughout the war, Washington would serve as an important rearguard position for troop encampments and supply operations. Among those who spent time here were local resident Matthew Brady, whose compelling photographs provide a vivid document of the war. Poet Walt Whitman was also a Washington resident then, volunteering at a makeshift hospital in the converted Patent Office – today the National Portrait Gallery; his poem 'The Wound Dresser' is based on his experiences tending the injured and dying. This building, incidentally, also hosted President Lincoln's inauguration ball, after his re-election in 1865.

Lincoln's second term would be short-lived. One month later – and five days after Confederate General Robert E Lee surrendered to Union General Ulysses S Grant at Appomattox – Lincoln was assassinated by John Wilkes Booth in downtown Washington at Ford's Theatre.

The Civil War had a lasting impact on the city. The war strengthened the power of the federal government, marking the first efforts to conscript young men into military service and to collect income tax from private households. Warfare brought new bureaucracies, workers and buildings to the capital. Between the war's start and end, the city's population nearly doubled to more than 130,000. One of the largest influxes of newcomers was freed blacks.

Vice-president Andrew Johnson, a southerner from Tennessee, assumed the presidency following Lincoln's death, but did little to help the freed African Americans; he even vetoed the first Civil Rights bill. Congress, however, did attempt to help blacks make the transition to free society, and in 1867 Howard University, the nation's first African American institute of higher learning, was founded. By this time, blacks composed nearly a quarter of the population.

Washington's economy was bolstered by a postwar boom. Although in some ways a Southern city, Washington was already part of the commercial networks of the north. The B&O Railroad connected the city via Baltimore to the industry of the northeast; while the Chesapeake and Ohio Canal opened a waterway to the agriculture of the Midwest. In 1871, President Ulysses S Grant appointed a Board of Public Works to upgrade the urban infrastructure and improve living conditions. The board was led by Alexander Shepherd, who energetically took on

Civil War Onscreen

Civil War (documentary; Ken Burns)

Glory (Edward Zwick)

Gods & Generals (Ronald Maxwell)

Gettysburg (Ronald Maxwell)

Gone With the Wind (Victor Fleming)

1916–19

WWI attracts thousands of people to Washington for the administration of the war. By war's end, the city's population is over half a million.

1919

Following the armistice, decommissioned soldiers and civilians look for work, and racial tensions lead to race riots in Washington and dozens of other cities.

1920

The 19th Amendment to the Constitution grants women the right to vote. Early activists such as Susan B Anthony (1820–1906) are instrumental in its success.

1920s

The '20s see an African American cultural boom, led by Ella Fitzgerald and native son Duke Ellington; U St becomes known as the Great Black Way.

the assignment. He paved streets, put in sewers, installed gaslights, planted trees, filled in swamps and carved out parklands. But he also ran over budget by some $20 million and was sacked by Congress, who reclaimed responsibility for city affairs. 'Boss' Shepherd was the closest thing that DC would have to self-government for 100 years.

TRAGEDY AT FORD'S THEATRE

In 1865, just days after the Confederate Army surrendered, one of the most beloved figures in America – at least the northern part – was gunned down in cold blood. Abraham Lincoln was dead.

John Wilkes Booth – Marylander, famous actor and diehard believer in the Confederate cause – had long harbored ambitions to bring the US leadership to its knees. A plot to kidnap the president the year prior had failed. Then, on April 14, Booth learned while stopping by Ford's Theatre to retrieve his mail that the president would be attending a play that evening. He knew it was time to strike. He met with his co-conspirators later that day, and hatched a plan: Lewis Powell would kill Secretary of State William Seward at his home, while George Atzerodt killed Vice President Andrew Johnson at his residence and Booth struck Lincoln and Grant – all would happen simultaneously around 10pm. As it turns out, only Booth would succeed in his mission.

Booth, who was well known in the theater, was questioned by no one as he strolled up to Lincoln's box. He crept inside and quietly barricaded the outer door behind him (Lincoln's bodyguard had apparently headed to a nearby pub at intermission and never returned). Booth knew the play well, and waited to act until he heard the funniest line of the play – '... you sockdologizing old man-trap!' As the audience predictably erupted in laughter, Booth crept behind Lincoln and shot him in the head. The president's lifeless body slumped forward as Mary Lincoln screamed and Major Henry Rathbone, also in Lincoln's box, sprang up and tried to seize the assassin. Booth stabbed him then leaped onto the stage. His foot, however, became entangled in the flag decorating the box, and he landed badly, fracturing his leg. He stumbled to his feet and held the bloody dagger aloft, saying '*Sic semper tyrannis!*' ('Thus to all tyrants!'), which was (and remains) Virginia's state motto. Booth fled the theater, mounted his waiting horse and galloped off to meet his co-conspirators.

Lincoln never regained consciousness. He was carried across the street to the Petersen House, where he died early the next morning. In a massive manhunt, Booth was hunted down and shot to death less than two weeks later; his alleged co-conspirators, including Mary Surratt, who some claim was innocent, were also discovered, brought to trial and executed on July 7.

The aftermath was devastating for the country. Millions gathered to see the slow funeral procession that carried the president's body from Washington to New York and back to Springfield, Illinois, where he was buried.

1922

The city experiences its worst natural disaster: heavy snowfall – 18 inches – causes the collapse of the roof of the Knickerbocker Theatre, killing nearly 100 people inside.

1931

The Great Depression devastates the country. In 1931, Hunger Marchers protest in the capital followed by encampments of 20,000 jobless WWI vets known as the Bonus Army.

1932–35

Roosevelt is elected president. His New Deal programs put people to work, and Washington sees a host of construction projects, including the National Archives and the Supreme Court.

Statue, Roosevelt Memorial (p94)

TURN OF THE AMERICAN CENTURY

In 1900, Senator James McMillan of Michigan formed an all-star city-planning commission to makeover the capital, whose population now surpassed a quarter-million. The McMillan plan effectively revived L'Enfant's vision of a resplendent capital on par with Europe's best cities. The plan proposed grand public buildings in the beaux-arts style (see p278), which reconnected the city to its neoclassical republican roots, but with an eclectic flair. It was impressive, orderly and upper class. The plan entailed an extensive beautification project. It removed the scrubby trees and coal-fired locomotives that belched black smoke from the National Mall, and created the expansive lawn and reflecting pools that exist today.

The Mall became a showcase of the symbols of American ambition and power: monumental tributes to the founding fathers; the enshrinement of the Declaration of Independence and Constitution in a Greek-style temple; and the majestic Memorial Bridge leading to Arlington National Cemetery. Washington had become the nation's civic center, infused with the spirit of history, heroes and myths. The imagery was embraced by the country's budding political class.

The plan improved living conditions for middle-class public servants and professionals. New 'suburbs,' such as Woodley Park and Mt Pleasant, offered better-off residents a respite from the hot inner city, and electric trolleys crisscrossed the streets. However, the daily life of many Washingtonians was less promising. Slums like Murder Bay and Swamppoodle stood near government buildings, and about 20,000 impoverished blacks still dwelled in dirty alleyways.

History Websites

Library of Congress (www.loc.gov)

National Archives (www.archives.gov)

PBS (www.pbs.org/topics/history)

Civil Rights Special Collection (www.teachersdomain.org/special/civil)

Americans at War (http://americanhistory.si.edu/militaryhistory)

A WORLD & A CITY AT WAR

Two world wars and one Great Depression changed forever the place of Washington in American society. These events hastened a concentration of power in the federal government in general and the executive branch in particular. National security and social welfare became the high-growth sectors of public administration. City life transformed from Southern quaintness into cosmopolitan clamor.

WWI witnessed a surge of immigration. The administration of war had an unquenchable thirst for clerks, soldiers, nurses and other military support staff. By war's end, the city's population was over half a million.

The 1920s brought prosperity to Washington and other parts of the country, but the free-spending days wouldn't last. The stock market crash of 1929 heralded the dawn of the Great Depression, the severe economic downturn that had catastrophic implications for many Americans. As more and more lost their jobs and went hungry, people turned

1941–44

The expanding federal government and its wartime bureaucracy lead to another population boom. More big projects are bankrolled, including construction of the Pentagon.

1954

The Supreme Court rules that segregation in public schools is 'inherently unequal' and orders desegregation. The fight to integrate schools spurs the Civil Rights movement.

1961

The states ratify an amendment to the Constitution that allows DC residents to participate (with three Electoral College votes) in presidential elections.

1963

Martin Luther King Jr leads the Civil Rights march on the National Mall. He delivers his 'I Have a Dream' speech at Lincoln Memorial before a crowd of 200,000.

to Washington for help. Thousands gathered in Hunger Marches on Washington in 1931 and 1932; they were followed by some 40,000 protesters who set up makeshift camps throughout the city, waiting for Congress to award them cash payment for service certificates issued in bonds – they became known as the Bonus Army. President Hoover ordered the US Army to evacuate them, and the troops attacked their encampments, killing several and wounding hundreds of others.

Franklin Roosevelt's New Deal extended the reach of the federal government. Federal regulators acquired greater power to intervene in business and financial affairs. Dozens of relief agencies were created to administer the social guarantees of the nascent welfare state. In Washington, New Deal work projects included tree planting on the Mall and the construction of public buildings, notably the massive National Archives and the Supreme Court.

The Great Depression didn't really end until the arrival of WWII, when Washington again experienced enormous growth. A burgeoning organizational infrastructure supported the new national security state. The US Army's city-based civilian employee roll grew from 7000 to 41,000 in the first year of the war. The world's largest office building, the Pentagon, was built across the river as the command headquarters. National Airport (today Reagan National) opened in 1941.

SUFFRAGETTES

Iron Jawed Angels (2005), starring Hilary Swank, is a moving docudrama about the struggles of early-20th-century suffragettes facing down the political establishment of Washington, with key events unfolding against the backdrop of Woodrow Wilson's presidency.

COLD WAR

The Cold War defined much of US foreign – and to some degree, domestic – policy in the decades following WWII. The USA's battle with the USSR was not fought face to face, but through countries including Korea, Vietnam, Cambodia, Mozambique and Afghanistan – all pawns in a geopolitical, economic and ideological battle. Red fever swept the US, as Washington organized witch hunts, like those investigated by HUAC (the House Committee on Un-American Activities), which aimed to blacklist communist subversives.

The Cuban Missile Crisis, which took place over 12 days in October 1962, brought the US and the Soviet Union perilously close to nuclear war, and some historians believe that without the effective diplomacy of John F Kennedy and Secretary of State Robert McNamara, the nation would have gone to battle.

During the Cold War, many covert battles were waged on foreign soil. Perhaps the most famous was the Iran-Contra affair in the 1980s, during Ronald Reagan's tenure as president. Staff in his administration, along with the CIA, secretly and illegally sold arms to Iran and then

1968

King is assassinated in Memphis; Washington and other cities erupt in violence. Twelve people are killed in the ensuing riots, with small businesses torched.

1969–71

As the war in Vietnam claims thousands of American lives, many citizens come to Washington to protest. Over 500,000 march in 1969, followed by many more in 1970 and 1971.

1974

Five burglars working for President Nixon are arrested breaking into the Democratic campaign headquarters at the Watergate Hotel. The ensuing brouhaha and investigation leads to Nixon's resignation.

1975

Following the Home Rule Act passed in 1973, disenfranchised Washingtonians are finally given the right to effectively govern themselves. Voters elect Walter Washington.

ESPIONAGE: A CAPITAL GAME

Near the hallowed halls of power, Washington, DC, has long played a role in the subterfuge world of intelligence operations. A few of the darker moments in cloak-and-dagger diplomacy:

On September 21, 1976, the Chilean diplomat Orlando Letelier and his American colleague Ronni Karpen Moffitt were killed by a car bombing in Sheridan Circle. Letelier served as the US ambassador appointed by President Salvador Allende before he was overthrown by General Augusto Pinochet. Several men were convicted for playing a role in the assassination, including the American Michael Townley, a former CIA operative, and Manuel Contreras, Chilean Secret Police Chief – both of whom implicated Pinochet for the role in the killing. Pinochet, who died in 2006, was never brought to justice for the assassination.

In the 1980s, the FBI and the NSA constructed a tunnel under the Russian embassy – right under their decoding room – on Wisconsin Ave. US operatives were never able to successfully eavesdrop, however, owing to a betrayal to the Soviets by FBI agent Robert Hanssen. The embassy incidentally, is where Vitaly Yurchenko, a former high-ranking KGB operative-turned CIA informant, re-defected after giving his CIA handlers the slip in a Georgetown restaurant. The KGB allegedly interrogated Yurchenko after his return, while he was under the influence of a truth serum, to ensure his return was not a CIA ploy.

Some historians suggest that Yurchenko's re-defection was really just a cover to protect one of the USSR's most important CIA informants. Aldrich Ames, a counterintelligence analyst in DC, began supplying secrets to the Soviets in 1985, and continued on a grand scale for some nine years. His betrayal led to the execution of at least 10 Soviet agents spying for the US and compromised scores of operations. In return the Soviets paid him over $4 million. The CIA slowly realized there was a mole in their organization and it took years before Ames was discovered – in part because he fooled several polygraph tests (although the $540,000 Arlington home purchased in cash was a slight tip-off). Ames, who narrowly avoided the death penalty, is serving a life sentence in a Pennsylvania penitentiary.

used the proceeds to finance the Contras, an anti-communist guerilla army in Nicaragua.

The Cold War furthered the concentration of political power in Washington-based bureaucracies, a trend that continued in the 1980s.

SEGREGATION & THE CIVIL RIGHTS MOVEMENT

In the early 20th century, Washington adopted racial segregation policies, like those of the South. Its business establishments and public

1976

Metrorail opens to serve the growing suburban community. Despite intense lobbying by the automobile industry, several freeway projects through the city are never realized.

1970s–'80s

Washington, like other American cities, enters a period of urban blight. Its population is falling as increased crime rates and social decay drive many residents out into the suburbs.

1981

Reagan survives an assassination attempt outside the Washington Hilton. The attack permanently disables press secretary James Brady, who becomes a leading advocate for gun control.

1990

In 1990, Mayor Marion Barry is arrested after being videotaped smoking crack. His arrest angers supporters, who decry the FBI 'entrapment.' Barry serves six months in prison.

spaces became, in practice if not in law, 'whites only.' The 'progressive' Woodrow Wilson administration reinforced discrimination by refusing to hire black federal employees and insisting on segregated government offices.

The Fifties (1993), by David Halberstam, explores an almost schizophrenic era: TV, civil rights, McCarthyism, Elvis Presley, suburbia and more coalesced into the decade that spawned modern America.

Following WWI, decommissioned soldiers returned en masse from the front, bringing to a head festering racial tensions in society. In the steamy summer of 1919, the tinderbox ignited when a white mob marched through the streets attacking at random black residents with bricks, pipes and, later, guns. In the following two days, whites and blacks alike mobilized and the violence escalated. President Wilson called in 2000 troops to put an end to the chaos, but by then nine people had been killed (dozens more would die from their wounds) and hundreds injured. It was but a foreshadowing for more chronic race riots in the future.

In response, organized hate groups tried, without much success, to organize in the capital. In 1925, the Ku Klux Klan marched on the Mall. Nonetheless, Washington was a black cultural capital in the early 20th century. Shaw and LeDroit Park, near Howard University, sheltered a lively black-owned business district, and black theater and music flourished along U St NW, which became known as the Great Black Way – Washington's own version of the Harlem Renaissance. Southern blacks continued to move to the city in search of better economic opportunities. Citywide segregation eased somewhat with the New Deal (which brought new black federal workers to the capital) and WWII (which brought lots more).

Civil Rights on Film

- *King* (Sidney Lumet)
- *Mississippi Burning* (Alan Parker)
- *Ghosts of Mississippi* (Rob Reiner)
- *Black Like Me* (Carl Lerner)
- *Long Walk Home* (Richard Pearce)
- *The Help* (Tate Taylor)

In 1939, the DC-based Daughters of the American Revolution barred the black contralto Marian Anderson from singing at Constitution Hall. At Eleanor Roosevelt's insistence, Anderson instead sang at the Lincoln Memorial before an audience of 200,000. That was the beginning of the growing movement toward equality – though the process would be long with demonstrations, sit-ins, boycotts and lawsuits.

Parks and recreational facilities were legally desegregated in 1954; schools followed soon thereafter. President John F Kennedy appointed the city's first black federal commissioner in 1961. The Home Rule Act was approved in 1973, giving the city some autonomy from its federal overseers. The 1974 popular election of Walter Washington brought the first black mayor to office. The capital became one of the most prominent African American–governed cities in the country.

Washington hosted key events in the national Civil Rights movement. In 1963, Reverend Martin Luther King Jr led the March on Washington to lobby for passage of the Civil Rights Act. His stirring 'I Have a Dream' speech, delivered before 200,000 people on the steps of the Lincoln

1992–94

Despite serving a prison term, Marion Barry quickly rejoins Washington political life; he is elected to the city council in 1992, then re-elected as mayor (his fourth term) in 1994.

1998

The Monica Lewinsky scandal breaks, with evidence of nine sexual encounters with the president. Bill Clinton becomes the first president since Andrew Johnson (in 1868) to be impeached.

1999

Barry's fourth term ends following a budgetary crisis inherited from his predecessor. A new Republican-controlled Congress overrules many of the mayor's fiscal decisions.

1999–2007

Washingtonians elect the sober, less-controversial Anthony Williams as the city's fourth mayor. During his two terms he helps restore the city's finances.

Memorial, was a defining moment of the campaign. The assassination of King in Memphis in 1968 sent the nation reeling. Race riots erupted in DC – and in over 100 other American cities. The city exploded in two nights of riots and arson (centered on 14th and U Sts NW in the Shaw district). Twelve people died, over 1000 were injured, and hundreds of mostly black-owned businesses were torched. White residents fled the city en masse, and downtown Washington north of the Mall (especially the Shaw district) faded into decades of economic slump.

The legacy of segregation proved difficult to overcome. For the next quarter-century, white and black Washington grew further apart. By 1970, the city center's population declined to 750,000, while the wealthier suburbs boomed to nearly three million. When the sleek, federally funded Metrorail system opened in 1976, it bypassed the poorer black neighborhoods in favor of linking downtown with the largely white suburbs.

In *The Souls of Black Folk* (1903), WEB Du Bois, who helped found the National Association for the Advancement of Colored People (NAACP), eloquently describes the racial dilemmas of politics and culture facing early-20th-century America.

DECAY & DECLINE

President Lyndon Johnson, until then lauded for his ambitious civil rights and social programs, sank his reputation on the disastrous war in Vietnam, which the US had entered in the 1950s. Towards the end of the 1960s hundreds of thousands of Americans had participated in protests against the continuing conflict.

The political upheaval that began in the 1960s continued unchecked into the next decade. The year 1970 marked the first time DC was granted a nonvoting delegate to the House of Representatives. Three years later the Home Rule Act paved the way for the District's first mayoral election in more than a century.

These were two rare positives in an otherwise gloomy decade. The city's most famous scandal splashed across the world's newspapers when operatives of President Richard Nixon were arrested breaking into the Democratic National Committee campaign headquarters at the Watergate Hotel. The ensuing cover-up and Nixon's disgraceful exit was not a shining moment in presidential history.

Meanwhile, life on the streets was no more glorious, as neighborhoods continued to decay; crack-cocaine hit District streets with a vengeance and housing projects turned into war zones. By the late 1980s, DC had earned the tagline of 'Murder Capital of America.' In truth, urban blight was hitting most American cities.

Jimmy Carter became president in 1977. A 'malaise' marked his tenure. Gas prices, unemployment and inflation all climbed to all-time highs. The taking of American hostages in Iran in 1979, and his perceived bungling of their release, effectively ended his political career. In

2000

Washington's real-estate boom is under way, with gentrification transforming formerly black neighborhoods. George W Bush is elected president in a much-disputed election.

2001

Hijacked planes destroy the World Trade Center in New York and crash into the Pentagon. A fourth plane, presumed intended for the capital or the White House, crashes in Pennsylvania.

2001

Less than a month after September 11, US armed forces invade Afghanistan. The stated aim of capturing Osama Bin Laden fails, and the war continues for over a decade.

2002–03

In the run-up to the Iraq invasion, mass protests against the planned war are held in Washington and other cities. An estimated 30 million protestors take part.

November 1980, Ronald Reagan, a former actor and California governor, was elected president.

Reagan, who was ideologically opposed to big government, nevertheless presided over enormous growth of bureaucratic Washington, particularly in the military-industrial complex.

Local politics entered an unusual period when Marion Barry, a veteran of the Civil Rights movement, was elected mayor in 1978. Combative and charismatic, he became a racially polarizing figure in the city. On January 18, 1990, Barry and companion, ex-model Hazel 'Rasheeda' Moore, were arrested in a narcotics sting at the Vista Hotel. The FBI and DC police arrested the mayor for crack-cocaine possession.

When Barry emerged from jail, his supporters, believing he'd been framed, re-elected him to a fourth and lackluster term. As city revenues fell under his term, Congress lost patience and seized control of the city, ending yet another episode in Home Rule.

2000 ELECTION

The film *Recount* (2008) dramatizes the events of the hotly contested 2000 US presidential election, including the issues surrounding voter fraud and disenfranchisement in Florida.

TWENTY-FIRST CENTURY

The 2000 presidential election went off with a history-making glitch. On election night, November 7, the media prematurely declared the winner twice, based on exit-poll speculations, before finally concluding that the Florida race outcome was too close to call. It would eventually take a month before the election was officially certified. Numerous court challenges and recounts proceeded, and the Supreme Court eventually intervened, declaring Bush the winner.

Bush's presidency unfolded during the nation's worst terrorist attacks. On September 11, 2001, 30 minutes after the attack on New York's World Trade Center, a plane departing Washington Dulles International Airport was hijacked and crashed into the Pentagon's west side, penetrating the building's third ring. Sixty-six passengers and crew, as well as 125 Pentagon personnel, were killed in the suicide attack.

In the wake of the attack, prominent media and political figures received lethal doses of anthrax in the mail. Several congressional staffers were infected and two DC postal workers died. Though unsolved, the anthrax mailings were eventually attributed to a domestic source.

Meanwhile President Bush's tenure in office was marred by controversy on many fronts. The war in Iraq – launched in 2003 to seize Iraq's (nonexistent) stockpiles of weapons of mass destruction – continued until the end of his second term, and sent the government deeply into debt. Bush was also criticized for the bungling of Federal relief efforts to victims of Hurricane Katrina, which devastated New Orleans in 2005.

2003

The Bush administration oversees a full-scale invasion of Iraq. The resulting war claims the lives of over 100,000 Iraqis and 4400 Americans.

2005

As Montréal weeps, Washington receives a new professional baseball team, the Washington Nationals (and former Expos). They eventually move into a custom-built stadium in 2008.

DENNIS JOHNSON / LONELY PLANET IMAGES ©

Baseball, Nationals Park (p137)

2005

President George W Bush is sworn in to his second term. His inaugural address emphasizes the spread of freedom and democracy.

The 2008 election featured one of the most hotly debated presidential contests in American history. In the end, Barack Obama became the nation's first African American president. Obama had run on a platform of hope and change in an era of increasingly divisive American politics. Following the financial meltdown in 2008, the Obama administration pumped money into the flailing economy. He also took on the growing crisis in Afghanistan, although his biggest challenge – an issue that some analysts say he's staked his presidency on – is the complicated issue of health-care reform.

As Obama went into the election of 2012, he continued weathering attacks from both liberals and conservatives: 'too much big-government spending' according to some Republicans, 'too much compromising to Republicans' according to some Democrats.

2008–09

Barack Obama becomes the first African American president. An estimated 1.8 million people attend his inauguration.

2008–09

The stock market crashes due to catastrophic mismanagement by major American financial institutions. The crisis spreads worldwide.

2011

In a surprise address, President Obama describes the covert raid in Pakistan that led to the death of Osama Bin Laden, ending a 10-year manhunt.

2011

The Martin Luther King Jr Memorial opens on the Tidal Basin. It's the first memorial in the mall area dedicated to a non-president and to an African American.

Arts & Media

Washington is the showcase of American arts, home to such prestigious venues as the National Theatre, the Kennedy Center and the Folger Shakespeare Theatre. The capital stages world-class performances, as well as edgier fare at smaller, more experimental venues. Loads of jewel box–sized art galleries and community theaters around the city contribute to the vibrant scene.

MUSIC

Only in the capital can national orchestras coexist with rebellious punk, all under the rubric of the local music scene. That military marches and soulful go-go both reached their peaks under the watchful eye (and attentive ear) of DC fans is tribute to the city's eclectic musical landscape.

In the early 20th century, segregation of entertainment venues meant that black Washington had to create its own arts scene. Jazz, big band and swing flourished at clubs and theaters around DC, particularly in the Shaw district. Greats such as Duke Ellington, Pearl Bailey, Shirley Horn, Johnny Hodges and Ben Webster all got their start in the clubs of U St NW. Today, this district has been reborn, with new clubs and theaters open in its historic buildings. After years of neglect, the renowned Bohemian Caverns reopened in 2000, and today hosts local soul-jazz music. Other venues in the area – such as the Black Cat and the 9:30 Club – have become mainstays of DC rock, blues and hip hop.

Washington Playlist

- *'Banned in DC' (Bad Brains)*
- *'Chocolate City' (Parliament)*
- *'Idiot Wind' (Bob Dylan)*
- *'I'm Just a Bill' (School House Rock)*
- *'Rock Creek Park' (The Blackbyrds)*

The scene at these venues is varied, but not unique to DC. The exception is where it builds on its local roots in go-go and punk. Go-go, which stomped into the city in the 1970s, is an infectiously rhythmic dance music combining elements of funk, rap, soul and Latin percussion. These days, go-go soul blends with hip-hop and reggae's rhythm. Clubs playing 1980s dance, and lounges with mellow house and trance, are equally popular.

DC's hardcore take on punk, embodied by such bands as Fugazi and Dag Nasty, combined super-fast guitar with a socially conscious mindset and flourished at venues in the 1990s. Arlington-based Dischord Records grew out of the punk scene and remains a fierce promoter of local bands. While punk is no longer the musical force it once was, its influence on grunge and other modern genres is undeniable.

Showing off its southern roots, DC has spawned some folk and country stars of its own, too, including Emmylou Harris, Mary Chapin Carpenter and John Fahey (who named his seminal folk record label, Takoma, for Takoma Park, his boyhood home).

The immensely talented Marvin Gaye was born in Washington and delved into music early on, singing in a church choir and performing with local groups before his discovery in a DC nightclub by Bo Diddley when he was 19. He later signed on with Motown records and created some of the unsurpassed hits of the 1960s and '70s, including 'What's Going On?,' 'Let's Get It On' and 'Sexual Healing'. His tumultuous life led him into troubles with drugs and the IRS (he lived in Belgium for a time), and in and out of marriages. During an argument following his return home, he was shot and killed by his father one day before his 45th birthday on April 1, 1984.

Popular African American R&B and soul artist Roberta Flack was raised in Arlington, VA. Before establishing her music career, she was the first black student teacher in an all-white school in posh Chevy Chase, MD. She was discovered at a respected Capitol Hill jazz club, Mr Henry's, where the owners eventually constructed an elaborate stage for her.

PERFORMING ARTS

The capital's most visible musicians are those from weighty cultural landmarks such as the National Symphony Orchestra and the Washington Opera. Repertoire and productions tend to lean toward the traditional, but are exquisitely performed. Former director Placido Domingo occasionally takes the stage, as does diva Denyce Graves, graduate of the local Duke Ellington School of the Arts.

A national orchestra of sorts is the Marine Corps Marching Band, based at the Marine Barracks in Southeast DC. Back in the late 19th century, military marching-band music reached its apotheosis (such as it was) in the work of John Philip Sousa, who directed the Marine Corps Marching Band for many years (and was born and is buried nearby). In this era of amped-up patriotism, this genre remains alive and well: the band still performs his work today.

For a look at the Washington punk scene of the 1970s and '80s, check out *Banned in DC*, a colorful photo book by Cynthia Connolly.

THEATER & COMEDY

Political comedy and theater are regular fixtures of the DC arts scene. Ford's Theatre – site of Lincoln's assassination – holds its place in time by presenting traditional, Americana-themed productions. For comedy,

THE DUKE

'My road runs from Ward's Place to my grandmother's at Twentieth and R, to Seatan Street, around to 8th Street, back up to T Street, through LeDroit Park to Sherman Avenue,' wrote DC's most famous musical son, jazz immortal Edward Kennedy 'Duke' Ellington (1899–1974), describing his childhood in Washington's Shaw district. In the segregated DC of the early 20th century, Shaw hosted one of the country's finest black arts scenes – drawing famed actors, musicians and singers to perform at venues such as the Howard Theatre and Bohemian Caverns – so the Duke took root in rich soil.

As a tot, Ellington purportedly first tackled the keyboard under the tutelage of a teacher by the name of Mrs Clinkscales. He honed his chops by listening to local ragtime pianists such as Doc Perry, Louis Thomas and Louis Brown at Frank Holliday's T St poolroom. His first composition, written at 16, was the 'Soda Fountain Rag'; next came 'What You Gonna Do When the Bed Breaks Down?' The handsome, suave young Duke played hops and cabarets all over black Washington before decamping to New York in 1923.

There, Ellington started out as a Harlem stride pianist, performing at Barron's and the Hollywood Club, but he soon moved to the famed Cotton Club, where he matured into an innovative bandleader, composer and arranger. He collaborated with innumerable artists, including Louis Armstrong and Ella Fitzgerald, but his most celebrated collaboration was with composer-arranger Billy Strayhorn, who gave the Ellington Orchestra its theme, 'Take the "A" Train,' in 1941.

Ellington's big-band compositions, with their infectious melodies, harmonic sophistication and ever-present swing, made him one of the 20th century's most revered American composers. His huge volume of work – more than 1500 pieces – is preserved in its entirety at the Smithsonian Institution in his old hometown.

For more on the Duke, check out his witty memoir *Music Is My Mistress*, which details his DC childhood and later accomplishments.

the Capitol Steps ('we put the mock in democracy') are kings, performing most Friday and Saturday nights at the Ronald Reagan Building. Living and working in the nation's capital provides an endless source of material for this comedy troupe's satirical pieces: the White House and Capitol Hill are favorite targets.

Most Broadway shows eventually find their way to the National Theatre or the Kennedy Center. The Arena Stage, home to one of the country's oldest troupes, was the first theater outside of New York to win a Tony and continues to stage diverse productions by new playwrights. Over the course of 25 years, smaller companies such as Studio Theatre have established a strong presence. For almost as long, the Source Theatre has hosted the Source Festival, a platform for new plays, workshops and the insanely popular 10-Minute Play competition in June. The Folger Shakespeare Library & Theatre gives new perspective to the Bard.

CINEMA & TV

Film fans who want the lowdown on every movie ever shot in DC should read *DC Goes to the Movies* by Jean K Rosales and Michael R Jobe.

Hollywood directors can't resist the black limousines, white marble, counterintelligence subterfuges and political scandal that official Washington embodies.

One of Hollywood's favorite Washington themes involves the political naïf who stumbles into combat with corrupt capital veterans. Such is the story of the Frank Capra film *Mr Smith Goes to Washington,* in which Jimmy Stewart and his troop of 'Boy Rangers' defeat big, bad government and preserve democracy for the rest of the country. This theme reappears in the 1950 hit *Born Yesterday,* as well as in *Dave, Legally Blonde 2* and *Being There.*

Another popular theme for DC-based cinema is the total destruction of the nation's capital by aliens (perhaps wishful thinking on the part of certain segments of the population). Along these lines, *2012, Independence, The Day the Earth Stood Still,* the spoof *Mars Attacks!* and the Cold War–era *Earth Vs the Flying Saucers* all feature DC on the edge of destruction.

Not surprisingly, DC is a popular setting for political thrillers: *In the Line of Fire* (Clint Eastwood as a savvy Secret Service agent protecting the president), *Patriot Games* (Harrison Ford as a tough CIA agent battling Irish terrorists) and *No Way Out* (Kevin Costner as a Navy officer out-racing Russian spies) are entertaining stories set against – sometimes erroneously placed – DC landmarks.

Must-See DC Cinema

- *Mr Smith Goes to Washington*
- *All the President's Men*
- *The Exorcist*
- *Good Night, and Good Luck*
- *Being There*

The finest satire of the Cold War is probably Stanley Kubrick's 1964 *Dr Strangelove.* Set inside the Pentagon, the plot revolves around a power-mad general who brings the world to the brink of annihilation because he fears a communist takeover of his 'precious bodily fluids.'

Real-life intrigue has been the subject of a handful of DC films, including the 1976 *All the President's Men,* which is based on Carl Bernstein's and Bob Woodward's firsthand account of exposing the Watergate scandal (Robert Redford and Dustin Hoffman play the reporters).

In 2005, George Clooney directed and starred in *Good Night, and Good Luck.* Shot in black and white, it is a stark account of how CBS reporter Edward R Murrow and his producer Fred W Friendly took on the widely feared red-baiting American senator Joseph McCarthy.

Curiously, films featuring a character in the form of a US president typically depict him with absurd idealism: *Air Force One, The American President* and *Thirteen Days* are all rather fanciful portraits of a good, if not downright heroic, Chief Executive. Variations on the theme include *Primary Colors,* a barely disguised account of Clinton en route to the White House, and the parody *Wag the Dog,* a story of a presidential advisor (Robert De Niro) who hires a Hollywood producer (Dustin

Hoffman) to 'produce' a war in order to distract voters from an unfolding sex scandal. Bizarrely, the film was released just a month before the Clinton-Lewinsky affair became headline news.

Only a select few films set in Washington, DC, are not about politics, espionage or cataclysmic destruction. The horrific highlight is undoubtedly *The Exorcist,* the cult horror flick set in Georgetown. The creepy long staircase in the movie – descending from Prospect St to M St in reality – has become known as the Exorcist Stairs. Another classic Georgetown movie is the 1980s brat-pack flick *St Elmo's Fire.* Demi Moore's and Judd Nelson's characters are supposed to be Georgetown graduates, but the college campus is actually the University of Maryland in College Park (although there is a key scene shot in the popular Georgetown bar Third Edition).

Slam, a 1998 docudrama, is a story about Ray Joshua, a gifted young (and jobless) MC trapped in a war-zone DC housing project known as Dodge City. Ray copes with the despair and poverty of his neighborhood by creating haunting poetry.

Over the years, DC has served as the backdrop to numerous TV series, including *Murphy Brown*, *The West Wing*, *Commander in Chief* and, less gloriously, *The Real Housewives of DC.* The latest show to feature the capital is *Veep*, a satirical look at the seemingly inconsequential duties of the vice-president, which stars the comedic Julia Louis-Dreyfus.

The first few seasons of *The West Wing*, which starred Martin Sheen as the beneficent, liberal president ('the best president we've ever had,' fans claimed), when Alan Sorkin was writing for the show, were truly brilliant and are well worth renting on DVD.

LITERATURE

Washington's literary legacy is, not surprisingly, deeply entwined with US political history. The city's best-known early literature consists of writings and books that hammered out the machinery of US democracy. From Thomas Jefferson's *Notes on the State of Virginia* to James Madison's *The Federalist Papers* and Abraham Lincoln's historic speeches and proclamations, this literature fascinates modern readers – not only because it is the cornerstone of the US political system, but because of the grace and beauty of its prose.

In the 19th century, Washington outsiders – who came here by circumstance, professional obligation or wanderlust – made notable contributions to the city's oeuvre. Walt Whitman's *The Wound Dresser* and *Specimen Days* and Louisa May Alcott's *Hospital Sketches* were based on the authors' harrowing experiences as Civil War nurses at Washington's hospitals. Mark Twain had an ill-starred (and short) career as a senator's speechwriter, memorialized in *Washington in 1868*.

Frederick Douglass (1818–95), the abolitionist, editor, memoirist and former slave, is one of Washington's most respected writers. His seminal antislavery works *The Life & Times of Frederick Douglass* and *My Bondage & My Freedom* were written in DC, where Douglass lived on Capitol Hill and in Anacostia.

Henry Adams (1838–1918), grandson of President John Adams, often invited DC's literati to salons at his mansion on Lafayette Sq, which became the literary center of the day. His brilliant *Democracy* was the forerunner of many political-scandal novels of the 20th century. His later autobiography, *The Education of Henry Adams,* provides a fascinating insider's account of Washington high society during this period.

In DC, the Harlem Renaissance is sometimes called the New Negro Movement, named after the famous volume by Howard University professor Alain Locke. *The New Negro* – the bible of the Renaissance – is a collection of essays, poems and stories written by Locke and his colleagues. The writing is energetic and subversive; as a snapshot of the Renaissance and the African American experience it is invaluable.

In the early 20th century, a literary salon took root at 15th and S Sts in Shaw. Artists and writers often gathered here, at poet Georgia Douglas Johnson's home, which became the center of the Harlem Renaissance in DC. Her guests included African American poets Langston Hughes and Paul Dunbar.

Throughout the 20th century, Washington literature remained a deeply political beast, defined by works such as Carl Bernstein's and Bob Woodward's *All the President's Men* (1974).

Native Washingtonian Gore Vidal often aims his satirical pieces squarely at his hometown. His six-volume series of historical novels about the American past includes *Washington, DC* (1967), an insightful examination of the period from the New Deal to the McCarthy era from the perspective of the capital.

Advise and Consent (1959) is Allen Drury's fictional account of Alger Hiss' nomination as Secretary of State under Franklin D Roosevelt. The novel brilliantly portrays the conflicting personal and political motivations of his characters – an eye-opening revelation of what goes on inside the US Senate.

Many more purely literary writers have appeared on the scene, too. Edward P Jones does a superb job of capturing the streets, sounds and sights of DC. His collection of stories *Lost in the City* (1992) is set in inner-city DC in the 1960s and 1970s, and portrays a raw and very real city, with characters grappling with the complexities of American life.

For a fine profile of the Washington literary scene, check out David Cutler's *Literary Washington: A Complete Guide to the Literary Life in the Nation's Capital* (1989).

Marita Golden writes about contemporary African American families dealing with betrayal and loss. *The Edge of Heaven* (1997) is about an accomplished 20-year-old student who must face uncomfortable truths following her mother's release from prison.

On a less elevated note, DC has also inspired hundreds of potboilers. Tom Clancy, a northern Virginia resident and creator of innumerable right-wing thrillers, has featured Washington in books such as *Debt of Honor* (1994) and *Executive Orders* (1996). Meanwhile, Dan Brown's *The Lost Symbol* (2009) brings his Harvard 'symbologist' to the nation's capital on a suspenseful – if formulaic – journey into the secrets of DC's coded (Freemason-filled) history.

MEDIA

Widely read and widely respected, the daily *Washington Post* is considered one of the nation's top newspapers. Its competitor, the *Washington Times,* is owned by the Unification Church and provides a more conservative perspective. The national newspaper *USA Today* is based across the Potomac in Arlington, VA. Several TV programs are also based in DC, including the PBS *NewsHour* with longtime host Jim Lehrer and all of the major networks' Sunday-morning news programs.

Also based in DC is National Public Radio (NPR), the most respected nonprofit, free-radio network in the nation. Popular shows include *Morning Edition, All Things Considered* and *The Diane Rehm Show.* NPR's offices are in the heart of the downtown redevelopment project.

ART GALLERIES

In addition to the massive holdings of famed art meccas such as the National Gallery of Art, a small, creative-minded gallery scene makes its home in Washington, DC. Many galleries are owned or operated by the artists themselves. This scene has blossomed since the 1990s, fuelled by DC's reinvigorated neighborhoods and increasingly cosmopolitan population. It is no longer a given that a talented artist will flee to New York to make it big. The largest assortment of galleries lies around Dupont Circle and in the downtown corridor. New in 2011, the massive gallery and film-performance space of Artisphere (p224) adds a dash of verve to often drearily minded Arlington. For more craft-focused works, visit the Torpedo Factory Art Center (p219) in Old Town Alexandria.

Another key Washington media organization is Politico (www.politico.com), which keeps its audience informed of breaking political stories via its free newspaper, radio show and website.

Washington has some excellent sources of independent media. The City Paper (www.washingtoncitypaper.com) keeps an alternative but informed eye on local politics and trends. Another valuable source for local and national events is the DC Independent Media Center (www.dc.indymedia.org). Smaller rags filled with juicy Hill gossip include the Hill (www.hillnews.com) and Roll Call (www.rollcall.com).

For some amusing but decidedly left-wing political cartoon humor, check out www.markfiore.com. The Pulitzer Prize–winning artist, whose work has appeared in newspapers across the country, pens weekly animated skits that take aim at the Washington ruling elite.

Architecture

Washington's architecture and city design are the products of its founding fathers and city planners, who intended to construct a capital city befitting a powerful nation. The early architecture of Washington, DC, was shaped by two influences: Pierre Charles L'Enfant's 1791 city plan, and the infant nation's desire to prove to European powers that its capital possessed political and artistic sophistication rivaling the ancient, majestic cities of the Continent.

L'ENFANT PLAN & FEDERAL PERIOD

The L'Enfant plan imposed a street grid marked by diagonal avenues, roundabouts and grand vistas. L'Enfant had in mind the magisterial boulevards of Europe. To highlight the primacy of the city's political buildings, he intended that no building would rise higher than the Capitol. This rule rescued DC from the dark, skyscraper-filled fate of most modern American cities.

In an effort to rival European cities, Washington's early architects – many of them self-taught 'gentlemen architects' – depended heavily upon the Classic Revival and Romantic Revival styles, with their ionic columns and marble facades. Federal-style row houses dominated contemporary domestic architecture and still line the streets of Capitol Hill and Georgetown.

Other fine examples from the Federal period are the Sewall-Belmont house and the uniquely shaped Octagon Museum. The colonnaded Treasury Building, built by Robert Mills in the mid-19th century, represented the first major divergence from the L'Enfant plan, as it blocked the visual line between the White House and the Capitol. Mills also designed the stark, simple Washington Monument, another architectural anomaly and not only because it is 555ft high, taller than the Capitol. Later, other styles would soften the lines of the cityscape, with creations such as the French-inspired Renwick Gallery, designed by James Renwick.

Ugliest Structures in Washington?

- *J Edgar Hoover Building (935 Pennsylvania Ave NW)*
- *Theodore Roosevelt Memorial Bridge*
- *HUD Federal Building (451 Seventh St SW)*
- *Lauinger Library (Georgetown University)*
- *Department of Energy Building (1000 Independence Ave SW)*

MCMILLAN PLAN

At the turn of the 20th century, the McMillan plan (1901–02) revived many elements of the L'Enfant plan. It restored public spaces downtown, lent formal lines to the Mall and Capitol grounds, and added more classically inspired buildings. During this period, John Russell Pope built the Scottish Rite Masonic Temple, which was modeled after the mausoleum at Halicarnassus, as well as the National Archives. Here are some of the best examples of this eclectic French-inspired design that has become so emblematic of Washingtonian architecture:

➡ **Historical Society of Washington, DC** Built with funds donated by Andrew Carnegie, the former main public library of DC occupies a majestic position at the center of Mount Vernon Sq.

➡ **Corcoran Gallery of Art** The Corcoran was once described by Frank Lloyd Wright as 'the best designed building in Washington, DC.' Fittingly, this grand building houses one of the nation's oldest art museums.

AMBASSADORIAL ARCHITECTURE & ANECDOTES

Some of Washington's most interesting buildings, by dint of design or history, are its embassies, mainly concentrated in the Dupont Circle area and Upper Northwest DC. Note that you'll generally have to appreciate these buildings from the outside; for an embassy walking tour, see p170.

Indonesian Embassy (2020 Massachusetts Ave NW) The extravagant 61-room former mansion of 19th-century gold-mining baron Thomas Walsh was built in a curving neo-baroque style, and originally contained a slab of gold ore embedded in the front porch. Not one for subtlety, Walsh once threw a New Year's Eve party where 325 guests knocked back 480 quarts of champagne, 288 fifths of Scotch, 48 quarts of cocktails, 40 gallons of beer and 35 bottles of miscellaneous liqueurs (according to a piece in the *New York Times*).

Embassy of Italy Chancery (3000 Whitehaven St NW) This odd, starkly geometric structure was actually fashioned to resemble the original 10-sq-mile plan of the District itself – its layout a giant diamond cut by a glass atrium, meant to represent the curving Potomac.

Danish Embassy (3200 Whitehaven St NW) Stark and simple, this 1960 modernist building, designed by Vilhelm Lauritzen, provides a dramatic counterpoint to a city of sometimes overwrought beaux-arts design.

Embassy of Kuwait Chancery (3500 International Dr NW) This sleek and geometrical cantilevered structure with stainless steel was designed in 1982 by Skidmore, Owings & Merrill, the well-known firm that also designed the Willis (Sears) Tower in Chicago, as well as the soon-to-be-completed One World Trade Center in New York.

Embassy of Bangladesh Chancery (3510 International Dr NW) Because water is such an important feature of the Bangladeshi landscape, the inverted roof gable atop this innovative structure is meant to resemble a water lily, while the interior, composed of different grades of slate and other materials, evokes a riverbed.

Embassy of Brunei Darussalam (3520 International Ct NW) With its post-and-beam construction and pitched roof, this deceptively modern-looking embassy is inspired by the rustic designs of traditional houses in Brunei Darussalam (a sultanate in Southeast Asia) – simple stilt structures built over water.

➡ **Meridian International Center** A limestone chateau by John Russell Pope.

➡ **Willard InterContinental Hotel** Fabled hotel where the term 'lobbyist' originated, from the men who prowled the lobby in search of political prey.

➡ **Union Station** The archetypical example of the neoclassical beauty and grandeur of beaux arts during the age of railroads.

WWII TO THE PRESENT

Classicism came to a screaming halt during and after WWII, when war workers flooded the city. Temporary offices were thrown onto the Mall and new materials that were developed during wartime enabled the construction of huge office blocks. Slum clearance after the war – particularly in southwest DC – meant the wholesale loss of old neighborhoods in favor of modernist boxes, such as the monolithic government agencies that currently dominate the ironically named L'Enfant Plaza.

Washington architecture today is of uncertain identity. Many new buildings, particularly those downtown, pay homage to their classical neighbors while striving toward a sleeker, postmodern monumentalism.

A handful of world-renowned architects have left examples of their work in the city. The National Gallery of Art is a perfect example. Franklin Delano Roosevelt opened the original building, designed by

Conspiracy theories abound about the secret symbols planted in the nation's capital by its masonic architects, builders and statesmen. Among the evidence: draw lines along the avenues between major DC points and you get key Masonic symbols – the pentagram, the square and the compass. To delve deeper, read *The Secrets of Masonic Washington* by James Wasserman.

John Russell Pope, in March 1941. Now called the West Building, Pope's symmetrical, neoclassical gallery overwhelms the eye at first glimpse. Two wings lacking external windows stretch for 400ft on either side of the main floor's massive central rotunda, which has a sky-high dome supported by 24 black ionic columns. In the center are vaulted corridors leading off to each wing, which end with an internal skylight and fountain and a plant-speckled garden court.

The East Building of the gallery is perhaps even more spectacular. Designed in 1978 by IM Pei, the ethereal structure is all straight lines that create a triangular shape. The building design was initially difficult to conceive, as Pei was given a strange shaped block of land between 3rd and 4th Sts. He solved the problem by making only the marble walls permanent. The rest of the internal structure can be shaped at will, according to the size of various temporary exhibitions. The design is striking, resembling the Louvre in Paris, with pyramidal skylights rising out of the ground (look up from the ground floor of the museum and you'll see a glassed-in waterfall).

Other famous buildings include Mies van der Rohe's Martin Luther King Jr Memorial Library and Eero Saarinen's Washington Dulles International Airport.

The architecture of this unique city tells much about American political ideals and their occasionally awkward application to reality. The National Mall of today is a perfect example. The western half contains a mix of sleek modern creations and neoclassical marble temples disguised as memorials. The eastern side is an entirely different story, a mishmash of sometimes awesome and sometimes appalling architecture.

One of the most successful 21st-century designs to grace the Mall is the National Museum of the American Indian, which opened in 2004. Designed by Canadian architect and Native North American Douglas Cardina, it is a curving, almost undulating building with a rough-hewn Kasota limestone facade that references the natural wind- and rain-sculpted rock formations of the southwest. The museum's garden has over 150 different species of plants and wildflowers that are native to the Atlantic coastal plain and the Appalachian Mountains, which add to the element of naturalism in the building and its landscape.

Another widely recognized building on the Mall is the Smithsonian Institution, locally known as the Castle, which dates from 1855. It was designed by James Renwick and features striking Gothic towers and battlements.

This Political City

It's hard to escape from politics in Washington. While LA attracts wannabe filmmakers and actors, and New York draws creative and financial types, DC draws folks wanting to be close to the corridors of power. So banter at cafes, restaurants and bars – at least downtown – tends to revolve around the latest gossip of Capitol Hill or the White House. Even those who have no professed interest in politics can't help but follow the decisions – which often have national or even global implications – being made just up the road. (You won't find many other cities where such a large number of cab drivers listen to NPR.)

Power, it must be said, has enormous appeal, which is perhaps why Washington exerts such a palpable buzz. It draws the best and brightest, from congressional staffers and foreign diplomats to policy analysts at think tanks, NGOs and the World Bank, to name but a few of many important offices headquartered here – every one contributing to the political pageantry in all its glory and shame.

Hand in hand with power comes corruption, and Washingtonians love a good scandal (particularly if it's happening to those who belong to the *other* party). And there's rarely a dull news day in this town. Congressional brawls, egregious abuses of power – and, of course, the mother lode: sexual scandals – are all par for the course in the ever-changing news cycle of US politics.

Not surprisingly, the denigration of federal politicians is a widely practiced pursuit – being called a Washington insider, after all, can ruin a career. Amid the current climate of anti-government sentiment – and the scandals that help fuel the resentment – sometimes it's easy to forget the momentous events precipitated by legislators, judges and presidents. Ending slavery, creating jobs during the darkest days of the Great Depression, sending astronauts to the moon, putting an end to institutionalized racial discrimination: all the work of so-called Washington insiders. US government at work is a messy business, but at times it has brought dramatic changes for the better to the lives of its citizens.

Comical Political Reads

America: A Citizen's Guide to Democracy Inaction (Jon Stewart)

I Am America (And So Can You!) (Stephen Colbert)

Parliament of Whores (PJ O'Rourke)

Dave Barry Slept Here (Dave Barry)

UNDERSTANDING US POLITICS: SEPARATION OF POWERS

Everyone knows Americans do things differently – spelling, measuring, sports – and the democratic process is no exception.

'What's the difference?' The best answer probably comes from journalist HL Mencken, who summed up many Americans' feelings toward a nanny state: 'The urge to save humanity is almost always a false face for the urge to rule it.' Americans are by and large paranoid about their government. The entire country was founded by anti-authoritarian colonists, while the Civil War was fought over how much power Washington, DC, could exert over the states (among other things). Obsessed with keeping government in check, the founding fathers devised a system that disperses power through three branches that keep each other in check.

You can visit those branches starting on Capitol Hill, where the legislative branch, better known as Congress, convenes. Put simply, Congress writes laws. There are two bodies assigned to this task: the House of Representatives and the Senate. In the House, there are 435 voting representatives, which are allotted proportionally by state population – Wyoming, the least populous state, has one, and California, with the largest population, has 53. There are 100 senators: two for each state, a way of giving smaller states equal footing with more populous ones. Congress not only writes laws, it can also impeach the president, determine the jurisdictional limits of courts and vote out its own members.

Behind the Capitol dome is the Supreme Court, whose 12 justices are appointed by the president to life terms. The court's job is to determine how true to the constitution laws are. Arguably the weakest branch, it nonetheless has a crucial role in the democratic process. While the public face of many causes in the USA are crowds of protesters, actual change is often practically affected through the courts, from the Supreme Court on down. This was the case with the Scopes Trial, which allowed evolution to be taught in public schools, the African American Civil Rights movement and the continuing bid for gay marriage.

WASHINGTON'S SITES OF SCANDAL

Washington media loves a good takedown. Here is a list of a few ill-fated sites where some of the big stories began:

➡ **The Gate of Gates** Watergate: Towering over the Potomac, this chi-chi apartment-hotel complex has lent its name to decades of political crime. It all started when Committee to Re-Elect the President operatives were found here, trying to bug Democratic National Committee headquarters; it ended with President Nixon's resignation.

➡ **Swimming for It** Tidal Basin: In 1974, Wilbur Mills, 65-year-old Arkansas representative and chairman of the House Ways & Means Committee, was stopped for speeding, whereupon his companion – 38-year-old stripper Fanne Foxe, known as the 'Argentine Firecracker' – leapt into the Basin to escape. Unfortunately for Mills' political career, a TV cameraman was there to film it.

➡ **Smoking Crack with Barry** Vista Hotel: It was in room No 727 that former DC mayor Marion Barry uttered his timeless quote: '...set up...bitch set me up!' when the FBI caught him taking a puff of crack cocaine in the company of ex-model (and police informant) Hazel 'Rasheeda' Moore. The widely broadcast FBI video of his toke horrified a city lacerated by crack violence, but didn't stop it from re-electing Barry in 1994.

➡ **Death in the Park** Fort Marcy Park: The body of Vince Foster, deputy counsel to president Clinton and Hillary Clinton, was found with a gunshot wound to the head in this remote McLean, VA, park in 1993. Investigations by the Park Police and the FBI determined that the death was a suicide, but conspiracy theories still proliferate among right-wing pundits.

➡ **Stool Pigeon Sushi** Pentagon City food court: It was by the sushi bar that Monica Lewinsky awaited Linda Tripp, her lunch date (and betrayer), who led Ken Starr's agents down the mall escalators to snag her up for questioning in the nearby Ritz-Carlton Hotel.

➡ **What's Your Position, Congressman?** Capitol steps: John Jenrette was a little-known South Carolina representative until he embroiled himself in a bribery scandal. Jenrette's troubles were compounded when his ex-wife Rita revealed to *Playboy* that she and her erstwhile husband used to slip out during dull late-night congressional sessions for an alfresco quickie on the Capitol's hallowed marble steps.

A little ways down Pennsylvania Ave sits the White House, where the president heads the executive branch. Unlike a prime minister, the president is both head of state and head of government, and possesses the power to veto (override) Congress' bills, pardon criminals, and appoint a cabinet, judges and ambassadors.

While the powers are separated, they are not isolated from each other. The founding fathers figured that each branch's ability to check its partners would generate a healthy tension. This uneasy equality makes compromise a necessity for movement on issues, and it is the true bedrock of US politics.

THE MEDIA & WASHINGTON

It's hard to imagine an area that packs so many journalists into such a small space. Politics is a game of public perception, and the gatekeepers of that opinion are the media. Politicians – even the ones who publicly lambaste journalists – must maintain a working relationship with the press corps. On the other hand, reporters must ostensibly be merciless, brutally honest and somehow removed from the politicians they cover. In reality, to gain access to the sources they require for their stories, relationships are forged between profiler and profiled.

And Washington can be a bubble. The same faces appear in the same hearings and conferences day after day, at lunches, after-work drinks and lectures. Politicians (although they'd rarely admit it) often become closer to reporters than their own constituents, and good journalism sometimes suffers as a result. Glenn Greenwald, a constitutional lawyer and columnist for Salon (www.salon.com), is perhaps the most prolific commentator on the DC press corps' reluctance to cover their backyard too critically.

Suspicious of political factoids? So are we – particularly during political elections. Turn to bipartisan www.factcheck.org to help discern truth from 'truthiness.'

LOBBYISTS

'Lobbyist' is one of the dirtiest words in the American political lexicon, yet its meaning is fairly innocuous. Essentially, a lobbyist is someone who makes a living advocating special interests. This isn't Europe, where causes form their own party and seek power through a parliamentary coalition (though there are lobbyists there, too, of course). Here the agenda-pushers directly thrust their message onto elected officials.

Lobbying is traditionally dated to the late 19th century, but it took off as a vital component of US politics during the money-minded 1980s. Most politicos see lobbyists as a necessary evil, and while it's the rare politician who admits to being influenced by them, everyone understands their importance: lobbyists are the go-betweens in a city built on client-patron relationships. For better or worse, they have become a vital rung on DC's power ladder.

Labor unions and tree-huggers, gun nuts and industrialists; every group gets its say here through the work of well-paid and connected advocates. Lobbying ranks, largely based on K St (to the point that the two terms are synonymous), are swelled by those who know how to navigate the complex social webs of the capital; some watchdogs estimate as many as 40% of former congresspeople rejoin the private sector as lobbyists. In a city where getting anything done is often based on personal relationships, a lobbyist can be worth far more than, say, an embassy with rotating staff. Indeed, many countries keep embassies for ritual value and leave the real legwork of diplomacy to DC lobbying firms.

Wining, dining, vacation packages and the art of giving all of the above without violating campaign contribution laws is a delicate dance.

MEDIA

Every year legislation is introduced to keep lobbyists off the floor of Congress (figuratively and sometimes literally), but lobbyists are probably too ingrained in the political landscape to ever be completely removed from it.

DEMOCRACY IN ACTION

One of the great paradoxes of US politics is how simultaneously accessible and impenetrable the system is. Visitors can walk into congressional hearings dressed in jeans and a T-shirt and address their elected representatives, in public, with minimal security screening. Mass protests have rocked the foundations of government and seared themselves on the national psyche forever. Yet most of the decisions that influence US government are made between small groups of well-connected policy wonks, lobbyists and special interests who are mainly concerned with perpetuating their own organizations.

Many Americans believe changing the system requires going to DC and coming face to face with their elected officials (there's even a cinematic subgenre devoted to the idea, from *Mr Smith Goes to Washington* to *Legally Blonde 2*). On a grand scale, the equation is partly true. Large protests, often held on the National Mall, can shift public perception a few points toward a particular cause. But smaller delegations usually require lots of money and clout to effect change.

MALL OF JUSTICE

The Mall has long provided a forum for people seeking to make their grievances heard by the government. Suffragists, veterans, peaceniks, civil-rights activists, sharecroppers and million-mom marchers, among many other groups, have all staged political rallies on the Mall over the years. Among the key events in history:

- Bonus Army (1932) – WWI veterans, left unemployed by the Great Depression, petitioned the government for an early payment of promised bonuses for their wartime service. As many as 10,000 veterans settled in for an extended protest, pitching tents on the Mall and the Capitol lawn. President Hoover dispatched Douglas MacArthur to evict the 'Bonus Army,' the violence of which helped cement Hoover's reputation as an uncaring president.
- 'I Have a Dream' (1963) – At the zenith of the Civil Rights movement, Reverend Martin Luther King's stirring speech, delivered from the steps of the Lincoln Memorial to 200,000 supporters, remains a high point in the struggle for racial equality.
- Anti-War Protests (1971) – In April 1971, an estimated 500,000 Vietnam veterans and students gathered on the Mall to oppose continued hostilities. Several thousand arrests were made.
- AIDS Memorial Quilt (1996) – Gay and lesbian activists drew more than 300,000 supporters in a show of solidarity for equal rights under the law and to display the ever-growing AIDS quilt, which covered the entire eastern flank of the Mall from the Capitol to the Washington Monument.
- Million-Mom March (2000) – A half-million people convened on the Mall on Mother's Day to draw attention to handgun violence and to demand that Congress pass stricter gun-ownership laws.
- Bring Them Home Now Tour (2005) – Led by families who lost loved ones in the war, this gathering of over 100,000 protesters demanded the withdrawal of American soldiers from Iraq.
- Barack Obama Inauguration (2009) – While not a protest, Obama's swearing in as president is believed to be the largest public gathering in DC history.

It's maddening, but the surface of the process is surprisingly open to travelers. Check www.house.gov and www.senate.gov to get the schedules for congressional committee hearings (see p132 for details on getting inside).

CURRENT ISSUES

US politics remains ever divided, with Republicans and Democrats rarely seeing eye to eye. One thing they do agree on, however, is the enormous challenges the US faces. One of the hot topics of the moment – dominating the airwaves both inside and outside the marble corridors of the capital – is the economic crisis.

What started as a collapse of the US housing bubble in 2007 then spread to the banking sector, with the meltdown of major financial institutions. Growth has since remained sluggish and unemployment high. Aiming to revitalize the economy, Congress passed an $800 billion stimulus package in 2009. The package was described by liberal commentators as too small to be effective and by conservatives as too large.

With the rise of the tea party and the demonization of government spending, neither party has had an appetite for passing another recovery package. The role of government is at the center of the ideological divide: those on the right believe fewer taxes, lower deficits and a smaller government will help spur economic growth, while those on the left believe government should take an active role in spending and in maintaining a social safety net.

Along those lines, the question of health care is front and center in the debate over government's role in society. Obama's health-care bill (the Affordable Care Act, nicknamed 'Obamacare'), which became law in 2010, aims to bring health care to more Americans, lower its cost and close loopholes that allowed insurance companies to deny coverage to individuals. Whether or not the bill is overturned, the economic pressure to change the system – for doctors and hospitals to care differently for more people at a lower cost – is undeniable.

Other major debates in the US that are unlikely to be resolved anytime soon revolve around immigration reform, gay marriage, gun control and the US role in the Middle East.

Americans vote most of their leaders into office, but not the president. Instead, they vote indirectly through the Electoral College. It is the College and its electors who actually pick the president every four years. This ensures geographically fair elections: even the small states can command election attention.

Survival Guide

Transportation

GETTING TO WASHINGTON, DC

Most visitors arrive by air. The city has two airports: Dulles International Airport is larger and handles most of the international flights, as well as domestic flights. Reagan National Airport handles domestic services plus some flights to Canada. Reagan is more convenient, as it's closer to the city and has a Metro stop. Baltimore's airport is a third, often cheaper option. It's connected to DC by commuter rail, though it's not handy if you're arriving at night.

Flights can be booked online at lonelyplanet.com/bookings.

Buses are a popular means of getting to DC from nearby cities such New York, Philadelphia and Richmond, VA. Tickets are cheap, the routes are direct to the city center, and the buses usually have free wi-fi and power outlets.

It's also easy to reach Washington by train from major east-coast cities. The fast, commuter-oriented Acela train links Boston, New York and Philly to DC's Union Station.

Ronald Reagan Washington National Airport

Washington National Airport (DCA; www.metwashairports.com) is 4.5 miles away in Arlington, VA. There's free wi-fi and a currency exchange (National Hall, Concourse Level). It's easy to reach:

Metro (www.wmata.com) National has its own Metro station on the Blue and Yellow Lines, which is fast (20 minutes to the center) and cheap (around $2). It connects to the concourse level of terminals B and C.

Supershuttle (☎800-258-3826; www.supershuttle.com; ⏰5:30am-12:30am) The door-to-door shared-van service goes downtown for $14. It takes 10 to 30 minutes, depending on traffic and where your hotel is in the drop-off order.

Taxi A taxi to the center takes 10 to 30 minutes (depending on traffic) and costs $12 to $20. Taxis queue outside the baggage-claim area at each terminal.

Washington Dulles International Airport

Washington Dulles International Airport (IAD; www.metwashairports.com) is in the Virginia suburbs 26 miles west of DC. It has free wi-fi and several currency exchanges throughout the terminals.

Metrobus 5A (www.wmata.com) Runs from Dulles to Rosslyn Metro station (35 minutes) and central DC (L'Enfant Plaza, 48 minutes); it departs every 30 to 40 minutes. The combo bus-metro fare is about $8.

Supershuttle (☎800-258-3826; www.supershuttle.com; ⏰5:30am-12:30am) The door-to-door shared van service goes downtown for $29. It takes 30 to 60 minutes, depending on traffic and where your hotel is in the drop-off order.

Taxi A taxi to the center takes 30 to 60 minutes (depending on traffic) and costs $56 to $64. Follow the 'Ground Transportation' or 'Taxi' signs to where they queue.

Washington Flyer (www.washfly.com) Dulles does not have a Metro station, but the Washington Flyer bus provides a link. It runs every 30 minutes from Dulles to West Falls Church Metro (Orange Line) for $10. Follow the 'Flyer' signs in the airport to the departure point. The total trip into the city (Flyer + Metro) takes 60 to 90 minutes. The Metro portion costs around $2.50.

Baltimore-Washington International Airport

Baltimore-Washington International Airport (BWI; www.bwiairport.com) is 30

CLIMATE CHANGE & TRAVEL

Every form of transport that relies on carbon-based fuel generates CO_2, the main cause of human-induced climate change. Modern travel is dependent on airplanes, which might use less fuel per kilometer per person than most cars but travel much greater distances. The altitude at which aircraft emit gases (including CO_2) and particles also contributes to their climate change impact. Many websites offer 'carbon calculators' that allow people to estimate the carbon emissions generated by their journey and, for those who wish to do so, to offset the impact of the greenhouse gases emitted with contributions to portfolios of climate-friendly initiatives throughout the world. Lonely Planet offsets the carbon footprint of all staff and author travel.

miles northeast of DC in Maryland.

Metrobus B30 (www.wmata.com) Runs from BWI to Greenbelt Metro station (last stop on the Green Line); it departs every 40 minutes from bus stops on the lower level of the international concourse and concourse A/B. The combo bus-metro fare is about $9. Total trip time is around 75 minutes.

Supershuttle (☎800-258-3826; www.supershuttle.com; ⏲5:30am-12:30am) The door-to-door shared-van service goes to downtown DC for $37. The ride takes 45 minutes to an hour.

Taxi A taxi to DC takes 45 minutes or so and costs $90. Taxis queue outside the baggage claim area of the Marshall terminal.

Train Both **Maryland Rail Commuter** (MARC; mta.maryland.gov; fare $6; 40 min) and **Amtrak** (www.amtrak.com; fare $14; 40 min) trains travel to DC's Union Station. They depart from a terminal 1 mile from BWI; a free bus shuttles passengers there. Note MARC does not run on weekends.

Union Station

Magnificent, beaux-arts **Union Station** (Map p324; www.unionstationdc.com; 50 Massachusetts Ave NE) is the city's rail hub. There's also a handy Metro station (Red Line) here for transport onward in the city.

➡ **Amtrak** (☎800-872-7245; www.amtrak.com) arrives at least once per hour from major east coast cities.

➡ Regular (unreserved) trains are cheapest, but pokey.

➡ Express Metroliners (reserved) between New York and DC are faster.

➡ Limited-stop *Acela* trains are fastest, traveling between Boston and DC (via New York, Philadelphia and Baltimore) in 6½ hours.

➡ **MARC** (Maryland Rail Commuter; mta.maryland.gov) trains run frequently to Baltimore ($7, 71 minutes) and other Maryland towns ($4 to $12), as well as Harpers Ferry, WV.

Bus Stations

Cheap bus services to and from Washington abound. Most charge around $20 for a one-way trip to NYC (it takes four to five hours). Pick-up locations are scattered around town, but are always Metro-accessible. Tickets usually need to be bought online, but can also be purchased at the bus itself if there is room.

Bolt Bus (☎877-265-8287; www.boltbus.com; 📶) The best of the budget options, Bolt Bus leaves from the upper level of Union Station (Map p324).

Greyhound (☎202-589-5141; www.greyhound.com; 1005 1st St NE) Provides nationwide service. The terminal is a few blocks north of Union Station; take a cab after dark.

Megabus (☎877-462-6342; us.megabus.com; 📶) Temporarily leaves from K St & N Capitol St NW. Call to verify location.

New Century (Map p326; ☎202-789-8222; www.2001bus.com; 513 H St NW) A Chinatown service.

Peter Pan Bus Lines (☎800-343-9999; www.peterpanbus.com) Travels throughout northeastern US; uses a terminal just opposite Greyhound's.

DC2NY (Map p330; ☎202-332-2691; www.dc2ny.com; 20th St & Massachusetts Ave NW; 📶) The bus stop is by Dupont Circle.

Vamoose Bus (☎877-393-2828; www.vamoosebus.com) Service to/from Arlington, VA.

WashNY (☎866-287-6932; www.washny.com; 1333 19th St NW; 📶)

GETTING AROUND

The public-transportation system is a mix of Metro trains and bus. Visitors will find the Metro the most useful option.

The District Department of Transportation's **goDCgo** (www.godcgo.com) is a useful resource for biking, bus, Metro and parking information and route planning. It even has a carbon calculator that compares different modes of local travel.

Bicycle

DC has become a cycling-savvy city with its own bike-share program. Lots of locals commute by bicycle.

➡ Riders can take bikes free of charge on Metro trains, except during rush hour (7am to 10am and 4pm to 7pm Monday to Friday) and on holidays. Bikes are not permitted to use the center door of trains or the escalator.

➡ All public buses are equipped with bike racks.

➡ The **Washington Area Bicyclists' Association** (www.waba.org) has information on recommended trails, expansions, bike advocacy and more.

Here are some options for rental:

Big Wheel Bikes (☎202-337-0254; www.bigwheelbikes.com; 1034 33rd St NW; per hr/day $7/35; ⏲11am-7pm Tue-Fri, 10am-6pm Sun) In Georgetown, near good trails.

Bike & Roll (☎202-962-0206; www.bikethesites.com; Union Station, 50 Massachusetts Ave NE; bikes per hr/day from $6/30; ⏲year-round) Other branches at the Old Post Office Pavilion and in Alexandria.

Capital Bikeshare (☎877-430-2453; www.capitalbikeshare.com) Modeled on bike-sharing schemes in Europe, Capital Bikeshare has a network of 1200-plus bicycles scattered at 140-odd stations around DC. To check out a bike, select the membership (24 hours is $7, three days is $15), insert your credit card, and off you go. The first 30 minutes are free; after that, rates rise exponentially ($2/6/14 per extra 30/60/90 minutes). Call or go online for complete details.

Boat

American River Taxi (www.americanrivertaxi.com; 1 way $11; ⏲mid-Apr–Oct) water taxis toodle along the Potomac from Georgetown's Washington Harbour to **The Wharf** (690 Water St SW) in southwest DC to The Yards by Nationals Park.

Bus

DC's public bus system has two main options:

Metrobus (www.wmata.com; fare $1.70) Operates clean, efficient buses throughout the city and suburbs. Have exact change handy.

DC Circulator (www.dccirculator.com; fare $1) Red buses link downtown DC to major tourism areas. Useful routes connect Georgetown to Union Station via K St and Massachusetts Ave, the Convention Center to the Waterfront, and Woodley Park and Adams-Morgan to the White House Area.

Car & Motorcycle

DC has some of the nation's worst traffic congestion. Bottlenecks are in the suburbs, where the Capital Beltway (I-495) meets Maryland's I-270 and I-95, and Virginia's I-66 and I-95. Avoid the beltway during early-morning and late-afternoon rush hours (about 6am to 9am and 3pm to 6pm). Clogged rush-hour streets in DC include the main access arteries from the suburbs: Massachusetts, Wisconsin, Connecticut and Georgia Aves NW, among others.

Parking

➡ Finding street parking is difficult downtown and in popular neighborhoods (Georgetown, Adams-Morgan and the U St area are particular nightmares), but it's reasonably easy in less-congested districts.

➡ Note that residential areas often have a two-hour limit on street parking. If you tempt the local traffic gods, you'll probably get ticketed.

➡ Parking garages in the city normally cost $15 to $30 per day.

Road Rules

➡ Certain lanes of some major traffic arteries change direction during rush hour, and some two-way streets become one-way. Signs indicate hours of these changes, so keep your eyes peeled.

➡ Except where otherwise posted, the speed limit on DC surface streets is 25mph (15mph in alleys and school zones).

➡ You must wear your seat belt and restrain kids under eight years in child-safety seats.

Auto Association

For emergency road service and towing, members can call the **American Automobile Association** (AAA; www.aaa.com). It has a branch in the White House Area: **AAA travel agency** (☎202-481-6811; 1405 G St NW).

Car Share

Zipcar (☎866-494-7227; www.zipcar.com), with its cute, eco-friendly Priuses and parking-friendly minis, is a popular commuting tool in this town. If you're on vacation, weekday rates run $8/74 hourly/daily and weekends $11.25/83 hourly/daily. That includes gas and insurance and good parking spaces around town. You need to become a member first ($60 annually).

Rental

All major car-rental agencies are in DC. Rates fluctuate radically. In general, airport rates are often better than those downtown. Gas is pricier inside the city than in Maryland and Virginia.

To rent a car you typically need to be at least 25 years old, hold a valid driver's license and have a major credit card.

Unless stated otherwise, these companies have outlets at both DC airports and Union Station:

Alamo (☎877-222-9075; www.alamo.com)

Avis (☎800-230-4898; www.avis.com)

Budget (☎800-527-0700; www.budget.com)

Enterprise (☎800-261-7331; www.enterprise.com) At the airports and downtown near McPherson Sq.

Hertz (☎800-654-3131; www.hertz.com)

National (☎877-222-9058; www.nationalcar.com)

Thrifty (☎800-847-4389; www.thrifty.com) At the airports.

Metro

DC's sleek modern subway network is the **Metrorail** (☎202-637-7000; www.wmata.com), commonly called Metro. It will get you to most sights, hotels and business districts, and to the Maryland and Virginia suburbs.

➡ Trains start running at 5am Monday through Friday (from 7am on weekends); the last service is around midnight Sunday through Thursday and 3am on Friday and Saturday.

➡ Machines inside stations sell computerized fare cards; fares cost from $1.85 (children under five ride free). Fares increase for longer distances and during rush hour.

➡ You must use the fare-card to enter *and* exit station turnstiles. Upon exit, the turnstile deducts the fare and returns the card. If the value of the card is insufficient, you need to use an 'Addfare' machine to add money.

➡ Unlimited travel passes are also available (one day/seven days from $9/33).

➡ If you're in DC for a week or more, you may want to get a SmarTrip card. This is basically a rechargeable fare card that's easier to carry than disposable Metro tickets; it also knocks 25¢ off each fare. Cards can be purchased at all Metro stations or online. The card itself costs $5, and you need to put a minimum of $25 on it.

Taxi

Lots of taxis prowl the district, but there never seems to be one when you need it. Locals grouse about it. Fares generally start at $3.50 at flag drop and increase at roughly 75¢ per half-mile – it's a pricey way of getting around. Add at least 10% for a tip and keep in mind rates increase at night and for radio dispatches. Look for taxis along major streets and adjacent arteries; hail them with a wave of the hand.

Reliable companies:

Capitol Cab (☎202-636-1600)

Diamond (☎202-387-6200)

Yellow Cab (☎202-544-1212)

TOURS

Tours are a great way to home in on DC's attractions. **Cultural Tourism DC** (www.culturaltourismdc.org) lists several quality tour operators, mostly for walking jaunts.

There used to be a hop-on, hop-off bus tour that zipped around the National Mall, Capitol, White House and out to Arlington National Cemetery, but the park service was looking for a new vendor at press time. Any visitor center should have details on the new service.

Bike & Roll (www.bikethesites.com; adult/child from $40/30; ⏰mid-Mar–Nov) Offers a handful of day and evening bike tours around the city (plus combo boat-bike trips to Mount Vernon) from branches at the Old Post Office Pavilion downtown and Alexandria, VA.

City Segway Tours (☎202-626-0017; http://citysegwaytours.com/washington-dc) Extremely popular and relaxing way of seeing the major sites along the Mall and in Penn Quarter ($75).

DC Metro Food Tours (☎800-979-3370; www.dcmetrofoodtours.com; per person $30-65) These walking tours take in the culinary riches of DC, exploring various neighborhoods and stopping for bites along the way. Offerings include Eastern Market, U St, Little Ethiopia, Georgetown and Alexandria, VA.

DC by Foot (www.dcbyfoot.com) Guides for this free, tip-based walking tour dispense intriguing stories and historical details on different walks covering the National Mall, Arlington Cemetery and Lincoln's assassination.

Old Town Trolley Tours (☎888-910-8687; www.trolleytours.com; adult/child $39/29) This open-sided bus offers hop-on, hop-off exploring of the major sights of DC. The outfit also offers a 'monuments by moonlight' tour and the DC Ducks tour, via an amphibious vehicle that plunges into the Potomac.

Potomac River Boat Company (☎877-511-2628;

www.potomacriverboatco.com) It offers a monuments cruise (one way adult/child $13/7) between Georgetown (dock at 31st and K Sts, Washington Harbour) and Alexandria (dock at corner of Cameron and Union Sts). From Alexandria, it also offers a Mount Vernon cruise (one way adult/child $14/7). Check the website for various packages and themed tours, as well.

Spirit of Mount Vernon (☎866-211-3811; www.cruisetomountvernon.com; adult/child $44/38) The large, flashy *Spirit of Mount Vernon* boat departs for George Washington's estate from Pier 4, at 6th & Water Sts SW in southwest DC. The day-long tour includes site admission.

Directory A–Z

Business Hours

The list below provides 'normal' opening hours for businesses. Reviews throughout this book show specific hours only if they vary from these standards. Note, too, that hours can vary a bit by season. Our listings depict peak-season operating hours.

Bars 5pm to 1am or 2am weekdays, 3am on weekends.

Nightclubs 9pm to 1am or 2am weekdays, 3am on weekends.

Offices and government agencies 9am to 5pm Monday to Friday.

Restaurants Breakfast 7am or 8am to 11am, lunch 11am or 11:30am to 2:30pm or 3pm, dinner 5pm or 6pm to 10pm Sunday to Thursday, to 11pm or midnight Friday and Saturday.

Shops 10am to 7pm Monday to Saturday, noon to 6pm Sunday.

Customs Regulations

For a complete list of US customs regulations, visit the official portal for **US Customs and Border Protection** (www.cbp.gov).

Duty-free allowance per person is as follows:

- 1L of liquor (provided you are at least 21 years old)
- 100 cigars and 200 cigarettes (if you are at least 18)
- $100 worth of gifts and purchases ($800 if a returning US citizen)
- If you arrive with $10,000 or more in US or foreign currency, it must be declared

There are heavy penalties for attempting to import illegal drugs. Note that fruit, vegetables and other food must be declared (whereby you'll undergo a time-consuming search).

Discount Cards

The following cards can net savings (usually about 10%) on museums, accommodations and some transport (including Amtrak):

American Association of Retired Persons (AARP; www.aarp.org) For US travelers aged 50 and over.

American Automobile Association (AAA; www.aaa.com) For members of AAA or reciprocal clubs in Europe and Australia.

International Student Identity Card (ISIC; www.isic.org) For students any age and nonstudents under 26.

Student Advantage Card (www.studentadvantage.com) For US and foreign travelers.

Emergency

Police, fire, ambulance: ☎911.

PRACTICALITIES

- The *Washington Post* (www.washingtonpost.com) is among the nation's top newspapers. Its competitor is the conservative *Washington Times* (www.washingtontimes.com).
- The *Washington City Paper* (www.washingtoncitypaper.com) is a free alternative weekly that scrutinizes DC politics and has great entertainment coverage. *Politico* (www.politico.com) is a free paper that covers DC's politics in-depth.
- The main TV channels are Channel 4 (NBC), Channel 5 (Fox), Channel 7 (ABC) and Channel 9 (CBS).
- National Public Radio (NPR) is headquartered in the District. Its programs can be found on WETA-FM90.9.
- Washington, DC, is entirely smoke-free in restaurants, bars and workplaces.

Electricity

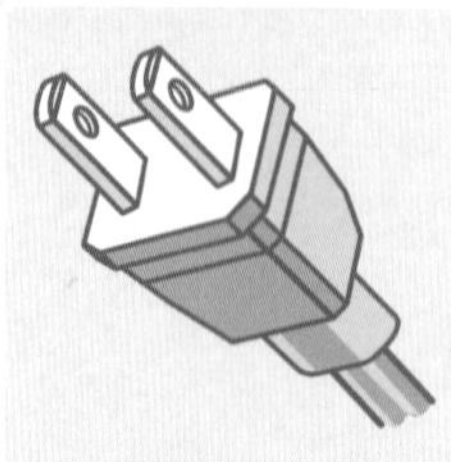

120V/60Hz

120V/60Hz

Embassies & Consulates

Nearly every country in the world has an embassy in DC. **Electronic Embassy** (www.embassy.org) offers links to all DC embassy homepages.

Australia (202-797-3000; www.usa.embassy.gov.au; 1601 Massachusetts Ave NW)

Canada (202-682-1740; www.canadainternational.gc.ca; 501 Pennsylvania Ave NW)

France (202-644-6000; www.info-france-usa.org; 4101 Reservoir Rd NW)

Germany (202-298-4000; www.germany.info; 2300 M St NW)

Ireland (202-462-3939; www.embassyofireland.org; 2234 Massachusetts Ave NW)

Mexico (202-728-1600; http://embamex.sre.gob.mx/eua; 1911 Pennsylvania Ave NW)

Netherlands (877-388-2443; http://dc.the-netherlands.org; 4200 Linnean Ave NW)

New Zealand (202-328-4800; www.nzembassy.com/usa; 37 Observatory Circle NW)

UK (202-588-6500; http://ukinusa.fco.gov.uk; 3100 Massachusetts Ave NW)

Gay & Lesbian Travelers

Home to more than 30 national gay and lesbian organizations and more than 300 social, athletic, religious and political support groups, DC is one of the most gay-friendly cities in the US. The community is most visible in the Dupont Circle and Capitol Hill neighborhoods, where there are many gay-friendly businesses. Resources:

Washington Blade (www.washingtonblade.com) Free weekly newspaper. Offers coverage of politics, information about community resources, and lots and lots of nightlife and meeting-place listings.

Metro Weekly (www.metroweekly.com) Free weekly news and events magazine available around town.

Capital Area Gay & Lesbian Chamber of Commerce (www.caglcc.org) Sponsors lots of networking events around town.

Gay & Lesbian Hotline (202-833-3234) Phone counseling and referrals.

Washington, DC GLBT Travel Guide (http://washington.org/visiting/experience-dc/pride-in-dc/glbt-home) The city tourism office's official guide.

Internet Access

- Wi-fi is common in lodgings across the price spectrum; many places also have a computer on site for you to use. This guide uses @ to indicate a place has a web-connected computer for public use and wi-fi icon when it offers wireless internet access, whether free or fee-based.
- Several bars and cafes offer free wi-fi.
- Outlets of the **DC Public Library** (www.dclibrary.org) offer free terminals for 15 minutes; to surf longer, you need to sign up for a free user's card.
- For a list of wi-fi hot spots (plus tech and access info), visit **Wi-Fi Alliance** (www.wi-fi.org) and **Wi-Fi Free Spot** (www.wififreespot.com).

Legal Matters

If you are arrested, you are allowed to remain silent, though never walk away from an officer; you are entitled to have access to an attorney. The legal system presumes you're innocent until proven guilty. All persons who are arrested have the right to make one phone call. If you don't have a lawyer or family member to help you, call your embassy or consulate. The police will give you the number on request.

The blood-alcohol limit is 0.08%. Driving under the influence of alcohol or drugs is a serious offense, subject to stiff fines and even imprisonment. Possession of any illicit drug, including cocaine, ecstasy, LSD, heroin, hashish or more than an ounce of pot, is a felony potentially punishable by lengthy jail sentences.

Medical Services

Washington, DC, has no unexpected health dangers and excellent medical facilities; the only real concern is that a collision with the US medical system might injure your wallet. Remember to buy health insurance before you travel. Check the Travel Services section of the **Lonely Planet website** (www.lonelyplanet.com) for more information. Recommended medical facilities:

George Washington University Hospital (☎202-715-4000; 900 23rd St NW; Ⓜ Foggy Bottom-GWU)

Howard University Hospital (☎202-865-6100; 2041 Georgia Ave NW; Ⓜ Shaw-Howard University)

Institute of International Medicine (☎202-715-5100; 900 23rd St NW, Suite G-1094; Ⓜ Foggy Bottom-GWU) Offers immunizations and health advice for travelers going anywhere on the planet; it's housed inside GWU.

Pharmacies

The most prominent pharmacy chain is CVS, with locations all around the city. These convenient branches are open 24 hours:

CVS Dupont Circle (☎202-785-1466; 6-7 Dupont Circle; Ⓜ Dupont Circle)

CVS Thomas Circle (☎202-628-0720; 1199 Vermont Ave NW; Ⓜ McPherson Sq)

Money

The currency is the US dollar. Most locals do not carry large amounts of cash for everyday use, relying instead on credit and debit cards.

ATMs

ATMs are available 24/7 at most banks, and in shopping centers, airports, grocery stores and convenience shops. Most ATMs charge a service fee of $2.50 or more per transaction and your home bank may impose additional charges. For foreign visitors, ask your bank for exact information about using its cards in stateside ATMs. The exchange rate is usually as good as you'll get anywhere.

Credit Cards

Major credit cards are almost universally accepted. In fact, it's next to impossible to rent a car or make phone reservations without one. Visa and MasterCard are the most widely accepted. Contact the issuing company for lost or stolen cards:

American Express (☎800-528-4800; www.americanexpress.com)

MasterCard (☎800-627-8372; www.mastercard.com)

Visa (☎800-847-2911; www.visa.com)

Money Exchange

Although the airports have exchange bureaus, better rates can usually be obtained at banks in the city.

American Express (☎202-457-1300; 1150 Connecticut Ave NW; Ⓜ Farragut North)

Thomas Cook (☎202-237-2229; 5335 Wisconsin Ave NW; Ⓜ Friendship Heights)

Tipping

Tipping is *not* optional; only withhold tips in cases of outrageously bad service.

Airport & hotel porters $2 per bag, minimum per cart $5.

Bartenders 10% to 15% per round, minimum per drink $1.

Hotel maids $2 to $5 per night.

Restaurant servers 15% to 20%, unless a gratuity is already charged on the bill.

Taxi drivers 10% to 15%, rounded up to the next dollar.

Valet parking attendants At least $2 when you're handed back the keys.

Photography

There are hundreds of stores throughout the district that sell both film and digital cameras along with supplies.

➡ CVS pharmacy and Ritz Camera are just two of many chains that transfer digital images to CD or make prints from either digital or film.

➡ You can photograph anything outdoors in DC, although video and still-camera use is restricted in airports and other high-security areas like the Pentagon. Depending on the terrorist-threat level in the United States at the time of your visit, photography and video use may be restricted in other public areas as well.

➡ If you are interested in photography, check out Lonely Planet's *Travel Photography* book.

Post

The **US Postal Service** (USPS; ☎800-275-8777; www.usps.com) is reliable and inexpensive. For first-class mail sent and delivered within the USA, postage rates are 45¢ for letters up to 1oz (20¢ for each additional ounce) and 32¢ for standard-size postcards. International airmail rates for postcards and letters up to 1oz are 80¢ to Canada and Mexico, and 98¢ to other countries. For awesome stamps, go to the post-office branch in the National Postal Museum.

Public Holidays

Banks, schools, offices and most shops close on these days.

New Year's Day January 1

Martin Luther King Jr Day Third Monday in January.

Inauguration Day January 20, every four years.

Presidents' Day Third Monday in February.

Memorial Day Last Monday in May.

Independence Day July 4

Labor Day First Monday in September.

Columbus Day Second Monday in October.

Veterans Day November 11

Thanksgiving Day Fourth Thursday in November.

Christmas Day December 25

Taxes & Refunds

Sales tax varies by state and county. Unless otherwise stated, prices given in this book don't include taxes.

DC restaurant tax 10%

DC room tax 14.5%

DC sales tax 6%

Maryland room tax 5% to 8%

Maryland sales tax 6%

Virginia room tax 9.5% to 10%

Virginia sales tax 5%

Telephone

The phone system mixes regional service providers, competing long-distance carriers and several mobile-phone companies. Overall, the system is efficient. Calls from a regular landline or cell phone are usually cheaper than a hotel phone or pay phone. Pay phones are thin on the ground. Local calls cost 50¢. Services such as **Skype** (www.skype.com) and **Google Voice** (www.google.com/voice) can make calling home quite cheap. Check the websites for details.

Cell Phones

Most of the USA's mobile-phone systems are incompatible with the GSM 900/1800 standard used throughout Europe and Asia (though some convertible phones will work). G3 phones such as iPhones will work fine – but beware of roaming costs, especially for data. Check with your service provider about using your phone here.

It might be cheaper to buy a prepaid SIM card for the USA, like those sold by AT&T, which you can insert into your international mobile phone to get a local phone number and voicemail. **Planet Omni** (www.planetomni.com) and **Telestial** (www.telestial.com) offer these services, as well as cell-phone rentals.

You can also buy inexpensive, no-contract (pre-paid) phones with a local number and a set number of minutes, which can be topped up at will. Virgin Mobile, T-Mobile, AT&T and other providers offer phones starting at $20, with a package of minutes starting at around $40 for 400 minutes. Electronics store chain **Best Buy** (www.bestbuy.com) sells these phones, as well as international SIM cards.

Phone Codes

All phone numbers within the USA consist of a three-digit area code followed by a seven-digit local number. Typically, if you are calling a number within the same area code, you only have to dial the seven-digit number; however, some places now require you to dial the entire 10-digit number even for a local call. If dialing the seven-digit number doesn't work, try all 10.

- Always dial '1' before domestic long-distance numbers and before toll-free numbers (☎800, 888, 877, 866). Some toll-free numbers only work within the US.
- Dial the international country code for the USA (☎1) if calling from abroad (the same as Canada, but international rates apply between the two countries).
- To make an international call from the USA dial ☎011 followed by country code, area code and phone number. Canada is the exception, where you just dial ☎1 plus the area code and phone number.
- Dial ☎00 for assistance making international calls.
- Dial ☎411 for directory assistance nationwide.
- Dial ☎800-555-1212 for directory assistance for toll-free numbers.

Phonecards

Private prepaid phonecards are available from convenience stores, supermarkets and pharmacies. AT&T sells a reliable card that is widely available in the District.

Time

DC is on Eastern Standard Time, five hours behind Greenwich Mean Time. Daylight Saving Time is observed between mid-March and early November. When it's noon in DC, it's 5pm in London, 6am the next day in Sydney and 8am the next day in Auckland.

Tourist Information

Washington, DC, operates several information centers in the city to help travelers arrange accommodations and develop itineraries.

DC Chamber of Commerce Visitor Information Center (Map p326;

202-347-7201; www.dcchamber.org; 506 9th St NW; 8am-5:30pm Mon-Fri; M Gallery Pl-Chinatown) Offers tours, maps, lodging brochures and events listings, and sells film, tickets and souvenirs.

NPS Ellipse Visitor Pavilion (Map p320; 202-208-1631; 8am-3pm) Books tours, sells snacks; located at the northeast corner of the Ellipse, south of the White House.

Smithsonian Visitor Center (Map p318; 202-663-1000; www.si.edu/visit; 1000 Jefferson Dr SW; 8:30am-5:30pm; M Smithsonian) Located in the Castle, it is a great resource with everything you ever wanted to know about the museum programs.

Destination DC (www.washington.org) DC's official tourism site.

Travelers with Disabilities

DC is an excellent destination for disabled visitors. Most museums and major sights are wheelchair accessible, as are most large hotels and restaurants.

➡ The **Smithsonian** (202-633-1000, TTY 202-633-5285) and many museums arrange special tours for people with visual, auditory or other impairments.

➡ All Metro trains and most buses are accessible to people in wheelchairs. All Metro stations have elevators, and guide dogs are allowed on trains and buses.

➡ If you cannot use public transit, you can use **MetroAccess** (202-962-2700), a door-to-door transport provider.

➡ Out of doors, hindrances to wheelchair users include buckled-brick sidewalks in the historic blocks of Georgetown and Capitol Hill, but sidewalks in most other parts of DC are in good shape and have dropped curbs.

➡ Unfortunately, only a handful of crosswalks, mostly near the Mall, have audible crossing signals.

➡ The **Washington DC Access Guide** (www.disabilityguide.org) has loads of information on accessible restaurants, hotels, tours and more.

➡ Hearing-impaired visitors should check out **Gallaudet University** (www.gallaudet.edu) in northeast DC, which hosts lectures and cultural events especially for the deaf.

Visas

Admission requirements are subject to rapid change. The **US State Department** (www.travel.state.gov/visa) has the latest information, or check with a US consulate in your home country.

➡ Under the US visa-waiver program, visas are not required for citizens of 36 countries – including most EU members, Japan, Australia, New Zealand and the UK – for visits of up to 90 days (no extensions allowed), as long as you can present a machine-readable passport and are approved under the **Electronic System for Travel Authorization** (ESTA; www.cbp.gov/esta). Note you must register at least 72 hours before arrival, and there's a $14 fee for processing and authorization.

➡ In essence, ESTA requires that you register specific information online (name, address, passport info, etc) prior to entering the US. You will receive one of three responses: 'Authorization Approved' (this usually comes within minutes; most applicants can expect to receive this response). It is also possible to receive 'Authorization Pending', in which case you can go back online to check the status within roughly 72 hours. The third response is 'Travel not Authorized'. If this is the case, it means your application is not approved and you will need to apply for a visa.

➡ Once approved, registration is valid for two years, but note that if you renew your passport or change your name, you will need to re-register. The entire process is stored electronically and linked to your passport, but it is recommended that you bring a printout of the ESTA approval just to be safe.

➡ Canadians are exempt from the process. They do not need visas, though they do need a passport or document approved by the **Western Hemisphere Travel Initiative** (www.getyouhome.gov).

➡ Those who need a visa should apply at the US consulate in their home country.

Behind the Scenes

SEND US YOUR FEEDBACK

We love to hear from travelers – your comments keep us on our toes and help make our books better. Our well-traveled team reads every word on what you loved or loathed about this book. Although we cannot reply individually to postal submissions, we always guarantee that your feedback goes straight to the appropriate authors, in time for the next edition. Each person who sends us information is thanked in the next edition – the most useful submissions are rewarded with a selection of digital PDF chapters.

Visit **lonelyplanet.com/contact** to submit your updates and suggestions or to ask for help. Our award-winning website also features inspirational travel stories, news and discussions.

Note: We may edit, reproduce and incorporate your comments in Lonely Planet products such as guidebooks, websites and digital products, so let us know if you don't want your comments reproduced or your name acknowledged. For a copy of our privacy policy visit lonelyplanet.com/privacy.

OUR READERS

Many thanks to the travelers who used the last edition and wrote to us with helpful hints, useful advice and interesting anecdotes:

Leyu Qiu, Tim Reilly.

AUTHOR THANKS

Karla Zimmerman

Many thanks to Ted Bonar, Lea Dooley, Kate Gibbs, Christie Lavigne and China Williams for good-heartedly answering my relentless questions. A great big heaping thanks to Adam Karlin for an awesome prior edition and cool-cat tips. Regis St Louis rocks and is a true co-author pal. Deep appreciation to Lonely Planeteers Cat Craddock-Carrillo, Jennye Garibaldi and Sarah Bailey for being paragons of patience. Thanks most of all to Eric Markowitz, the world's best partner for life, who indulges my insane job.

Regis St Louis

Thanks to Eve and friends for top tips in Washington and to co-author Karla Zimmerman for all of her hard work. Thanks also to Adam Karlin for fine work on the previous edition. Big hugs to Cassandra, Magdalena and Genevieve for joining me on the big capital road trip. I'm also indebted to my father, who always loved visiting DC and filled my head with wanderlust as a boy.

ACKNOWLEDGMENTS

Illustrations pp88-9 and pp102-3 by Javier Martinez Zarracina.
Cover photograph: Capitol, Jean-Pierre Lescourret/Alamy.

THIS BOOK

This 5th edition of Lonely Planet's *Washington, DC* guidebook was researched and written by Karla Zimmerman and Regis St Louis. The previous edition was written by Regis St Louis and Adam Karlin. This guidebook was commissioned in Lonely Planet's Oakland office, and produced by the following:
Commissioning Editors Jennye Garibaldi, Catherine Craddock-Carrillo
Coordinating Editors Sarah Bailey, Carolyn Boicos
Coordinating Cartographers Xavier Di Toro, Julie Dodkins
Coordinating Layout Designer Carlos Solarte
Managing Editors Bruce Evans, Anna Metcalfe
Senior Editors Andi Jones, Susan Paterson
Managing Cartographers Anita Banh, Alison Lyall
Managing Layout Designer Chris Girdler
Assisting Editors Paul Harding, Trent Holden, Anne Mulvaney, Saralinda Turner
Assisting Layout Designer Paul Iacono
Cover Researcher Naomi Parker
Internal Image Research Nicholas Colicchia, Rebecca Skinner
Illustrator Javier Martinez Zarracina
Thanks to Shahara Ahmed, Ryan Evans, Larissa Frost, Heather Howard, Trent Paton, Raphael Richards, Gerard Walker

See also separate subindexes for:

- EATING P311
- DRINKING & NIGHTLIFE P313
- ENTERTAINMENT P313
- SHOPPING P314
- SPORTS & ACTIVITIES P315
- SLEEPING P315

Index

Sights 000
Map Pages **000**
Photo Pages **000**

Sights 000
Map Pages **000**
Photo Pages **000**

D

E

F

Sights 000
Map Pages **000**
Photo Pages **000**

EATING

Sights 000
Map Pages **000**
Photo Pages **000**

DRINKING & NIGHTLIFE

ENTERTAINMENT

SHOPPING

Sights 000
Map Pages **000**
Photo Pages **000**

SPORTS & ACTIVITIES

SLEEPING

Washington, DC Maps

Map Legend

Sights
- Beach
- Buddhist
- Castle
- Christian
- Hindu
- Islamic
- Jewish
- Monument
- Museum/Gallery
- Ruin
- Winery/Vineyard
- Zoo
- Other Sight

Eating
- Eating

Drinking & Nightlife
- Drinking & Nightlife
- Cafe

Entertainment
- Entertainment

Shopping
- Shopping

Sleeping
- Sleeping
- Camping

Sports & Activities
- Diving/Snorkelling
- Canoeing/Kayaking
- Skiing
- Surfing
- Swimming/Pool
- Walking
- Windsurfing
- Other Sports & Activities

Information
- Post Office
- Tourist Information

Transport
- Airport
- Border Crossing
- Bus
- Cable Car/ Funicular
- Cycling
- Ferry
- Metro
- Monorail
- Parking
- S-Bahn
- Taxi
- Train/Railway
- Tram
- Tube Station
- U-Bahn
- Other Transport

Routes
- Tollway
- Freeway
- Primary
- Secondary
- Tertiary
- Lane
- Unsealed Road
- Plaza/Mall
- Steps
- Tunnel
- Pedestrian Overpass
- Walking Tour
- Walking Tour Detour
- Path

Boundaries
- International
- State/Province
- Disputed
- Regional/Suburb
- Marine Park
- Cliff
- Wall

Geographic
- Hut/Shelter
- Lighthouse
- Lookout
- Mountain/Volcano
- Oasis
- Park
- Pass
- Picnic Area
- Waterfall

Hydrography
- River/Creek
- Intermittent River
- Swamp/Mangrove
- Reef
- Canal
- Water
- Dry/Salt/ Intermittent Lake
- Glacier

Areas
- Beach/Desert
- Cemetery (Christian)
- Cemetery (Other)
- Park/Forest
- Sportsground
- Sight (Building)
- Top Sight (Building)

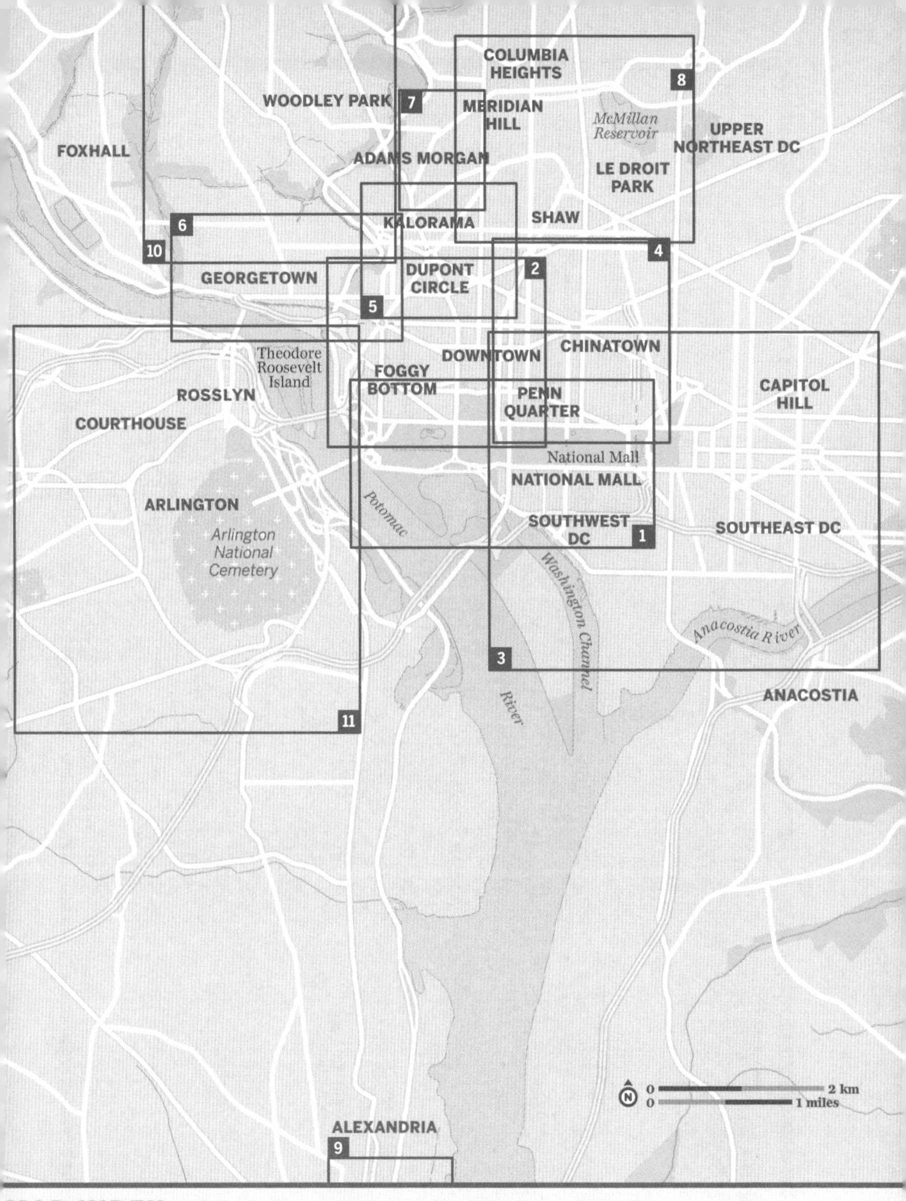
COLUMBIA HEIGHTS
8
WOODLEY PARK
7
MERIDIAN HILL
McMillan Reservoir
UPPER NORTHEAST DC
FOXHALL
ADAMS MORGAN
LE DROIT PARK
KALORAMA
SHAW
6
10
4
2
GEORGETOWN
DUPONT CIRCLE
5
Theodore Roosevelt Island
DOWNTOWN
CHINATOWN
FOGGY BOTTOM
ROSSLYN
CAPITOL HILL
PENN QUARTER
COURTHOUSE
National Mall
NATIONAL MALL
ARLINGTON
Potomac
SOUTHWEST DC
1
SOUTHEAST DC
Arlington National Cemetery
Washington Channel
Anacostia River
3
River
ANACOSTIA
11
0 2 km
0 1 miles
ALEXANDRIA
9

MAP INDEX

NATIONAL MALL

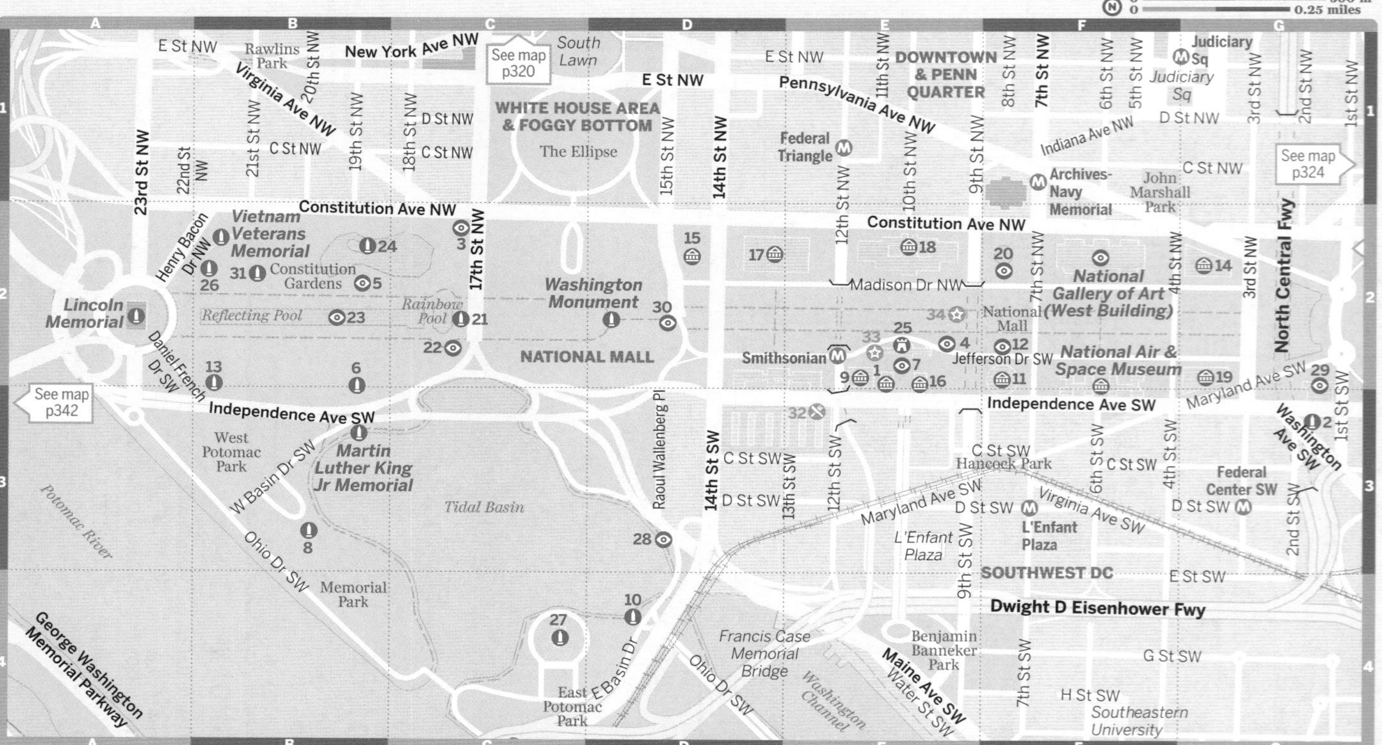

NATIONAL MALL

Top Sights (p82)
- Lincoln Memorial ... A2
- Martin Luther King Jr Memorial ... B3
- National Air & Space Museum ... F2
- National Gallery of Art (West Building) ... F2
- Vietnam Veterans Memorial ... B2
- Washington Monument ... D2

Sights (p90)
1 Arthur M Sackler Gallery ... E2
2 Bartholdi Fountain ... G3
3 C&O Canal Gatehouse ... C2
4 Carousel ... E2
5 Constitution Gardens ... B2
6 District of Columbia War Memorial ... B2
7 Enid A Haupt Memorial Garden ... E2
8 Franklin Delano Roosevelt Memorial ... B3
9 Freer Gallery of Art ... E2
10 George Mason Memorial ... D4
11 Hirshhorn Museum ... F2
12 Hirshhorn Sculpture Garden ... F2
Ice Rink ... (see 20)
13 Korean War Veterans Memorial ... B2
14 National Gallery of Art - East Building ... G2
15 National Museum of African American History and Culture ... D2
16 National Museum of African Art ... E2
17 National Museum of American History ... D2
18 National Museum of National History ... E2
19 National Museum of the American Indian ... G2
National Museums of Asian Art ... (see 1)
20 National Sculpture Garden ... F2
21 National WWII Memorial ... C2
22 National WWII Memorial kiosk ... C2
23 Reflecting Pool ... B2
24 Signers' Memorial ... B2
25 Smithsonian Castle ... E2
26 The Three Soldiers ... B2
27 Thomas Jefferson Memorial ... C4
28 Tidal Basin Boathouse ... D3
29 United States Botanic Garden ... G2
30 Washington Monument Ticket Kiosk ... D2
31 Women in Vietnam Memorial ... B2

Eating (p96)
Cascade Cafe ... (see 14)
32 Farmers Market ... E3
Mitsitam Native Foods Cafe ... (see 19)
Pavilion Cafe ... (see 20)

Entertainment (p97)
33 Discovery Theater ... E2
Jazz in the Garden ... (see 20)
34 Screen on the Green ... E2

Key on p322

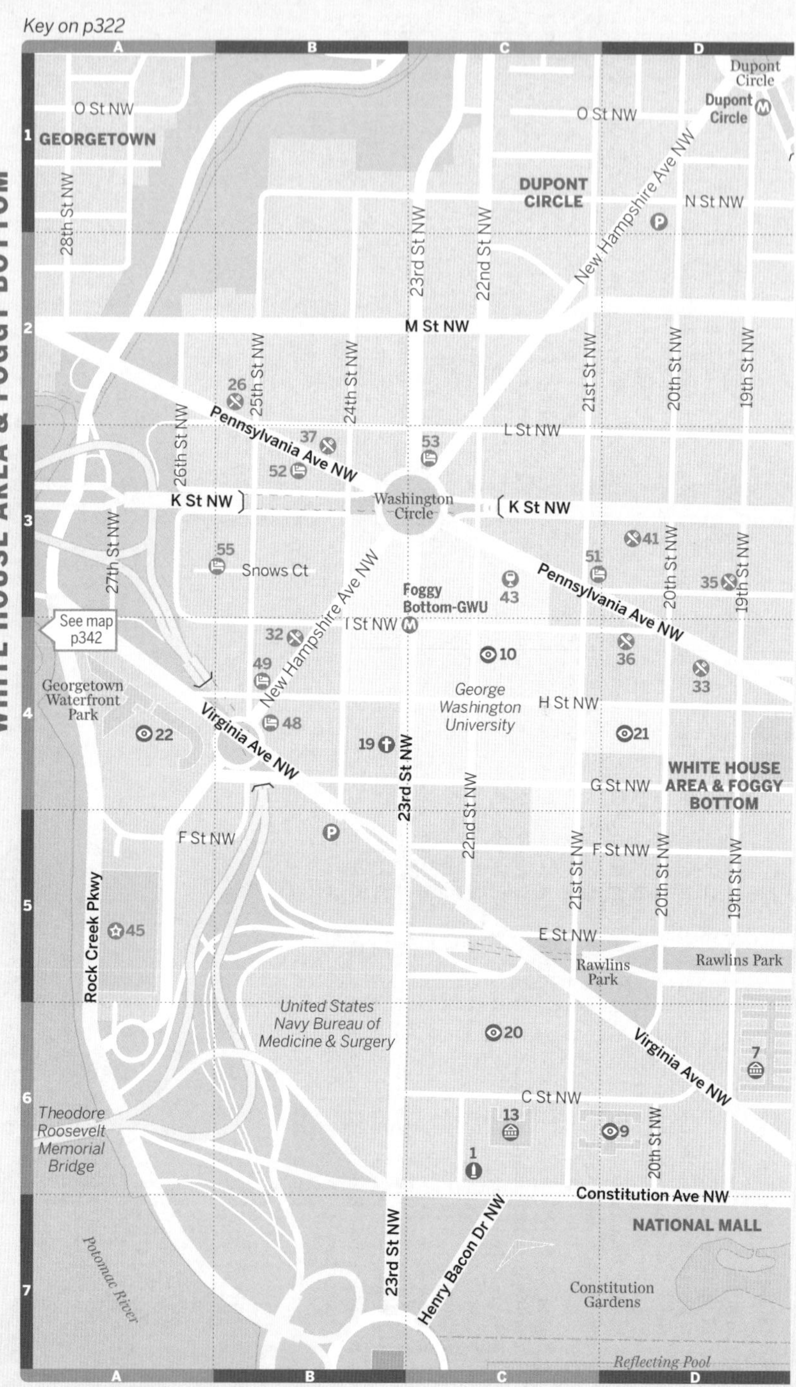

A
B
C
D
1
2
3
4
5
6
7
O St NW
GEORGETOWN
28th St NW
Dupont Circle
Dupont Circle
O St NW
DUPONT CIRCLE
New Hampshire Ave NW
N St NW
23rd St NW
22nd St NW
M St NW
26
25th St NW
24th St NW
21st St NW
20th St NW
19th St NW
Pennsylvania Ave NW
37
53
L St NW
26th St NW
52
K St NW
Washington Circle
K St NW
41
27th St NW
55
Snows Ct
51
20th St NW
New Hampshire Ave NW
Foggy Bottom-GWU
43
Pennsylvania Ave NW
35
19th St NW
See map p342
I St NW
32
10
36
33
49
Georgetown Waterfront Park
George Washington University
H St NW
22
Virginia Ave NW
48
19
23rd St NW
21
G St NW
WHITE HOUSE AREA & FOGGY BOTTOM
22nd St NW
F St NW
F St NW
21st St NW
20th St NW
19th St NW
Rock Creek Pkwy
45
E St NW
Rawlins Park
Rawlins Park
United States Navy Bureau of Medicine & Surgery
20
Virginia Ave NW
7
Theodore Roosevelt Memorial Bridge
C St NW
13
9
1
20th St NW
Constitution Ave NW
Henry Bacon Dr NW
NATIONAL MALL
23rd St NW
Potomac River
Constitution Gardens
Reflecting Pool

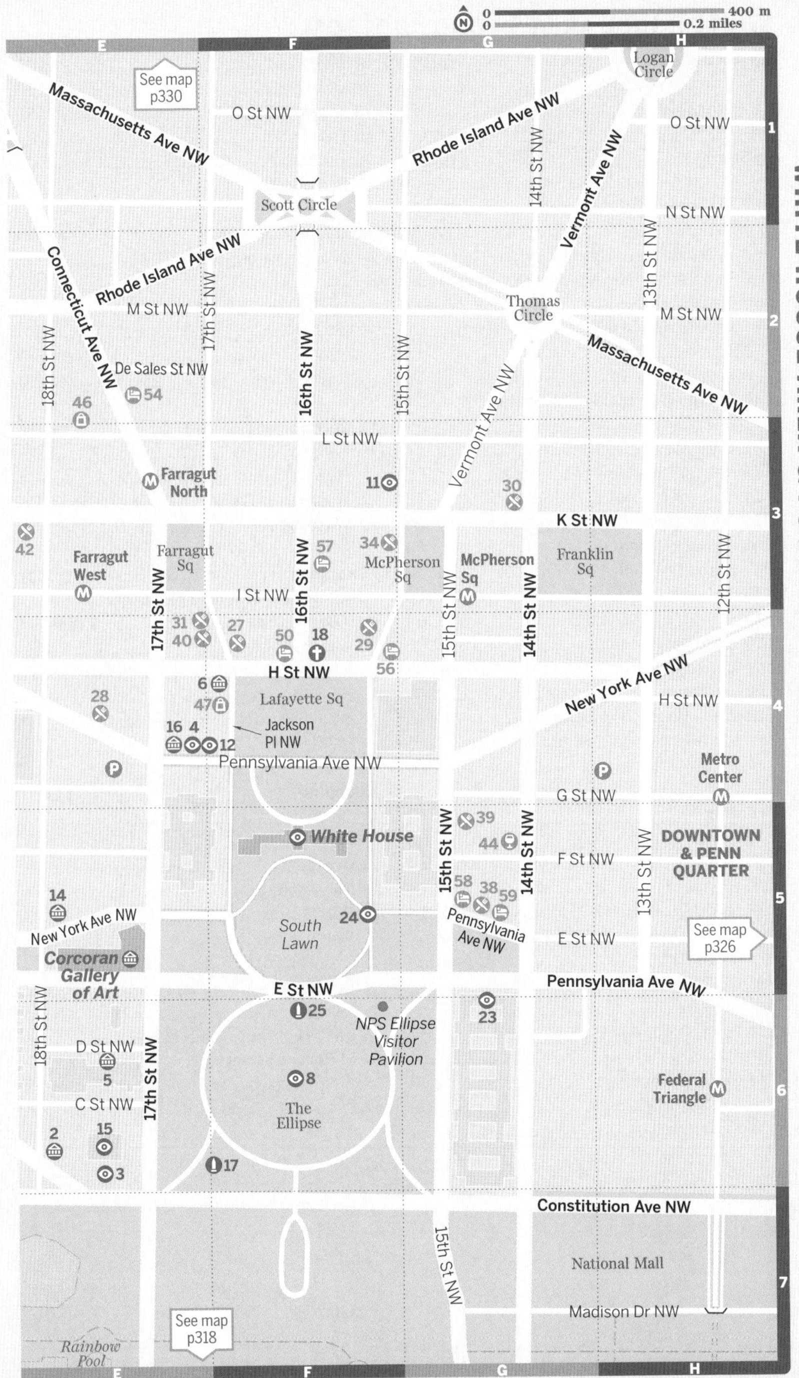

See map p330
See map p326
See map p318

WHITE HOUSE AREA & FOGGY BOTTOM *Map on p320*

CAPITOL HILL & SOUTHEAST DC *Map on p324*

Key on p323

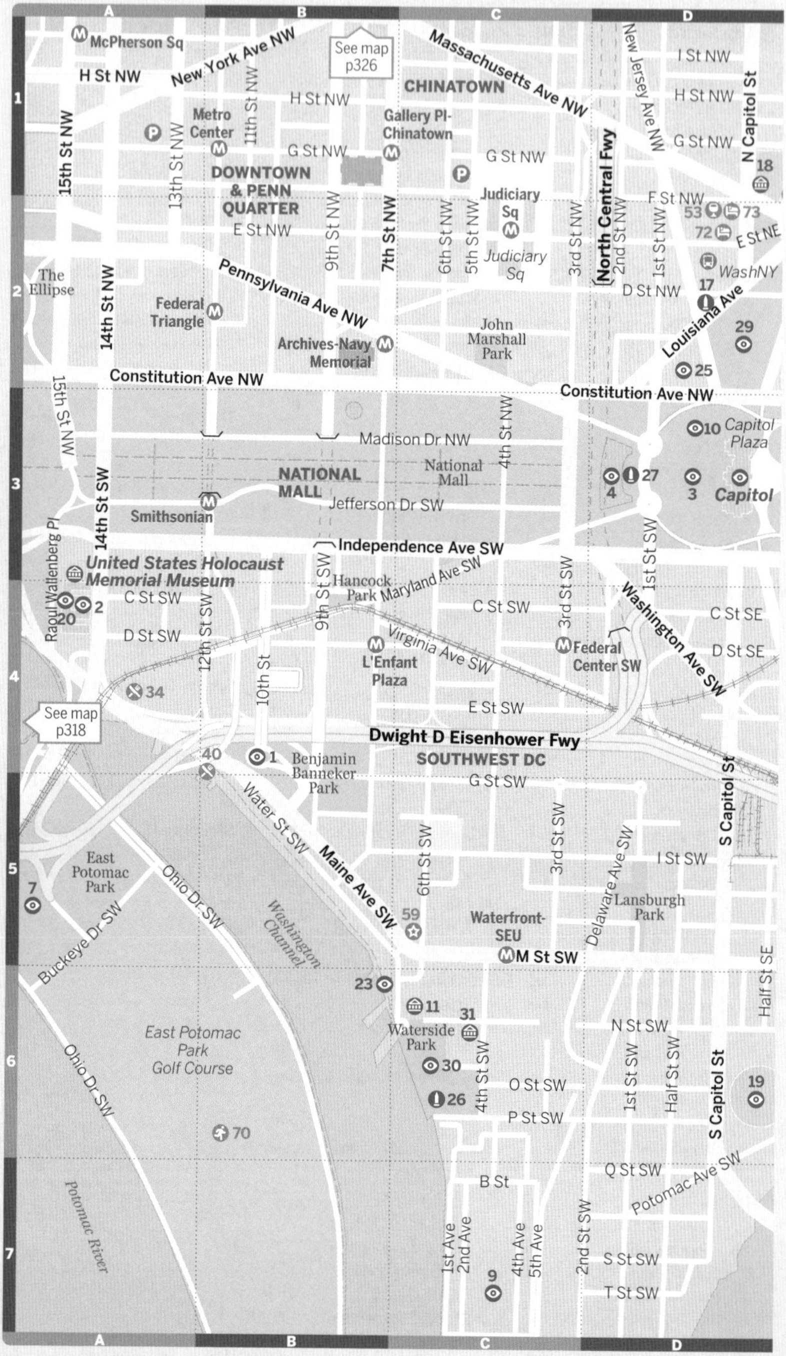

CAPITOL HILL & SOUTHEAST DC

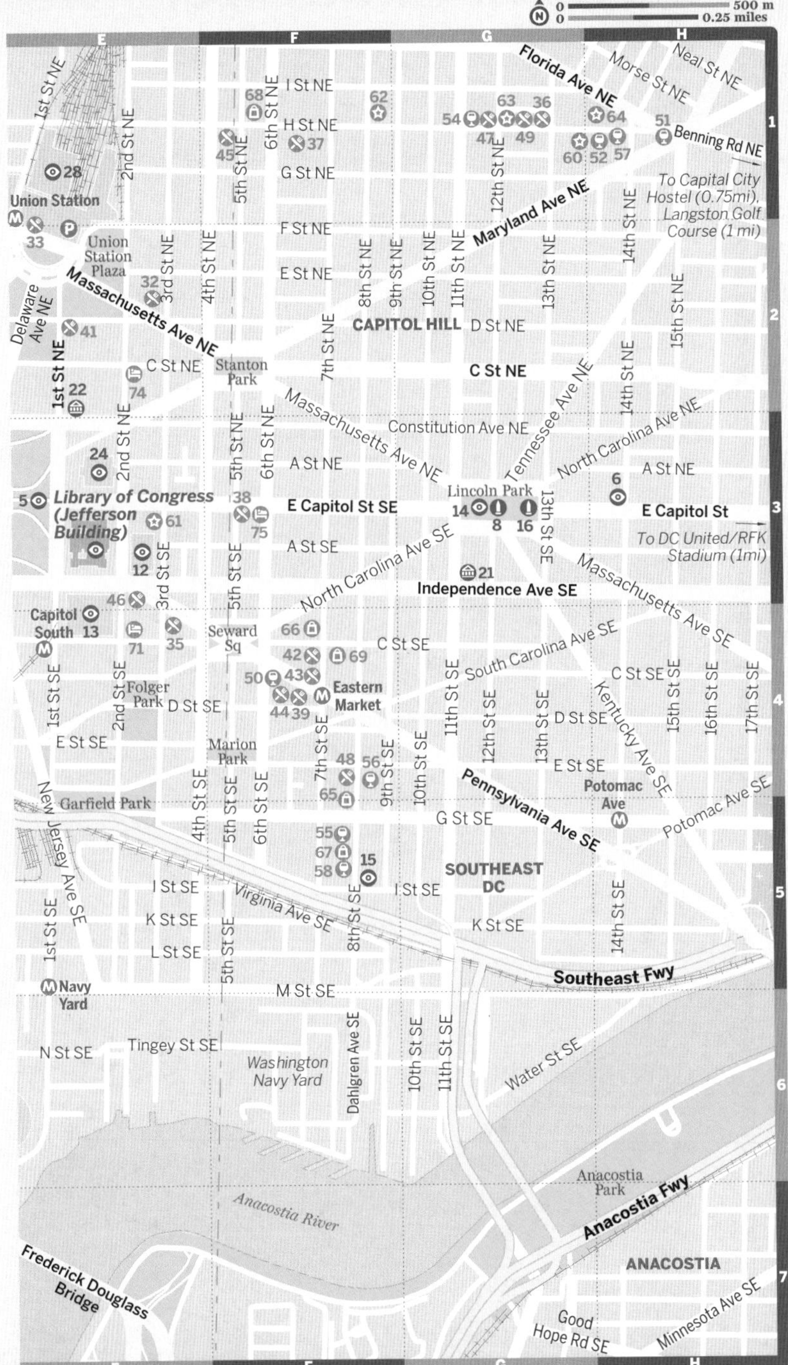
CAPITOL HILL & SOUTHEAST DC
500 m
0.25 miles
CAPITOL HILL
SOUTHEAST DC
ANACOSTIA
Union Station
Union Station Plaza
Library of Congress (Jefferson Building)
Stanton Park
Lincoln Park
Seward Sq
Folger Park
Marion Park
Garfield Park
Eastern Market
Capitol South
Potomac Ave
Navy Yard
Washington Navy Yard
Anacostia River
Anacostia Park
Frederick Douglass Bridge
Southeast Fwy
Anacostia Fwy
Florida Ave NE
Maryland Ave NE
Massachusetts Ave NE
Massachusetts Ave SE
North Carolina Ave NE
North Carolina Ave SE
South Carolina Ave SE
Tennessee Ave NE
Kentucky Ave SE
Pennsylvania Ave SE
Potomac Ave SE
Virginia Ave SE
New Jersey Ave SE
Delaware Ave NE
Independence Ave SE
Constitution Ave NE
E Capitol St SE
E Capitol St
Benning Rd NE
Water St SE
Good Hope Rd SE
Minnesota Ave SE
Dahlgren Ave SE
Tingey St SE
To Capital City Hostel (0.75mi), Langston Golf Course (1 mi)
To DC United/RFK Stadium (1mi)

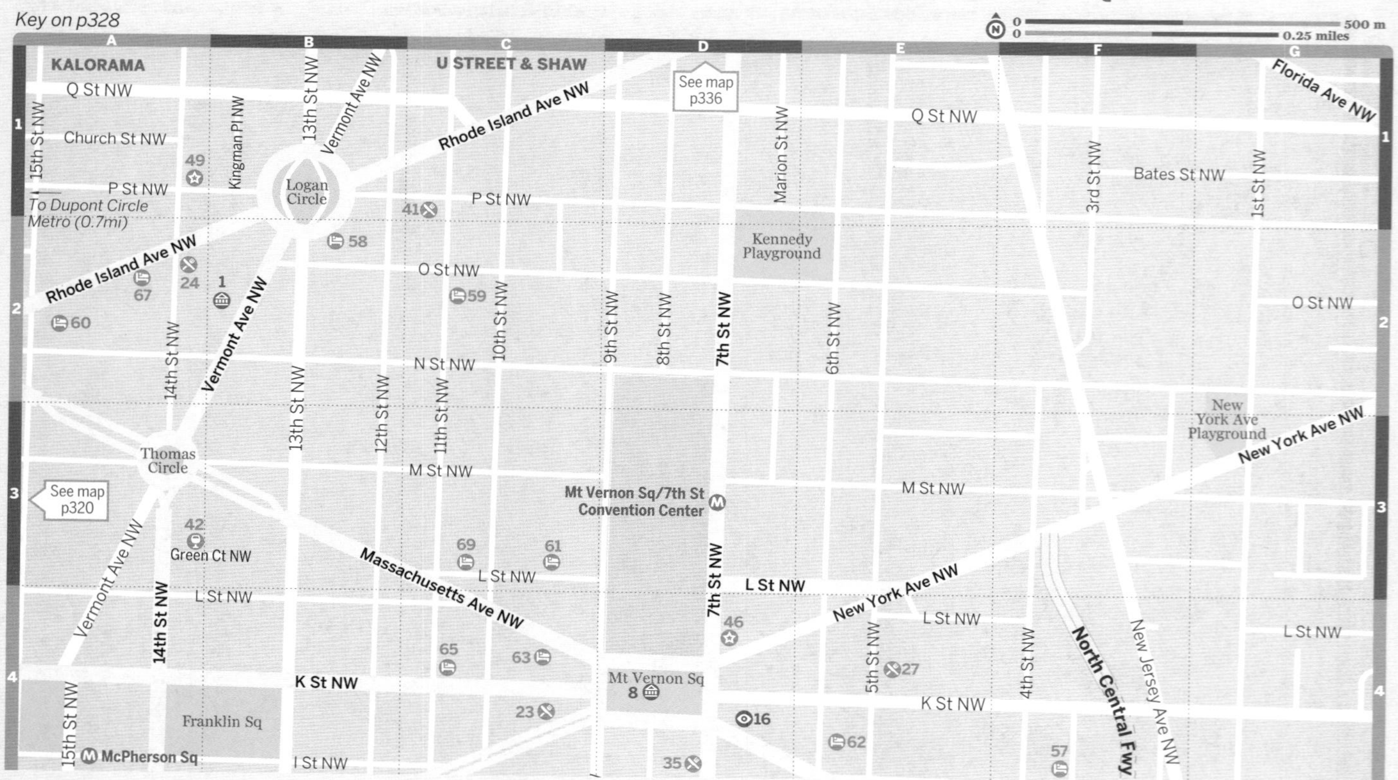
Key on p328
500 m
0.25 miles
KALORAMA
U STREET & SHAW
See map p336
See map p320
To Dupont Circle Metro (0.7mi)
Florida Ave NW
Rhode Island Ave NW
Vermont Ave NW
Massachusetts Ave NW
New York Ave NW
New Jersey Ave NW
North Central Fwy
Q St NW
Church St NW
P St NW
Bates St NW
O St NW
N St NW
M St NW
L St NW
K St NW
I St NW
Kingman Pl NW
Marion St NW
Green Ct NW
15th St NW
14th St NW
13th St NW
12th St NW
11th St NW
10th St NW
9th St NW
8th St NW
7th St NW
6th St NW
5th St NW
4th St NW
3rd St NW
1st St NW
Logan Circle
Thomas Circle
Kennedy Playground
New York Ave Playground
Mt Vernon Sq/7th St Convention Center
Mt Vernon Sq
Franklin Sq
McPherson Sq

DOWNTOWN & PENN QUARTER

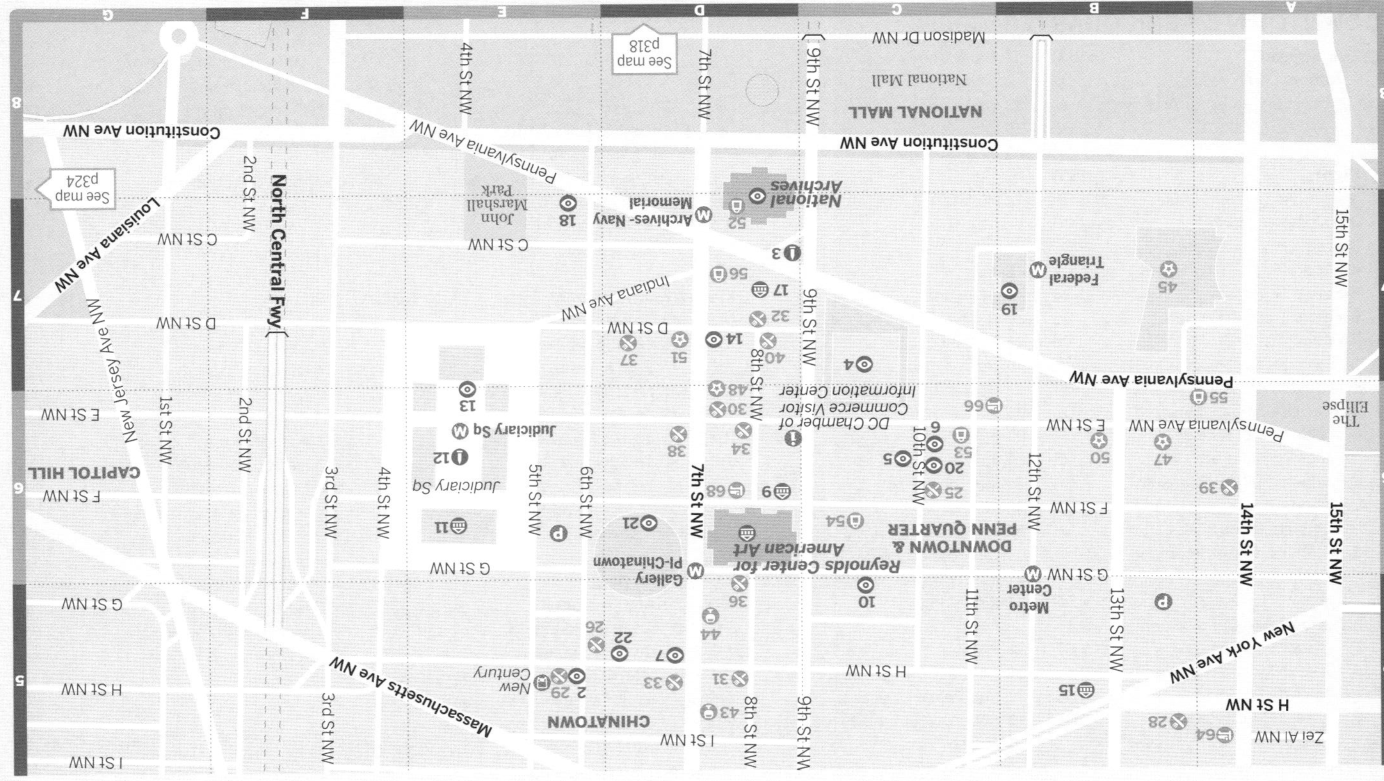

DOWNTOWN & PENN QUARTER *Map on p326*

Top Sights (p153)
National Archives ... D7
Reynolds Center for American Art ... D6

Sights (p155)
1 Bethune Council House ... B2
2 Chinatown Market ... E5
3 FDR Memorial Stone ... D7
4 Federal Bureau of Investigation ... C7
5 Ford's Theatre ... C6
6 Ford's Theatre Center ... C6
7 Friendship Arch ... D5
8 Historical Society of Washington, DC ... D4
9 International Spy Museum ... D6
10 Martin Luther King Jr Memorial Library ... C5
11 National Building Museum ... E6
12 National Law Enforcement Officers Memorial ... E6
13 National Law Enforcement Officers Museum (Future Site) ... E6
14 National Law Enforcement Visitors Center ... D7
15 National Museum of Women in the Arts ... B5
16 National Public Radio ... D4
17 Navy Memorial & Naval Heritage Center ... D7
18 Newseum ... E7
19 Old Post Office Pavilion ... B7
20 Peterson House ... C6
21 Verizon Center ... D6
22 Wok & Roll (Surratt House site) ... D5

Eating (p158)
23 Acadiana ... C4
24 Birch & Barley ... A2
25 Bistro D'Oc ... C6
26 Burma ... E5
27 Busboys & Poets ... E4
28 Cafe Mozart ... B5
29 Full Kee ... E5
30 Jaleo ... D6
31 Matchbox Pizza ... D5
32 Minibar ... D7
33 Nando's Peri Peri ... D5
Old Post Office Pavilion ... (see 19)
34 Penn Quarter Market ... D6
35 Ping Pong ... D4
Poste ... (see 68)
36 Proof ... D5
37 Rasika ... D7
38 Red Velvet Cupcakery ... D6
39 Shops at National Place ... A6
40 Teaism ... D7
41 Veranda ... C1
Zola ... (see 9)

Drinking & Nightlife (p161)
Churchkey ... (see 24)
42 Green Lantern & Tool Shed ... A3
Poste ... (see 68)
43 RFD Washington ... D5
44 Rocket Bar ... D5

Entertainment (p162)
45 Capitol Steps ... B7
46 Civilian Art Projects ... D4
Ford's Theatre ... (see 5)
47 National Theatre ... B6
48 Shakespeare Theatre ... D6
49 Studio Theatre ... A1
Touchstone Gallery ... (see 23)
50 Warner Theatre ... B6
51 Woolly Mammoth Theatre Company ... D7

Shopping (p163)
52 Archives Shop ... D7
53 Coup de Foudre ... C6
54 Cowgirl Creamery ... C6
International Spy Museum ... (see 9)
National Building Museum ... (see 11)
National Museum of Women in the Arts ... (see 15)
Old Post Office Pavilion ... (see 19)
55 Political Americana ... A6
56 Pua Naturally ... D7
Teaism ... (see 40)

Sports & Activities (p164)
Bike & Roll ... (see 19)
Washington Capitals ... (see 21)
Washington Wizards ... (see 21)

Sleeping (p247)
57 Capital View Hostel ... F4
58 Chester Arthur House ... B2
59 DC Lofty ... C2
60 District Hotel ... A2
61 Eldon Suites ... C3
62 Hampton Inn ... E4
63 Henley Park Hotel ... C4
64 Hilton Garden Inn ... A5
65 Hostelling International – Washington DC ... C4
66 Hotel Harrington ... C6
67 Hotel Helix ... A2
68 Hotel Monaco ... D6
69 Morrison-Clark Inn ... C3

DUPONT CIRCLE & KALORAMA *Map on p330*

Key on p329

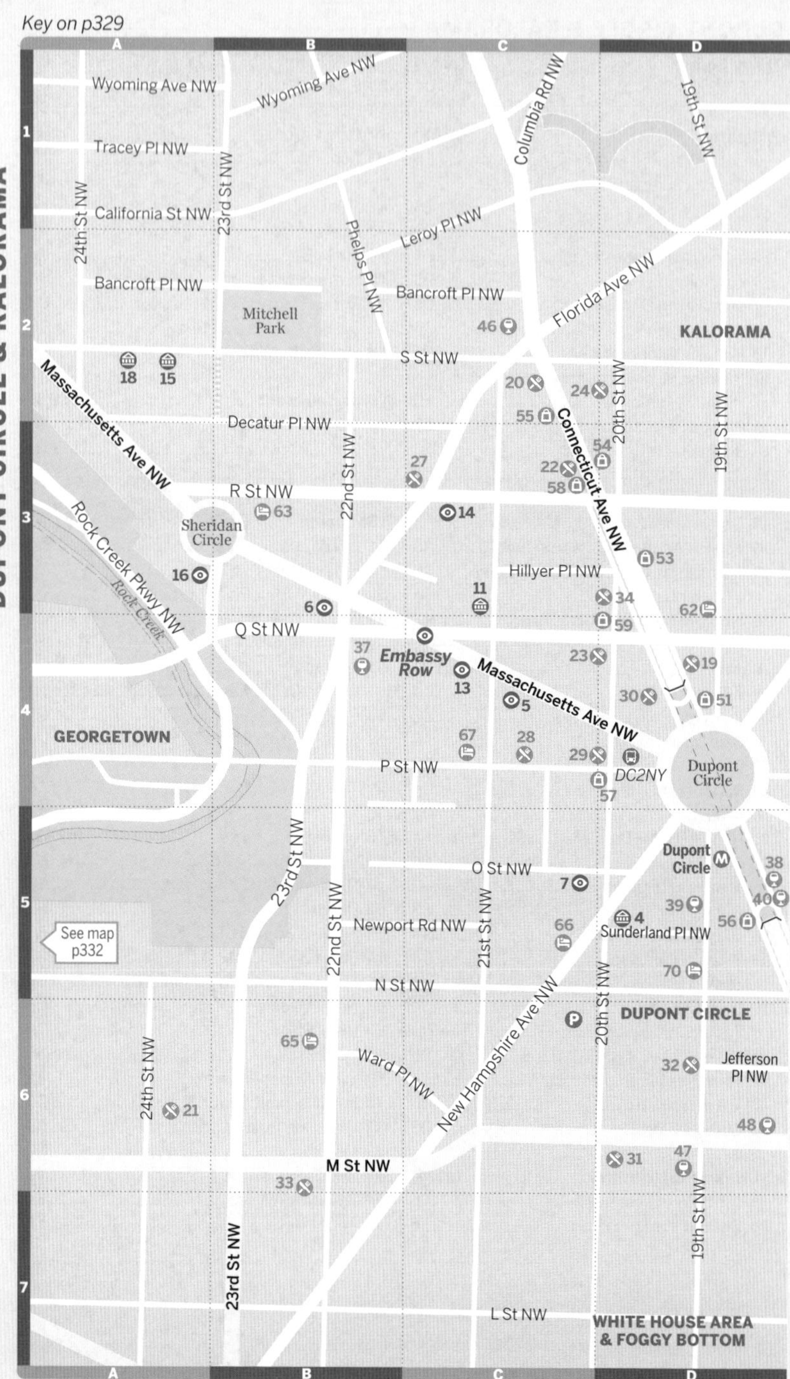

Wyoming Ave NW
Tracey Pl NW
California St NW
Bancroft Pl NW
24th St NW
23rd St NW
Phelps Pl NW
Leroy Pl NW
Columbia Rd NW
19th St NW
Florida Ave NW
Mitchell Park
KALORAMA
S St NW
Massachusetts Ave NW
Decatur Pl NW
22nd St NW
20th St NW
Connecticut Ave NW
R St NW
Sheridan Circle
Rock Creek Pkwy NW
Rock Creek
Hillyer Pl NW
Q St NW
Embassy Row
GEORGETOWN
P St NW
DC2NY
Dupont Circle
O St NW
21st St NW
Newport Rd NW
Sunderland Pl NW
See map p332
N St NW
New Hampshire Ave NW
DUPONT CIRCLE
Ward Pl NW
Jefferson Pl NW
M St NW
L St NW
WHITE HOUSE AREA & FOGGY BOTTOM

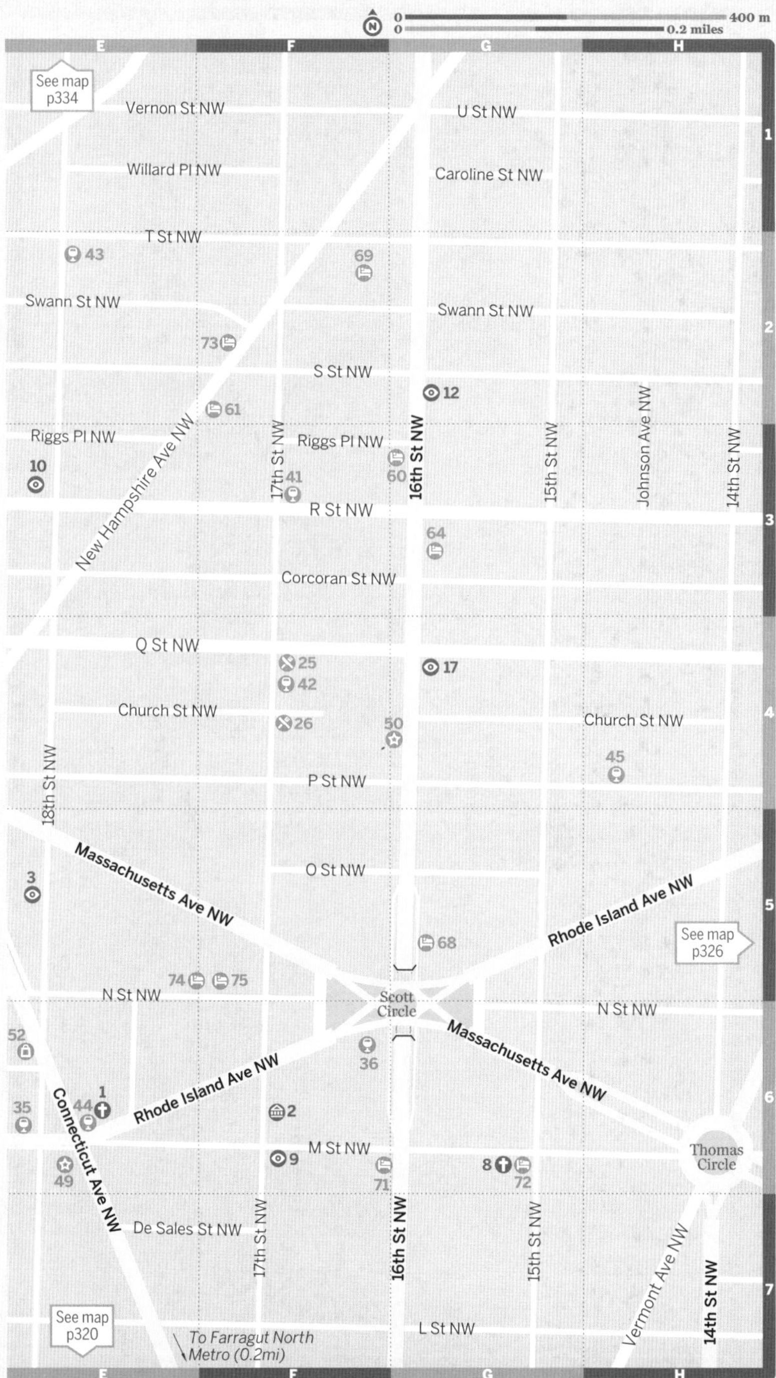
0
0
400 m
0.2 miles
E
F
G
H
See map p334
Vernon St NW
U St NW
Willard Pl NW
Caroline St NW
T St NW
43
69
Swann St NW
Swann St NW
73
S St NW
12
61
New Hampshire Ave NW
Riggs Pl NW
17th St NW
Riggs Pl NW
16th St NW
15th St NW
Johnson Ave NW
14th St NW
10
41
60
R St NW
64
Corcoran St NW
Q St NW
25
42
17
Church St NW
26
50
Church St NW
45
P St NW
18th St NW
Massachusetts Ave NW
O St NW
3
Rhode Island Ave NW
68
See map p326
74
75
N St NW
Scott Circle
N St NW
52
36
Massachusetts Ave NW
1
35
44
Rhode Island Ave NW
Connecticut Ave NW
2
M St NW
9
8
72
Thomas Circle
49
71
De Sales St NW
17th St NW
16th St NW
15th St NW
Vermont Ave NW
14th St NW
See map p320
To Farragut North Metro (0.2mi)
L St NW
1
2
3
4
5
6
7
DUPONT CIRCLE & KALORAMA

GEORGETOWN

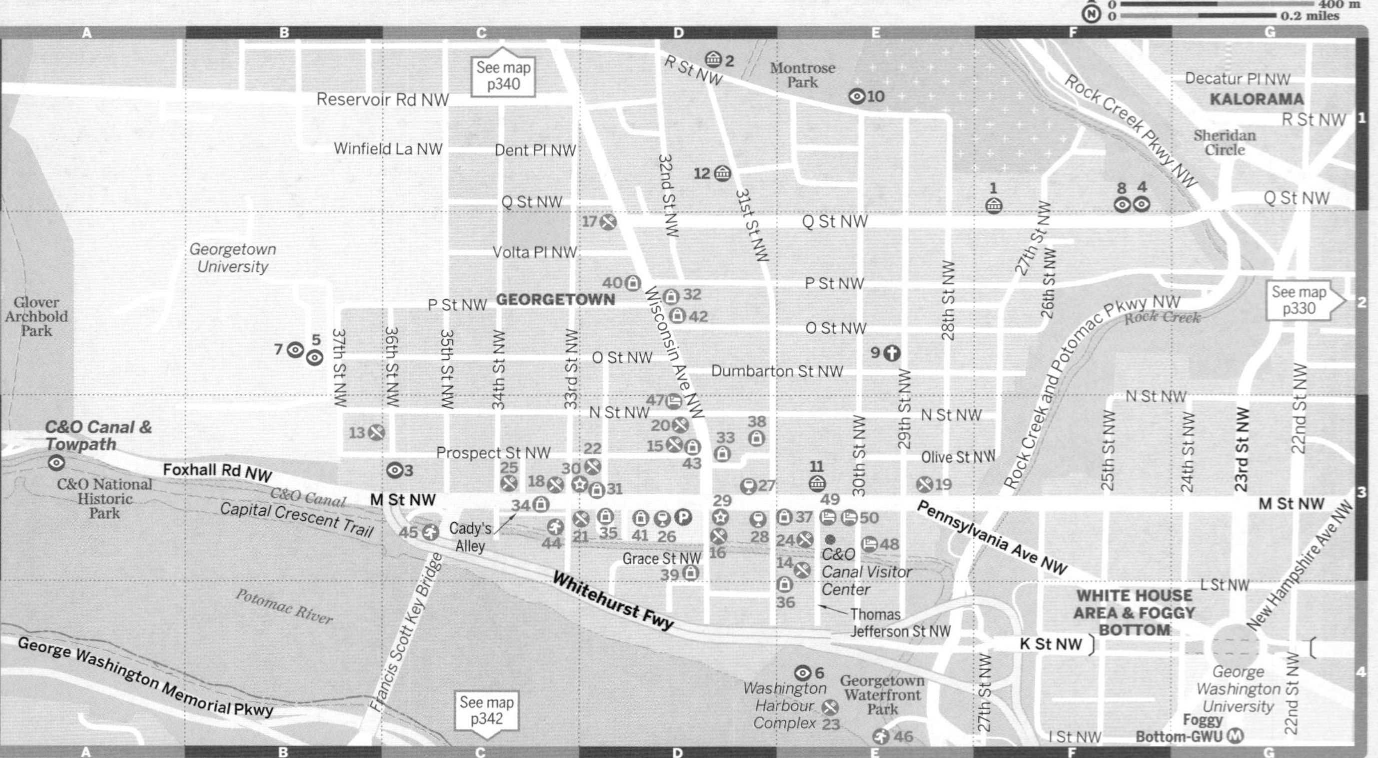

0 400 m
0 0.2 miles
See map p340
See map p330
See map p342
Reservoir Rd NW
Winfield La NW
Dent Pl NW
Q St NW
Volta Pl NW
P St NW
O St NW
N St NW
Prospect St NW
M St NW
Foxhall Rd NW
Grace St NW
Dumbarton St NW
Olive St NW
Pennsylvania Ave NW
Whitehurst Fwy
K St NW
L St NW
I St NW
Thomas Jefferson St NW
New Hampshire Ave NW
Rock Creek Pkwy NW
Rock Creek and Potomac Pkwy NW
Rock Creek
Decatur Pl NW
R St NW
Wisconsin Ave NW
37th St NW
36th St NW
35th St NW
34th St NW
33rd St NW
32nd St NW
31st St NW
30th St NW
29th St NW
28th St NW
27th St NW
26th St NW
25th St NW
24th St NW
23rd St NW
22nd St NW
GEORGETOWN
KALORAMA
Sheridan Circle
Montrose Park
Georgetown University
Glover Archbold Park
C&O Canal & Towpath
C&O National Historic Park
C&O Canal
Capital Crescent Trail
Cady's Alley
C&O Canal Visitor Center
Potomac River
Francis Scott Key Bridge
George Washington Memorial Pkwy
Washington Harbour Complex
Georgetown Waterfront Park
WHITE HOUSE AREA & FOGGY BOTTOM
George Washington University
Foggy Bottom-GWU

GEORGETOWN

Top Sights **(p117)**
- C&O Canal & Towpath ... A3

Sights **(p118)**
- Dalghren Chapel ... (see 7)
- 1 Dumbarton House ... F1
- 2 Dumbarton Oaks ... D1
- 3 Exorcist Stairs ... C3
- 4 Female Union Band Cemetery ... F1
- 5 Georgetown University ... B2
- 6 Georgetown Waterfront Park ... E4
- 7 Healy Building ... B2
- 8 Mt Zion Cemetery ... F1
- 9 Mt Zion United Methodist Church ... E2
- 10 Oak Hill Cemetery ... E1
- 11 Old Stone House ... E3
- 12 Tudor Place ... D1

Eating **(p120)**
- 13 1789 ... B3
- 14 Baked and Wired ... E3
- 15 Café Milano ... D3
- 16 Ching Ching Cha ... D3
- Citronelle ... (see 50)
- 17 Dolcezza ... D2
- 18 Georgetown Cupcake ... C3
- 19 La Chaumiére ... E3
- 20 Martin's Tavern ... D3
- 21 Pizzeria Paradiso ... D3
- 22 Quick Pita ... D3
- 23 Sequoia ... E4
- 24 Snap Café ... E3
- 25 Sweetgreen ... C3

Drinking & Nightlife **(p125)**
- Birreria Paradiso ... (see 21)
- 26 J Paul's ... D3
- 27 Mie N Yu ... D3
- 28 Mr Smith's ... D3
- Tombs ... (see 13)

Entertainment **(p126)**
- 29 Blues Alley ... D3
- 30 Rhino Bar & Pump House ... D3

Shopping **(p126)**
- 31 Annie Cream Cheese ... D3
- 32 Appalachian Spring ... D2
- 33 Apple Store ... D3
- As Seen on TV ... (see 41)
- 34 Cady's Alley ... C3
- 35 Dean & DeLuca ... D3
- 36 Lost Boys ... E4
- 37 Lush ... E3
- 38 Old Print Gallery ... D3
- 39 Patagonia ... D3
- Relish ... (see 34)
- 40 Secondhand Rose ... D2
- 41 Shops at Georgetown Park ... D3
- 42 Tugooh Toys ... D2
- 43 Zara ... D3

Sports & Activities **(p127)**
- 44 Big Wheel Bikes ... C3
- 45 Capital Crescent Trail (Start) ... C3
- Jack's Bathouse ... (see 45)
- 46 Thompson Boat Center ... E4

Sleeping **(p246)**
- 47 Georgetown Inn ... D3
- 48 Georgetown Suites ... E3
- 49 Hotel Monticello ... E3
- 50 Latham Hotel ... E3

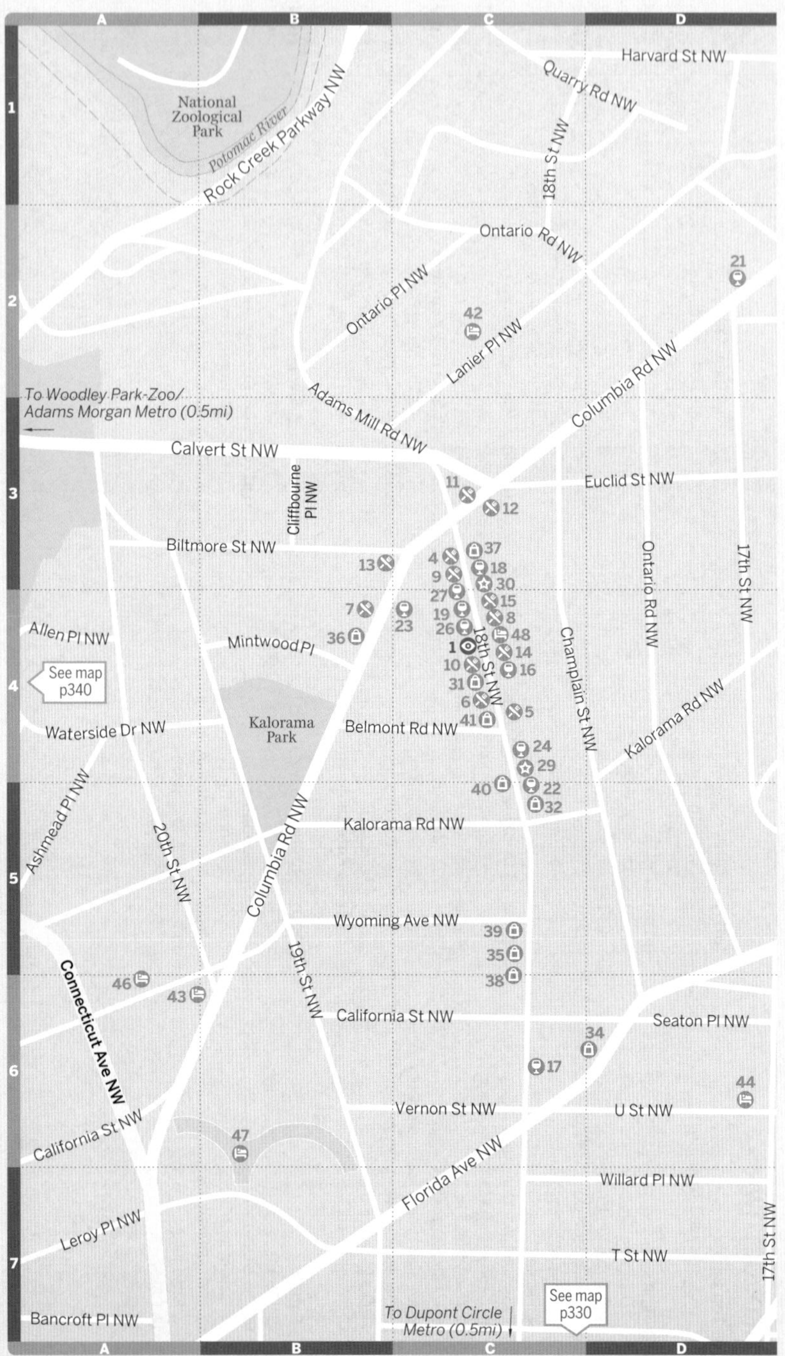
National Zoological Park
Potomac River
Rock Creek Parkway NW
Harvard St NW
Quarry Rd NW
18th St NW
Ontario Rd NW
Ontario Pl NW
Lanier Pl NW
Adams Mill Rd NW
Columbia Rd NW
To Woodley Park-Zoo/ Adams Morgan Metro (0.5mi)
Calvert St NW
Euclid St NW
Cliffbourne Pl NW
Biltmore St NW
Allen Pl NW
Mintwood Pl
See map p340
Waterside Dr NW
Kalorama Park
Belmont Rd NW
Champlain St NW
Ontario Rd NW
17th St NW
Kalorama Rd NW
Ashmead Pl NW
20th St NW
Wyoming Ave NW
19th St NW
Connecticut Ave NW
California St NW
Seaton Pl NW
Vernon St NW
U St NW
Florida Ave NW
Willard Pl NW
Leroy Pl NW
T St NW
Bancroft Pl NW
To Dupont Circle Metro (0.5mi)
See map p330

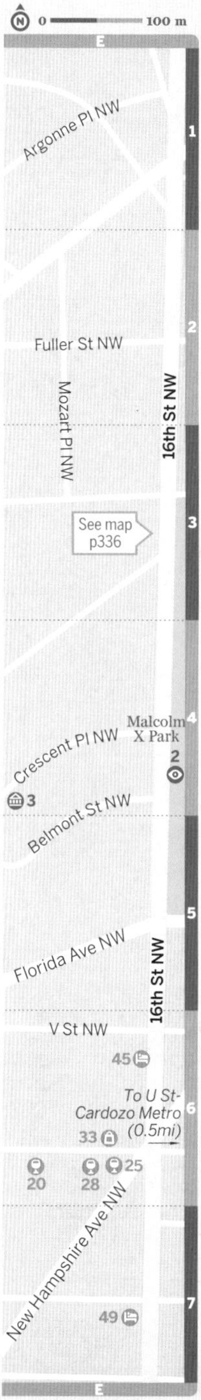

0 — 100 m

E

1 2 3 4 5 6 7

Argonne Pl NW
Fuller St NW
Mozart Pl NW
16th St NW
See map p336
Malcolm X Park
Crescent Pl NW
Belmont St NW
Florida Ave NW
V St NW
To U St-Cardozo Metro (0.5mi)
New Hampshire Ave NW

Sights (p180)

1 District of Columbia Arts Center C4
2 Malcolm X Park E4
3 Meridian International Center E4

Eating (p180)

4 Adams-Morgan Farmers Market C3
5 Amsterdam Falafelshop C4
6 Bardia's C4
7 Cashion's Eat Place B4
8 Diner C4
9 Julia's Empandas C3
10 Meskerem C4
11 Mixtec C3
12 Pasta Mia C3
13 Perrys B3
14 Rumba Cafe C4
15 Tryst C4

Drinking & Nightlife (p182)

16 Black Squirrel C4
17 Blaguard C6
18 Bossa C3
19 Bukom C4
20 Chi-Cha Lounge E6
21 Chief Ike's Mambo Room D2
22 Dan's Cafe C5
23 Habana Village C4
24 Heaven & Hell C4
25 Local 16 ..... E6
26 Millie & Al's C4
27 Reef C4
28 Stetson's Famous Bar & Grill E6
Tryst ..... (see 15)

Entertainment (p186)

29 Columbia Station C4
District of Columbia Arts Center ..... (see 1)
30 Madam's Organ C3

Shopping (p186)

31 B&K Newsstand C4
32 Brass Knob C5
33 Caramel E6
34 Commonwealth D6
35 Crooked Beat Records C5
36 Fleet Feet B4
37 Idle Times Books C3
38 Meeps Vintage Fashionette C6
39 Skynear Designs Gallery C5
40 Smash! C5
41 Toro Mata C4

Sleeping (p252)

42 Adam's Inn C2
43 American Guest House A6
44 Bed & Breakfast on U Street D6
45 Meridian Manor E6
46 Taft Bridge Inn A6
47 Washington Hilton B6
48 Washington International Student Center C4
49 Windsor Inn E7

Key on p338

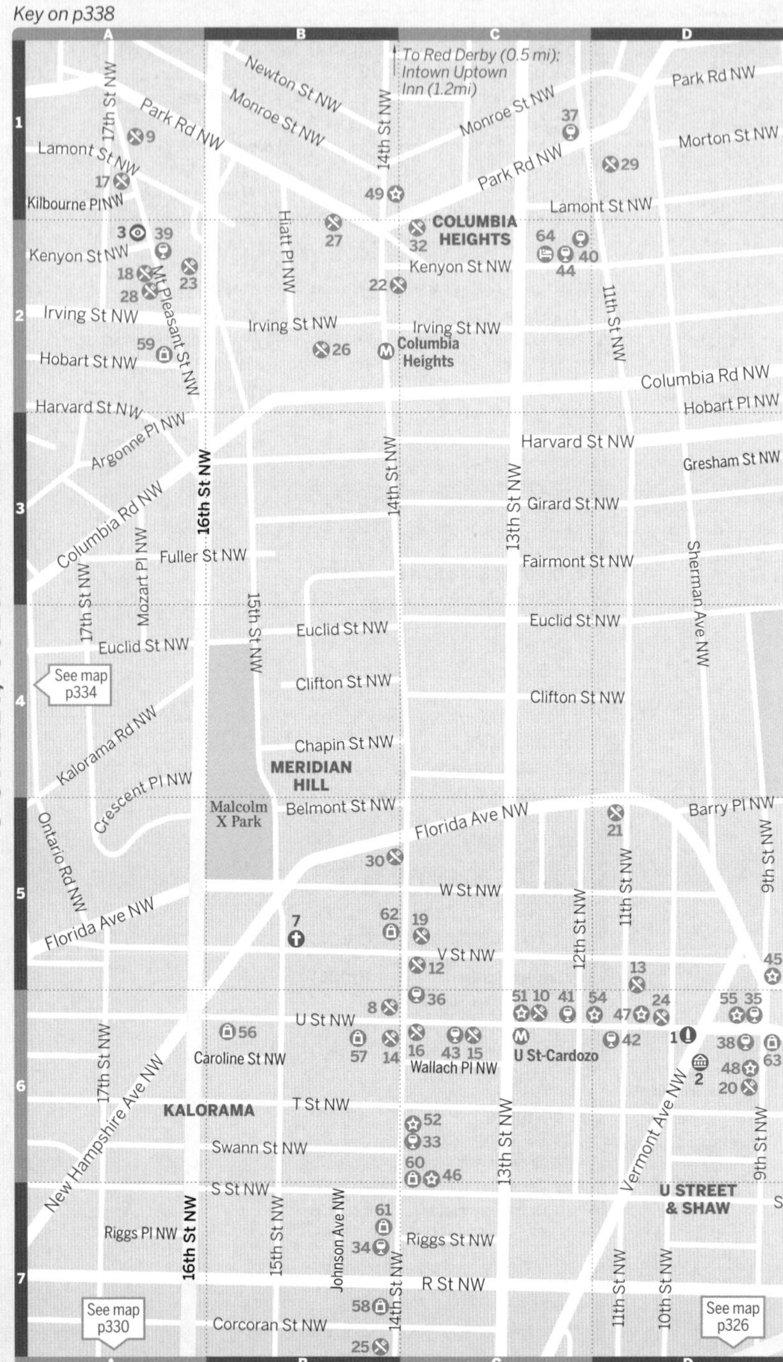
To Red Derby (0.5 mi); Intown Uptown Inn (1.2mi)
COLUMBIA HEIGHTS
Columbia Heights
MERIDIAN HILL
Malcolm X Park
KALORAMA
U St-Cardozo
U STREET & SHAW
See map p334
See map p330
See map p326
Newton St NW
Monroe St NW
Park Rd NW
Lamont St NW
Kilbourne Pl NW
Kenyon St NW
Irving St NW
Hobart St NW
Harvard St NW
Argonne Pl NW
Columbia Rd NW
Fuller St NW
Euclid St NW
Kalorama Rd NW
Crescent Pl NW
Ontario Rd NW
Florida Ave NW
Mt Pleasant St NW
17th St NW
16th St NW
15th St NW
14th St NW
13th St NW
12th St NW
11th St NW
10th St NW
9th St NW
Hiatt Pl NW
Mozart Pl NW
Morton St NW
Hobart Pl NW
Girard St NW
Gresham St NW
Fairmont St NW
Sherman Ave NW
Clifton St NW
Chapin St NW
Belmont St NW
Barry Pl NW
W St NW
V St NW
U St NW
Caroline St NW
Wallach Pl NW
T St NW
Swann St NW
S St NW
Riggs Pl NW
Riggs St NW
R St NW
Corcoran St NW
New Hampshire Ave NW
Vermont Ave NW
Johnson Ave NW

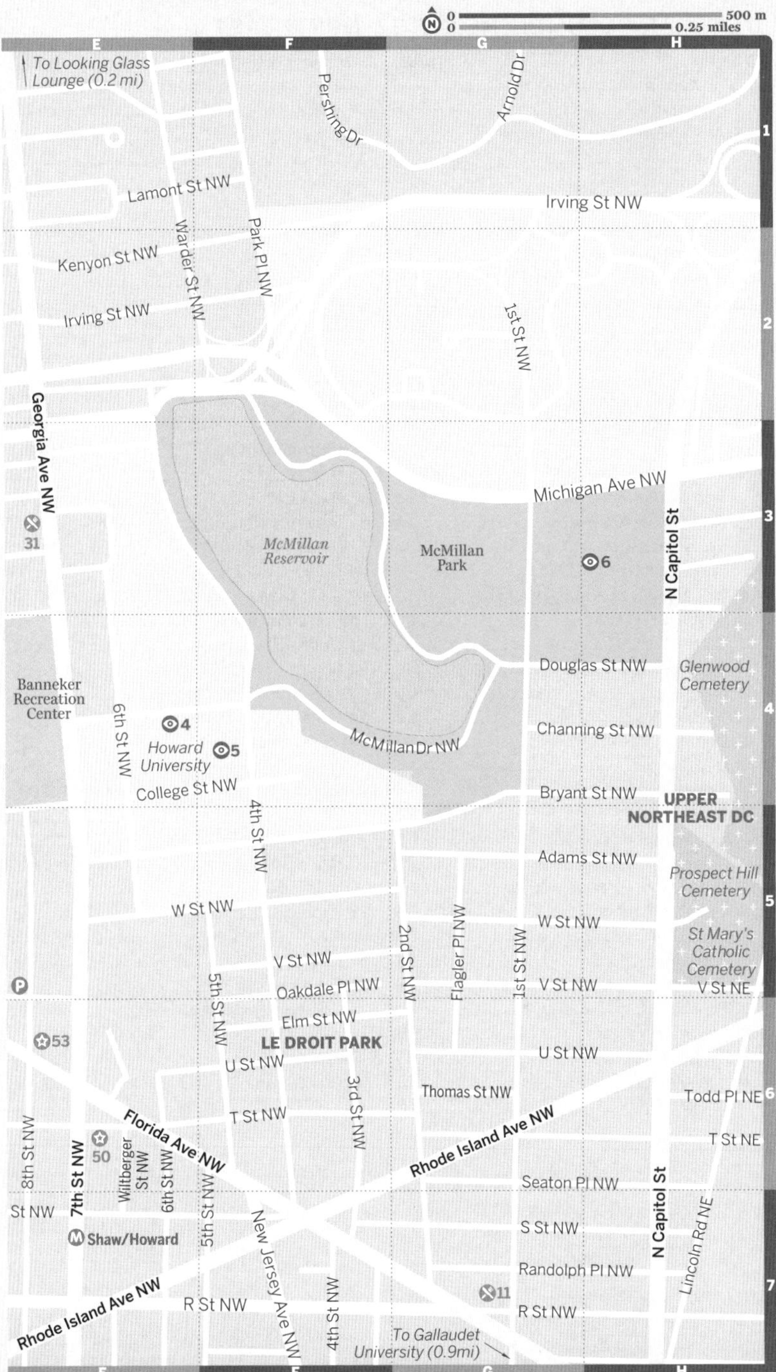

0 500 m
0 0.25 miles
To Looking Glass Lounge (0.2 mi)
Pershing Dr
Arnold Dr
Lamont St NW
Irving St NW
Kenyon St NW
Warder St NW
Park Pl NW
Irving St NW
1st St NW
Georgia Ave NW
31
McMillan Reservoir
McMillan Park
Michigan Ave NW
N Capitol St
6
Douglas St NW
Glenwood Cemetery
Banneker Recreation Center
6th St NW
4
Howard University
5
McMillan Dr NW
Channing St NW
College St NW
Bryant St NW
UPPER NORTHEAST DC
4th St NW
Adams St NW
Prospect Hill Cemetery
W St NW
W St NW
St Mary's Catholic Cemetery
2nd St NW
Flagler Pl NW
1st St NW
V St NW
Oakdale Pl NW
V St NW
V St NE
5th St NW
Elm St NW
53
LE DROIT PARK
U St NW
U St NW
3rd St NW
Thomas St NW
Todd Pl NE
T St NW
Florida Ave NW
Rhode Island Ave NW
T St NE
8th St NW
7th St NW
50
Wiltberger St NW
6th St NW
5th St NW
Seaton Pl NW
St NW
N Capitol St
S St NW
Shaw/Howard
New Jersey Ave NW
Lincoln Rd NE
Randolph Pl NW
Rhode Island Ave NW
R St NW
11
4th St NW
R St NW
To Gallaudet University (0.9mi)

U STREET, COLUMBIA HEIGHTS & NORTHEAST *Map on p336*

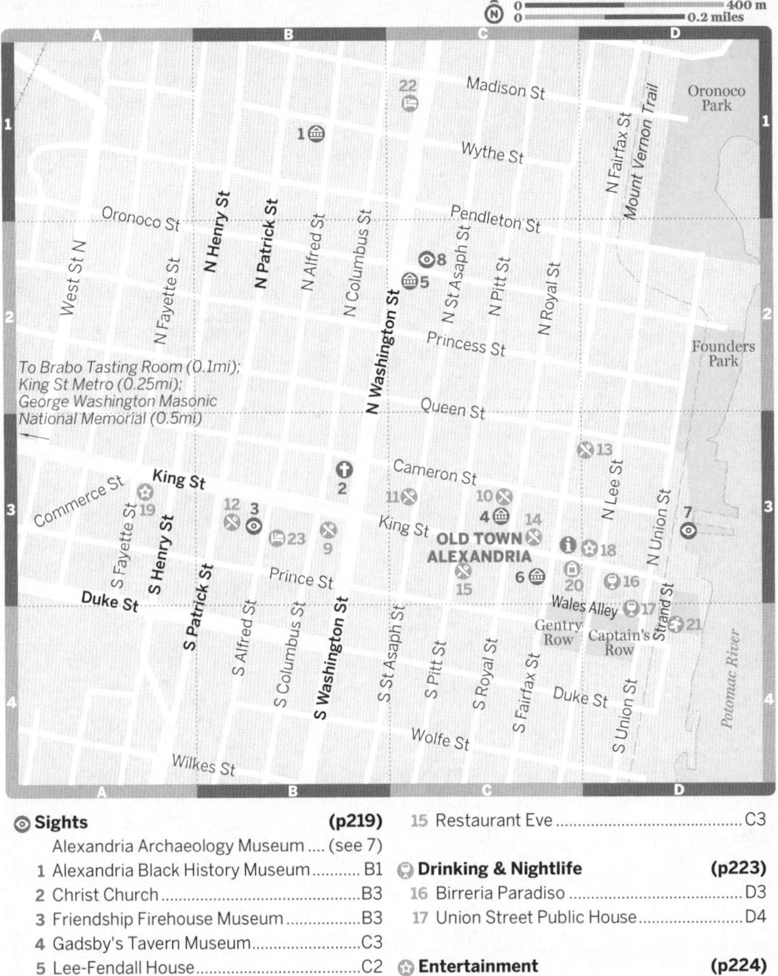

Sights (p219)

Alexandria Archaeology Museum .... (see 7)
1 Alexandria Black History Museum B1
2 Christ Church B3
3 Friendship Firehouse Museum B3
4 Gadsby's Tavern Museum C3
5 Lee-Fendall House C2
6 Stabler-Leadbeater Apothecary Museum C3
7 Torpedo Factory Art Center D3
8 Town House (Robert E Lee's Childhood Home) C2

Eating (p222)

9 Eamonn's Dublin Chipper B3
10 Gadsby's Tavern Restaurant C3
11 King Street Blues C3
12 Misha's Coffee Roaster B3
13 Momo Sushi & Café D3
14 Old Town Farmers Market C3
15 Restaurant Eve C3

Drinking & Nightlife (p223)

16 Birreria Paradiso D3
17 Union Street Public House D4

Entertainment (p224)

18 Basin Street Lounge D3
19 Tiffany Tavern A3

Shopping (p224)

20 Principle Gallery C3
Torpedo Factory Art Center .... (see 7)

Sports & Activities (p225)

21 Bike & Roll D4

Sleeping (p254)

22 Alexandria Travel Lodge C1
23 Morrison House B3

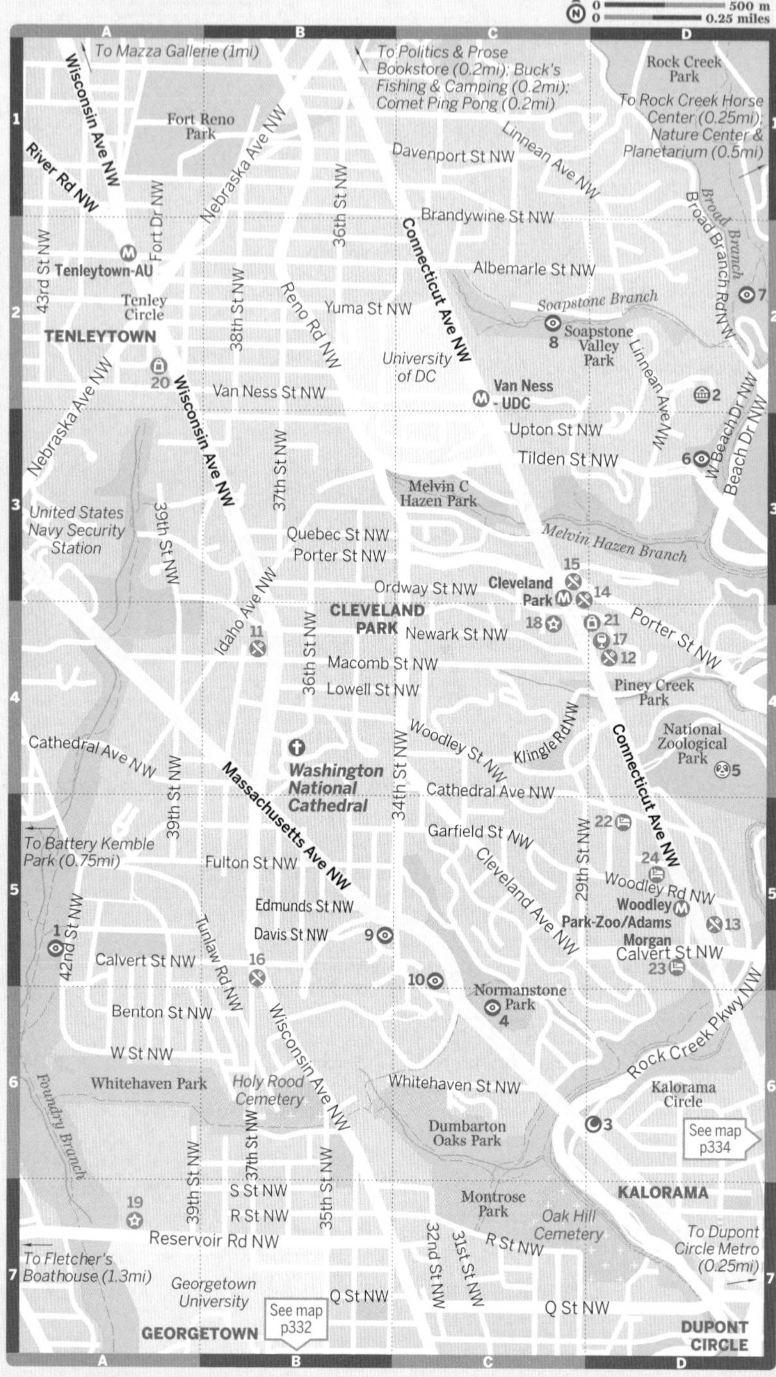

To Mazza Gallerie (1mi)
To Politics & Prose Bookstore (0.2mi); Buck's Fishing & Camping (0.2mi); Comet Ping Pong (0.2mi)
Rock Creek Park
To Rock Creek Horse Center (0.25mi); Nature Center & Planetarium (0.5mi)
Fort Reno Park
Wisconsin Ave NW
River Rd NW
Nebraska Ave NW
Davenport St NW
Linnean Ave NW
Fort Dr NW
36th St NW
Connecticut Ave NW
Brandywine St NW
Broad Branch
Broad Branch Rd NW
43rd St NW
Tenleytown-AU
38th St NW
Albemarle St NW
Tenley Circle
Reno Rd NW
Yuma St NW
Soapstone Branch
Soapstone Valley Park
TENLEYTOWN
University of DC
Van Ness St NW
Van Ness - UDC
W Beach Dr NW
Beach Dr NW
Upton St NW
Tilden St NW
37th St NW
Melvin C Hazen Park
United States Navy Security Station
39th St NW
Melvin Hazen Branch
Quebec St NW
Porter St NW
Ordway St NW
Cleveland Park
Idaho Ave NW
CLEVELAND PARK
Newark St NW
Porter St NW
Macomb St NW
Lowell St NW
Piney Creek Park
Woodley St NW
Klingle Rd NW
National Zoological Park
Cathedral Ave NW
Massachusetts Ave NW
Washington National Cathedral
34th St NW
Cathedral Ave NW
Garfield St NW
29th St NW
To Battery Kemble Park (0.75mi)
Fulton St NW
Cleveland Ave NW
Woodley Rd NW
Edmunds St NW
Woodley Park-Zoo/Adams Morgan
42nd St NW
Tunlaw Rd NW
Davis St NW
Calvert St NW
Calvert St NW
Normanstone Park
Benton St NW
Rock Creek Pkwy NW
W St NW
Whitehaven Park
Holy Rood Cemetery
Whitehaven St NW
Kalorama Circle
Foundry Branch
Dumbarton Oaks Park
See map p334
S St NW
R St NW
35th St NW
Montrose Park
KALORAMA
Reservoir Rd NW
Oak Hill Cemetery
To Dupont Circle Metro (0.25mi)
R St NW
32nd St NW
31st St NW
To Fletcher's Boathouse (1.3mi)
Georgetown University
Q St NW
Q St NW
See map p332
GEORGETOWN
DUPONT CIRCLE
500 m
0.25 miles

UPPER NORTHWEST DC

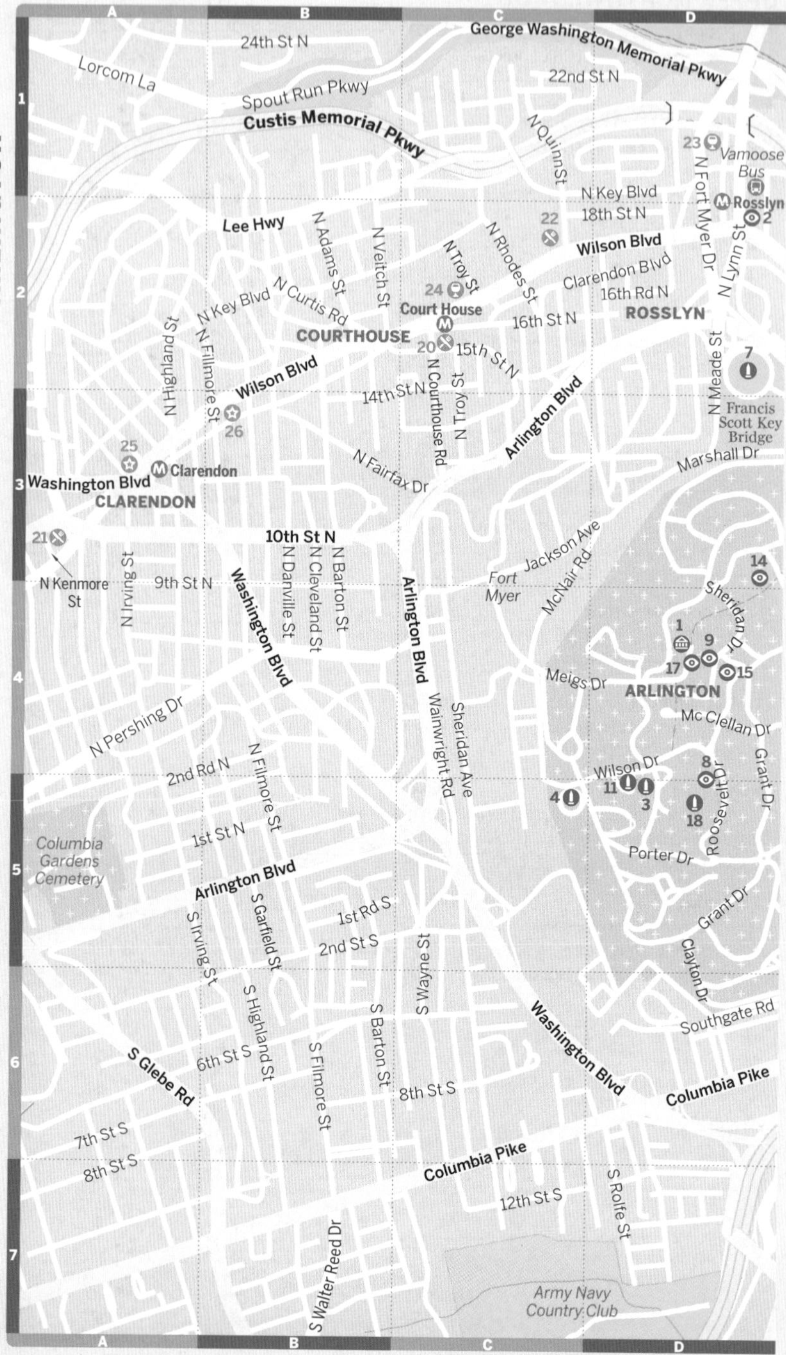
A
B
C
D
1
2
3
4
5
6
7
George Washington Memorial Pkwy
24th St N
22nd St N
Lorcom La
Spout Run Pkwy
Custis Memorial Pkwy
N Quinn St
23
Vamoose Bus
N Fort Myer Dr
N Key Blvd
18th St N
Rosslyn
2
22
Lee Hwy
N Adams St
N Veitch St
N Troy St
N Rhodes St
Wilson Blvd
Clarendon Blvd
16th Rd N
N Lynn St
24
Court House
N Key Blvd
N Curtis Rd
16th St N
ROSSLYN
N Highland St
N Fillmore St
COURTHOUSE
20
15th St N
N Meade St
7
Wilson Blvd
14th St N
N Courthouse Rd
N Troy St
Arlington Blvd
Francis Scott Key Bridge
26
25
Clarendon
N Fairfax Dr
Marshall Dr
Washington Blvd
CLARENDON
21
10th St N
N Kenmore St
N Irving St
9th St N
Washington Blvd
N Danville St
N Cleveland St
N Barton St
Arlington Blvd
Fort Myer
Jackson Ave
McNair Rd
14
Sheridan Dr
1
9
17
15
Meigs Dr
ARLINGTON
N Pershing Dr
Wainwright Rd
Sheridan Ave
Mc Clellan Dr
2nd Rd N
N Filmore St
Wilson Dr
8
Grant Dr
4
11
3
18
Roosevelt Dr
Columbia Gardens Cemetery
1st St N
Porter Dr
Arlington Blvd
S Garfield St
S Irving St
1st Rd S
2nd St S
Grant Dr
Clayton Dr
S Wayne St
S Highland St
S Barton St
Washington Blvd
Southgate Rd
S Glebe Rd
6th St S
S Filmore St
8th St S
Columbia Pike
7th St S
8th St S
Columbia Pike
12th St S
S Rolfe St
S Walter Reed Dr
Army Navy Country Club

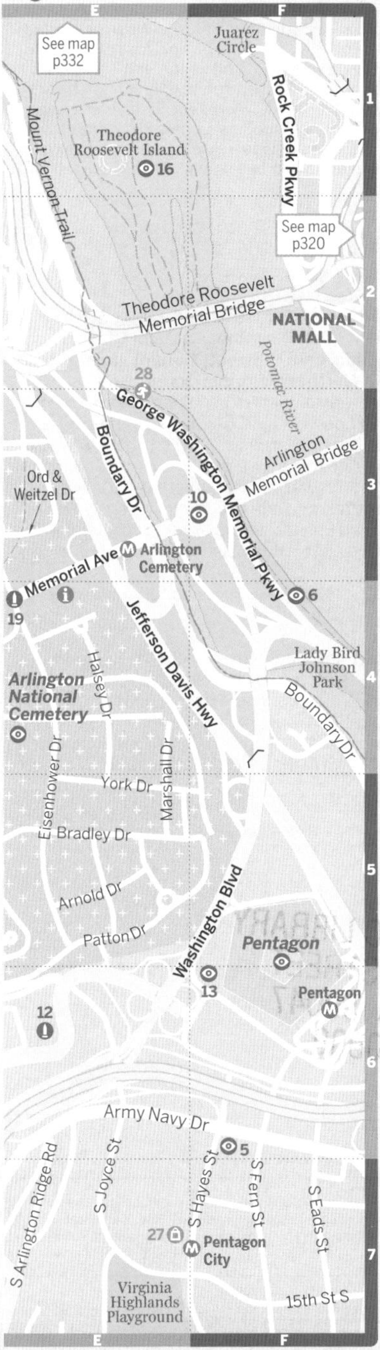

Top Sights (p216)

Arlington National Cemetery E4
Pentagon F5

Sights (p218)

1 Arlington House D4
2 Artisphere D2
3 Challenger Memorial D5
4 Confederate Monument C5
5 DEA Museum F6
Freedom Park .... (see 2)
6 George Washington Memorial Parkway F4
7 Iwo Jima Memorial D2
8 Joe Louis Gravesite D4
9 Kennedy Gravesites D4
10 Lady Bird Johnson Park F3
11 Mast of the Battleship USS Maine D5
12 National Air Force Memorial E6
13 Pentagon Memorial F6
14 President William Howard Taft Gravesite D3
15 Rear Admiral Richard Byrd Jr Gravesite ... D4
16 Theodore Roosevelt Island E1
17 Tomb of Pierre L'Enfant D4
18 Tomb of the Unknowns D5
19 Women in Military Service for America Memorial E4

Eating (p221)

20 Arlington Farmers' Market C2
21 El Pollo Rico A3
22 Ray's Hell Burger C2

Drinking & Nightlife (p223)

23 Continental D1
24 Ireland's Four Courts C2
Whitlow's on Wilson .... (see 26)

Entertainment (p224)

Artisphere .... (see 2)
25 Clarendon Ballroom A3
26 Iota B3

Shopping (p225)

27 Fashion Center at Pentagon City E7

Sports & Activities (p225)

28 Mount Vernon Trail E3

Our Story

A beat-up old car, a few dollars in the pocket and a sense of adventure. In 1972 that's all Tony and Maureen Wheeler needed for the trip of a lifetime – across Europe and Asia overland to Australia. It took several months, and at the end – broke but inspired – they sat at their kitchen table writing and stapling together their first travel guide, *Across Asia on the Cheap*. Within a week they'd sold 1500 copies. Lonely Planet was born.

Today, Lonely Planet has offices in Melbourne, London and Oakland, with more than 600 staff and writers. We share Tony's belief that 'a great guidebook should do three things: inform, educate and amuse'.

Our Writers

Karla Zimmerman

Coordinating Author; National Mall; White House Area & Foggy Bottom; Georgetown; Capitol Hill & Southeast DC; Downtown & Penn Quarter; Dupont Circle & Kalorama; Adams-Morgan; U Street, Columbia Heights & Northeast; Upper Northwest DC; Northern Virginia During her Washington travels, Karla devoured an embarrassing number of half-smokes, swirled a Scotch in the Round Robin, admired bongs at the DEA Museum and gaped unabashedly at the Declaration of Independence in the National Archives. The city will always be her first love, the one that unleashed her wanderlust. Walking up the steps of the Lincoln Memorial at night as a five year old, and seeing big ol' white-gleaming Abe, is her first magical travel memory. Karla has since trekked to more than 55 countries, and authored several Lonely Planet guidebooks covering the USA, Canada, the Caribbean and Europe. She lives in Chicago and writes travel features for newspapers, books, magazines and websites. Karla also wrote the book's Plan Your Trip and Survival Guide sections.

Read more about Karla at:
lonelyplanet.com/members/karlazimmerman

Regis St Louis

An avid news junkie and admirer of all things strange and political, Regis was destined for a long and tumultuous relationship with Washington, DC. No matter the season, he never tires of exploring the city of grand design and big ideas (if sometimes small-minded bureaucrats). A longtime travel writer, Regis has contributed to dozens of Lonely Planet titles, including the previous edition of *Washington, DC* and *USA*. When not down in the capital, he resides in Brooklyn, New York. Regis wrote the Day Trips from Washington, DC, chapter and the Understand section.

Read more about Regis at:
lonelyplanet.com/members/regisstlouis

Published by Lonely Planet Publications Pty Ltd
ABN 36 005 607 983
5th edition – Nov 2012
ISBN 978 1 74179 951 4

10 9 8 7 6 5 4 3 2 1
Printed in China